THE FORGING OF BUREAUCRATIC AUTONOMY

PRINCETON STUDIES IN AMERICAN POLITICS:
HISTORICAL, INTERNATIONAL, AND COMPARATIVE PERSPECTIVES

SERIES EDITORS

IRA KATZNELSON, MARTIN SHEFTER, THEDA SKOCPOL

*A list of titles in this series appears
at the end of the book*

THE FORGING OF
BUREAUCRATIC AUTONOMY

REPUTATIONS, NETWORKS, AND
POLICY INNOVATION IN
EXECUTIVE AGENCIES, 1862–1928

Daniel P. Carpenter

PRINCETON UNIVERSITY PRESS   PRINCETON AND OXFORD

Library of Congress Cataloging-in-Publication Data

Carpenter, Daniel P., 1967–
The forging of bureaucratic autonomy : reputations, networks, and policy
innovation in executive agencies, 1862–1928 / Daniel P. Carpenter.
p.   cm. — (Princeton studies in American politics)
Includes bibliographical references and index.
ISBN 0-691-07009-1 (alk. paper) — ISBN 0-691-07010-5 (pbk. : alk.
paper)
1. Executive departments—United States—History.   2. United States.
Congress—History.   3. Bureaucracy—United States—History.
4. Government executives—United States—History.   5. Political
planning—United States—History.   I. Title.   II. Series.
JK585 .C37   2001
351.73'09'034—dc21   2001036260

British Library Cataloging-in-Publication Data is available

This book has been composed in Times Roman

Printed on acid-free paper.∞

www.pup.princeton.edu

Printed in the United States of America

10   9   8   7   6   5   4   3   2   1

10   9   8   7   6   5   4   3   2   1
(Pbk)

To Kathleen Ellen Carpenter and John Edward Carpenter

Contents

Ten

Illustrations _____

Tables

Acknowledgments _____

THIS BOOK began as a political science dissertation at the University of Chicago. There were moments (some of them extended) when I thought the project would be infeasible or worthless, but the people I thank here made valuable contributions toward its completion. Often the very severity of their criticism convinced me of the inherent significance of the project. More often it was their support and friendship that made the countless hours of theorizing, of archiving, of running statistical analyses, and of writing seem worthwhile.

In this respect I particularly thank my dissertation committee, including Bernard Silberman and Andrew Abbott. I was helped immensely by John Mark Hansen, who shared his vast knowledge of agricultural history and politics, his long study of interest groups, of Congress, and of the bureaucracy, and, not least, his warm friendship. My dissertation chair, John F. Padgett, has been an inspiration. When the ideas here were inchoate, John provided structure, guidance, and support. He also taught me that the best social science lies neither in narrative methods nor in quantitative research alone, but in a theoretically informed combination of the two.

This book is large in scale and scope—my research effort included the collection or perusal of more than fifty thousand primary source documents from federal, state, and private archives; five thousand federal personnel files; hundreds of executive and congressional prints; and many secondary sources. I thank William Bassman and Victoria Gross of the National Personnel Records Center; Frank Scheer of the Railway Mail Service Library; Aloha South and Richard Fusick of the National Archives; Douglas Bowers, Wayne Rasmussen, and Vivian Wiser of the United States Department of Agriculture; Megaera Ausman and Jim Meyer of the United States Postal Service; Timothy Carr of the National Postal Museum; and numerous specialists in state and local archives. For data I thank Sarah Binder, Elizabeth Sanders, and the Interuniversity Consortium for Political and Social Research. Todd Austin, Sharon Barrios, Sanford Gordon, and Michael Morley provided excellent research assistance.

The Department of Politics at Princeton University was a supportive and stimulating place to begin this book. Doug Arnold, Larry Bartels, Sheri Berman, John DiIulio, Jameson Doig, Mark Fey, Fred Greenstein, Jeffrey Lewis, Tali Mendelberg, Tom Romer, Howard Rosenthal, Kenneth Schultz, and Keith Whittington offered helpful comments. At the Governmental Studies Program at the Brookings Institution, Sarah Binder, Carrie Hennefeld, Robert Katzmann, Jon Oberlander, R. Kent Weaver, and Margaret Weir shared their collegiality and insightful remarks. For financial support I thank the Alfred D. Chandler Dissertation Fellowship from Harvard Business School, the Iowa State Historical Society, the Princeton University Committee on Research in the Humanities and the Social Sciences, Princeton's Center for Domestic and Comparative Policy Studies, and the University of Michigan's Julia Lockwood Award.

The Department of Political Science at the University of Michigan has been a wonderful place to complete the book. Nancy Burns, John Campbell, Michael Cohen, Martha Feldman, Rick Hall, Donald Kinder, Ken Kollman, and Ann Chih Lin have provided critical and appreciative commentary.

I am also privileged to have received incisive feedback from the diverse network of scholars that comprises contemporary political science. I thank R. Michael Alvarez, Jeffrey Banks, Jonathan Bendor, William Bianco, Carles Boix, Delia Boylan, David Brady, John Brehm, Charles Cameron, Michael Dawson, Kevin Esterling, Tom Hammond, Jonathan Katz, J. Morgan Kousser, Keith Krehbiel, David Lazer, John Londregan, David Mayhew, Lawrence Rothenberg, William Sewell Jr., Stephen Skowronek, and Barry Weingast.

Ken Meier and Alice O'Connor provided excellent comments on my study of the Reclamation Service, and Sidney Fine, Sam Kernell, David Mayhew, Michael McDonald, and Sunita Parikh provided helpful criticisms of my Post Office study. Daniel Kryder, Debra Reid, and Mary Summers offered critical reactions to my work on the USDA. Two historians—Richard John and Donald Pisani—offered enthusiastic and voluminous commentary, and both saved me from numerous errors. Richard Bensel, Ira Katznelson, Elizabeth Sanders, Martin Shefter, and Theda Skocpol provided helpful encouragement and advice throughout. At Princeton, Malcolm Litchfield encouraged a timely and sound submission, and Chuck Myers offered his flexible and gentle style in getting the book in print. Dalia Geffen's fair and meticulous copyediting smoothed the text and excised many mistakes. The flaws that remain are mine alone.

Gerald Mara's college guidance gave me reason to believe that an academic career in political science could incorporate my diverse interests. And numerous friends have smoothed this effort, among them Chris, Dan, Greg, Harry, Jeff, Peter, and Richard of the Sunday Gang, Timothy Chafos, Ann Davies, David Hooper, Chris Jordan, Steven Laymon, Gia Pascarelli, David Savio, and Chris Yannelli.

I finally thank those friends and family who complete my life, including John Breslin, S.J., Mark Gammons, and John McCormick. My sister Rebecca Carpenter has been a constant source of support and humor. My wife, Rita Butzer-Carpenter, *lived* this project and infused it with her love, from our dating days in graduate school to our wonderful marriage now. And, of course, none of my travails would have been possible (or worthwhile) were it not for the support of my parents, Kathleen Ellen Carpenter and John Edward Carpenter, to whom this book is dedicated.

Abbreviations

AAAS American Association for the Advancement of Science
AFBF American Farm Bureau Federation
AOAC Association of Official Agricultural Chemists
B Box
BAE Bureau of Agricultural Economics, United States Department
    of Agriculture
BANC Bancroft Library Collections, University of California, Berkeley
BPI Bureau of Plant Industry, United States Department of Agriculture
C Container
CR *Congressional Record* (usually followed by Congress
    and session numbers)
DFH David F. Houston, secretary of agriculture, 1913–21
E Entry, under RG (Record Group) and NA (National Archives)
EMC Ellwood Mead Collection, Water Resources Library,
    University of California, Berkeley
F Folder
FCDW Farmers' Cooperative Demonstration Work (agricultural
    extension program)
FTC Federal Trade Commission
GFWC General Federation of Women's Clubs
GLO General Land Office, Department of Interior
GNH Gilbert N. Haugen Papers, Iowa State Historical Society
GP Gifford Pinchot Papers, Library of Congress
HCW Henry Cantwell Wallace, secretary of agriculture, 1921–24
HED House Executive Document
HWW Harvey W. Wiley Papers, Library of Congress
ICC Interstate Commerce Commission
JSW James S. Wilson, secretary of agriculture, 1897–1913, or,
    in italics, James S. Wilson Papers, Iowa State University
LOC Library of Congress, Manuscript Division, Washington, D.C.
NA I National Archives, Washington, D.C.
NA II National Archives, College Park, Maryland
NAL National Agricultural Library, Beltsville, Maryland
NARPC National Association of Railway Postal Clerks
NFU National Farmers' Union
NPRC National Personnel Records Center, Saint Louis, Missouri
NYSSV New York Society for the Suppression of Vice
POD Post Office Department

RFD   Rural Free Delivery, Post Office Department
RG   Record Group, in conjunction with National Archives
RMA   Railway Mail Association (RMS labor union)
RMS   Railway Mail Service, Post Office Department
RPO   Railway Post Office (in italics, the RMA's official journal,
            Railway Post Office)
SED   Senate Executive Document
SRS   States Relations Service, United States Department of Agriculture
USDA   United States Department of Agriculture
USPSL   U.S. Postal Service Library, Washington, D.C.
V   Volume (National Archives)
WCTU   Women's Christian Temperance Union

THE FORGING OF BUREAUCRATIC AUTONOMY

Introduction

"UNCLE JOE" Cannon was fuming.

It was 1905, and Cannon, the Republican Speaker of the U.S. House of Representatives and arguably the nation's most powerful politician, had just been beaten by a bureaucrat. Gifford Pinchot, chief forester in the U.S. Department of Agriculture, had quietly and methodically persuaded Cannon's House colleagues that the nation's forest reserves should be transferred from the Department of Interior to his own Agriculture Department. Pinchot's aim was to put the reserves under a much tighter regimen than Cannon and his Republican allies would allow, introducing user fees and grazing restrictions. Just two years earlier Cannon had taken control of the House floor to denounce the transfer scheme, tarring Pinchot's bureau as a "cheat and a fraud." But now Pinchot had turned the tables. By leaning on his friends in professional and scientific circles and by massively publicizing his bureau's accomplishments, he had convinced much of the nation's press that his organization possessed unique and unparalleled expertise on forestry matters. Moreover, Pinchot had built himself a coalition. He had wedded numerous groups together in his transfer crusade, including the General Federation of Women's Clubs, the Audubon Society, the Sierra Club, western ranchers' organizations, the National Board of Trade, and even pivotal members of the House Public Lands Committee who just two years earlier had applauded Cannon's tirade and had voted with the Speaker. Such diverse groups had little in common before and after 1905, but that year they were united in their zeal for land regulation.

Cannon's anger at Pinchot was hardly misplaced. Republicans (especially in the West) would soon rue the day that Pinchot's bureau took over the reserves. Pinchot imposed numerous user fees on logging, mining, and ranching interests, fees that were never contemplated in the 1905 act. Cannon's allies angrily denounced Pinchot and his power as a lawmaker. "History is challenged to instance anything," cried one, "approaching such audacious Departmental assumption of power in a legislative capacity." One senator marveled at how Pinchot had gotten the "right to legislate as to how lands shall be preserved." Another politician complained of Pinchot's hold over public opinion, denouncing the "publicity machine" he had erected in the Forest Service, which mailed out more than 9 million circulars annually. "Congress usually undertakes to ascertain what the people want and legislate accordingly," he grumbled. "Pinchot reverses the proceeding." Against the publicly recognized expertise and political clout of Pinchot's bureau, Congress could do little but stand by and watch. Thus, one of the central acts of American environmental history came from the political entrepreneurship of a bureaucrat.

It was not the last time that Speaker Cannon would find himself outflanked. A year after Pinchot's triumph, Harvey Wiley, chief of the USDA's Chemistry Bureau, successfully completed a twenty-year campaign for a national pure food and drug law. Wiley's bill had also been voted down by Republican Congresses in the late 1890s and early 1900s, again with opposition from Cannon. In 1906, however, Wiley's bureau reversed this pattern and recorded a political triumph that probably outranks Pinchot's. Like the chief forester, Wiley and his associates deluged Congress with data from his studies and lectured around the country. By 1905, in fact, "Dr. Wiley" was a household name in America. Yet Wiley's coalition was much larger and more varied than Pinchot's, and it stands as perhaps the first national "consumer protection" coalition in American political history. Backing Wiley's bill was a stunningly diverse league of more than one hundred organizations, including the General Federation of Women's Clubs, the American Medical Association, the Grange, the Women's Christian Temperance Union, a new coalition of state officials, the Association of Official Analytic Chemists, and the National Board of Trade. With this broad coalition, Wiley and his USDA associates turned to the legislative process, where they broke decisively from nineteenth-century precedent by writing the 1906 act. Cannon and other opponents saw their allies drop away, one by one, into a numbing approval of the Wiley bill. After the act passed, the constituents of Wiley's coalition defended his bureau at every turn, beating back attempts to restrict the USDA's range of activity. Like the 1905 Transfer Act, the Pure Food and Drugs Act of 1906 bears an immense institutional legacy. It authorized the regulation of food and pharmaceutical products now carried out by one of the nation's most powerful federal agencies, the Food and Drug Administration (FDA).

The Department of Agriculture was not the only federal agency to forge new policies in this way. The Post Office—that supposedly tradition-bound, patronage-dripping behemoth—authored immense shifts in national policy from the 1870s to the First World War. Postal officials were the prime movers behind the "Comstock" anti-pornography law of 1873 and the Anti-Lottery Law of 1890. Under Anthony Comstock and his associates, the Post Office became the most feared and powerful moral police agency the nation had yet known. With a varied collection of moral reform groups backing him—prohibitionists in the Anti-Saloon League, social elites in vice-suppression societies, and abortion opponents in the American Medical Association—Comstock became a legislative force unto himself, pressing numerous extensions of his authority through Congress. When President Theodore Roosevelt and congressional Republicans tried to turn Comstock's force on their political opponents after 1905, postal officials brazenly refused, wielding their own power on their own terms.

The Post Office also inaugurated the rural free delivery system, which began in 1891, the Postal Savings Act of 1910, and the parcels post plan of 1912. In the early 1890s Congress had initially balked at these ideas, citing the department's high operations deficit at the time. As postal officials reduced the deficit, and as the department fortified its ties to the media, Progressive moralists, agrarians, and business interests, the momentum for policy change grew. In postal savings, the department capitalized on the Panic of 1907 and European immigrants' distrust of private banks, framing its campaign in terms of the economic virtue of increased savings for the lower classes. When opposition arose, the Post Office joined with Progressive welfare advocates, journalists, and organized agrarians to beat back the attempts of bankers' associations to limit the scope of its discretion. From 1910 onward, the department operated savings banks out of virtually every post office with money order services. Postal officials also geared postal savings institutions toward European immigrants, gaining their participation and cementing legitimacy among a growing portion of the American electorate. In the parcels post system, established two years later, Congress gave the postmaster general unprecedented pricing authority over package delivery. By 1913 the department was able to make deep inroads into markets once dominated entirely by private enterprise.

Although the Post Office and Agriculture Departments triumphed at bureaucratic policymaking, the Interior Department remained an enigmatic failure. Given hold over vast reserves of the public domain and empowered by the Arrears Act of 1879 to distribute billions of dollars in pensions to Civil War veterans, the Interior Department seemed better equipped for autonomous policymaking than any agency of the time. Its policies had beneficiaries across classes, of both sexes, and in every state. Yet for all its formal authority, the Interior Department was perhaps the most politically feeble agency in American government before the New Deal. In managing Civil War pensions, the Interior Department was confined to do the bidding of congressional Republicans and the Grand Army of the Republic. Department proposals to centralize the pension system met, like its other ideas, with silence. The Reclamation Act of 1902—which gave the department more than $100 million in discretionary spending to develop arid lands in the West—promised to reenergize the Interior Department. Yet just a decade after its creation, the department's Reclamation Service had squandered its funds, forcing Congress to subject all of its projects to external review and tight appropriations control. Forest policy, meanwhile, marked Interior's truly crowning embarrassment. The department had been the principal regulator of the public domain in the nineteenth century, but in 1905 the Interior Department lost control of the national forests to the USDA and Pinchot.

Why Bureaucratic Autonomy?

Narratives of this sort—bureaucrats building reputations for their agencies, erecting coalitions behind their favored policies, and securing the policies that they favor despite the opposition of the most powerful politicians—are not isolated occurrences in American political development. Stories like these abound in the Progressive Era. Such cases raise important questions of democratic governance, not least the specter of unelected officials with broad policymaking power. Yet the primary query that these narratives raise is one of empirical bewilderment: Why and how does such autonomy happen? Why are some agencies autonomous, whereas others lie dormant? Why did the USDA and the Post Office Department succeed where the Interior Department failed? Why did the USDA and Post Office Department succeed in the Progressive Era and not before?

Bureaucratic autonomy occurs when bureaucrats take actions consistent with their own wishes, actions to which politicians and organized interests defer even though they would prefer that other actions (or no action at all) be taken. (A more extended definition appears in chapter 1.) Bureaucratic autonomy so defined is a common feature, though far from a universal one, of American government in the twentieth century. Agencies have at times created and developed policy with few, if any, constraints from legislative and executive overseers, and they have frequently coordinated organized interests as much as responded to them. To suggest that bureaucracies have policymaking autonomy may strike some readers as a controversial if not outlandish claim. Surely agencies lack the ability to take any action they desire in our system of representative government and rule of law. Yet I contend here that bureaucratic autonomy lies less in *fiat* than in *leverage*. Autonomy prevails when agencies can establish political legitimacy—a reputation for expertise, efficiency, or moral protection and a uniquely diverse complex of ties to organized interests and the media—and induce politicians to defer to the wishes of the agency even when they prefer otherwise. Under these conditions, politicians grant agency officials free rein in program building. They stand by while agency officials do away with some of their cherished programs and services. They even welcome agencies in shaping legislation itself.

Reputations, Networks, and Autonomy

A bureaucracy is an organization, and its autonomy (or lack of it) is premised on its organizational reputation and the networks that support it. When bureaucracies in turn-of-the-century American politics gained a lasting esteem for their ability to provide unique services, author new solutions to troubling national dilemmas, operate with newfound efficiency, or offer special protection to the public from economic, social, and even moral hazards, bureaucratic autonomy usually followed. The reputations that autonomous agencies established were diverse. Some agencies became known for their ability to conserve the nation's natural resources. Others were celebrated for protecting American consumers from the hazards of adulterated food and medicines. The Post Office earned esteem for moral guardianship (a powerful role in the culturally conservative Progressive Era), that is, for shielding American families from the evils of pornography and gambling. Whatever their specific content, organizational reputations had two common traits. First, they were grounded in actual organizational capacity. Agencies with strong reputations possessed greater talent, cohesion, and efficiency than agencies with reputations for weakness, corruption, or malfeasance. Second, organizational reputations were not ethereal but socially rooted. They were grounded in diverse political affiliations maintained by career bureaucratic officials. Reputations that were embedded in multiple networks gave agency officials an independence from politicians, allowing them to build manifold coalitions around their favored programs and innovations.

Two features of bureaucratic legitimacy—reputational *uniqueness* and political *multiplicity*—are crucial in the pages that follow. Autonomous agencies must demonstrate uniqueness and show that they can create solutions and provide services found nowhere else in the polity. If politicians can easily find compelling policy alternatives to an agency's plans, then agency autonomy will not be stable. Autonomous agencies also have a legitimacy that is grounded—not among the voters of one party or one section, not in a single class or interest group, but in multiple and diverse political affiliations. Agencies are able to innovate freely only when they can marshal the varied forces of American politics into coalitions, coalitions that are unique and irreducible to lines of party, class, or parochial interest. Network-based reputations as such are the very essence of state legitimacy in modern representative regimes.

Autonomy and the State: A New Look at American Political Institutions

The phenomenon of autonomy is fascinating not merely for academic purposes but also because the form of autonomy I consider in this book—independent policymaking power—has forcefully shaped the political institutions of the twentieth-century United States. Chief among these is what is called (with affection or disgust) the modern state. The advance of the bureaucratic state is one of the most wrenching and controversial changes of the twentieth century. However considered—by its capacity for war-making and policing, by its regulation of commerce and private life, by the enormity of its public expenditure—our national bureaucracy has grown ever more formidable and complex. Yet there is an entirely different characteristic of our modern state, one that heralds its arrival more than any other, one unique to the last century, for nothing so distinguishes twentieth-century bureaucratic government from its predecessors as its ability to plan, to innovate, and to author policy.

Bureaucratic policymaking is the hallmark of modern American government.

Our national bureaucracies routinely collect and analyze information, and they systematically forecast economic and social outcomes. Our agencies write regulations and draft legislation based on this information. At times, they apply influential political pressure for the passage of the laws they draft. They administer with considerable discretion the resulting rules and statutes, in accordance with their own standardized routines and procedures. This pattern holds sway in programs ranging from pharmaceutical regulation to defense procurement, from highway construction to welfare assistance, from counterterrorism to grant allocation. We may celebrate or bemoan the expanded role of our bureaucracies, but the story remains the same. The brute fact of modern politics is that myriad national programs begin and end in the hands of federal agencies.

The advance of the policy state is a narrative of organizational evolution and bureaucratic entrepreneurship. Operating within the rigid confines of the American institutional order—the primacy of elected officials, the constraints of American political culture, and the dominance of parties—administrative leaders in the USDA and the Post Office Department slowly carved out pockets of limited discretion by starting small experimental programs. By nurturing local constituencies and by using their multiple network affiliations to build broad support coalitions among professionals, agrarians, women's groups, moral crusaders, and congressional and partisan elites, they won for their young programs both political currency and administrative legitimacy. Fledgling experiments with dubious survival prospects at the turn of the century became, by the close of the 1920s, established policies. At almost every step in the development of these programs, the institutional authorities of the American order—Congress, the president, the parties, the courts, and organized interests—assented to greater and greater administrative innovation. Through reputation building, federal agencies won the capacity to innovate. In American political development, bureaucratic autonomy was not captured but earned.

This argument joins a time-honored dialogue on the evolution of American bureaucracy, a dialogue enriched by scholars as diverse as Stephen Skowronek, Theda Skocpol, Richard Bensel, Terry Moe, Richard John, Martin Shefter, Elizabeth Sanders, Samuel Kernell, Ronald Johnson and Gary Libecap, Scott James and Brian Balogh. My argument also departs subtly but significantly from these accounts. In its focus on bureaucratic development in "pockets" of the American state—and with its analysis of the varied evolution of capacity and reputation across agencies and over time—this book offers a different view of institutional change from that advanced by Skowronek.[1] An emphasis on organizational reputations in addition to organizational capacities distinguishes this narrative from the capacity-based arguments of Skocpol, John, and Kenneth Finegold.[2] With its argument that strong states are not simply embedded in society but must have durable reputations that are seated in multiple and diverse networks, this book diverges from numerous accounts that connect American state formation to sectional conflict and social movements (Bensel and Sanders), partisan coalitions (Shefter, Kernell, and James), organized federal employees (Johnson and Libecap), professions (Balogh), presidents (Moe, James), or some combination of these forces (Moe).[3]

Sovereign Stories of the Policy State

In important and novel ways, this story differs from the two sovereign narratives of American state building. For casual observers and scholars alike, the first story is very simple. According to received historical wisdom, the policy state we know today in America is a legacy of the New Deal. In response to the mass economic crisis of the Great Depression and unified under Democratic rule, the government launched a wide array of programs designed to counter the disastrous consequences of the business cycle and to shore up an aging national infrastructure. To stabilize industrial production, President Franklin D. Roosevelt offered the National Recovery Act, the most far-reaching attempt at government-coordinated industrial regulation our nation has known. To boost employment and build public works projects, Roosevelt created the Works Progress Administration and the Civilian Conservation Corps. To ease farmers out of the price depression of the 1930s, Roosevelt tendered a massive price support program in the Agricultural Adjustment Act. And to solidify the retirement income of elderly Americans, the government offered the first entitlement-based guaranteed income program, Social Security. In addition, Roosevelt and the Democrats created and extended numerous regulatory agencies responsible for moderating industries as diverse as banking, communications, and pharmaceuticals. Floating massive programs and creating agency upon agency from scratch, the story goes, Roosevelt and the New Deal Democrats launched the discretionary bureaucratic state we know today.[4]

As a story of the accretion of bureaucratic power, the New Deal narrative is persuasive. As an account of the origins of the modern policy state, however, it suffers from two critical flaws. The first is that many New Deal creations lacked institutional permanence. Social Security, much of the Agricultural Adjustment Act, and several New Deal regulatory agencies endure today, but few of the programs and bureaucracies created in the New Deal survived to 1950. This is particularly true for the more ambitious attempts to plan and coordinate economic production or mass public construction—the National Recovery Act and the public works programs.

The genuine poverty of the New Deal narrative, however, consists in its lack of accuracy and nuance. In America, our bureaucratic state did not evolve all of a piece. Some bureaucracies developed the capacity to innovate and plan decades before 1933, whereas many agencies that were created anew in the New Deal never exhibited this ability. Consider, for instance, the Agricultural

Adjustment Act, the foundation of twentieth-century farm policy. The durability of this act, as Finegold and Skocpol have shown, was due largely to the exceptional administrative and organizational capacities of the U.S. Department of Agriculture in the 1930s. Yet few factors in New Deal politics can account for why the USDA developed its organizational capacity before 1930. Alternatively, the demise of the National Recovery Act may be traced in large measure to the inability of the agency implementing it—the National Recovery Administration—to achieve administrative stability. What requires explanation is why one agency was possessed with greater capacity and political legitimacy than the other. Stark differences across agencies such as these abound in American administrative history.

Others have alighted on the fact that the critical steps in American state building took place before the Depression. During the last two decades, numerous scholars—Skowronek, Skocpol, Bensel, Sanders, and James—have hewn out a rough consensus over the proposition that between the end of the Civil War and the New Deal, a national state was constructed in America that was genuinely distinct from the feeble structure of the nineteenth century. To the federal government there accrued a variety of new formal powers ranging from taxation of income to regulation of railroads and foods to the programmatic delivery of benefits to veterans and poor mothers. The American military was transformed from a loose, federated collection of state militia into a centralized bureaucratic machine. Reform movements and political leaders struggled and converged to overhaul the prevailing mode of governmental operations, placing the civil service under a merit standard and transforming the federal budget process. And, of course, the volume and expanse of national governmental operations exploded.[5]

Three features are common to these Progressive narratives, features that also mark their critical flaws. First, these stories focus principally on the rise of a new creature of bureaucracy: the independent commission. In the Interstate Commerce Commission (the ICC, created in 1887) and the Federal Trade Commission (the FTC, created in 1914), scholars of the Progressive narrative see the genuine state-building achievement of the early twentieth century. As Skowronek proclaims, the ICC

> emerged in 1920 as the signal triumph of the Progressive reconstruction. Here, the old mode of governmental operations was most completely superseded, and the reintegration of the American state with the new industrial society most clearly consummated. The agency . . . acquired the responsibility for supervising all aspects of the national railway system in accordance with the most advanced precepts of scientific management. . . . It was all the promises of the new American state rolled into the expansion of national administrative capacities.[6]

The independent commissions marked a departure from the large-scale departments of the nineteenth century. In theory, at least, they smacked less of bureaucracy and more of expertise. Born after the Pendleton Act of 1883, they were insulated from patronage, freed in principle from party control. In landmark pieces of legislation, they were charged with governing vast segments of the American economy—from the transportation sector (under the ICC) to antitrust and fair industrial competition (the FTC). And they were a uniquely American state-building achievement. In a literature still wedded to American "exceptionalism," the fact that the independent commissions were not institutional copies of the European state but homegrown remedies to industrialization has been their most powerful lure.

Although certainly worthy of the immense historical attention they have received, the independent commissions figured little in the development of the American policy state. First, commissions have occupied a relatively diminutive place in twentieth-century state formation. Over the last one hundred years, the vast share of nonmilitary state activity, government employment, and public expenditure in the United States has been borne by executive departments.[7] This brute fact of administrative politics was no less true in the Progressive Era and the New Deal. Compared with the impact of executive departments— the regulation of American trade and financial markets by the Treasury Department; the governance of agriculture, pharmaceuticals, and forests by the Department of Agriculture; the management of western lands, Indian affairs, pensions, and patent law by the Interior Department; the persistence of a multibillion dollar economy in the Post Office; voting rights and antitrust enforcement in the Department of Justice; and numerous activities in the Departments of Commerce and Labor—the political, economic, and social implications of ICC and FTC activity in the early twentieth century were small.

Beyond this, the Progressive commissions never exhibited the core properties of the twentieth-century policy state—planning and discretionary innovation. As historians have repeatedly shown, neither commission was capable of sustained policy creation. Both the ICC and FTC took their orders from the dominant Progressive and Republican coalitions in Congress. And the ICC was particularly ill equipped to carry out the aims of the Progressives. Where new programs required it to plan or to innovate, the commission failed miserably. In 1913 Congress passed the Valuation Act, charging the ICC with a massive study of railroad assets and liabilities. The act doubled the size of the commission, but it only exposed its feeble organizational structure and lack of analytic talent. Although Progressive politicians expected completion of the valuation project in a decade, the crudest asset estimates were not available until 1933. An even greater failure of planning followed upon the Transportation Act of 1920, Skowronek's "signal triumph" of Progressive state building. The Transportation Act charged the ICC with setting forth a broad national plan for railroad consolidations. The commission began consolidation planning in May 1920 but did not adopt a plan until 1929. So hapless was its administrative organization that for three successive years, from 1926 to 1928, the commission appealed to

Congress to remove the consolidation burden from its shoulders. Two students of the commission summarize its experience with planning in the 1920s.

> Having originally programmed the ICC to reflect congressional bidding, Congress gave the commission authority to determine policy, but the ICC was unwilling to innovate bold plans or to generate power to support its policies. To solve the railroad problem and provide a rational transportation system, the ICC needed to plan, shape, innovate and act, but it continued merely to reflect power and respond to pressure from other sources.[8]

A second form of the Progressive narrative emerges in the work of Skocpol, who has paid the most scholarly attention to state-building developments outside the commissions. Skocpol's *Protecting Soldiers and Mothers* details the evolution of early forms of social provision in the United States. The explosion of Civil War pensions after Reconstruction provided a far-reaching system of social distribution. Later, the diffusion of mothers' pensions across the states and the creation of the Sheppard-Towner program constituted the earliest forms of governmental aid to single mothers. Arguing from a "polity-centered" perspective, Skocpol credits party structure, reformist professionals, and gender-driven, locally rooted women's movements for forging early American social policy.

Still, Skocpol herself admits that the promise of Progressive social policy lay more in its historical possibilities as a social program than in its bureaucratic achievements. Bureaucratic planning and agency entrepreneurship play a lesser role in Skocpol's narrative than do the coalition strategies of party officials and far-flung women's organizations. As successful as Civil War pensions were, they never engendered any sustained administrative innovation in the Interior Department's Pension Bureau. Instead, pension administration further debilitated the Interior Department from a state-building standpoint, as I discuss in chapter 2. Nor did mothers' pensions inaugurate bureaucratic planning in American social policy. In summary, neither veterans' benefits nor mothers' pensions added materially to the organizational capacities of American bureaucracy.

The third and by far the most prevalent misperception among state-building narratives is that civil service reform was a historically sufficient condition for the emergence of unique bureaucratic preferences. In contrast to Bensel and Skowronek,[9] I argue that civil service professionalization through the construction of a merit-based system of hiring and promotion does not suffice to render the state autonomous of parties, legislative coalitions, and interest formations. Instead, the development of statist identities in the federal bureaucracy evolved agency by agency, often through network-based hiring that was specific to particular agencies. Skowronek's narrative itself demonstrates the limits of merit reform, insofar as genuine enforcement of the Pendleton Act was completed only from 1908 to 1920, a quarter-century after its enactment in 1883.[10] But the primary reasons for the insufficiency of merit reform lie in well-established arguments about how bureaucracies can be captured by organized interests or dominated by legislatures, for the Pendleton Act did not suppress the opportunities for organized interests to influence agencies by shaping the character of appointments to positions of political leadership in them, appointments made by the president and confirmed by Congress. Nor were agencies that were released from the strictures of patronage any less likely to witness their discretion constrained in acts of federal courts and in rigid legislative specification, as Skowronek's "reconstitution" of economic regulation demonstrates.[11]

Unpacking the Politics of Bureaucracy

With rare exceptions, analyses of American state building share one other flaw. They study bureaucracy only through the legislation that creates agencies, the presidents who govern them, or the court decisions that check or enable their decision making. Skowronek's narratives of state building place presidents (particularly Theodore Roosevelt) at the center of the story, presaging his landmark book on executive power, *The Politics Presidents Make* (1992). Bensel, Sanders, and James study bureaucratic development through the passage of laws, focusing their analyses primarily on roll-call votes. Although administrative agencies undoubtedly occupy a smaller place in American political institutions than in other nations, the neglect of bureaucratic organizations in studies of administrative development is unfortunate. First, it reduces political development to institutional *creation,* to the neglect of institutional *transformation.* Second, it leaves the most important political outcomes—the impact of policies on citizens—unstudied. Only by focusing on administrative outcomes can transformations in the relationship between state and society be properly analyzed. As the narratives in this book show repeatedly, legislation cannot hard-wire administrative outcomes. Scholars must examine the ongoing relationship between politicians, citizens, and bureaucrats.

From the vantage point of ease of analysis, the neglect of bureaucracy in American political development is easy to understand. Congressional debates, roll-call votes, presidential biographies, and court decisions are readily available to researchers in American politics. Administrative documents are not. Whereas scholars have made rich and ingenious use of congressional and executive materials and refer occasionally to agencies' annual reports, they have almost uniformly ignored other primary sources: agency memorandums, records of administrative decisions, civil service records, and correspondence between agencies, members of Congress, and the president.

I hope that this book eschews the limitations of earlier analyses without neglecting the important role of politicians and courts. I have tried to unpack American bureaucracy by collecting more than fifty thousand pages of pri-

mary-source documents, including data on more than seven thousand civil servants and hundreds of official government prints. I have also consulted a rich
secondary literature on the development of these three executive departments.
In addition, I have incorporated the reports and archival files of the House and
Senate committees that oversaw these agencies, as well as the papers of influential members of Congress, of presidents, and of several state archives where
the relationship between the executive departments and state-level institutions
was illuminated. I admit that the research here does not exhibit the exhaustive
specificity of particular studies such as Richard John's treatment of the antebellum postal system, Donald Pisani's analyses of western reclamation, or
James Harvey Young's history of the Pure Food and Drugs Act of 1906 (all
cited in later chapters). As a comparative study of agencies, however, I hope
that it breaks new ground and offers at least a partial template for other social
scientists.

Why the Post Office, Agriculture, and Interior?

I chose the three departments I examine in this book with a view to illuminating the dynamics of bureaucratic autonomy in domestic policy arenas. Each of
these agencies was created at least a generation before 1900 and was neither
disassembled nor merged during the period under study. Although all three organizations experienced fargoing transformations between 1860 and 1930, they
kept their titles and a core set of functions. I also include short discussions of
the Department of Treasury and the Department of Commerce and Labor (later
split into separate departments, as they exist today) in various chapters.

    Readers will also note that this analysis excludes the military and the De-
partment of State. I leave these agencies to other scholars, principally for the
reason that foreign policy introduces constitutional issues that would complicate my theoretical purposes. Because the president carries greater institutional
authority in foreign policy under our Constitution, the relative autonomy of
military and diplomatic agencies from politicians is an altogether different matter from its status in domestic agencies. Because the bureaucratic structure of
the American military changed materially from the Civil War to the New Deal,
moreover, it would be difficult to analyze the military as a single executive department. In addition, a focus on domestic agencies narrows the factors that
can explain the divergent historical outcomes observed across agencies and
over time. In this sense, my exclusion of military and diplomatic agencies
amounts to a form of historical control. For a similar reason, my analysis of the
Department of Interior excludes its management of Native American populations, a fascinating episode in bureaucratic policymaking, which I leave to
other scholars.

    What the three agencies I analyze here do offer are differences in tasks and structure which render their divergent paths of evolution all the more intriguing. Both the USDA and the Post Office, I claim, developed a degree of relative autonomy from politicians and organized interests. Yet these agencies had little in common that differentiated them from the Interior Department. The Department of Agriculture was the dominant scientific agency of the federal government; postal officials exhibited few scientific or professional credentials of note. The USDA was the official representative organ of farmers in the executive branch, though as I show, the department's support from organized agrarians was weaker than has commonly been supposed. Meanwhile, the vast share of postal employment was in cities, and the most earnest lobbyists of the department were moral reformers, merchants, and railroads. If anything, the Interior Department's strong embedment in the West and in rural communities should have disposed it to receiving greater favor from rural interests than it did. Nor can agency size or patronage explain the outcomes. The Agriculture Department continued through the Progressive Era as among the smallest of executive departments, dwarfed by the Post Office, Interior, and Treasury.

Only bureaucratic legitimacy—the evolving belief among politicians and the organized public in the problem-solving capacities of a select few agencies—explains the evolution of conditional autonomy in the Post Office and Agriculture Departments. Rooted in the arrival of a new generation of officials with novel talents and a distinct ideological view of the proper role of their bureaucracies, bureaucratic legitimacy crystallized in the Progressive Era and was cemented during the the First World War and the 1920s. I offer a theoretical account of this process in chapter 1, and in chapter 2 I explain why it did not arise for most departments, especially the Department of the Interior. I organize the remaining eight chapters into three distinct sections. In chapters 3, 4, and 5, I narrate the rise of bureaucratic autonomy in the Post Office Department. In chapters 6 through 9, I discuss the trajectory of autonomy in the USDA. In chapter 10 I show how the Interior Department lost wide-ranging bureaucratic discretion in federal reclamation policy. I offer a concluding note on the political nature of bureaucratic autonomy and consider the meaning of these patterns for the larger interpretation of Progressivism.

One

Entrepreneurship, Networked Legitimacy, and Autonomy

WHETHER CELEBRATED or lamented, bureaucratic autonomy prevails when politically differentiated agencies take sustained patterns of action consistent with their own wishes, patterns that will not be checked or reversed by elected authorities, organized interests, or courts. So conceived, bureaucratic autonomy emerges only upon the historical achievement of three conditions.

- Autonomous bureaucracies are *politically differentiated* from the actors who seek to control them. They have unique preferences, interests, and ideologies, which diverge from those of politicians and organized interests.
- Bureaucratic autonomy requires the *development of unique organizational capacities*—capacities to analyze, to create new programs, to solve problems, to plan, to administer programs with efficiency, and to ward off corruption. Autonomous agencies must have the ability to act upon their unique preferences with efficacy and to innovate. They must have bureaucratic entrepreneurs.
- Bureaucratic autonomy requires *political legitimacy,* or strong organizational reputations embedded in an independent power base. Autonomy first requires demonstrated capacity, the *belief* by political authorities and citizens that agencies can provide benefits, plans, and solutions to national problems found nowhere else in the regime. These beliefs must also be grounded *in multiple networks* through which agency entrepreneurs can build *program coalitions* around the policies they favor.

Legitimacy is the foundation of bureaucratic autonomy in democratic regimes. Only when politicians and broad portions of the twentieth-century American public became convinced that some bureaucracies could provide unique and efficient public services, create new and valuable programs, and claim the allegiance of diverse coalitions of previously skeptical citizens did bureaucratic autonomy emerge. These reputations surfaced slowly, and they varied widely across the agencies of the American executive branch. In the main, the departments bearing strong reputations for innovation and service were distinguished by two characteristics from those that did not. First, these agencies had political and organizational capacity. They were possessed of the ability to plan, to innovate, and to control and modify their own programs. They also had bureaucratic entrepreneurs who could assemble broad coalitions to push their innovations into law, coalitions that are necessary in our system of divided and federated powers. Second, the reputation-bearing departments were embedded in political and social networks that reduced their dependence on elected officials. They were able to demonstrate their capacities and sell their ideas to the media and a diverse set of organized interests. They were influenced by numerous economic, social, and political interests but controlled by none.[1]

My understanding of bureaucratic autonomy as conditioned upon organizational legitimacy departs in two respects from previous scholarship. It departs first and foremost from arguments advanced by Richard Bensel, Samuel Kernell, Elizabeth Sanders, Barry Weingast, and others that minimize the role of bureaucratic action in American political development. Sanders in particular has argued that bureaucratic autonomy was a "dubious proposition" in the Progressive Era and the 1920s, as these periods were characterized not by bureaucratic choice but by "legislative specification" that was "explicit and discretion-limiting." In contrast, I argue that agencies with established reputations and independent power bases can change the terms of legislative delegation. These agencies can initiate and manage programs without statutory authorization. They regularly make program innovations that elected officials did not direct them to take. At times, they can even make sustained policy choices that flout the preferences of elected officials or organized interests.[2] Yet the dominant form of bureaucratic autonomy exists not when agencies can take any action at will but *when they can change the agendas and preferences of politicians and the organized public*. Political legitimacy allows agencies to change minds through experimentation, rhetoric, and coalition building.

Second, this book offers a more guarded set of claims about bureaucratic autonomy than has been made by most scholars who believe it is possible. I do not claim that bureaucratic autonomy amounts to total administrative freedom. Although I concur with Eric Nordlinger that bureaucrats can achieve the "translation of state preferences into public policy," I doubt that bureaucracies can always take these authoritative actions at will, even with the many strategies available to them. Indeed, bureaucratic autonomy requires a pattern of deference by elected officials who see it as in their long-run interest to do so. More important, bureaucrats who value their autonomy will act in measured ways to preserve it, refraining from strategies of consistent fiat or defiance. The notion of reputation-based autonomy transcends the often-hollow debate between believers in strong autonomy like Skocpol and Nordlinger and partisans of legislative dominance like Sanders, Bensel, Weingast, and many legislative scholars.[3]

1. Autonomy as a Historical Variable

The development of bureaucratic autonomy in America has not been uniform. It has emerged in pockets of our administrative state, but the larger whole remains dormant. The three conditions for bureaucratic autonomy—the condition of political differentiation, the condition of organizational capacity, and the condition of political legitimacy—have rarely been achieved in American political history. As the introduction suggests, however, the twentieth century offers historical exceptions to this pattern. If these "exceptional" agencies amount to a rule of sorts—if they constitute a historical pattern worth explaining—then some intriguing puzzles must be addressed:

- How did American bureaucracies become differentiated from congressional majorities, from partisan and presidential elites, and from organized interests? How did they develop preferences of their own?
- How did agencies in America develop the capacity to plan and innovate? How did they develop the organizational capacity for rational program administration, for program learning?
- How did bureaucratic agencies acquire political legitimacy? How did they develop reputations that transcended our cultural antipathy toward bureaucracy? How did they build stable and invulnerable coalitions behind their favored innovations?

In the rest of this chapter I develop generalizable answers to these questions. I lay out a theory of bureaucratic autonomy and the process of its forging. I begin in section 2 by elaborating my definition of bureaucratic autonomy. In section 3 I outline the concept of bureaucracy as I discuss it in this book, paying heed to organizational structure and culture and clarifying their relationship to capacity, innovation, and bureaucratic reputation. Then in sections 4, 5, and 6 I discuss the three conditions for bureaucratic autonomy—differentiation, capacity, and reputation.

2. The Concept of Reputation-Conditioned Autonomy

In American politics, institutional power flows from the three constitutional authorities—Congress, the president, and the federal courts. Congress has been the Article One branch of this institutional order of power. Bureaucracies are created, empowered, and funded by the legislature; they owe their very existence to Congress. Presidents also powerfully shape the size and structure of agency budgets, and they can often direct bureaucracies at will through executive order and appointment. And federal courts often play the role of ultimate arbiter over agency choices, as they are in the best position of the three constitutional actors to overturn bureaucratic decisions. The formal powers of these constitutional authorities are formidable, and they are strengthened by other, informal powers. As numerous scholars have argued, political authorities (presidents, legislative coalitions, and courts) can constrain patterns of bureaucratic decision making by resorting to legislative specification, administrative procedures, budgetary control, and various other measures.[4] In representative systems where bureaucracies receive their authority and resources from the national legislature, administrative officials can rarely (if ever) carve out autonomy by fiat, shirking, or defiance. This is particularly so in the United States, where politicians and judges guard their institutional prerogatives with caution and even jealousy.

Instead, bureaucratic autonomy in American government is a form of deference. *Bureaucratic autonomy prevails when a politically differentiated agency takes self-consistent action that neither politicians nor organized interests prefer but that they either cannot or will not overturn or constrain in the future.* Self-consistency here means that the agency is taking actions consistent with its own preferences. Because these preferences are, by construction, distinct from the preferences of politicians and organized interests, these actions depart from the preferred actions of these actors.[5]

Bureaucratic autonomy so defined emerges not from fiat but from legitimacy. It occurs when political authorities see it as in their interest to defer to agency action, or when they find it too problematic to restrict it. They defer to the agency because (1) failure to do so would forfeit the publicly recognized benefits of agency capacity and/or (2) the agency can build coalitions around its innovations that make it costly for politicians to resist them. These coalitions are part of the agency's reputation; reputations are not ethereal but are embedded in network-based coalitions.[6]

Autonomy versus Discretion

The notion of "discretion" common to political science and administrative law is only a bare tendril of autonomy as I define it here. Discretion is part of a contractual arrangement between politicians and an agency they establish; a statute may give an agency discretion or leeway to interpret and enforce a law within certain bounds. Bureaucratic autonomy, by contrast, is external to a contract and cannot be captured in a principal-agent relationship. Indeed, when agencies have autonomy, they can bring their political legitimacy to bear upon the very laws that give them power. They can change the terms of delegation. They can even alter the electoral strategies of their principals in the legislature, the presidency, and the parties.

Whereas discretion is much more likely when an agency governs a highly uncertain and complex policy domain,[7] the key prerequisite for autonomy is bureaucratic reputation. High uncertainty and task complexity are insufficient conditions for bureaucratic autonomy if politicians and organized interests doubt that an agency will execute its tasks competently, provide innovative solutions to reduce uncertainty, or command the allegiance and confidence of citizens. Absent both complexity and perceived agency efficacy, bureaucratic autonomy will not prevail.[8]

A semantic dilemma remains. Can an agency be truly autonomous when its latitude of operation and choice depend on legislative, presidential, and judicial recognition of its capacity and political power? For several reasons, I believe so. First, autonomy cannot be defined in absolute terms if it is to be helpful in studying political history. If autonomy demands that a bureaucracy can take any conceivable action without possible restraint, then I would question whether any agency (indeed, any actor) has ever been autonomous in this sense, even in monarchical, communist, and totalitarian regimes. Autonomy so defined is the stuff of deities, not political actors.[9] Second, the institutional persistence of legislative and presidential decisions is a critical factor lending stability to autonomy. When politicians defer to agencies, they often do so through funding and legal mechanisms that are not easily changed or reversed on short notice. Third, strong bureaucratic reputations are relatively stable phenomena. What cements autonomy is the stability of an agency's reputation and the coalition that it can assemble behind its favored policies. Given wide recognition of an agency's capacity and legitimacy, politicians and organized interests simply have no better choice than to defer to agency wishes.

3. Managers and the Mezzo Level: Organizational Aspects of Bureaucracy

Most theories of state building have defined the administrative state in terms of organizations. For Skocpol, the state is a "set of administrative, policing, and military organizations"; for Skowronek, it is an "integrated organization of institutions, procedures and human talents"; for Charles Tilly, it is an "organization which controls the population occupying a definite territory." Yet none of these authors have placed organizational aspects of the state at the core of their analysis. Developments in organization theory in political science, sociology, psychology, and economics remain curiously absent from most studies of state formation.[10] As a result, scholars are unable to answer the question: What is organizational about the state? For we cannot understand the state apart from the bureaucratic organizations that compose it. These organizations are not mere sets of administrative actors. Organizations differentiate among actors, they structure the relations and contracts among actors, and they give actors an identity. The way that bureaucracies conduct this differentiation, this structuring, and this identifying powerfully affects their capacity and their autonomy.[11] The organizational theory of bureaucratic autonomy in this book explains three patterns: why durable bureau and division chiefs are the decisive actors in the forging process, why organizational structure places middle-level managers and monitors at the center of change, and the role of department executives and organizational culture.[12]

The theory I offer invokes precepts of rational choice but is not fully wedded to rationalist theory. Quite certainly, many of the choices made in the development of the bureaucratic policy state were strategic ones. In the narrative of the following chapters, Congress, presidents, party elites, and courts were rational, learning actors; they were able, through repeated interaction with administrative agencies, to identify where the capacity was. In addition, administrative actors were characterized by an intelligent pursuit of relatively well defined aims. Bureau chiefs and middle-level officials sought expanded discretion while pursuing greater control over subordinates. This narrative differs from most rational choice accounts, however, in that few, if any, of the outcomes here were the product of design. Many of the core properties of turn-of-century bureaucracies—career systems, administrative organization, agency culture, capacity, and bureau chiefs' access to multiple networks—were not the product of strategic design. To account for these properties, I turn to organization theory in political science and sociology, which emphasizes evolution (rather than design), hierarchy and networks, and the properties of learning by historical actors with limited rationality.

Bureau Chiefs and Division Chiefs as Crucial Bureaucratic Actors

No single actor or set of actors drove or controlled the forging of bureaucratic autonomy in America. The process could not have occurred, however, without the decisive action of federal bureau and division chiefs. Each of the three conditions for bureaucratic autonomy in the United States was met at the bureau or division level—political differentiation through bureau-led hiring, capacity growth through program experimentation and accumulation of expertise, and reputation-building through propaganda and coalition formation. In the Progressive Era, bureau and division chiefs were the durable managers most capable of program innovation and organizational reputation building.

Crudely speaking, executive departments are composed of three types of actors, each at a different level of the agency hierarchy. At the executive level are department secretaries, their assistants, and their executive staff. At the mezzo level are bureau or division chiefs, program planners, and monitors. At the operations level are the officials who carry out the root-level actions of the agency.[13] Figure 1.1 portrays these actors in a simplified hierarchy.

In American history, bureau and division chiefs have been the most durable actors with official authority. Neither departmental executives nor program operators have exhibited both durability and authority in tandem. Executive department secretaries have always been political appointees in the United States; they are usually members of the president's Cabinet. For this reason, they have played a small role in administrative development. They do not occupy their offices for long—rarely serving even a full four-year tenure—and their talents and experiences have been loosely matched to the departments they govern.

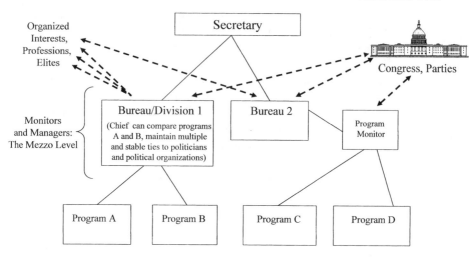

Figure 1.1 The centrality of the mezzo level in executive department politics. *Note:* Solid lines indicate multiple political ties that are stable across shifts in partisan and presidential control of government.

Lower-level administrators, meanwhile, have been patronage appointees through much of American history. Even under the merit system, although they have administrative discretion, operators have little ability to shape the agencies for which they work.[14]

Through most of American administrative history, bureau chiefs have had durability, official authority, and the capacity to learn about individual programs and operations. Before the New Deal, bureau chiefs were not sufficiently status-laden to qualify for partisan or symbolic appointments. Nor were they so numerous in the federal bureaucracy as to render them integral to the patronage designs of party leaders. The parties focused their political and symbolic appointments on secretaries, reserving patronage for the legions of lower-level workers in the federal bureaucracy: postmasters, customs collectors, and land agents. The unique durability of bureau chiefs translated into an important political and administrative asset: constancy. They were the only administrative actors who maintained stable relations with the oversight and appropriations committees of Congress. This stability enhanced their ability to build reputations and trust with members of Congress and party elites and allowed them to engage in program entrepreneurship—the rhetorical selling of innovations and new program ideas to legislators and interest groups. Even in the "party period" of American political development (1830–90), bureau chiefs were often stable repositories of administrative talent, accumulated expertise, and political trust.[15]

If bureau chiefs are uniquely capable actors in American politics, what are their aims? As a historical generalization, most bureau chiefs seek maximal long-term control over the programs and offices under their direction. This maximal control requires two elements. First, bureau chiefs need discretion from above, the latitude (given by Congress, the president, and the department head) to run programs as they wish. As salaried and relatively durable officials, bureau chiefs are interested more in long-run autonomy than in short-term power. Second, bureau chiefs want control over their subordinates. Latitude from above is of little utility unless bureau chiefs can translate it into program results they desire. And preferred results depend on the control and cohesion of their bureaus.[16]

Learning and Innovating through Hierarchy: The Structural Power of the Mezzo Level

The advantages of political durability are complemented by the logic of organizational structure. In the pyramidal arrangement of executive departments, mezzo-level actors possess crucial powers: the ability to learn and the authority to innovate.

Hierarchy and the Power of Organizational Comparison. The hierarchical structure of many bureaucracies—a structure depicted in figure 1.1—leaves middle-level bureaucrats in the best position to experiment, learn, and innovate. For this reason, the presence of a discretionary mezzo level is a core factor separating departments with strong organizational learning capacities from departments without them.[17]

Administrative learning is a form of active experimentation, or learning by doing. An agency that manages numerous programs and offices is, in a sense, conducting a number of experiments. Some divisions administer programs with efficacy; others do not. Some offices succumb to corruption; others show resistance. Some programs prove politically popular; others wither. The key to bureaucratic learning is proper inference from the ongoing "tests" of everyday administrative operations. Learning requires structured comparisons; bureaucrats must distinguish those decisions, plans, and programs that succeed politically and programmatically from those that fail.

The power of mezzo-level bureaucrats is that their positions best allow for cross-divisional and cross-office comparisons. This point may not be clear prima facie. Department executives can also make organizational comparisons. Indeed, as figure 1.1 shows, executives are the only officials in pyramidal organizations with an all-encompassing span of authority. The problem, as Herbert Simon recognized four decades ago, is that the span of authority is not equivalent to the *span of control.* The effective purview of an executive is curtailed by two factors. First, time constraints limit the effective span of executive attention. Beyond a certain number of individuals whom a superior can govern, the credibility and efficacy of control declines. So, too, does the "stability" of attention to any one program.[18] Second, the specific information needed to monitor an office or a program effectively declines as one moves up the hierarchy. In a large bureaucracy that administers multiple programs, program information is specific and is known best at the "bottom." Specific program information thus flows upward in a hierarchy, whereas decisions filter downward. The resulting pattern is known in organization theory as ecological control.[19]

Hierarchy, Networks, and the Authority to Innovate. Bureau chiefs, division chiefs, and monitors at an agency's mezzo level, then, are optimally positioned to learn. They are sufficiently elevated to observe differences across offices but low enough to know the necessary details about programs. Yet by the logic of ecological control, mezzo-level actors are also uniquely positioned to innovate. For two reasons, organizational innovation requires more than observation. First, innovation requires sufficient authority to make spot changes in a program—to engage in experimental *doing* as well as inferential *learning*—and the ability to act on what has been learned. Mezzo-level administrators have authority sufficient for experimentation, combined with the program-specific information necessary to learn from their experiments. By tweaking the programs or offices under their direction and by discovering the factors that differentiate success from failure, bureau and division chiefs are able to offer innovations and to improve the programs under their direction.

Second, innovation requires the political capacity to build coalitions behind new ideas, and few actors in an agency are better positioned than bureau chiefs to know both political elites and the grass-roots constituents of an agency's programs (potential and actual). This position is enhanced by the greater durability of middle-level program leaders. With greater experience and structural access to numerous organizations and individuals outside the agency, middle managers in executive departments are in the best position to build durable and diverse coalitions from the multiple network affiliations in which they are involved.

The conclusion here is simple yet powerful. In the organizational structures of many nineteenth- and early-twentieth-century executive departments, program learning and innovation were more likely to occur at the mezzo level of bureaucratic hierarchy—among managers and program monitors—than at either the executive level or at the program/operations level.[20]

My argument for the primacy of mezzo-level bureaucrats is not entirely new. Nor is its strength limited to government agencies. At the center of Alfred Chandler's classic argument in *The Visible Hand* is a claim that middle-level managers made possible the efficiency gains in the multidivisional business enterprises that dominated late-nineteenth-century industry in the United States. As Chandler argues, "[T]he producing and distributing units within a modern business enterprise [were] monitored and coordinated by middle managers." Without a mezzo level, Chandler argues, a "multiunit enterprise . . . remains little more than a federation of autonomous offices." Chandler also emphasizes the organizational distinctiveness of the middle managers. Much like mezzo-level innovators in the federal bureaucracy, middle managers in American railroads "had the time, the information, and, above all, the long-term commitment to the road in a way that was not often true of the investors and their representatives on the board."[21]

Bureaucratic Culture and the Role of Executives

Incentives and organizational structure surely account for many bureaucratic outcomes. Yet these factors do not exhaustively explain the forging of bureaucratic autonomy. The identification of bureaucrats with their organizations rather than with parties, localities, or professions, the steps through which agencies acquired reputations among political elites, and the constraints on bureaucratic autonomy—these critical elements of the forging process cannot be properly understood without reference to organizational culture.

Bureaucratic culture is the metaphorical complex of language and symbols which defines the self-understanding of an agency as well as the view of the agency which prevails among those actors who oversee and interact with it. In bureaucratic culture internal organizational communities and external bureaucratic reputations are fused. The same metaphor informs both.[22]

A bureaucracy's culture is a metaphor or set of metaphors that constructs an analogy between the actual organization and a model organization. The analogy allows members, clients, overseers, and others who interact with the organization to understand it in a simplified way. These actors can reconceptualize the actual organization as another, simpler entity: a team, an army, a school, a church, a brotherhood, a machine, or a business. The conceptual structure of organizational metaphors is more complicated than this simple analogy, however. In particular, the model organization has an implied hierarchy, and it carries a portrait of the ideal-typical member, a portrait constructed of ideal-typical traits or organizational "virtues."[23]

As a clarifying example, consider the most common metaphor prevailing in late-twentieth-century organizations: the athletic team. The team metaphor is powerful for two reasons: it is simple and it holds enormous social currency. The statement "this organization is a team" connotes a participatory ethic in which all members of the organization share in its processes and in its outcomes (the whole team plays, and the whole team wins or loses). This is an enormous and inaccurate simplification of the decision-making patterns in contemporary organizations, of course, but the team metaphor's power is a direct (and largely increasing) function of this crudity. Its force is only enhanced by the pervasive cultural presence of athletics in American society. In addition, the team metaphor carries two other sets of implications: authority and virtue. Teams have coaches, captains, and quarterbacks—they carry an implicit hierarchy in which some members lead and others follow. Moreover, team membership demands virtues such as persistence (as in "winners never quit") and a sacrifice of individual aims, such that the ideal member of the organization as team is a "team player."

In contrast to others who have written on this subject, I do not believe that every organization is characterized by a culture. A culture results when a sufficiently large number of organizational members "buy into" a metaphor such that their identification with the organization is governed by it. A bureaucracy may then lack a culture if employees and clients do not feel inclined to "consume" any of the available metaphors, or when there are so many contending metaphors that none of them can take hold. In other words, metaphors alone cannot create organizational cultures. Two other factors—executive leadership and the institutional and structural foundations of culture—determine the variation in the strength of cultures across agencies.[24]

No bureaucratic actors are better positioned than department executives to articulate organizational metaphors. Department executives set the agenda in culture building. Their leadership consists of finding and articulating metaphors that work in diverse organizations, symbols that invoke the common good of the agency and the nation. Beyond this, executives also team with bureau and division chiefs to form policy coalitions with organized interests, party elites, members of Congress, and the press. Department executives are critical in the rhetorical and network-based selling of their agencies' program innovations.

Organizational structure matters because metaphors require a receptive audience. Where departments are characterized by a high degree of social homogeneity, and where career similarity leads bureaucrats to perceive themselves as having common pasts and common expected futures, cohesive organizational cultures are more likely to arise. The personnel recruitment process—the institutional rules and networks that shape who gets hired by an agency—determines the kinds of individuals who select themselves (and who are selected) into employment. And the features of the agency's career system determine the extent to which an agency's employees will have similar or disparate career experiences.

If the presence of culture and its strength vary across bureaucracies, what, then, is the force of this culture for bureaucratic outcomes? What do cultural metaphors do? Organizational metaphors have differentiating and enabling properties. First, these metaphors demarcate bureaucracies from one another and from other organizations in their policy domain. Second, they can strengthen bureaucracies by the cohesion, coordination, and commitment they foster among agency personnel. These dual features of bureaucratic culture account for its causal relationship to bureaucratic autonomy and administrative capacity. The differentiating properties of culture help satisfy the first necessary condition, political distinction. The enabling properties of culture help satisfy the second condition, organizational capacity. The degree to which bureaucratic cultures either differentiate or enable is an increasing function of their simplifying power. By intimating that "this agency is an army" or "this department is a university," bureaucratic culture allows the diverse people who work for or interact with agencies to make sense of bureaucracies.

The differentiating properties of bureaucratic culture have another important role in organizational change, one that figured critically in the forging of bureaucratic autonomy in the United States. Because important bureaucratic entrepreneurs who altered the preferences of their organizations could not remain forever in their positions, bureaucratic culture was an important mechanism of stabilizing and locking in these preferences for the future. In different ways, Gifford Pinchot and Anthony Comstock understood that culture can stabilize preference change in organizations.[25]

4. Selection, Socialization, and Political Differentiation

Bureaucratic autonomy is a hollow proposition if the preferences or interests of administrative actors are reducible to those of the legislative, executive, and organized political interests who may attempt to control agencies. Numerous scholars—from Skocpol, Skowronek, Nordlinger, and Offe to many formal theorists—have observed that state autonomy requires that the preferences of state officials not be mapped cleanly to those of "society"—of powerful social interests and organized groups. As Skocpol lucidly argues, states are

> sites of autonomous action, not reducible to the demands or preferences of any social group. Both appointed and elected officials have ideas and organizational and career interests of their own, and they devise and work for policies that will further those ideas and interests, or at least not harm them.[26]

Political Differentiation as the Irreducibility of Preferences

Bureaucratic preferences are irreducible only if they are distinct both from societal preferences and from the preferences of elected officials. Historically, such a divergence of interests is rare. The problem with Skocpol's argument is that in modern representative governments, organized interests have many tools with which to shape the composition of the bureaucracy. It is precisely because agencies have the authority and resources that they do that organized interests expend so much time, money, and effort in influencing bureaucratic choice and in securing favorable appointments. In representative regimes, the authority and resource endowments of state organizations are, by themselves, insufficient conditions for the emergence of preference irreducibility.

Yet when conceived as a necessary condition for bureaucratic autonomy, preference divergence is rather helpful. To the degree that bureaucratic ideologies can be reduced to those of dominant social classes, organized interests, or legislative coalitions, any bureaucracy is less autonomous from these entities in the range of actions we can expect it to consider and take. How then can agencies become politically differentiated? My argument points to three factors—the multiple networks of bureau chiefs, administrative selection, and the cultural socialization of career officials.[27]

Merit Reform, Multiple Networks, and the Ascendance of Bureau Chiefs in Recruitment

The differentiation of American bureaucracies begins with bureau chiefs, and nowhere more significantly, as they occupy a central role in hiring, innovation, and political coalition building. Their possession of this role is due to civil service reform, a pattern of institutional changes that substituted merit criteria (such as competitive examinations) for partisanship in government hiring. The United States adopted such a merit system in the Pendleton Act of 1883.[28]

The key facet of merit reform is not that it replaces partisanship with test-passing "neutrality," but that it substitutes decentralized bureau-based hiring for centralized, party-based hiring. In the United States, as elsewhere, merit criteria rarely, if ever, dictate the exact choice of employees for agencies. Instead, civil service exams and entrance requirements merely narrow the pool of applicants from which agency leaders will eventually select. This procedural power over agency hiring allows career agency leaders to mold bureaus according to their preferences. Moreover, merit reform has another feature that stabilizes any drift of agency preferences: tenure. Once bureau chiefs have hired an employee, civil service protections restrict politically based dismissals. The tenure provisions of merit reform mean that any degree of differentiation in agency leadership will stick.[29]

In few agencies, however, do bureau chiefs translate their authority into differentiated bureaus. In many cases, bureau chiefs do not have preferences that depart from those of an agency's governing politicians and organized interests. Yet even when bureau leaders' preferences are distinctive, they need two mechanisms to shape a bureau to their liking. First, bureau chiefs must have access to networks that differ from those of the agency's governing coalition. Numerous scholars in bureaucratic politics have noted how bureau chiefs seek out potential applicants through educational, professional, class, and friendship networks. Officials look in their communities of origin, in the schools they have attended, and in the companies for which they have worked. By these means, bureau chiefs influence the self-selection and entry of individuals into the agency's applicant pool. Second, these hiring networks must be supported by an agency culture that can serve as a screening mechanism to ensure that new hires will behave in ways that agency leaders want them to. Bureau chiefs can define ideal-typical employees according to their "fit" with the dominant agency culture. Potential employees can then assess their fit with the agency by the same cultural criteria.[30]

Career-based socialization can reinforce the political differentiation of an agency. Herbert Kaufman's *Forest Ranger* offers an excellent example of how agency leaders can shape careers so as to enhance loyalty to their bureaucratic objectives. Upon their entrance into the Forest Service, new employees are gradually steeped in a culture of identification with the agency. The Forest Service consciously observes a pattern of seeking and hiring younger applicants, and these entering officials perform apprenticeship work in a mentoring relationship with their superiors. This process continues in the form of career development where career tracks and status rewards encourage employees to identify and remain with their agencies.[31]

These patterns of network selection and socialization will hardly surprise students of comparative bureaucratic development. At the dawn of the twentieth century, the state bureaucracies of industrialized democracies recruited extensively through class and educational networks. In France the system of *grandes écoles,* inaugurated in the Napoleonic period but legally entrenched in the Third Republic (1871–1900),[32] became the principal supplier of higher-level civil servants to national ministries. The *écoles* narrowed the pathways of entry into the civil service and produced a corps of officials with similar educational and career experiences. In Meiji Japan (1868–1900), as in France, formal educational-career trajectories restricted entry into the national ministries. Although a system of open competitive examinations was instituted in 1894, political leaders had already established "an almost total dependence on Tokyo Imperial University as the source for new recruitment to the upper civil service after 1887." Yet unlike the French Third Republic, as Bernard Silberman has argued, the recruitment of higher civil servants was also network based. Meiji elites recruited through class and local acquaintance networks to find officials with ideologies similar to their own. They forged a leadership structure with a high degree of consensus.[33] A similar pattern prevailed in nineteenth-century Britain, where recruitment through elite "public school" networks and through Oxford and Cambridge Universities gave to the national ministries a "generalist" outlook and a broadly conservative ideology. As in Japan (but unlike France), these recruitment patterns were not formalized. In all three nations, according to scholars, these selection patterns strongly affected public policy.[34]

5. Networks and the Genesis of Organizational Capacity

The capacities of modern states are diverse and numerous. States are defined by their monopoly over the power of coercion, as well as by their abilities to extract and to appropriate resources. Yet it is plain that bureaucracies in America and elsewhere now engage in patterns of action that no state could have fathomed two centuries ago. Bureaucratic states forecast, plan, gather, and analyze intricate statistical information, and they execute complex programs. To form, twentieth-century agencies have depended most critically on two types of capacity: *analytic* (or informational) and *programmatic* (or planning). Informational capacity is the power to analyze social problems, what Hugh Heclo has called the ability to "collectively puzzle" over national dilemmas. For Heclo, informational capacity is the basis of administrative power in modern states.

> Even [successful] increases in administrative power have had as their basis less the ability to issue authoritative commands than the capacity to draw upon administrative resources of information, analysis and expertise for new policy lessons and appropriate conclusions on increasingly complex issues.[35]

For other programs, such as welfare administration, the informational demands of bureaucratic tasks may be less daunting. When national bureaucracies engage in service delivery—postal services, benefit and insurance programs, and the like—significant programmatic complexities can emerge in addition to those posed by informational complexity. Programmatic capacity is the ability of the bureaucracy to carry out programs in accordance with a previously specified plan. It is the ability to utilize information and forecasting to plan and to execute plans in rationalized form. In a sense, programmatic capacity is the agency's knowledge of its own capabilities and limitations, the efficacy and flexibility of its standard operating procedures.[36]

Why do these capacities differ so starkly across agencies and over time? Surely administrative design by elected authorities provides one answer to this question. Some agencies are designed to be providers of information, others to be distributors of tangible benefits to powerful constituencies. Some agencies are created to respond to national crises, others to satisfy the demands of organized interests. Some agencies have sufficient fiscal resources, given by Congress and the president, to expand programs and hire technical experts.

There are limits, however, to the ability of elected authorities to hard-wire capacity into an agency. Bureaucratic capacity is first and foremost a function of organizational evolution. Neither formal authority nor spending suffices to create an organizational ability to discover and solve problems. Simply put, bureaucratic problem solving and policy analysis require that the agency attract problem solvers and analysts to its ranks and retain them for long periods. Neither law nor appropriations alone can attract such officials to an agency or keep them there. Historical examples abound of agencies with all the formal and resource-based components of capacity—rapidly growing budgets and workforces, statutory requirements to hire more technicians or scientists, or a statutory provision to execute a feasible plan or study in order to improve a program —which nonetheless lacked planning capacity, innovation, and administrative cohesion. The Department of Interior in the late nineteenth century, the Inter-state Commerce Commission after 1900, and the Department of Commerce in the 1920s are several examples of these cases.[37]

If strategic design cannot account for historical differences in bureaucratic capacity, then what about organizational evolution does? I point to the emer-gence of two factors: a mezzo level of managers and inspectors that integrated turn-of-century bureaucracies, and organizational networks that assisted re-cruitment and reduced turnover among personnel.

The Attraction and Retention of Analytic Capacity

Informational and programmatic capacity depend on the ability of bureaucra-cies to attract, keep, and secure the commitment of skilled technical and ad-ministrative personnel.[38] Although many agencies suffer from too little turnover and the rigidity that may result from this stasis, high turnover is usu-ally more damaging. Among policy analysts, experts, and technicians, high turnover can be quite damaging to agency capacity. Officials with longer tenure, rising to authority within their bureaus (with experience at many different lev-els), possess enhanced leadership skills and the ability to solve organizational dilemmas. Longer-tenured officials possess a better sense of the history of their programs and are better able to make comparisons over time. In other words, bureaus with lower turnover rates are usually better equipped to learn.

The Solution of Networks

Because they compete with private-sector and nonprofit firms for skilled offi-cials, government agencies often face acute challenges in attracting and keep-ing talent.[39] For some agencies, however, a solution to this dilemma emerges from a network-based employment rotary among universities, professional as-sociations, corporate industry, and middle-level bureaucrats. Where profes-sions, guilds, or certain schools hold a monopoly over particular forms of ex-pertise, their acquaintance ties (or "weak ties") to government bureaucracies can be an important well of talent for the state. As Skocpol has argued, state ca-pacity depends on "historically *evolved* relationships among elite educational institutions, state organizations, and private enterprises that compete with the state for educated personnel." Again, because they are the durable career offi-cials in federal agencies, middle-level managers and monitors hold the central positions in these networks.[40]

Networks of attachment also reduce turnover, but less through "weak-tie" circuits of acquaintance than through "strong-tie" patterns of collaboration. Co-operative work patterns forged through informal apprenticeships—such as a re-

search venture, cooperative manual labor, or political teamwork when building
a new program—can inspire organizational attachments. When officials establish long-term working relations with their colleagues, they develop attachments both to their fellow officials and to their bureaus as structured contexts
of collaboration.[41]

6. Entrepreneurship, Experiment, and Coalitions of Esteem

The greatest obstacle to bureaucratic autonomy lies in American political culture. Before 1900, most Americans simply did not believe in the capacity of
most government agencies to ameliorate national economic and social dilemmas. The transcendence of this cultural constraint began with bureaucratic entrepreneurship: the incremental selling of new program ideas through experimentation and piecemeal coalition building.

Bureaucratic Entrepreneurship through Coalition Building
and Incremental Program Expansion

Delegation is a risky venture. For politicians to empower an agency to launch
a new program, or to defer to its ongoing policy innovations, is to invite political jeopardy. Funds may be wasted. A program with ambitious aims may fall
prey to corruption or capture. Agencies may take a program aimed at one constituency and redirect its benefits to another. Or a program may succumb to bureaucratic inertia.[42]

The development of bureaucratic program innovation, and eventually autonomy, requires the transcendence of these doubts. Agency leaders must persuade politicians to take risks. In practice, this institutional trust building requires one of two beliefs. First, politicians must believe that the agency can
organize a system of administration that will satisfy their wishes, at least in part.
Whether the aims of the program are distributive or collective, legislators and
the organized public need to be convinced that the agency can deliver on the
promises of its innovations. Second, the agency is further empowered when
politicians and organized interests believe that it is capable of creating new programs that better their fortunes in previously unforeseen ways. In the early 1900s,
this faith in bureaucratic "progressiveness" was crucial to program evolution.

Bureaucratic entrepreneurship is the process by which agency leaders experiment with new programs or introduce innovations to existing programs and
gradually convince diverse coalitions of organized interests, the media, and
politicians of the value of their ideas and their bureaus. It consists of two components: incremental program development and the assembly of network-based
political coalitions for the passage of program laws. As Richard Bensel has ar-

gued, independent coalition building is a central feature of bureaucratic autonomy and state capacity.

> [W]hen the structural principles associated with bureaucratic autonomy are satisfied, state bureaucracies are said to possess "administrative capacity." State agents within such bureaus are theoretically able to effectively exploit political opportunities for further societal penetration by, for example, creating and leading political coalitions that support further enhancement of central state authority.[43]

The Strategy of Incrementalism. Bureaucratic entrepreneurship appears in many contexts but has a common narrative. Agency officials frequently use program "experiments" to erect slowly two bases of autonomy: (1) beliefs in program efficacy and agency uniqueness and (2) coalitions of diverse actors who value the agency's services and who support agency moves.[44] When officials launch experimental programs, incrementalism is wise because it reduces the risks of trial and error. When officials take small steps in building a program, any errors they make are correspondingly smaller and more reversible. Rapid program expansion early in the life of a new idea, by contrast, risks program death by dint of early errors that are magnified by the program's larger scope. Incrementalism, then, allows an otherwise "good" idea to fail early on and still survive.

Incremental program development, then, allows bureau leaders to demonstrate the capacity of their organizations. Yet demonstrating capacity forms only part of the story of entrepreneurship. Incrementalism also helps build the multiple networks that support agency reputations and coalitions for new program ideas. If an idea flows from an agency's truly differentiated preferences, then it is not likely to have support early on. Program managers need time to bring different organizations and individuals aboard the coalition and to publicize the unique services their agency offers. Indeed, the greater the multiplicity of the networks that eventually underlie an agency's innovation, the more time it will take to build these networks. For an agency to round up all relevant business groups on a given issue takes some time; to round up farm groups, women's groups, *and* business groups surely takes more. Multidimensional politics takes more time (and more steps) than single-issue politics.[45]

Because incremental entrepreneurship takes time, it is hardly surprising that its most common and successful practitioners lie at the middle (or upper "careerist") level of the bureaucracy. Bureau chiefs, when they have sufficiently long tenures and ties in multiple networks, acquire the power to assemble coalitions around their fledgling programs. The durability of these leaders allows them to build trust-laden relations with civic organizations, political elites, professions, congressional committees, and presidents. After sustained political experimentation, agency officials seek allies in the presidency and the legislature who will introduce legislation to give their burgeoning programs statutory permanence. Their authority and their access to the president, Congress, party officials, and organized interest groups give them a unique ability to sell their program ideas over a long period. With voluminous reports to bolster their claims of value, and with emboldened constituencies who value the experimental programs, agency leaders are able to shepherd their ideas into law.

Reputations as Beliefs Embedded in Networks. In the process of bureaucratic entrepreneurship, Progressive-Era agencies slowly created their greatest asset: reputations for innovation, service, and moral protection that were embedded in multiple networks. In some measure, this conception of bureaucratic reputations resembles the understanding of abstract estimates or "beliefs" common to studies in positive political theory. Politicians observed agency capacity and made rational inferences about the likelihood of agency success or failure. Yet alone, Bayesian best guesses about the capacities or intentions of an organization clearly do not suffice to portray historical reputations. For although the successes and failures of agencies were observable, some citizens and some groups clearly understood their import better than others did. For this reason I suggest that agency reputations were beliefs embedded in networks.

Multiple Networks, Program Coalitions, and Political Deference to the Bureaucracy. The network affiliations undergirding strong bureaucratic reputations must be multiple and diverse. In a system of federated and divided powers, in a universe of parties and organized interests, the authority of bureaucracies depends on their linkages to the numerous power bases of American politics. At their strongest, these ties cut across established lines of class, partisanship, and ideology. Officials who hold numerous and varied ties of this sort are able to ground their agency's reputation in a broader embedment in society. The broader this embedment, the more legitimate the agency appears. An agency whose activities and innovations have only monolithic support—the backing only of farmers, only of the wealthy, only of one trade—will appear captured. Multiple and crosscutting networks support the mien of bureaucratic neutrality, the image of public-spirited service.[46]

Just as important, crosscutting ties help bureaucratic officials to build a stable and inviolable coalition behind a new program. An agency without any external affiliations will depend entirely on politicians or on the beneficiaries of its programs for political support. An agency with ties to a single clientele group, however strong that group, is not autonomous but more likely to be captured because it depends all the more on that clientele. A coalition formed of network ties to multiple, diverse organizations, however, renders the agency less dependent on politicians and less dependent on any one of the partners in this coalition. A coalition that includes Democrats and Republicans—particularly a coalition that includes Democrats of many sorts and Republicans of many sorts—is one that politicians can neither control by dint of party affiliation nor break apart by invoking principles of partisanship. Networks that are merely epiphenomenal to party, class, section, or other political cleavages will not support bureaucratic autonomy.

The reputational basis of bureaucratic autonomy, then, is equivalent to agency coalition building. If an agency's aims differ from those of the coalition that created it or the coalition that governs it, then the agency has incentives to try to create a new coalition of its own to push policy in its own direction. It has good reasons, in other words, to "end-run" the representative process and take its ideas directly to voters. As economist Gary Becker has noted, "[V]oter preferences are frequently not an *independent* force in political behavior"; strategic actors can and will try to change these preferences. The key here is that autonomous bureaucracies will court these voters not through party, and not through one clientele organization, but through numerous affiliations. When experiment and network building are most successful, bureaucratic entrepreneurship shifts the preferences of voters and citizens, and hence politicians.[47]

How, finally, do network reputations engender the consistent deference of politicians and organized interests to agency moves? For bureaucrats to have autonomy, politicians and organized interests must believe that it will be costly to resist the agency's innovations even when they are not preferred. First, the general *belief* in the agency's expertise, neutrality, and public-spiritedness must be sufficiently high that politicians will be reluctant to challenge the agency's claims. These beliefs impose *generalized* public costs on any political actor who may attempt to restrain the bureaucracy. Second, the *coalition* behind the agency's reputation must include a sufficient number of members of the society—particularly "swing" actors whose electoral loyalties are unclear—such that to restrain the agency would be electorally unwise. Hence the networks underlying bureaucratic legitimacy impose numerous *specific* costs on any political actor who would restrain the agency. The combination of these general and specific costs can constrain even the most powerful actor, including the very presidents who oversee executive agencies.

7. Methods: The Narrative Panel, Counterfactuals, and Statistics

Organizational legitimacy, I claim, decisively separates those bureaucracies that enjoy policymaking autonomy from those that do not. Yet if my argument is correct, what should the historical character of bureaucratic autonomy look like? What differentiates reputation-conditioned autonomy from momentary discretion? How, moreover, can such an argument be assessed rigorously, if at all?

Innovation, Persuasion, and Discretion: Historical Markers of Bureaucratic Autonomy

The primary marker of bureaucratic autonomy is entrepreneurial policy innovation. Bureaucratic entrepreneurship results in two forms of autonomy. First, entrepreneurs in legitimized agencies are able to inaugurate and manage programs without statutory authorization. Recognizing the capacity and political currency of these bureaucracies, politicians allow agency officials to create programs out of new fiscal instruments, even when these programs are not entirely in line with congressional preferences. A second form of autonomy surfaces in agencies' ability to induce national politicians to consider (and in many cases pass) laws that otherwise would never have been entertained. Innovation serves as a historical marker of autonomy, but it is also the very demonstration of bureaucratic capacity on which reputations are built. Innovation is as much a prelude to autonomy as it is its outcome. A dual relationship prevails between innovation and autonomy.[48]

A second hallmark of reputation-conditioned autonomy emerges in program transfer. Where a valued program falls prey to inefficiency or corruption, and where these problems can be traced to the program's administration, politicians often seek to transfer the program to a more publicly legitimate agency. Program transfer suggests clearly that interagency differences in capacity matter to legislators. Moreover, program transfer illustrates the larger dynamics of jurisdictional competition. Up to a point, agencies seek new programs and position themselves to administer the most popular and stable innovations. Indeed, bureaucrats frequently seek to wrest programs away from other agencies or to protect new programs that other agencies desire. The ultimate choices lie with elected politicians, who reward high-capacity agencies and avoid those with reputations for corruption and slack.

Third, autonomous agencies are characterized by discretionary administration. When these agencies inaugurate new programs, they often garner stable and generous leeway with which to direct resources and operations. In some cases agencies earn the rare authority to set prices for commodities they control or regulate. In other cases, bureau leaders are awarded the ability to conduct their operations with new and discretionary fiscal instruments. The essence of stable discretion, as mentioned earlier, is that agencies consistently take actions that politicians do not prefer but that they are not willing to overturn, given the political currency of the agency and the long-run benefits of deferring to its legitimacy.

Incrementalism, Coalitions, and the Changing of Minds. Policymaking by bureaucratic innovation and entrepreneurship has several unique features. First, the political historian should observe *incremental* policy change when bureaucratic entrepreneurship is driving program development. Programs built all at once are not likely to have been created by administrative innovation, with its pace of trial-and-error experimentation and piecewise alliance building. A second characteristic of reputation-driven policy reform is that *minds change* due to bureaucratic persuasion and coalition building. The decisive events that allow new laws to be passed or policies to change are not new presidential administrations, new congressional majorities or rule changes, but a process of political persuasion. Finally, a central feature of bureaucratically driven policy change is that middle-level agency officials lead or anchor coalitions that favor new or altered programs. Recognizing the political power of autonomous bureaucrats in fact leads to a highly counterintuitive result. *Bureaucratic autonomy in its most powerful form prevails when it appears that politicians and bureaucrats are politically aligned.* The appearance of control and fidelity can mask bureaucratic autonomy.

The Comparison of Histories: Narrative Panel Analysis. The primary method of analysis in this book is comparative history. In the following pages, I compare not three cases but three narratives. This comparison offers two advantages over the standard "comparative method" used in historical social science. First, much like a statistical panel analysis, comparative histories offer variation *over time* as well as across cases. A crucial part of my story is why the USDA and the Post Office became autonomous when they did. Second, as Ira Katznelson has argued, historical narratives transcend mere cases, for they embed conjunctures of events, crucial sequences of action (or inaction), and complex processes. Narratives have value precisely because they can show us what theory tends to cloud: historical change is contingent and rarely foreordained.[49]

Counterfactuals. To demonstrate the existence of bureaucratic autonomy and to provide further purchase on the narratives, I also employ counterfactuals. I claim it sufficient for a demonstration of bureaucratic autonomy in a given narrative if the following counterfactual holds.

> In the absence of the self-consistent action of a preference-irreducible bureaucracy, a nontrivial and counter-institutional policy shift (1) would not have *occurred,* (2) would not have occurred *when* it occurred, or (3) would not have eventuated *in the form* it did.

Although counterfactuals usually support causal inference, the aim here is to demonstrate autonomous bureaucratic influence on policy. As a result, I attach several important conditions to the counterfactuals here. As before, the agency must satisfy the irreducibility condition. Further, the agency's action must be "self-consistent" or coherent with its own preferences—the action in question cannot be induced by administrative procedures or simply taken on orders from Congress. Moreover, the policy change must be counter-institutional, in the sense that it is not the most preferred alternative of relevant politicians and organized interests.[50] Finally, notice that agencies can take autonomous action in several ways, by innovating (or preventing the innovation of) new policy, by influencing the timing of policy change, and by shaping the form of policy.

Counterfactuals of this sort appear throughout this book, particularly in chapters 4 through 10. They are crafted to satisfy the most common requirements

Two

The Clerical State: Obstacles to Bureaucratic Autonomy in Nineteenth-Century America

> The administration of government, in its largest sense, comprehends all the operations of the body politic, whether legislative, executive, or judiciary; but in its most usual and perhaps in its most precise signification, it is limited to executive details, and *falls peculiarly within the province of the executive department.* The actual conduct of foreign negotiations, the prepatory plans of finance, the application and disbursement of the public moneys in conformity to the general appropriations of the legislature, the arrangement of the army and navy, the direction of the operations of war—these, and other matters of a like nature, constitute what seems to be most properly understood by the administration of government.
> —Alexander Hamilton, *Federalist* 72

ALEXANDER HAMILTON'S vision for an administrative state did not, for most of the nineteenth century, come to fruition. The Constitution that Hamilton defended mentioned bureaucracies only once, allowing the heads of "the executive Departments" to submit their mere "Opinion . . . upon any subject relating to the duties of their respective Offices." Nor did Hamilton's hope for "prepatory" planning agencies materialize in the century after its articulation. The political culture and institutions of the United States systematically disabled federal bureaucracies and hindered the possibilities for bureaucratic solutions to national problems.[1]

As Massachusetts parliamentarian Fisher Ames would have put it, the nineteenth-century American national state was "a government not of men but of laws." A strong reaction to regal authority under colonialism led the framers of the American constitutional order to put a stranglehold on executive power in domestic affairs. The domestic range of federal bureaucratic action during the nineteenth century consisted primarily in the conquest and management of interior lands, the operation of the postal network, and a minute role in the regulation of interstate commerce. Moreover, administrative organizations figured little in the development of these powers. With sparse exceptions, such as the Post Office before 1830, executive departments were only quiet and quiescent spectators in national debates over policy or legislation. Instead, the power of the state lay in legislative acts and their judicial construction. The share of public authority left to national administrators in the American institutional order was "so feeble and so restricted" as to offer to Alexis de Tocqueville the impression that the nation governed itself. For Tocqueville, administrative decentralization and debility most distinguished American state institutions from their European counterparts. Whereas other nations endowed administrative organizations with significant autonomy, and whereas their national political cultures bestowed status on administrative careers, in the United States political culture and institutions conspired to create a feeble bureaucratic state.[2]

American bureaucracy in the 1800s was a regime of clerkship. In law and in practice, federal agencies existed only to carry out with a minimum of forethought the laws that Congress had passed and that the courts had legitimized and interpreted. At the core of this regime lay three political legacies: the culture of autonomy and agrarian ideology that Thomas Jefferson represented, the institutional framework that James Madison had envisioned, and the institutional constraints that Andrew Jackson had bestowed. The clerical state owed to Jeffersonian ideology its roots in American political culture. The Madisonian constitutional order placed national administration in a state of servile dependence on Congress. Yet it was Jacksonian democracy and its practice of "rotation in office" that vanquished for a half century the development of rationalized bureaucratic organizations that could command public legitimacy and secure a stable flow of talented personnel.

This chapter documents the absence of the historical conditions for bureaucratic autonomy in nineteenth-century American government. By and large, nineteenth-century federal agencies were neither politically distinctive, nor possessed of analytic or managerial talent and the ability to plan, nor legitimate in American political culture. The Jacksonian patronage system rendered federal agencies mass receptacles for the votaries of the Democratic and Republican Parties. In so doing, it functioned as a remarkably effective instrument of political control. The incapacity of agencies was also due to their curious organizational construction—usually a mixture of formally centralized authority in a bottom-heavy department—which trampled any chance of mezzo-level discretion. I conclude by discussing why federal departments rarely and only temporarily achieved political legitimacy, and why the absence of trust in bureaucracy reduced the otherwise favorable impact of late-century agrarianism on bureaucratic state building. In this chapter I discuss several executive agencies, focusing on the Interior Department.

It is worth remarking that in recent years scholars have begun to chip away at this "stateless" portrait of nineteenth-century American bureaucracy. Richard

John has shown how the antebellum Post Office was a thriving political institution that exerted a profound influence on American economic, political, and social affairs. William Novak and Colleen Dunlavy have in different ways portrayed American state governments as forceful regulators and investment leaders that powerfully enabled and constrained the rise of American industry. Patricia Nelson Limerick and Donald Pisani, among others, have detailed the century-long presence of the federal government in the western states and territories. Merritt Roe Smith has shown how federal armories at Springfield, Massachusetts, and Harpers Ferry, West Virginia, were harbingers of mass production decades before it became an economic fact. These authors and many others have demonstrated the political and social importance of bureaucratic institutions before the Civil War.[3]

Despite the value of their lessons, these works remain qualifications rather than fundamental challenges to the prevailing portrait of the political weakness of federal agencies in the early and middle nineteenth century. Federal agencies undoubtedly played important roles in shaping American society and industry, yet their *independence* in doing so is a question that few of the works just mentioned address in detail. Administering significant policy is rather different from innovating in such a way as to create new policy that politicians would either have not considered or not fully desired. The ability of federal officials to shape agencies in ways different from the predilections of elected politicians, the ability to build administrative capacity without complete dependence on Congress, and the ability to build coalitions behind their new ideas—these traits were extremely rare, if indeed witnessed at all, in antebellum federal agencies. Certainly mid-nineteenth-century politicians did not doubt this portrait, as they believed that executive departments were predominately clerical organizations shot through with patronage and inefficiency.

Reputations or Rules? Explaining Administrative Weakness in the United States

The account of administrative weakness in this chapter is unique in one important respect: it focuses on reputations rather than on rules. The traditional explanation for the debility of American bureaucracy, one embraced by scholars ranging from Elizabeth Sanders and Scott James to Stephen Skowronek and Barry Weingast, is primarily institutional because its explanatory power is based on rules. In this view, the Constitution's limiting power on administration derives from the legal constraints it places on executive power. The spoils system, meanwhile, defined rotation in office as a rule of political engagement, thus depriving agencies of stability, talent, and efficiency. Whatever the public's beliefs about American bureaucracy, and whatever the actual capacities of agencies, bureaucratic autonomy would not emerge in the nineteenth century because the rules of American government got in the way. There is considerable force in this story. Yet as the development of American bureaucracy makes clear, the relaxation of these institutional strictures did not suffice to create autonomous bureaucracies in the United States.

The limited success of institutional reform suggests that the obstacles to a discretionary bureaucratic state were more than just institutional. For three reasons, reputational and cultural hurdles were just as potent. First, the entrenched symbols of nineteenth-century American political culture disabled bureaucracy by casting doubt on governmental careers and bureaucratic effectiveness. By exalting the study of law as the quintessential prerequisite to a career in public life, and by defining the labor of government as essentially clerical in function, nineteenth-century political culture weakened the prospects for administrative capacity. Second, the most important set of rules in American politics—the Constitution of 1787—treated the question of bureaucracy not with constraints but with silence. As Stanley Elkins and Eric McKitrick have pointed out,

> In the beginning there were no executive departments—no Treasury, no State Department, no War Department, or any others—nor was there any clear idea what such departments might be like once they were organized, or who would really control them, or to whom they would be finally responsible. The Constitution had said nothing about any of those questions, and there was no automatic way of settling them.[4]

Finally, institutional obstacles hobbled the administrative state in ways that have not yet been acknowledged. In part because institutional constraints weakened administrative capacity, the reputations of federal agencies suffered. As a result, American politicians—and the citizens they represented—harbored severe doubts about the ability of bureaucratic organizations to address national problems. Indeed, Americans regarded bureaucracies as brute administrative units, not planning or policymaking organizations.

The Political Reducibility of American Bureaucracy

Bureaucracies in nineteenth-century America were rarely, if ever, politically distinct from the reigning ideology and distributive focuses of the dominant party in national politics. At their center, agencies were partisan reflections of the presidential administration in power. At their periphery, they were captured creatures of local elites and organized economic interests.

Patronage, Rotation, and the Clerical State

As the American government settled into operation after 1800, federal agencies began to burgeon. Aside from the creation of the congressional committee system, the signal institutional development in the Jeffersonian period of American history (1801–29) was the explosion of a structurally static executive bureaucracy. Under brisk economic growth and in the aftermath of the War of 1812, the major executive departments—the Post Office, Treasury, and War—all burgeoned, adding new offices and functions. It was this system that Democratic president Andrew Jackson inherited in 1829. In matters of fiscal policy, administrative practice, and management, Jackson and his successors did not introduce lasting innovations. But over the course of two decades they gradually constructed a personnel system—party patronage—that shaped the national state and party politics more than any other development, save perhaps the Civil War.[5]

The patronage, or spoils, system was an integrated structure of ties between party and bureaucracy, a structure designed to distribute the offices of state to party loyalists and to extract from those loyalists the votes and funds necessary to compete for electoral supremacy. Beginning in the Jackson administration and solidifying under Buchanan, the spoils system was founded on two mutually sustaining institutional pillars: rotation in office and party assessments. Rotation was the executive practice of staffing administrative offices with the members of one's party. At every change in presidential administration, much of the federal bureaucracy would flush itself out through the rotation of party members in and out of executive departments. In the first term of Democratic president Grover Cleveland (1885–89), more than 40,000 Republican postmasters shuffled out of the Post Office Department, the vast majority either removed outright or asked to resign. They were summarily replaced by Democrats. Four years later, under Republican president Benjamin Harrison, more than 50,000 Democratic postmasters resigned or were removed to make way for Republicans. In the span of eight years, almost 100,000 men and women had staffed the nation's 56,000 post offices. Moreover, presidents usually rewarded the most active party members with more lucrative and reputable posts. The postmaster general was usually the reigning party's campaign chairman. The rotation system thus set into place an incentive structure that accorded money and status to party activists and contributors, boosting the payoffs to energetic partisanship.[6]

Yet the contributions of rotating partisan bureaucrats did not stop with ardent campaign efforts. Party assessments were the institutional glue that bound party to state in the nineteenth century. Officeholders were required by the major parties to contribute a substantial percentage of their annual salaries—usually several hundred dollars or more per person at a time when most federal employees made less than $1,000 annually—to the party coffers. Those who refused to pay the annual assessments were promptly dismissed from office. In this way, the spoils system bore curious similarities to the medieval European notion of property-in-office, which Max Weber found so intriguing. Assuming the president was a member of the party, a party member had an effective claim on administrative office holding if he maintained a steady habit of contributing his time, energy, and money to the machine.

Thus the twin institutional practices of rotation and assessments enacted something of a political equilibrium that was remarkably self-sustaining, for assessments and party contributions were premised on party members' expectations of having a government job when their party took over the presidency. Had one of the Jacksonian-era presidents simply left the partisans of the previous administration in place upon taking office, party assessments and contributions would have plummeted. By the same token, the careers of individual party members were heavily dependent on the totality of their contributions to the national party organization.

Jacksonian patronage had wide-ranging effects. Rotation brought citizens of all classes to government service. By connecting the operations of the state to national elections, the spoils system invigorated American democracy by creating the world's first nationwide mass parties.

In two ways, patronage also transformed the federal bureaucracy. First, rotation in office ensured partisan control of administration. After 1850, virtually the entire apparatus of policy execution in the United States was in the control of the party holding the presidency. Whether in the postal service, in customs collection, in land allocation, in patent administration, or in agricultural research, politicians aligned with the president could rest assured that federal programs were being implemented according to their party's view. Of course, neither the Republicans nor the Democrats were much inclined to expand administrative discretion before 1900. Yet the ideological similarity of the parties did not prevent party leaders from using patronage-based control over administration to enact real changes that would not have occurred had their opponents been in power. It was shocking from a legal standpoint, but hardly surprising from a partisan one, when Postmaster General Amos Kendall allowed his postmasters to restrict the distribution of abolitionist publications in the Southern states after 1835. Indeed, Southern postmasters such as Charleston's Alfred Huger took the lead in this practice. Kendall and his Jacksonian associates did not have to compel their subordinates to suppress abolitionist materials; they merely allowed the postmasters' preferences to operate freely. Partisan control through patronage also facilitated the sectional and class distribution of federal largesse. In programs ranging from pension distribution to cattle regulation to stagecoach contracting to land grants, Republican bureaucrats rewarded Republican loyalists, and Democrat-filled agencies did likewise for reliably Democratic states and localities.[7]

Local capture of federal positions was a second mechanism through which federal agencies became politically reducible to political interests. Field appointments in federal agencies were controlled by party notables and civic elites with strong ties to local interests. This practice shaped the character of personnel in the nation's rural periphery—the South, the Great Plains, and the mountain West—and was nowhere better entrenched than in the Interior Department. Land officers (in the department's General Land Office) were hired upon the recommendations of local business leaders, often the very speculators to whom the officers would disburse the land. In the Pension Bureau, local pension examiners—who were charged with verifying military service by those desiring Civil War pensions—were frequently involved in the same social networks as the individuals whom they examined. Even after civil service reform in the early 1880s, Interior Department employees were appointed under a strict system of congressional apportionment and presidential recommendations. States were allotted an effective quota over Interior positions, and the department's Appointments Division kept close tabs on the distribution of hiring from states. The division collected statistics on the number of women and blacks hired from each state and even tallied "Persons from Indiana (Who Served in the Union Army)" in the department's ranks.[8]

From 1830 to the 1890s, party rotation and local capture established the Jacksonian structure of state legitimacy. Under this system, national authority was present in local affairs only through the mediation of state and local public officials who answered to the party machine. Complementing and reinforcing the tendencies of American federalism, the patronage system so thoroughly yoked national officers to state and local party machines as to render the national state invisible in community life. Federal officers lacked both a permanent presence in their posts and an enduring statist identification. In lieu of permanence there reigned constant partisan turnover, a volatility so severe as to move Tocqueville to remark that in America a "revolution" of state occurred every four years. Daniel Webster decried this state of affairs, arguing that in a genuine administrative system no bureaucracy is "either the mere instrument of the [presidential] administration for the time being, or of him who is at the head of it. The Post Office, the Land Office, the custom-house, are in like manner, institutions of the country, established for the good of the people." But Webster's laments fell on deaf partisan ears. In the daily lives of most Americans, federal agencies appeared not as representatives of the national will but as auxiliary creatures of local rule maintained by the parties. As Tocqueville observed, the national government lacked a standing human presence in local communities. The refraction of national authority retarded "the flood of the popular will."

> As the state has no administrative officers of its own, stationed at fixed points in its territory, to whom it can give a common impulse, it seldom tries to establish general police regulations. . . . There are some enterprises of the whole state which cannot be carried out because there is no national administration to control them. Left to the care of townships or elected and temporary officers, they lead to no result, or nothing durable.[9]

Bureaucrats as Clerks: The Symbolic Residue of Patronage. In addition to launching the spoils system, the Jacksonians inaugurated a clerical understanding of mass bureaucracy, an enduring ideology that allowed them to open the federal bureaucracy to mass party entry. Not until the symbolic concept of the government worker as a discreditable clerk dominated American political discourse did the spoils system truly come to an institutional roost. For the introduction of the patronage system was first and foremost a matter of presidential initiative. And the succession of presidents from Jackson to Buchanan relied increasingly on clerical imagery in order to support their patronage policies. As Leonard White, whose survey *The Jacksonians* remains the classic work on the patronage system, has shown, not until the administration of President James Buchanan (1853–61) did the spoils system grip the entire executive branch. Yet the idea of bureaucratic operations as primarily clerical was clear even in Jackson's rhetoric. Jackson himself provided the most eloquent and sustained defense of patronage in his inaugural address of 1829.

> The duties of all public officers are, or at least admit of being made, so plain and simple that men of intelligence may readily qualify themselves for their performance; and I can not but believe that more is lost by the long continuance of men in office than is generally to be gained by their experience. I submit, therefore, to your consideration whether the efficiency of the Government would not be promoted and official industry and integrity better secured by a general extension of the law which limits appointments to four years.[10]

At the center of the Jacksonian theory of rotation were three arguments. The first was that office corrupts. No person could properly be trusted to spend a lifetime in administration because without the discipline of elections, the temptations of power—"the influence of feelings unfavorable to the faithful discharge of . . . public duties"—would sour his virtue. The second was that in a democracy, administrative office is a civic entitlement. The system of tenure in office—and, by implication, the Federalist and Jeffersonian practice of appointment through elite networks of local notables—deprived the American citizen, particularly the producer, of his vested right to serve the nation in a public office.[11]

The third argument undergirding the theory of rotation relied on yet another bulwark of American political culture: the government worker as a clerk executing perfunctory tasks. The embryo of this symbol clearly lies in Jackson's confidence that intelligent men could easily perform the "plain and simple" duties of administrative office. Jackson and his followers believed that any citizen could perform the brute and simple tasks of "Government" as well as any other, and that there were few, if any, public gains to be had from seeking the best talent and intellect for administrative positions. This understanding was a theoretical prerequisite to rotation. Only in a government of perfunctory tasks could one citizen perform as well as the next. As Jackson reasoned later in his speech, private citizens and public officers were fluidly and immediately interchangeable: "He who is removed has the same means of obtaining a living that are enjoyed by the millions who never held office."[12]

Clericalism was the symbolic foundation of the Jacksonian patronage system. By Jackson's second term, Democratic defenders of the system repeatedly invoked the simple, clerical work of government in defense of the spoils regime. Senator Isaac Hill of New Hampshire argued in 1835 that rotation actually liberated the clerk from a debilitating dependence on government employment, compelling those employees in the losing party to seek private work. To him, the Jeffersonian system of tenure in office "degraded many who have spent their whole lives as clerks in the Departments, and died leaving destitute families." Even early opponents of patronage such as George Bancroft appropriated the spoilsmen's rhetoric, deriding the executive departments in 1831 as "full of the laziest clerks." Yet the full flowering of clerical imagery came in the administration of President James Buchanan (1857–61). Even before his presidency, Buchanan exalted private employment as "a much more honorable & independent vocation than to be hanging around the public offices here as a subordinate clerk." His treasury secretary Thomas Corwin warned a young office seeker not to risk the infirmity of federal employment: "[A]ccept a clerkship here, and you sink, at once, all independence; your energies become relaxed, and you are unfitted in a few years for any other and more independent position." The Buchanan administration departed from Jacksonian precedent in explicitly adopting clerical rhetoric and by rejecting the citizen's claim to office, maintaining that a mere clerk, even a fervent partisan, did not merit such vested rights.[13]

In these respects, Jackson and his successors differed sharply from the Federalists and Jeffersonians. The early presidents and their department heads saw office not as an entitlement but as a privilege, a noblesse oblige position that embodied intelligence and patriotic virtue. Postmaster General John McLean (1821–29) held that "[a]dministration . . . should rest on the virtue and intelligence of the people. The motives of its supporters should arise from pure patriotism and high moral principle." Like McLean, other Federalist and Jeffersonian writers pointed to both intelligence and patriotic virtue in discussing the requirements of national administrative office. Even Tocqueville worried that patronage promoted a desire for the perks of officeholding that would stifle "the manlier virtues."[14]

The Futility of Merit Reform. The Pendleton Civil Service Act of 1883 and subsequent laws promised to change many of these patterns. Beginning quietly in the 1870s and reaching a crescendo after the 1881 assassination of President James Garfield by a disgruntled office seeker, the civil service movement succeeded in 1883 in passing genuine reform legislation. By requiring federal office seekers to pass a competitive examination, and by protecting federal employees from dismissal for reasons other than inefficiency, civil service reform legislation aimed to reshape a more independent and efficient bureaucracy. Having been crippled in law, the spoils system was left to be extinguished by executive action, a process not fully completed until after the New Deal. As Stephen Skowronek and others have argued, however, the effect of merit reform was limited and slow in coming. Initially, merit reform did little to alter the pattern of local capture. For two decades after the Pendleton Act, hiring in the Interior, Treasury, and Post Office Departments continued primarily on a local basis. Whether their positions were "covered in" under the merit law or not, most middle- and lower-level employees in federal agencies sought and received their jobs through affiliations to local elites. Civil service tests barely touched this practice, because federal agencies were not required to hire the highest-scoring applicants. At the Interior Department, the civil service test removed only one-half of job seekers from consideration in 1892. As a result, agencies hired applicants based on "presidential recommendations," congressional advice, and geographic apportionment for decades after the Pendleton Act.[15]

Second, merit reform did little to induce organizational or national identification among career bureaucrats. Of the twin components of the Jacksonian structure of legitimacy—the impermanence of federal officials and the mediation of their presence through local authority—civil service reform changed only the first. Moreover, merit reform made no progress in cleansing away the decisive cultural residue of the Jacksonian period: the absence of any statist identification among national administrative officials. Merit reform could turn administrative officials away from their party, but it could not lead them to embrace the state.

Another shortcoming of civil service reform is that it offered the greatest protection to those positions where significant discretion over federal programs was least likely to be exercised. As Skowronek has written, "Merit service was restricted to technical and clerical workers, whereas those jobs holding the most interest for the new professionals remained securely in the hands of party elites." The first positions covered in under the Pendleton Act were clerical positions in Washington. Although most scientific jobs were quickly covered in, some highly discretionary positions remained under presidential appointment well after 1900. From 1885 to 1901, presidents of both parties removed 315 land registers and money receivers in the General Land Office—ostensibly for reasons of "misconduct," but more likely (as a 1913 report found) for reasons of partisanship. These were the most discretionary positions in the Land Office at the time. Even in the Post Office Department, first- and second-class postmasters in the largest cities were covered in twelve years after most fourth-class postmasters (who ran the smallest rural offices) and three decades after the mass of city carriers and clerks. In other departments, bureau and division chiefs were still subject to political appointment well into the New Deal Era, and many upper-level federal positions are still filled by the White House.[16]

In part these limitations were built into the Pendleton Act and subsequent laws, but the more important constraint lay in the organizational structure of federal agencies. As I detail in the following section, what little discretion existed in nineteenth-century federal agencies was concentrated at the top levels of executive departments. The lack of a discretionary mezzo level in federal departments rendered civil service reform impotent in protecting or enhancing sites of discretion in the federal bureaucracy. Only when discretion grew for bureau and program leaders at the middle levels of executive bureaucracy in America—a pattern that evolved in some departments and not in others and that was quite unrelated to civil service reform—did meaningful discretion become entrenched among political appointees.

The Incapacity of American Bureaucracy: The Dissolution of Power in the Interior Department

> The Interior Department is the most dangerous branch of the public service. It is more exposed to corrupt influences and more subject to untoward accidents than any other. To keep it in good repute and to manage its business successfully requires on the part of its head a thorough knowledge of its machinery, untiring work and sleepless vigilance. I shall never forget the trials I had to go through during the first period of my Administration, and the mistakes that were made before I had things well in hand. It is a constant fight with the sharks that surround the Indian bureau, the General Land Office, the Pension Office and the Patent Office, and a ceaseless struggle with perplexing questions and situations, especially in the Indian service. Unless the head of the Interior Department well understands and performs his full duty, your Administration will be in constant danger of disgrace.
> —Carl Schurz, secretary of the interior
>   under President Hayes

Through most of the 1800s, administrative capacity in the United States—the collective talent of bureaucracies to perform with competence and without corruption or malfeasance—was the minimally sufficient ability to distribute federal largesse to electorally favored constituencies. The possibility of employing bureaucracies to address national problems, the possibility of bureaucratic planning, was almost entirely removed from the American political imagination.

These limitations were nowhere more evident than in the three mainstays of domestic administration—the Departments of the Interior, Treasury, and Post Office. The limits of American administration lay at the core of executive agencies—their human talents (or lack thereof) and their formal structures. Within the civil service itself, American national bureaucracies at the turn of the century lacked the organizational communities found in many other national civil services. The Pendleton merit system governing selection into these agencies, although it required the passage of formal entrance examinations, never prescribed a formally fixed or informally legitimized path of education to the bureaucracy as existed in every one of the rationalized states discussed earlier. Nor did established networks of recruitment exist such as the *han* cliques in Japan and the professional-public school nexus in Britain. And finally, unlike virtually every other rationalized state at this time, America's national bureaucracy was, until the Classification Act of 1923, starved of a career structure that could prescribe standardized career ladders and foster predictability and similarity of experience among career state officials.[17]

The Problem of Recruitment

Where they required talent, nineteenth-century agencies were usually unable to attract it. As Skowronek summarizes the nineteenth-century dilemma, "[P]romising young students were actually being advised by their mentors against planning careers in government. For those who did come, clerical work provided merely short-term employment in preparation for a career in the private sphere." Even the unfinished work of civil service reform could not compensate for the low status of government employment. In the United States— where law was king, where *bureaucrat* and *clerk* were culturally equated, where government employment could not promise stability, and where administrative tasks were dominated by distributive policies that restricted discretion— Alexander Hamilton's hope for strong talent in civil administration remained unfulfilled.[18]

Complementing the image of bureaucrats as clerks, nineteenth-century political culture defined law and its study as the essence of statesmanship. The cult of law exalted the legal career as the quintessential expression of political leadership. The root of this status was law's mythic role in the creation of the American institutional order. As Robert Ferguson has noted,

> The centrality of law in the birth of the republic is a matter of national lore. "In America the law is king," Thomas Paine the prophet of revolution proclaimed in 1776, and so it has remained ever since in the political rhetoric and governmental councils of the nation. Revolutionary orators and pamphleteers like John Dickinson, James Otis, John and Samuel Adams, Patrick Henry, Thomas Jefferson, James Wilson and Arthur

Lee were members of the profession. Their writings were heavily scored with the citations and doctrines of legal study and contributed decisively to what historians have called the conceptualization of American life. Twenty-five of the fifty-six signers of the Declaration of Independence, thirty-one of the fifty-five members of the Constitutional Convention, and thirteen of the first sixteen presidents were lawyers.[19]

The pursuit of law projected a mythic hold on the nineteenth-century conscience. Correspondingly, civil service and administrative labor were delegitimized. Though the Federalists and Jeffersonians had established strong patrician links between administrative offices and local notables, few, if any, trappings of an administrative career arose during this period. Instead, political elites such as John Marshall and Daniel Webster defined a new status archetype in American politics: "the lawyer as patrician-statesman." The early legal profession had established a socially vested claim to high political office and judicial authority and, increasingly, the power to make "policy." The gulf of status and legitimacy separating judicial from administrative pursuits was further widened by the constitutional granting of life tenure to federal judges. In comparison, national civil servants enjoyed no such institutional protection, which only widened the gulf between a permanent judiciary and a transient bureaucracy in the 1800s.[20]

Rotation in office only worsened the general opprobrium surrounding administrative careers. The effect of the rotation system at the Interior and Treasury Departments was not unlike its effect at the Post Office, where, John concludes, it "sapped the esprit de corps of the staff and blunted the spirit of innovation." The image of federal employees also suffered from the perception that administrative employment was insecure. As Tocqueville reasoned, "When official appointments are few, ill-paid, and insecure, while at the same time industry offers numerous lucrative careers, all those in whom equality is daily breeding new and impatient desires naturally turn their attention to industry, not to administrative work." Nathaniel Hawthorne compared rotation in office to a "guillotine," which took not merely sustenance but "pride and sensibility" from men when the inevitable change of administration came.[21]

The cultural constraints on recruitment were compounded by the lack of networks through which agency leaders could hire. Even if their jobs offered status and stability, most agencies did not have established affiliations to colleges, businesses, or social organizations from which they could attract talent. In other words, nineteenth-century agencies lacked the mediating institutions found in Europe and Japan, institutions that could screen and prepare private citizens for public work. Certainly the absence of these institutions accounts in part for the prominence of hiring through party, locality, and Congress in the nineteenth century. Patronage, local capture, and congressional apportionment were, in the absence of professional and technical recruitment networks, relatively efficient institutions for staffing the bureaucracy.

The end result left federal agencies talent-starved. If Andrew Jackson had been right that federal positions did not require talent, then this dilemma would not have affected federal programs. Yet available evidence from the Interior Department suggests that recruitment constraints profoundly hampered the most elementary program operations. The Pension Bureau was staffed by "old soldiers" who were, for all their honesty, unable to process the thousands of applications and to distinguish worthy from undeserving applicants. By 1889 one in six (24 of 150) "special examiner" positions in the bureau was vacant, and the bureau was forced to fill another one in six by promoting clerks from other offices in the Interior Department. At the periphery of the agency, examining surgeons made decisions on whether applicants' injuries were war related, but the Pension Bureau required few observable talents from these doctors, and as Theda Skocpol suggests, they were embedded in the same social networks as the applicants they examined. Nor was the bureau able to hold on to its personnel, many of whom left for more lucrative private-sector positions, often representing pension applicants. Like Charles F. Diggs, a pension law specialist who departed the bureau in 1902, most officials found the Interior Department a "confining" place from which they hoped to be "emancipated."

> If, sir, I had not within me ambition's spark, I might be content to accept the four walls of this Bureau as the arena in which to win such victories as are permitted here, but the field is far too small to encompass my hopes, and, hence, sir, I shall leave the subtle influence and ease of governmental life and pitch my camp in the broad field which lies beyond the confines of this narrow structure. By your leave, I will fix January 5, 1903, as my date of my emancipation.

The Pension Bureau's lack of talent in information gathering and analysis left it wholly unable to manage the massive rise in pensions after 1880. Powerless to verify pension applicants' claims to Civil War service, the bureau summarily approved most requests. The bureau's examiners could drop fraudulent claims, but during the 1870s fewer than 1 percent of claims were dropped for this reason, even though as many as 40 percent of the claims may have been fraudulent, according to the bureau's own estimates.[22]

Recruitment problems also plagued the General Land Office, which managed lands in the public domain. The GLO employed land officers, surveyors, funds receivers, and, after the creation of national forest reserves, forest rangers. By 1888 the office was divided into 110 land offices scattered throughout the territories, each with a register of lands (who managed the office) and a receiver of monies (who conducted financial transactions). These positions were central sources of patronage, especially for the Republican Party's western wing. Even after merit reform classified many GLO positions, a facile civil service test removed only three in ten job applicants from consideration. Historian Everett Dick argues that for most of the 1800s, land surveyors were chosen "often with almost no technical training" and "without examination of any kind." Inspectors, too, were chosen through local networks and were friends and even business associates of the very interests whose claims they surveyed and judged. Most inspectors' positions—forty of seventy special agent slots in 1889—went unfilled, even though the department had the appropriations to hire them. To make matters worse, Land Office clerks—who made the vast majority of decisions in the Land Office, and whose decisions were almost invariably accepted by the commissioner of public lands and by office review boards—departed their organization at an increasing rate. By the early 1880s, Commissioner Willis Drummond lamented that he could not get the bureau's "more competent clerks to remain." Clerks left before they could acquire a good knowledge of land law and office precedents. Instability in the Washington office deprived review boards and Washington officials of the wherewithal to challenge or inspect the clerks' decision making. Almost every position in the Land Office experienced high turnover, and new talent was increasingly difficult to recruit.[23]

The Land Office's talent drain led to organizational delinquency. The office was thoroughly unable to guard against deception and fraud in land transactions and to protect public lands from trespass, illegal use, and depredation. Washington clerks could give land claims only "a pretence of a review," according to an 1881 congressional report. Part of the problem was an immense backlog of pending cases—276,670 of them by 1887. When special agents did discover fraud and decide to pursue a case, nothing substantial came of the findings. A suspect's political connections could often get the special agents dismissed entirely from the department. More often, the local-level operations of the office were subject to no inspection whatsoever. In many cases, Treasury Department officials learned of Interior Department corruption before the secretary of the interior did. Local GLO officers, often recruited from the very communities whose livelihoods they affected, were left to their own devices. By the 1880s fraudulent land claims, illegal logging and grazing, and speculation schemes illegally run by Land Office employees were commonplace in frontier communities throughout the western United States.[24]

Organizational Structure and the Crippling of Mezzo-Level Innovation

The other organizational dilemma suffocating administrative capacity at the Interior Department was a feature of its organizational structure. In some respects, the Interior Department's structure, displayed in figure 2.1, represented what Leonard White has called the "Great Miscellany," a kit bag of programs and bureaus that bore no relation to one another—land management, patent administration, pension distribution, Indian affairs. From a different vantage point, it is clear that the structure of the Interior Department reflected the constituency basis of the late-nineteenth-century Republican Party. The Land Office repre-

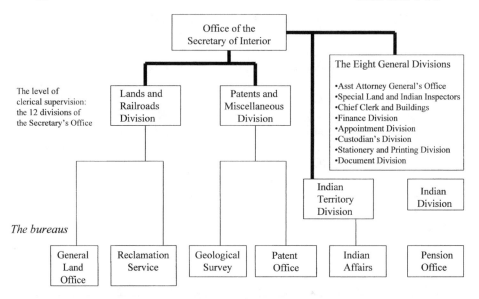

Figure 2.1 The structure of the Interior Department in 1905. *Note:* Solid lines indicate descending authority relations and ascending flow of information. Even though the Reclamation Service and the Geological Survey have overlapping operations, there is no communication between the two bureaus except through the Secretary's office. The Bureau of Education is excluded here.

sented the interests of the logging and mining West, the Pension Office embodied the program of the Grand Army of the Republic, the Bureau of Indian Affairs was enmeshed in ties to contractors for Indian supplies, the Bureau of Education advanced Republicans' aim of a "Christian civilization" among Native Americans, and the Patent Office assisted the cause of large, technologically intensive corporations and northern inventors. In truth, the essence of Interior's organization lay somewhere between the Great Miscellany and the Republican holding tank. Neither the Republicans nor any other coalition of politicians, after all, had designed the Interior Department all at once. White rightly noted that Interior's structure reflected less the rationalized design of a partisan agency and more the agglomeration of programs that were originally housed in other departments.[25]

In fact, the Great Miscellany of the Interior Department lay not in its diffuse programs but elsewhere. It lay in a system of "clerical organization" that subdued bureaus and compelled bureaucrats making the most routine administrative decisions to gain approval from several (if not five or more) administrative checkpoints in the Secretary's Office. Beginning in 1850, the Office of the Secretary of Interior spawned divisions that exerted greater and greater control over the work of the department's bureaus and offices. An assistant attorney general approved all legal features of department decisions, an Appointments Division governed all hiring in the department, and a Stationery and Printing Division authorized all publication decisions.[26]

Not until 1905 was systematic thought given to the Interior Department's clerical organization. That year President Theodore Roosevelt appointed five men to the Commission on Department Methods, named the Keep Commission for its chairman, Charles Keep, then assistant secretary of the treasury. Among these five, James R. Garfield, the son of the assassinated president, stood as the most able and energetic reformer. When Roosevelt directed the commission to investigate executive departments, Garfield turned his critical eye toward Interior's organization, issuing a summary report to Roosevelt that autumn.[27]

Garfield found "grave defects" in the administrative organization of the department. As Garfield saw it, the department consisted essentially of three parts. Like other departments of this period, Interior had an executive level where the secretary and assistant secretary were positioned. Garfield also praised the seven "great Bureaus" that carried out the operations of the department. What was unique about Interior, however, was its "clerical supervision"—a set of twelve divisions within the Secretary's Office which were responsible for the oversight of the bureaus and communications between these and the secretary.

> As is the case with no other Secretary, the Secretary of the Interior is surrounded by a number of clerical Chiefs of Division, whose duty it is to examine and criticize practically all the recommendations, reports and requests transmitted to the Secretary of Interior from his Bureau Chiefs.
> . . . The essential effect of this form of organization is to create . . . a body of intermediaries between the Secretary and his Bureau Chiefs and to submit the recommendations of the latter to the censorship and approval of a number of clerical advisers to whom, in effect, the Chiefs of Bureau are subordinate.[28]

In Garfield's analysis, two features differentiated the clerical supervisors in the twelve divisions from Interior's bureau chiefs. First, the divisions possessed unique authority in the department, exercising power over the bureaus and acting as intermediaries between the bureaus and the secretary. The leaders of the General Land Office and the Reclamation Service could communicate to the secretary only through the Lands and Railroads Division. Indeed, bureau chiefs could conduct official transactions with any other bureau of the government, including others in the Interior Department, only through the division. As Garfield concluded, "in effect the Commissioner of the General Land Office and the Director of the Reclamation Service are subordinate to the Chief of this Division." Second, and more problematic from Garfield's vantage point, the chiefs of the divisions were "*clerical* supervisors." Not only was an excessive layer of administration placed over the bureaus, but the men in charge of the divisions had little, if any, scientific, technical, or administrative training. In an agency second only to the Agriculture Department in its dependence on scientific talent, the organization of the Interior Department had placed its most important decisions in the hands of elevated clerks.[29]

The structure that Garfield disdained had a number of deleterious consequences for program administration. First, as Garfield recognized, the eight nonsupervisory divisions—including the Assistant Attorney General's Office, the Division of Stationery and Printing, and the Appointments Division—combined to hinder the quick and unified disposition of departmental affairs. Interior's organizational structure placed the most basic operations of its bureaus under clerical supervision. Virtually every decision of legal import made at the bureau level was subject to review by the Office of the Assistant Attorney General *before* its transmission to the secretary. Similarly, any requisition for printing studies or reports had to pass through the Stationery and Printing Division. Even though Roosevelt's executive order of January 23, 1906, had demanded "practical experience in editing and printing" for any publications chief in an executive department, Garfield found the committee governing the Stationery Division "without proper technical qualifications for its work." As a result, clerks without scientific education were controlling publication decisions for the Geological Survey, the Reclamation Service (staffed with hydrologists and civil engineers), and the Patent Office.[30]

Perhaps the most crippling aspects of clerical supervision for the bureaus lay in the reduction of their authority and discretion within the department. In Garfield's view, the clerical supremacy of Interior's structure rendered the bureaus not "agents of the Secretary" but "foreign organizations." Because bureau chiefs could communicate to the secretary only through their departmental clerical supervisors, they had little ability to sell programs and administrative innovations to the secretary. Moreover, the internal regulations of the department prevented bureau chiefs from communicating directly with other agencies of the government. All such correspondence had to pass first through the clerical supervisory level, then through the secretary. The monitoring functions charged to bureau chiefs and program managers in other executive departments were, in Interior, given to the clerical supervisors. As Garfield noticed, this arrangement reduced the incentive for bureau chiefs to run a clean ship: "The responsibility for mistakes rests with the Chiefs of Bureau and should be left with them." Garfield concluded that the basic organizing principle of the Interior Department was deeply flawed.

> The central fact in the organization of the Inteior [*sic*] Department is the clerical supervision of executive officers. The waste of time and effort which arises from this clerical form of organization is serious enough in itself, but it sinks into complete insignificance when compared with the blighting effect of clerical control over the work of the great Bureaus. This burdensome and unproductive form of supervision has deprived the Chiefs of Bureaus of autonomy in their work, while it has wholly failed ei-

ther to demand initiative on their part or to supply to them the leadership of which, by its action, they were deprived.[31]

By institutionalizing the supremacy of the clerk, the Interior Department had shackled its bureau chiefs. The department had a mezzo level of administration in formality, but middle-level program leaders were deprived of discretion through the clerical divisions. The chiefs' restricted ability to promote their own programs and ideas provided them scant incentive to innovate. For the Reclamation Service—established in 1902 to implement an ambitious policy of damming and diverting water to new western farmsteads—clericalism made interaction with the department's other bureaus more costly and rendered every decision subject to the second-guessing of the Division of Lands and Railroads (see chapter 10). The ability of program leaders to forge coalitions around their innovations and ideas—a core feature of state formation, as identified by Richard Bensel—was almost impossible under this system.[32]

The other tragedy of clerical supervision, as Garfield discovered, was its subversion of organizational learning. All of the learning advantages of a bureau-based system of administration were forfeited because program leaders could not communicate directly with the secretary or with one another. "Faulty conditions, which demand immediate and thorough remedy, have been allowed to continue notwithstanding the most complete submission of details to the scrutiny of the Secretary's office. Any adequate form of control would have discovered these conditions and reformed them. Clerical supervision, as was natural, did not."[33]

Interior lacked one other strength of middle-level organization. The department had only a handful of inspectors who could mediate between the Washington office and the local level of program operation and who could help root out program malfeasance or corruption. For the tens of millions of dollars in land managed by the General Land Office in the 1880s, there were only three inspectors based in Washington. A larger force of "special agents" was assigned to the field, but again, forty of the seventy special agent positions were vacant in the 1880s. Even these agents had little discretion within the Land Office— several were even dismissed outright after gathering evidence on well-connected western firms. None of the GLO's timber agents were investigated, and reports of depredations on the public domain lands were advanced to the Treasury before they reached the Interior Department.[34]

The clerical supervision of the Interior Department defies both partisan and rationalist explanations. One reason for its persistence is that it seemed to afford interior secretaries a good opportunity to exercise formal control over their subordinate bureaus. In the 1880s interior secretaries continually suggested an increase in salaries for the supervisory force in the divisions of their office but withheld salary increases and personnel boosts for the department's bureaus.[35] Yet it is difficult to see how the clerical supervision system could possibly have advanced the interests of the Republican Party. Interior's programs were already overseen by the secretary and by congressional committees, and clerical supervision served only to delay the distribution of benefits and rewards to valued Republican constituencies—veterans, Indian contractors, western farmers, and inventors. Like the collection of bureaus in the department, clerical supervision was not designed all at once but evolved gradually through the agglomeration of divisions in the Office of the Secretary. Indeed, as the following pages detail, Republican members of Congress targeted with severe criticism the administrative delays and inefficiencies of the Land Office in the 1880s.

The Interior Department—the administrative bulwark of the Republican Party after the Civil War—typified the clerical state. A department that required a more diverse array of talents than any other before 1900—knowledge of patent and land law, statistics in census administration, medical expertise for pension claims, finance in pension and land administration, hydrology, forestry and civil engineering in land management, and scientific expertise for patenting innovations—left its most important decisions to newly hired clerks. It was a bureaucracy run neither by planning nor by expertise but by rote administration and clerical supervision.

The Reputational Legacy of Bureaucratic Failure

Late-nineteenth-century politicians in the United States hardly lost sleep over the incapacity of their largest agencies. At first glance, few programs seemed to ask much of the executive departments running them. Yet even patronage-fed and pork-happy politicians sought solutions to national problems. Financial standards, agricultural production, communications efficiency, and land conservation were just a few. As the limits endemic to American administration became clear after the Civil War, the organizational reputations of executive departments suffered. Reconstruction exposed the debility of the Treasury Department in managing the national money supply. Scandals in land administration evinced the weaknesses of the Interior Department. And as the following chapter shows, a climbing postal deficit renewed politicians' doubts about trusting the Post Office Department with new authority or programs. Even where programs were purely distributive in character, as in the administration of Civil War pensions, the weak reputations of agencies stood in the way of a genuine planning role.

Scandal and Depredation: The Legacy of the General Land Office

The General Land Office was perhaps the most tarnished agency in the entire executive branch. As early as Andrew Jackson's presidency, one observer thought it was "a den of thieves and robbers, a curse to the nation, and the destroyer of morals." The office began in the Treasury Department but was transferred to Interior in 1849. It enforced the provisions of the Preemption Act of 1841 and the Homestead Act of 1862, and its mission was the divestiture of public lands with a view to individual settlement. When concern about grazing, logging, and depredations on public lands grew after Reconstruction, Congress passed two other acts that charged the office with protecting the domain—the Timber Culture Act of 1873 and the Timber and Stone Act of 1878. As the century progressed, however, the office became enmeshed in local ties to speculators and large land holders, and the aims of all of this legislation were defeated. As Fred Shannon concludes, "In its operation the Homestead Act could hardly have defeated the hopes of the enthusiasts of 1840–1860 more completely if the makers had actually drafted it with that purpose in mind."[36]

As Everett Dick concludes, the central failures in late-nineteenth-century land programs were administrative. "The most serious scandals of the post–Civil War period occurred when moneyed interests, such as timber barons, railroads, or mining companies [,] secured covert control of land offices, put in 'their men,' and ran the public business as an auxiliary of their own." Local capture meant widely divergent interpretations of the law across localities and a frustration of the aims of the Homestead Act. Settlers of limited means were repeatedly denied public lands, and masses of the best land were monopolized by large speculator concerns (which later sold their plots to arriving settlers at higher prices). As anecdote after anecdote of settler frustration and land fraud reached Congress and the press, the troubled and haphazard disposal of the public domain became a topic of national dialogue. Settlers' land claims were continually subject to delays of several years. Moreover, Congress was convinced that Land Office inefficiency was more to blame than a dearth of clerks. "It seems strange that the plan of more and better work by the employés has never suggested itself to the General Land Office," reported the cynical Cockrell Committee on governmental reform in 1888. Numerous committee reports on the Land Office's failures appeared in the 1880s, 1890s, and early 1900s. Indeed, the very institution of special investigative committees (by both presidents and Congress) seems to have been directed mainly at the Interior Department.[37]

In some respects, the tirades of congressional committees at the Interior Department amounted to blame shifting. There were deep problems in the Homestead Law and in public land programs, as numerous resource historians have emphasized. Yet in other respects, the committee reports of the 1880s were acute. They were not wide barrages against "bureaucracy" writ large, nor mainly against the Land Office employees, but against the managerial failings of the Office, its *organization*. "The condition of the business in the General Land Office for many years past has been and now is chaotic, and has resulted and now exists from a want or lack of plain, correct, business methods, and requirements, promptly, rigidly, and uniformly enforced upon the local land officers and the employés," the Cockrell Committee lamented. Cockrell's committee accused the Interior Department headquarters of "gross carelessness and negligence" in record keeping. The committee further blasted the "failures, omissions, neglects, and carelessness" of the land registers and receivers of monies, pinning the blame for delay on these officers. The committee pointed to the lack of a mediating layer of organization between Washington and the local offices.[38]

Nor was Congress convinced that delay resulted in sound choices. The Committee on Public Lands knew fully well that the Land Office's most important decisions were not being rendered by knowledgeable officials: "[T]he great body of those cases are in fact decided by the division clerks, many of whom are not educated lawyers." The collective doubt about the management of the office cooled legislators' willingness to fork over needed funds. Even conservation-minded Progressives scoffed at the prospect of boosting the Land Office's resources or authority. Montana senator Paris Gibson and George Maxwell of the National Irrigation Association said that any attempt to correct abuses of the land laws "by an increased field force as recommended by the Commissioner of the General Land Office [W. A. Richards] is simply foolish."[39]

As public land frauds swelled, and as several major Land Office scandals hit the national press in the 1880s and 1890s, it became increasingly clear that the Interior Department was powerless even to constrain the behavior of its local offices. Congress heard of intoxicated funds receivers working out of saloons, fighting with claimants, misappropriating money, and "visiting houses of ill repute" during working hours. Reports came of land registers "totally unfamiliar with the office work and without training for it." When Charles F. Conrad, a special agent in the General Land Office, discovered survey frauds in California in the early 1880s, the office's delinquency was exposed in national press outlets from California papers to the *Washington Post*. Secretary John W. Noble later dismissed Conrad, only fueling the rage of Mugwumps who with growing accord saw the Interior Department as the very incarnation of corrupt government.[40]

The Interior Department's reputation took a plunge just as middle-class and professional interest in the nation's forests was cresting. A burgeoning conservation movement stemmed from broad concern about deforestation at the hands of the logging and railroad industries. Harvard University's Charles Sargent and the Agriculture Department's forester Bernhard Fernow discussed the problem with several leading leisure and news journals with wide circulation, including *North American Review, American Garden, Popular Science Monthly,* and *Forest and Stream.* By the early 1890s, the previously academic concerns of the conservationists reverberated in the urban and rural presses of the country. The *Norfolk Landmark* worried aloud that "[o]ur forests are disappearing," and the

Farm Implements News warned of a "treeless country." Petitions and letters expressing concern about the future of America's forest resources poured into Congress.[41]

Eventually, the Interior Department lost the trust of conservationists, who by and large turned their hopes to the Agriculture Department. It was an unfortunate development. By 1880 the General Land Office was arguably the agency best suited to satisfying emerging demands for better management of the public domain. In law after law and edict after edict—the Reclamation Act of 1902, the Forest Transfer Act of 1905, the establishment of park reserves—turn-of-the-century politicians repeatedly snubbed the Land Office and delegated authority to other agencies. Even when more energetic land commissioners such as William A. J. Sparks campaigned to transform federal land policy with a ready-made plan to repeal the Timber Culture Act, establish standards for the land agents and lawyers representing claimants, and limit grazing and fencing on public domain lands, his cries fell on an untrusting audience. Sparks was dismissed by Interior Secretary Lucius Q. C. Lamar in 1888, a stark reminder of the servitude of bureau chiefs in the department.[42]

The Limits of Pension Administration

The Pension Office ran, by all accounts, an operation smoother than any managed by the General Land Office. With hundreds of thousands of claims for war pensions descending annually upon Washington, the office did have difficulty in processing claims with celerity. Yet congressional investigations and scandals were less severe in pensions than in land. As Skocpol has written, the Civil War pension program represents an early entry of the United States into social welfare policy, albeit a limited precedent to future state builders. Civil War pensions began as supplements to antebellum military pensions but mushroomed after the Arrears Act of 1879. The Arrears Act authorized a lump sum of payments to any Union veteran, a sum equivalent to the total benefits he would have received from the date of his honorable discharge from Union service. After 1879, soldiers could apply for a lump sum of fifteen years of pension payments, an amount totaling several thousand dollars (or several years' wages) for many soldiers. The act spawned an industry of pension lawyers and agents, not to mention the Grand Army of the Republic, the veterans' group that arguably was the most powerful congressional lobby in the late nineteenth century.[43]

The stability of pension administration belied the organizational weakness of the Pension Bureau. The bureau was a purely administrative actor, an agency entirely powerless to influence the shape and size of the programs it administered. The reason, as reviewed earlier, was the lack of an effective mediating link between the Washington office, which decided on the pension claims, and examining doctors and agents at the local level. In the late 1870s Commissioner of Pensions J. A. Bentley (1876–81) offered a reform proposal to centralize the claims process. Bentley offered to divide the nation into numerous pension districts. Each district would have an examining surgeon and a clerk who would conduct hearings and examine witnesses and, upon gathering sufficient evidence, forward the case to Washington for judgment. Bentley's ideas were encoded into the "Sixty Surgeon Pension Bill," which was considered at the same time as the Arrears Act was under review by Congress. Yet congressional Republicans ignored Bentley's plan. Administrative innovation in the war pension program was not a possibility.[44]

From the perspective of the twentieth century, Bentley's call for reform, like Land Commissioner Sparks's proposals of the 1880s, was an overture for bureaucracies to enter uncharted territory: policy innovation by planning. Bentley and Sparks had separately stumbled on a historical possibility: allocation of resources at least partly according to administrative preference and wholly according to bureaucratic plan. Yet these episodes also reveal the limits of the bureaucratic role in the nineteenth century. As Richard McCormick has summarized, "A paucity of planning also characterized government in the party period. . . . 'Policy' was little more than the accumulation of isolated, individual choices, usually of a distributive nature." Nineteenth-century politics commissioned a state equipped to perform little more than the delivery of mail, the routine taxing of imported goods, and the rote distribution of pensions and public lands. Bureaucrats as clerks did not innovate; they took orders.[45]

Financial Management and the Roots of Organizational Distrust

Administrative discretion was quite possibly broader in matters of finance than in any other area of nineteenth-century government. Hamilton envisioned a strong role for the Treasury Department, aspiring to make it the center of innovation and executive management in the federal government. Yet over the course of the 1800s, national bureaucracies also fell into disfavor with financial constituencies and the public. The financial failures of government agencies became raw lessons that impeded bureaucratic policymaking well after 1900.

Bureaucratic disaster in national finance originated not with the Treasury Department but with a quasi-public entity: the second National Bank of the United States, perhaps the most powerful financial organization in the early Republic. Chartered in 1816 with a twenty-year term, the bank held $35 million in capital, one-fifth of it Treasury funds, and served as the repository of public funds in the United States. Significantly, these funds were removable at the discretion of the secretary of the treasury. The second bank was, for all intents and purposes, run by Philadelphia financier Nicholas Biddle after 1823. Biddle exerted near-authoritative control over the twenty-five-member board of directors. His policies were generally conservative, aimed at sound credit and "hard money," but many business interests and speculators found his credit unduly restrictive, and many eastern bankers resented the control that the bank in general, and Biddle in particular, had over the general money supply. In 1832 Biddle asked for a recharter of the bank, buoyed by a resolution of confidence passed in the spring by the legislature of Pennsylvania, a crucial state in the upcoming general elections. Both the House and the Senate passed a bill for a fifteen-year recharter, but in one of the boldest and most stunning moves of his presidency, Andrew Jackson vetoed the bill. The veto was also unpopular outside the South, for many eastern and western state legislatures and banks had supported recharter.[46]

Biddle's response to this move so drastically damaged the bank's reputation and so rapidly eclipsed its future that Jackson himself could not have planned a more fanciful scenario. Biddle began a deliberate policy of monetary contraction in order to compel recharter, a policy destined economically to destabilize the young republic. In early 1834 he began to curtail the bank's discounts and to call in its loans. The result was to weaken the already crumbling confidence of eastern financial and business interests in the bank. As the year and the battle wore on, Biddle's confidants began to tell him that any hope of recharter had vanished. That very summer he abandoned the attempt.

The irony is that the principal casualty of the bank war was not Biddle but public confidence in executive organizations. Business interests frowned both on Jackson's veto and on Biddle's egocentric and maniacal attempt to save it by disturbing the American economy. Biddle had lost the battle for recharter when he demonstrated to American financiers that no large organization should be trusted with governance of the American money supply. Beyond this, a pervasive distrust of large corporate institutions became a credo of the representatives of the working class. No one summarized the Jacksonian distrust of organizational power as well as Treasury Secretary Roger Brooke Taney: "It is a fixed principle of our political institutions to guard against the unnecessary accumulation of power over persons and property in any hands. And no hands are less worthy to be trusted with it than those of a moneyed corporation." That Taney directed his suspicion not to moneyed individuals but to a moneyed organization was critical. The official and symbolic links between the bank and the national state—perpetuated in the writings of Hamilton and Biddle—further weakened distrust for the federal bureaucracy. There was no more resonant charge against the bank than Jackson's own declaration that "the Bank of the United States is in itself a Government which has gradually increased in strength from the day of its establishment."[47]

Yet even the president could not escape the damage done to public bureaucracies as a result of his battle. After the bank war, when Jackson and his associates restored specie—the "hard money" of the Jacksonians—to the center of American economic life, they were compelled to use the Treasury and the General Land Office to do so. Jackson was successful in specie resumption, but only by enforcing hard-money policy through the federal bureaucracy. The exercise of presidential power through administrative organs left even ardent Jacksonians such as the Catholic social critic Orestes Brownson feeling uneasy. In one of the earlier uses of the word *bureaucracy* in American political discourse, Brownson expressed his fear of Jackson's "tendency to Centralization and his evident leaning towards *Bureaucraticy*. . . . We are making more rapid strides towards. . . . Centralization and to the Bureaucratic system than even the most sensitive nullifier has yet suspected."[48]

Although the Treasury emerged from the bank war in a more powerful position, seen as a more established store of proficiency than the bank, the turmoil of Reconstruction three decades later damaged its reputation. After the Civil War, when gold and greenbacks together circulated in the national economy, the responsibility for sound financial management fell to the secretary and the assistant treasurer of the New York subtreasury. These officers wielded broad control over the burgeoning financial sector that had sprung up in the war. By discretionary sales and purchases of gold on the market, they established the relative prices of gold and greenbacks and hence regulated the nation's money market. But few eastern financiers felt that the Treasury did this job well. As Bensel reports, "[T]he administrative capacity of the Treasury . . . was a continual preoccupation of finance capitalists." *Hunt's Merchant's Magazine,* an eminent New York financial paper, decried the "despotism" and arbitrariness of the Treasury. A series of mishaps in the 1860s and 1870s confirmed the worst fears of finance capital interests. Several bungled purchases of greenbacks and sales of specie led to small-scale panics in New York money markets, and the department earned the unmitigated scorn of powerful New York financial journals.[49]

The problem, according to analyses by Richard Bensel and Gretchen Ritter, was that treasury secretaries "were products of the intense partisan competition and politicization of policymaking that characterized the period." That said, the lack of competence in the Treasury Department was not principally due to the patronage system, because financial discretion lay in the secretary's office, which was before and after the 1880s a nonmerit appointment. The failure of the Treasury was less a failure of individual errors by treasury secretaries than a failure of *organizational capacity*. Almost nowhere in the Treasury Department did there exist a permanent cadre of officials with knowledge of monetary policy. The Treasury Department and the Comptroller of Currency lacked a mezzo level of organization just as the Interior Department did. Ultimately American finance capital turned against the department wholeheartedly, advocating a full-scale resumption of the gold standard and a restriction on Treasury discretion in specie purchases and sales on the market. Financial conservatives fully doubted the capacity of the Treasury "to try to perform the functions of a bank of issue." The Treasury Department's foibles and radical Republicans' support of greenbacks eventually led finance interests to turn against Reconstruction altogether, a decision that in Bensel's interpretation severely impeded American state expansion.[50]

The collective doubts about finance strongly influenced American debates over finance policy well after 1900. During the 1908–10 debate over postal savings bills—proposals to allow the Post Office Department to manage a system of savings banks out of its money-order offices—opponents repeatedly reminded Congress of the legacy of bureaucratic failure in financial management (see chapter 5). Banking officials who stood to lose business to the Post Office pointed to the second National Bank, the failures of the Treasury Department, and even the financial mismanagement of the Freedmen's Bureau during Reconstruction. Arguments against new government programs continually pointed not to the mistakes of Congress, not to the power of the president, but to the foibles of bureaucracies.

The Jacksonian Structure of State Legitimacy

The dismal reputation of the Interior and Treasury Departments in the late 1800s resonated with a general disfavor for bureaucracies, a distaste imparted by patronage. The "tide of mediocrity" that beset Jackson's administration defeated bureaucratic efficiency as surely as the foes of spoils had said it would. The deterioration of service was most evident in the Post Office Department, in customhouses, and in the government-run navy yards. The inefficiencies in service became ever more obvious after the Civil War, when a burgeoning national economy relied heavily on the fluid operation of customhouses and post offices. These problems generated an increasing volume of complaints from business concerns in the East, and these interests later helped set in motion the forces of reform. Although measuring the exact inefficiencies of patronage is difficult, documenting the plummeting reputation of American bureaucracy after 1830 is not. Year after year in the mid-nineteenth century congressional committees heard an ever-growing litany of complaints about the performance of executive departments: piles of undelivered mail, sloth and graft in duties collection and land distribution, the glacial pace of naval construction. In this respect, the adverse reputational effects of the spoils regime were concentrated geographically and in class terms. The principal laments came not from the emerging financial sector, nor from the western agrarian interior, but from eastern and mid-Atlantic mercantile interests dependent on steady trade flows and communications and logistics networks.[51]

The Jacksonian structure of state legitimacy also limited the political rootedness of bureaucratic reputations. The presence of national bureaucracy in mid-nineteenth-century America was mediated almost entirely through state and local elites. Generally speaking, agencies did not have reputations that were geographically or communally situated. The goods and services that federal agencies provided were attributed largely to the programs of the parties. By starving the bureaucracy of officials who would identify with the interests of the national state, and by yoking national officials to local party machines, the spoils system minimized the presence and reputation of national authority in local affairs. In contrast, federal courts (with lifetime-tenured judges) had proliferated and extended into the nation's interior during the Jeffersonian period. As Richard Ellis has documented, political struggles over the reach of the federal judiciary in the early 1800s resulted in a multiplication of federal and state courts in bellwether states such as Kentucky, Pennsylvania, and Massachusetts. The Jeffersonian period created "conditions which allowed for the eventual establishment of an efficient, dependable, and uniform system of justice which could adapt to the rapidly changing requirements of American life during the nineteenth century." There would be no such consistent, nonpartisan, and uniform presence on the part of any American bureaucracy.[52]

The nineteenth-century American state was not simply a regime of "courts and parties," as Skowronek has detailed. A bureaucratic state existed, but it was predominantly a clerical outfit. The American national bureaucracy was assigned and delegated distributive tasks fit only for organizations of mediocre talent and routinized duties. The bureaucratic apparatus was imaged in American culture as a regime of stenographers, copyists, and record keepers. All of these tendencies were powerfully reinforced by the Jacksonian spoils system.

Three

The Railway Mail, Comstockery, and the Waning of the Old Postal Regime, 1862–94

> I traveled through part of the frontier districts of
> the United States in a sort of open cart called the
> mail coach. We went at a great pace day and night
> along roads that had only just been cleared
> through immense forests of green trees; when the
> darkness became inpenetrable, our driver set fire
> to branches of larch, by whose light we continued
> our way. From time to time we came to a hut in
> the forest; that was the post office. The mail
> dropped an enormous bundle of letters at the door
> of this isolated dwelling, and we went galloping
> on again, leaving each inhabitant of the neighbor-
> hood to come and fetch his share of that treasure.
>   —Alexis de Tocqueville, *Democracy in America*

FOR MUCH OF THE NINETEENTH CENTURY, the American postal system was the one Tocqueville knew. It was a system dominated by two features that emerge clearly in the French traveler's account—the stagecoach and the isolated rural office. Although formally administered from Washington, postal operations were profoundly shaped and limited by the available mode of transportation. To form, the nineteenth-century Post Office relied thoroughly on the stage-coach. As Tocqueville's reminiscences remind us, the early mail coaches carried passengers and goods in addition to the mails. More significantly, stage-coaches were private. They were neither built, nor managed, nor driven by employees of the government. They dropped mail in plain view before post of-fices that were visited only once per week (or less often) by rural citizens. And these "offices" bore a dubious identity as spaces of the state. The rural post of-fice was usually housed in a general store or woods outpost, with only a vague relationship to the department.

Yet Tocqueville's portrait obscures as much as it clarifies. The antebellum Post Office was a thriving institution. The "enormous bundle of letters" dropped in the woods on that dark night of Tocqueville's ride was indicative of the tens of millions of letters that coursed yearly through a network that spanned the entire United States. Under the leadership of Postmaster General John McLean (1823–29), antebellum postal officials orchestrated a highly effective and celebrated system of national communications. Antebellum Americans marveled at the efficiency of a system whose "progress . . . has been so rapid as almost to stagger belief," and in which "time and distance are annihilated." Postal officers were renowned national officials with a strong organizational community centered in Washington. What Tocqueville observed in the hinterland, furthermore, was scarcely characteristic of postal operations in the cities and larger villages, where the department's presence was strong and where the Post Office was widely regarded as efficient and systematic.[1]

Indeed, the limitations of the nineteenth-century Post Office would be much more apparent *after* the Civil War than before. As the postal network exploded—as rural offices and stagecoach routes multiplied, as tens of thousands of party loyalists flowed through postal jobs under the spoils regime, and as the department's monitoring structure withered—the system broke down. A system that experienced its first fiscal shortfall in 1833 ran twenty consecutive multimillion-dollar deficits at the close of the century. The esprit de corps that marked the McLean years crumbled away. The consequence was a thorough dissolution of the hard-won esteem and efficiency of the 1820s.

More than any other agency, the Post Office Department of the late nineteenth century embodied the Jacksonian equation of bureaucracy and clerkship. Although a continent-wide mail network was complete, the department exercised ever less authority over it. Presidents and parties appointed personnel far less for service than for electoral fidelity. The widening organizational gulf between Washington headquarters and rural offices made effective supervision impossible. As Postmaster General John Wanamaker admitted in 1891, the "touch" of the department on local operations was "slight." Even the well-traveled assumption that the Post Office was the "face" of nineteenth-century government—the only state organization that interacted with all citizens—is inaccurate. As late as 1890, just one in seven Americans received his or her mail by government carrier. The vast majority of Americans rarely saw officials whose primary allegiance in their employment was to the government as opposed to their party or their private business.[2]

From the Civil War to the Gilded Age, this ancien régime crested and disintegrated under the weight of new organizational challenges. A new cadre of officials arose, typified by the moral crusader Anthony Comstock, proposing to transform not only the mail but also the very terms of American culture. Whereas war-fired partisan loyalists had filled the Post Office for half a century, a generation of officials who embraced their department as much as their party surfaced. The railway mail car revolutionized postal operations, both by speeding mail delivery and by giving Washington officials a penetrating and ceaseless watch over local offices. Finally, midlevel postal leaders struck chords of alliance with two vital organized movements: agrarians and "antivice" Progressives. The Post Office quickly became the moral arbiter of national culture and the innovator of choice for commerce-hungry farmers. Although the death knell of the Jacksonian regime had yet to toll by century's end, the outlines of a new postal system—a centrally managed and morally infused realm of exchange—appeared in the 1890s in the vision of John Wanamaker.

The Old Regime as a Spoke of Contracts

The antebellum Post Office was a nexus of private contracts for the delivery of mail through a geographically exploding distribution network. In his landmark book on the early postal system, *Spreading the News,* Richard John richly narrates the development of this institution. Many of its early characteristics—a government monopoly over letters, the practice of local rate-setting, private control over parcel and newspaper distribution, and reliance on citizen contractors to carry the interstate mails by horse and stage—were inherited from royal practice under the colonial governments. Not until three years after the ratification of the Constitution did Congress agree to restructure the fundaments of postal institutions. The Post Office Act of 1792 "broke radically and irrevocably with the inherited traditions of the past," as John concludes, admitting newspapers into the mails for the first time and laying down a framework for the relentless extension of the national mail service.[3]

The achievement of 1792 was unique and lasting. The act allowed every willing newspaper into the national mails for a modest fee, thereby subsidizing the rapid and profitable expansion of the print press. As John astutely observes, the act underwrote the creation of a national market for information fully two generations before the emergence of a national market for consumer goods. The 1792 legislation also relaxed the earlier constraint that every new route should be self-supporting. It created a petition-based procedure of postal route allocation, requiring communities that sought routes to collect and advance signatures directly to Congress. Over the ensuing two decades, thousands of petitions deluged the national legislature. Responding to popular demand that stemmed primarily from the South and West, Congress authorized hundreds upon hundreds of new routes. By 1830 the United States possessed a denser and more extensive network of postal facilities and routes than any other nation by far. Americans could count 75 post offices for every 100,000 inhabitants, compared with 17 for Great Britain and 4 for France. The existence of a far-flung circuitry of distribution, combined with generous government subsidies for the press and the franking privilege, fueled the petition- and periodical-driven politics of the nineteenth century. The political and social effects of the massive Federalist expansion of the postal system were felt well into the New Deal Era.[4]

Before 1828, the department was governed by fiscal self-sustenance, resistance to patronage employment, and rigorous inspection. Self-sustenance amounted to an implicit yet steady congressional commitment. Up to the point of breaking even, Congress funneled profits from operations on the eastern seaboard to newer, less remunerative routes in the West and South, a policy made easier by the department's steady surplus between 1792 and 1833. In addition, early postal officials such as Postmaster General McLean steadfastly refused to use the growing labor force at their disposal for mass patronage, even with strong temptations to do so.[5]

It was McLean who, more than any official before the Civil War, forged the efficient national organization that became the envy of Europe. As John remarks, McLean committed the Post Office to a "gospel of speed," ensuring that the postal system would transmit information more quickly than any other institution or competitor. The rapid transmission of news and information sponsored a "communications revolution" that stands, in retrospect, as a necessary (or at least facilitating) historical condition for some of the early nineteenth century's most notable features—the Sabbatarian controversy and the Second Great Awakening, the rise of abolitionism, and the creation of the mass party. McLean was the most highly regarded postmaster general of the antebellum period, and his agency was the best-known and most revered department of the government, perhaps any government. So widely recognized were his improvements in postal service that in 1829 Congress took the unprecedented step of voting to increase his salary.[6]

The Evolution and Limits of Jacksonian Postal Administration

In the years from the victory of Andrew Jackson to the end of the Civil War, the basic outlines of late-nineteenth-century postal administration—patronage, a generous urban free delivery program, and the railway mail—were established. The structure founded in these decades would shape postal operations into the New Deal and beyond. In the wake of the act of 1792, the Post Office quickly became the largest government agency, and politicians could no longer ignore the vast reserves of jobs the department offered. The announced patronage policy of the Jackson and Van Buren administrations was aimed particularly at the Post Office Department, and the Whigs and Democrats quickly inaugurated a six-decade contest over the spoils of electoral victory. The patronage system quickly trashed whatever efficiency was established under McLean's tenure. Less than five years after the arrival of patronage to the postal system, the department was running its first annual deficit and had amassed a debt equaling almost one-third of the annual revenue.

The Eclipse of the Mezzo Level. The mid-nineteenth-century Post Office was mired in difficulties rooted in the organizational dilemmas of a system that Jackson had created. The department was without a genuine mezzo level of organization, it could not organize an effective system of inspection, it was unable to control the transportation of the mails, and it made less and less claim on the allegiance or national identification of the mass of postal officials. Together, these organizational control dilemmas crippled the postal service after Reconstruction.

The mid-nineteenth-century Post Office Department consisted of two general classes of employees. First, an administrative class operating from Washington and larger city offices attempted the coordination of operations, the management of contracts, and the setting of postal rates. Larger city offices, also known as distributing offices, employed handlers and other clerical workers who routed interstate mails. The primary functions of the central office were awarding and monitoring stage contracts and setting and enforcing rates. Second, a vast cadre of local postmasters in rural areas and smaller municipalities was responsible for receiving and organizing postal matter for citizens to retrieve at the local office. John has suggested that a third, middle level of management existed in the Post Office, consisting of the distributing postmasters. John characterizes the antebellum system as a "hub-and-spoke" method of distribution, in which the mezzo-level role was played by the distributing postmasters and their staffs at larger city offices. So integral were the distributing offices in John's scheme that he portrays the distributing postmasters as the Chandlerian middle management of the department. "Like the modern middle manager," John reasons, "the distributing postmaster acted as the principal intermediary between the general office and the offices in the field."[7]

After the Civil War, a weak and ever-thinning organizational tissue connected the Washington administration to local offices. John's argument for the importance of the distributing postmasters is sound, yet it is clear that by the 1860s at the latest, they were no longer effective middle managers. Compared with the managers of the nineteenth-century business enterprise, distributing postmasters held limited responsibilities. In the corporate enterprises that Chandler portrayed, monitoring and management were fused at the middle level of the organization. Meanwhile, most managerial tasks in the mail network—regulating stage contract auctions, running the inspection service, and monitoring local finance—remained in Washington. In the far-flung, bottom-heavy web of postal distribution, stagecoach operators were the only officials who regularly interacted with distributing offices and local offices alike. As late as 1835, the number of persons employed in stagecoach mail transport (more than 20,000) was almost twice that of postmasters (10,693). Stage transportation remained in private hands, only loosely regulated by the department. Stages carried no authority to direct or monitor local offices, and they could not transmit information reliably from one level of the network to another. In short, the mid-nineteenth-century Post Office Department lacked a mezzo level of administration—a class of officials who could monitor local operations with stability, oversee the delivery of mails between post offices, and serve as detail-hungry intermediaries between the central office and local postmasters. The distributing postmasters possessed too narrow a span of control to fulfill this role effectively.[8]

The mid-nineteenth-century Post Office also struggled to organize a stable and effective corps of inspectors. The department had employed special agents since the War of 1812 and had set aside an office for them in 1830. Hailed as the eyes and ears of the postal system, inspectors rivaled the Pony Express in their capacity for inspiring mythic tales of valor and peril. The agents' imaginative accounts of their travails—James Holbrook's *Ten Years Among the Mail Bags* (1855), P. H. Woodward's *Secret Service of the Post Office Department* (1886), and even David B. Parker's *Chautauqua Boy in '61 and Afterward* (1912)—sold widely and were models of nineteenth-century literature. Holbrook's memoirs, which helped to establish the genre of the modern detective story, are filled with the inspectors' methods, including lengthy interrogations of suspects and "decoy letters" to tempt thieves.[9]

Yet by the 1850s, special agents were too sparse, too little coordinated, and too little connected to the distributing postmasters to wring economies from local offices. The limits of mid-nineteenth-century inspection are manifest in the letters of special agents such as Quincy A. Brooks, Amos Foster, John Frey, John B. Furay, C. G. McHatten, David Bigelow Parker, and George Plitt. Brooks, who worked in Oregon during Reconstruction, kept tabs on stage contractors, postmasters, and mail theft. He took his position without previous experience in the department and with only a dim knowledge of postal laws and regulations. Echoing Duff Green's complaints in the 1840s, Brooks grumbled of the department's tardiness in sending updated regulations and information, a notable flaw given the incessant overhaul of postal laws begun in 1864. Brooks's letters also show that inspection was essentially independent of the distributing postmasters. Brooks wrote almost half of his letters to two top-level officials in the Washington office—First Assistant Postmaster General Alex W. Randall and Second Assistant George W. McLellan. Although Brooks wrote often to Postmaster General William Dennison, he corresponded rarely with the distributing postmasters in his region in San Francisco and Portland, Oregon. Postal inspection cleaved tightly to headquarters, yet Washington officials were slow to introduce new regulations and methods to the special agents.[10]

They were also slow to pay them. From the 1840s through the 1880s, special agents routinely complained that slow reimbursement was leaving them "broke dead." Tardy payments drove Plitt to insolvency. "Will not the Postmaster General do something for my relief?" Plitt pleaded in January 1842. "I have been employed night and day for the benefit of the Dept., without having received a single dollar for months." Even U.S. marshals, who were employed on a contractual basis for arrests and investigations, reprimanded the department in the 1840s for slow payments, several intimating that they would ask their superiors to refuse the department's future requests for help. By the late 1800s, payment issues had soured the fidelity of many special agents. John B. Furay, a confidant of Woodward and a thirteen-year veteran of the force, angrily protested in 1883 when Chief Inspector A. G. Sharp refused to pay a reimbursement that had already been delayed for months. Sharp responded by dismissing Furay, infuriating his friends among the special agents.[11]

There is also reason to believe that mid-century inspectors did not comprise the affable corps that Holbrook and others had depicted. Partisan politics was partly to blame. During the era of intense party competition from the 1830s to the 1880s, special agents were employed to spy on the opposition and whip laggard postmasters into partisan loyalty. Postmaster General Jacob Collamer, in a rare moment of official candor, admitted this in an 1850 letter to the inspectors. Special agents, he warned, "will always be viewed by the party in opposition with jealousy and distrust," not least because the public believed that inspectors, "while professedly employed in the public service, are in fact busy as political emissaries, and in the propagation of party doctrines." The blatantly political work of inspectors winnowed their loyalty to Washington officials and to each other. Plitt was galled by Inspector Samuel Beach's dismissal of Philadelphia postmaster Robert Oliver Lowry in 1842, smelling partisanship. When he confronted Beach about the matter, Plitt received a nasty reply, prompting him to ask Postmaster General Charles Wickliffe whether "you, knowingly, will allow any of your officers to so grossly insult a person making a respectful application for official information?"[12]

For several reasons, these affairs were damaging to the Post Office. First, the department did not have the luxury of a large inspection corps; in 1860 there were only sixteen. This figure tripled during the Civil War, but many of the agents were assigned to war-related duties such as monitoring the Union postal system for Confederate disruptions. Thus any departure was costly. Second, the department found it difficult to retain quality agents, at least until the distinguished tenure of Chief Inspector David Parker (1878–83). Between the war and 1890, most chief inspectors departed after a year or two, with Parker alone serving four years or more. Another problem is that the aptitude of mid-century inspectors was not what Washington leaders had hoped it would be. Woodward and Furay agreed in 1875 that senior inspectors had "nothing to work with" in the way of talented junior agents.[13]

Stages and the Deficit. The debility of inspection and the growing structural gulf between Washington and the localities led to enduring difficulties with stage contractors after the Civil War. Through most of the nineteenth century, contracts were awarded through a competitive bidding process with roots in the act of 1792. Contracting opportunities were advertised in Washington and in local papers three months in advance of a published deadline for the arrival of all bids. Routes were awarded to the firm that bid the lowest price to carry out the mail runs for the department. The 1792 act thus spawned a large, profitable, and politically entrenched stagecoach industry, and the department's attempts to control it became ever more futile as the national postal network grew. A partial victory was secured in 1845, when Congress allowed the postmaster general to let postal routes to any means of transportation that would guarantee "celerity, certainty and security." By depriving stage companies of their monopoly, this act struck what John calls "the deathblow of the industry."

The success of 1845 notwithstanding, nothing in the new act prevented stagecoach contractors from securing virtual monopolies over routes in their locale, particularly in the western states and territories. Contractors rigged auctions by scaring off or colluding with potential bidders. In the 1860s Pacific Coast stage companies circulated rumors that the department had awarded them all routes for four years (a lie, since bids were taken annually). Brooks tried in vain to dispel the rumors but became so exasperated by the attempt that he lobbied Postmaster General Dennison for the authority to relet all northern California routes himself. Postmaster General James Campbell admitted "much confusion" in northern California's contracting operations in 1853, and twenty years later Furay wrote Chief Inspector Woodward that the Pacific Coast "contract service has been and is now reeking with rottenness." David Bigelow Parker, the most esteemed agent of his time, was required to spend months in the West trying to clean up affairs there. Yet even where auctions were clean, few bidders summoned the courage or the capital to challenge an existing contractor. Before the advent of railway mail, stage service in Sioux City, Iowa, was dominated by the Western Stage Company, which managed all four of the city's westbound routes. The department asked its special agents to encourage local competition in the bidding process, but with thousands of auctions per year and few agents, this strategy failed. The absence of reliable information about service left the Post Office without any basis for demanding that contractors reduce costs below the level of their bids. As department attorney T. A. Spence admitted in 1873, "[T]he bids for the new service become and are to the Department the only reliable basis upon which the compensation can be estimated."[14]

Mid-century stage contractors were also prone to malfeasance and unanticipated cost excesses. Stages frequently carried passengers and other cargo, and "hangers-on" were habitually permitted to handle the mails, in stark violation of postal law. These practices slowed delivery, resulted in lost and stolen mail, and inflated aggregate costs. In effect, the Post Office subsidized the transport of nonpostal matter on stages for decades. It also subsidized mass theft. So dismal was the oversight of contract service in the western states, lamented Furay, that "very many thousands of letters [had] been plundered in that section" in the early 1870s. Then there was the further dilemma of contract alterations. Stage companies frequently changed the terms of the contract several years after receiving routes. These "extra allowances" usually implied more expenditures for the department, which permitted them for politically favorable contractors. Between 1829 and 1833 the department lost $1.5 million to contractors' alterations, and after 1834 the annual losses from allowances matched almost perfectly the size of the postal deficit. Moreover, the persistence of mail transportation in private hands prevented reformers from solving any of these problems through civil service reform. Civil service regulations could not touch contractors.[15]

The Post Office's fiscal dilemma transcended stages and worsened as the century progressed. The new profligacy stemmed in part from the rural network expansion. From 1829 to 1836 Jacksonian Democrats from rural districts succeeded in propelling through Congress a series of bills that increased the number of post roads in the states and territories. The total mileage in the postal network increased from 13,610,418 at Jackson's inauguration to more than 20 million in 1833, creating a postal deficit of $250,000 to $450,000. This pattern of largely unregulated expansion continued throughout the nineteenth century. From an institutional perspective, the massive expansion of the postal network occasioned the "communications revolution" of the nineteenth century. From a fiscal perspective, at least after 1850, network expansion puffed up the department's costs and did little for its revenues. Postal officials were powerless to halt the expansion. Although thousands of new offices were created, only a handful were closed in any year. As late as 1893, postal official Marshall Cushing could write that the department almost never closed a post office where there lived a postmaster willing to manage it.[16]

The Withering of Control. As offices and routes proliferated, and as stage contractors became ever more elusive, the department's grip on the postal network weakened. In two ways, the Post Office's centralized but feeble monitoring apparatus crumbled at mid-century. First, a system that depended heavily on local reporting lost credibility. The department required voluminous record keeping by postmasters, but as John reports, the central office staff "found itself overwhelmed by the sheer volume of information with which it was deluged." Washington officers let sit thousands upon thousands of local office reports. As postmasters learned of the scarcity of monitoring, they willfully disobeyed department regulations (often in plain view of special agents). As Plitt reported in 1841, there was "no *effectual check* upon a single post office in the Union." This dire situation would not change in the succeeding four decades. As Chief Inspector William West stated in 1888, "[P]revious to 1886 no general inspection of the post-offices of the country had ever been undertaken," and only the large city offices received attention.

Second, postmasters and stage firms began to maintain a collusive silence about each other's practices, crushing McLean's hope that the two would keep mutual tabs on their operations. Brooks found postmasters who belonged "soul and body to the stage company" in their region, but he was essentially powerless to remove them. The sum total of these factors was an institutionalized defiance of national authority in postal operations. So bold were postmasters in the West that they openly took commission-paying positions with express companies, placing them in a direct conflict of interest with postal revenues. Brooks could only "remonstrate," with "seldom . . . an abatement of the evil." Eventually, Oregon postmasters grew so intolerant of Brooks that they unabashedly petitioned Congress for his removal. Elsewhere, postmasters continued to exercise discretion in rate administration, a practice that was supposed to have been fixed by law under Blair's tenure.[17]

Although Brooks was a novice, his experience was not isolated. Atlanta-based special agent John Frey complained incessantly of outright lawlessness among Georgia postal workers and of the limited resources with which he could track them. Frey discovered numerous postmasters who regularly rifled federal pension payments, embezzled postal funds, and opened letters without authorization. Just as Brooks had discovered in Oregon, Frey found postmasters in Florida and Georgia serving in dual capacities as representatives for railroad or express companies. Echoing Brooks's frustration, he reported that "Railroad & Express Agents invariably make the postoffice a secondary affair to be attended to always last." Throughout the late nineteenth century, in fact, express companies surreptitiously plied for postal business, using double-agent postmasters to advertise their covert services. In midwestern states such as Illinois and Ohio, express companies were in the habit of allowing their agents to carry letters over the rails, outside the postal system. Railroad employees were performing a similar courier service. Even federal officials in the Freedman's Bureau, it was discovered in 1867, used the Adams Express Company to send and receive mail. So widespread had the practice become that the Post Office brought suit against the company in 1868.[18]

Meanwhile, southern postmasters demonstrated an absolute defiance of department authority, colluding with mail thieves and conspiring against other postmasters (particularly blacks) by encouraging citizens in their villages to deposit their mails with the passing trains, thus depriving their enemy postmasters of rightful revenue. In Texas, where special agents did not patroll the network before 1876, mail robberies were rampant. Nor were arrests a credible deterrent to postal crime. As a frustrated Frey wrote to Postmaster General David M. Key in 1879, "Our success in securing convictions in this State [Georgia] have [sic] been so disastrous, and our Agents, who are all gentlemen, have been treated with so much contempt, that they, with great reluctance, investigate cases in this State, and on account of which I have directed them to make no arrests in the State of Georgia if it can possibly be avoided." Noting that the inspectors tried their cases alone in court, often against a bevy of well-paid, locally revered lawyers, Chief Inspector William West echoed Frey's lament in 1886, bemoaning the public humiliation that several inspectors experienced at the hands of defense attorneys.[19]

The Distillation of National Identity. In no single facet was the post–Civil War postal network less unified, less imbued with "stateness," than in the absence of a cohesive organizational culture. Not until 1890 did a solidary organizational community begin to reemerge in the Post Office, re-creating the corporate identity among Washington clerks in the McLean era. The postwar system was bifurcated between the central officers on the one hand and rural postmasters on the other, and the department's culture consisted largely in the distinct partisan identities to which these two classes cleaved. The bifurcation followed from the Jacksonian structure of legitimacy. Central officers were affiliated with executive leaders and members of Congress, whereas postmasters and letter carriers sought favor with local elites and party machines. When a Republican president assumed office, Republican representatives were more likely to receive their requests for positions from constituents who had migrated to the capital than from aspiring postmasters still in their district. Washington office seekers also patronized the postmaster general and other top-level postal officials. From the very day that Lincoln nominated him postmaster general, Montgomery Blair was besieged with requests for clerical and administrative positions. In contrast, local postmasters identified with community elites and leaders of the county or state party organization. Between these classes lay the clerks and officials of city post offices, who directed their allegiance neither to Washington nor to state party leaders but to urban machines. A department under Republican governance for most of the nineteenth century was in fact separated occupationally and geographically by party structure.[20]

There were structural reasons that these two classes remained separate. The first was institutional permanence. High turnover prevailed among rural postmasters and city letter carriers, whereas administrators and clerks in Washington spent longer terms in the department. Whatever outlook developed in the central office was unlikely to be shared for long (if at all) among postmasters and letter carriers. The second structural factor lay in the obscurity of the organizational middle. For most of the nineteenth century, Washington administrators were linked to the periphery of postal operation only through the stage. Only rarely did postal administrators interact personally—other than by letter—with postmasters. As a result, no general department-oriented identification could arise among the postmasters and the administrators.

The flip side of this dilemma is that the Post Office failed to project a unified identity in the late nineteenth century. The structure of legitimacy engendered by the Jacksonian patronage system limited the presence of the national state in townships. The individuals stationed in these locales, although national officers in a titular sense, identified with state and local party machines. Jacksonian politics thus mediated the presence of the national state in these localities.

This dilution of national presence was reinforced by stagecoaches. Until the use of larger Concord coaches in the 1820s—with the insignia "U.S.M." or "U.S. Mail" appearing crudely on the side of the coach—few stages were even recognizable as carriers of the mail, even though the stage industry depended for its livelihood on the postal subsidy. Even the insignia were highly variable, with many stages and passenger wagons forgoing them in the Gilded Age. Nor could the Post Office compel symbolic allegiance from the stages. Its attempt in the 1870s to require stage contractors to observe an oath of allegiance to the nation and the Constitution failed. Observers and clients of the postwar postal system saw, like Tocqueville did in the 1830s, that it bore few of the affects or symbols of national authority.[21]

After the Civil War, the diffusion of a "postal army" metaphor enhanced the stratification of the Post Office. Military symbolism and rhetoric spread throughout the department, most visibly in the Railway Mail Service, as I discuss shortly. Yet although the military idiom could have served to unite the Post Office, or at least to give its diverse employees a common referent for understanding the organization, it only furthered the department's balkanization, for the American understanding of *army* in the nineteenth century was conditioned by the Civil War experience of armies as federated militias. War veterans remembered their military experience as a decentralized, state-specific campaign. As a result, most employees of the department tended to eschew any systemic interpretation of the postal army. Whereas Washington officials envisioned a unified military body, postmasters who had volunteered in the war saw their participation in the postal army as much more locally centered. The multiply refracted meanings of *army* served to coalesce the identities of officers within some subdivisions, but the department as a whole remained detached.[22]

The Coming of the Railway Army

As with other national bureaucracies during the war, the Post Office was a beneficiary of the removal of southern congressional opposition to central state expansion.[23] Montgomery Blair, Lincoln's postmaster general, used the southern absence to call for a program of urban free delivery. From a contemporary standpoint, the virtual absence of governmental mail delivery was a glaring feature of antebellum postal service. In cities, delivery was privately conducted where it existed at all. After 1825, the department contracted with commercial carriers under the "penny post" system, which allowed the carriers a charge of two cents per letter per recipient. For the rest of the nation, mail circulation was much as Tocqueville described it. There was no mail delivery to domiciles; citizens rather traveled to the local office to retrieve and deposit their letters. Local mail matter was delivered to the post office box of the addressee, usually located in the same building—a general store or the postmaster's own home— where the stages had deposited the mails.[24]

Blair abhorred the penny post. In the absence of any administrative coordination of the carriers, the system generated considerable inefficiencies. In many cities, carriers' routes overlapped and considerable malfeasance was suspected, though little documented in light of a weak inspection system. In his second *Annual Report* (1862), Blair urged Congress to abolish the penny post and create in its place a city free delivery service employing government carriers, establishing post boxes for urban patrons and regulating operations by daily schedule. Blair also decried the "depredations" of mail theft and declared "that money should be as far as practicable excluded from the mails." He then rec-ommended a money-order system using registered mail to secure the contents of valuable mail matter. Congress obliged in 1864. In free delivery and the money-order service, Blair inaugurated two hallmarks of the twentieth-century postal system.[25]

The Post Office tendered one other proposal during Blair's tenure. It garnered the least attention of any of his reforms in 1862, yet more than any other inno-vation—merit reform, free delivery, and institutionalized inspection—it marked a fundamental departure from the postal past. The inauguration of the Railway Mail Service offered to re-create a genuine postal system from the increasingly hamstrung mail network of the Civil War period. With the rise of railway mail transportation, the trademarks of the old regime—the dominance of the stage-coach, the autonomy of the local postmaster, the debility of inspection—began to wane.

Railway mail transport began informally in 1837, when Postmaster General Amos Kendall (1835–40) authorized "Route Agents" to ride aboard trains in makeshift "mail cars" shuttling between Washington and Philadelphia. The agents sorted "through mail" matter while the train proceeded to its terminal destination, and by the time the war began the route agents were employed on numerous mid-Atlantic routes and on some southern routes, though their sched-ules were not regularized and there was usually only one agent per car. It later fell to George B. Armstrong, assistant postmaster at Chicago, to champion the idea of the railway post office as a systematic alternative to existing trans-portation approaches. In 1862 Armstrong established an experimental railway post office on the Hannibal and St. Joseph (Missouri) Railroad. As postal offi-cials (principally Armstrong) considered the Hannibal experiment successful, they expanded the trials by administrative order in 1864. Prefiguring the me-chanical metaphors that would dominate postal discourse three decades later, Armstrong vouched for the simplicity of his idea in a May 1864 letter to Wash-ington. "To carry out the true theory of postal service," Armstrong reasoned, "there should be no interruption in the transit of letters in the mail, and, there-fore, as little complication in the necessary internal machinery of a postal sys-tem as possible." Armstrong was deeply dissatisfied with the distributing post offices and wished that his new system would replace them entirely. He pointed to the distinct efficiency of railway post offices, "the work being done while the cars are in motion." By 1865 Armstrong had sold Congress on this logic, and the railway post office received annual statutory appropriations.[26]

Sorting mail was a continuous process between two terminal stations on a run (or line). All letters and packages were collected, sorted, and distributed in a railway mail car, usually owned by the railroad company that owned the track. All mail going out from the station of origin arrived at the beginning of the run, was dumped into large bins (or frequently on the floor of the traveling car), and

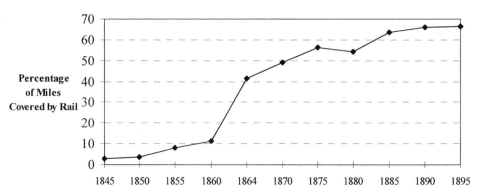

Figure 3.1 The percentage of annual postal mileage covered by the railroad from 1845 to 1895.

was sorted by one to four clerks as the train moved. When the train approached a station, the mail intended for the local community was off-loaded and the incoming mail destined for communities farther down the line was piled on. Mail intended for localities hundreds of miles (and several lines) down the track was transferred from line to line until it reached its destination. The distribution of mail along the principal trunk lines of the American rail system required a force of workers sufficiently informed to know the communities along a certain route and capable of sorting quickly enough so that all the mail sent on a train could be organized by the time it arrived at the terminal station of the run.

Railway mail cars quickly deposed the private stage and the steamboat in mail transport. Blair and his successors—William Dennison (1864–66), Alexander Randall (1866–69), and John A. J. Creswell (1869–74)—authorized the construction of hundreds of railway mail cars, greatly expanded the number of lines on which mail cars traveled, and succeeded in encouraging an otherwise fiscally conservative Congress to provide the necessary appropriations. In Sioux City, Iowa, the Northwest Stage Company went out of business just three years after the first railway mail run to the city. As figure 3.1 shows, the percentage of annual postal mileage traveled by railroad increased from just above 10 percent in 1860 to 50 percent in one decade, leveling at about two-thirds of postal mileage by the end of century.[27]

In July 1869 Creswell organized the Railway Mail Service, parceling it into six geographical divisions, and named George Armstrong as its general superintendent. Armstrong was succeeded by George S. Bangs, who is commonly credited with establishing the "fast mail" service in 1875. Bangs discovered that by securing a train between New York and Chicago and by avoiding the numerous shorter trunk runs between these two nodes, much of the nation's mail could be distributed in half of the previously required time. At first, the New

York and Chicago Railway Post Office stopped only in Albany. All other collection was accomplished by means of "catcher" devices that allowed the speeding train to snag waiting mail bags as it passed by "through stations."

Craft Pride, Metaphor, and Organizational Community

In 1882 Congress recognized the Railway Mail Service by law and designated job classifications and salaries. This act marked the beginning of the RMS as a modern administrative organization. The workers in the Railway Mail Service were hereafter known in the government's *Official Register* as railway postal clerks, and the RMS was elevated to the status of a bureau in the Post Office Department. As one student of the RMS describes the law, it established "the professional autonomy of railway postal clerks." What the law did not change was the militaristic partisan fidelity of the RMS. Although the clerks were subject to political removal until 1889, when they were covered in by order of President Harrison, most of them at the turn of the century were Republican loyalists and Union veterans. The partisan bent of the service had been secured for at least a generation after 1890.[28]

Railway postal runs demanded uniquely exacting and perilous work. Perhaps the most onerous task was mental. Railway clerks had to memorize thousands of post office addresses and the railway line routes that led to them. The service required the clerks to memorize 4,000 post office addresses, but if estimates from the 1920s are accurate, most clerks had an active and operational memory of anywhere from 5,000 to as many as 12,000 addresses and route numbers. Moreover, because the sorting of the mail was done en route to its destination, these addresses could not be looked up one by one; rote memorization was an essential demand of the job. For this reason, the RMS periodically tested clerks for the speed and accuracy of their sorting, using a practice case made up of numerous cubbyholes like those in the mail car. Mail clerks often kept such a case at home and practiced sorting in their spare time. So difficult was the test, even for experienced clerks, that the practice case quickly became known as "the sweat box."[29]

However, no test could replicate the working conditions of the railroad—the ceaseless tipping and swerving of the mail car, the inability of the clerks to anticipate oncoming curves, the intense heat and stench occasioned by the requirement that the doors and windows to the mail car be kept closed so that mail would not be lost en route, and the dense black smoke that constantly belched from the steam engine just one car ahead. Veteran clerks who were interviewed usually reported severe nausea and fainting on their first run. Postal historian William Dennis wrote in 1916 that the first run was a more effective weeding tool for the RMS than the civil service exam and the "sweat box" test combined.[30]

Then there was the peril of rail travel. With safety regulations loose and poorly enforced, and with traffic direction and railway construction in their infancy, devastating railroad accidents were frequent. The Interstate Commerce Commission reported that in 1894 more than nine thousand people lost their lives in railroad accidents. When trains pulled a railway mail car, this unit usually fared the worst in any wreck. Because it was supplied by the contracting railroad, the mail car was usually of the cheapest possible construction, often retooled from a wooden freight car. Moreover, the mail car was almost always sandwiched between the engine in the front and a steel car called the combine car in the rear. In any collision the wooden mail car was invariably crushed. And because oil lamps were employed for the mail car's lighting system, fires consuming the wooden car usually followed wrecks. Little wonder that the clerks' union, the National Association of Railway Postal Clerks (later the Railway Mail Association), lobbied for decades to have the department and Congress require that the railroad companies supply the Post Office with cars of steel construction to replace the wooden "death traps." As the *Peoria Star* lamented in April 1904, "[T]he liabilities of the postal railway clerk are much greater than the dangers of being shot in battle."[31]

Such comparisons between the railway service and battle were frequent in Gilded Age newspapers, and the service welcomed them. Stark military imagery comprised the central idiom of the nineteenth-century RMS. Most early railway postal clerks were Union veterans and often had worked for one or more of the burgeoning railroad companies before coming to the Post Office. Contemporary observers described a "discipline" among the clerks that was "almost military in efficiency." Indeed, numerous aspects of the Railway Mail Service invited ready comparison with Union Army organization. Armstrong had parceled the service into eight (later fifteen) divisions, similar to the army structure that had previously been witnessed only in the Washington office, which McLean had split into seven divisions in 1823.[32] All germane rules and regulations were compiled into a small volume called *The Black Book*. Military rhetoric even informed Armstrong's desired nomenclature of authority ("Superintendents" and "General Superintendents"), and it counseled the display of the United States coat of arms on the side of select "fast mail" cars. This last move clearly distinguished the RMS from other postal operatives, for no other agency of the department—neither stages nor steamboats—displayed such an obvious symbol of national identity. The symbolic contrast with stage firms, whose employees took no oath of allegiance to the government and whose wagons customarily printed "U.S. Mail" on their doors at best, could not have been clearer.[33]

The military idiom also suffused administrative discourse. Service leaders cast their organization as an army, with the clerks as "soldiers" and "warriors." Even the clerks' union—the Railway Mail Association—actively promoted military imagery in its writings, implicitly advancing the service's official rhetoric. RMA officials extolled the clerks as a "grand army of men who daily go forth in the midst of danger and death to a duty most severe and exacting," and "a great army of faithful and efficient postal railway clerks." In political debates and union appeals alike, RMA officials appealed to clerks as "Comrades" and to the senior generation as "The Old Guard."[34]

The army metaphor carried organizing force for two reasons. First, it accorded strongly with the ubiquity of military rhetoric in national culture. In the wake of the Civil War, parties, interest groups, trade unions, and businesses were all drawing on military symbolism in their rhetorical practice and in the design of organizational structure. And police forces, labor unions, industrial managers, and government agencies adopted the trappings of military life—uniforms, badges, coats of arms, and the like. The symbolic framing of business or labor leaders as "warrior heroes" was a common rhetorical stratagem throughout the Gilded Age.[35] Second, the military idiom had clear implications about authority relations and exemplar categories exalting ideal-typical performance and character. Among the principal virtues of combat soldiers, many RMS veterans maintained, were fraternity and loyalty to fellow workers and (significantly) to organizational authority. Comparing the clerks to "comrades in the fierce shock of battle," one RMA member appealed to his fellow clerks for "a genuine spirit of fraternity" in making demands upon the administration, especially among those "who stand shoulder-to-shoulder in the same clattering charnel house of postal car."[36]

The military metaphor also implied schemes of authority. At a time when the railway clerks were agitating for several benefits from Congress—increased salaries, reclassification, eased transfer among lines, and more liberal travel allowances—service officials chose to focus on salary issues and urged the unions to keep their members solidly behind this effort (and no other). For the association, military fraternity implied obedience to department and union leaders alike, especially RMA president George Kidwell and Service Superintendent James E. White, known as Captain White to the men. Clerk George M. Whitson wrote to his fellow association members expressing his hope that the union would assist the department's efforts: "[L]et us hope that with a united postal fraternity doing its full duty, the cause championed by our grand old Captain will triumph." RMS veteran Clark E. Carr observed that White had imparted a military spirit to the service. "Captain White was a patriotic Union soldier in the Civil War and was wounded in his country's service," Carr wrote. "In his career as a postal official, through the grades of the railway mail service, he has imbued and maintained among all those in his department an *esprit de corps*."[37]

The Railway Mail Service, then, evinced a unique organizational solidarity in the national postal system. As the service grew stronger after Reconstruction, the self-understanding of its members took on the flavor of institutional arrogance. Railway postal clerks saw their work as fundamentally distinct from, if not superior to, the tasks of other department employees. After all, they reasoned, did postmasters risk their lives on a daily basis in their work? Did clerks in larger city offices sort mail while their workplace was moving at sixty miles per hour? Who else in the department put in ten- and twelve-hour shifts on a regular basis? Like all late-nineteenth-century postal workers, railway postal clerks lobbied for increased salaries. Unlike others, they argued explicitly and at length that they deserved more money and status than postmasters, clerks, and carriers. Their letters and communications show an increasing disregard for the political power and facile jobs of postmasters and office clerks. Railway workers spoke of their work as exhibiting an optimal balance of mental acuity and physical strength, and they lamented their lack of public recognition relative to postmasters, who were embedded in local communities and enjoyed much more facile jobs. Denver-based clerk W. H. Coulter wrote to RMA secretary George A. Wood in November 1904, proclaiming that the clerks "represent one of the highest forms of labor ever created by man, blending evenly both the manual and the intellectual."[38] The blending of manual and mental labor provided the basis for a status claim. RMS clerks were unlike "clerks" and unlike other postal operatives. D. W. Young, a veteran with the Detroit and Saint Louis RPO line, lamented that "little is known of the requirements and vicissitudes of our calling. . . . The profession is not accorded the intellectual recognition it deserves; in short, the art of being a postal clerk does not stand as high in the list as it should, because too little is known of it or its exponents." Ever so slowly, railway mail workers were transcending the clerical identity of nineteenth-century bureaucracy.[39]

Beyond its unique internal cohesion, the Railway Mail Service brought government officials permanently into mail transportation. After 1864, the role of private firms in the postal system would decline inexorably. Railway mail also established for the first time genuinely bureaucratic links between Washington officials, the larger city offices, and the rural postmasters. Postmasters and local patrons who deposited their mail with the railway car interacted directly with national postal agents. The railway clerks, furthermore, were unique among department employees in their consistent and patterned interaction with officials at all levels of the system. This integrating capacity derived from the service's geographic division of labor. Armstrong's divisional system allowed Washington officials to establish centralized control over the transportation network through a regionally based system of superintendents whose sole responsibility was the management of railway post offices. Nothing resembling this system had ever existed in the department, even among the distributing postmasters.[40]

The social and political cohesion of the Railway Mail Service had one other effect that would reverberate powerfully in postal politics after 1900. When the precursor of the RMA—the National Association of Railway Postal Clerks—formed in 1891, it solidified a three-way split among the department's laborers:

clerks, carriers, and railway workers. This division of postal union strength among occupational lines would continue through the Progressive Era. I treat this issue at greater length in chapter 5, but two legacies warrant mention here. First, the fracture of the postal labor force was an immense advantage to the department (and to Congress) in labor negotiations. The labor unions almost never saw fit to coordinate their efforts for increased pay, reclassification, or benefits. The sharply defined organizational identity of the railway clerks would not have allowed it. Second, the contending labor unions succeeded only in institutionalizing an intra-organizational competition that postal workers had long feared and begrudged. Railway clerks in the Gilded Age knew that their own Republican Party was treating postmasters with increasing favor (and salaries), and all the while reclassification (the only hope of increased pay for railway workers) lay dead in Congress. For this reason, the disregard of RMS workers for postmasters and office clerks would only intensify.[41]

Comstockery and the Evolution of Inspection

Outside of the RMS, railway mail enhanced the power of Washington administrators by expanding the reach of inspection over the network. Special agents such as Quincy Brooks and George Plitt relied almost entirely on stage transport to visit post offices, yet as early as 1864 special agents were riding aboard mail cars and systematically using them to monitor postal operations. Inspectors could now see hundreds of offices per month by traveling on railway lines. They could gather information from RPO clerks, inquiring about offices that seemed less efficient or more prone to mail theft or loss. Moreover, because postal transport was now a department function, mail depredations were much easier to ferret out. It was much simpler to trace thefts to a guilty railway mail clerk than to one of the many people who might have handled the mail for a short stage run in the antebellum period. Atlanta's John Frey continually noted how the vast knowledge of the RMS "Route Agents" facilitated his own work in tracking postal crime.[42]

Within the inspectors' corps, a slow transformation was bringing in more and more men whose careers had started in the Railway Mail Service. This pattern had its roots in the institutional arrangements of 1864, when Blair abolished the Office of Inspection and put the special agents under the second assistant postmaster general, who also had control of the railway mail. Postal officials from the Civil War onward then established an implicit policy of choosing inspectors from among the elite ranks of RMS clerks. The rationale for this policy was evident to any postal official of the time. Unlike the Quincy Brookses and John Freys of the antebellum period, RMS clerks carried a deep knowledge of the network and its regulations at all levels of operation. Assessing a new recruit for Chief Inspector P. H. Woodward in 1875, special agent John B. Furay could say little, but he knew from the recruit's "long association with the Railway Mail service" that he was "not green at all." Special agents had for decades relied on RPO clerks to provide them with information they could secure nowhere else. It was straightforward to begin hiring service men into the Division of Inspection.[43]

By 1896 at least 46 of the 132 inspectors on the department's rolls (or 35 percent) had been appointed from the Railway Mail Service. Moreover, as many as 30 RMS officers, including all of the regional superintendents, were routinely given special agent commissions that accorded them the full powers of inspectors. Yet the RMS-led overhaul of postal inspection transcended sheer personnel numbers. In the 1880s the inspectors were organized along the lines of the Railway Mail Service and cleaved into fifteen field divisions. Somewhat less formally, Gilded Age inspectors laid claim to the title *service*—as in the "Inspection Service" or "Secret Service."[44]

Postal inspectors also turned their attention to new problems. The antebellum and Reconstruction-Era special agents were prized for their ability to detect and ward off mail theft, yet they did little else of note. All of this changed with the arrival of Anthony Comstock, the Connecticut-born farmer's son who permanently altered the relationship of the Post Office Department to American society. In 1870 Comstock was invisible to American culture, a dry goods clerk who had served with the wartime Christian Commission in Florida. Two years later the New York Young Men's Christian Association (YMCA) appointed him to lead its newly established Committee for the Suppression of Vice. By 1872 Comstock had founded the New York Society for the Suppression of Vice and had gathered a coalition of New York social elites, religious leaders, and politicians to press for new anti-obscenity legislation. The result of Comstock's endeavors was the most sweeping anti-obscenity statute in the nation's history: the Comstock law of 1873. The 1873 law provided that

> no obscene, lewd or lascivious book, pamphlet, picture paper, print, or other publication of an indecent character, or any article or thing designed or intended for the prevention of contraception or the procuring of abortion, nor article or thing intended or adapted for any indecent or immoral use or nature, nor any . . . book, pamphlet, advertisement or notice of any kind giving information, directly or indirectly, where, or how, or of whom, or by what means either of the things before mentioned maybe obtained or made . . . shall be carried in the mail.[45]

The Comstock law defined any attempt to mail such matter as a misdemeanor. President Ulysses Grant was reportedly unwilling to sign the bill unless he was assured that Comstock himself would be enforcing it. Soon after Grant signed the act, members of Congress asked Postmaster General John A. J. Creswell to appoint a special agent for anti-obscenity work. Comstock volunteered for the position, and Creswell promptly obliged. Soon after, the NYSSV was incorporated by the New York State legislature. Comstock was named enforcing agent of the society and assumed simultaneous state and federal authority. Under the power of the federal and state laws in his name, Comstock prosecuted book dealers and pornographers, harassed and imprisoned doctors and midwives who performed abortions, jailed art dealers who sold and displayed representations of nudes, regulated public libraries, and even secured a ban on a new edition of Walt Whitman's *Leaves of Grass.*[46]

Comstock's attempts to regulate American sexuality have been thoughtfully detailed by sociologist Nicola Beisel. Beisel shrewdly connects Comstock's anti-obscenity drive to the social and economic fears of upper-class easterners. She shows that vice-suppression societies in New York and Boston were composed overwhelmingly of wealthy Protestant men with elite college backgrounds and the most distinguished pedigrees. Comstock succeeded, Beisel concludes, because he persuaded these elites that the reading of obscene literature was "the boon companion of all other crimes," as he would write in his 1883 monograph *Traps for the Young.* He deftly stoked upper-class fears of the loss of privilege through the corruption of rich youth and the sexual intermingling of the classes.

Although the anti-vice societies were undoubtedly crucial to Comstock's campaigns, Beisel and most historians have neglected the relationship of Comstock and the anti-vice societies to the Post Office Department. Comstock is depicted as a solo artist whose titular association with the federal government was merely instrumental. It is worth remembering, however, that none of Comstock's federal prosecutions—including his famed pursuit of free-love advocate Ezra Heywood—would have been possible without his status as a postal officer. The same can be said of Comstock's state prosecutions, many of which were carried out with explicit assistance from postal officials. Beyond this, Comstock was one of many department officers in the anti-vice crusade. He enlisted other inspectors in his campaigns, both as prosecutors and as political organizers. For three decades, the Western Society for the Suppression of Vice was led by R. W. McAfee, a postal inspector in Saint Louis. As head of the Western Society, McAfee led the anti-vice societies in Cincinnati, Chicago, and Saint Louis. Comstock, pressing his own efforts northward, also established the Boston-based New England Society for the Suppression of Vice, later named the Ward and Watch Society. By the 1880s the dominant vice-suppression societies of the North and West were either led or established by a postal official.[47]

Administrative records illustrate, moreover, that the mustachioed crusader received considerable help from department leaders. Chief Inspector Parker enthusiastically supported Comstock's activities, openly expressing his sympathies with Comstock's work after a string of arrests in the western states in September 1876. In the 1870s Comstock reported every one of his arrests to Parker in handwritten letters of excruciating detail. Comstock continued the practice with Parker's successors, A. G. Sharp and William A. West. The letters, written on Comstock's official department stationery, reveal the wide swath of police activity in which the Post Office was now engaged. Postal inspectors clearly targeted many "crimes" in which the mails were never used, including the provision of abortion, the manufacture of contraceptive devices, the display of paintings of nudes by barroom owners, pickpocketing, and even alleged indecent exposure (Comstock himself admitted that the last matter was "a little out of my line"). In some of these cases, Comstock took his prosecutions to state court. Yet at the state level, too, the assistance of department officials was undeniable. Parker, for example, asked Comstock to keep him fully informed of the progress of *all* arrests and prosecutions, state or federal. Comstock did so, and his operations were itemized in the Inspection Division's *Arrest Book.* Washington officials detailed special agents to New York for Comstock's cases, and Comstock used New York City postmasters as witnesses and interrogators in many of his arrests.[48]

By the 1880s it was hardly clear where the Post Office's role in anti-vice crusades ended and where that of the YMCA, NYSSV, and New York City officials began. In reporting arrests, New York papers such as the *New York Times* bequeathed a dual identity to Comstock, labeling him "Special Agent of the Post Office Department and Secretary of the Society for the Suppression of Vice." Special agents continued to accompany Comstock on many of his high-profile arrests, including those of university professor Charles Gaulier, Manhattan socialite Dr. Calvin Halstead Wetmore, and his mistress Elsie Hallenbach. Comstock was also the chief figure and driving force in the antivice movement's political lobbying efforts. It was he who, with his detailed knowledge of postal laws and regulations, repeatedly approached congressmen of both parties in the 1880s and 1890s with proposals for strengthening anti-obscenity and anti-lottery laws. He admitted to Chief Inspector West in May 1887 that he had spent the better part of the previous nine months politicking in Albany and Washington for expanded authority under state and national anti-obscenity statutes. Perhaps never before in the history of the Republic had a career federal officer so openly (and successfully) lobbied for the expansions of his authority, not only in Congress but also in state legislatures.[49]

Although he was roundly criticized for entrapment and his distasteful methods, Comstock was spectacularly successful in his campaigns. Contemporary observers agreed that for three decades, he effectively shut down a large fraction of the previously burgeoning pornography industry in New York and Boston. Under Comstock's direction, the New York Society from 1873 to 1892 seized more than eight hundred thousand "obscene" pictures, more than 1.5 million circulars, more than 2 million lottery tickets, and more than twenty tons of books. As historian John Mohr reports, no individual in the United States arrested more abortion providers in the 1870s. Abortion and pornography were forced further underground during Comstock's reign, becoming less and less available to many urban dwellers.

Yet the sheer weight of Comstock's efforts conceals his institutional legacy, for Comstock reinvigorated the Post Office Department. The 1873 statute and subsequent laws gave to postal officials a powerful political rationale for boosting the inspection force. The force had been stagnant for most of the century, even with the proliferation of offices and mail routes, yet it quintupled from just over twenty during Reconstruction to one hundred by 1897. In the absence of Comstock and the anti-vice campaign, it is indeed likely that the number of inspectors would have declined in the 1870s, as Democrats in Congress sought deep cutbacks in the force. Taking his anti-vice activity nationwide, Comstock also infused new energy into the inspectors' corps. To a degree that historians have not appreciated, Comstock's reach extended well beyond the East Coast. Before Comstock traveled westward to Chicago in 1874, postal arrests in the burgeoning city averaged about one per month. On February 7, 1874, Comstock arrested thirteen individuals in one day. The rate of arrests then accelerated in Chicago in 1874, almost triple the total of any previous year. By the 1880s inspectors' arrests in Illinois were greater than in any other state. Moreover, Comstock achieved an organizational permanence in the department and was seen as a figurative leader among inspectors. None of the twenty-two postmasters general from 1873 to 1910 thought twice about recommissioning him when they assumed office.[50]

Beyond this, Comstockery enhanced the department's reputation as the guardian of American purity. Comstock and McAfee garnered national recognition with their arrests and convictions of Ezra Heywood, a Boston pamphleteer and organizer of the New England Free Love League; D. M. Bennett, author of the controversial tract *An Open Letter to Jesus Christ;* and Kansas pornographer Moses Harman. As their campaigns received ever-increasing coverage in the *New York Times* and other newspapers, the notion of postal inspectors as moral regulators took on an air of familiarity. Bennett's arrest opened a legal conflict culminating in *U.S. v. Bennett* (1878), a Supreme Court decision that widened the postal enforcement of anti-vice laws. Along with *ex parte Rapier* (1892), *Bennett* and its aftermath further established the department as the anti-vice policing authority of the federal government.

This reputation was much more than a literary or media construct. The department's reputation for moral protection was embedded in the inspectors' cooperative ties to the anti-obscenity leagues. Rightly or wrongly, the Post Office received much of the credit (or the blame) for the work of the vice-suppression societies. Postal officer Marshall Cushing observed in 1892 that the New York Society "has been so closely identified with the Postal Department that it is almost part of it." Through Comstock and McAfee, the inspectors and the societies explicitly coordinated their efforts. The New York Society's widely read annual reports publicized and tabulated the department's arrests, and the vice leagues vigorously backed the expansion of postal discretion. Outside the societies, the Post Office's anti-vice work brought it newfound respect from some of Progressive America's most esteemed and powerful quarters. The YMCA, for example, vigorously supported Comstock's work, a tie that would only strengthen once lifelong YMCA member John Wanamaker became postmaster general in 1889. Comstock's anti-abortion arrests brought letters of congratulations from officers of the American Medical Association, who looked with disgust upon free-wheeling abortion providers who were operating outside the confines of established medicine. Not the least of Comstock's allies were the anti-Tammany forces in New York City, including anti-vice philanthropists in the prominent Committee of Fifteen, district attorneys and judges in the city's justice system, and a young police commissioner named Theodore Roosevelt. As I discuss in the following chapter, these bonds would only strengthen at the turn of the century. At a time when Victorian sexual mores were an integral part of the American cultural fabric, this reputation generated considerable political capital. At the behest of organized moral reformers, Congress continually strengthened the Comstock law in the 1880s and 1890s, giving the inspectors the explicit power to open envelopes and broadening their ability to make arrests. One senator questioned why "all the morals of the people must be directed from this central point by agents" of the department. Contemporaries may have questioned the department's tactics but not its effectiveness or resolve.[51]

Wanamaker, the Reform Coalition, and the Limits of Military Idiom

By the time Benjamin Harrison appointed Philadelphia department-store magnate John Wanamaker to the keep of postmaster general in 1889, the Post Office presented a split identity. For many postal employees and patrons, witnessing the spoils-ridden city operations, the fourth-class post offices dotting the rural countryside, and the stage contractors that knit many rural offices to the larger network—little had changed since the 1830s. As Wanamaker lamented in 1890, "The post-offices throughout the country bear little relation to one another. The touch of the Department upon them is very slight. The machinery is set up and then let alone." Yet in Washington headquarters, on the railway lines, and in the Division of Inspection and Depredations, a new vision of the department as a progressive enterprise and as a moral arbiter of national communications emerged. Wanamaker faced the challenge of negotiating this organizational divide. Yet his legacy was to widen it.[52]

Wanamaker entered the department with celebrity and controversy. Ostensibly, he earned his term as postmaster general because he raised unprecedented corporate funds for Benjamin Harrison's successful election campaign of 1888. Newspapers and contemporaries equated Wanamaker's appointment with the purchase of administrative office. Although appointed as a reliable and wealthy Republican, Wanamaker managed to disappoint, if not enrage, some of the party's most reliable constituencies. His plan for parcel delivery by the government set express companies on the defensive. His proposal for a governmental takeover of the nation's telegraph network brought cries of pure socialism, as did many of his other ideas. Whether Wanamaker's job represented compensation for his fundraising prowess is not clear, but Harrison found himself puzzled and angered over his appointee's choices. What *is* clear is that Harrison did not hire Wanamaker to the department because he thought the industrialist would reform it.[53]

Wanamaker and the Armstrong-Bangs Generation

Wanamaker also entered with verve. He proposed at least ten reforms or programs in his first annual report to Congress, and his tenure quickly galvanized a reform coalition that slowly yet firmly dedicated itself to the eradication of the Jacksonian order. He spoke a language that the RMS favored, he lionized the inspectors and sought to elevate their status and authority, and he pressed vigorously for program expansion at the department. Among Washington officials, railway clerks, special agents, and many county-seat postmasters, he commanded a degree of allegiance unseen since McLean. He excited older identifiers with the department, among them RMS superintendent White, Comstock and McAfee, Assistant Attorney General James Tyner, August Machen, and others whose allegiance to the department transcended partisanship. Members of the new reform cadre were usually midlevel officials such as chief inspectors, RMS leaders, and attorneys; they had customarily served through several changes in presidential administration. Wanamaker's well-known religiosity— he was a lifetime member of the YMCA, a major contributor to anti-vice leagues, and a builder of Presbyterian churches worldwide—suited him well for a culturally conservative agency.

Tyner typified the new cadre. Even though he had served for twenty years in the department before Wanamaker's arrival—he began his career as a special agent in 1861 as an understudy of Parker and served a nine-month stint as Grant's postmaster general—Tyner was an enthusiastic prosecutor of the anti-obscenity cases and aimed his forces at state lotteries as well. He was Comstock's most solid ally outside the inspectors' corps. Reformers like Tyner allied with Progressive moralists and urban journalists and some farm papers, but against the old regime of stage contractors, clerks, and fourth-class postmasters. Wanamaker also infused new talent into the Post Office, hiring more inspectors and creating program offices staffed by his chosen reformers.[54]

Wanamaker's reformism was enthusiastically received among top postal officials, less because the business magnate was a persuasive boss than because the career leadership of the Post Office Department had been decisively, if quietly, reshaped in the late 1800s. The understudies of George Armstrong and George Bangs had come to leadership positions throughout the department, not simply in the Railway Mail Service, but also in post offices in large cities and in Washington. Table 3.1 shows the heights to which the Armstrong generation and the Bangs generation had reached in the 1890s.

In November 1889 Wanamaker articulated an overhaul of the department in which the efficiency and technocratic zeal that characterized the Railway Mail

TABLE 3.1
The Armstrong Generation and the Bangs Generation in the 1890s

Armstrong Cohort (entered RMS 1869–73)

James E. White	General Superintendent, RMS (served from 1866 to 1907)
James E. Stuart	Post Office Inspector in Charge, Chicago
M. J. McGrath	Superintendent of Free Delivery Service, Chicago Post Office
E. W. Alexander	Superintendent of Mails, Philadelphia Post Office
Jerome B. Johnson	Superintendent of RMS in San Francisco
J. L. Wilder	Superintendent of Mails, Milwaukee Post Office
Charles Harrison	Manufacturer of the Harrison Postal Bag Rack, Fond du Lac, Wisconsin
Bradford Williams	Post Office Inspector in Charge, Saint Louis, Missouri, retired from the service in 1888
C. A. Vickery	Superintendent of RMS, Washington, D.C.
W. P. Campbell	Assistant General Superintendent, RMS
J. A. Montgomery	Superintendent of Mails, Chicago Post Office
John B. Furay	Inspector in Charge, Omaha, Nebraska, retired 1885
R. C. Jackson	Superintendent of RMS, New York

Bangs Cohort (entered RMS 1873–76)

C. J. French	Superintendent of RMS, Cincinnati; later headed Bell Telephone in Boston
Theodore N. Vail	General Superintendent, RMS (1876–78); left to become head of Bell Telephone Service
Louis Troy	Superintendent of RMS, Chicago
W. B. Thompson	Second assistant postmaster general before his retirement in 1886
L. M. Terrill	Superintendent of RMS, Atlanta, Georgia

Source: George Armstrong Papers, Chicago Historical Society.

Service would come to dominate every aspect of postal operations. Wanamaker envisioned a fully integrated postal system. He saw a dichotomy between the clerical administration of the past and the planned programs of the future. He felt that the lack of middle management saddled the department's leadership with administrative details that were better devolved. Regional administrators could handle these burdens more efficiently, being in closer contact with postmasters and rail transport, and the resulting organization would radiate the progressive spirit of the times.

> The Postmaster-General . . . could intelligently exercise the functions of an administrative officer. He could apply the inventive and creative power of a mind freed from minor things, to the larger work of executive management of greater organization. He would do the planning, originate new ideas and inaugurate new methods, revise and make more practical and effective the regulations, study the systems of other countries, superintend the heads of departments, and give constantly the touch of life to the entire system, making it more representative of the commercial energies and social requirements of the American people. He would ascertain by investigation, study, and experiments, and by encouraging invention, possible improvements that would make the postal organization an agency of larger service and greater convenience. . . . He would . . . push forward American mails as the forerunner of the extension of American commerce; lift the entire service into a larger usefulness for the people and a larger increase for itself.[55]

Wanamaker also lucidly perceived the main obstacle to his reforms: the attachment of postal employees to clerical function and idiosyncratic tradition. "The venerable clerk who is always with us, faithful to tradition and proudest of all in remembering precedents, should not worry and retard a progressive Department in this progressive age by making a wall of an opinion delivered in 1823 or citing a precedent that governed in 1848." Wanamaker's ideal organization would have subjugated both Washington clerks and postmasters to regional superintendents. The model of his dreams lay in the Railway Mail Service, which alone had developed a regional organization with superintendents. As Wanamaker saw it, "[T]he railway mail is the spinal column of the service." Wanamaker was the first postmaster general to elevate the RMS above the post offices, a rhetoric unimaginable before his keep.[56]

Wanamaker's vision transcended structural reorganization, however. He wanted the department to play a broader role in the nation's political economy. He proposed that the department transport larger parcels, deliver mail to rural citizens just as it did to city dwellers, manage a national telegraph system, and operate postal savings banks. His call for postal expansion came at the crest of the Populist movement, and as Wayne Fuller remarks, "the very years his proposals were more likely to get a hearing in the nation than at any previous time."[57]

Yet apart from a small experiment in rural free delivery, Wanamaker's proposals met with silence from Congress and the major parties. Wanamaker pressed diligently for the expansion of rural delivery, knowing that rural denizens would support other departmental initiatives once they had a taste of its best services. But even here, Congress appropriated a fraction of what Wanamaker had requested—$10,000 versus Wanamaker's $1 million. As I discuss in the following chapters, the institutional hurdle to Wanamaker's aim was a deeply entrenched doubt about the department's capacities, for instance, the fact that it was losing money. For all of the Post Office's progress, national politicians had grave concerns about its fiscal stability. All of Wanamaker's proposals involved fiscal risk, new administrative authority, and appropriations, and congressional committee leaders were simply unwilling to turn over the power or the money. Yet the department was also losing mail. In 1889 Wanamaker pointed to several companies that had taken out insurance policies on lost mail matter and admitted, "The losses in the transit of mails are so many and large as greatly to impair the reputation of the Department."[58]

Wanamaker left the department in 1893 having energized an organization but without having achieved any of his policy goals. The postal deficit undergirded congressional concerns. In the decade following the Pendleton Act, the deficit shot from zero to $10 million, or 13 percent of revenues. Although members of Congress knew that the expansion of free delivery was a contributing factor, they also carried an abiding sense that the quintessential agency of the Jacksonian state was not to be trusted with an expansive reach of authority.

As Wanamaker's successors struggled to reduce the deficit in the 1890s, they saw the department's core dilemma in much the same terms that Wanamaker had described it. The department lacked structural integrity. Increasingly, the army metaphor was seen less as an ideocultural description of postal operations and more as a model of what the department was *not*. Wilson S. Bissell, who followed Wanamaker under Grover Cleveland, complained of the department in 1893 that it lacked an institutional medium linking Washington administrators and local postmasters.

> I think that any business man assuming charge of the Post Office Department feels the weakness of its organization at one point, and that is in the relation of the heads of the Department to its postmasters and other local officers. . . . As a general proposition, it may be said that this great army is organized in companies, without regiments or brigades, so that the company captain makes his report to the general commanding officer; or, in railroad management, it would be like organizing a company with a president and four vice-presidents, but without superintendents, either general or local, the station agents making their reports directly to the one or the other of the general officers. This is a strange anomaly, and is without parallel in any business institution that I have any knowledge of.[59]

Bissell's successor, William L. Wilson (1895–97), addressing Congress in 1896, complained of departmental organization that it appeared "as if each private soldier in a great and growing army reported directly to the commanding general, received orders from him and had little other supervision than what was possible from army headquarters."

The Post Office Department closed the century perched on the edge of transformation. No regional management system existed or was forthcoming. The department was unable to establish a hold over the practices (or costs) of local offices or stage contractors. Oversight committees were unwilling to grant new program authority. Yet in the expansion of the Railway Mail Service and growth of the inspection corps, the foundation had been established for the structural integration of the national postal system. In the railway and inspection factions of the new system, Congress found functions that the Post Office could perform well. The nation's vice wars were now fought less over the definition of rights than over the turf of administrative discretion. The railway post office had evinced a degree of organizational cohesion and efficiency that no one, not even the department's most jaded detractors, could deny. Finally, in the inspection division, in the railway mail car, in county-seat offices, and among a growing cadre of Washington administrators, postal bureaucrats had become politically distinct from the Old Guard Republicans that now ruled Congress. Although it lacked demonstrable capacity and the ability to plan, the Post Office had broken the decisive grip of Jacksonian clericalism.

Four

Organizational Renewal and Policy Innovation in the National Postal System, 1890–1910

> Such business as the post-office now does in car-
> rying fourth-class mail should be done by private
> enterprise. If I had my way, the post-office would
> give no more facilities than it gives today—it
> would give fewer.
> —Eugene Loud, chairman of the House
>   Post Office Committee

IN THE TWO DECADES commencing with John Wanamaker's tenure, the U.S. Post Office Department thoroughly transformed itself. An agency still heaving under the weight of patronage in 1890 had, by President William Howard Taft's inauguration in 1909, achieved impressive gains in service efficiency. An organization previously marked by local-level control now centralized virtually every aspect of its operations, standardizing daily operations and making the inspectors a routine presence in the life of the postmaster. A system propelled by ceaseless expansion witnessed for the first time an aggregate decline in the number of post offices, as the department eliminated unnecessary offices in small towns and consolidated operations in larger cities. An agency that had established itself as the guardian of American purity now took its moral crusade to the American economy, tackling consumer fraud and alcohol advertising. The department's managers and operators alike, heavily immersed in military idiom before 1900, began to speak an entirely new administrative discourse—one that the press echoed—of the department as a machine.

The crux of these transformations lay in policy innovation. Despite Eugene Loud's best efforts, nothing further separated the new Post Office from its nineteenth-century past than its ability to inaugurate experimental programs that would later become institutionalized, containing broad and lasting grants of discretion from Congress and the presidents. In 1896 department executives launched a rural free delivery system that would carry mail to the doorstep of virtually every domicile in America. In 1910 the department launched its newest initiative in finance: postal savings banks. In 1912 the department wrested control of parcels post delivery from the nation's express companies, obliterating private carriers in less than a decade. In idea and in experiment, all three of these programs found their origin in the department. All three were characterized by significant operational autonomy. All three became trademark features of the twentieth-century state.

As entrenched as these features of the post office may appear to twenty-first-century Americans, they appear puzzling in light of nineteenth-century politics. Civil service reform, the motive force that most scholarly histories ascribe to American state development, made little, if any, contribution to postal efficiency between 1890 and 1910. The department remained until the 1920s the primary bastion of the patronage system, and what progress there was in the extension of the merit system had already been attained by 1896. Two other forces commonly cited in state-building histories—agrarian social movements and the increasing power of committees in Congress—also played a largely reactive role in these developments. Agrarians were internally divided over many postal innovations and cared little, if at all, about postal efficiency. Whereas citizen-farmers vigorously supported the department in its campaign for rural free delivery, their support did not precede but rather followed the department's overtures for rural delivery and its calls for petitions.

I reach a similar conclusion concerning the roles of the House and Senate Post Office Committees. If anything, as Loud's remonstrance demonstrates, the Post Office Committees favored service retrenchment during this period. The committees withheld authority and funds on occasion, and they favored the wishes of postal officials, particularly when experimental results warranted it. At few points after 1890, however, did the department do Congress's bidding. The department set the agenda for rural free delivery, implementing the program according to its own schedule. It also used the popularity of the rural delivery program to compel congressional Republicans to accept its massive closure of fourth-class post offices, preempting President Theodore Roosevelt's reclassification of fourth-class postmasters in 1908.

Only an account that focuses on organizational politics, the administrative pursuit of autonomy, and bureaucratic reputation building can explain the emergence of an integrated and discretionary postal system in the United States. The achievements in centralization, program innovation, and cost efficiency were driven by middle-level postal officials—August Machen, Anthony Comstock, James Tyner, William Vickery, and others—who desired two results above all others: discretion from above and control over those below. These middle-level administrators emerged in three areas of the department: the Railway Mail Service, the Division of Inspection, and first-class city offices. In concert with the continued expansion of the Railway Mail Service, the advance of the postal inspectors allowed the department to establish a durable link between the center of postal operations in Washington and the remotest local office.

As the regime of inspectors grew, the basic nature of postal operations was irreversibly altered. The launching of the rural free delivery system at century's end displaced the local postmaster as the center of rural postal politics. In the place of the postmaster, two figures with greater allegiance to the department—the rural carrier and the special agent—arose to occupy this important community niche. As the local presence of the postal state expanded and the array of its services widened, the department's reputation and presence in national social and economic life grew. The Post Office became an independent player in small towns and large cities alike. Its weight was increasingly felt in the very policy debates it had authored, by experimenting with new programs and by building coalitions around them. And the department's expanded reputation provided strong political capital for its attempts to introduce packages into the general mails and to create postal savings banks, developments I leave for the following chapter.

Nothing more truly marked these transformations than the succession of mechanical imagery, replacing military idiom in the department's culture—its internal discourse and the image it presented externally. The imagery of machinery acquired new currency in the department and in the nation because it expressed the emerging realities of postal labor and operation at the same time that it symbolized the structural integration of the department. Mail and parcel transportation had become a unified and routinized apparatus. The machine metaphor also powerfully intimated that postal work was no longer clerical or distributive. The metaphor suggested complexity of organizational tasks and smoothness of operations. It also projected administrative reliability in a nation increasingly dependent on fueled machines for transportation, the cultivation of land, the synthesis of products, and the generation of usable energy. The rise of the machine metaphor in national postal administration transcended the primary residue of Jacksonian symbolism: the distributive state operating primarily through clerical function.

The Crystallization of the Reform Coalition

Despite his failures in persuading Congress, John Wanamaker succeeded mightily in assembling and leaving intact a multilevel organizational coalition bent on the renewal of the Post Office Department. In speeches and reports, he steadily articulated his dual vision of railway-style efficiency and inspection. He also brought new elements of the department in line with his conception, splitting the nation's postmasters along status lines. In 1890 he asked Congress for $50,000 to establish a trial system of twenty-five to thirty postal districts in which a head postal expert would continually monitor local offices. Congress recoiled, doubting the aggregate payoff of such a trial. Undaunted, Wanamaker appealed to the voluntary spirit of county-seat postmasters and sent to each of the 2,807 officials a sixteen-part questionnaire to be used for inspecting the offices in the postmaster's county. The response surpassed officials' grandest hopes. A total of 2,142 of the county-seat postmasters, having visited more than

45,000 post offices, returned the survey. Tens of thousands of detailed recommendations for service improvements and cost reductions were tabulated from the reports. Wanamaker learned that in one in six post offices, accounts and reports were not "properly and promptly written up," in the judgment of the visiting postmaster. In more than 1 percent (409 of 36,930) of the reports tabulated, the county-seat officials recommended the discontinuance of the office inspected, an almost inconceivable suggestion at any previous time in the century.[1]

The county-seat survey stimulated a new planning imperative in the Post Office. By granting temporary inspection authority to the postmasters, it gave them a new institutional identity and built favor for wider reform in the department's ranks. It reoriented the postmasters who had looked with suspicion on inspections and standardization of operations. Wanamaker then capitalized on the organizational momentum of the survey and called two conferences in the spring of 1892. In the first he invited thirty-two first-class postmasters to Washington for a discussion of the results of the county-seat survey and of planned improvements to the service. The conference produced no fewer than fourteen bills, all of them firmly in the reformers' vein—postal savings banks, rural free delivery, increased use of pneumatic tubes, and others. The House and Senate Post Office Committees reacted furtively to the department's agenda-setting move, inviting many of the officials to testify in a patchwork set of hearings. In the second conference, Wanamaker gathered seven second- and third-class postmasters in the capital, and in the impromptu gathering they agreed to continue the practice of "visiting postmaster" inspections. Significantly, there is no evidence of any conference of fourth-class postmasters from 1890 to 1910. Quite simply, fourth-class offices did not fit well into the new vision of the reformers, as Wanamaker envisioned a reduction of their numbers.[2]

In gathering the congresses, Wanamaker tapped into the ideas of an ascendant generation of postmasters who looked quite different from the Republican loyalists who came before. Many had worked for railroad enterprises or for urban newspapers before coming to the department, and their industrial and journalistic experience had given them lasting doubts about the Jacksonian mode of operations. Many postmasters were active in progressive religious societies as well. Wanamaker's secretary Marshall Cushing, the de facto spokesman of the postal reform wing, venerated the new first-class postmasters, casting them as exemplars of the postpatronage regime: "They were actually of the opinion that they really had no right to their post offices unless they did better than their predecessors." C. W. Ernst, assistant postmaster at Boston, epitomized the new type. A German émigré and Lutheran pastor, Ernst brought a fifteen-year career in journalism to the Boston office. He was also one of the leading Republican intellectuals of his generation, a member of the AAAS who had published a widely cited tract on national tariffs, biographical essays on Martin Luther, and several reflections on European politics. So prominent was Ernst in Boston society and Mugwump politics that Wanamaker invited him alone among *assistant* postmasters to the March 1892 conference. In Maine, Walter D. Stinson (postmaster at Augusta) and John Chase Small (Portland) came to their positions from railroad enterprises. In Philadelphia, assistant postmaster Benjamin Franklin Hughes had edited two Pennsylvania newspapers before his appointment in the 1880s.[3]

The new postmasters were usually Republicans, and many could boast of Union service decades earlier. Although many of the officials at Wanamaker's conference were his own party appointees, many others were not. Stinson spent ten years in the Augusta office before Benjamin Harrison's election, serving through three changes of administration. Ernst came to the department not through patronage but through nepotism; he was the son-in-law of Boston postmaster Thomas Hart. Tennessee postmaster G. H. Slaughter had been in the department for more than forty years, but he most clearly articulated the reformist vision in his *Stage Coaches and Railroads* (1894), a widely read tract that identified the department's future with the RMS. What united this cadre was not the party but an increasing commitment to local reforms. Hughes and his superior, Philadelphia postmaster John Field, pioneered the use of special agents to root out fraud in almshouses. Baltimore postmaster William Waters Johnson standardized his office's accounts and created a level of administrative assistants in the city office. Many of the urban postmasters' moves were not directed by Wanamaker, even though they were clearly in line with his broader vision of the Post Office. Where Wanamaker supplied an organizational ideology, the postmasters offered concrete innovations and ties to the urban press. In Boston and Philadelphia chiefly, but in other cities as well, a progressive movement gained a foothold in the Post Office Department fully two decades before coming to power in Congress.[4]

The Railway Postal Machine

The core of the postal reform movement still lay in the Railway Mail Service. The service's leadership was characterized not by political appointees but by organizational loyalists, most of them appointed a decade or more before the Pendleton Act. As in the larger city offices, many of these officials left railroad enterprises to take positions in the department. Second Assistant Postmaster General J. Lowrie Bell, who managed all mail transportation and contracting, worked as a train dispatcher before joining the department as a railway clerk. He ascended through the RMS to general superintendent before his appointment under Wanamaker. Bell's assistant, George F. Stone, worked as a telegraph operator for the Lehigh Valley Railroad before entering the second assistant's office at a low-level clerkship and ascending to the highest administrative positions in the office. RMS superintendent Captain James E. White began his forty-year career as a clerk under George Armstrong in 1866. White's assistant,

William P. Campbell, entered the RMS in 1868 as Armstrong's secretary. Careers such as these, spanning numerous partisan shifts in the presidency and congressional majorities, were extremely rare in Gilded Age bureaucracy.[5]

After Wanamaker gathered RMS division superintendents to Washington in the 1890s, the service began holding conferences under its own auspices. These meetings further cemented the service's self-understanding as the promise of twentieth-century postal administration. They also heightened the guildlike identity of the railway clerks. At the Second Annual RMS Banquet in Saint Louis in November 1904, D. W. Young of the Detroit and Saint Louis RPO mingled reformism with professional self-understanding.

> It is true that little is known of the requirements and vicissitudes of our calling. . . .
> The profession is not accorded the intellectual recognition it deserves; in short, the
> art of being a postal clerk does not stand as high in the list as it should, because too
> little is known of it or its exponents. . . . He will endure because without him there
> could not be that indispensable adjunct of modern civilization, the fast mail; *he is the
> motive power of commercialism;* without him there could not be scores of things
> which today exist and make for the welfare, happiness and prosperity of our nation.[6]

Young's metaphor of the service as a "motive power," a well-oiled machine, accorded well with the national experience of railroad-driven industrialization. To be a part of a vast machine was, for railway postal workers, not to be a lifeless "cog in the wheel" but an active participant in a finely tuned and intricate system that was at the center of national development. The machine was not inhumane but alive and organic.[7] For this reason, the service workers' metaphor differed substantially from other late-nineteenth-century images of industrial work such as Carroll D. Wright's moral lionization of the factory, Jane Addams's portraits of industrial monotony, and the bleak forecasts of the industrial betterment movement. Postal officials felt that the Railway Mail Service, as a vast mechanical apparatus connecting the post offices of thousands of local communities, could make a unique contribution to the national interest. As RMA secretary George A. Wood argued in 1904,

> *The railway postal clerk is but another mite, but the railway mail service is the whole
> great system; a vast machine so accurately adjusted in all its parts that it is a marvel
> to all.* The railway mail is not alon[e] in New Hampshire or Louisiana, it is not the
> "local" affair of one community; but rather does [*sic*] the senses build up a picture of
> shining steel and throbbing locomotives with hundreds of cars hurrying hither and
> thither upon their allotted routes, covering with a vast network of conveyance for the
> ready intercommunications of every person in the land.[8]

The mechanical idiom also found a steady home in the organizational myth-making of Clarence E. Votaw, assistant superintendent of the RMS after Campbell. Votaw was another reformer who had entered the service in 1881, two years before civil service reform. His popular *Jasper Hunnicutt of Himpson-*

hurst (1907) lucidly reveals the coalescing identity of the service. The book is a fictional autobiography of Hunnicutt, a young railway clerk from New Jersey, but the recollections are undoubtedly Votaw's. The narrative follows Hunnicutt as he leaves his hometown and experiences his "first run," where "after sixteen days flying back and forth [between Pittsburgh and Kansas] I began to feel like a shuttle." Though weary from constant travel, Hunnicutt works steadily, following the injunction of his coworker that "no part of the machine must stop." Hunnicutt's romantic interest in New Jersey, young Stella Coyner, later announces that "the mail service is a big machine that never stops, night or day. So, if one clerk should fail, many people might be disappointed. . . . Business would suffer, love affairs be broken off." For many, Hunnicutt articulated in the most familiar and understandable terms the vision of national prominence to which D. W. Young had aspired in 1904.[9]

The machine metaphor slowly came to dominate postal administration. Few voiced it more zestfully than Wanamaker's secretary, Marshall Cushing, who penned *The Story of Our Post Office*, a one-thousand-page tome about the department. Cushing, who arrived to the department with Wanamaker, marveled at "the intricate machinery" of the postal service and claimed that "this immense machine, this stupendous, delicate, all-pervading business, is everywhere impecunious and restive." Cushing glorified the department's reform wing, devoting a chapter to it entitled "The Wonderful Railway Mail Service." Mechanical imagery such as Cushing's also affirmed a rapidly emerging Taylorism in RMS management. The dreaded "sweat box" test was administered yearly, and clerks were given incentives to do well. A stellar performance carried an almost certain promise of career advancement. In 1890 Superintendent White instituted a national competition in which clerks vied for the honor of being "most efficient," the winners being announced in the department's *Daily Bulletin*. The winner for 1891 had sorted 32,195 practice cards in nineteen hours and ten minutes, with just thirteen mistakes in that time, for an accuracy rate of 99.96 percent.[10]

At no level, however, did postal officials abandon entirely the army metaphor. The department was still home to many Old Guard loyalists, and none of the reformers wanted to antagonize this favored class, at least not yet. Superintendent White was still called Captain, and in 1894 the Post Office attempted to standardize postal uniforms, which had not changed since Congress had authorized them in 1868. The department briefly compelled city carriers to wear semimilitary uniforms and heavy blue helmets. The changes in postal apparel were noticed in locales as diverse as New Orleans, where they occasioned sympathy for the overburdened (and overheated) carriers, and Cedar Rapids, Iowa, where one newspaper later remarked that they made the carriers look more Confederate than Union. The helmets gave way to lighter hats, but the uniforms remained. For twenty years, then, two metaphors governed the department's culture, as the mechanical gradually displaced the military. This metaphorical succession followed the generational dynamics of the service. The earliest RMS workers were Union veterans, but the second wave of entrants in the 1890s had little or no military experience. For later entrants, the machine metaphor held greater meaning; they thought the military idiom applied to the older generation of clerks, whom they called "those old war horses of the service."[11]

The new generation also expressed growing dissatisfaction with the title "clerk," a relic of army identity. Secretary Wood argued that "[w]e all admit that the old name [National Association of Railway Postal Clerks] had become very dear, for many hard battles had been fought and won under it." Yet for Wood and others, the title "railway postal clerk" evoked too easily a comparison between railway labor and the work of postmasters and carriers whose labor they found disgustingly facile. The railway workers were also well aware of the gendered implications of their change in title. For the most common new "clerks" in government employment were now women, as the Progressive civil service had feminized the clerical realm in government work.[12]

The Machine as Model and as Reputation

The political force of the mechanical idiom lay in two facets of its symbolism. First, it testified to the growing concern of postal reformers with administrative efficiency. The advance of mechanical discourse clearly paralleled the amplified discussion of the postal deficit in Progressive political and administrative circles. From economist H. T. Newcomb's book in 1900, to Rep. W. W. Moody's shocking statistics showing the deficit to be 30 to 50 percent larger than officially estimated, to the testimony of University of Michigan professor Henry Carter Adams before Congress, numerous Progressive scholars were turning their attention to the postal deficit and trying to explain it. For postal officials and optimistic reformers alike, then, the mechanical idiom suggested that the department aspired to the industrial efficiency of the modern corporate enterprise. Cushing said as much when he called the department a "business" and a "machine" in the same sentence, and Postmaster General Charles Emory Smith echoed Cushing in his monograph *Greatest Business Organization in the World: The United States Postal Service.*[13]

Journalists and their reading public also imbibed the rhetoric of postal "machinery" and postal "business." Two articles in leading Progressive-Era magazines—Forrest Crissey's "Traveling Post-Office" (*World's Work,* 1902) and Earl Mayo's "Post Office Work and Methods" (*The Outlook,* 1903)—offered a stunning new portrait of the department to their readers. Crissey's monograph offered seven photographs of the railway mail system, including some of the first widely published pictures of the interior of the mail car. Yet it was Mayo who, more than any other writer of his time, cemented the mechanical understanding of the Post Office. No branch of the federal government was "more efficient or arduous in its requirements," he concluded. Mayo's article was accompanied by nine still photographs showing the latest contraptions of mail operations: the stamping machine, the pneumatic tube, the interior of the railway mail car, a speeding mail express train. It was a journalistic portrait of the postal system unlike any other before it. After Crissey's and Mayo's portrayals, mechanical and corporate images of the Post Office abounded in Progressive journalism. A 1910 *World's Work* editorial trumpeted "A National Opportunity—a Business Postal Department." Nebraska congressman George W. Norris likened the department to "a great corporation" in a 1912 essay in the *Editorial Review*. The *Review*'s editors, in announcing Norris's essay, stated that "[t]he Post Office Department represents the greatest working machinery in the world." *Watson's Magazine* writer David Gates marveled at the quietude of the Railway Mail Service, "this machine that runs so smoothly and makes so little noise that we seldom think of it running at all."[14]

The second effect of the mechanical idiom was to simplify a complex and burgeoning organizational structure. Over the course of four decades the number of RMS divisions had grown from six to eleven, obfuscating lines of authority and loyalty. The railway mail clerk was ultimately responsible to the Post Office Department and to *The Black Book*. But clerks also had responsibilities—including orderly behavior and cooperation—to the railroad lines they inhabited. The growth of the Railway Mail Association further problematized lines of authority, as union members were implicitly encouraged not to "check" one another's sorting efficiency on a run, even though *Black Book* regulations required it. To the degree that postal workers bought into the model of the new Post Office as a machine, then, they implicitly sympathized with the reformers' aims. As with the army metaphor of the Gilded Age, the machine model was a centralizing force.

The Regime of Inspectors

In 1893 postal inspectors set a forceful (albeit disturbing) precedent. Rumors had been swirling for several years that urban letter carriers were inflating their hours on their weekly work sheets. The department decided to take action. For months thereafter postal inspectors spied on the letter carriers, clocking their work patterns and comparing these with the carriers' own reports. Repeatedly the carriers turned in time sheets reporting hours worked well above the inspectors' estimates. The Post Office Department used the information to prosecute a number of letter carriers that year. House Republicans criticized the inspectors' behavior as tyrannical and warned the department to halt such spying tactics. Yet Congress refrained from prohibiting the practice.[15]

The 1893 "spotting" incident was no isolated case of postal hubris. At the turn of the century, congressional committees, presidents, and organized interests deferred consistently and broadly to the brazen political advance of postal inspectors. Emboldened by a liberal judicial interpretation of the Constitution's "postal powers" clause, and supported at virtually every turn by organized Progressive moralists who took their principal cues from Anthony Comstock, postal inspectors took a place among the most powerful Progressive-Era political figures. Even wary postmasters general did not hinder the inspectors' advance. As Chief Inspector William J. Vickery concluded in 1905,

> An inspector's territory has practically no bounds, the variety of his work has no limit. . . . He is a traveling auditor, to check up offices and collect shortages; a postal expert, to decide where an office should be located, how fitted up or how many clerks or carriers it may need. He passes on postmasters' bonds, negotiates leases for post-office premises . . . he displaces postmasters and sometimes must assume control of the office himself . . . find[s] the criminal and evidence to convict him . . . assist[s] the United States attorney. . . . He inquires into all things that demand personal attention and handles many cases where the property, position, reputation, or even the liberty of a citizen is affected by his report.[16]

The organizational ideology of the inspectors was shaped by two factors. The first was an expanding pattern of recruitment from the Railway Mail Service. In 1896 just over one-third of postal inspectors had identifiable RMS backgrounds, but by 1910 the proportion exceeded one-half and in some divisions approached two-thirds. In the Philadelphia division, the percentage of inspectors appointed from the RMS rose from 14 in 1896 to 53 in 1902, settling at 46 percent by 1909. In the New Orleans office, the percentage rose from 55 in 1896 to a 1908 peak of 67 percent. The career experience of inspectors was also growing. Where Philadelphia-based inspectors averaged less than ten months' experience in 1896, they averaged more than three years' tenure in 1910, even with dozens of new hires during a quadrupling of the inspection force (from seven to thirty men). The naturalization of a railway-to-inspection career track gave the inspectors a reform-minded identity attached to the RMS.[17]

The second factor was the continued progress of Comstockery. Comstock remained in the department until his death in 1915, and his continued presence energized the socially conservative inspectors' corps. He grew ever more repressive after 1890, turning his ire toward lotteries, counterfeiters, gamblers, art galleries, belly dancers, and Progressive contraception advocate Margaret Sanger. Comstock's political power began to surge in the late 1880s, when he took an active role in recommending stringent legislation against mail fraud. When Rep. Benjamin Enloe of Tennessee offered a bill that only weakly bolstered the 1873 law, Comstock publicly hammered Enloe's measure. Department officials then drafted a substitute that immediately deposed the Enloe bill and passed "with no real debate," as one contemporary put it. Later, when the department prompted the Fifty-second Congress to consider stronger anti-obscenity legislation (S. 2825 and H.R. 5067), Comstock coordinated a writing campaign by the New York Society for the Suppression of Vice and the Women's Christian Temperance Union, depositing numerous petitions with the House Post Office Committee. New legislation passed both chambers easily. With the NYSSV in his pocket and with strong support from women's groups, Comstock was a legislative force unto himself.[18]

Doctors, Anti-Salooners, and Enemies of the Lottery: The Inspectors' Multiple Affiliations

Comstock's ties to a diverse set of anti-vice reformers would only expand and strengthen after 1890. Having driven the circulation of pornography underground through much of New England and the Great Lakes region, Comstock turned to new vices: sexual hygiene and abortion, alcohol advertising, and lotteries. In each case, he was aligning the Post Office Department with a new facet of the Progressive moral reform movement—"Progressive physicians" and the American Medical Association, prohibitionists, and anti-lottery enthusiasts.

The Inspection Division's foray into sexual hygiene and abortion was in some respects a slight extension of its anti-vice work in the 1870s and 1880s. With public concern about venereal disease growing at the turn of the century, a number of companies began advertising remedies for sexually transmitted diseases. In the 1890s inspectors began to suppress these advertisements, at first targeting them for "fraudulent advertising." Comstock, of course, had been targeting abortionists from the earliest days of enforcing the Comstock law of 1873. The new departure in anti-vice work began when U.S. attorneys declined to prosecute the inspectors' arrests, citing unclear authority. In many of these cases, the inspectors ruled the matter "indecent," requiring the companies to revise their ads. Yet clearly Comstock, Tyner, and others felt that new legislation was necessary. Enter the American Medical Association (AMA) and Charles A. L. Reed. The AMA was the institutional center of a "Progressive physician" movement that disdained abortion providers as lower-class butchers who brazenly masqueraded as doctors. In November 1905 Reed, who chaired the AMA's Committee on Medical Legislation, approached Postmaster General George Cortelyou with an open-ended gift. Noting that he would gather the AMA's legislative committee and its National Legislative Council in December, he offered support for any "medical legislation" that the department had to offer. Reed concluded his letter by expressing his hope that his organization "may prove of benefit in promoting *any legislation in which you may be interested.*" Prodded by Comstock and department attorney general James Tyner, Cortelyou wasted no time in taking advantage of the opportunity. He requested that Reed's committee recommend legislation prohibiting hygienic and abortion advertisements, and the AMA promptly obliged.[19]

Comstock and his associates had hardly forgotten pornography and the vices of the 1870s, of course. Arrests for the mailing of obscene matter continued apace in the 1890s and early 1900s, and they spread from the East Coast and Great Lakes to virtually every section of the country. Yet most of the work was carried out not by Comstock and McAfee but by a new generation of inspectors who had been steeled in the vice battles of the previous decades, not least William Vickery, who would become chief inspector in 1904.[20]

Alcohol was not one of Comstock's targets in the 1870s and 1880s, but after 1900 postal inspectors considered and pursued thousands of fraud violations against alcohol advertisers. A conservative estimate suggests that from 1905 to 1921, alcohol-related matters composed at least 80 percent of the Inspection Division's correspondence with civic organizations, business firms, and state officials. These cases brought the division into a cooperative discourse with two forces in the emerging prohibition campaign—state and local officials who were enforcing prohibitionist statutes in dry regions and the Anti-Saloon League. Much more than the anti-pornography and anti-abortion drives had ever done, the Post Office's anti-alcohol operation connected its officers with moral reformers throughout the country—to Anti-Saloon Leagues in Idaho and Texas, to state officials on the Pacific Coast, and to established Washington lobbies.[21]

The department's most visible enemy was the Louisiana Lottery. All but three states (Louisiana, Delaware, and Vermont) had prohibited lotteries before 1900, and Louisiana ran the most profitable operation, accounting for 45 percent of the business of the New Orleans post office. With pressure from Tyner and Comstock, Wanamaker wrote to President Benjamin Harrison on June 28, 1890, asking him to pressure Congress for new legislation prohibiting lotteries from the mails. The Louisiana Lottery, Comstock argued, "could not exist but for the use of the postal machinery of the Government." He also included a typewritten legal analysis of the department's powers over lotteries, a document almost surely written by Tyner. The memorandum concluded that discretion to exclude lotteries from the mails was consistent with the legal history of the department's power over mail matter but that explicit authority was needed to contradict earlier administrative interpretations of the law. One month later, after continued persuasion from department officials, Harrison wrote the Senate in strong support of a federal anti-lottery statute. The president called the lottery "an evil of vast proportions" and warned that "the general government, through its mail system, is made the effective and profitable medium of intercourse between the lottery company and its victims." Soon after, a department-drafted bill was introduced into Congress that declared lottery tickets and advertisements nonmailable matter.[22]

Harrison's letter pointed subtly to the moral high ground that the department was taking. In seeking to rid the postal system of lotteries, it was willingly forfeiting millions of dollars in revenue. No politician could claim that the department had its own interests in mind when tackling the lottery issue. Nonetheless, an intense opposition arose to the bill, funded by the lottery, whose "money bags jingled in the very corridor of the Capitol." Enigmatically, agrarian legislators spearheaded the opposition, led by Walter I. Hayes of Iowa, who wrote the House committee's minority report. Hayes claimed that the measure was unconstitutional and warned of government espionage. Still, Comstock, Tyner, Wanamaker, and the anti-vice societies carried the day. The bill passed the House and flew through the Senate with no recorded debate. Biographers have disputed whether the final legislation was a child of Comstock's 1885 draft or whether Tyner wrote it. The striking fact of the 1890 anti-lottery law, ultimately, is that two career postal officials wrote an agenda-setting bill that significantly expanded the department's inspection power. They also pushed the bill through Congress over the wishes of a well-heeled lobby and over the fears of divided agrarians, not to mention an unsure White House and postmaster general.[23]

Comstock, Tyner, and Wanamaker immediately gave enforcement authority to the Inspection Division, headed by Chief Inspector E. G. Rathbone. In the first year of the act Rathbone's division compiled 202 arrests, 653 indictments, and 59 convictions. Comstock and McAfee directed none of these efforts; the moral reform impulse now drove the inspectors' corps by autopilot. The business of the New Orleans post office plummeted by one-third in the two months after the act's passage. The Post Office secured a reputation for moral dynamism. As the *North American Review* summarized in 1907, "The war against lottery schemes, waged vigorously for twenty years by the Department, has been measurably successful in excluding that gigantic swindle from the mails."[24]

The institutional legacy of the Anti-Lottery Act lay not just in the robust enforcement record of Rathbone's force but also in the constitutional and legislative momentum that it gave to the expansion of postal inspectors' powers. The Supreme Court upheld the act in *ex parte Rapier* (1892), *Streep v. U.S.* (1895), and *John H. Durland v. U.S.* (1896). Then, nine years after Congress broadened the terms of the act in 1895 to include all first-class mails, the Court again sanctioned department enforcement in *Public Clearing House v. Coyne* (1904). Dorothy Fowler, who has written the broadest work on the "postal powers" clause, concludes: "By 1900 the Post Office Department had received almost plenary power for dealing with attempts to use the mails to defraud." Strikingly, this power came from one of the most conservative Supreme Courts in the history of American jurisprudence, a Court that consistently rendered the equal protection clause so narrowly as to protect not civil rights but corporate property.[25]

Inspectors and the Mail

Fueled by Comstockery, the inspection force grew steadily through the turn of the century—from 100 in 1897 (on a budget of $300,000) to 390 in 1912 (with more than $1 million). While Congress was appropriating money for the inspection of mail frauds and obscenity, department officials were using the inspectors primarily to wring greater economies from postal operations. Through the inspectors' actions, the presence of executives in Washington and Chicago such as Frank Hitchcock, J. Louis Ball, G. F. Stone, M. D. Wheeler, and James Stuart was enhanced. As Cushing remarked, "the great bulk" of inspection lay in "investigations of simple irregularities in the mail service." Much as in urban locales in 1893, postal inspectors engaged in a form of espionage. They detailed fraudulent stamp cancellations by postmasters, the rigging of delivery contract auctions, violations of the civil service laws, slack in local offices, and even the moral character and drinking behavior of postal employees. Officials saw boosting the inspection force as the best way to heighten efficiency. Though apparently small in their numbers—there were just under 400 special agents in 1912, compared with a total postal labor force of more than 250,000—postal inspectors established common expectations about the costs of shirking and corruption throughout the postal system. Inspectors could now use the national railway mail network to visit numerous offices per week, conducting unannounced inspections. Moreover, the railway experience gave most inspectors an intimate familiarity with the modern technology of mail delivery. And because they were not drawn from the localities for which they were responsible, the department was able to minimize the capture of inspectors by localities and their postmasters.[26]

In practice, the inspectors performed three supervisory functions for the department—monitoring system performance, assessing the moral "character" of local officials, and surveying political sentiment. The first category subsumed most inspection work. Here the department aimed its resources at three bastions of the old regime: the stagecoach contractors, first-class post offices in large cities, and fourth-class offices in small towns. As if to express its wish that the Railway Mail Service eclipse entirely the role of the stage in postal transport, the department employed not its regular inspectors but RMS agents to inspect stagecoaches. J. M. Masten, an assistant superintendent of the RMS, investigated numerous stage contractors in the 1890s. He had impressive powers at his disposal in case he found that the messenger service was not being run "properly." He could dissolve the contract on the spot and immediately begin to receive bids from other stage operators for a new one. Inspectors searched out lapses in service, and they vigorously regulated subcontracting among stage companies. An even more powerful strike at the power of stage contractors was the department's newfound ability to monitor stage auctions. These auctions had been subject to considerable collusion before 1890, but with inspectors traveling more widely and frequently, the department could more easily invalidate the results of an auction, deeming these "too high for acceptance," and demand lower, more "reasonable" bids.[27]

If the stage contractors were subject to invasive monitoring, local postmasters received insidious, sometimes harassing treatment. Department officials viewed third- and fourth-class postmasters as the primary holdovers of the cumbersome postal regime of the nineteenth century. The majority of the postal labor force having been covered in by 1896, postmasters were the only local-level officials who did not depend on savory efficiency reports for their jobs. As a result, conflicts between the Washington administration and the local postmasters were frequent and drawn out. Desiring to curtail the power and autonomy of the postmasters, Washington officials saw close monitoring by special agents as the ideal strategy. In 1888 Chief Inspector William A. West reported that postal inspectors had achieved a stunning precedent: the first systematic, office-by-office examination of post office accounts in the history of the department. The 1887–88 survey was directed, furthermore, at fourth-class offices. Special agents visited offices by the thousands, subjecting every aspect of local operations—accounts and log books, hiring, contracting, supplies, and equipment—to ruthless scrutiny. In cases of dispute between postmasters and mail messengers, or between postmasters and the RMS, the inspectors usually questioned the postmasters' stated version of the facts. Although they could not remove local postmasters except in cases of fraud (a rare but successfully employed tactic), they could make a postmaster's occupation abjectly miserable. Arkansas Democrat William Leake Terry—among the fourth-class postmasters' best allies in Congress—complained on the House floor in 1897 that "these petty post-office inspectors . . . are constantly, in order to secure a record of efficiency, hounding the hard-worked and poorly paid fourth-class postmaster, and deviling him with all kinds of petty criminalizations and charges."[28]

The special agents also traveled to determine the desirability and feasibility of new routes and contracts for carrying the mail. As the department projected its delivery network deeper into the nation's interior, it relied strongly on the recommendations of special agents as to which new routes to create for mail delivery and which to abandon. The agents offered their recommendations for both stage delivery routes and railway delivery routes.[29] By the turn of the century, field agents were privy to every aspect of postal operations—the railway delivery system, the stage auctions, route planning, hiring and firing at rural post offices, and even local workers' hours. By providing to Washington officials a previously unavailable view of local operations, and by supplying an independent assessment of bids in local auctions, the inspectors' corps became the informational glue of the department to a degree unwitnessed at any other period in American history.

A second function that special agents performed entailed moral judgment. In the new postal machine, the primary virtue was "reliability." Anything that detracted from a smooth, orderly performance—tardiness in the payment of debts, the use of alcohol, evidence of "shiftlessness"—was to be rooted out. For this reason, the department's agents assumed the role of judging "suitable character" and "reliability" for the department in the bidding of mail messenger and stage contracts. They offered character assessments for letter carriers, clerks, and even postmasters.[30]

Finally, the agents performed one function earlier provided by postmasters under the patronage system: monitoring local political sentiment. When local offices were eliminated, when one community (and not another) was chosen for free delivery service, when routes were changed or service terminated for a time, communities expressed varying levels of dissatisfaction. The department maintained an ongoing calculus of the political costs and benefits of these actions, even if the moves were administratively minute. What the special agents brought to the equation, again, was information. The department could propose the elimination of a delivery route or a local office, and the agents could provide an estimate of the local reaction. In addition, the special agents were instructed to arrange lines "without giving rise to complaint" from affected communities.[31]

The Political Autonomy of the Inspection Division

In Washington the Inspection Division saw continued success in moving Congress to enact favorable legislation. In the 1890s Comstock and John Ashe, inspector in charge at the New York Post Office, became frustrated by their inspectors' inability to make arrests without a prior warrant. In November 1895 Ashe instructed Comstock to draft a bill that would give postal inspectors the status of peace officers, with all of the powers then granted to U.S. marshals. The bill as written by Comstock gave the inspectors not only arrest powers but also the authority to summon a *Posse Comitatus* (which would consist, undoubtedly, of other inspectors) to aid in making arrests. Comstock's bill received the enthusiastic support of the departmental hierarchy, including Fourth Assistant Postmaster General R. A. Maxwell and Assistant Attorney General John Mouros.[32] Comstock then had a highly unlikely ally introduce his bill into the House of Representatives in January 1896: California Republican Eugene Loud. Why did Loud, an acknowledged opponent of postal expansion, act as Comstock's surrogate?

In pressing for full arrest powers, Comstock used a two-dimensional rhetorical strategy. He argued that arrest powers would help not only to combat fraud and vice in American culture but also to render postal inspection a more credible deterrent to mail crime, thereby enhancing the efficiency of the postal system. The second argument was key, for it appealed to business and media interests who were increasingly concerned about the department's mounting deficit. It was this argument that persuaded Loud. Not coincidentally, Comstock's bill as introduced by Loud was entitled "A Bill to Increase the Efficiency of the Postal Service." The dual rhetoric of anti-vice and efficiency was rehearsed almost verbatim by the House Judiciary Committee, which reported the bill. Both arguments were on display on the House floor in February 1897 when the chamber debated the measure and passed it by 117 to 94.[33]

Two features of the arrest powers law warrant notice. First, the House Post Office Committee never saw the bill, as Loud referred the bill to the Judiciary Committee. This referral alone suggests the success of Comstock's multidimensional rhetoric. The bill was no longer a postal matter alone but one that concerned the coercive power of the state. This brought fresh opposition from otherwise favorable Republicans, but it also brought new support from business-minded Republicans and anti-vice Democrats. Second, in the House debate and subsequent vote on February 25, 1897, standard sectional and party divisions inexplicably broke down. Whereas Loud, a clear Old Guard Republican, spoke in favor of the bill, House Speaker "Uncle Joe" Cannon, clearly of the same party wing, spoke in opposition and voted against it. Indeed, of the 94 votes against the arrest bill, 38 came from Republicans. On the other side of the aisle, 7 Democrats from all regions broke ranks to support Comstock's winning majority. Missouri representative Champ Clark—who later became Democratic Speaker of the House—also voted for the bill. Although the Democratic support was not crucial for the passage of the bill, unified Democratic opposition might clearly have doomed it, especially if many Democrats had not abstained. A statistical analysis of the House vote on the "Comstock arrest bill" supports this account. During the heyday of party voting as identified by David Brady and Philip Althoff, party was insignificantly associated with the Comstock arrest bill vote.[34]

For all of Comstock's legislative power, his fanaticism in enforcing statutes began to sour his reputation in the media. With growing frequency newspapers and social observers viewed Comstock's methods as entrapment. Allegations of physical abuse toward two women he had arrested—particularly Anna Rieble, a nineteen-year-old bookkeeper at the Art Students' League of New York— brought wide condemnation in the New York press. The *New York Times* and *Herald Tribune* vented their frustrations with increasing frequency after 1900. A growing torrent of criticism led to rumors in December 1906 that Postmaster General Cortelyou was about to dismiss Comstock. Comstock visited Cortelyou in Washington, and the NYSSV pleaded with Cortelyou to keep their agent on the department's rolls. Cortelyou once again sided with the mustachioed crusader, promising his "hearty support" in all of his efforts. More than anything else, the episode demonstrated the near-total reliance of the New York Society on Comstock's inspection powers.[35]

Even as Comstock began to incur public and media ridicule for his excessive stands, his division continued to assume new powers, successfully resisting executive and legislative attempts to rein it in or use it for partisan purposes. The division began by pushing for a codification of the postal laws and regulations so that conflicting regulations could be reconciled. In January 1901, when the

Senate blocked a House recodification bill, the department brazenly codified the laws and regulations on its own, creating for the first time in three decades a unified set of procedures that functioned as a blueprint for the regulation of mail matter. Under this codification, the department continued using "fraud orders" to prosecute and effectively disable firms that in the inspectors' judgment had violated the nonmailable statutes. The department had averaged more than 100 fraud orders per year in the 1890s but began to step up enforcement even more after 1900. In 1904 and 1905 inspectors issued 630 fraud orders, 71 more than during any other *four*-year period. Nor could mailers find any solace in the federal courts; in 1905 every single application to enjoin postal enforcement of a fraud order was summarily denied. Members of both parties in Congress watched the department's new momentum with concern. When Rep. Edward Crumpacker of Indiana introduced a bill that would require the Post Office to give notice of intent to issue a fraud order (with a fifteen-day window for a response by the accused), the House Post Office Committee passed it unanimously. The committee report included Alabama representative Henry Clayton's sharp criticism of the department's fraud order procedures. The bill passed the House in January 1907.[36]

The Crumpacker bill was a frontal attack on the power of Tyner and the inspectors' corps, and it set the department into action. Tyner and Comstock found a ready ally in the former postmaster general and then treasury secretary George Cortelyou, who had begun his public career in the inspectors' office. At the prompting of Tyner, Comstock, and others, Cortelyou launched a public campaign against the bill. Cortelyou published an essay in the April 1907 *North American Review* arguing that discretionary fraud orders were necessary for the Post Office to combat "fly-by-night" mail-order firms who could instantly disassemble their operations. The campaign worked, and the department "was successful in getting the bill buried in the Senate committee."[37]

Indeed, no postal legislation, no matter how popular, passed Congress against the wishes of the department from 1900 to 1910. The Post Office succeeded in killing off Pennsylvania senator Boies Penrose's bill to deny second-class mailing privileges to magazines declared nonmailable, and it secured the pigeonholing of other bills that imposed due process restrictions on the exclusion of newspapers from the mails. A bill by Rep. Charles Bartlett (Georgia) to provide for mandamus proceedings against the postmaster general when he denied second-class mailing privileges was tabled, like other attempts to rein in the department's inspection power.[38]

The department's most impressive show of political independence came when it resisted congressional and presidential attempts to use mail exclusion for partisan ends. When Roosevelt's nemesis and Socialist Party leader Eugene V. Debs angered the president in a 1906 article in the socialist weekly *Appeal to Reason*, Roosevelt asked the department to ban the paper from the mails. The department sat silently on Roosevelt's request. In 1908 Roosevelt again sought enforcement against the "enemies of mankind" at *La Questione Sociale* of Paterson, New Jersey. The department again declined, with Attorney General Charles Bonaparte holding that legislation would be needed for administrative action against socialist papers. Finally, on April 9, 1908, Roosevelt wrote Congress asking for a statute that would permit the postal exclusion of any paper advancing "anarchistic opinions." The Senate Post Office Committee added the necessary proviso as a rider to the 1908 postal appropriations bill. Yet the department again refused to use its new statutory authority. Twice more, in 1907 and 1908, the Post Office rebuffed presidential and congressional attempts to dictate its enforcement agenda. Postal officials focused neither on partisan papers nor on sensationalistic media reporting but on what they deemed to be "mail fraud" and "obscenity." They succeeded in 1912 in getting Congress to extend their authority to films, and their decisions met with uninhibited approval from the federal judiciary.[39]

By 1900, then, Washington officials and postal inspectors were the power ascendant in the Post Office Department. The days of local independence had passed. By harnessing the technology of modern postal delivery and employing it for purposes of organizational monitoring, by vaulting the inspectors to new posts of prestige and authority, and by cultivating an outlook among the inspectors that favored the RMS vision of a postal machine, Washington officials such as Perry Heath, Chief Inspector Wheeler, Tyner, Stuart, Rathbone, and others fundamentally altered the everyday pattern of operations in their favor. In the realm of Progressive politics, the Inspection Division became an independent actor. Postal inspectors pressed their anti-obscenity campaigns as far as Comstock and his associates wished to carry them, and they resisted the attempts of Roosevelt and congressional Republicans to push them into partisan espionage.

The Transformation of Postal Operations: Inspection, Turnout, and City Free Delivery, 1896–1910

Growing an inspection force was one matter. Translating inspection and RMS-style efficiency into postal efficiency was another. Politicians and press critics still decried the department's yearly deficit. The causes mentioned were numerous—from second-class mail privileges to congressional franking to overpayments to railroads for carrying the mail—but the annoying fact of multimillion-dollar shortfalls would not disappear. With little control over railway mail payments or the franking privilege, postal officials knew that any deficit-reduction strategy would have to come from within. And their first targets were the large first- and second-class offices of cities and towns. City free delivery operations, extended willy-nilly by Congress in the late nineteenth century, constituted the meat of the postal deficit. From 1883—the year after the department ran its last surplus of the nineteenth century—to 1896, city free delivery costs almost quadrupled, jumping from $3.5 million to $12.7 million in inflation-adjusted (1900) dollars. The postal deficit tracked this increase almost dollar for dollar, rising from $3.4 million to $10.2 million. As free delivery ballooned, urban offices proliferated without bound, carriers were hired by the tens of thousands, and the department's ability to compel efficiency from its forces withered.

The booming deficit of the early 1890s stood as a statistical mockery of the department's new mechanical self-image. For all of the fear that special agents struck in the hearts of postmasters and clerks, it is questionable whether centralization and inspection truly lowered the department's costs. Did the department's centralizing efforts make a difference?

If measured by the political discomfort that they raised, the success of the reformers is undeniable. With newfound certainty, the department, for the first time in the history of the national postal network, began systematically to consolidate offices and curtail urban services. In 1898 the department reduced free delivery service in Boston, New York, and Philadelphia and other first-class offices by eliminating carrier positions. The moves brought petitions to Congress from numerous business groups, including the selectmen of Brookline, Massachusetts, the Philadelphia Grocers' and Importers' Exchange, and the Wilkes-Barre Board of Trade. In New York a protest organized by the Merchant's Association gathered ex–postmaster general Thomas L. James, ex-senator Warner Miller, the Catholic Club's John Rooney, and Rep. Amos J. Cummings. The association's petition to Congress was signed by hundreds of New York luminaries, including Rabbi Gustave Gottheil, Archbishop Michael Corrigan, Louis Stern, George Clinton Batchellor, and Arthur Sullivan.[40]

The protests of eastern cities against postal consolidation were loud but unsuccessful. Postal officials displaced urban carriers and clerks with streetcar railway post offices (RPOs). The cars could quicken mail delivery and reduce the role of clerks by combining sorting with delivery. Saint Louis postmaster Major John B. Harlow, himself a former railway mail clerk under Armstrong, started street rail service in 1891, and by 1895 fourteen cities had streetcar offices. Unlike urban carriers, streetcars could stick closely to published schedules. And the streetcars carried an important title that demarcated them from previous urban operations: United States Railway Post Office. The streetcar office was a moving emblem of reform, presaging the railway-modeled overhaul of city delivery.[41]

The new regime relentlessly standardized numerous aspects of postal operations. In the 1870s and 1880s, most accounts in post offices were written in whatever form the postmaster wished to record them. Money-order books for Cedar Rapids in 1870 were organized according to daily receipts, whereas the books for Garrison, Iowa, in 1887 contained a separate entry for every individual order. The only commonality for both offices is that the books were loosely scribbled in the postmaster's hand. Such disparities across offices were a primary target of the postal inspectors at the turn of the century, as Marshall Cushing noticed. After the department issued a new set of regulations in 1893, however, uniform accounting procedures quickly took hold in the nation's post offices. Postmasters no longer jotted down receipts according to their discretion or their personal organizational style. Instead, they completed standard account forms issued by the central office. The department also targeted postmarking, or imprinting stamps with the date and place of postage. Accurate postmarking was essential for inspectors who sought stolen mail or fraudulent businesses. In 1897 First Assistant Postmaster General Perry S. Heath, a holdover from the Wanamaker era, issued a circular that standardized the practice. Heath's circular warned postmasters that the Post Office was "determined to secure a radical reform in the method of postmarking," demonstrating the reformers' commitment to a thorough overhaul of even the most minute operations.[42]

Statistical evidence suggests that these moves were not merely symbolic. The turn of the century recorded a sharp decline in the postal operations deficit from more than 10 percent of revenues in the 1890s to a fiscal balance by 1912 (see figure 4.1). Moreover, table 4.1 shows that the decline in the postal deficit was almost certainly driven by increased efficiency in city free delivery. The answer surely *cannot* lie in rural free delivery, which only increased costs after it began in 1896 (though it did not really begin on a large scale until 1902). Even though RFD boosted postal revenues, revenue growth cannot account for the department's improved fiscal state. Real revenue growth during the period of deficit expansion (1883–96) was almost *double* the revenue growth when the deficit was shrinking (1897–1910). Nor can the deficit reductions be explained by two

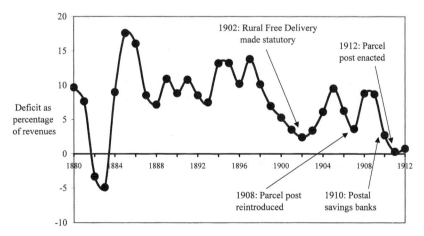

Figure 4.1 The rise and eclipse of the postal deficit from 1883 to 1912.

TABLE 4.1
City Free Delivery and the Postal Deficit from the Pendleton Act to 1910

	1883–1896	*1897–1910*
Movement in deficit over period	From: 4.8% surplus (1883) To: 10.2% deficit (1896)	From: 13.1% deficit (1897) To: 2.3% deficit (1910)[a]
Average annual percentage increase (API) in total revenues	8.6%	4.6%
Average API in total costs	9.7	3.9
Average API in city free delivery costs[b]	16.1	4.0

Source: "Statistics of the Postal Service from 1862 to 1910," in *Postal Policies and Problems,* address by Daniel Roper (Washington, D.C.: GPO, 1913); also in Albert S. Burleson Papers, Library of Congress.

[a]The deficit was fully erased in 1912.

[b]City free delivery statistics exclude payments to railroads. All figures are calculated from raw figures in 1900 dollars, using price deflators from *Historical Statistics of the United States.*

other factors to which the postal system's scourges constantly pointed— second-class mail privileges and railway mail payments. The department carried second-class mail (primarily magazines, catalogs, and newspapers) at a consistent loss from the early 1800s on—essentially subsidizing these by overcharging letter writers—but the fundamental payment scheme was unaltered between 1890 and 1910. Similarly, the basic scheme for paying railroads was also unchanged during this period. The key to the department's fiscal health was a robust reduction in *spending.* Some of this was due to reduced payments to railroads for carrying the mails, which leveled off at about $49 million from 1907 to 1910. In the absence of city free delivery efficiencies, however, the plateau of railroad payments would not have been sufficient to eliminate the deficit. The largest declines were in city free delivery, where the department achieved a 75 percent reduction in annual spending increases from 1897 to 1910.[43]

The deficit reductions received favorable attention from journals of opinion, including *The Outlook, The American Review of Reviews,* and *World's Work.* As *The Outlook* noted in 1907, the deficit had previously been considered the prime example of why the Post Office should not manage either a parcels system or savings banks.

> But it is worth while noting that this argument against the Government's engaging in business is losing force year by year. Fifty years ago the deficit was forty-three per cent of the receipts of the Department; ten years ago it had dropped to thirteen percent; in 1906 it was but a little over three and one-half per cent; while in the year just

passed it was a little over three and one-half percent. If the progress which has been continued so steadily since 1857 continues, it should be but a very few years before the post-office will show a profit on its yearly business.

Astute observers also noted a grand institutional irony in the deficit drop. As Congressman George W. Norris asked in his essay "Why Not Take the Post Office Department Out of Politics?" the deficit reductions were occurring at a time when civil service rules still allowed thousands of political appointments to important, discretion-laden positions. Although supporting further reforms, Progressives were not congratulating the Pendleton Act for a more profitable Post Office.[44]

A Statistical Analysis of City Free Delivery, 1896–1910

Whereas the cost reduction in city delivery tracks the growth of inspectors after 1890, a thorough analysis of the Progressive transformation of postal operations requires attention to local operations. Fortunately the National Archives holds a detailed source of information. In part because information about first- and second-class operations was so elusive, in 1896 the Post Office began to track their behavior in a multiyear survey of costs and receipts. The initial survey collected data on costs and revenues, the population served and square miles covered in the delivery program, the number of deliveries and collections per week (for businesses and residences, separately), expenditures for stock and contracting, the number of letter boxes maintained by the office, and the average yearly hours tolled by postal carriers. The very execution of the survey and the richness of its data evince the growing power of postal headquarters to investigate local-level operations.

To examine the determinants of cost reduction at the local level, I have selected all post offices of the first and second class for three states: Iowa, Pennsylvania, and Texas. I chose these three states for several reasons. First, the combination represents some geographic and socioeconomic diversity. Of the three, Pennsylvania was the most populous state during this period, with a strong manufacturing sector and a developed primary-sector economy. Iowa represents a Plains state and a relatively advanced agricultural economy, and Texas represents the South, with its relatively depressed agricultural economy (combined with emergent mining sectors) at the turn of the century. The second reason is political diversity. Iowa was among the most reliable states of the post-1896 Republican stronghold in the Plains, whereas Texas remained firmly in the southern Democratic fold. Pennsylvania mixed coalitions of both parties, combining a more electorally competitive industrial core with a solidly Republican hinterland.

By a variety of indices, the cost of free delivery declined in all three states from 1896 to 1908. State-level summaries of office data for Pennsylvania, Texas,

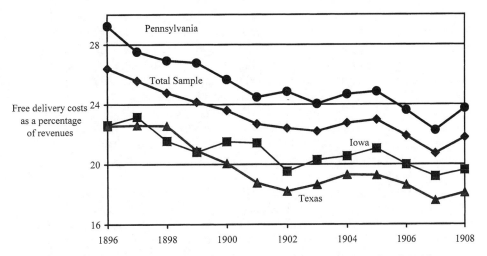

Figure 4.2 The cost reductions in free delivery from 1896 to 1908. (National Archives data from post offices in Iowa, Pennsylvania, and Texas)

and Iowa show that they reasonably track the department's aggregate measures in official reports. As figure 4.2 shows, offices in all three states reported consistent declines in costs as a percentage of receipts.[45]

At the level of individual offices, the National Archives data also permit a statistical analysis of the factors driving the department's cost reductions. Accordingly, I analyzed the determinants of office-level costs—the very object of postal officials' efforts—in a three-state panel regression. The department's survey includes a number of useful measures. The estimated population served by the office and the number of square miles in a service zone measure the population- and geography-based demand for free delivery. The number of postal carriers employed measures the brute labor requirements of free delivery. The institutional and political determinants of the demand for mail are measured by the log of program receipts, the number of business deliveries per week, the number of residential deliveries per week, the number of business collections per week, the number of residential collections per week, and the number of letter boxes in the postal zone.

The survey also yielded two variables—carriers' office time per ten days and carriers' total time per ten days—which evince the reach of the department's data collection efforts. If, as Richard John has argued of the nineteenth-century system, the efficiency of postal operations depended more on logistics than on the speed of actual delivery, that is, if it depended more on coordination than on execution per se, then office time should be a critical determinant of efficiency. Both terms should be negatively associated with costs, especially the office time measure.

There is reason to suspect, however, that partisan strategy was also at work. Even though first- and second-class carriers were covered in, their bosses were not. City postmasters had impressive political leverage at their disposal. They could employ carriers to canvass for the party, press for greater hiring of clerks and carriers during election years, and use the power of contracting to spend more in areas where the party most needed an infusion of pork. All three strategies inflated costs. As a result, costs were probably greater where Republicans were the majority party. Higher costs might also have prevailed where localities supported the Republicans with greater turnout—less important for House races but critical in newly popularized Senate and presidential contests.

Finally, National Archives data on postal inspectors permit an assessment of whether the department's inspection efforts met with success. If increased inspection reduced postal spending, then costs should be negatively associated with the number of inspectors overseeing an office. Yet the factional conflict between the Railway Mail Service and the free delivery operations suggests that the sheer number of inspectors is a poor measure for the force or presence of inspection. For this reason, I include the percentage of inspectors overseeing an office who were promoted from the Railway Mail Service. And consistent with the intuition that better-paid and longer-tenured inspectors were, on average, more likely to discover inefficiencies at the local level, I include aggregates of the percentage of inspectors paid more than $2,000 and the average employment duration of inspectors. I expect all four of these inspection variables to be negatively associated with cost.[46]

Using these unique data, I estimate several "cost function" regressions to determine which factors were positively or negatively associated with costs across offices and over time. The models are fixed-effects panel regressions in which dummy variables are assigned to each post office and each year. In table 4.2 I split the sample into three separate state-level regressions. In table 4.3 I combine the state-level samples and estimate the cost function for all 153 offices. Table 4.3 also includes a model of costs as a percentage of receipts for an easier interpretation of the results.

The results of panel estimation in tables 4.2 and 4.3 show that cost reductions in free delivery were driven by the advance of inspection and the decline in voting turnout. For proper interpretation, negative coefficients indicate cost reductions and hence greater efficiency. This efficiency is a nonlinear function of population—large cities had cost margins almost as efficient as those of the smallest cities. The results also show that two services of the free delivery program—business deliveries and residential collections—visibly boosted postal spending. Moreover, estimates for the hours-worked measures are consistent with intuition; in most cases, costs were systematically lower where self-reported hours were higher.

One of the strongest results of the statistical analysis appears in the turnout variable. In Pennsylvania and Iowa, electoral turnout consistently inflated free

TABLE 4.2
Inspection and Cost Efficiency in the Free Delivery System

Variable	Pennsylvania (90 offices)	Iowa (36 offices)	Texas (27 offices)
Constant	1.988** (0.567)	3.758** (0.556)	4.734** (0.945)
ln(Receipts)	0.6030** (0.0372)	0.5155** (0.0520)	0.3366** (0.0889)
Population served	0.0000060** (0.0000011)	0.0000178** (0.0000040)	0.0000295** (0.0000055)
(Population served)^2	-1.834 E-10** (2.642 E-11)	-2.105 E-08** (4.391 E-09)	-2.465 E-08** (4.563 E-09)
Square miles in service zone	-0.0015 (0.0028)	0.0050 (0.0030)	0.0135* (0.0054)
Number of postal carriers	-0.0018* (0.0009)	0.0032 (0.0046)	0.0156** (0.0049)
Business deliveries per week	0.0518** (0.0125)	0.0506** (0.0138)	0.0569* (0.0233)
Residential deliveries per week	-0.0052 (0.0133)	-0.0068 (0.0208)	0.0174* (0.0043)
Business collections per week	0.0052 (0.0063)	-0.0021 (0.0081)	-0.0027 (0.0091)
Residential collections per week	0.0193* (0.0085)	0.0103 (0.0102)	-0.0588^+ (0.0321)
Number of letter boxes in zone	-0.0002 (0.0003)	0.0025** (0.0008)	-0.0010 (0.0009)
Carriers' office time per 10 days	-0.0315 (0.0236)	-0.0540* (0.0237)	-0.1003* (0.0403)
Carriers' total time per 10 days	-0.0593 (0.0472)	-0.1739** (0.0357)	0.0560 (0.0386)
County illiteracy rate (percentage of adults)	0.0221$^+$ (0.0141)	0.0117 (0.0010)	0.0014 (0.0061)
Percentage of county vote for Republican congressional candidate, previous election	0.0002 (0.0010)	-0.0043** (0.0013)	0.0017 (0.0013)
Percentage voter turnout, previous election	0.0040** (0.0010)	0.0087** (0.0012)	-0.0011 (0.0016)
Absolute percentage difference between Republican and Democratic Party, previous election	0.0013 (0.0010)	0.0018 (0.0012)	0.0004 (0.0008)
Number of inspectors	0.0061* (0.0027)	0.0073** (0.0016)	-0.0122* (0.0057)
Percentage of inspectors trained in RMS	-0.0048** (0.0014)	-0.0190** (0.0035)	-0.0058 (0.0057)

(*continued*)

TABLE 4.2
(*Continued*)

Variable	Pennsylvania (90 offices)	Iowa (36 offices)	Texas (27 offices)
Percentage of inspectors paid over $2000	−0.0075* (0.0020)	−0.0037 (0.0040)	−0.0097+ (0.0054)
Average tenure (in years) of inspectors	0.0599** (0.0156)	0.1011** (0.0305)	−0.0204 (0.0232)
$\rho[e_t]$	0.6919**	0.7038**	0.7610**
n (df)	1061 (934)	440 (369)	307 (245)
Hausman [Pr]	155.67 [0.0000]	111.08 [0.0000]	26.81 [0.1408]
Var(e_t) [Var(u_t)]	0.033 [0.073]	0.015 [0.035]	0.029 [0.093]
Adjusted R^2	0.85	0.91	0.91

Dependent variable is the natural log of free delivery costs of office i in year t. Two-factor fixed effects panel estimation; includes office and year dummies. Standard errors in parentheses.

*Significance at $p < 0.05$.
**Significance at $p < 0.01$.
+Significance at $p < 0.10$.
(All tests are two-tailed).

delivery costs. The only null estimate for turnout appears in the one state where Republicans did not wish to reward voting—Democratic Texas. The historical implications of this finding offer novel interpretations of the oft-noted "efficiency gains" of the Progressive period.[47] One reason that city post offices spent less for free delivery in the Progressive period is that after 1896, the decline in turnout gave Republicans less reason to reward voters with tangible incentives. On average, electoral turnout in the three states declined by 21 percentage points from the election of 1896 to the election of 1908. This aggregate drop accounts for a decline of 1.3 percentage points in costs as a percentage of revenues, or fully 28.1 percent of the department's free delivery cost reduction during the period covered by the sample.

The estimates for inspection variables tell a complicated story. When other inspection variables are excluded, the size of the inspection force is associated with cost reductions (and weakly so) only in Texas. Indeed, in table 4.2, the number of inspectors is positively related to costs in Pennsylvania and Iowa. Once cross-state differences are taken into account in table 4.3, however, the coefficient for this variable becomes negative. The results suggest that growth of the department's inspection force had its greatest effects in the western states such as Texas where the force was absent before 1890.

TABLE 4.3
Inspection and Cost Efficiency in the Free Delivery System: Full National Archives Sample
of 153 Post Offices from 1896 to 1910

Variable	ln (costs)	Costs as percentage of receipts
Constant	1.964** (0.345)	35.9386** (4.8088)
ln(Receipts)	0.6406** (0.0257)	—
Population served	0.0000049** (0.0000008)	0.000010** (0.000014)
(Population served)^2	−1.560 E-10** (2.018 E-11)	−5.46 E-10 (3.40 E-10)
Square miles in service zone	0.0024 (0.0020)	−0.0729* (0.0348)
Number of postal carriers	−0.0019* (0.0008)	0.0026 (0.0137)
Business deliveries per week	0.0550** (0.0095)	0.7531** (0.1575)
Residential deliveries per week	0.0039 (0.0115)	0.1668 (0.1916)
Business collections per week	0.0069 (0.0045)	0.0422 (0.0737)
Residential collections per week	0.0184* (0.0069)	0.2099$^+$ (0.1147)
Number of letter boxes in zone	−0.00005 (0.00028)	−0.0019 (0.0049)
Carriers' office time per 10 days	−0.0471** (0.0169)	−0.4438 (0.2784)
Carriers' total time per 10 days	−0.0746** (0.0245)	−2.0361** (0.4059)
Average wage in county, 1900	0.00038 (0.00034)	−0.0023 (0.0072)
Average salary in county, 1900	0.00022* (0.00009)	—
County illiteracy rate (percentage of adults)	0.0030 (0.0035)	0.0739 (0.0798)
Percentage of county vote for Republican congressional candidate, previous election	0.0011** (0.0004)	−0.0045 (0.0065)
Percentage voter turnout, previous election	0.0038** (0.0006)	0.0617** (0.0107)
Absolute percentage difference between Republican and Democratic Party, previous election	0.0009* (0.0004)	0.0112$^+$ (0.0059)
Number of inspectors	−0.0023* (0.0010)	−0.0226$^+$ (0.0163)
Percentage of inspectors trained in RMS	−0.0047** (0.0008)	−0.0686** (0.0137)

(*continued*)

TABLE 4.3
(*Continued*)

Variable	*ln (costs)*	Costs as percentage of receipts
Percentage of inspectors paid over $2000	−0.0020* (0.0009)	−0.0335 (0.0150)
Average tenure (in years) of inspectors	−0.0091 (0.0080)	0.0766 (0.1304)
$\rho[e_t]$	0.6476**	0.7932**
n (df)	1808 (1633)	1904 (1716)
$\sigma(e_t)$ $[\sigma(u_t)]$	0.35 [0.23]	6.36 [3.48]
Adjusted R^2	0.86	0.07

Dependent variable is free delivery costs of office i in year t. Standard errors are in parentheses. Two-factor fixed effects panel estimation; includes office and year dummies.
*Significance at $p < 0.05$.
**Significance at $p < 0.01$.
+Significance at $p < 0.10$.
(All tests are two-tailed).

Yet if the effects of a growing inspection corps are muddled, the force of a new generation of railway-trained inspectors is not. The most powerful factor in the department's efficiency was the twenty-point increase in the percentage of inspectors who were trained in the Railway Mail Service. This variable is negatively associated with delivery costs in all regressions. In the aggregate, increased RMS training contributed to a 1.34-point decline in costs as a percentage of revenues, making it more powerful than any other variable in boosting the department's efficiency. Using the coefficient estimates from table 4.3, three inspection variables—the growth of the inspection force, the prevalence of RMS veterans, and the presence of well-paid inspectors—account for 55 percent of the free delivery cost reductions from McKinley to Taft.

Perhaps the starkest evidence for the force of inspection appears in the standardization of office operations. Figure 4.3 plots the standard deviation across offices of cost margins and hours worked from 1896 to 1908. The standard deviation of total hours worked fell by 10 percent during this period, whereas the standard deviation of office time plummeted by almost half. Moreover, the cost margins of local offices became much more predictable, as the standard deviation of costs as a percentage of revenues fell by over a full point. With the advance of inspection, first- and second-class offices looked (and worked) more and more like one another.

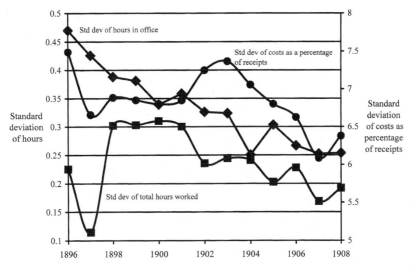

Figure 4.3 The standardization of free delivery operations from 1896 to 1908.

The answer to the riddle of declining delivery costs, then, rests less in the *numerical* than in the *procedural* and *ideological* advance of inspection. Investigation by railway-trained special agents rendered post offices everywhere less costly and more uniform. Not only were inspectors in greater force, boosting the likelihood of monitoring for all offices, but their interests and ideology were now clearly aligned against those of postmasters. Where inspectors once displayed a tacit ignorance of local-level problems, their factional energy now wrought new economies from city offices. Standard procedures were adopted with much greater uniformity than before. Large city offices were consolidated for the first time in the history of the network. And the eyes of the department—particularly its reform wing in the inspection corps and the RMS—were ubiquitous, compelling local self-consciousness. With an aggressive local presence cemented after 1890, the department gained the upper hand in its decades-long struggle with local shirking.

Rural Free Delivery: Experimentation, Reputation, and the Demise of Local Rule

No genuine transformation of the postal system could proceed without a full institutional rewiring of rural operations. The loose nexus of contracts among stagecoach operators, mail messengers, star route carriers, and country postmasters remained essentially unchanged since the Jacksonian era. The slow implementation of rural free delivery was the final step in system integration, to which the postal reformers had aspired for two decades. RFD was no mere extension but an overhaul of the entire national delivery network. Precisely as its departmental proponents wished, RFD buried the last vestiges of the nineteenth-century postal regime. The department employed buggy drivers and route riders to deliver the mail directly to the homes of rural denizens. It trained drivers to file mail matter inside the stage as they drove their routes, creating a "travelling post office" modeled after the railway mail cars. As the role of the country postmaster was eclipsed, two figures with greater allegiance to the department—the rural carrier and the special agent—arose to occupy this important community niche.

The reigning story of the Rural Free Delivery program—its origins and its operation—relegates the Post Office Department to the role of bit player in an agrarian policy drama. In the most recent work on the program, Samuel Kernell and Michael McDonald argue that the principal movers behind rural free delivery were farm groups and their representatives in Congress. Kernell and McDonald even suggest that the department opposed RFD, relenting to congressional pressure to create the program after several years of recalcitrance. The authors marshal and analyze an impressive fund of data on RFD route allocations to show that congressional Republicans strategically placed delivery routes to stabilize the congressional majority they had won in 1894. Spawned by agrarian demands for parity with cities, and shrewdly managed to cultivate Republican votes in the agrarian interior, the rural free delivery system is depicted in this analysis as a movement creation and a partisan tool.[48]

In this section I offer a different interpretation of the decade-long struggle for rural free delivery. RFD was the essential step toward centralization and program expansion, fervently sought by postal reformers in the department who wanted increased jurisdiction and control over local offices. Indeed, no accurate portrait of RFD can ignore the integral role of the department in its creation. Postal officials conceived, planned, lobbied for, and secured the passage of RFD as did no other actor or force in the United States. More to the point, the emergence of rural delivery illuminates the dynamics of reputation-based autonomy, as the timing of the program's growth depended critically on the department's ability to demonstrate its fiscal stability. An initial period of administrative experimentation was followed by a heightened departmental reputation for efficacy. Combined with network-based lobbying among rural presses and Progressives for the program, legislative perceptions about postal efficiency drove the passage of RFD. To be sure, Wayne Fuller properly suggests that organized farmers helped to push the system into statutory existence. So, too, Kernell and McDonald rightly point to the partisan electoral logic governing route allocations. The difficulty, as I will show, is that neither agrarian petitioning nor strategic route allocation can be considered independent of the Post Office. As with other cases of Progressive policy reform, the deluge of agrarian sentiment was orchestrated by the bureaucracy. Agrarians wrote en masse to Congress and the department in support of RFD only after the department had asked them to. And route allocations were managed not by Congress but by the department, and they served the designs of postal officials just as much as (if not more than) those of legislators.

However RFD is conceived, there is little doubt or discord that it marked a grave departure from postal business as usual in the 1890s. For rural postmasters and star route contractors—the last holdouts of the nineteenth-century Post Office—rural free delivery presented a mortal threat to their power and their livelihood. Even with the rapid expansion of railway delivery routes into the nation's rural interior, the structure of postal delivery before 1896 remained little altered from the antebellum postal network. Rural citizens did not receive their mail; instead they made weekly trips to the nearest post office to retrieve it from a post office box located in a general or common store owned or managed by a fourth-class postmaster. These travel patterns allowed the postmaster to augment his store business with postal patrons and conferred community status and political power on the postmaster, often the central political figure in nineteenth-century rural locales. Fuller argues that fourth-class postmasters were the central institutional actors of the old regime. "In the rural America of the 1890's and early 1900's, country postmasters were virtually institutions. With their little combination stores and fourth-class post offices, they had been the heart of the old rural mail system from George Washington's day to the beginning of rural free delivery."[49]

RFD also promised (or threatened) to truly nationalize the postal system. For star route riders were, like stage managers, private employees of the department operating under the terms of delivery contracts. And neither the star route riders nor the private stages had adopted and displayed the seal of the Post Office Department or, much less, the insignia "U.S. Mail." The symbolic quality of these agents was to some members of Congress exceedingly poor. "Of all the disgraceful, damnable things that undertake to *represent* the United States, this [contract] service is . . . the worst," said one Georgia congressman.[50] By 1890 only 10 million of 76 million American citizens received their mail directly from officials of the United States government.

Coordinating Pressure through Multiple Networks

Scattered demands for rural delivery had surfaced in the 1870s, beginning perhaps with the journalist John Stahl, who claimed in his 1920s memoirs that he had conceived the idea as early as 1879. Yet as Fuller notes, it was the Post Office that coordinated pressure for RFD: "[U]ntil Postmaster General John Wanamaker began to agitate for rural free delivery in 1891, few people had ever heard of it." Extending the free delivery system to rural villages and towns was one of Wanamaker's chief concerns upon taking office. In November 1889 he opened his tenure with a call to extend the free delivery system to "all places of a population not less than 5,000, or where the post-office has shown a gross revenue of $7,000 for the previous fiscal year," an umbrella that included 350 towns. New Jersey Republican C. D. Beckwith promptly followed Wanamaker's lead. He wrote the postmaster general's proposal into a bill in February 1890 and requested Wanamaker's advice throughout in selling and modifying the expansion. The Senate proposed to take Wanamaker's suggestion one step further, proposing free delivery for towns with a population of five thousand but a revenue of only $5,000. Yet in a letter to Pennsylvania Republican Henry Bingham, chair of the House Post Office Committee, Wanamaker carefully outlined the fiscal reasons for a more limited and incremental measure. The postmaster general's revenue statistics, displayed at length but ably summarized, made a powerful case for an aggressive but limited delivery expansion. The House found it impossible to disregard the informational advantages of Wanamaker's office. Bingham's committee bowed to Wanamaker's expertise, and Congress authorized the more limited extension of the free delivery system that the department had requested. From the very first steps of rural free delivery, Wanamaker and the department assumed control of its expansion.[51]

The following year, Wanamaker began to sketch a new plan for experimentation, a proposal far bolder than even Bingham could fathom. Wanamaker suggested extending free delivery to towns with just five hundred persons or more. He asked for appropriations to begin testing the feasibility of the idea, and Senator Philetus Sawyer, a Wisconsin Republican, obliged, attaching a resolution to the postal deficiency bill that authorized $10,000 for experimental rural delivery. In the department's annual report for 1890–91, Wanamaker took the decisive step in the inauguration of RFD. In two widely read essays—"Rural Free Delivery" and "Free Delivery on Star Routes"—he proposed a comprehensive rural free delivery system, a nationwide network with divisional status in the department, and he requested further experimental funds to begin its construction. The department's experience with previous free delivery experiments had convinced Wanamaker that a full-fledged system of delivery could be inaugurated. Before 1890 rural free delivery had been an opaque vision; now Wanamaker offered to make it an organizational and administrative reality.[52]

Wanamaker expected that RFD would secure its principal support from rural constituencies, but RFD split farm communities. Fourth-class postmasters, the central figures in rural towns, lobbied heavily against rural delivery, and star-route contractors, whose jobs were even less secure, raised a loud cry in favor of the old regime. The centrality of these figures in the Republican Party left many representatives split between ushering in a new postal system and retaining the old one. In addition, wholesalers, rural store owners, and other commercial middlemen saw RFD as a threat to their businesses—they knew that once RFD was inaugurated, it would be only a matter of time before the rural carriers transported not just letters but packages too. As Hal Barron shows in

his recent survey *Mixed Harvest,* there was a sustained anti-mail-order movement in the rural North from the 1890s through the 1910s, and many rural businesses—including village newspapers and local merchants—reacted to talk of
free delivery with muddled feelings. To complicate matters, Charles Burrows,
who championed small wholesalers, offered a powerful policy alternative to
RFD—one-cent postage. Burrows's plan promised to reduce the farmers' mail
bill by half while fending off RFD's threat to wholesalers, fourth-class offices,
and star routers. His alternative found favor with the National Board of Trade
and with some agrarian papers, including the *Farm Journal,* which castigated
Wanamaker: "The *Farm Journal* wants, and the people want, Mr. Wanamaker,
1 cent postage. We don't want our country roads overrun with half-paid federal
officials delivering 2 cent letters at a cost of 10 cents a letter."[53]

Wanamaker and his officials knew they had a selling job to do. So they
shrewdly cultivated agrarian support through their ties to farm leaders and
presses. Throughout 1891 Wanamaker and his subordinates met with leaders of
the National Grange, the National Farmers' Congress, and the numerous state
Farmers' Alliances, outlining RFD's benefits and nudging them to press for the
program. He publicly summoned rural communities to petition Congress to
grant the department experimental funds to enlarge the program. And he collected his thoughts in an article of the November 1891 issue of the *American
Agriculturist,* an essay that was widely read, circulated, and excerpted in the
rural press. The support of farmers—through the Grange, the alliances, and the
petitions—placed rural free delivery permanently on the congressional agenda.
In Congress, their voices were channeled through the agrarian radical Rep.
Thomas E. Watson of Georgia. The National Grange organized a massive petition drive in 1891 and 1892, one extending throughout the Plains states and
New England. The *Philadelphia Bulletin* noted that "the Farmers' Alliance and
the Patrons of Husbandry are using all their influence to further the scheme."[54]

For all of their strength, farmers did not come to RFD advocacy alone. The
department had welcomed their participation and had made the Grange and Alliance coalition partners in the campaign. In this respect, the crucial initiating
moves for RFD were made not by agrarians but by the Post Office. Broad and
consistent grassroots support for RFD among farm organizations and their representatives did not precede but *followed* Wanamaker's proposals in 1890 and
1891. Only after Wanamaker provided his "official blessing" did the organized
clamor for RFD begin. After his meetings and communications with farm editors and movement leaders, an avalanche of petitions descended on Congress
and the department. Most were form petitions with ledgers for signatures,
printed and distributed by farm journal editors. Accordingly, little mention is
made of rural free delivery in congressional debates or hearings until May 1892,
when the Committee on Post Offices and Post Roads reported "a large number
of petitions from several states asking Congress to extend free delivery of mails
to rural districts. The demand has been so great that we have given the subject

full consideration." Through skilled appeal to organized rural opinion, Wanamaker had set the agenda of the Post Office Committee for the ensuing decade.[55]

Wanamaker also lectured widely to business and civic associations in support of rural delivery. He began in September 1891 by taking the idea before a friendly audience: the Manufacturer's Club of Philadelphia, a group of elites whom he knew well from his career as a chain-store magnate. Other manufacturing and commerce groups would soon follow. These were wise overtures. Wanamaker had hoped to split apart Charles Burrows's coalition by energizing mail-order houses and manufacturers who sought lower delivery costs and pitting them against rural wholesalers and express companies who monopolized the transport of consumer goods to farmers.[56]

The Post Office also dominated the fiscal debate over RFD. With the $10,000 appropriation, the department had begun experimental rural delivery from 46 post offices in February 1891. By April 1892 Wanamaker could report "the most satisfactory and gratifying results"—RFD had increased post office revenues in 40 of the 46 experimental sites. The experiment was profiting the department at a rate of almost $10,000 per year, or the amount of the original appropriation. Ever in pursuit of more agrarian support for the department's plan, Wanamaker trumpeted the revenue statistics in a letter to the *American Agriculturist* in November 1891, a full six months before presenting the numbers to Congress. Hundreds of newspapers mentioned the statistics in their advocacy of rural free delivery, reporting that the experiments had "awakened widespread interest" in the program, having been "successful to the point of creating a demand for more."[57]

The department's role in inaugurating the program is not merely of academic interest. Whatever historians may suggest, nineteenth-century contemporaries were united in their belief that RFD was the invention of Wanamaker and his departmental officers. The Accotink (Virginia) Farmer's Club resolved to "approve the recommendation of the Postmaster General in reference to the establishment of . . . the free delivery service in rural districts." The Farmer's Institute of Luzerne County, Pennsylvania, passed a resolution in the fall of 1891 affirming that "the feeling of this Institute is in favor of increased mail facilities in rural districts, and we heartily support the Postmaster-General in his efforts in this direction." The Summit County (Ohio) Farmer's Alliance even tendered to "Brother Wanamaker" a "vote of thanks for his suggestions in regard to free delivery throughout the rural districts."[58]

While farmers' resolutions lauded Wanamaker and his department for inventing rural free delivery, the national press crowned the postmaster general as father of the program. Editorial after editorial pronounced RFD as "Mr. Wanamaker's pet scheme" or "comprehensive scheme." The *New York Press* hoped that Wanamaker would "persevere in this work, of which he will finally be classed as a pioneer." The *Butler (Miss.) Record* minimized Congress's role in RFD. The national legislature had merely been "induced by the Postmaster

General to make an appropriation" for the program. The praises spanned the nation's small presses over a period of two years.

> The agitation for the extension of the post office free-delivery system to the rural districts is a natural outcome of the turning of the public imagination in that direction by the calculations and experiments of Postmaster-General John Wanamaker. Should the improvement be instituted, the credit would belong not to the Farmers' Alliance, who are trying to shine by the reflected light of a borrowed idea, but to the Republican Postmaster-General. (*Milwaukee Journal,* October 21, 1891)

> The farmers of the country have made no mistake in securing the cooperation of Postmaster-General Wanamaker in the free mail delivery scheme in the country.
> ... When the measure is introduced into Congress and referred to the Committee on Post-Offices and Post Roads, the chairman of that committee could do no wiser thing than consult Mr. Wanamaker upon the legislation necessary to make the scheme thoroughly practicable, and take his advice.
> ... It is progression of high order, and Mr. Wanamaker deserves great credit for adding to his already onerous duties his intelligent advocacy of this scheme. (*Philadelphia Item,* October 22, 1891)

> The plan recently outlined by the Government's Post-Office Department for enlarging the facilities of the Department by giving a service of free delivery in the rural districts is certainly a good scheme. (*Athens (Ga.) Banner,* December 5, 1891)

> One of the many enterprising schemes of Postmaster-General Wanamaker has been his effort to extend the free-delivery system to the whole country, the small villages and even country districts, as well as the big cities. ... To help him in carrying out his plans the Postmaster-General asks the farmers of the country to petition Congress to grant him the funds at least to make the experiment and prove that it can be made a success. (*Spokane Spokesman,* February 5, 1892)[59]

The opinions of these papers represent a far broader pattern of press support for Wanamaker and the department. In his report to the Senate in the spring of 1892, Wanamaker attached 472 newspaper editorials from across the nation supporting free delivery in rural districts. A simple tabulation of the editorials, presented in table 4.4, shows that of editorials assigning credit for the RFD idea, more than two-thirds gave it to Wanamaker and the department. Few of the editorials even mentioned farmers' organizations or Congress (except to urge it to expand the program).[60]

These editorials manifest the enhanced reputation for program innovation that Wanamaker's efforts were bestowing on the department. Presses both urban and rural rained accolades on the department for originating the idea, for the care and success of the experiments, and for its newfound ability to innovate. The *Emporia (Kansas) Republican* conveyed delight that "the Government can inaugurate a system so useful to the people without entailing any con-

TABLE 4.4
Newspapers' Assignment of Credit for the Rural Free Delivery Program,
1890–92: An Analysis and Tabulation of 479 Editorials

Category	Number	Percentage of total
Editorials mentioning Congress, the parties, or a member	165	34.4
Editorials crediting Congress, the parties, or a member with origination of RFD	36	7.5
Editorials mentioning farmers' organizations or movements	91	19.0
Editorials crediting RFD to farmers' organizations or movements	73	15.2
Editorials mentioning the POD or the postmaster general	340	71.0
Editorials crediting the POD or the postmaster general with the origination of RFD	224	46.8

Source: SED 92, 52ᵈ Cong. 1st sess., May 3, 1892, pp. 10–180.

Note: The principal method of marking credit assignment is by marking assignment for the institution (Congress, groups, or the POD) mentioned *first* in the editorial, *combined* with the editorial's indication that the institution is advancing or advocating RFD. For methodology, see Daniel Carpenter, "State Building through Reputation Building: Policy Innovation and Coalitions of Esteem at the Post Office, 1880–1912," *Studies in American Political Development* 14, no. 2 (Fall 2000): 121–55.

siderable expenditure of the public funds." "We trust the Department will carry out the plan that has been promisingly mapped out," assured the *Athens (Ga.) Banner*. The department had become "a public educator," characterized by "progressiveness." Indeed, "No Government service has been more progressive than the Post-Office Department," as the *Utica Press* declared.[61]

His confidence brimming, Wanamaker asked Congress for $1 million in RFD funds for fiscal year 1893. He followed this with a $6 million request the year after. Under the weight of uncertainty, however, Congress continued to appropriate only $10,000 for the program. Experimental free delivery might have proven a one-year success, but statutory establishment would be a politically irreversible outlay. The House committee harbored "doubts as to the expediency of providing free delivery in all the country districts at this time, owing to the probably great expense." Inflating members' concerns was the department's operations deficit of $7 million—almost 12 percent of revenues. Newspapers across the land echoed congressional fears. The otherwise enthusiastic editor of the *Steubenville (Ohio) Star* admitted, "[T]he Government Post-Office, it is true, is far from being self-sustaining." The *Bangor (Maine) Commercial* would offer its support only "if free rural delivery of mails can be made to a large degree self-sustaining." Even in the face of the department's impressive revenue statistics, Congress refused to expand the young experiment. The Post Office's reputation for profligacy and inefficiency, a child of the Jacksonian era, now limited its reach. Wanamaker closed his tenure in 1893, having established only an infant program in rural delivery.[62]

End-Running Congressional Opposition: Machen's Petition Plan

Historians who narrate the story of rural free delivery as a purely agrarian creation frequently point to the department's impoundment of RFD funds from 1893 to 1895. Postmaster General Wilson Bissell refused to spend $10,000 in experimental appropriations. Kernell and McDonald argue that "the department balked" at administering the program. Yet in equating the department's stance on the RFD program with Bissell's opposition, these scholars neglect the organizational realities of the Post Office. Lower-level postal officials continued their support for RFD even as Bissell prevented experimentation. Moreover, Bissell was perhaps the most antistatist ideologue to occupy the position of postmaster general in the nineteenth century. Even so, he had understandable reasons for refusing to spend the experimental funds. One reason was that Congress had provided a paltry, laughable sum for a policy experiment—$10,000 when Wanamaker had asked for $6 million. To continue to run so small a pilot program when Wanamaker had already demonstrated RFD's value, Bissell stated, would waste valuable administrative resources. Bissell found his most compelling doubts in finance, however. A decade-long string of postal deficits, all of them incurred while the free delivery system was expanding, had convinced many postal critics that "a general introduction of the service might prove a tax upon the postal revenues too burdensome to be even thought of." Before Congress, reluctant officials, and the public would consent to further expansion of the free delivery system, the pro-RFD forces in the department would need to demonstrate its fiscal stability and profitability.[63]

Bissell did make one choice that perhaps more than any other before 1896 advanced rural free delivery. He appointed to the position of superintendent of free delivery a career postal officer, August Machen, who would become RFD's truest patriot. Machen had commenced rural delivery experiments in the spring of 1893, but these were abruptly halted by Bissell's impoundment. When William L. Wilson took over in 1895, Machen prepared to resume the experiments even before Congress provided him with the money to do so. Most critically, he cemented a relationship of trust with California Republican Eugene Loud, chair of the House Post Office Committee from 1896 to 1902. Loud opposed postal expansion and on occasion questioned the very existence of the department, but he was willing to let Machen run and expand the rural delivery system with no interference. Fuller, who has written the most exhaustive history of RFD, regards Machen as "the key figure in the development of rural delivery" and the genuine "father of RFD."[64]

Bissell resigned and was replaced by Wilson, who echoed Machen's and other officials' support for RFD. The program garnered new attention in 1896, when the general election pitted populist orator William Jennings Bryan, the Democrat, against Old Guard Republican William McKinley. Knowing that the Plains agrarian vote would be up for grabs, and with the Republicans trying to protect the House majority they had won in 1894, both major parties saw electoral returns in the program. Although historians regard 1896 as RFD's year of birth, in reality Congress assented only to an expansion of the brief experiments of 1891–92. RFD still lacked a statutory identity (existing only in appropriations granted for "experiments"). It was without an administrative foothold in the department, and it fell vastly short of a complete delivery network.

After McKinley's victory, it fell to two department officials—Machen and Perry Heath, McKinley's first assistant postmaster general—to launch the service administratively. Postmaster General James A. Gary, in expanding the RFD experiments, kept Machen (who had joined the department during Cleveland's administration) and made him RFD superintendent, in part out of an explicit recognition that he would have the administrative expertise to manage the program in its early years of expansion. The RFD experiments of 1896–1900 provided just the opportunity that Machen needed to demonstrate the fiscal sufficiency of RFD. Beginning in the fall of 1896, Machen and Heath erected eighty-two routes with the experimental funds. Then they employed inspectors and special agents to monitor systematically the returns to the RFD system. The early results satisfied neither RFD's enthusiasts nor its critics; the experimental routes ran about even.[65]

Then in 1898, as if taking cues from Wanamaker, Machen devised a brilliant stratagem to advance RFD. He suggested to Postmaster General Gary that the department propose publicly that any group of farmers desiring RFD petition their member of Congress for a route. If the member assented and the department approved the route upon inspection, the community would receive a route. Gary followed Machen's recommendation and inserted the announcement in the department's annual report for 1898. Machen and Perry repeated Gary's call in departmental bulletins. In one respect, Machen's move was risky. RFD appropriations would not permit all of the requesting communities to obtain routes. But Machen and Perry knew that once flooded by petitions, Congress would have no choice but to expand the RFD route network.[66]

American farmers rewarded Machen and Perry's prescience. A massive volume of petitions soon descended on Washington. Significantly, many, if not most, petitions to Congress cited the results of the department's early experiments. The Pomona Grange of Vandergrift, Pennsylvania, opened its resolution by reminding Rep. E. E. Robbins that Heath's most recent report provided evidence in favor of RFD expansion: "[T]he experiments as reported by the First Assistant Post Master General on free rural mail delivery has [*sic*] proven a success." So, too, the Meigs County (Ohio) Farmers' Institute began its petition by declaring that "[e]xperiments made by the Post Office Department have proven Free Rural Mail Delivery to be practicable and in many cases self-supporting."[67]

The Carroll County Experiment

RFD still had its fiscal skeptics, however, and quelling their doubts necessitated a different kind of experiment. The late 1890s had been a period of growth, and RFD routes were established alongside conventional fourth-class offices and star routes. It was difficult to separate the effects of RFD from the operations of these other offices. Concerned that the experimental RFD routes established in different sections of the country were laid out haphazardly, Machen set out in 1899 to devise a bold new policy test. He asked Postmaster General Charles Emory Smith and Congress for authoritative control over the postal service of a single county—Maryland's Carroll County—and reengineered its postal networks. In a move starkly revealing of his aims for rural free delivery, Machen's Carroll County experiment dispensed with 63 of the county's 94 fourth-class post offices and discontinued 33 star routes and 2 messenger services. These were replaced by 4 postal wagons and 26 letter carriers. The postal wagon lay at the core of Machen's vision for the administrative burial of the old regime; it performed "all the functions of a postmaster or superintendent of a postal station." For Machen, the experiment's core purpose lay in determining how well RFD could "feasibly displace or supersede fourth-class post offices and star routes."[68]

Machen's landmark report—"Rural Free Delivery in Carroll County, MD" —documents a classic exercise in administrative entrepreneurship. The report at once routed the critics of RFD and offered a stentorian rebuttal to any and all concerns that the department opposed the program. So careful was Machen's execution of the experiment and so decisive were the report's findings that the full-scale explosion of the rural free delivery system was a foregone conclusion upon its publication. Machen opened the report by declaring proudly that "the results achieved are far beyond the expectations of the most enthusiastic advocates of rural free delivery." Postal revenues in Carroll County increased by 23 percent during the year of the experiment, and the net cost of the service was $236. RFD had cost "practically nothing" and would return a "snug profit" to the government. Moreover, RFD had "successfully supplanted the old system, embracing fourth-class post offices and star routes." Machen closed the report by pointing less to RFD's fiscal benefits than to its promise for the *institutional* transformation of the national postal system.[69]

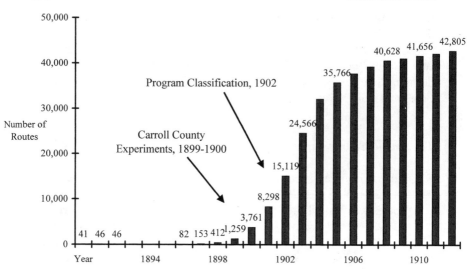

Figure 4.4 The expansion of RFD routes between 1890 and 1912.

Combined with the avalanche of petitions after 1898, the Carroll County experiments decisively propelled the institutionalization of RFD. The experiments received broad notice in the press, and a year after the publication of Machen's report, the House and Senate committees took steps to make RFD a permanent part of the postal system. These moves culminated in April 1902, when Congress authorized Postmaster General Henry C. Payne to classify the Rural Free Delivery Service under the civil service system and regulate it by departmental rules. Payne established a superintendent of Rural Free Delivery and immediately gave the post to Machen. Machen proceeded to organize the service according to his designs. This act marked the real beginning of RFD. Historians often mark the birth six years earlier, but in 1896 the halted experiments of 1891 and 1892 were merely resumed. As figure 4.4 shows, the explosion of RFD routes occurred not in 1896 but after 1900, when the Carroll County experiments had been completed and their results published. In the five years following Machen's report, more than thirty-two thousand routes were established, or 72 percent of the system's eventual route network after 1913. It is also worth noting that RFD's explosion began several years before the founding of the principal business organization in favor of postal expansion—James Cowles's Postal Progress League. M. G. Cunniff of *World's Work* marveled in 1903 at how RFD had exploded without statutory existence.

No institution is more closely shackled with antiquated laws than the United States Post-Office, yet no law governs rural free delivery—it expanded to its present compass as an "experiment." Officially, it is still an "experiment." August W. Machen . . .

had the experiment in charge. Under him it grew. Under him it secured its appropriations.[70]

The Carroll County experiments also established a template for the expansion of RFD. Noting the "effective" and "telling" work of the special agents, Machen moved to grant them more authority. After battling the concerted opposition of the postmasters and star route contractors, he knew that his political efforts could proceed not lithely around these actors but rather straight at them. By Machen's design, the future administration of rural free delivery would take as gospel the lessons of Carroll County. Machen believed firmly that progress in rural delivery would require the gradual attenuation of the three institutional stalwarts of the Jacksonian past—the fourth-class postmaster, the star route carrier, and the mail messenger. After 1901 Machen would pursue these aims relentlessly, sculpting more than any other individual the new structure of the twentieth-century Post Office.[71]

The Operation of RFD: A Portrait of Administrative Politics in Iowa

The institutional parameters of rural free delivery left enormous discretion in the hands of the Post Office Department. In part because its experiments had evinced a newfound capacity for management, in part because Congress was largely unable either to micromanage or procedurally to regulate the administrative expansion of the system, the department assumed control of virtually every aspect of rural operations—the selection and mapping of routes, the recruitment of carriers, and, most critically, the termination of fourth-class post offices. Even when the House Post Office Committee, under the leadership of California Republican Eugene Loud, attempted to assert control over the RFD Service and contract out many of its operations, its recommendations were voted down by the House after department officials announced their opposition to its schemes.

The organization of the Rural Free Delivery Service consciously reflected the signal traits of the Railway Mail Service. Machen and Perry established a set of eight geographic divisions for the RFD Service, creating regional superintendents as in the RMS. These divisions were responsible for establishing thousands of routes per year. Yet a far more significant reflection of the new postal regime was the reliance of RFD on railway-trained inspectors. All new routes required approval by the department; members could not simply legislate these into existence as in the case of private bills or works projects. Because the demand for routes outstripped supply, the department was compelled to decide which communities deserved routes and which did not. Doing so required information on the economic feasibility of routes in communities about which

few in Washington had knowledge. Accordingly, departmental procedures gave
to the RFD special agent the decisive role in this decision.

The first step toward obtaining a new route was an informal application from
an individual or local postmaster, supported by a petition signed by 150 families on the proposed route. The department then referred the route decision to
the Division of the Chief Inspector. The division assigned an inspector to visit
the route, map it out, report on any existing star routes, and recommend for or
against establishing a route. Rural agents (or inspectors) had near-total discretion in route selection and management. If the special agent recommended
against a route, it was nearly impossible for a community to obtain one, even
where the representative strongly favored it. Agents also had the authority to
alter routes, and if they suggested discontinuance, the department almost always followed suit.[72]

At the community level, a triangular flow of information developed between
the RFD inspector, the congressional representative, and department officials.
A rich portrait of the relations among these three actors emerges from the collected papers of Gilbert N. Haugen, the Republican representative of Iowa's
Fourth District from 1900 to 1928. The agents assigned to the post offices in
Haugen's district were Gilbert Guttersen and George Olson. Before advancing
their recommendations to the department, Guttersen and Olson sought Haugen's advice and support, knowing it would strengthen their hand in Washington. Guttersen in particular became a close correspondent of Haugen's and an
active supporter of the congressman's career. He frequently wrote to Haugen
on private stationery, informing him of the latest developments in appointments, position vacancies, RFD routes, and the like. According to departmental custom, Haugen offered recommendations for the reappointment of postmasters at third-class offices, many of which managed their own RFD
networks. When new routes were established, Guttersen asked Haugen for his
"wishes" as to which carriers to appoint. When Haugen did not supply these,
Guttersen selected "active" and "strong" Republicans. Guttersen even campaigned informally for Haugen in his visits to the Fourth District, reporting: "I
made it a point to tell everyone I saw that I had 189 applications from Iowa and
that yours were the first ones I took up because you were pushing them."[73]

In addition to Haugen, the agents maintained a broad network of contacts in
Iowa. Guttersen talked frequently with Willard Eaton, chairman of the Iowa
House Ways and Means Committee and one of the most powerful Republicans
in the state. Olson appears to have known a number of bank cashiers in the
towns whose routes he had inspected. Like fourth-class postmasters, cashiers
were central elites in rural locales, for they saw virtually the entire population
frequently and regularly. They also commanded prestige as country professionals and rural businessmen. And both Guttersen and Olson met with numerous farmers along the routes they inspected and knew many other notables

in the towns they toured. In other counties special agents were close associates of newspaper editors and Republican county committee officials.[74]

As closely intertwined as the agents were with Haugen and the communities in his district, their relationship consisted not of capture but of mutual dependence for information and political support. The agents ultimately answered not to Haugen but to the department. In particular, the special agents rejected many of Haugen's requests for the establishment or alteration of routes, despite Guttersen's statement of favor. In 1900 the towns of Calmar and Ossian in Winneshiek County petitioned for routes. Haugen recommended both routes, as important notables in both towns (including the cashier of Calmar's bank) had written to him for support. Olson inspected the two routes and wrote to Machen recommending against their establishment. He noted that "[t]hese two applications cover a good share of the same territory as Route #2 established from the Decorah Post Office." The department approved Olson's report, marking the cases "Adverse" and closing them. Obedience to Machen's rules constrained Guttersen as well. The postmaster at Osage complained in 1900 that Guttersen had altered the town's route so as to depart significantly from the one petitioned for. Guttersen wrote with a firm rejection of the town's request for remapping and a warning to cease protest.

> Mr. Haugen also kicks about this and wants me to have it changed so as to satisfy you and some other friends he has on that north road, this I cannot do and if you and Mr. Hougen [sic] knew what our orders from the department were you would not ask me to do it, for under the conditions that exist in this case you would not then get a route, for the Department would see as I did that by changing it, Dixie P.O. and star route would be discontinued and that expence saved the department.[75]

The rural carriers were also a political force in their own right. In daily conversations with the citizens of any locality, the RFD carrier was a powerful local politician. Graham Romeyn Taylor of *The Survey* noted in 1916 that not even a congressman would dare cross the opinion of rural carriers in his district. "[O]ne observer has pointed out that the men engaged in the rural free delivery are able to exert much greater political influence than city carriers. They have a relation or personal acquaintance or friendship with nearly every family on their route and no congressman from a rural region would dare vote contrary to the sentiment which the rural free delivery man can easily arouse among his constituents." Beyond this, the department's unencumbered authority to create and terminate routes allowed it to compel cooperation from Haugen and other members. When the Decorah post office lost its two letter carriers to resignation in February 1901, Machen wrote Haugen and asked that he suggest names for hiring. Haugen was perfectly eager to supply names of his choosing, but in case he was not, Machen added a powerful incentive clause to the letter: "[I]f a suitable person cannot be secured to serve as rural carrier the route will necessarily have to be abandoned." In 1905 Fourth Assistant Postmaster General Peter V. DeGraw chastised Haugen and other rural members for their tardiness in responding to department requests for names for postmaster appointments. Concerned that the delays in appointments were subjecting the department to "embarrassment and criticism," DeGraw instituted a new system requiring recommendations within sixty days of request; otherwise the department would exclude members from the selection process.[76]

Rural carriers were generally selected from among local notables, according to "character" standards promulgated by the department. Selecting "men of character" and maintaining "moral purity" in the RFD Service were important strategies of reputation building in local communities. The department wanted carriers who possessed not simply "the necessary ability to perform the service" but also "the confidence of the patrons of the route." Postal officials openly solicited the opinions of households on the route on the suitability of any person applying for a carrier position. Moreover, the service was governed by regulations on private and on-duty conduct that restricted the use of alcohol and the pattern of interactions with route patrons. There were also minimum standards of dress, which, although they did not mandate the wearing of uniforms, compelled a "tidy" appearance.[77]

The department employed two criteria—partisanship and literacy—in selecting the communities that were given routes. Postal officials used the first criterion informally, and the second publicly. Partisanship was a salient factor separating the wealth of routes in northern districts from the dearth of routes in the South. McKinley and Roosevelt Republicans saw immense political advantage in expanding routes to the satisfaction of the rural interior communities that had been essential in the victories of 1896 and 1900. The stark differential was not lost on congressional Democrats. One noticed that Kansas, "as rock-ribbed and everlasting in her republicanism as South Carolina in her democracy," had over one thousand more routes than South Carolina. In response, the department admitted the geographic differential but attributed it to the necessity of placing routes where literacy and readership were high. Yet the force of partisanship is undeniable. In an innovative analysis of the distribution of routes across districts, Samuel Kernell and Michael McDonald show that the department allocated routes so as to strengthen the congressional majority that Republicans had won in 1894. Republican districts received more routes than Democratic incumbents did, of course, but the effects depend critically on the electoral competitiveness of races. Republican incumbents in recently acquired districts received more than ten times the routes of Democratic incumbents in swing districts.[78]

Literacy was also a crucial factor in route allocation. Readership meant consumption, and department officials desperately needed to show profits to persuade Congress to fund RFD expansion. Accordingly, special agents such as Guttersen and Olson repeatedly pointed to literacy in their investigations of proposed routes. Olson denied Haugen's request for RFD at Calmar because the proposed route would have left "two-thirds of the most intelligent Citizens and patrons unserved." Olson then approved service at Decorah because its post office was "one of the very best in this part of the state, doing a very large business for its size." Rural citizens knew of the department's preferences for high literacy rates and incorporated them into their petitions. Hardin County, Iowa, residents advertised their "distinguished honor of having the smallest per cent of illiteracy of any county in the nation. It is the exception to find a home without a newspaper and other valuable reading matter."[79]

From an institutional perspective, of course, the central and most neglected story of RFD concerns not route allocation but the displacement of fourth-class post offices. Reform-minded department officials had long pointed to England, where rural office consolidation had heightened service quality and reduced costs. After 1900, with full administrative control of RFD, Machen proceeded to eliminate the country postmaster. He secured Postmaster General Charles Emory Smith's consent to issue a departmental regulation requiring the closure of at least one fourth-class post office in each community served by a new route. Aiming for efficiency and the undermining of nineteenth-century tradition, Machen's officials targeted long-entrenched postmasters in small towns. In some respects, the department's patterns of choice amounted to outright age discrimination. In December 1908 First Assistant Postmaster General C. P. Grandfield eliminated the post office at Hustad because "the postmaster, who is about eighty years of age, is unable to look after the office."[80]

The postmasters fought back with passion and tact. Even where new routes did not snuff out their offices, RFD promised to bypass their role in mail distribution, reducing the number of through customers for their general supply stores and limiting their influence in the local community. The postmasters joined with star route carriers in petitioning members of Congress to pressure the department to delay or obstruct the introduction of rural free delivery in their localities. They also befriended the rural agents, persuading them to draw routes that would originate with or intersect their offices, to preserve their role in the new scheme of distribution.[81]

Wayne Fuller, surely the best-known historian of the rural free delivery system, has argued that RFD resulted in less uniformity and efficiency than national postal officials would have liked. In a thorough study of RFD operations in Hardin County, Iowa, Fuller claims that Machen's efforts to eliminate fourth-class post offices were largely unsuccessful. Fuller argues that few post offices were destroyed, due largely to local capture of the special agents and the resistance of fourth-class postmasters. The postmasters "cajoled and argued and threatened," putting members of Congress in the unhappy predicament of having to choose between routes for their constituents and the livelihoods of the most powerful local elites. Fuller concludes that the members were usually able to secure both. He finds that in Hardin County three of forty-two—or less than

10 percent—of fourth-class post offices were terminated after the introduction of RFD.[82]

Although Fuller's study of Hardin County remains valuable, evidence from elsewhere in Iowa suggests that the department's efforts were far more successful. Roy Atwood intimates as much in his survey of RFD's effects on communities in southeastern Iowa. Atwood reports "numerous accounts of post office closures in the small communities of southeastern Iowa," as many as 207 fourth-class closures in 1909 alone. Haugen's papers allow even more precise estimates, as he kept a personal notebook of all the post offices in his district. Haugen's notes report every change of postmaster, the population served by the office, its services (such as money orders) and date and cause of any office termination. Analyses of a six-county sample of these records appear in table 4.5. The rate of termination for fourth-class post offices appears far higher than Fuller's article on Hardin County would suggest. Of 132 post offices sampled from Haugen's district, 49 (or 37.1 percent) had closed by 1908. Moreover, a duration analysis shows that the life span of a fourth-class post office was starkly decreasing in the tenure of the postmasters who had managed them when RFD was introduced. In other words, the more entrenched the postmaster, the greater the probability of a quick office termination after RFD. Clearly Machen's unit was targeting the old regime.[83]

The patterns of Haugen's district were replicated nationwide. Between Machen's report in 1900 and the inauguration of President Woodrow Wilson in 1913, the department rid itself of more than twenty thousand fourth-class postmasters. The number of offices in the national postal system peaked in 1901 at 76,945; in 1910 the number had dropped to 59,580. Machen and his associates had completed a 22 percent trimming of the postal bureaucracy in less than a decade. The immense popularity of RFD made this process easier, of course. So too did the Republican leanings of many rural carriers. The carriers' civil service test was commonly regarded as an easy one, and combined with the Republican leanings of many special agents, RFD often presented itself as a patronage system in the clothing of Progressive efficiency.[84]

Yet the popularity of RFD goes only so far in explaining why congressional Republicans were willing to part ways with the fourth-class postmasters. Kernell and McDonald argue that "nearly everybody" understood the necessity of office closure as RFD expanded, but they offer no evidence. Indeed, as Fuller reports, the department alone floated the rule for the closure of fourth-class offices in 1901. It was no committee chair and no agrarian group but Machen and First Assistant William Johnson who forced Congress to choose between routes and offices. Moreover, with RFD running a clear surplus by 1905, and thus posing no threat to the department's fiscal discipline, it is not clear why congressional Republicans could not have stemmed the bleeding of their old (and continued) friends. Also, the opposition of the postmasters and star route contractors was intense. Why then did the fourth-class office die such a quick

TABLE 4.5
The Elimination of Fourth-Class Offices in Iowa: Estimates from the Papers
of Gilbert N. Haugen

Analysis 1: The Aggregate Rate of Termination

Sample	Offices Terminated	Rate (% of Total)
Hardin County (from Fuller)	3	7.1
Six-county sample (Haugen Papers)	49 (8 per county)	37.1

Analysis 2: The Determinants of Termination
Proportional Hazards Model of Post Office Duration for 132 Offices in Iowa's
    Fourth District

Variable (no constant term)	Termination of Post Offices
Tenure of postmaster serving in 1896	0.0407* ($t = 2.107$)
Percentage of county vote for Republican, 1900	0.0584 ($t = 0.910$)
Percentage of county vote for Bryan, 1896	0.0247 ($t = 0.728$)
Number of office patrons	-0.0007** ($t = 3.114$)
Money order office	-0.6288** ($t = 3.221$)
Number of offices/postmasters analyzed	131
Chi-squared (Pr)	23.20 (0.0003)
Log-likelihood function	-482.374

    Source: Post Office Notebook of Gilbert N. Haugen, 1900–1930; Gilbert N. Haugen Papers, State Historical Society of Iowa, Iowa City. Voting data are from Inter-University Consortium for Political and Social Research.
    Note: Dependent variable is the hazard rate of post office termination after the introduction of RFD, or the rate of termination in year t, given existence until year t.
    *Statistical significance at $p < .05$.
    **Statistical significance at $p < .01$. (All tests are two-tailed).

death? No adequate explanation can ignore the entrenched pattern of deference that prevailed between the House committee and the department. Whereas the committee constrained office elimination, its members were more interested in which offices got axed, not how many. Machen's officials could terminate more offices than efficiency counseled simply because they were better informed. And where members such as Haugen were opposed to elimination, the department bought them off by hiring more carriers to cover the routes of the eliminated office. Carriers were less costly than offices for POD officials but still politically valuable. Most important, however, was Congress's growing institutional trust in the department to run the system well, a confidence seated firmly in the House committee and its leaders Eugene Loud, John Wadsworth, and John Weeks. The department had invented RFD, it had issued and secured compliance with scores of regulations to make the system efficient, it had done so without upsetting the majorities of 1896 and 1900, and the long-criticized postal deficit had begun, for the first time in a generation, to disappear. To acquiesce in Machen's and the department's overhaul, to grant them lasting and relatively unencumbered hold over the system, was a rational reward for services rendered.[85]

In the development of American political institutions, RFD is important less for extending mail delivery to the agrarian interior than for displacing nineteenth-century administration. Rural delivery was not an extension but a transformation of the postal system. It made the Post Office Department an integrated projection of the American state once and for all.

More to the point, rural free delivery evinces bureaucratic autonomy. Its development conforms neither to narratives of legislative dominance nor to narratives that place presidential action at the center of national policy innovation. In the saga of RFD, experimentation and the reputation of the Post Office decisively conditioned the program—its existence, the timing of its development, and the form of its administration. It is impossible to conceive of RFD without the agency of the department, particularly of middle-level officials such as Machen and the special agents. Without Wanamaker and Machen's advocacy and experimentation, without Machen's astute political management of the program after 1893, and without Machen's appeal for petitions in 1898, it is questionable whether RFD would have been established by 1910 if not later. RFD was established not in 1896 for electoral concerns but in 1902, following Machen's decisive experiment in Carroll County. It was managed not at the will of the Committee on Post Office and Post Roads but by Machen and Perry, to whom Congress repeatedly deferred. While members of Congress received creditable service in rural free delivery, Machen and the railway-raised inspectors' corps eventually saw in the program the fruition of their designs—the administrative burial of the fourth-class postmaster.

Although his program triumphed, Machen's career ended in scandal. The affair—which also tripped up Tyner and Heath—entailed the mass purchase of unnecessary supplies at exorbitant prices and the permission given to otherwise fraudulent concerns to use the mails (with postal officials taking the kickbacks). The public ramifications of the contracting scandal were brief, but they energized reformist voices who pressed for the full divorce of the postal service from partisan politics, including the entire removal of the department's leadership from political appointment. Whatever they were pointing to, contemporaries were fully aware that the new efficiencies of the Post Office Department had little to do with civil service reform. Yet in retrospect, the most notable aspect of the scandal is that it was discovered, detailed to the public, and fully prosecuted by postal inspectors, who were led by Fourth Assistant Postmaster General Joseph Bristow. As a *World's Work* editorial made clear, the scandal was confined to two bureaus and did not touch the department's reform wing— the Inspection Service and the Railway Mail Service. The insularity of the contracting scandal of 1907 was the department's greatest protection against a loss of reputation. In Machen's fall, the triumph of the regime of inspection came at the expense of its architects.[86]

Five

The Triumph of the Moral Economy: Finance, Parcels, and the Labor Dilemma in the Post Office, 1908–24

> Why should we have a system of postal savings?
> Primarily, because as a nation we need to cultivate
> the quality of thrift. Thrift is an old-fashioned,
> homely virtue not so highly regarded, perhaps, as
> by our fathers. . . . Thrift is the exercise of sound
> judgment, not the deprivation of necessary and
> useful things for the sake of a useless bank ac-
> count. Thrift implies the strengthening of charac-
> ter, the sacrifice of smaller pleasures for larger.
>   . . . The postal savings bank is absolutely safe,
> it provides for the smallest sums, it involves no
> advance decisions about purchases, it pays a mod-
> erate rate of interest, and it is at hand wherever a
> postage stamp can be bought. Moreover, even if
> all the existing agencies for the promotion of thrift
> were above criticism, they are not sufficient.
> —"Postal Savings," *The Survey*

IN THE FIRST two decades of the twentieth century, the United States Post Office Department became an integral participant—perhaps the central player—in the Progressive moral reform movement.[1] No other agency of government was as involved in regulating and suppressing pornography and other erotic literature, "green-goods" schemes and consumer fraud, lotteries and gambling, the provision of abortion and contraception, and the cultural subversion of Victorian morality, including the free-love tracts of Margaret Sanger and the plays of George Bernard Shaw. Indeed, no private or ecclesiastical contributor to moral reform was engaged in such a wide swath of activity, and none had attacked moral reform's detractors with such teeth. Few, if any, organizations lay more squarely at the movement's center, with ongoing affiliations to its most powerful members—the vice-suppression societies, the Women's Christian Temperance Union, the Anti-Saloon League, the American Medical Association, the YMCA, and consumer advocates such as Florence Kelley. This legacy, which historians and political scientists have all but ignored, was the source of immense political legitimacy and power. Combined with an increasing esteem from American manufacturers and commercial interests, and steady favor from agrarians who favored postal expansion at every turn, the department in 1910 lay atop a curious, multidimensional coalition, a nexus of political affiliations that crossed lines of party, class, region, ethnicity, and gender.

In this chapter I show how this unique complex of ties supported political autonomy for the Post Office Department and how it maintained this network with new program offerings, with skilled public appeals, and by streamlining its internal affairs. From 1908 through the First World War, postal officials articulated a new vision, a slow shift from the ideology of an anti-vice machinery to a prophecy that cast the national postal system as a moral economy. Postal officials now proposed to use the unique power and appeal of the department to end parcel monopolies, to cultivate thrift among immigrants and the working poor, to expand national communications with new technology, and to unify nationalistic sentiment during the war. The vision of a moral economy functioned both as a culture integrating the department and as an external image clarifying its unique capacities and services. The symbol of the department as machine gave way to a more humanized metaphor of the department as a morally spirited commercial entity. Officials hoped that Americans would see in the Post Office not simply a market or a system but a unique arena of discourse and commercial activity, one that protected republican virtue (especially of new citizens) and promoted national unity.

Eventually, this vision ran up against the stark reality of late Progressive politics. The immense expenditure of the world war, combined with the government's retrenchment after 1917, left the department with deficits of more than $50 million. With the efficiency gains of the early 1900s surrendered, the department's business identity met ridicule in press accounts depicting it as a "charitable enterprise," giving over millions of dollars to support a communications infrastructure. The department's brief wartime experience in managing the national telegraph system would end quickly after the Treaty of Versailles. Washington officials encountered new resistance from its labor unions, even in the once reliable Railway Mail Service. And the department's efforts in enforcing wartime press constraints jeopardized its long-standing relationship of warmth with the national media.

This chapter treats the evolution of the department from the financial panic of 1907–8, which engendered sustained pressure for postal savings banks, to 1924, when the department's labor relations finally stabilized. By the 1920s the growth of the department's autonomy was curtailed, but it retained a new set of functions and programs it had acquired during the previous decade. The labor problem was muted, and the spirited commercial machine culture was successful in stunting any widespread radicalism in the postal labor movement.

Maintaining Reputation: The New Surplus, the Postal Progress League, and the Turn to Fraud

The new decade began auspiciously. In 1911, for the first time since the Pendleton Act of 1883, the department ran a surplus. "THE POSTAL SERVICE WAXES PROFITABLE," exclaimed the oft-skeptical editors of *The Outlook*. Expenditures were $237,648,926.68, revenues, barely more: $237,879,823.60. Nonetheless, Postmaster General Frank Hitchcock trumpeted the news in his 1911 and 1912 annual reports. The disappearance of the postal deficit was a boon to the department in its attempts to build a reputation of businesslike efficiency. As early as 1907 *The Outlook* had noted "an acknowledged increase of efficiency at the Department." The *American Review of Reviews* took "pleasure" in the fact that "the postal service itself has been growing more efficient." Five years later, with the surplus still intact, *The Survey*'s Graham Romeyn Taylor approvingly noted the "daily efficiency and administrative economies" that characterized national postal operations. These economies, Taylor observed, were based on "the short cuts and new devices that are rapidly being developed" at urban offices, which had become "try-out places for innovations" in the service.[2]

For all of their happiness with the fresh economies of the department, contemporaries still found fault with two aspects of postal organization: the partisan appointment of top officials and an alleged overpayment to railroads for carrying the mails. The department would never become a true business organization, these voices concurred, until its officials were appointed independently of their party affiliation. During a time of national phobia over corporate "trusts" moreover, the millions of dollars forked over to the railroads for mail pay drew considerable ire. Yet Progressives could not help but notice that the department's fiscal ills had been subdued while these two "causes" were still in place. "The postal deficit," as *Twentieth Century Magazine*'s James Babcock huffed, "was reduced twelve million dollars in one year [1910] at the expense of employes and public service, while the real cause for the immense deficit—the railroads—was untouched." Babcock worried that the Post Office was balancing its books on the backs of the railway clerks and letter carriers. Whether they agreed or not with Washington's moves, Progressives were pointing not to new postal laws, not to railway mail pay, and certainly not to civil service reform, but to the department's own moves as the reason for the deficit's eclipse.[3]

Progressive admiration for the Post Office Department had another dimension. At a time when the collective labor of social work was a chief concern of Progressive reformers, the Post Office was viewed as a force capable of massive social improvement. The agency's ubiquitous presence in American commerce, politics, and culture was not lost on a generation of intellectuals who saw extraordinary promise in the programs floated and administered by postal officials. The veneration of *The Survey* was typical. Founded in the 1890s as "a house organ of the charity organization movement," by 1913 *The Survey* had become, in historian Daniel Rodgers's view, a "general clearinghouse of progressive social reforms." Published by municipal housing advocate Robert W. De Forest, it boasted a governing council with the likes of settlement house matron Jane Addams, New York Charity Organization Society leader Edward T. Devine, department-store philanthropists V. Everit Macy and Julius Rosenwald of Sears, Roebuck, and "social insurance" advocate Lee Frankel of the Metropolitan Life Company. De Forest's magazine took note of the new ideas emanating from the department—it supported parcels post and postal savings banks, plus departmental ownership of the national telegraph network—remarking in 1916 that "an open mind toward every sort of modern improvement is making the post office the spriest sort of public servant." Publishing reports almost monthly on the department, *The Survey* cast a warm light on postal officials, displaying them in flattering photographs. One adoring picture captured a smiling letter carrier and presented him to *The Survey*'s readers as "SOCIAL WORKER EXTRAORDINARY."[4]

The goodwill of Progressive social reformers was hardly an unforeseen bequest. Postal officials had been cultivating it for decades. At the core of this effort was the diversity of the department's clienteles and the corresponding diversity of the Progressive movement. Commercial giants Rosenwald and Macy had been associated with the department from the days of John Wanamaker, and both men profited immensely from the rural delivery service and the department's new efficiencies. Fashioning its campaign for postal savings, the department eagerly courted Progressive voices favoring national insurance programs, even corporate spokesmen like Frankel. The department also sought (and found) favor from two other voices of Progressive reform: municipalization advocates in James Cowles's Postal Progress League and conservative neo-Victorian moralists.

Cowles's league was perhaps the loudest voice in the postal reform chorus. Founded in 1902 and officially led by Frederick Beach (editor of the *Scientific American*), the league was a steady backer of various ideas being pressed by the department's reform wing. Cowles's family wealth and social ties as a Boston elite helped make his fledgling organization cohesive. Among its contributors were mail-order concerns Woodward and Lothrop, William Thorne of Montgomery Ward, and Rosenwald of Sears, Roebuck; agrarian publishers Orange Judd Company and the *Farm Journal;* publishers Frank Doubleday of Doubleday, Page and Company, W. H. Gannett, and Simon Brentano; even the Burpee Seed Company. It would be erroneous, however, to see Cowles's outfit as simply a front for businesses that stood to gain from postal expansion. AFL president Samuel Gompers, United Mine Workers' president John Mitchell, and officials of the American Association for Labor Legislation were also donors and allies in league policy campaigns. Not the least of the advantages of Cowles's efforts was his conscious linkage of postal reform to wider currents of the municipalization movement. ICC commissioner Charles Prouty and former mayors Seth Low of New York and Josiah Quincy of Boston each lent their voices and their wallets to Cowles's efforts, giving over thousands of dollars when Cowles fell into financial trouble in 1914. To all of these social connections Cowles added an aggressive schedule of pamphlet mailings and public outreach—thousands of letters, pamphlets, and postcards sent monthly to elected officials, newspapers, civic organizations, and businesses—on issues ranging from nationalization of the telegraph to the parcels post plan.[5]

Accompanying these labors with social reform advocates and postal progress enthusiasts was the continued endeavor of Washington officials and postal inspectors to render the postal economy a "pure" realm of communication and exchange. The new weapon of choice for the postal inspector was the fraud order. The department's modern enemy was less the producer of obscenity or contraceptives, even less the lottery, than the "crooked promoter," the "quack," and the "Get-Rich-Quick-Wallingfords." The most celebrated of these actions was the department's pursuit of oil frauds in Texas and the Southwest in the early 1920s. Pressed by Chief Inspector Rush Simmons, a career official who had started with the RMS in 1889, agents rooted out fake mergers and ghost investment schemes with names such as the Revere Oil Company and the General Lee Development Interest. Inspectors amassed 731 indictments against oil concerns in two years. At a time when Interior Secretary Albert Fall was tripped up in the Teapot Dome scandal, the Post Office's prosecution of oil fraud offered a vivid public contrast with the Interior Department's problems. Less visible than the oil cases but warmly cheered by Progressive social reformers was the department's attack on medical fraud. Supported by the American Medical Association and assisted by USDA pure food crusader Harvey Wiley, the Post Office began after 1906 to issue fraud orders shutting down patent-medicine and spiritual healing concerns. Liberal-minded Progressives eagerly supported these moves, as did state officials whose grip over interstate commerce was dwindling in the new economy.[6]

Fraud arrests—with their detailed portraits of "marauding" stock advertisers and "wily, scurrilous" medicine promoters—became a press favorite during the 1910s and 1920s. Simmons and Postmaster General Harry S. New were regularly invited to contribute articles to all manner of journals and newspapers. A series of *World's Work* articles in 1923 presented a kindly portrait of "the experienced post office inspectors who work quietly and unostentatiously but persistently and effectively" to abolish fraud from the burgeoning American economy. All in all, the department issued tens of thousands of fraud orders from 1910 to 1924, investigating more than 200,000 cases per year, averaging more than 3,500 arrests and 2,000 convictions annually by the 1920s. In a development that has been all but ignored by economic historians and political scientists, postal officials made the fraud order one of the most powerful forms of economic regulation in the new, advertising-driven economy. The department's reputation for moral vigor—one celebrated by many (albeit not all) Progressive liberals, by prohibitionists, and by conservative physicians—would serve it well in debates over its favored policy innovations.[7]

Experimentation, Coalitions, and the Struggle for Postal Savings Banks

On October 22, 1907, a run began on the Knickerbocker Trust Company in New York City, depleting its cash reserves by noon of the twenty-third. In the ensuing panic, twelve other banks closed their doors, the stock market plunged, and several railroads went into bankruptcy. Although a limited recovery began in January 1908, the first "Panic" of the twentieth century was under way, and it had wide-ranging effects: increased cash hoarding, an industrial recession, and a retrenchment in bank loans. For the first time, proposals for a postal savings system of the sort that John Wanamaker had floated in 1890 received sustained consideration on the floor of Congress. In 1908 all major party platforms included a plank favoring a postal savings system. Within two years, the Post Office Department was in the banking business. At thousands of post offices across the country, depositors could open interest-bearing postal savings accounts with just one dollar.[8]

Existing narratives of the postal savings campaign of 1908–10 emphasize the demands of organized agrarians for government financial institutions in the bank-dry rural South. These populist-centered accounts, the most recent of which is an illuminating legislative history of the Postal Savings Act of 1910 by Jean Reith Schroedel and Richard Snyder, tie the act to the breakdown of the conservative Republican wing of the House that originated in the Cannon revolt. With conservative procedural hurdles to statist legislation removed after 1909, postal savings legislation could pass. Southern and western representatives offered most of the postal savings bills, the authors claim, and established cheap and widely available savings institutions for a massive rural populace that was previously ignored by eastern banking concerns.[9] As comfortable as this narrative may seem, it leaves a number of questions unanswered. Where did the plan for postal savings come from? Why did postal savings not receive sustained executive and legislative consideration (including floor debate) before 1908? Finally, did the administrative development of postal savings conform to this populist narrative? Did southern and western farmers take advantage of the system that their representatives purportedly fought to create?

The Genesis of Thrift

By 1908 most European nations had been running a postal savings system for decades. Great Britain had established a system in 1861, Canada in 1868, Italy in 1876, Sweden in 1884, and Russia in 1889. During the very years that the Panic struck American banks, deposits in the Japanese postal savings system surpassed the equivalent of $50 million. Activity in the United States was silent until 1873, when postal inspector M. La Rue Harrison offered a detailed plan for taking the existing apparatus of the department and transforming it into a financial institution. Whereas most of the early proposals to create a postal savings system included a vaguely defined "postal depository" as a new branch within the department, Harrison's idea proposed to use the "existing machinery" of the money-order system established in 1865. In 1880, ten years before Wanamaker tried to popularize postal savings in an executive report, Harrison published his plan, by far the most complete of any yet considered. Harrison offered nine arguments for a savings system, rationales that starkly revealed the ideology of the inspectors' corps.

> **1ˢᵗ.** It would encourage economy and habits of thrift among the laboring classes by the certain protection that would be afforded thereby to their surplus earnings, which, for the want of a reliable cache, are now intrusted to insecure private banks or investments, or are secreted beneath floors, in chimney crevices, under stumps in the fields and forests, or in other equally unsafe hiding places, *or worse still, wasted in extravagance and dissipation.*
>
> **2ⁿᵈ.** It would accommodate all classes in the many sections where no banks exist. . . .
>
> **4ᵗʰ.** It would promote loyalty and patriotism. Each depositor would have a direct and substantial interest in the stability and prosperity of the Government intrusted with the safe-keeping and safe return of its treasure.
>
> **5ᵗʰ.** It would protect a class unable to protect itself—the toiling millions—against swindlers and robbers, fire and flood, unsafe investments and unsound banks; *against improvidence, recklessness and dissipation.* . . .
>
> **9ᵗʰ.** It would be a bulwark of defense against panics and financial crises. Runs would not be made upon post-office banks. . . . Their funds would constitute a reserve upon which the masses could implicitly rely in times of financial disaster and business depression.[10]

Over the next thirty years, the arguments for a postal savings system strayed little from Harrison's first overture. At the core of the campaign—Harrison's first rationale and the dominant theme coursing through officials' arguments— was the salutary effect a postal banking system would have on the saving habits of "the laboring classes," "the masses," "the toiling millions." Absent a savings system, the fiscal behavior of the working poor would be driven by "extravagance," "improvidence," "recklessness," and "dissipation." Such explicit class rhetoric characterized the department's campaign from 1880 onward.

Postal officials at all levels backed the postal savings drive. In 1899 R. F. Lawson of Illinois founded *The Country Postmaster: A Journal for Postmasters and the People Advocating Rural Free Delivery and a Postal Savings System.* Lawson's monthly journal printed dozens of letters—it was unable to print hundreds of others—from postmasters, inspectors, carriers, and others who favored postal savings banks. Postmaster General George von L. Meyer, the most ardent advocate of postal savings among those in his position after Wanamaker, was firmly sympathetic with the reform wing's program and was, not coincidentally, a man of independent wealth who contributed money and time to the YMCA. Still, it merits attention that postal savings arose from the ranks of inspectors. Harrison was a contemporary of Anthony Comstock, whose anti-pornography campaigns were also aimed at the moral transformation of the poor. Along with the RMS, moreover, the inspectors' corps was a central participant in the department's post-Reconstruction reform coalition. It is difficult to find a major transformation in early-twentieth-century postal policy that was not first pressed by the railway-inspection reform wing of the department.[11]

The fact that the postal savings idea had undergone a lengthy trial overseas was a sure advantage. As historian Daniel Rodgers has emphasized, the policy innovations of the Progressive period were bandied about in a dense and energetic network of cross-Atlantic intellectual exchange. Meyer developed his interest in the program while serving as Theodore Roosevelt's ambassador in Italy first, then in Russia. Beyond this, four decades of experience in continental Europe were repeated by postal savings advocates and reform-minded journalists throughout the debate. Readers were reminded of "Holland's Care for Its Poor" and of the steady trust of Greeks, Italians, Japanese, and Russians in their nations' postal savings systems. "Practically all the leading nations except our own," *The Outlook* scolded in 1908, "have postal savings banks."[12]

A number of proposals spun off from Harrison's scheme over the ensuing three decades. Six bills were reported to Congress as early as 1882. Yet the Panic of 1907–8 ushered postal savings into new favor. The financial crisis starkly revealed the limits of Americans' trust in private savings banks. For several decades before the crisis, Americans living near the northern border avoided private banks and deposited their funds in Canadian post offices. Far more troublesome to financial experts was the fact that European immigrants were using international money orders to send their wages to postal savings banks in their home country for safekeeping. In fiscal year 1907 the department sent more than $72 million to European countries through international money orders.[13] The immigrants were clearly expressing their fear of private savings banks, but postal officials also interpreted their behavior as a vote of confidence in postal institutions in America and abroad, for immigrants were sending funds *through* the international money order system and *to* the postal banks of their home country.[14]

Department officials gestured emphatically to the immigrants' behavior. They argued that the immigrants' fear, although understandable, was a drain on domestic capital and that postal savings would return to circulation millions of dollars that were currently being hoarded or sent overseas. Again, the officials' most powerful argument was not economic but cultural. If trustworthy savings institutions could be established throughout the country, they would promote thrift—a cardinal virtue of American citizenship and a staple of republican virtue. Americans of all classes, the officials held, saved and invested little. The American Banking Association (ABA) noted what it called "an unfortunate currency situation." The department's argument came at an auspicious time in American culture, when the ABA and banks were conducting a nationwide "education" and advertisement campaign touting the virtues of saving. Because postal savings institutions were voluntary, moreover, the department could promote virtue without the compulsion that was characteristic of early Comstockery.[15]

By 1897 the debates and bills in Congress were explicitly reflecting the department's arguments. Rep. Jeremiah Botkin's bill of July 1897 was entitled "A bill to establish postal savings departments, to encourage savings among the people, to furnish them a safe and reliable place to deposit their idle funds, and to put into actual use the money of the country." Senator Thomas Carter described his 1908 bill as intended "to place at the disposal of people of small means the machinery of the Post Office Department to aid and encourage them to save their earnings." In March 1910 hearings before the House Post Office Committee, headed by John Weeks of Massachusetts, members of Congress worried aloud about immigrants sending their deposits to "their old country." Martin B. Madden of Illinois stated that as much as $500 million of "hidden money" existed in the United States. He told the Weeks committee that in allowing the department to erect a postal savings system, "you are creating a new class of enterprise among the citizens of the United States. You are encouraging them in the habit of thrift and frugality . . . you are encouraging them to learn the habit of saving and investing money." The major party platforms, both of which offered a postal savings plank in 1908, also echoed the thrift question. As the Republican plank intoned, "We favor the establishment of a postal savings system for the convenience of the people and the encouragement of thrift." In 1917 Princeton University finance professor Edwin W. Kemmerer—an expert on postal savings who wrote frequently on the subject in the 1910s—recalled that "the avowed object of the establishment of postal savings banks in the United States was the encouragement of thrift."[16]

The principal outlines of the department's proposed postal savings system as encoded in one exemplary bill—S. 6484, by Senator Thomas Carter of Montana—were as follows. The postmaster general would, at his discretion, name various post offices throughout the United States as "postal savings depositories." Any citizen over ten years of age would be eligible to open a savings account at a depository with a minimum deposit of $1.00. All accounts would bear 2 percent annual interest, and no more than $500 could be kept in any one account. As an incentive clause to attract deposits, fourth-class postmasters would receive the equivalent of one-quarter of 1 percent of all savings deposits as annual salary. Postmasters would take their customers' savings and deposit them in the nearest national banks, thereby keeping the investments in the community of origin. Of these provisions, the minimum deposit, interest rate, and community reinvestment provisions were the most debated.[17]

The Opposition and the Response. With the momentum for postal savings growing, a well-financed opposition—led by the American Banking Association—emerged and attempted to allay fears about private savings institutions and cast doubt on the Post Office Department. The association's representatives tried at length to reframe the immigrant question. Cleveland banker William Creer dismissed the hoarding problem as "infinitesimal" and argued for the financial assimilation of the foreign-born: "[W]hat we need, gentlemen, is to Americanize our immigrants, not to Italianize our Post-Office Department."[18]

Opponents of postal savings also expressed their doubts about the department's capacity to manage a system. L. B. Caswell of Wisconsin argued that postal savings "would load the Postmaster-General, already overburdened, with duties and responsibilities never contemplated for that department." John Rhoades pointed to the $17 million deficit of 1908 and asked why the department would seek to "shoulder new responsibilities" when its existing services were out of balance. E. R. Gurney, a Nebraska bank vice president who appeared before the Weeks committee on behalf of the ABA in 1910, offered a frontal attack. First he astutely recognized that the bill gave virtually all program discretion to the department and warned the committee that "you are treading on dangerous ground in thus centralizing the control of the vast sums as will be derived." Then the Nebraskan slammed the department for its absurdly low rate of compensation to postmasters; it showed, he openly ridiculed, "that the men who have drafted this measure have no comprehension of the expense involved in doing business." Such poor planning raised the certain specter of a "succeeding deficit." The deficit formed only one component of the doubts about the Post Office Department's capacity. The fact that the Post Office was better able to manage its mail operations was not in doubt. As Gurney recognized, however, a new financial system required knowledge of much more than mail delivery: "[A] banking business requires some little measure of skill and reliability and knowledge of the business; it takes some appliances of safety and so on."[19]

Whatever doubts finance capitalists harbored about postal savings were only magnified by the prospect of government writ large managing a nationwide banking system. Advocates of postal savings were suggesting something radical: a bureaucratic intrusion into private finance, "a species of socialism," as Gurney called it. Lucius Teter of the Chicago Savings Bank and Trust Company evoked the distant but still fresh memory of previous government banking failures in the United States. Reminding committee members of the First and Second Banks of the United States and of the Reconstruction-Era Freedmen's Savings and Trust Company, he queried rhetorically: "Has the Government ever tried banking before? Yes. Three times—and failed."[20]

With all of the detail in which opponents of postal savings laid out their arguments, a broad array of organizations voiced their favor. As Schroedel and Snyder emphasize, the National Farmers' Union weighed in positively. Nahum Bachelder of the National Grange corresponded regularly with Meyer and promised unwavering support for the plan. Georgia farmer F. D. Wimberly appeared before the House Post Office Committee and offered an hour of homespun testimony. He promised to "hit the bankers a lick" and asked the committee to embrace a noble cause—politics as "the making of laws for folks." He stated that "the farmers of the South and the West are tired of being so utterly dependent on Pierpont Morgan and Rockefeller." He thought that southern hoarding was widespread and would be reduced considerably under a postal savings system. He also offered some abjectly racist testimony to the effect that white families who hoarded money were subject to savage attacks by ax-wielding black men who sought to steal it. Wimberly seemed to imply that postal savings would reduce these threats to the white family by diminishing hoarding.[21]

Arthur E. Holder of the American Federation of Labor also spoke in favor of the bill, but Weeks muted his testimony by speaking at length in opposition. After Holder, Cowles appeared on behalf of the Postal Progress League. Cowles spoke forcefully for postal savings, reciting the citizenship arguments that Harrison had made three decades earlier, and secured the admission of Weeks that no private savings bank could back a deposit with the security offered by the government. Declaring the Post Office "a commercial business," Cowles stated that the purpose of his league was "the widest possible extension of the sphere of the post-office, its most economical and efficient administration." He pronounced his organization in favor of postal savings, parcels post, a Post Office Department role in road building, and other functions. Although he eschewed direct contact with postal officials, Cowles coordinated his rhetoric and his lobbying with the department's officers throughout his career as league secretary, particularly during the postal savings campaign. As he wrote to Meyer in 1909, "You will be glad to know that the Postal Progress League is at last beginning to receive substantial support. The enclosed program is proving exceedingly popular. We will have a system of postal savings banks and a cheap merchandise post in this country within the next twelve months."[22]

Cowles's support was echoed by two other political forces. Supporters and opponents agreed that the vast majority of Progressive journals and newspapers favored postal savings. Teter of the ABA intimated as much when he said that his association had been unfairly sullied in the press as having spent millions of dollars to defeat postal savings legislation. As a frustrated Teter lamented to the Weeks committee: "The newspapers, which are not always kind either to you or to us, have seemingly been determined at all times to put us in the wrong light on this question." *The Survey*'s slamming was characteristic: "Never was the issue between selfish interests and the public good more clearly drawn than in the demand for a system of national postal savings and the counter-demand

that the banks shall be allowed to play the traditional part of dog in the manger."
Because the new generation of postal officials had strong ties to Progressive
journalists, however, news and opinion writers were firmly behind postal savings, many taking it upon themselves to lobby skeptical congressmen.[23]

Consumer advocates Florence Kelley and Marcus M. Marks provided another supportive voice. Reformers for immigrant populations had petitioned the
House Post Office Committee for postal savings since the early 1880s. They insisted that private savings banks inadequately served the working poor and
first-generation immigrant populations. Kelley maintained that "immigrants
urgently need the banks," and she echoed the department's officers in emphasizing the moral benefits of postal savings for the rural poor: "Drinking, gambling, petty speculation in wildcat stocks . . . all these widespread practices of
country people are fostered by their cruel, needless lack of accessible safe
places for small savings." It is worth remembering that Kelley's concern for the
"morals of the poor" kept her from supporting other Progressive reforms, including old-age pension schemes. Precisely because postal savings banks were
seen as a device to improve the morals of the poor, they survived in this self-
consciously moralistic age. Other advocates argued that much of bank-rich
New England's immigrant and rural population was ill served by the status quo.
Marks, a frequent correspondent with Meyer, lionized the department. He
praised Meyer, "our present efficient Postmaster-General," and repeatedly
pointed to the department's "existing machinery" for postal savings: more than
forty thousand post offices with money-order capacity.[24]

In pointing to "existing machinery," Marks rehearsed a decades-old claim of
department administrators: that the Post Office was uniquely qualified to run
banks due to its half-century of experience with the money-order system. Such
claims dated from Postmaster General Creswell's time in 1871 and were reverberated by Wanamaker and dozens of other postal officials before 1910.
These pronouncements were not mere rhetoric. Postal administrators consciously nursed the money-order system in order to build capacity for new policy functions. The department had zealously protected its money-order offices
while closing others (see table 4.5), and it took advantage of the Panic of 1907–
8 by designating thousands of new money-order offices. By increasing national
familiarity with the money order, the department was "market-testing" postal
savings. As Rep. David Finley admitted, furthermore, the money-order expansion was not Congress's doing but was "the policy of the Post-Office Department within the past year [1909–10]." By 1910 Hitchcock could tell Carter of
51,824 money-order offices that were ready to serve as postal savings banks if
the department saw fit to designate them as such. Money orders were also successful merchandise, revenues having almost tripled from 1896 to 1906. The
Senate Post Office Committee took clear note of the department's argument,
citing the money-order system as a "valuable preliminary step" toward postal
savings.[25]

The second sustained drop in the department's operations deficit—to less than 3 percent of revenues in 1907—put to rest any remaining doubts about the department's general capacity. Journals of opinion soon began to predict the deficit's disappearance. Hitchcock was therefore able to address the concerns that the department, by virtue of its inefficiency, would inevitably run the savings program at a loss. Throughout the debate over postal savings, officials indicated their intention that postal savings be a "success from a financial standpoint," as Hitchcock put it. As Kemmerer remarked in 1911, "The debates in Congress show clearly that it was the intention of the advocates of the postal savings-bank system to make it self-supporting."[26]

In 1910 the House and Senate Post Office Committees favorably reported postal savings bills. The Senate committee reported the Carter bill with few details other than a minimum deposit and an interest rate. "A rigid rule of law," the committee declared, "might greatly hamper administrative work, detract from the efficiency of the system, increase its cost, and greatly retard improvement." Accordingly, the Carter bill left most of the savings system's parameters to the postmaster general and to a board of trustees composed of the postmaster general, the secretary of treasury, and the attorney general. The House committee's endorsement came less easily, in part because Chairman Weeks opposed postal savings. The House committee was keenly aware of the major departure in institutional and constitutional precedent that postal savings would bring. Throughout the March 1910 hearings, Weeks asked: "Are you in favor, under ordinary conditions, of the Government going into business?" In response to this question, Creer noted the strange administrative jurisdiction of postal savings legislation. The Founders, he said, no more intended that a banking system be put under the Post Office Department "than that we would have an automobile factory established under that department." Even Cowles said the bill was "dangerous" because of the power it gave to "the Executive," and he proposed more legislative control over the postal savings system.[27]

Even with these reservations, most legislators in 1910 acknowledged that postal savings was a foregone conclusion. Debate centered not on the passage of the plan or on administrative discretion but on its financial details. The arguments of skepticism the ABA advanced faded into institutional silence. The Senate passed the Carter bill in a 50-to-22 party-line vote, with only one Democrat voting in favor. In the House, Carter's bill was amended thoroughly by Insurgents who favored community reinvestment of postal savings. The House amendments mandated that 60 percent of the funds be invested by local banks, subject to withdrawal for "exigencies" by the president. Yet the course of legislation took an unexpected turn when Speaker Joseph G. Cannon, still chastened by the revolt of the Insurgents, persuaded the House to debate both the unamended Carter bill and the fully amended Weeks committee measure under restrictive rules. The House approved a version of the original Carter bill—one more conservative on financial details, allowing a 2 percent rate of return and a $500 maximum deposit. After President Taft threatened to veto any pending legislation until the House bill was passed, the Senate and the House agreed on the more conservative version, and Taft signed the Postal Savings Act into law on June 9, 1910.[28]

First-Generation Immigrants and Postal Savings

In some respects, the board of trustees functioned as an important constraint on the administrative discretion of the Post Office. Yet this constraint was short-lived. In March 1911, just nine months after it passed the Postal Savings Act of 1910, Congress placed virtually full control of postal savings in the Post Office Department. The postmaster general now had full authority over the designation of postal savings depositories and rules regarding the deposit and withdrawal of funds. Given that the new Democratic House changed nothing else about postal savings—the deposit and reinvestment provisions of the 1910 act were untouched—it was an important recognition of departmental capacity. Two years later Postmaster General Albert S. Burleson relinquished much of his own authority over the postal savings system, making the program even more bureaucratic. By creating the Division of Postal Savings in the Bureau of the Third Assistant Postmaster General, Burleson's order of May 1, 1913, placed authority over postal savings squarely in the middle levels of the department's career bureaucracy. Carter B. Keene—whose previous post was, not trivially, chief post office inspector—became the sovereign of the postal savings system.[29]

Despite opponents' predictions that postal savings would run at a loss, the system erased an early deficit in 1913 and thereafter returned a healthy profit to the department. By 1917, with the maximum deposit having been raised to $1,000, Americans had entrusted more than $100 million of their money to the Post Office. As the Senate committee reported in 1916, "Deposits and profits of the service are running up constantly and operating expenses are falling off. . . . The Post Office Department is equipped to transact double the present postal-savings business with comparatively little additional outlay." Schroedel and Snyder conclude that postal savings "provided a means to equalize the distribution of savings depositories throughout the country, affording rural, especially southern, residents a safe place to keep their money." Yet evidence from the administrative placement and the popular utilization of the banks suggests that if farmers pressed for a postal savings system, they did not take much interest in it after its erection in 1910. In a 1916 speech before the American Banking Association, Keene gleefully noted that departmental predictions about the enthusiasm of first-generation immigrants for postal savings banks turned out to be correct. As early as 1915, 59 percent of all postal savings depositors were foreign-born, and they owned 72 percent of the deposits. Russian immigrants alone had deposited more than one-fifth of all postal savings by World War I. The pattern was repeated within states. After Detroit, no city in Michigan had more postal savings deposits than Ironwood, a mining town in the Upper Peninsula with large numbers of Russian and Scandinavian immigrants. A similar pattern was observed in Wisconsin, where the postal deposits in the copper enclave of Superior were exceeded only in Milwaukee. The force of foreign-born investors left immigrant-rich states such as Washington and New Jersey with far more than their proportional share of postal savings banks and depositors. As Senator John Hollis Bankhead of Alabama said, immigrant depositors "will patronize no savings institution that does not have the Government directly back of it."[30]

The distribution of banks and deposits across states corroborates these narrative impressions. Table 5.1 shows the results of three regression analyses of the distribution of postal savings banks, depositors, and deposits across the forty-eight states in 1916. The variables of interest are banks, depositors, and deposits per population of 100,000. I estimate the presence of farmers and farm groups in states by using four variables: the percentage of the state's population living in rural areas, the percentage of state farms that were rented for a share of the crop, and Grange and Farmers' Union membership. It turns out that none of these variables is consistently and significantly correlated with postal savings across the states. Banks were positively associated with the rural population, but postal depositors were negatively associated with this variable. What all three regressions show is that the presence of foreign-born citizens powerfully boosted savings banks, deposit activity, and deposits. Even controlling for the presence of postal savings banks, postal savings activity was larger in states with more foreign-born citizens. A five-point increase in the percentage of a state's citizens that were foreign-born was associated with three more savings banks, 414 more depositors, and $69.90 additional deposits per population of 100,000. No other variable in the analyses comes close to matching these effects.[31]

Read differently, table 5.1 also demonstrates the autonomy of the department. The Postal Savings Act and the 1911 appropriations act gave sole discretion to the department to choose the post offices that would be established as savings banks. For all the power of agrarian representatives in the postal savings campaign—and in light of agrarian Democrats' rise to power in the Democratic Party in 1912—it is interesting to note that the distribution of savings offices across states did not strongly favor agrarian or Democratic constituencies. Instead, the department directed savings offices to the constituency that it sought most to influence: first-generation European immigrants. The department actively invited immigrants into the system, as by 1917 postal officials designed twenty-three foreign-language circulars describing the system (see figure 5.1). Kemmerer noted "the democratic atmosphere which pervades most post offices, in contrast with the aristocratic one that pervades most banks."[32]

TABLE 5.1
The Determinants of Postal Savings, 1916

	Savings Banks per 100,000 State Population	Depositors per 100,000 State Population	Deposits per 100,000 State Population
Mean of dependent variable	11.8	602.8	$89.60
(standard deviation)	(6.4)	(618.80)	($106.70)
Constant	4.22	309.79	214.01
	(4.23)	(346.60)	(70.94)
State population (1916)	−2.59**	−25.51**	−36.86**
(in millions)	(0.65)	(6.64)	(11.83)
(State population)^2	1.9 E-07**	3.4 E-04**	5.2 E-05**
	(8.0 E-08)	(1.0 E-04)	(1.6 E-05)
Percentage of state population	20.069$^+$	0.76	−0.80
black	(0.040)	(4.05)	(1.14)
Percentage of state population	0.649**	81.17**	13.70**
foreign-born	(0.227)	(20.76)	(4.60)
Grange family memberships,	4.6 E-03	−7.2 E-03	24.5 E-03
1910	(3.7 E-03)	(5.1 E-02)	(7.9 E-03)
Farmers' Union family	7.7 E-03	3.1 E-02	26.1 E-03
memberships, 1916	(7.1 E-03)	(6.6 E-02)	(1.1 E-02)
Percentage of state population	−0.21**	12.26	3.66
illiterate	(0.08)	(09.71)	(2.52)
Percentage of state population	0.14**	−5.17	0.25
living in rural areas	(0.04)	(3.23)	(0.65)
Percentage of state farms rented	−0.005	4.38	0.32
for share of crop	(0.055)	(5.03)	(1.09)
Residuals from savings banks	—	7057.81**	1397.11**
regression		(2306.63)	(485.36)
N (df)	48 (38)	48 (37)	48 (37)
Adjusted R-squared	0.74	0.68	0.57

Sources: Kemmerer, *Postal Savings;* Robert Tontz, "Membership of General Farmers' Organizations, United States, 1874–1960," *Agricultural History* 38 (June 1964): 143–56; Census of 1910.

Note: Ordinary least squares regressions with White heteroscedasticity-corrected standard errors in parentheses.

*Significance at $p < .05$.

**Significance at $p < 0.01$.

$^+$Significance at $p < 0.10$.

(All tests are two-tailed).

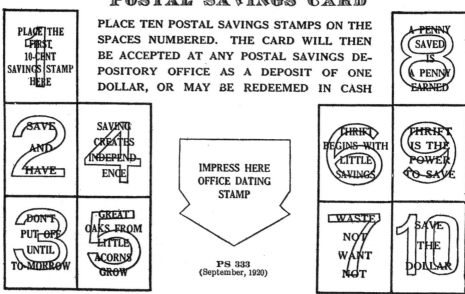

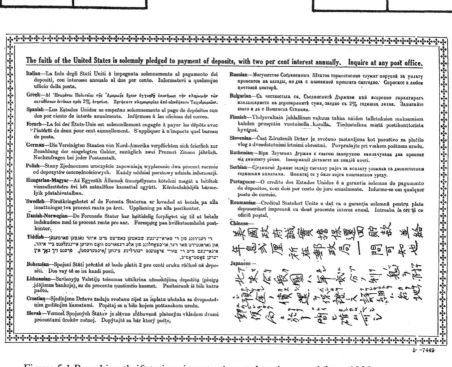

Figure 5.1 Preaching thrift to immigrants. A postal savings card from 1920.

One might attribute this pattern to the Democratic Party's attempts to capture the elusive immigrant vote in industrial and mining centers, a campaign dating from Grover Cleveland. Scott James has advanced a similar explanation of the Interstate Commerce Act and the Democrats' support of state-building measures after 1910. Although this explanation seems plausible, the legislative and administrative history of postal savings defies it. In the campaign for savings only postal officials consistently emphasized its benefits for foreign-born citizens, and they did so under Democratic *and* Republican administrations for four decades before the act of 1910. When Democrats weighed in at all for postal savings, they emphasized the benefits for farmers. Moreover, none of the Democrats from industrial districts—including Francis Dodds of Michigan and William Cox of Indiana, both on the House Post Office Committee—took active roles in the postal savings debate. Finally, among the immigrant groups who relied most heavily on postal savings—Italians, Russians, Greeks, Scandinavians, and others—only the Italians carried sufficient political weight (less than Irish immigrants) to occupy the attention of national Democrats. With their influence in city machines, the Irish had less need for the department's savings institutions.[33]

A better explanation for the tilt of postal savings toward immigrants lies not in partisan strategy but in administrative coalition building. The department, after all, had emphasized immigrants' savings and the moral benefits of thrift for a full decade before Cleveland's presidency. The department's advocacy of the program advanced its legitimacy among moralist Progressives and among foreign-born citizens. For the Division of Postal Savings in particular, immigrants had become a powerful ally. Their enthusiasm for the system tempered the opposition of finance-state Republicans, kept the savings banks afloat, and deflated concerns that the department could not manage the program without a deficit. Steeped in the post-Victorian republican virtue of thrift and supported heavily by charity reformers, the department had built a program that would undoubtedly last for generations. The postal savings program, in retrospect, stands alongside well-known Progressive attempts to shape the behavior and the culture of the working poor, including the Children's Bureau and mothers' pensions.[34]

Farmers and Immigrants: Explaining Postal Savings

What requires explanation in the emergence of a postal savings system is not conflict but consensus. Why did agreement coalesce so quickly around postal savings? Undoubtedly Schroedel and Snyder are correct to emphasize the "agitation" of western and southern "periphery" representatives who offered most of the postal savings bills. Yet although sectional and partisan divisions strongly characterized the congressional votes over postal savings, it is noteworthy how few substantive issues were even subject to vote by 1910. After 1908, with postal savings firmly entrenched in the platforms of all major parties, and with Taft firmly committed to the department's plans one year later, the erection of a postal savings system was never in doubt. Instead, the parties and sections warred over financial details, such as community reinvestment and the maximum deposit.

Nor is the Postal Savings Act strongly attributable to changes in Congress. The act was passed in June 1910, *before* the Democratic takeover of the House. The Cannon revolt undoubtedly assisted the savings campaign by reducing the Old Guard's ability to strangle the bill. Yet the decentralization of power within the House could not have boded well for postal savings, as Post Office Committee chairman John Weeks was opposed to the bill and worked actively to defeat it.

As powerful as the agrarian logic behind postal savings may appear, it leaves two significant historical lacunae. First, it pays insufficient attention to the role of the Post Office Department in promoting and shaping the savings idea, and it ignores the centrality of concerns about postal efficiency in Congress's reluctance to authorize postal banks before 1910. The department had been the principal font of ideas for postal savings since Harrison's plan in 1871, producing numerous drafts of legislation. The department also protected its money-order functions as a way of demonstrating that it could manage large cash flows. Combined with deficit reduction, the growing success of the money-order system was the critical hurdle to the erection of a postal savings system.

The second foible of the populist narrative is more severe. European and Asian immigrants, not western and southern agrarians, were the most important component of the political coalition behind postal savings. Agrarian-centered accounts of the postal savings debate ignore this crucial force altogether. Beyond this, the *administration* of postal savings flouts standard sectional and agrarian-centered accounts. The most powerful determinant of the administrative creation and economic use of postal savings banks in a state was the presence of first-generation immigrants in its population. Immigrants, like the postal savings banks they favored, established a presence on both coasts and in midwestern and Ohio Valley states with mining towns.

The postal savings system—arguably the most intrepid bureaucratic intrusion into private finance since the Second Bank of the United States—was driven by the Post Office Department's desire to shape the moral and economic behavior of working Americans. The campaign for postal savings was undoubtedly aided by other energies, including agrarian statism and the enthusiasm of Taft. Yet the department's strategy of tailoring the system to the needs of immigrants was a necessary condition for the emergence of a postal savings system. Kemmerer, writing of the campaign in 1917, came to the same inescapable conclusion, namely, that the postal savings system had the "primary object of encouraging thrift among the poorer classes." Its success in doing so, far surpassing even Wanamaker's expectations, was a further source of political esteem for the department in the early twentieth century.[35]

Reputation, Program Expansion, and Discretion: The Parcels Post Debate

The novel feature of postal savings was that it represented an explicit bureaucratic intrusion into private markets. An agency of state now competed with established private firms on a local basis throughout the country. Two years after the Postal Savings Act of 1910, the department would once again tread upon the previously hallowed ground of private enterprise. This time, the department competed not with small local firms but with large parcel delivery companies.

As in the case of rural free delivery, parcels post transcends any mere extension of the national delivery network. As Richard Kielbowicz has argued, Congress's decision to allow the department to deliver parcels was an institutionally novel grant of permission. It allowed the government to enter markets and compete where before only private entities had reigned. As an idea, parcels post descended from antebellum politics. As a policy vision, however, parcels post entered the national stage during the heady days of the agrarian depression after 1880. Accordingly, many writings on the struggle for parcels post have stressed its origins in agrarian ideology. Kielbowicz suggests that Populist supporters of parcels post saw the program as a potential collectivization of the nation's communication and transportation infrastructure. The Grange had demanded parcels post in 1887, and in December 1889, the Southern Farmers' Alliance joined with the Knights of Labor to call for "universal ownership of the means of communication and transportation," with the department as a model.[36]

The irony here is that agrarian demands for parcels post fell silent on Capitol Hill in the 1890s. Even in the Populist heyday of 1892 to 1896, the parcels post plan led to little public and almost no congressional discussion. Why then was parcels post enacted more than two decades after its appearance in Populist platforms?

Certainly the concentrated opposition to parcels post had much to do with its delay. Parcels post threatened to bankrupt commercial middlemen, wholesalers, and rural merchants by establishing a virtually direct link from the factory to the farm. Under the leadership of Charles William Burrows—president of Cleveland's Burrows Brothers Company and first vice president of the National Board of Trade—these interests organized quickly and loudly in opposition to parcels post, just as they had come together against RFD. They made their voices heard through the National Association of Retail Grocers, the American Hardware Manufacturers' Association, and the American League of Associations.

These interests allied with railroad and express company interests, who greatly feared postal competition. The express companies, who dominated the parcel market before 1912, anchored the antipostal coalition. As Wanamaker remarked waggishly in 1891, "[T]here are four reasons against the establishment of a parcels post: the American Express Company, the Adams Express Company, the United States Express Company, and the Wells Fargo Express Company." Six of these companies controlled 90 percent of the parcel business before World War I, and they financed and organized a well-heeled opposition. In a bow to the diversity of interests that supported postal expansion, the companies shrewdly and secretly financed the Chicago-based American League of Associations, an umbrella federation of businesses that would suffer under a parcels post system and the expansion of mail-order trade that it would spur. Many of these businesses were wholesalers, and their concerns were voiced recurrently by Burrows, who proposed an alluring substitute for parcels post: one-cent postage. Together, the plaintive cries of wholesalers and express concerns caught the ear of Old Guard Republicans, who were favorable to their cause. After the demise of the Old Guard leadership in the Cannon revolt and the midterm elections of 1910, Democrat John Moon of Tennessee took over the House Post Office Committee, and Congress became an institution more propitious for parcels post.[37]

Although the presence of concentrated opposition and partisan hurdles helps to account for the delay of parcels post, it is insufficient. If wholesalers were opposed to rural free delivery as well as parcels post—Burrows spoke and wrote against RFD in the 1890s—then why did parcels post fail before 1910 while RFD grew? Why would a Congress that was unwilling to pass parcels post have nurtured RFD, which, as wholesalers knew all too well, was a necessary condition for parcels post? In short, if RFD came so early, why did parcels post come so late?

The fiscal health of the department, tracked in figure 4.1, provides a clue. The most persuasive argument against parcels post from the 1890s to 1910 emphasized the inability of the department to manage a parcel delivery system. This claim appeared in many forms—in statistical summaries, in arguments from principles of political economy, in broadsides against bureaucratic inefficiency. The *Chicago Dry-Goods Reporter* warned of "the enormous annual deficit which the parcels business cannot fail to create in the postal department," and the National Board of Trade and the National Hardware Association also warned about an "enormous loss to the Government." Petitions from rural communities echoed these fears. A 1908 essay in the *Journal of Political Economy* tarred the department's operations and concluded that it "would be utterly unable to compete with express companies on a business basis." Burrows, the most eloquent of parcels post's detractors, pointed to program losses in the special delivery service and RFD and claimed that "the service is blow-holed, full of inaccuracy and fraud upon which there is no efficient check." He cautioned that "any Parcels Post Service must result in enormous loss to the Government." Even as the movement gained momentum after 1908, its leader, Maryland representative David Lewis, complained that "talk of postal deficits is indulged in" by its opponents. It was an argument accepted by the House and Senate Post Office Committees, which refused to report parcels post bills before 1908.[38]

After 1900, as the department's deficit gradually diminished, parcels post became a legislative possibility. The deficit reductions received favorable attention from journals of opinion, including *The Outlook, The American Review of Reviews,* and *World's Work. The Outlook* noted in 1907 that deficits had previously been cited as a reason against programs such as parcels post.

> But it is worth while noting that this argument against the Government's engaging in business is losing force year by year. Fifty years ago the deficit was forty-three per cent of the receipts of the Department; ten years ago it had dropped to thirteen percent; in 1906 it was but a little over six per cent; while in the year just passed it was a little over three and one-half percent. If the progress which has been continued so steadily since 1857 continues, it should be but a very few years before the post-office will show a profit on its yearly business.[39]

As in the case of rural free delivery, a public campaign by the department lit the momentum for legislation. The first of the department's moves was clandestine. Since the 1902 law creating the RFD Service left the department to regulate it entirely, postal officials allowed rural carriers to augment their salaries by contracting with farmers to deliver unmailable packages. Under pressure from express companies fearful of postal expansion, Congress prohibited parcel delivery for pay in 1904, terminating the impromptu experiment after two years. Yet because the 1904 law did not prohibit parcel delivery altogether, many rural carriers still toted packages for free. Departmental rulings even encouraged the practice, as long as carriers kept records of deliveries. For thousands of rural patrons, the department had given an administrative taste of parcels post a full decade before Congress authorized a system.[40]

The department also engaged in advocacy, which became ever louder as its deficit declined and its organizational confidence crested. Prodded to speak publicly for parcels post by lower-level officials, Postmaster General Meyer traveled to Boston in October 1907 and supported an incremental approach to parcels post. Meyer's plan, which reflected the beliefs of the career cadre, advocated package delivery through a more liberal definition of fourth-class matter. George S. R. Miles, president of the National Retail Hardware Association and a powerful rural voice against parcels post, admitted that Meyer "was the first man, so far as I know, to define our present fourth-class mail service as a parcels post, and as such to advocate its extension."[41]

Parcels post's supporters included Cowles's Postal Progress League. Many of its member businesses stood to gain from the implicit subsidization of package delivery under parcels post. Yet the public ownership enthusiasts in the league also held firm with their faith that the department was capable of managing a parcel system efficiently. Colonel Albert Pope, owner and president of his manufacturing company and a well-established Progressive, pointed to the rural carriers' unofficial deliveries and surmised that "[i]f barrels of flour and sacks of grain can be carried on our rural postal machinery outside the post office, . . . they can be carried at far greater advantage . . . under the post office." By 1908 Postmaster General Meyer was explicitly coordinating mass mailings with Cowles and with Farmers' National Congress lobbyist John Stahl. He also corresponded frequently with editors of publications ranging from the *Boston Evening Transcript* to *Advertiser's Magazine* to the *American Review of Reviews,* all of whom enthusiastically endorsed parcels post, even more so when Meyer personally asked them to chime in. Throughout the entire parcels debate, Meyer cultivated a mien of neutrality, meeting with Cowles and these editors only privately.[42] By 1905 major business and academic interests in the league were well aware of the department's capacities. As the *North American Review* observed in 1902, "An influential clientele now clamors for the parcels-post." The reputation of the Post Office was firmly rooted in its economic and political network ties (see table 5.2).[43]

The final step in the department's reputation building was the reduction of the deficit to post-Depression lows. Maryland representative David Lewis publicized the department's new economies repeatedly in special reports to the House committee. He cited statistics showing that in 1900 the per-employee efficiency of the department surpassed that of the French, English, and German systems. As of 1910, the department's efficiency was almost double that of its British and German counterparts. Lewis also trumpeted the department's cost statistics, suggesting that the department's surplus would have been even larger without congressional franking. Of course, Lewis's reports had the sympathetic ear of the House committee under Tennessee Democrat John Moon. Yet the new tenor of arguments about the department's capacities and the deficit was remarkable. Opponents who once pointed to the deficit as a reason not to enact parcels post now argued that the program would erase the department's successes.[44]

In 1911, with the clamor for parcels post in full crescendo, the Senate and the House began hearings. While agrarian groups demanded a government takeover of the express market, the department presented a more cautious front. When asked by the Senate committee how the department would proceed, James Britt, third assistant postmaster general, spoke in workmanlike prose of the logic of incremental expansion and experiment-based delegation.

> My own view is that we should commence with the rural routes; that we should commence almost at the same time with some large city delivery in experimenting; that we should go to studying the transportation in relation to this enlarged parcel post, and in a careful, cautious way, in order that the Congress might have the benefit of information obtained in the most accurate way. I think that next year we would enlarge upon this year and next year upon that year until within a few years any citizen of the United States can mail his parcel.[45]

TABLE 5.2
The Multiple Network Affiliations of Postal Officials

Corporate Ties	Media, Publishing, and Municipalization Ties	Moral Reform and Consumerist Ties	Agrarian Ties
Julius Rosenwald, Sears, Roebuck & Company	Simon Brentano *Advertising American*	American Medical Association, Charles Reed	John Stahl, Farmers' National Congress
John Wanamaker, Wanamaker's (Philadelphia)	*The Survey* (social welfare advocates)	Women's Christian Temperance Union	National Grange (Nahum Bachelder)
Macy's	*Boston Evening Transcript*	Florence Kelley, National Consumers' League	James Cowles's Postal Progress League
Woodward & Lothrop	Doubleday, Page & Co.	Anti-Saloon League	Orange Judd Co. (farm journal publisher)
James Cowles (ties to numerous business firms, including Montgomery Ward)	Funk & Wagnalls	Prohibition United	
	Josiah Quincy, ex-mayor, Boston	New York Society for the Suppression of Vice	
	Seth Low, ex-mayor, New York		

Britt's testimony was more prescient than he let on. The creation and expansion of parcels post would take almost exactly the form he presaged. As in rural free delivery and postal savings banks, the department never proposed to create a new service all at once. Progressive-Era postal officials always asked for the chance to prove the efficacy of their schemes to the committees. And whether committee leaders were as skeptically predisposed as Eugene Loud and John Weeks or as enthusiastic as John Wadsworth, Jonathan Bourne Jr., or John Moon, they all assented to greater and greater discretion and program jurisdiction for the department.

The Reputational Significance of the Deficit: A Counterfactual. Parcels post was passed as a rider to an appropriations bill in 1912. In the end, the balance of beliefs and doubts about the department's efficacy drove its passage. As Kielbowicz concludes, "Much of the campaign for parcel post turned on beliefs about the capacity of the Post Office Department to handle new tasks." Consider, then, the following historical counterfactual: what if the department had maintained its nineteenth-century reputation for inefficacy? Had the postal deficit been 10 percent of revenues instead of 0 in 1912, had the experiments with rural parcel delivery failed, and had RFD proven a fiscal loser, it is inconceivable that parcels post would have passed in 1912, if at all by the First World War. Although the Cannon revolt and the 1910 elections certainly paved the way for statutory parcels post, they were hardly sufficient to empower the program on their own. For even under Cannon's reign, the House and Senate committees had allowed the department to experiment with package delivery. And absent the taste of postal parcel delivery from these trials, rural communities would never have pressed for the program in such force. From 1902 onward, the department's experiments and efficiencies left its detractors with hollow predictions and its enthusiasts with hope.

The best evidence that reputation shifts underlay parcels post is the fact that Congress resorted to new institutional forms in creating it. As Kielbowicz writes, the Bourne legislation "harbored one other innovation: Congress left considerable latitude to the chief administrator." Under the 1912 legislation, the postmaster general had sole authority to set parcel rates. This capacity would persist even though Congress retained its control over stamp prices. It was the boldest and most direct delegation of commodity pricing authority to any bureaucracy before the First World War.[46]

From Gags to Co-optation: The Struggle with Labor

From 1908 to 1912, just as the department's productivity crested, the very basis of that productivity slowly began to crumble. Postal efficiency had been achieved through the RMS-led transformation of the system, through civil service reform, and through the relentless expansion of the institutions and ideology of postal inspection. The markers of this transformation were longer hours for post office clerks, reduced shirking from greater inspection, and the austere efficiency of the Railway Mail Service. By the summer of 1909, clerks in the Chicago post office were working, on average, ten hours a day, with a maximum rest of thirty minutes; railway mail clerks were commonly putting in twelve-hour shifts in rotting, tuberculosis-infested wooden cars that had been introduced during Wanamaker's tenure two decades earlier; and postal workers everywhere were increasingly aware that their salaries were being outpaced by their colleagues in the private sector. The wage scale for the clerical grades of the federal workforce had not changed since 1854.[47]

Together, these forces created an impetus for union formation in the department's ranks. Scattered and largely temporary labor organizations had cropped up since the Reconstruction period, mainly in the form of mutual benefit associations. Compared with other unions at the turn of the century, however, postal unions were docile. Like other government workers, postal workers had no liberty to strike, a handicap maintained in part by the unions' sheepish reluctance to fight for striking rights. Another debilitating factor was the federal government's open-shop rule dating from 1903. Yet the primary reason for the weakness of the postal labor organization relative to other governmental workers was its balkanization along craft lines. By 1910 there were separate unions for letter carriers, rural free delivery carriers, and post office clerks and two labor unions for RMS clerks.[48]

At first the department responded harshly to worker organization, issuing gag orders and attempting to dissolve the unions. The unions were showing political muscle in electoral contests—culminating in the 1902 defeat of House Post Office Committee chairman Eugene Loud, who had opposed reclassification measures that would have made whole cadres of clerks and carriers better off—and Republicans began to view them with suspicion. The department had restricted workers' political activities in 1895, but after Loud's defeat, the issue became tinged with partisanship. Theodore Roosevelt issued his infamous gag orders of 1902 and 1906, prohibiting workers from lobbying or communicating with Congress on any reclassification or salary issue. The department also issued a "wreck-gag" in August 1906 that proscribed workers from publicly discussing the role of the Post Office or railroad companies in train accidents. The unions were officially silenced, but they only grew stronger, securing the cooperation of Samuel Gompers of the AFL, organizing the RFD carriers in 1903, and forming a new, more powerful union, the National Federation of Post Office Clerks, in 1906. The Railway Mail Association took a leftward turn under the leadership of John Kidwell after 1905, and two radical postal labor weeklies—*The Post Office Bundy Recorder* and *The Harpoon*—surfaced.[49]

Labor activism now split the reform wing of the department. Railway mail clerks had long forsaken collective organization, but with working conditions deteriorating and reclassification long delayed, the wreck-gag of 1906 and a new gag order by Taft in 1909 proved intolerable. RMS workers knew they could not turn to the Railway Mail Association. Even with more aggressive leadership under Kidwell, the association was dominated by the department. Instead, a new union—the Brotherhood of Railway Postal Clerks—formed, infused by the ideology of *The Harpoon*. *The Harpoon*, published in Phoenix by retired clerk Urban A. Walter and therefore not subject to the gag, had ten thousand subscribers in 1912. In January 1911 RPO clerks on the "Tracy (Minnesota) to Pierre" line refused to perform extra duties (or "take-up-the-slack") as the department had recently ordered. The department suspended the ten men and the line fell into chaos. More than one thousand unsorted mailbags piled up on the Tracy station platform. Soon the RPO clerks on the "Elroy to Tracy" line were refusing extra work, and more than two hundred clerks in Saint Paul, Minnesota, threatened to resign en masse. To make matters worse, discord between Taft and Wisconsin senator Robert M. LaFollette resulted in a congressional investigation of the RMS, which cast the service's troubles in stark relief. LaFollette's offensive on behalf of railway clerks eventuated in the passage of the Lloyd-LaFollette Act of August 1911, which gave organizing and petitioning rights to all federal employees.[50]

Postal administrators were far more concerned about railway labor unrest than about workers' rights, however. Because railway mail work required detailed knowledge of routes that could be learned only through on-the-job training, the department could ill afford to lose its RPO clerks. Although the administration came out in official opposition to reclassification measures, Hitchcock privately supported reclassification as a way to ease the department's troubles. Congress, seeking favor with the postal unions in a highly unpredictable election year, gave the railway clerks a summary reclassification in the Reilly Act of 1912.[51]

Whatever goodwill prevailed between the department and its labor unions under Hitchcock quickly eroded under the administration of Albert S. Burleson, postmaster general under Woodrow Wilson. Formerly an eight-term House representative from Texas, Burleson commenced an explicit antilabor campaign that lasted the full course of his administration. He aimed his ire not simply at the labor radicals and *The Harpoon* but at the mainline unions as well. In 1914 Burleson asked Congress to scale back the provisions of the Reilly Act so that the department could compel postal workers to work more hours and could cut salaries. When the mainline unions initiated opposition in 1917, the department dismissed the presidents of the RMA and the Rural Letter Carriers' Association. First Assistant Postmaster General Daniel Roper described Burleson's attitude: "Organizations of postal employees have no official status which may be recognized by the Department. They are not per se a part of the postal service, nor are they essential to its conduct or welfare. They are purely unofficial." Ironically, Burleson's attack on the mainline unions succeeded only in relegitimizing them. Railway workers who were previously estranged from the RMS now pledged new allegiance to it. When the American Federation of Labor called for Burleson's dismissal in June 1919, the association brazenly endorsed the AFL resolution at its national convention in Saint Louis.[52]

Burleson's labor troubles were magnified by his tepid relations with the press and by concerns that his economy program was hurting the quality of service. Reports surfaced that delivery time for mail traveling between Washington, D.C., and New York had doubled during the early years of Burleson's tenure. Unlike the nineteenth century, however, it was Burleson's reputation, and not the department's, that suffered a public hit. As *The Providence Journal* reminded its readers, "[T]he carriers and clerks are not responsible for the lack of administrative capacity at the head of the department." At the core of Burleson's negative publicity were two actions he had taken that outraged newspaper owners and editors. To begin with, Burleson enforced anti-espionage press restrictions during the war, propelling him into a nasty public spat with the now-retired Theodore Roosevelt. Yet nothing struck at the press more than Burleson's attempt to raise the second-class mail rates in 1917. For decades the department had artificially suppressed the mailing rate on second-class matter—mail-order catalogs, newspapers, and journals—thereby subsidizing the press by covering losses on second-class matter with "profits" on first-class matter (standard letters). Burleson later estimated the annual cost of this subsidy at $72 million. His decision to raise rates earned him the unrestrained enmity of many eastern city papers. The *Philadelphia Ledger* called him "loco-minded," and the *New York World* waged a two-year campaign to oust him.[53]

Co-opting the RMA. Even though many workers and newspapers greeted his departure with glee, Burleson had established a stable basis for departmental autonomy. The postal service, the parcels post, and the postal savings banks were running at a healthy surplus. Burleson had reduced the department's rate of pay to railroad companies who transported RPO cars, ensuring cost savings for the future. Perhaps the most secure legacy of Burleson's keep was the opposite of his aims. Burleson's attack on the mainline unions had unwittingly reunited the railway postal employees under the RMA. When Republicans took control of the department after 1920—under Harding's postmaster general Will H. Hays—the RMA once again became the conduit for official attempts to rein in labor radicalism and squeeze more efficiency from the postal labor force. This transformation, as it turns out, was less an institutional change than a cultural one.

After 1920, the mechanical idiom that shaped the Railway Mail Service was "humanized," "spirited," and characterized by "cooperation." In numerous respects, the service assumed the trappings of a commercial outfit`. Citizens became "patrons" and postal operations became a "postal business" and "enterprise." The mechanical idiom melded with an emerging commercial idiom. The RMS, like the department, became a business machine.[54]

The emergence of this business metaphor is traceable to the more frequent interaction of postal officials with commercial and manufacturing firms. An alliance with Cowles's Postal Progress League and the launching of parcels post brought postal officials into greater contact with mail-order houses such as Sears, Roebuck and Company. RMS administrators met often with Sears executives to coordinate Sears's distribution plans and RMS operations. Perhaps more important was a series of tours of the Ford Motor Company's plants by department officials (organized as the Parcel Post Committee) in the early 1920s. R. J. Harris, superintendent of the Fourth Division of the RMS, in a letter to Riddell describes the practical lessons he took from a "profitable" 1923 tour of the Ford plant in Detroit.

> From an economic sense and a scientific production standpoint, I feel that our trip through the Ford plant was the most impressive and instructive experience that any of us have ever had, and I am convinced that great good will come of the trip. The unparalleled activities and congenial manner in which the executives and employees function [at Ford] serve as an example as to the constant needs in our service for sound logical thoughtout economic and effective service improvements by all employees of the Post Service [*sic*].
>
> The successful mechanical devices used and the systematic and automatic manner in which the men respond and carry on their work in my opinion . . . is traceable to orderly mental processes and comprehensive application by a large number of students who make a study of such problems with the underlying thought of reducing overhead charges and the saving of man power.

Postal officials learned powerful and replicable lessons at Ford. They discovered a "congenial manner" and admired the "orderly mental processes" and "systematic and automatic manner" of Ford laborers. They also ascribed Ford's success to its managerial design rather than to its talent.[55]

From these meetings postal officials took the rudiments of the new business discourse. To foster a more "congenial" labor force, RMS officials embarked on a dual strategy. First, they monitored the morale of clerks. In weekly newsletters sent to Washington headquarters, divisional superintendents reported on the emotive state of their employees. They detailed the "sentiment" of the clerks, their potential agitation over matters of salary and reclassification, and the like. And administrative officials held their own meetings to discuss morale; one meeting in Nebraska left a divisional superintendent "very well satisfied with reports as to the feeling of the clerks." The increasing concern for employee morale was also seen in the department's organizational structure. Hays placed a new welfare director just below himself and outside the assistant postmasters general. Department officials penned new tracts for the business community, typified by Herman Blackman's *Business Mail,* a booklet on how firms could make profitable use of the postal system.[56]

Second, the department asked regional officials to promote a variety of interservice meetings and to monitor "sentiment" at them. These varied from regional postal conventions to auxiliary dinner-and-dance functions to weekend "leisure" trips. At a Cleveland, Ohio, auxiliary dance a divisional officer noticed that "the feeling of harmony between the office force and the clerks was very pronounced." An outing of Florida railway clerks to the Sulphur Springs pleasure resort was attended by administrative officials, one of whom reported that the event created "feelings of good will and fellowship" and would have a "wholesome effect for cooperation." Even the railway clerks noted the new "humanism" of their machine. As one labor leader wrote to Hays, "It is extremely gratifying to feel that the employees are to be considered as partners in the great postal administration and that the 'human element' is to receive proper consideration." A *New York Times* writer found himself "marveling at the enthusiasm" in the 1920s Post Office and noticed that the "brains of the Post Office" were placing more emphasis on "the human element." Sterling Denhard Spero, writing what remains the definitive book on postal unions in 1927, remarked on the "humanizing" character of Hays's administration. The department even revisited Wanamaker's practice of bringing postmasters to Washington for the purpose of learning about technological and administrative breakthroughs. Divisional officers were also pleased by the apparently "conservative" and "harmonious" tone of RMA meetings they attended. R. J. Harris of the Fourth Division reported that

> after attending a number of Postal Conventions held in the Fourth and Twelfth Divisions, . . . I feel sufficiently qualified in saying to Departmental officials that these "get-to-gether" Postal Conventions will reflect credit to the Department in the eyes of the business world and will make for a more thorough and systematized service throughout the country. . . . [T]he mere fact of the high officials from Washington moving around in the field among their patrons and their employees is in my judgment one of the best examples of good fellowship and will serve to establish a fine precedent, not only for the employees of the Postal Service, but for the business world in general as well.[57]

Like much of Progressive-Era organizational culture, the new culture of the department counseled the rationalization of administrative structure. Yet the concept of efficiency—the central theme of Progressive and 1920s rationalization—is absent from the administrative discourse of the RMS. Department officials instead emphasized "harmony," "cooperation," and "performance." To back its commitment, the department assiduously avoided the Taylorist stopwatch methods that Burleson had favored. This "spirited" nature of the "business machine" distinguished the organizational culture of the Post Office from the larger current of Progressivism.

The new emphasis on organizational "spirit" meshed well with the enduring moral reform lens of the department's careerists. During the Southern States Convention Tour of 1923, postal officials held many of their interservice conventions in churches. The Postal Conference-Convention of Georgia of January 20, 1923, was held in Atlanta's Baptist Tabernacle. The Reverend Richard Orme Flinn, pastor of Atlanta's North Avenue Presbyterian Church, presided over the convention and offered the opening invocation. At Atlanta and elsewhere, interservice convention schedules included organized prayers.[58]

The new cooperative ethic entered the RMS at a time when the department most needed it. As part of an effort to fend off a new deficit, postal officials in the 1920s authorized reorganizations entailing the mass transfer of clerks among RPO lines, the overhaul of service schedules, and the redrawing of geographic and hierarchical lines of authority within the service. The moves initially met with stiff opposition from rank-and-file clerks whose lives were being thrown into turmoil and whose working patterns and social ties to other clerks were being disrupted, if not altogether destroyed. Clerks wanted the stability that private railroad employees had come to expect. Yet the threat of turmoil was doused by none other than the clerks' union, the Railway Mail Association.

In the 1910s the department began to promote selected RMA officials to administrative and investigative positions in the service, thereby securing their loyalty and establishing a chain of expectations that altered the incentives of the union members up and down the hierarchy. Not coincidentally, association leaders supported the reorganization efforts, enjoining the cooperation of their members. The officials used the metaphor of the department as business to elaborate their appeals. John Kringel, president of the RMA's Fourteenth Division, wrote to his members in 1922, directing them to offer prompt and effective job performance. He euphemistically described the reorganization as a "reconstruction" and asked the clerks for a "spirit of cooperation," a central trope in the business metaphor. Then Kringel elaborated a business metaphor much richer than had existed in official department discourse. In a letter, Kringel lucidly spelled out the crucial characteristic of any organizational metaphor: the implicit division of labor embedded in the idiom.

> The postal establishment of this country is a great industry. The post offices are the branch houses, the post office clerks are the clerks, the post office carriers are the deliverymen, and the railway postal clerks are the travelling salesmen. The travelling salesmen are the most important adjunct of any business. We, therefore, have a very important mission, and the prosperity of the concern depends a great deal on the manner in which we deliver the goods. ARE WE DOING IT? . . . ARE WE USING EVERY OPPORTUNITY TO THINK ABOUT AND SUGGEST IMPROVEMENTS TO THE POSTAL SERVICE? Let us do our work a little better every time we go to work.[59]

In Kringel's department-as-enterprise notion, the railway workers were not clerks but "travelling salesmen." The moral crux of the letter is the enjoinder to "deliver the goods" securely, a role that Kringel had delegated to the postal "deliverymen." This commercial-industrial division of labor and the idea of postal offices as "chain stores" were echoed widely in 1920s administrative communications. Second Assistant Postmaster General E. H. Shaughnessy argued for more centralization, to the degree found in national chains: "We have the greatest system of 'chain stores' in the country. We haven't taken the first step toward making them alike from an efficiency standpoint." RMS superintendents told local postmasters that they served as "advertisers" for the department. RMS clerks were counseled to discuss proper packing procedures with postal "patrons." And the *Richmond Times-Dispatch* echoed Kringel's portrait when it stated that the RMS "is the silent salesman for the manufacturer and jobber, the runners for the great banking system and above all the coupers of the people."[60]

A metaphorical division of labor was one legacy of the commercial-mechanical idiom; organizational conservatism was the other. Kringel finished his letter by pointing optimistically to the upcoming conference between the union and department officials and asking for moderation and consideration in the making of demands. "It is time," he warned, "to be thinking also about the coming conference between the Post Office Department and the Executive Committie [*sic*] of the Railway Mail Association. . . . In your discussions be careful to look at both sides of the question. We are playing a 50–50 game. Do not be selfish in your views." Kringel went on to list an exceedingly moderate set of demands for the conference, including a "retention of present salary," defending this proposal against a mock threat of reduction, and "very little change" in the seniority rules. The association continued this moderation of salary demands at a time when pay levels were a broad concern among railway clerks; postwar wage inflation led many of them to opt for private railroad work. In light of this, Kringel's was a thoroughly conservative address, one that unified the interests of Washington administrators and the union.[61]

In fact, RMS officials explicitly promoted conservative tendencies in their dealings with the RMA. A Texas superintendent, asked by the local association branch to provide entertainment for an upcoming event, wrote to Washington and vowed to use the opportunity "to keep down anything like radicalism in the division." A Georgia official was pleased that the RMA meetings he attended were "characterized by dignity and decorum as well as by intelligent and conservative action on all questions that may arise." It is hardly surprising, in light of this portrait, that the RMA repeatedly turned down opportunities to join the American Federation of Labor. A conservative labor union was an invaluable managerial asset to the RMS administration. For this reason the department strongly favored increased association membership, a situation almost unimaginable under Burleson. Divisional superintendents lauded clerks for signing up additional RMA members. They found meeting places and provided entertainment for events at local association branches. And they continued an enthusiastic pace of attendance at RMA meetings, a presence and a "plan of cooperation" that the association welcomed. In the Railway Mail Association, the department had found the perfect mouthpiece for its metaphorical reshaping of the postal operations and its centralizing strategies.[62]

The payoff of the department's efforts came not only in peaceful labor relations but also in a growing willingness of railway workers to assume leadership roles characteristic of the older clerks. Whereas railway workers from 1910 through the Burleson administration actively resisted attempts to "take up the slack," the department could now call upon the RMS to relieve overworked post offices. When a temporary operations crisis engulfed the Detroit and Cleveland post offices in 1923, the department called clerks from the Detroit Terminal RPO to step in and solve the problem. The clerks did so without balking, earning accolades in the local papers as "the mail squad." According to the *Cleveland Plain Dealer,* "[T]he Cleveland postoffice yesterday found an ally in the railway mail service."[63]

By 1924 the Post Office had achieved a pacific accord with the unions. Only a sliver of radicalism remained. The result of two decades of struggle with railway workers was the co-optation of the union by departmental administration. Burleson had made the RMA the only alternative, but by "cooperation" and rigorous attention to the workers' needs, postal administrators in the early 1920s were able to win back the loyalties of the workers and to stunt radicalism. As the Post Office made efforts to centralize labor authority in the general superintendent, it found assistance from the increasingly moderate association. In other words, the route to administrative centralization in the Railway Mail Service went through, not around, the Railway Mail Association. Organizational culture prevented the Post Office from forfeiting its core capacities and efficiencies derived from the Progressive period. Organizational culture allowed postal administrators a means of stabilizing administrative capacity, in part by lengthening careers, but even more by reducing organizational dissensus and by preserving the reform coalition.

Conclusion: The Puzzle of Postal Development

By the 1920s the fundamental outlines of the twentieth-century postal system were established. Free delivery was essentially universal. Postal inspection was institutionalized, and inspectors maintained their status-laden careers. Parcels post and postal savings were lasting and profitable components of the department. Even as air and automobile transport displaced railway mail, they only furthered the nationalization of the postal system that the RMS had perfected. Not until the 1960s would these features of the postal system wane from record.

The real puzzle in the development of the Post Office is why pathbreaking advances in national state power would come to a department that represented the bastion of the patronage system well into the New Deal. Historians are familiar with state formation as a movement away from bureaucracies such as the Post Office and toward more "expert" agencies and independent commissions. Yet it is worth questioning whether any independent commission before the New Deal held a fraction of the capacity, the political independence, and the market power of the Post Office Department. Labor organizations enabled the Post Office even as they constrained it. Postal unions were politically powerful and supported policy expansions and opposed retrenchments in service or autonomy. On classification and salary issues, the department was able to play *divide et impera* with worker organizations.

The trajectory of policy development suggests that changes in Congress and the committee system account poorly for program innovation at the Post Office. Rural free delivery (1902), postal savings (1910), and parcels post (1912) emerged under three completely different Congresses. Whereas savings made its way through the House Post-Office Committee under John Weeks, who opposed it, parcel delivery passed the committee under a favorable John Moon. No *unified* explanation for these policies can be constructed from standard institutional explanations emphasizing congressional rules changes, party balancing, or coalition building. Moreover, any unified explanation must include the preferences of the reform wing of the Post Office Department—its bent for incremental policy expansion, its focus on cost efficiency after 1890, and its bold attempt to reshape the market morals of first-generation European immigrants.

It is not a necessary feature of this account to lionize or revere the power of the postal reform wing as a praiseworthy development in American history. Many of its policies were patronizing toward the working classes. Historians of Comstockery have lamented many of its lasting adverse effects on American dialogue. Moreover, postal reformers were hardly immune to broader currents of Progressive "enlightened racism," and they clung to an insular, fraternal, and white male identity. Whatever the reformers' legacy for American culture, however, it is undeniable that they achieved a political triumph in their time. Praiseworthy or not, the forging of bureaucratic autonomy, and much of American state building, was premised on moral, social, and religious movements whose effects remain ethically problematic today. What empowered bureaucratic autonomy in national postal administration is that such advocates found a home in the bureaucratic face of the Progressive state.

To suggest that all of the crucial state-building developments in the Post Office Department occurred during the period 1880–1920 would, of course, be an unwarranted conclusion. Important developments in mail service occurred before 1880, and significant changes have occurred since 1920. Nothing resembling the vast expansion of the postal system that occurred during the four decades after the Post Office Act of 1792, with its institutional seeding of a vast communications network, to name one such development, would occur during these years. Program expansion and bureaucratic autonomy were not unique to the Progressive Era; they indeed echoed the triumphs of John McLean almost a century earlier. Yet during the Gilded Age and Progressive Era, postal officials commenced an entrepreneurial style of program innovation, striking chords of alliance with a diverse assortment of civic organizations, in a way that was unprecedented and has not been witnessed since. The consolidation of the national postal system from 1890 to 1910 was, moreover, unique; never before had the postal system so drastically pared back and refined its services. The path of state building for the early-twentieth-century Post Office, with its reliance on entrepreneurship through innovation and the building of multidimensional coalitions of esteem, was a distinctly Progressive triumph.

Six

Science in the Service of Seeds:
The USDA, 1862–1900

A NATIONAL AGRICULTURE DEPARTMENT was the brainchild of George Washington, who recommended its creation in his final address to Congress in 1796. Washington echoed the agricultural fundamentalism of Jefferson. "It will not be doubted that with reference either to individual or national welfare, agriculture is of primary importance," he intoned. Yet the very farm idolatry with which Washington shaped his vision of an agricultural state became, by century's end, a curse as well as a blessing to the United States Department of Agriculture. For the first four decades of its existence, the USDA was conceived by its supporters and its overseers as the clerical servant of American farmers. The department existed to cater to the distributive wishes of the nation, most visibly in the pork-style distribution of common seeds, the dominant federal agricultural program of the nineteenth century.

The late 1800s saw a prolonged attempt by division leaders at the USDA to transcend these limitations. Beverly Galloway, Bernhard Fernow, and Harvey Wiley aimed to expand their range of action and to claim status for the USDA as the paternal organization of American agriculture. At every turn, they met resistance from Congress and received only lukewarm support from organized farmers. Farmers were predisposed to pursue their ends with the scepter of legislation; they generally saw the USDA as a distributive tool. Yet where USDA leaders failed in creating administrative latitude, they succeeded in organizational renewal. By 1890 the Department of Agriculture was the strongest voice for scientific policymaking in the federal government, if not the entire nation. While constrained politically, the USDA had broken ideologically from the parties and had distinguished itself from the agrarian revolt. It occupied a unique space in turn-of-century national politics.

Seeds versus Science: The Rise of Organizational Tension

The USDA evolved from the Interior Department's Patent Office, established in 1836. The first commissioner of patents, Henry Leavitt Ellsworth, was a student of scientific farming and a believer in mechanized agriculture. Scientific farmer Elkanah Watson, Ellsworth's acquaintance, piqued the commissioner's interest in seed importation and distribution. Ellsworth started a seed distribution program in the Patent Office, which in 1849 was transferred to the newly created Interior Department. He quickly lent his voice to a growing chorus of Interior officials and farm societies who sought a separate department of agriculture. The United States Agricultural Society, organized in 1852, pressed for five years for a farmers' department, as did the state societies of Maryland and Massachusetts. Ironically, opposition came from the Midwest, the very section that would furnish the USDA with most of its personnel after 1880. Senators Stephen Douglas of Illinois and Edgar Cowan of Pennsylvania opposed the creation of an agriculture bureau. The stalemate continued through the 1850s until Southern secession produced the rump Thirty-seventh Congress. In December 1861 President Lincoln endorsed the idea of an agricultural bureau, and one month later, Rep. Owen Lovejoy of Illinois wrote Lincoln's recommendations into a bill. Congress then created a department of agriculture without a Cabinet-level appointee to run it. Lincoln penned the department into existence on May 15, 1862.[1]

The creation of the USDA was in some respects consistent with the "developmental" imperative that Richard Bensel and Eric Foner have attributed to the Republican Party of the 1860s. While fiercely protective of property rights, Republicans also believed in national institutions such as land grants, limited regulation, and educational organizations. Congress also passed the Morrill Act in 1862, granting federal land to states for the establishment of agricultural colleges. Yet in comparison with their eagerness for land-grant colleges, both the Republicans and most agricultural societies were lukewarm on a new bureaucracy. For instance, the very author of the land grant bill, Maine senator Justin Morrill, did not favor the department, and he proposed several severe cuts in its appropriations after 1862. Farm societies also preferred land-grant monies to USDA funding. More generally, Republicans' vision for the USDA fell far short of the establishment of a research agency. The act of 1862 emphasized the practical services that an agricultural agency could offer. Embedded in the act was tension between a clientele service to farmers and investment in scientific discoveries for the advancement of agricultural productivity. The new agency was envisioned more as a library than as a researcher. The USDA's mission was not so much to create knowledge as to gather it and disseminate it; its business was the distribution of new seeds rather than their discovery.

> [T]here is hereby established at the seat of the Government of the United States a Department of Agriculture, the general designs and duties of which shall be to acquire and to diffuse among the people of the United States useful information on subjects connected with agriculture in the most general and comprehensive sense of that word, and to procure, propagate, and distribute among the people new and valuable seeds and plants.[2]

One year later, the appropriations act of 1863 spelled out this practical agenda. Congressional Republicans stated their wish that the department direct its labors not toward pure research and discovery but toward tangible results.

> For the collection of agricultural statistics, investigations for promoting agriculture and rural economy, and the procurement, propagation and distribution of cuttings and seeds, . . . sixty thousand dollars: *Provided however,* That in the expenditure of this appropriation, and especially in the selection of cuttings and seeds for distribution, due regard shall be had to the purposes of general cultivation and the encouragement of the agricultural and rural interests of the United States.[3]

Only a year after creating the department, congressional Republicans were devoting most of their attention to seed distribution. In the 1863 appropriations law and elsewhere, Republicans sought to direct the USDA away from pure scientific discovery and toward "general cultivation." Their emphasis was echoed by agrarian coalitions in Congress, which emphasized applied research whose results could be implemented quickly and easily in the field, to the farmer's immediate benefit. By and large, nineteenth-century politicians wanted USDA scientists to serve in a merely advisory capacity to farmers, analyzing soil and product samples and answering questions about the weather and pests. The department quickly became a lending library and a growing farm for plants, most of which were already common variants in American soils. The USDA's few foreign consuls—including the celebrated abolitionist Zebina Eastman, who served for four years on the department's payroll in England—did little more than collect gardener's magazines for the USDA library. The department's seed research, moreover, was closely tied to American planting cycles, which compelled Eastman and other officials to search only for readily available seeds that could be shipped to the United States for immediate planting. The department's "experimental farm" merely housed general plant varieties, most of which were already common in the United States. As Harold Faulkner summarizes, "Under the stimulus of Congressional appropriations and the demands of farmers, the research of the department was of a decidedly practical type."[4]

Building Capacity from Within

Agency leaders were negotiating two divides: the conflict between distribution and science, and the conflict *within* scientific programs between an applied focus and pure research. Nineteenth-century politicians—especially agrarian representatives, as I detail shortly—favored distributive programs over scientific policy, and to the degree that they wanted scientific research at all, they favored a strong applied focus. Yet among USDA scientists, a preference for pure research evolved. Department scientists had been trained in traditional research disciplines such as biological chemistry and plant physiology. Their interests lay in an autonomous research program and the provision of facilities to carry it out.[5]

Before 1862, government agricultural research was directed by the renowned entomologist Townend Glover. Glover worked in the Patent Office in the 1850s and returned to serve the department from 1863 to 1878. Perhaps Glover's most enduring gift to the USDA was the nexus of personal ties to county elites and to foreign scientists and seed companies he had maintained during the 1850s. Much agricultural research during the nineteenth century, primitive in comparison with that of the early 1900s, was exhibited at county and state agricultural fairs. Glover had attended these fairs for almost twenty years—in Ohio, Buffalo, Rochester, New York's Genesee Valley, Philadelphia, and Maine—cataloging the different products in each county and collecting specimens for the Patent Office.[6] But Glover's exploits were not confined to domestic soil. He had also procured a large number of seeds and specimens from overseas and had made some critical connections to English, French, and German seed companies—including the famed Vilmorin-Andrieux exporters of Paris—affiliations that endured well into the twentieth century.[7]

In part because agricultural science was just getting off the ground in the United States in the 1860s, the department's early scientists hailed from Europe. Glover and Isaac Newton, the first commissioner of agriculture (1862–67), drew strongly on their overseas ties in assembling the government's first body of agricultural scientists. Newton appointed William Saunders, a horticulture graduate of the University of Edinburgh, as superintendent of the propagating garden. Charles Wetherill, a student of the pioneering agricultural chemist Justus Von Liebig, was employed as the first chemist. Wetherill was succeeded by Henri Erni, who had trained in Switzerland in the methods of Liebig. Many of the USDA's assistant chemists and plant specialists during Reconstruction were also trained in Europe.[8]

The department encountered difficulty in assembling a lasting scientific workforce, however. The USDA experienced high turnover among scientific personnel. Many European-trained division chiefs and scientists left the department to return to their home country. And the patchwork system of recruiting through ties to foreign universities produced a cadre of division chiefs that was not well integrated internally. Few of the chiefs knew one another well or were familiar with their colleagues' work, though Glover remained a considerable exception to this pattern. Further, the lack of prestige attached to scientific and division chief positions meant that scientific talent fluidly passed through the department during Reconstruction. Ryland T. Brown was appointed chief chemist under Commissioner Frederick Watts (1871–77) in January 1872, only to resign eleven months later to tend to his "private affairs in the West"—a cattle ranch.[9]

Another mass departure of USDA personnel was responsible for creating the dominant agrarian organization of the nineteenth century—the Patrons of Husbandry, or the Grange. When Commissioner Newton sent Minnesota farmer Oliver Kelley on a tour of southern farms in 1866, Kelley discovered that farmers needed a fraternal organization. Upon his return, he joined with Saunders and department librarian Rev. Aaron B. Grosh to form the Grange of Washington, D.C. Kelley's plan for the Grange included explicit assistance from the department, including a schedule of USDA lecturers who would tour the various Granges and offer addresses to local groups. Yet Kelley became disillusioned with his employer, angry that its scientific talents were not being put to use for the farmer. He left the USDA in 1868, and other Grange members soon followed.[10]

Scientists could hardly be faulted for leaving their agency so quickly, for the program that garnered most of the attention, prestige, and resources of the department was not a research venture but a seed giveaway. Congressional Free Seed Distribution became a favorite program of farm-state representatives, who could curry favor with their constituents by unloading bulk quantities of free seeds to their fields and gardens. When the department answered the seed request of West Virginia representative H. Goff in March 1888, for example, its shipment filled seven mail sacks. It was only one of several seed requests Goff made that year. The usual seed varieties included rhubarb, potato, grass, and alfalfa, but by far the most frequent seeds appearing in USDA distribution lists were "vegetable seeds" and "garden seeds." In the three weeks from January 16 to February 3, 1888, the USDA provided Rep. James Blount, a Georgia Democrat, with 7,372 papers of common vegetable seed and 335 papers of flower seed. Another frequent practice was to distribute large quantities of crop seeds commonly available from domestic supply houses, thus promising farmers a cheap distributive benefit yet little or no gain in technology. In short, the seed distribution program was funding not scientific discovery but sustenance gardening and crop expansion.[11]

Congressional free seed distribution was the dominant agricultural program of the late nineteenth century. In 1870 the appropriations for the seed distribution program were $45,000; by 1880 they had risen to $102,000, comprising almost one-half of the USDA's total budget of $212,000. By contrast, the department's entire allowance for distributing scientific publications and bulletins was $26,000. Not until the meat inspection laws of 1885 did any single USDA activity approach the level of funding or priority given to seed distribution. Congress maintained these prerogatives through the end of the century. In 1893 the department mailed seeds to 1.8 million farmers, and by 1900 the number of recipients may have reached 3 million. As late as 1900, with a budget approaching $200,000, the seed distribution program outspent the Divisions of Chemistry, Forestry, and Soils combined.[12]

The fact that the seed program grew so quickly in the late nineteenth century may seem surprising, given the rising power of reform-minded farmers' organizations such as the Grange and the Alliance. These movement-based organizations disdained the political status quo of rotation in office and congressional pork. Yet no organizations benefited as consistently from the largesse of the seed distribution program as did the Grange and the Alliances.[13] Although comprehensive statistics on the seed distribution program are not available, National Archives records indicate that Congress rained tens of thousands of dollars and millions of seed packets annually upon local Granges and Alliance clubs, and the Grange and Alliance welcomed them. Grange founder Kelley, for example, was one of the first farmers in the nation to utilize Patent Office seeds, and he actively distributed USDA seeds in Minnesota in the 1860s. He frequently professed his excitement for the free seed program. By the 1880s and 1890s, moreover, the Alliance was receiving even more seeds than the Grange. The USDA sent "a liberal supply of seed" to Alliance clubs such as the Decatur Alliance of Bainbridge, Georgia, and to the Smith Springs Alliance No. 2531 of Texas (on behalf of agrarian senator John Reagan). Although there are no records of the total volume of seeds sent to all Alliance clubs during this period, particular requests filed by the department suggest an astonishing transfer of "seed pork." In May 1890, for instance, the department sent one thousand packets of seeds to almost every Alliance club in South Dakota (see table 6.1). In one shipment alone—on behalf of Rep. J. A. Pickler—this included 164 Alliances for a total of *164,000 seed packets* in one month. If the May 1890 shipment is representative, the USDA distributed many millions of seed packets to Alliances in 1890. It is hardly surprising, then, that in the 1890s, Populists and Grangers petitioned the Senate Post Office Committee for reduced rates on the free seed distribution program so that the USDA could mail more seeds and bulbs.[14]

A broader portrait of the demand for seeds can be gleaned from National Archives correspondence between the USDA and Congress. In response to every request for seed or information from a member of Congress, the department was required to send a letter to the member or senator notifying him of the fulfillment of the request. The vast majority of letters sent from the USDA to Congress (82.5 percent) from 1886 to 1893 and contained in the National Archives are letters detailing the department's compliance with one of two requests—for seeds or for information. The distribution of these requests across states, districts, and counties can therefore be used as a rough measure of the geographically based demand for the department's services. Table 6.1 shows a surprising pattern when the requests are tabulated at the county level. Requests for seeds were *positively* associated with the percentage of a county's vote for Populist presidential candidate James B. Weaver in 1892. By contrast, county-level requests for information were *negatively* associated with the Weaver vote. Regressions also show that neither the demand for USDA information nor the demand for USDA seeds was associated at the county level with the Republican vote from 1892 to 1904. In other words, counties where Populist sentiment ran higher were more likely to support the distributive programs of the USDA and less likely to support scientific programs. Combined with the anecdotal evidence, table 6.1 suggests that whatever their official pronouncements, nineteenth-century agrarian organizations were firmly established feeders at the free seed trough.[15]

Indeed, relations between the USDA and the major agrarian groups were frequently strained. The Grange recommended the abolition of the department for four successive years, retrenching only after an 1880 meeting with USDA officials in Richmond, Virginia.[16]

For all of its political appeal, the seed program brought the disfavor of the department's scientists. The common heritages of the new scientists—their training in Europe, in land-grant colleges of the United States, and in agricultural experiment stations—produced a class of investigators with a strong interest in basic research and the expansion of research facilities. The expenditure of vast sums on already discovered seeds was an affront to these scientific ideals. The department tried frequently (with limited success) to discontinue common or unpromising varieties (such as coffee, turnip, alfalfa, and rhubarb) in the free seed program when the shipments did not prove to be of scientific value. Nonetheless, maintenance of congressional and clientele support compelled the agency to bankroll and administer the program, to the visible detriment of scientific research.[17]

Of course, the tension between applied and pure science was rooted in nineteenth-century agrarian culture; the suspicion of most farmers for "book farming" was well known.[18] And so department executives understood the need to appease agrarians by emphasizing the practical aspects of their scientific endeavors. For this reason USDA leaders continually launched new initiatives of official rhetoric in order to demonstrate the utility of their research to the farmer and the ease with which it could be translated into improved yield.[19] Agriculture's executives first commenced an aggressive publication strategy. Initially this entailed a limited distribution of the *Farmers' Bulletin* and an unsuccessful attempt to popularize the agency's annual report.[20] Then, in 1890, at the initiative of Secretary Jeremiah Rusk, the department established a publications room, which quickly assumed the status of a departmental division. And shortly after the USDA ascended to the Cabinet level in 1889, executives launched an annual yearbook, admittedly a "popular form" of the annual report but a volume that Assistant Secretary Edwin Willits hoped would evolve into "the almanac of American agriculture." Unlike the annual report, the yearbook quickly gained favor with the USDA's clientele groups and support coalitions in Congress, and it became the largest single government publication within five years of its inauguration. Departmental leaders also continued a schedule of attendance at agricultural fairs, city conventions, and national expositions.[21]

A clearly deferential mode of expression marked the agency's public discourse, however. The department's leaders were careful to emphasize that a scientific transformation of agriculture—including the bearing of empirical scrutiny on existing modes of production—would not render older forms of farming (or social life) irrelevant. Agriculture had always been and would for-

Grant	14	14,000
Hamlin	5	5,000
Hansen	5	5,000
Total	164	164,000

Statistical Relationships between County-Level USDA Program Demands and the County-Level Presidential Vote for Weaver in 1892

County Demand Variable	County Percentage Vote for Populist Presidential Candidate James B. Weaver, 1892 (Average = 8.7%)	Average Presidential Vote for Republican Candidate, 1892–1904
An additional letter requesting seeds was associated with →	1.03% additional percentage points for Weaver (statistically significant; $t = 6.3$)	0.11% additional percentage points for Republican presidential candidate (insignificant; $t = 0.7$)
(standard deviation = 1.63 letters)		
An additional letter requesting information was associated with →	0.64% fewer percentage points for Weaver (significant; $t = -3.0$)	0.25% fewer percentage points for Republican presidential candidate (insignificant; $t = 1.2$)
(standard deviation = 1.27 letters)		

Sources: Requests for seeds and information compiled from USDA-congressional correspondence, 1886–93, NA II, RG 16, E 4. Voting data are from Inter-University Consortium for Political and Social Research.

Note: Vote regressions control for county population and its square, logged manufacturing capital, logged average farm land values and their square, logged fertilizer and machinery use, the percentage of county farms rented for cash and share-cropped, and a South dummy.

ever remain "an art and a science."[22] The essential practices and mores of agrarian social life would not alter. Thus the department's leaders carefully (and defensively) cultivated an image of its place in American agriculture, an image designed to eschew any hint of elitism.

Merit Reform, Networks, and the Internal Transformation of the USDA

As the USDA expanded after Reconstruction, its personnel split into two rather distinct blocs: a core of clerical and administrative functionaries and a growing scientific force. Clerical and mechanical functionaries who performed paperwork duties, operated the department's experimental gardens, and staffed the all-important Seed Supply Division were hired from the mid-Atlantic states nearest the capital—Virginia, Maryland, and Delaware. In contrast, the department began to recruit fewer scientists from overseas and more from the emerging land-grant colleges—Michigan Agricultural College (later Michigan State), Iowa State Agricultural College, Kansas State Agricultural College, Cornell University, Clemson University, and the University of Wisconsin. The colleges offered a steady supply of graduates trained in scientific agriculture, individuals who were raised on more advanced, mechanized, and progressive farms.[23]

Before the Pendleton Act, the USDA's selection process was governed almost entirely by patronage considerations. Three years after the Pendleton Act passed, USDA commissioner Colman could still complain that partisan pressure for USDA jobs was intense. "The pressure has never been so great upon me as it has been in the last few months," Colman wrote. "I come to the Department with about the same reluctance that a criminal goes to jail. Knowing that I shall be appealed to by dozens, many of whom are actually in need of bread to eat." To make Colman's life worse, most personnel decisions lay outside his purview. By entrenched custom, agriculture commissioners referred all job applications for consultation to the member of Congress for the applicant's district. A favorable recommendation from a member of Congress was a critical prerequisite to a USDA job. The representative was the principal intermediary between prospective applicants and the department.[24]

The resulting selection pattern rendered the Department of Agriculture only remotely agricultural. As a brute demonstration of this pattern, table 6.2 presents a statistical analysis of the number of USDA employees from each state in 1883. The independent variables are the log of the state's population, the log of manufacturing capital, and the log of the total value of farm products for that state. Whereas the amount of manufacturing capital in a state was positively related to USDA selection in 1883, the value of farm products was negatively related.

TABLE 6.2

Merit Reform, Bureau Chiefs, and the Transformation of USDA Recruitment, 1880–1900

A. Negative Binomial Regression Analyses of State-Level Selection into the USDA, Before (1883) and After (1897) Merit Reform[a]

Variables	1883 Selection (Negative Binomial)	1897 Selection (Negative Binomial)
Constant	−7.23* (1.94)	−11.55* (1.24)
ln(state population)	0.79* (0.35)	0.49* (0.23)
ln(total capital in manufacturing)	0.28* (0.11)	0.19 (0.12)
ln(total value of agricultural product)	−0.42[+] (0.25)	0.35* (0.11)
Dispersion	0.00 (0.10)	0.13* (0.05)
n (df)	38 (33)	45 (40)
LLF	−71.94	−290.06
χ^2 (Prob)	83.23 (0.0000)	225.18 (0.0000)

B. Selected USDA Bureau/Division Chiefs and Their Tenure, 1880–1910[b]

Bureau/Division	Chief	Year of Appointment as Chief	Tenure as Chief (or as "Principal" with Hiring Authority)	College Degree (LG = Land Grant)
Animal Industry	Daniel Salmon	1884	20 years (to 1905)	Cornell (LG)
Biological Survey	C. Hart Merriam	1889	20 years (to 1910)	Yale
Botany	F. V. Coville	1888	49 years (to 1937)	Cornell (LG)
Chemistry	H. W. Wiley	1883	30 years (to 1912)	Purdue (LG)
Plant Industry	B. T. Galloway	1887	26 years (to 1914)	Missouri Agricultural (LG)
Soils	Milton Whitney	1894	33 years (to 1927)	

Summary: Of bureau chiefs serving in 1895, average chief served through

✓ six presidents

✓ four partisan presidential transitions (Democratic to Republican or vice versa)

✓ four partisan majorities in the House of Representatives (or three partisan transitions)

✓ five USDA secretaries (or commissioners)

[a]Dependent variable: number of USDA employees from state i. Poisson regression was also used for 1883 data because distributional assumption of equivalent mean and standard deviation could not be rejected.
*Statistical significance at $p < .05$.
[+]Significance at $p < .10$. (All tests are two-tailed.) Standard errors appear in parentheses after coefficient estimates.
[b]Source: NA II, RG 16, E 185. Tenure figures are rounded.

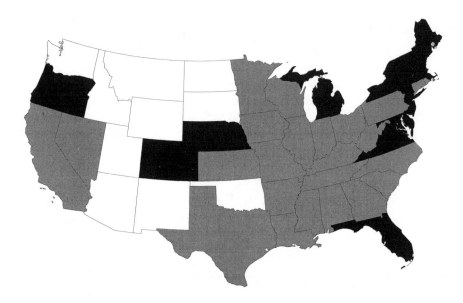

Figure 6.1 The dominance of Northeastern states in USDA recruitment before Merit Reform, ca. 1883. Geographic selection ratios (GSRs) for USDA. GSR = (USDA Employees from State/Total USDA Employees)/(State Population/U.S. Population). White area: Territory (10); crosshatched area: GSR < 1 (24); black area: GSR > 1 (14).

This surprising pattern is replicated in figure 6.1, which presents the geographic selection ratio (GSR) of USDA employment for each state in 1883. The GSR is obtained by dividing the portion of people from each state in the USDA by the portion of people from each state in the total population. When this statistic is greater than one, the state is "overselected" (relative to random selection); when the GSR is less than one, the state is underselected.[25] Figure 6.1 maps the crude variation in this statistic for 1883; it shows that, before merit reform, USDA employees came mainly from northeastern states with weak agricultural sectors and strong manufacturing sectors. The reason for this aggregate relationship stems from the logic of patronage. Under the patronage system that governed USDA appointments from 1861 to 1884, USDA commissioners meticulously managed appointments so as to please as many members of Congress as possible. As a result, agency selection favored states with greater power in the Republican Party and in Congress, precisely the industrial states such as Massachusetts, New York, and Pennsylvania.

Selection after Merit Reform

The Pendleton Act of 1883 sought to bring a new standard of efficiency and neutrality to American government. Among other provisions, the act required most applicants for government positions to pass a competitive examination to qualify for federal employment. As Stephen Skowronek has emphasized, the legislation formally ended the spoils system but left it to presidents to implement the law agency by agency, position by position. By President Cleveland's executive order of December 10, 1884, more than half of the positions in the USDA were brought under the Pendleton Act. By 1889 virtually the entire agency was under the merit law, making the USDA among the very first agencies to be covered in under the act.[26]

Four stages composed the structure of the personnel recruitment process after 1889. First, any prospective applicant for a USDA job had to file an application and register with the Civil Service Commission. Second, the applicant needed to pass the necessary civil service examination. All applicants who passed this examination were then placed on a "roster of eligibles" for USDA positions, which the Civil Service Commission would send to the USDA. Third, the secretary of agriculture sent this roster of eligibles to the relevant bureau and solicited the bureau chief's recommendation as to whom to appoint. The secretary then chose one or more individuals from this roster, depending on the number of administrative vacancies in the bureau.

For two reasons, the critical stage in the agency selection process was the third. First, by an entrenched pattern of deference, the secretary of agriculture always followed the appointment recommendation of the bureau chief. As a result, USDA bureau chiefs assumed the role of principal gatekeeper to department positions. The bureau chiefs identified preferred employees through their contacts in land-grant colleges, experiment stations, and their home counties. In many cases, the bureau chiefs would contact preferred individuals *before* they had passed the civil service examination. They would also hire preferred younger employees as "scientific aides" before they took the civil service examination, promoting these employees to the higher levels of the USDA after they had passed the examination.[27] Second, the well-known preferences of bureau chiefs for scientifically inclined employees led to a pattern of expectations among USDA job applicants which reinforced the chiefs' selections. This is because the bureau chiefs themselves managed much of the department's recruitment. As a result, both the self-selection and recommendation stages favored the interests of USDA bureau heads.

An excellent example of the power of the bureau chiefs in the USDA selection process emerges in National Archives documents from the Division of Soils. In September 1896 the division needed to fill the position of soil expert, which had just been vacated owing to an interdepartmental transfer. Only two applicants passed the civil service examination for the position, a Northwestern University physics professor named Hiram Loomis, who had scored 95.81 out of 100 on the exam, and a twenty-two-year-old college graduate named Lyman Briggs, who had scored 76.54. The formal qualifications of Loomis were clearly superior, but Division Chief Milton Whitney recommended Briggs. In a letter to Assistant Secretary Charles Dabney he explains why:

> I have examined the two sets of papers very thoroughly and have no hesitation in saying that the papers prepared by Mr. Loomis are far abler than those of Mr. Briggs. In fact the papers of Mr. Loomis are exceptionally fine and show a thoroughly well trained mind as well as vast intimate knowledge of all the subjects of the examination.
>
> There is another element, however, which must be considered in making a selection of this kind; that is the personal equations . . . . Mr. Briggs is still young, twenty-two years old. He was brought up on a farm in Michigan, and his father is still a farmer there. He was educated in the Michigan Agricultural College, and was engaged while there in agricultural investigations. . . . His early training gives him a very thorough appreciation of the value of scientific work to practical problems, which his University education has not yet neutralized. He is not settled into any groove, but is in a formative period in his life. . . .
>
> Mr. Loomis, on the other hand, is a very much older man, thirty-three years of age. . . . It seemed to me that his early classical education [at Trinity College] was not well adapted to the work of this Division and would not give him the knowledge or interest in practical agriculture that is essential to the carrying on of the investigations in the right spirit. From his age and long experience in teaching I judge that he must be somewhat set in his ways and already be in a groove which it would be hard for him to leave. If this is so, then he would not be likely to be satisfied at the Department or to remain long with us.[28]

USDA Secretary Julius Sterling Morton adopted Whitney's recommendation and hired Briggs over Loomis. Whitney's main criterion of choice—the "personal equations"—reveals his vision of the ideal USDA employee. First and foremost, Whitney wanted someone young. As Whitney had reminded Dabney, "[I]t was distinctly understood that in organizing the Division [of Soils] we should take young, untrained men and try them." Second, Whitney wanted an individual with farm experience and a land-grant education, not because these ties imparted a set of skills, but because they conferred a specific research ideology, "the right spirit" of agricultural science. In this respect the preferences of USDA leaders for scientific minds were not absolute; even university physicists could be rejected in favor of applicants who knew the soil better. Nonetheless, USDA leaders wanted personnel from advanced farming areas who would share their preferences for a tilt toward scientific policy in the department. (Briggs would become just such a votary of scientific policymaking for the next twenty years.) Individuals with the "right spirit" of agricultural science would be less likely to favor the distributive demands of Congress and more likely to ally themselves with the informational policy leanings of bureau chiefs.[29]

The merit reforms of the 1880s, then, established USDA bureau and division chiefs as the new intermediaries for bureaucratic recruitment. The power of personnel selection shifted from Congress to the middle levels of the USDA. Yet these were precisely the personnel whom the department was losing so quickly during the Reconstruction period. As the second half of table 6.2 shows, however, the USDA in the nineteenth century was fortunate to have a long-tenured cadre of bureau chiefs. Most of the chiefs serving in 1900 were appointed in the 1880s and, on average, served through six presidents and four congressional majorities into the 1910s and 1920s.[30]

From 1884 to 1900 and later, then, USDA bureau chiefs established an informal policy of preferential selection. The department recruited increasingly from the nation's land-grant agricultural colleges and their associated state agricultural experiment stations. These institutions acted as funnels through which educated farm youth descended on the department throughout the 1890s and early 1900s. This bureau-based selection created a much more agriculturally homogeneous personnel base by 1897. In the third column of the first half of table 6.2, a statistical analysis of state-level recruitment patterns in 1897 shows a *positive* relationship between agricultural product value and USDA employees. And the state-level variation in geographic selection, mapped in figure 6.2, shows that by 1897 the department overselected from Great Lakes and Plains farm states.[31]

A Statistical Analysis of USDA Recruitment at the County Level. A more detailed analysis of USDA selection patterns is possible using county-level data. Until 1905 USDA employee rosters in the *Official Register of the United States* listed the legal county residence of every single employee before his or her arrival to the USDA. In table 6.3 the number of USDA employees from each county has been tabulated and regressed upon a number of county-level variables in an attempt to sort out economic, social, and political influences on bureaucratic recruitment.[32]

The analyses in table 6.3 include a number of census variables reflecting educational and mobility dynamics in the late 1800s. From county-level aggregates in the census of 1900, it is possible to control for population, literacy, and the geographic size of the county. The analyses also control for manufacturing capital in the county (a measure of industrialization), and the average county wage and salary to measure the local opportunity costs of USDA employment. Regional dummy variables for the South, East, and Midwest are also included.

Even after the Pendleton Act, it is possible that partisan and congressional factors were involved in USDA recruitment. Republican politicians, who remained in the majority through most of this period, undoubtedly preferred to have Republican-leaning individuals staff USDA positions. The regressions in

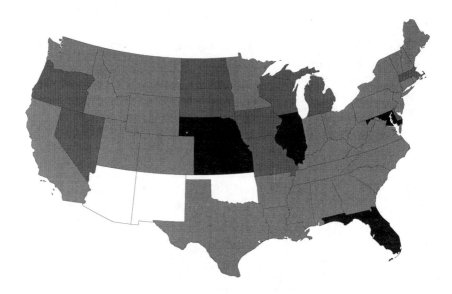

Figure 6.2 The dominance of Plains states in USDA recruitment after Merit Reform, ca. 1897. Geographic selection ratios (GSRs) for USDA. GSR = (USDA Employees from State/Total USDA Employees)/(State Population/U.S. Population). White area: Territory (3); light crosshatched area: GSR < 1 (30); dark crosshatched area: GSR > 1 (10); black area: GSR > 2 (5).

table 6.3 therefore include (1) the county's average percentage vote for the Republican presidential candidate from 1892 to 1904[33] and (2) the number of congresses in which the county was represented by a Republican House member from 1897 to 1905. If Republicans continued to shape bureaucratic hiring, then both of these variables should correlate positively with USDA recruitment. To test for committee-based recruitment, I tally the number of congresses in which a county was represented by a member of the House or Senate agriculture committees from the Fifty-third to the Fifty-eighth Congress (1893–1905). If the USDA recruited from Populist areas, then county-level recruitment should be positively associated with the 1892 vote for presidential candidate James B. Weaver. And finally, because county-level membership data are not available for farm groups in this period, table 6.3 includes measures of the strength of two agrarian groups—the Grange and the National Farmers' Union (NFU)— by an instrumental variables procedure.[34]

If the USDA recruited from advanced farm communities, county-level recruitment should be directly related to measures of technologically advanced farming, such as mechanization and fertilizer use. To measure these I use the natural log of total county machinery and fertilizer expenditures, respectively. Since these technologies were characteristic of more productive farms, I include the average (per-acre) agricultural land value in the county and its square as measures of the productivity of land in counties. And since larger farms were—controlling for land valuation—generally more advanced in the nineteenth century, I include the county average farm size and its square. Consistent with this class-based dynamic, selection should be negatively correlated with the county percentage of farms rented for cash or the percentage rented for a product share (tenancy) as opposed to percentage owned (the reference category), as tenancy and renting were characteristic of less advanced farms.

The seeds-versus-science dilemma may also have affected recruitment. If in fact bureau chiefs recruited young workers who favored the scientific leanings of the bureau chiefs, then USDA matriculation should be positively associated with the county's requests for information and perhaps negatively associated with the county's demand for free seeds. The requests tabulations employed in table 6.1 are used in the analyses of table 6.3 as measures for two demands from each county: the demand for distributive goods and the demand for informational goods.

Perhaps the most important variables in table 6.3 are those that attempt to measure the *network basis of USDA recruitment.* If the USDA was recruiting from land-grant colleges, then county matriculation should be higher in land-grant counties that contained agricultural colleges and experiment stations. And network selection and agency-driven selection would both suggest that employees would be more likely to come from bureau chiefs' counties.

Results from County-Level Recruitment Analyses

Table 6.3 displays the results of the county-level analysis in four columns. The leftmost column offers variable definitions, the second column reports a full model in which all variables are included, and the third column reports a "reduced" model in which statistically insignificant variables are excluded. The fourth (rightmost) column reports the marginal effects of the variables: the expected number of additional USDA employees from a county, given a one-unit increase in the variable in question for that county.

The analyses in table 6.3 suggest that the turn-of-century USDA recruited mainly from wealthier and scientifically advanced farming communities. Controlling for numerous other variables, the number of USDA employees from a county is positively and significantly associated with average land values and fertilizer use. Mechanization is negatively correlated, but given that the equation controls for land values, this means only that less productive mechanized farms sent fewer individuals to the department. Moreover, counties with higher

TABLE 6.3

Negative Binomial Regression Analyses of County-Level Matriculation into the U.S. Department of Agriculture, 1905

Variable	Model 1 Full Model	Model 2 Reduced Model	Marginal Effects from one-unit ↑ in variable
Constant	−10.6158** (1.4516)	−9.1347** (0.7111)	
ln(County population)	1.0516** (0.1674)	1.0968** (0.1154)	1.93 (USDA employees from the county)
ln(Size of county [square miles])	0.2065** (0.0472)	0.0440 (0.0284)	0.38
ln(Capital in manufacturing)	−0.0208 (0.0330)	—	
Percentage of farms rented for crop (tenancy)	−0.0875** (0.0177)	−0.0931** (0.0124)	−0.16
Percentage of farms rented for cash	−0.0341** (0.0088)	−0.0334** (0.0067)	−0.06
ln(Total farm land values) [valuation in acres]	0.9882** (0.1475)	0.8718** (0.1101)	1.82
ln(Total machinery expenditures)	−0.4167 (0.0858)	−0.2947** (0.0521)	−0.76
ln(Total fertilizer expenditures)	0.1068** (0.0196)	0.1037** (0.0167)	0.20
Percentage of county families on farms	−0.0196** (0.0023)	−0.0196** (0.0019)	−0.36
ln(Average farm size in acres)	0.3181 (0.4908)	—	
(ln(Average farm size in acres))^2	−0.0328 (0.0375)	—	
ln(Avg. manufacturing wage)	0.0392 (0.0682)	—	
ln(Avg. manufacturing salary)	0.0411** (0.0139)	0.0408** (0.0123)	0.76
Literacy rate (percentage of county population)	−0.1323** (0.0344)	−0.1342** (0.0239)	−0.24
East	1.7876** (0.3592)	1.5838** (0.2710)	3.29
Midwest	0.6340** (0.1777)	0.4704** (0.1553)	1.16
South	0.5762* (0.2642)	0.5484** (0.1518)	1.06
House Republican representation, 1893–1905	0.0098 (0.0079)	—	
Senate Republican representation, 1893–1905	0.0037 (0.0216)	—	
Average percentage vote for Republican presidential candidate, 1896–1904 (instrumented)	−0.0060 (0.0128)	—	

TABLE 6.3
(*Continued*)

Variable	Model 1 Full Model	Model 2 Reduced Model	Marginal Effects from one-unit ↑ in variable
Percentage vote for Populist presidential candidate James B. Weaver, 1892 (instrumented)	0.2546** (0.0582)	0.2699** (0.0411)	0.47
Senate Agriculture Committee representation, 1893–1905	0.0130 (0.0156)	—	
House Agriculture Committee representation, 1893–1905	0.0354 (0.0359)	—	
ln(Peak Grange membership, 1875–77) (instrumented)	0.080 (0.0641)	—	
ln(National Farmers' Union membership, 1908) (instrumented)	0.0450+ (0.0270)	0.0512* (0.0214)	0.08
Land-grant county (*network recruitment*)	1.3672** (0.1968)	1.4095** (0.2191)	2.52
Bureau chief or division chief county of origin (*network recruitment*)	0.7620** (0.1754)	0.7571** (0.1256)	1.40
District requests for seeds (*distributive coalition*)	−0.2576** (0.0621)	−0.2817** (0.0432)	−0.47
District requests for information (*science coalition*)	0.2958** (0.0611)	0.3210** (0.0461)	0.54
n (df)	2437 (2407)	2565 (2545)	
Overdispersion parameter	0.57** (0.04)	0.65** (0.04)	
χ^2	1180.3	1532.7	
χ^2 Probability	Pr = 0.00	Pr = 0.00	
Log-likelihood	−3489.51	−3689.35	

Source: Census of 1900, County Election Data (from Inter-University Consortium for Political and Social Research), *Official Congressional Directories,* and *Official USDA Roster,* 1905. All variables expressed in units (dollars, members, acres, etc.) are logged, except for seed and information requests (which often take zero values), and variables expressed as percentages. (Dependent variable is number of USDA employees from county *i*. Mean count = 2.072. Standard errors in parentheses.)

**Implies significance at $p < .01$.

*Implies significance at $p < .05$.

+Implies significance at $p < .10$. (All tests are two-tailed).

tenant (share) farming, where farmers were poorer and scientific agriculture was slow to catch on, produced fewer USDA employees. The land value and fertilization results explain why matriculation was *decreasing* in the percentage of county families on farms. Generally, the greater the percentage of county families on farms, the greater the density of farms, and the less advanced the county's agricultural sector. The results are nuanced: The USDA selection process favored not farming regions per se but only relatively advanced and science-prone farm communities.[35]

There appears to be little association between USDA selection and partisan- and committee-based factors. Neither Republican voting patterns nor Grange membership nor representation on the House and Senate Agriculture Committees was significantly associated with USDA selection. At the same time, the analysis does display a surprising effect of populist voting. The county-level vote for James Weaver is positively and significantly correlated with USDA hiring; a two-percentage-point increase in a county's 1892 vote for Weaver is associated with an additional USDA employee from that county. This is surprising, given the high seed demand of Weaver constituencies shown in table 6.1. Given that the analysis in table 6.3 controls for seed demand, however, the Weaver variable probably captures those Weaver constituencies who also favored a scientific USDA. National Farmers' Union membership also appears to be positively associated with USDA matriculation. The National Farmers' Union was more radical than the Grange, but at least by 1900 it was also more scientifically oriented and open to changes in farm structure such as agricultural cooperatives.

The most stunning findings from the analyses in table 6.3 show that division chiefs were systematically leading their agency away from the wishes of Progressive-Era political majorities. First, selection was positively associated with the demand for scientific *information* but negatively associated with the demand for *seeds*. An increase in the demand for information, represented by two more letters requesting scientific assistance or advice from the USDA, is associated with the arrival of another employee from that county. A two-letter boost in a county's demand for seeds, however, is associated with one less USDA hire. USDA recruitment was higher where the county-level demand for information was higher but not where the demand for distribution was higher.

Table 6.3 also shows evidence of network-based recruitment, as bureau chiefs' counties and land-grant counties sent more of their citizens to the USDA than did other counties. The computed marginal effects in the fourth column indicate that, on average, bureau chiefs' counties of origin generated 1.4 more employees, and land-grant counties 2.5 more employees, than the average county in 1905. Together, these two marginal effects estimates account for more than 200 USDA employees in 1905. In short, the late nineteenth century solidified the scientific outlook at the USDA even as seed pork largesse became firmly entrenched in Congress and among major agrarian groups.[36]

The Stunting of Science: The USDA under Julius Sterling Morton (1893–97)

The USDA's scientific leanings came under increasing congressional criticism in the late nineteenth century. As early as 1867, when Commissioner Horace Capron closed the seed room, lamenting that it had "attached onto the Dept and grown like a fungus, sapping its vitals," Congress responded by freezing scientific salaries. Secretary Jeremiah Rusk's initiative to ship departmental scientists to international conferences was met by congressional lamentations of sending "broken-down professors to Europe."[37]

The subservience of the USDA was embodied and maintained in departmental symbolism and official rhetoric. In annual reports, the common referent to the department as a "servant" of American farmers was telling, for the agency was beholden to the short-term distributive imperatives of the Seed Division, agrarian interests, and their legislators. Similarly, department executives after 1880 ended their letters to members of Congress and agricultural groups with "Your obedient servant," a common nineteenth-century salutation, to be sure, but generally uncharacteristic of agriculture secretaries after 1897 such as James S. Wilson or David F. Houston. In letters to William Allison, chairman of the Appropriations Committee, and William H. Hatch, chairman of the House Agriculture Committee, leaders such as Norman Colman quite patently begged for scientific funding while promising to keep the seed program flush.[38]

The conflict came to a head under Secretary J. Sterling Morton (1893–97), a "gold Democrat" from Nebraska whose conservatism rankled agrarians even as his budget cutting angered USDA scientists. Morton took dead aim at the seed distribution program. Morton had attempted to introduce a number of economies at the department, requesting less in funds and personnel during each successive year of his tenure. Yet the seed distribution program quickly became the object of his greatest ire. He noted that the original purpose of the program was experimental, and that the recipients of free seed were, in principle, supposed to report the results obtained to the department, and these were to be published in the annual report. Yet in 1893 he noted that only 940 of the 1.8 million farmers receiving seeds had bothered to report to the department. The distributive utility of the program had eroded all promise of the scientific and informational benefits for which it was launched.

> In view of the above, it is difficult to see how any practical statesman can advocate an annual disbursement of $160,000 for such a purpose. Educationally, that sum of money might be made of infinite advantage to the farmers of the United States if it were expended in the publication and distribution of bulletins showing, in terse and plain language, how chemistry, botany, entomology, forestry, vegetable pathology, veterinary, and other sciences may be applied to agriculture.
>
> If in a sort of paternal way, it is the duty of this Government to distribute anything

gratuitously, are not new ideas of more permanent value than old seeds? Is it a function of government to make gratuitous distribution of any material thing?

Morton's expression of sentiment against the program is noteworthy for its concern about paternalism. The department's provision of any service to American farmers, distributive or informational, was, in essence, a paternal practice. Morton thus cleaved tightly to Democratic and conservative agrarian faith in doubting the capacity of bureaucracy to offer viable solutions to the dilemmas of American cultivators. For this reason, he ordered reductions in scientific funds and services as well as seed distribution within the department. Morton quickly translated his dismay into budgetary action. In preparing his fiscal estimates for 1895, he proposed and authorized a $100,000 reduction in the seed distribution program.[39] When Congress responded by reappropriating the monies for 1895, Morton effectively impounded them, rejecting all bids for the purchase of seeds. Congress passed a joint resolution directing Morton to distribute the seeds, thereby compelling Morton to administer the program. Morton thereafter became a target for congressional criticism of the post of secretary of agriculture in general. The ugly specter of clerical symbolism again made its appearance, with North Dakota senator Henry C. Hansbrough deriding Morton as little more than a "high grade clerk." Congress then enacted a statute curbing the growth of scientific salaries in the department, a law unaltered until 1909. Legislators also reduced research and regulatory funds drastically during Morton's keep. The Seed Division, the rogue bureau in an otherwise scientific department, was victorious. The Department of Agriculture had been subjugated to clientelism.[40]

If Morton's seed war demonstrated the weakness of departmental executives with respect to Congress, his internal problems magnified the lack of executive reach in the agency. Morton's economies provoked resentment among personnel who felt that the cost cutting had gone too far. Several division chiefs and head scientists resigned during the secretary's tenure, some intimating that their resignations were requested. Younger scientists began leaving the agency in droves, opting for the relative comfort of private and academic work. Those who stayed were resentful of a program and a division whose funding dwarfed their own. In 1896 the average length of service for assistant scientists was only two years and four months. Divisional and bureau chiefs were highly reluctant to support the secretary in his fight with Congress over seed distribution when Morton had cut their staff and funds. In short, Morton did not have a receptive audience within or without the department during his stormy tenure. When he tried to discharge employees, they began reporting their status and salary positions to congressional committees and to the Civil Service Commission to protest the move. Morton had to prohibit this practice by executive order. His frequent reliance on stopgap measures and internal orders evinced the low degree of control in the Secretary's Office.[41]

Bureau Building in Chemistry, Forestry, and Plant Science

USDA division and bureau chiefs were doing more than simply transforming the nature of agency personnel. They were also organizing talent at the divisional level within the USDA, creating small but forceful organizations of scientists within their divisions and forging crucial ties outside of them to professional associations, Mugwumps, politicians, women's associations, and moral reformers.

From Alternative Sugar to Pure Food: Harvey Wiley and the Division of Chemistry

When Harvey Washington Wiley came to the Department of Agriculture in 1883, he turned his attention to the question that had occupied his predecessor, Peter Collier: the promise of sugar. Having completed nine years of teaching at Purdue University, Wiley was professionally established as an analyst of sugar and was well known among sugar growers and state chemists in the Midwest. Indeed, he was recruited after meeting Collier and Commissioner George B. Loring at the Mississippi Valley Cane Growers' convention of 1882 in Saint Louis. Whereas Collier's analyses were restricted to sorghum, Wiley focused on both sorghum and beet sugar, and he also hoped to increase the efficiency of cane sugar production. Wiley was convinced that sugar needed not just analysis but advocacy through experimentation. He proposed to erect factories where his methods could be tried. Within two years Wiley had established two experimental stations—a sorghum factory in Kansas and a cane sugar station in Louisiana.[42]

In the highly volatile agricultural economy of the late 1800s, sugar was a promising but uncertain crop. Consumer demand for sugar was rapidly growing in urban households, yet sugar was hard to produce cheaply, and outside of southern cane production, most sugar was imported and remained expensive. As John Heitmann has richly detailed, the Louisiana sugar industry was technologically reshaped in the late nineteenth century, and Wiley's division played an important role in this technological overhaul. Wiley's experiments with new refining methods for cane sugar spurred Louisiana producers to experiment with alternative technologies. In his cane sugar venture Wiley was also fashioning alliances with the Louisiana Sugar Producers' Association, a powerful actor in national Democratic politics. When Wiley, a self-styled Republican, became the target of scientific and political criticism during the 1880s, the Louisiana Producers came to his aid and helped him keep his position during Grover Cleveland's two presidencies. Democrats like Rep. Theodore Wilkinson, who despised the Republicans' resistance to a sugar tariff, bellowed their praise for Wiley on the House floor.[43] Yet Wiley's ties to sugar growers had more than partisan implications. The chemist was also eliciting admiration among Gulf State farmers for his division. The division's bulletins were widely cited in sugar trade journals in the 1880s and 1890s, and southern state chemists praised the "intelligent cooperation" of the Agriculture Department. The USDA would continue a tight relationship of cooperative research with Louisiana and Florida sugar growers into the 1930s.[44]

Along with department agent J. M. Hines, Wiley also toured the Ohio Valley and Great Lakes states to promote the sugar beet. In dozens of small towns— to audiences of hundreds, packed with a mix of investors and farmers—he spoke of an agricultural-industrial "Empire" of beet farming.[45] In economic respects, Wiley's sugar campaigns met with limited success. Many of the technological innovations he suggested were too costly or slow to be implemented. The dream of sorghum never materialized, and the sugar beet industry, although healthy, was slow to establish itself, in part because the 1880s brought renewed price increases for cane sugar. Nonetheless, the sugar campaigns established Wiley as "the father of the sugar beet industry in the United States," according to the *Elmira (N.Y.) Advertiser*. Wiley built lasting alliances with planters, investors, state chemists, and college officials throughout the Midwest and Gulf States. Wiley and Hines also established a close rapport with agrarian newspapers; in the 1880s the *Country Gentleman* began to publish the Chemistry Division's intermediate results. Throughout his travels, Wiley was now announced as "Chemist of the United States."[46]

Wiley's sugar campaigns were revolutionary in one other respect. They comprised the most forceful attempt of any agricultural scientist in the nineteenth century to preach crop changes to American farmers. Wiley had previously agreed with his predecessors that the mission of the Chemistry Division was to provide dispassionate analyses of soil samples and prompt answers to farmers' written queries. After 1885, however, Wiley led his division into crop proselytizing. As the *Troy (N.Y.) Daily Times* observed in December 1897, the "Department of Agriculture . . . was never before so suggestive as now to the farming interests." Wiley had trained in Europe and at Harvard and was firmly established in the tradition of Justus Liebig's agricultural chemistry. He believed in a mode of farming governed by "competition, which is science reduced to practice." Scientific agriculture lay not simply in soil analysis but also in the consistent preaching of superior over inferior crops. In this way, Wiley championed the didactic and policy implications of chemistry.[47]

Yet the stagnation of the chemist's sugar campaign was undeniable. At a time when the Chemistry Division was losing ground and prestige to other organizations in the USDA—particularly the Bureau of Animal Industry (entrusted in 1885 with broad meat inspection powers) and the Seed Division—Wiley sought another cause to bring prestige to his fledgling organization. He would find it in pure food.

Wiley's interest in food adulteration stemmed from his research in Indiana and Europe, and it continued that of his predecessors. Thomas Antisell had warned Congress of fertilizer adulteration in 1869, and a decade later Peter Collier had conducted analyses showing significant amounts of lead in common food coloring. Yet Wiley went far beyond any previous government chemist in his advocacy for reform, even before 1900. His leadership role was cemented during his involvement with the Association of Official Agricultural Chemists (AOAC). The AOAC was a broad group of state officials and professionals who gathered informally in 1880 and 1881 for the purpose of setting uniform state standards for fertilizers. In 1884 Wiley and several chemists officially formed the association with an explicit view to projecting the utility of government chemistry well beyond fertilizer analysis. With Chemistry Division monies, Wiley and his associates gave the AOAC a home for meetings, a journal, and printed stationery. Wiley also served as the association's second president (1886–87) and for twenty-five years thereafter as the AOAC secretary. He consciously led the association into uncharted territory and toward food adulteration in particular. He marshaled the chemists into unprecedented unity in their advocacy for national uniform food standards. Wiley's dominance of the association in the 1880s put him at the center of the government chemistry network.[48]

Wiley's alliances with state chemists were politically shrewd, for the earliest anti-adulteration statutes gave them powerful authority in their states. New York and New Jersey passed pioneering laws in 1881. Their statutes reflected a draft law promoted by the National Board of Trade (NBT), an organization of civic trade groups and chambers of commerce. In 1882 Massachusetts passed a National Board law, yet the state-level movement waned thereafter. What remained was a confusing patchwork of state laws. If their institutional legacy lay incomplete, however, state-level campaigns in the 1880s did usher government chemists into new roles of political advocacy. The statutes established state health boards whose chemists were empowered to establish standards and to enforce them.[49]

In the late 1880s, with support from the association, Wiley turned his office's microscopes on butter, syrup, milk, spices, coffee, tea, sugar, lard, and preservatives. Wiley had requested and received funding from Congress to study drug adulteration, but instead he spent the monies on analyses of food. The division's studies were collected in a ten-part administrative bulletin, which, in retrospect, stands among the most influential publications of nineteenth-century American government: *Division of Chemistry Bulletin 13: Foods and Food Adulterants*. Wiley's staff found water added to commercial milk, cottonseed oil and stearins mixed with lard, tin chloride added to molasses, peas colored with copper sulfate, and copious amounts of glucose in syrup advertised as "pure." Yet the Chemistry Division's studies were also tempered by moderation. The bureau's scientists found no problems with commercial beer or baking powder. In *Bul-*

letin 13, the Division of Chemistry had published the only scientific treatise on food adulteration in America. It raised a voice of caution without striking a pose of radicalism or unwarranted excess.[50]

The moderate tone in Wiley's advocacy reaped political dividends, earning his outfit a reputation for neutrality. As early as 1891, Algernon Paddock had persuaded his Senate colleagues that the Division of Chemistry was "as nearly nonpartisan in its work as an institution can be under our system," assuring them that Wiley's office was "purely a scientific force."[51]

Wiley feared, however, that *Bulletin 13* appealed only to technocrats. It powerfully led state chemists to agitate for food regulation—the AOAC soon drafted a bill that Congress adopted as a model for legislation—but moving public sentiment would require a more popular report. So Wiley hired farm journal editor Alexander Wedderburn to write a popular version of *Bulletin 13,* and in 1890 the division published *Bulletin 25: A Popular Treatise on the Extent and Character of Food Adulteration. Bulletin 25* was a clarion call for federal legislation, arguing that the patchwork of existing state laws was woefully inadequate to rein in adulterations that "impaired the health of the consumer" and "frequently caused death."[52]

The Chemistry Division came more slowly to the issue of proprietary medicines. Commonly but falsely known as "patent medicines," proprietary drugs were protected by trademark. There were virtually no limits on their advertising. Papers ranging from dime rags to the *Journal of the American Medical Association* (*JAMA*) carried patent medicine advertisements in their columns. Fly-by-night companies promised that their sweet or mild-tasting nostrums offered swift cures for any ailment. The majority of these remedies were sound and, if of no medicinal value, at least innocuous. Many others were not. Patent medicine promoters sold alcohol-laden "soothing syrups" for children and babies, liver pills, "lost-manhood" tonics, and fever reducers laced with opium. In the 1890s organized physicians began to warn the public about the dangers of these "pseudoethicals." The political positioning of the American Medical Association was compromised, however, by its reliance on proprietary firms for advertising revenue for *JAMA.* The association wavered back and forth between permitting and banning patent drug advertisements.[53]

National politicians were not unaware of the adulteration and advertising problems. Between 1879 and 1905, more than 190 anti-adulteration measures were introduced in Congress. The best chances for passage came when the Senate Agriculture Committee, under Algernon S. Paddock of Nebraska, reported a bill in 1891. The Paddock bill was backed by more than ten thousand petitions and received official support from the National Dairy Association, the National Association of Retail Druggists, the National Grocers' Association, and other business groups. The Senate passed the Paddock measure in March 1892, but opposition prevented a vote in the House. Other than the Paddock measure, pure food bills rarely received even a committee report in either chamber of

Congress. The resulting lacuna in federal law, combined with the confusing patchwork of state regulations, left pure-food enthusiasts wondering how to surmount the status quo. Anti-adulteration bills had received the enthusiastic endorsement of numerous state officials, organized scientists, and farmers' and business groups. Yet these voices, powerful in the abstract, lacked political harmony. The multitude of voices fell far short of a coalition. No national pure-food movement existed, and no national law could pass.[54] Put differently, the USDA's Bureau of Chemistry had divergent preferences over regulatory policy, and it possessed unique administrative capacity, but its reputation was not politically grounded.

As he completed his first decade in government service, Wiley had made a mark. He had created a bureaucratic agenda, one that even the most visionary of the department's creators could not have imagined in 1862. He had also built an organization within an organization, a division of loyal workers that was gaining esteem within the USDA. Whereas the department at large was taking its orders from Congress and the nation's love affair with free seeds, Wiley was taking neither orders nor agendas from anyone but himself.

Conservation and Planning: The Divisions of Forestry and Biological Survey, 1880–97

The conservationist impulse in American government has commonly been associated with Gifford Pinchot, the wealthy Progressive Republican who was Theodore Roosevelt's confidant and who completed a weighty and contentious career as chief forester of the United States in 1910. Yet when Pinchot arrived to head the Forestry Division in 1898, a talented corps of foresters had already been recruited by Bernhard Fernow, and an even closer friend of Roosevelt, C. Hart Merriam, had led the USDA's Biological Survey for nine years. In the 1890s Fernow, Merriam, and Pinchot were busy establishing fiscal and organizational stability for their tiny divisions, and they succeeded in much the same manner that Wiley did, by assembling talent and by forming durable affiliations with newspapers, business associations, professional scientists, and political elites across regions, classes, and parties.

Fernow was the first government official in the United States to lay out a vision for a scientific and managerial forestry program—most lucidly in his 1891 paper "Need of a National Forest Administration." Born in Prussia, Fernow was trained in the Prussian Forestry Department at the renowned Muenden Academy. He believed firmly in the Prussian system of centralized planning and forest management, in part because he had seen it adopted by several nations, including British India and Japan. Fernow was also well known in late-nineteenth-century scientific circles. He traveled prominently in the American Association for the Advancement of Science, serving as secretary of its Section of

Economic Science and Statistics. He was also the dominant figure in the short-lived American Forest Congress, formed in 1873. In Fernow, the bureaucratic and organizational bases of Gilded Age conservationism were fused. Simultaneously, he became the secretary of the American Forestry Association and the head of the Division of Forestry. He continued to draft legislation for the association during his tenure with the USDA.[55]

Upon his arrival in 1886, Fernow found the Division of Forestry staffed by two men: a political appointee and Fernow's predecessor Nathaniel Egleston, whose knowledge of forestry amounted at best to an arboricultural hobby. Egleston's division had produced four small reports in a decade. Fernow immediately commenced an aggressive program of publications, mailing division bulletins, forestry circulars, and reports to hundreds of newspapers, as well as replying to thousands of queries from private foresters, university botanists, and state officials. His *Bulletin No. 5: What Is Forestry?* was distributed to twenty-five thousand farmers and lumbermen in the early 1890s and excerpted by hundreds of newspapers. *Bulletin No. 5* helped to popularize the concepts of forestry to a nationwide audience. By lending his professional expertise and his organizing talents, moreover, Fernow actively sponsored the development of forestry in the United States. As early as 1888, state forestry associations eagerly sought Fernow's help in assembling their organizations, and land-grant universities asked Fernow to devise curricula in forestry for their campuses. In addition, state governments actively sought the forester's ear in devising "plans" for their own state lands.[56]

Far more than historians of conservation have recognized, Fernow took steps to enlarge the forestry role of the national government and of his division in particular. It was Fernow who in 1888 first drafted a bill giving the government the power to create and administer forest reserves within the public domain. The bill was not immediately passed, but it established the model for most of the subsequent reserve bills, including section 24 of the Forest Reserves Act of 1891. Section 24, which Pinchot later called "the most important legislation in the history of Forestry in America," gave the president the power to define reserves in the public lands. Fernow was, as John Ise has discovered, the moving force behind section 24. Beyond this, Fernow offered two arguments that would later become linchpins of Pinchot's campaign to grab the national forest reserves from the General Land Office. In his 1891 annual report to Congress, Fernow noted the "incongruity of having a Division of Forestry in a Department of the Government to preach rational forest management, while such is entirely absent from the Government timber lands." He also argued that rational forest management would require "strong administrative capacity," including civil service protection and a high level of discretion for foresters.[57]

Fernow also connected the Division of Forestry to the wider dialogue of conservation. He struck up affiliations with Samuel Trask Dana, Charles Sargent, Carl Schurz, forestry researcher Franklin B. Hough, Pinchot, and other concerned citizens. These were important moves. As Samuel Hays and Donald Pisani have argued, the late-nineteenth-century conservation movement was not centered entirely in the government. Instead, it grew out of post–Civil War civil society and cleaved as much to emotive and culturally based argumentation as it did to planning. Gilded Age Americans heard not rational caution of the exhaustion of natural resources but "moralist" warnings of the coming "timber famine" and the consequent drought. Popular writers and magazines advanced this rhetoric as powerfully as did government administrators. By the close of the 1890s, however, Fernow's ties rendered the division a central locus of American conservation. The division became the preeminent source of conservationist publicity when in 1897 Sargent ended his journal *Garden and Forest.*[58]

Despite his successes, Fernow was passed over in 1898 for the position of forester, as Wilson opted instead for another German-trained scientist, Gifford Pinchot. Pinchot brought a different set of interests and connections to the department. The Yale-educated Brahmin was respected in Republican circles but paid less allegiance to President William McKinley than to independent Mugwumps. He came to the department from his post as secretary of the National Forest Commission, where he developed a hunger for a comprehensive approach to national forest management. Pinchot was appointed to the classified civil service, which insulated him, for a time, from partisan politics. He also had free reign over hiring and division operations. After 1898, Pinchot quickly embarked on two organization-building strategies. First, he sought to demonstrate the utility of the division to private foresters and state officials by lending out his foresters for management planning on private and state reserve lands. Some of the largest timber owners in the country quickly embraced Pinchot's offer, including Weyerhaeuser Lumber Company in the Pacific Northwest, the Northern Pacific Railroad, and the Kirby Lumber Company of Texas. Second, Pinchot began to recruit aggressively from the Cornell School of Forestry, snapping up the very students whom Fernow (the school's new dean) was training.[59]

Conservation had another voice in the Gilded Age USDA. C. Hart Merriam was a biologist who in the 1880s commenced a lifelong campaign for wildlife preservation through the creation of game preserves. In 1886 Merriam organized the Division of Ornithology and Mammology, and four years later he recruited the young ornithologist Theodore S. Palmer from Berkeley. Palmer and Merriam built one of the most productive research organizations in the nation. With a staff of ten or fewer, they published dozens of reports that were much in demand by leisure conservationists and foreign officials. Merriam's studies of birds—particularly the crop-ravaging English sparrow—were widely read, both by naturalists such as John Audubon and by agricultural leaders looking to rid their fields of pests. Merriam's active involvement in Washington's nature societies (including the Boone and Crockett Club) made him friends with many federal scientists and sport-minded politicians. One such individual was a rising Republican named Theodore Roosevelt. Beginning in 1887, Roosevelt and Merriam carried on a four-decade friendship. By 1896 Roosevelt was regularly lobbying members of Congress, including House Speaker Thomas Reed, for Merriam's favored bills.[60]

With Pinchot taking up Fernow's agenda for a unified program of bureaucratic forestry, and with Merriam and Pinchot linked to so many conservationists, in the 1890s the Department of Agriculture became an organizational center (perhaps *the* center) of American environmentalism. No other organization could boast such expertise in mammology, ornithology, *and* forestry, to say nothing of soil expertise, insect research, and dozens of other problems in which a growing swell of nature enthusiasts was interested. Nor were the consumers of the department's research interested in mere sports and hobbies. The publications of Merriam and Pinchot were also getting increasing attention from the House and Senate Public Lands Committees and Agriculture Committees, who were receiving a growing volume of petitions related to nature and forest protection—petitions from the very organizations in which Merriam, Fernow, and Pinchot were so centrally involved.[61]

Beverly Galloway, David Fairchild, and the Science of Seeds

The USDA's last foray into science in the nineteenth century was, ironically, into seeds. When Beverly Galloway took over the Section of Plant Pathology in 1887, he began hiring young plant explorers. By recruiting through family and academic associates in land-grant colleges, Galloway brought a series of young plant scientists—Mark Carleton, Palemon Dorsett, David Fairchild, Walter T. Swingle, and Merton Waite—to the department. With these men, Galloway began a quiet campaign to build scientific capacity through the seed program.

Fairchild, whom Galloway had met at Kansas Agricultural College, began his studies in Naples, Italy, in 1893. There he met Barbour Lathrop, a wealthy Chicago industrialist who was so impressed by Fairchild's erudition that he instantly offered the young scientist a $1,000 "investment" to travel to Southeast Asia to gather plants. Fairchild asked for a delay so that he could learn more about the region, but by 1895 Fairchild was traveling throughout the Philippines, Micronesia, Japan, and Java in search of indigenous plants that could be grown profitably in American soils. Lathrop frequently traveled with Fairchild on these tours and gave Fairchild money with which to purchase products and export samples to the United States for growing in the USDA's experimental gardens. With Lathrop's largesse, Fairchild introduced hundreds of viable plant varieties to the United States, including strains of Egyptian cotton, Sumatran tobacco, alfalfa from Turkestan, and Bavarian hops. Just as important, Fairchild set up enduring linkages to foreign seed houses (in Finland, Germany, and England) and elite farms in Asia.[62]

Perhaps the single most famous USDA import was not Fairchild's but Carleton's. Conducting grain research in Russia in 1898, Carleton imported new red durum wheat—also known as Russian winter wheat—which was ideally suited to American soils. By 1903 American farmers were growing 20 million bushels of Carleton's import, and it was established throughout the Great Plains. By 1919 the varieties Carleton introduced accounted for 98 percent of all wheat grown in Kansas.[63]

Ultimately, Fairchild's brilliance lay not merely in his ability to procure new seeds and plants but in his penchant for getting others to pay for them. With weak congressional interest in seed and plant introduction, Fairchild was compelled to make do with limited funding, usually less than $10,000 per year (from which he also had to pay for his travel expenses). Many of his overseas discoveries were purchased not with federal monies but with Lathrop's donations, by bartering USDA bulletins and yearbooks (read enthusiastically by European and colonial officials), and, on occasion, by clandestine purchases from thieves (thereby allowing the division to purchase plants well below the market price). Fairchild employed the last strategy in obtaining Bavarian hop cuttings that were later adopted by American brewers. He wrote to his Washington associates that he felt "like a dog in this business . . . but am acting under my government's instructions."[64]

Conclusion

By 1895 the USDA's Division of Chemistry had moved from soil analysis to political advocacy for pure food, the Division of Forestry had metamorphosed from a botany outfit to the central node in American forest conservation, and Beverly Galloway and David Fairchild were articulating and administering a new vision of seeds based not on pork but on rational experimentation. In all three of these ventures, USDA scientists were following ideas and agendas that were substantially their own. It was not Congress or President Cleveland but Wiley who turned the Division of Chemistry toward food adulteration studies. It was Fernow and Pinchot, not John Muir or the Public Lands Committees of Congress, who began preaching a national bureaucratic forestry program in the 1890s and farming out the Forestry Division's talents to create goodwill among Weyerhaeuser and others. It was Galloway and Fairchild, not the Grange or the Alliance, who commenced an aggressive plan of seed exploration in Asia. At the Department of Agriculture, merit reform and bureau-based selection had parented a unique voice for scientific policymaking in the United States. USDA bureau chiefs were clearly much more enthusiastic about agricultural science at the department than Congress, the presidents, or the major farming organi-

zations and movements. They had also come to favor unique policy alternatives—a federal pure food law, rational and centralized forest management, and
a scientific seed program.

Each of these USDA leaders was backed by hundreds of employees who
shared their policy aims. The mechanism that allowed division chiefs to reshape
the ideology of their organizations was civil service reform. Merit reform
shifted the gatekeeping role in USDA hiring from congressional representatives
to USDA bureau chiefs. As the statistical analyses of this chapter show, USDA
leaders took shrewd advantage of this opportunity and hired people who shared
their preference for a scientific USDA. They recruited disproportionately from
advanced, wealthy, and technological farming communities. Most striking, the
USDA was more likely to recruit from those areas where the demand for USDA
scientific information was higher but less likely to hire from areas with a higher
demand for free seeds.

The department also maintained a reservoir of highly visible scientific and
programmatic capacity. In addition to the discoveries and publications of the
Chemistry Division, the Forestry Division, and Fairchild's seed office, the
USDA had come visibly to the aid of American livestock farmers. In 1889
USDA researchers tackled Texas cattle fever, which had killed millions of cattle in more than seven hundred thousand square miles of southern grazing lands.
Their discovery that cattle ticks transmitted the disease propelled land-grant
college researchers toward finding a cure. In 1903 Marion Dorset discovered
an effective vaccine for hog cholera, saving the hog industry hundreds of millions of dollars annually.[65]

It would be inaccurate to maintain that the USDA alone favored agricultural
science in the late nineteenth century. The Grange and Alliances helped to sponsor farmers' institutes and, in principle at least, supported scientific funding for
the USDA. These organizations also supported the creation of federal experiment stations and kept a close eye on land-grant colleges to ensure that they remained faithful to their farm-based missions. Yet no voice cried as loudly for
scientific policymaking in agriculture as did the USDA. The specific policy
thrusts of the department in the 1890s—food adulteration, forestry management, and foreign plant importation—were issues in which the agrarians were
not very involved. The major farm organizations instead focused on monetary
reform and on industrial regulation. Further, as John Hicks and other students
of the Populists have argued, agrarian radicals focused not on bureaucratic solutions to policy problems but upon *legislative* remedies. This theme of legislative solutions to farm dilemmas coursed through late-nineteenth-century
agrarian discourse—from Oliver Kelley's early Grange to William Jennings
Bryan's antigold crusade. For all of their professed support for scientific agriculture, the major agrarian groups were, in the final analysis, severely compromised by their love affair with free seeds.[66]

In the USDA a budding mezzo-level administration arose not through institutional design but in a patchwork fashion and through division-level entrepreneurship. The promise of agricultural state building lay not in Cabinet status, not primarily in movement affiliations, and not really in civil service reform. It lay elsewhere, in the small divisions where Harvey Wiley, Bernhard Fernow, C. Hart Merriam, Gifford Pinchot, Beverly Galloway, and David Fairchild had already hewn out the rudiments of scientific capacity. Every one of these individuals except Pinchot came to the department before its ascension to the Cabinet level. Nor did office creation at the USDA follow any well-established institutional or partisan logic. In the 1890s the department had the Divisions of Statistics, Chemistry, Forestry, Animal Industry, Illustrations, and Publications. Not once in the 1800s did any secretary or congressional committee attempt to relate these divisions to one another systematically. The young agency was at once a clientele-based organization, a functional organization, and a publishing house.

By 1899 the U.S. Department of Agriculture had for a decade possessed all of the attributes commonly associated with strong bureaucracies—status as a Cabinet-level department, a broad-based and politically active clientele, and a merit-based civil service. Yet none of these conditions sufficed to create autonomy, at least not yet. Without a strong middle-level structure and a set of supportive networks for its more unconventional ideas, the USDA remained a feeble actor in agricultural politics. The promise of an agricultural state was growing, but it remained invisible to all but a few organizations and scientific communities. Absent a set of diverse affiliations to support the department's visions, esteem for the USDA remained ethereal and mainly limited to enthusiasts of progressive agriculture. The USDA's scientific and administrative capacity was undeniable, indeed unique in the federal government. Autonomy would await the coalitions that only manifold networks could bring.

Seven

From Seeds to Science: The USDA as University, 1897–1917

The Americans' Department of Agriculture is now
the most popular and respected of the world's
great administrative institutions.
   —Horace Plunkett, 1910

I became his devoted disciple. I embraced his
teachings and philosophies without reserve and
with the ardor and enthusiasm of youth.
   —Rep. Asbury F. Lever, speaking of USDA
     official Seaman Knapp

THE REPUBLICAN landslide election of 1896 brought William McKinley to the presidency and James S. Wilson of Iowa to the perch of secretary of agriculture. Beginning in January 1897, Wilson's watch lasted sixteen years, the longest tenure of any Cabinet-level officer in American history. Wilson's tenure was marked by an expansion of administrative authority and capacity the likes of which, arguably, no executive department had ever seen. From a backwater seed-distribution agency with declining support for the scientific missions that its personnel supported, the Department of Agriculture strode boldly into a new policymaking role. From 1900 onward, the USDA established a reputation par excellence as the principal scientific agency of American government. It also became an authority in the policymaking process, an unrivaled supplier of drafts and amendments for Congress and the president. The department's officials did not merely participate in the legislative process. They directed the course and the terms of significant bills, transforming their organization into a firm gatekeeper of farm legislation in the United States.

The central organizational shift in the Progressive Department of Agriculture was the cementing of scientific policy ideology. The department's recruitment of science-minded farm youth from land-grant colleges continued, but much more important to capacity building in the USDA were its internal networks of affiliations and cooperation. Departmental officials inhabited a dense web of social and professional interactions that were new to early-twentieth-century Washington. They traveled together to the same professional meetings, collaborated in research and inspection ventures, spent long hours in discussion with each other at Washington's Cosmos Club, and developed abiding friendships within the department.[1]

Autonomy emerged in several forms. The department won a *programmatic autonomy* through its policy innovations, often launched with the use of discretionary lump-sum funds. Lump-sum monies funded several USDA programs in 1900, most notably congressional seed distribution. In taking free seed monies and allocating them to a pressing new farm crisis in the early 1900s—the rise of the cotton boll weevil in the South—USDA leaders built the county-based farm advising program known today as agricultural extension. This brilliant exercise in bureaucratic entrepreneurship was duplicated in other programs—in food and drug regulation, scientific forestry, and agricultural economics. After developing the administrative rudiments of a program with lump-sum funds, USDA bureau chiefs nurtured clients in rural localities, urban centers, the media, and Congress. Congress then legislated and institutionalized the programs, largely along the lines desired by the department. The cycle of experimentation and institutionalization then continued with the steady expansion of lump-sum funds throughout the Progressive Era.

The department's liberation from nineteenth-century politics received its most profound expression in *metaphorical autonomy*. Through the rhetorical strategies of its executives, principally Wilson, the USDA won a symbolic freedom from its subdued past. The department discarded the rhetoric of "servitude" to Congress and negotiated for itself a scholastic self-understanding as a "university" in the newly defined "Empire" of "American Agriculture."

The transformation from seeds to science was nowhere more visible than in the USDA's radical conversion of seed distribution largesse into a fledgling farm education program in 1903, a program that within one decade became the agricultural extension system that has dominated twentieth-century farming in the United States and dozens of other nations. Two other policy transformations that illustrate the bureau-level basis of the USDA's autonomy—the rise of national food and pharmaceutical regulation and national forest conservation—are discussed in the following chapter. Yet the rise of agricultural extension also impressively displays the political autonomy of the Department of Agriculture. From 1903 to 1914, the department championed a form of extension that no other actor in agricultural politics had envisioned—the county-agent system. This form of education was actively opposed by many agrarians and land-grant colleges, who preferred college-based farmers' institutes instead. In the Smith-Lever Act and its aftermath, the USDA buried the institute model—not through fiat, nor through elitist imposition, but by the irrepressible political logic of policy experimentation and coalition building through diverse networks.

Careers and Culture: The Department as University, 1897–1913

Wilson was not McKinley's first choice for secretary of agriculture, but his arrival in Washington marked a new aggressiveness for his department. Wilson brought a diverse pedigree to the USDA. He was familiar both to agrarian radicals and to established western farming elites. An early member of the Farmers' Protective Association in Iowa with "Uncle" Henry Wallace and Seaman Knapp, Wilson had considerable experience in antimonopoly and agrarian campaigns. He had served on the House Agriculture Committee from 1873 to 1877, and again from 1883 to 1885. After his departure from the House, he sat on the Iowa Railway Commission and came to the department from his post as director of the agricultural experiment station at Iowa State College. His involvement in agricultural politics was patently deep, his commitment genuine.[2]

Wilson opened his tenure by replacing the previous discourse of deference with a much more assertive rhetoric centered thematically on the promotion of agriculture as an essentially scientific practice. Wilson spoke with certainty about the department's mission in his opening annual report:

> The Department of Agriculture was organized to help farmers to a better knowledge of production and its tendencies at home and abroad, so as to enable them to intelligently meet the requirements of home and foreign markets for material that may be profitably grown or manufactured on American farms. It was also intended that the Department should organize a comprehensive system of means by which the sciences that relate to agriculture should become familiar as household words among our farmers.[3]

Significantly, Wilson offered not a word about seed distribution. The job of the USDA was to produce and distribute not seeds but knowledge. It was to formulate, institute, and spread a new language of intelligent and science-informed agriculture to America's farmers. Moreover, Wilson emphasized repeatedly to Congress that the department had the singular capacity to perform this service for the nation. It was a message he rehearsed in nearly every annual report until his departure in 1913.[4]

Wilson's didactic framing of the USDA's mission meshed well with his metaphor of the department as a corporate body of scientists instructing and advancing American agriculture. In numerous speeches to commerical congresses, university faculty, and convention gatherings, Wilson spoke of the transformation of American agriculture by scientific education. On several occasions Wilson exalted the agency as a "university" and a "great educational institution," a referent unheard before 1897. He lauded repeatedly the department's "corps of experts" or "corps of scientists."[5] His conscious use of this corporate terminology to transform the agency's culture is evident in his remarks of 1900.

> The future success of the Department will depend in large measure on each man being made to feel a personal responsibility as to the details of his work, and at the same time that he must lend his full support to matters of general policy which concern the division of which he is a member and the Department as a whole. The broader plan

... has for its object the arrangement of the work in such a close cooperative way as to bring the strongest support from every Division interested. ... [T]he intimate relation of the various allied groups will bring the investigators into more sympathetic union.[6]

The danger in such language, of course, was that it radiated a paternalistic, even elitist stance. To talk of science and expertise as the essence of the department was to risk alienating or offending agrarian support by suggesting that the American farmer somehow had to be led by the hand toward more efficient production. In 1893 Secretary Julius Sterling Morton had warned against such rhetoric: "As organized, the Department of Agriculture offers opulent opportunities for the exercise of the most pronounced paternalism."[7]

Wilson countered this jeopardy by advancing yet another corporate metaphor, one somewhat more diluted than the first. He integrated the notions of agriculture and research and recast agriculture as a form of science. He spoke of "the science of dairying" and of the various scientific disciplines as "parts of a single great problem which is primarily agricultural." He capitalized on the momentum of the movement for "domestic science," which he defined as a systematic exercise of "the arts which are practiced in the home" and which stood "in the same category with medicine, engineering and agriculture." No more would the department parse science into "basic" and "applied" modes or distinguish between scientific and practical activity in agriculture. For Wilson, agriculture was intrinsically a scientific practice, and "[s]cience that is not applied is dead."[8]

In departmental discourse, employees at all levels began to refer to "Agriculture" as a proper noun—a distinct realm and arena of practice—much more frequently after 1900. Wilson himself referred to "American Agriculture" and "practical Agriculture" in his letters, a practice uncharacteristic of previous executives. Lower-level employees who described themselves as "teachers" and "economic scientists" on 1890s personnel forms now thought of themselves as "Agriculturists" pursuing "Agricultural Science." And during his nationwide campaign to boost sugar beet cultivation, Chemistry Bureau chief Harvey Wiley envisioned an "Empire of Agriculture" in America.[9] Just as Wilson spoke of the various scientific disciplines as "parts of a single great problem which is primarily agricultural," his employees and successors perceived "Agriculture" as a field incorporating subordinate pursuits such as biology, (plant) physiology, and chemistry.

These statements evoked a metaphorical hierarchy. They construed scientists and their research as contributing to a select field of study (biophysics, for example). These fields of study were corporately organized as a university, and collectively they advanced "Agriculture" as a scientific practice and as a national good. In this way, Wilson was capitalizing on the long-standing agrarian imagery that portrayed farming as fundamental to commerce and manufacturing in the United States. For as the department's seal maintained, "Agriculture Is the Foundation of Manufacture and Commerce," and to serve "Agriculture" in working for the department was implicitly to serve "the Nation" by putting it upon better foundations. Crucially, Wilson reminded his employees that these foundations were moral in character. He waxed homiletic in 1897: "[T]he farmer's home is becoming more and more the seat of comfort, the centre of intelligence, virtue, and happiness, the source of strong men for all vocations, and sure safeguard of the Republic." The force of Victorian moral progressivism was not lost on Wilson. In summary, then, a complex structure of concepts and symbols was entailed in the university / agriculture-as-science metaphor. It offered a portrait of the ideal employee, the ideal bureau, the ideal department, and relationships between each of these entities and the nation.[10]

The Disciplinary Meaning of Bureaucratic Work

One of the most powerful effects of the university metaphor was its implied portrait of the ideal bureaucrat as a researcher and scholar. The ideal, typical portrait of the USDA worker emerged frequently in bureau chiefs' recommendations for employee salary boosts and promotions. If they were praised, USDA scientists were described as "a collegiate of high degree" or "a natural research worker" with "a fertile imagination and an open mind for new principles." If they were faulted, USDA scientists were scorned for their lack of "collegiality" and inability to understand the broader implications of their work for department policy and farming in general. Bureau leaders particularly admired employees who could help develop a collegial atmosphere. One food and drug inspector was singled out for "developing his men into a strong corps of efficient and loyal workers and carr[ying] on the work in the utmost harmony with State officials."[11]

In the USDA's scholastic culture, the ideal employee was a scholar, a colleague, one who displayed the bureaucratic virtues of loyalty to office and persistence in research. Moreover, the essential "spirit of cooperation" and the ability to foster loyalty and efficiency were highly prized talents. The ideal employee was also a male, a "practical man" who understood that his disciplinary pursuits were performed in the advancement of "Agriculture." Particularly talented and dedicated individuals were perceived as central to the department's performance, without whom the corps of researchers would be "crippled."[12]

The exemplary USDA bureaucrat also displayed "virility" and "vigor" in his research. These tandem virtues coincided neatly with Progressive-Era gender roles. At a time when women were increasingly relegated to clerical work, the concept of "vigorous" and "virile" performance was a metaphorical way of separating the male realm of research and administration from the "female" realm of clerical labor. For this reason, the notion of promoting women to research and administrative positions within the department was often contentious. Many women worked in the department as librarians, but the management of the department's collections and libraries was left to men. When Josephine Clark was nominated head librarian in 1900, department executives feared that it was inappropriate for women to be in management positions. Wilson was willing to advance Clark only on the condition that she demonstrate that she was a "thorough business woman," and that in no way would "her sex . . . handicap her usefulness in the slightest degree." For the USDA as for other agencies, the Progressive shedding of clerical stigma was a gendered transformation. The new "disciplinary" work of the state in the USDA was men's; the old "clerical" work, women's.[13]

In part because it embodied so many symbols of the Progressive Era—agrarian rebirth, the hierarchy of science, remapped gender relations—the university culture took hold in the USDA and dominated the department's thinking until at least the New Deal. In their 1940 book on the department, John Gaus and Leon Wolcott argue that a "corporate atmosphere" emerged in the department during Wilson's tenure: "This atmosphere of an institution devoted almost exclusively to scientific studies and the diffusion of information about them remained a powerful factor in the Department's life. There is an obvious likeness in it to a university." Significantly, Wilson boasted in 1912 that the department had become a "great agricultural university for postgraduate work," comparing the larger mission of the department to its fledgling graduate training programs. Leonard White also remarks on an esprit de corps prevailing among departmental scientists during this period, a corporate identity that suffused the web of scientific and professional associations surrounding the department.[14]

The corporate culture that Wilson shaped did not by itself meld USDA workers together. The power of rhetoric was bolstered by a number of institutional and structural conditions, and Wilson controlled only some of these. Not the least of these was the fact that Republican hegemony in presidential electoral politics allowed Wilson to stay at the executive perch for sixteen years. Moreover, the ascendance of the department to Cabinet-level status in 1889, an institutional advance for which the National Grange had been a strong advocate, gave the secretary a tall place from which to speak to Congress and to clientele groups.[15]

Nor was Wilson unattuned to the importance of satisfying congressional wishes. He departed from the confrontational stance of his predecessor Morton and commenced his tenure with effusive praise of the seed-distribution program. He spent nearly all of the money allocated by Congress for the purpose of free seed distribution. Indeed, to demonstrate the value of science to congressional concerns, he even placed a scientist at the head of the Seed Division—the post had previously been occupied by a clerical civil servant—fearing that "much of this work has been done in the dark."[16]

From the perspective of the USDA as a whole, Wilson's new corporate metaphor had internal and external meanings. Within the USDA, the scholastic idiom unified the various scientific and applied activities of the department in a concentrated mission. In the USDA as university, the various bureaus—Biological Survey, Chemistry, Forestry, Statistics, Plant Industry, and Weather—were conceived as disciplinary research specialties. The department took on the shape and the image of the emergent German research university.

Externally, the university metaphor projected a new identity for the USDA. It amounted to a singular claim to the professorial expertise that was increasingly valued in Progressive-Era politics. Notably, urban and rural journalists took up Wilson's cue, pronouncing the department the "National University of Agriculture." Urban newspapers from the *New York Times* to the *Pittsburgh Gazette* marveled at the size, complexity, and usefulness of the department's annual reports. Others noted the stunning diversity of the new policies with which it was experimenting. Still others, such as the Democratic *Daily Express* of San Antonio, Texas, equated the department's scientific leanings with absolute policy neutrality. "There is no politics, of course, in the Agriculture Department, and there should be none." Wilson's department looked after interests in "every section of the country, without the slightest indication of partiality in any direction." In a highly partisan era, the USDA's visible stance of neutrality was a stunning feat.[17]

The Emergence of Mezzo-Level Administration

The university metaphor was not simply a rhetorical construct. It also affected the department's organizational structure. In 1901 Wilson reshuffled the USDA's salary schedules and bureau organization. With both moves he furthered a scientific definition of the USDA's mission. The overhaul of salary schedules was necessary to help retain the analytic personnel who could find better and better salaries in the private sector. Wilson and his bureau chiefs requested and secured salary raises for head and assistant scientists, successfully placed the department's land-grant college graduate students in the classified civil service, and promoted many head scientists to administrative divisions. The result (displayed in table 7.1) was a salary boost for the department's scientists, a raise not experienced by the USDA clerical force. It skewed the department's pay distribution sharply in favor of analytic labor.[18]

The stratification of bureaus along functional lines made concrete the model of the department as university. Before Wilson, as Gaus and Wolcott have written, "the basis of the Department's organization . . . had been either a [single] scientific research activity or a commodity." In 1901 Wilson reorganized the department along scientific lines, promoting almost every scientific division to bureau status and leaving major clerical divisions with important clientele ties (Seed, Supply, Experiment Stations, Publications) unadvanced. Congress then

TABLE 7.1
Wilson's Reorganization and the Emergence of Mezzo-Level Bureaus at the USDA

Divisions	Status of Head
Official USDA Organization in 1892	
Bureau of Animal Industry	Chief of Bureau
Division of Chemistry	USDA Chemist
Division of Entomology	Entomologist
Division of Ornithology and Mammalogy	Chief of Division
Division of Botany	USDA Botanist
Division of Vegetable Pathology	Chief of Division
Division of Pomology	USDA Pomologist
Division of Forestry	Chief of Division
Office of Fiber Investigations	Special Agent
Division of Statistics	USDA Statistician
Seed Division	Chief of Division
Division of Illustrations	Chief of Division
Division of Records and Editing	Chief of Division
Division of Accounts and Disbursements	Chief of Division
Office of Experiment Stations	Director of Office
Weather Bureau	Chief of Bureau
Official USDA Organization in 1909	
Supply Division	Chief of Division
Weather Bureau	Chief of Bureau
Bureau of Animal Industry	Chief of Bureau
Bureau of Plant Industry	Chief of Bureau
Forest Service	Chief Forester
Bureau of Chemistry	Chemist and Chief
Bureau of Soils	Soil Physicist and Chief
Bureau of Entomology	Entomologist and Chief
Bureau of Biological Survey	Biologist and Chief

(*continued*)

TABLE 7.1
(*Continued*)

Divisions	Status of Head
Division of Accounts and Disbursements	Chief and Disbursing Clerk
Division of Publications	Editor and Chief
Bureau of Statistics	Statistician and Chief
Library	Librarian
Office of Experiment Stations	Director of Office
Office of Public Roads	Director of Office

Note: Scientific divisions became full bureaus, and head scientists were given administrative authority. Major clerical divisions remained in divisional status or were removed from official department organization. The organization of scientific activity was consolidated along functional/disciplinary lines.
Source: Secretary of Agriculture, *Annual Report,* 1892; USDA, *Yearbook,* 1909.

sanctioned Wilson's restructuring in the following year's appropriation act. Recognizing that Seed Division employees desired continuity and stable funding and that scientific employees valued status and autonomy most, Wilson made a brilliant restructuring move that appealed to both and that elevated science in the hierarchy of the USDA. Further, the university metaphor carried an implicit division of labor. Wilson's new structure arrayed USDA scientists along disciplinary lines—chemistry, plant science, biology, and forestry—with each discipline contributing to the departmental "product": knowledge for dispersion. Table 7.2 encapsulates the transformation.[19]

The rhetorical and structural articulation of the university metaphor was part of a broader pattern of centralization. Wilson undertook several other centralizing moves during his tenure, including the rationalization of the USDA's budgetary system and the concentration of expenditure authority in the Secretary's Office.[20] At the same time, he continued to allow his bureau chiefs to operate as they pleased, even when he disagreed with their policies. Unlike his predecessor Morton, Wilson's moves met not with organizational resistance but with praise. The university metaphor accomplished cultural centralization within the USDA even as Wilson formally delegated authority to his subordinates. Wilson portrayed the department as functioning with a singular purpose, and the background that Wilson shared with the bloc of department analysts lent him legitimacy and certainly facilitated his extension of executive reach. If there is anything revolutionary about Wilson's tenure, it is that he brought together these diverse tools to unify his organization (as well as American agriculture) under a common symbolic scheme.

TABLE 7.2
The Transformation of USDA Salary Structure, 1900–1910

Position	1900 Salary	1909 Salary	Percentage Change
Example One: The Bureau of Chemistry			
USDA Secretary (Wilson)	$8,000	$12,000	+50%
Chief of Chemistry Division (H. W. Wiley)	2,500	5,000	+100
Assistant Lab Chief (W. D. Bigelow)	1,600	3,500	+119
Assistant Chemist (maximum)	1,600	2,500	+56
Class 1 Clerk (maximum)	1,200	1,400	+17
Example Two: The Forest Service			
Chief Forester (Gifford Pinchot)	$2,500	$5,000	+100%
Assistant Foresters	1,600	2,500–3,500	+56 to 119
Class 1 Clerk (maximum)	1,200	1,400	+17

Note: Net shift: Whereas class 1 clerks made little more in 1909 than they did in 1900, bureau chiefs (now scientists) doubled their salaries, and staff chemists/foresters and lab operators received double or more what they received in 1900. This was accomplished through (1) absolute salary increases for scientists and (2) more complex schematization of analytic labor but not of clerical labor.

Source: Report of the Secretary of Agriculture, 1900; *Expenditures of the Department of Agriculture,* 1909, House Documents, vol. 71, 61st Cong., 2d sess.

Wilson's ideal of corporate attachment was that each employee would be attached to his or her functional position, bureau, and the department as a unified entity. He explicitly recognized the importance of creating autonomous subcultures within the bureaus of the USDA. The identity of USDA employees was based on their participation in a scholastic institution functioning as the catalyst in the ongoing scientific transformation of American agriculture. Through the incessant but nuanced use of corporate metaphors such as the university, harmony among bureaus was maintained. Each bureau was assigned a role to play in the greater departmental mission of information production. A similar strategy was employed within individual bureaus.[21]

Moreover, the metaphor implied a central authority for the organization. At the head of the scholastic corpus was Wilson, an Iowan and a farmer, but also a former professor and president of a state agricultural experiment station. He could personify the institution and its aims.

Internal Networks and Bureaucratic Careers. The generation of individuals who arrived at the department in the 1890s and early 1900s were thrust into characteristic career paths, many of them experiencing a stable progression in status and income for the first time in their lives. USDA chemists in the 1870s had remained as assistant chemists for ten years or more. After 1901, the cohort of new recruits in Wiley's Bureau of Chemistry usually started working as "Assistant Chemist[s] at $1,200." Most chemists moved within two years to the position of "Assistant Chemist at $1,400," then to "Assistant Chemist at $1,600," then to "Assistant Chemist at $1,800." These changes were not mere salary boosts; each position carried a different set of responsibilities in the bureau. Chemists who were paid $1,800 annually were expected to take a greater lead in publishing than were assistant chemists paid $1,200, who were essentially apprentices. After ascending to the $1,800 position, chemists often became laboratory chiefs in Washington or in the inspection laboratories that the Chemistry Bureau maintained around the nation. USDA scientists moved from informal apprenticeships through assistantships to senior research positions, and from these to the perches of lab, division, and bureau chiefs. The scientific careers of those employed in the early USDA paralleled those in the emergent German-form research universities of the United States. Not only was a generation of civil servants living the novelty of a modern career, but many of them were experiencing the same job ladders.

The forces of career dynamics and organizational structure were combining, then, to produce a personnel force with a great deal of attachment to fellow workers and to the department. As Gaus and Wolcott argued in their Social Service Research Council book on the department, corporate attachment was based on this underlying commonality of background and experience.

> During the early years of the Wilson secretaryship there was developing in the Department a characteristic personnel, derived from the increasing number of civil servants recruited from the land-grant institutions which had now become more firmly established in the educational system of the country. . . . Many civil servants were farm-bred; they were natural scientists by training; they were conditioned both by the period of expanding economic activity that prevailed in general throughout the nation and by the ideals of the individual farm-owner-occupier.
>
> . . . A certain unifying sense of corporate life was derived in part from the rural background and interests of so many of the civil servants and from their training in the new types of institution that had undergone a period of struggle and opposition.[22]

The portrait Gaus and Wolcott offer suggests that the USDA's corporate atmosphere was a function of the common educational, familial, and occupational heritages shared by department employees, particularly scientists. Graduates of land-grant institutions who shared similar organizational positions frequently wrote to each other and spoke of the "attachment" they felt toward other members of their bureau, an "intimate connection" they wished not to "sever."[23]

Still another factor in the USDA's cohesive culture was the nexus of social networks among the department's scientific personnel, networks that also created mutual attachments among departmental scientists. Most of the department's chemists, employed in the Bureau of Chemistry, were members of the American Chemical Society and the Association of Official Agricultural Chemists and regularly attended annual meetings and regional functions. In addition, USDA scientists shared social club memberships in Washington, D.C., including the now infamous Cosmos Club.[24]

Backgrounds or Networks? A Statistical Analysis of Career Duration at the USDA, 1891–1907

One important effect of the USDA's cohesive culture was its low turnover rate. Whereas the Departments of Interior and Justice regularly lost 10 percent or more of their personnel on an annual basis after 1900, the USDA's turnover averaged less than 5 percent during the Progressive Era. In some respects, the "background similarity" argument of Gaus and Wolcott (echoed more recently by Finegold and Skocpol) and the "internal networks" argument complement one another in explaining the USDA's ability to retain its talent. In other ways, they point to different organizational processes. Given an abundance of National Archives data on federal employees at the turn of the century, these arguments can be tested. Was the USDA's esprit de corps traceable mainly to common heritages or to networks within the USDA?[25]

This question can be addressed by using USDA employees' employment duration—net of the standard economic and social factors that can be invoked to explain it—as a measure of their organizational attachment. Controlling for gender, education, work experience, salary, sickness, and a battery of other variables, I assess the relative merit of the "background similarity" hypothesis and the "internal networks" hypothesis with two variables. If Gaus and Wolcott were right about the importance of common heritages, then USDA employees who were educated at land-grant colleges—namely, employees who had the background most common in the USDA—should have exhibited longer tenures than those who did not. If, however, internal networks mattered more, then employees who were members of professional societies would have been more likely to stay at the department.

Whether or not career duration is a sound measure of organizational attachment today, it was certainly a sound measure in the Progressive period. For after 1890, USDA employees worked for the department at a steadily increasing opportunity cost. Private-sector pay for clerical workers, mechanical laborers, and scientists alike was uniformly greater than what the department could afford to pay. One chemist who had left the Bureau of Chemistry told his former colleagues: "I would not have left the Bureau had it been able to pay me $4000 per annum, and *I suspect that many of my associates who have left feel the same way.*"[26] Examples of individuals voicing their decisions in these terms abound in the personnel files of the National Archives. Throughout this period, the USDA employee knew that, eventually, other employers (even other federal agencies) would promise greater financial rewards than the department could offer. After 1900, the acceleration in private-sector pay was greater than the growth rate of USDA employment value. In almost no case could the decision to stay with the USDA be attributed to the economic value of department employment.

The data used to address this question are taken from the personnel files of 856 USDA employees who worked in the department at some time during the years 1891 to 1907. The data were collected from personnel files at the National Personnel Records Center in Saint Louis, Missouri. Specifically, the files include information on race, gender, age, place of birth, marital status, the state and congressional district from which the employee was appointed, whether the employee was raised on a farm, dates of any sickness experienced (and any sick leave taken) while the employee worked for the USDA, all educational information (places and dates of attendance from high school through doctorates), full prior employment and military service histories, and data on whether the employee's parents served in the U.S. military or in the federal civil service. Finally, the data include a battery of efficiency ratings (usually scored by bureau chiefs), including a general efficiency rating and scores for quantity of work done, quality of work done, cooperativeness, and punctuality/reliability. The files also include network data on cooperative publishing and membership in more than twenty professional organizations and interest groups such as the American Chemical Society, the Grange, and the American Farm Bureau Federation and, occasionally, data on whether the employee actively attended professional or annual meetings sponsored by these groups. And for analyses of career duration, the files contain date of entry and exit for employment.

The results of a statistical analysis of the career duration of 856 USDA employees appear in table 7.3. These results suggest that long career tenures at the USDA were traceable more to the USDA's unique web of professional societies than to land-grant college backgrounds. Once hired, USDA employees with land-grant degrees were no more likely to remain with the agency than were employees without these affiliations. The reason, although unclear from the statistical analysis, can be gleaned from employees' personnel files. Land-grant education made USDA employees more susceptible to private and academic offers. Frequently, land-grant college graduates were hired away from the USDA by their former colleges and associated experiment stations. What kept the longer-tenured employees at the USDA was the web of scientific associations

TABLE 7.3

Networks and Status Rewards as the Historical Solution to the Dilemma
of Retaining Experienced Talent

A. Weibull Analysis of Career Duration for USDA Employees Entering between 1891
and 1907

Variable	Coefficients (Standard Errors in Parentheses)
Farm experience	−0.2953+ (0.1410)
Land-grant college education	0.1855 (0.1639)
Doctoral degree	0.5936+ (0.3073)
Previous civil service	−0.4024** (0.1451)
Previous professional employment	−0.5380** (0.2322)
Entering salary (1926 dollars)	−0.000067 (0.000060)
Age at entry	−0.0166** (0.0061)
Pay frequency (salaried = 1; 0 otherwise)	0.4385** (0.1442)
Professional society membership	0.6208** (0.1644)
Bureau/Division chief	0.8199* (0.3344)

B. Summary of Variable Effects on Employment Duration at the USDA

Effect of land-grant college education	No statistically distinguishable effect on work duration
Effect of professional society membership	4.77 years longer tenure
Effect of bureau or division chief status	3.62 years longer tenure

Note: Dependent variable is the log of employees' career length in months. Number of employees = 856; 667 for these estimations. Analysis shows negative duration dependence; the longer employees stayed, the more likely they were to leave.
  *Significant difference from zero at p < .05.
  ** Significant difference from zero at p < .01.
  +Implies significant difference from zero at p < .10. (All tests are two-tailed).
  Marginal effects are calculated at mean of independent variables.

there. More than 67 percent of USDA scientists belonged to one of the professional associations and science clubs in the department, and the benefits of collaboration and scientific fellowship moved members of these organizations to remain in the USDA. Controlling for education, income, position, and other variables, professional society members stayed for four years and nine months longer at the department than employees without professional memberships. Moreover, the department was successful in getting its mezzo-level leaders to remain; bureau and division chiefs stayed three years and six months longer at the USDA than did the average employee.

Significantly, many societies in which USDA employees participated were either unique to the department or located within its walls. The Bureau of Chemistry, for instance, was home to the dominant agricultural chemistry association of the late 1800s and early 1900s—the Association of Official Agricultural Chemists. Fully 76 percent (59 of 78) of the Chemistry Bureau's research scientists in 1905 were AOAC members. USDA employees also created the Rural Economics Club (see chapter 9) and the Washington Botanical Society. These internal organizations mirrored a wider pattern of "joinership" among USDA employees. USDA personnel files from 1905 indicate that in five bureaus alone—Biological Survey, Chemistry, Soils, Plant Industry, and the Secretary's Office—there were 105 members of the American Academy of the Arts and Sciences, 82 members of the American Chemical Society, 54 members of the American Botanical Society, 29 members of the National Geographic Society, and 25 members of Washington's elite Cosmos Club. By contrast, only 13 of the employees in this five-bureau sample were Grange members. As a result, the benefits of membership in scientific organizations were enhanced by staying at the USDA, where fellow group members were abundant.[27]

The Extension of the University: Seaman Knapp, Seed Introduction, and the Rise of Extension

As Wilson pieced together his model department based on autonomous, disciplinary bureaus bound together in the scholastic-corporate idiom, USDA bureau chiefs launched new programs to extend the reach and reputation of the department into the nation. Without coordination, these officials—Beverly T. Galloway in Plant Industry, Harvey Wiley in Chemistry, C. Hart Merriam in Biological Survey, Milton Whitney in Soils, and Gifford Pinchot in Forestry—founded a common method of entrepreneurial administration. The chiefs experimented with new programs, often discovering monies for their initiatives in lump-sum budget funds. These discretionary appropriations were generally freed from statutory limitations on spending.[28] They allowed bureau chiefs to employ workers for whatever purposes were not currently specified in legislation. Experimenting with their ideas and drawing on their unique amalgam of social contacts, these officials mounted quasi-public campaigns for legislation favorable to their bureaus. Some sought broad new grants of federal authority, entailing new functions of state. Others lobbied for authority that had been previously reserved for the states. Some sought existing programs that were housed in other agencies. The unique marker of autonomy, one founded on political legitimacy, was that in nearly every case the bureau chiefs succeeded in expanding their missions.

The symbolic triumph of bureaucratic entrepreneurship occurred after 1901, in the newly organized Bureau of Plant Industry. In 1902 the bureau began a program of cooperative extension—county-based agricultural advising, surveying, and demonstration work—that would come to employ more personnel than any other USDA activity. Although agricultural historians have written myriad works on the subject of extension, they have ignored two facets of its evolution. First, before 1914 extension survived for more than a decade without any statutory funding from Congress. Second, the maturation of the extension program was closely intertwined with the seed exploration efforts begun by Galloway, Wilson, and David Fairchild. In agricultural extension, the USDA transformed nineteenth-century "seed pork" into twentieth-century scientific proselytizing.[29]

The transformation of the seed program had begun under Fairchild in the nineteenth century. By 1900 the department was using different states as experimental plots for its plant introduction program. Mark Carleton tried out durum (macaroni) wheat in Kansas and Missouri, eventually persuading midwestern farmers of its value and launching a crop worth $40 million annually by 1910. In New Mexico the department started growing the nation's first breeds of Egyptian cotton on an experimental plot near La Huerta. The results were sufficiently impressive to induce the operators of a Texas cotton gin to relocate to Carlsbad in 1903. As a result, Egyptian cotton became a staple crop in New Mexico and Arizona after 1905. Some of Galloway's most sustained plant introduction and seed testing efforts were in California. There the Berkeley Experiment Station provided USDA seeds to fruit growers and surveyed private plots in order to assess where imported varieties of seed would grow best. Whereas experimentation was decentralized, control over knowledge, procedure, and information was not. The bureau stood at the center of seed experimentation, distributing experimental capital (seeds), regulating procedure, and serving as a repository of scientific information. All experimental seed varieties were given a number by the department, and in commercial discourse the seed number quickly became the effective name of the seed. The bureau also provided guidelines for proper experimentation and education. Watching these events, the *New York Nation* anticipated the death of congressional free seeds as early as 1902: "The Department of Agriculture no longer plays this farce."[30]

Wilson and Galloway were pleased with the progress of seed introduction in the northern dry Plains region and the West and wanted to expand the program in the South. Yet the department was poorly established in this section of the United States, with few personnel and a reservoir of institutional distrust. The solution to the USDA's southern dilemma came in the person of Professor Seaman A. Knapp (1833–1911), a part-time USDA statistical agent in Louisiana who would become the father of federal agricultural extension. Knapp—Wilson's friend from his days at Iowa Agricultural College—came to the USDA before Wilson's arrival in 1897 and in 1898 proposed to Wilson that he help with fruit and rice introduction in the South. Knapp brought far more than a knowledge of seeds to the department. He also brought a reputation and social ties. He had acquired national renown in agrarian circles for his experiments in growing rice in Texas and Louisiana. He had also written and spoken extensively on the cultivation of rice in the South.

More significantly to department executives, Knapp was deeply embedded in two interstate networks. First, having served as president of Iowa Agricultural College, he was familiar to land-grant college officials. Knapp's experience in political advocacy for federal experiment stations reveals the considerable esteem in which he was held and his centrality in the land-grant college network. Knapp had served as professor of agriculture at Iowa Agricultural College since 1879 and briefly served as its president in 1884. He drafted an experiment-station bill, introduced in the House by C. C. Carpenter of Iowa in 1882, which became a prototype for the Hatch Act of 1887. As chairman of the USDA agricultural convention in 1884, he sponsored a resolution in favor of the Carpenter bill. Second, Galloway, Fairchild, and Wilson recognized that Knapp lay "at the center of the new rice region's activities." Knapp came to power in southern rice-growing networks through his management of a plantation at Lake Charles, Louisiana, beginning in 1886. He superintended the cultivation of rice by northern farmers at Lake Charles and, by force of his spectacular results there, induced thousands of northern farmers to settle in the region and plant rice fields. Many of these farmers joined Knapp's fledgling Rice Association of America in the winter of 1894–95. Later, when the group became the Rice Growers' Association of America, Knapp served as its president. Finally, to teach the lessons he learned at Lake Charles, in December 1897 Knapp founded an agrarian monthly called the *Rice Journal and Gulf Coast Farmer.* Knapp was well known in the Gulf Coast as well as the dry Plains region. He traveled broadly in educational circles and in the network of agricultural journalists and farmers' organizations.[31]

Knapp recommenced correspondence with Wilson in early 1898 and proposed to the secretary that he travel to Japan and collaborate with Fairchild in introducing seeds and fruits. Wilson obliged and hired Knapp full-time as a plant explorer in 1898, using lump-sum funds. Knapp returned with Kiushu rice from Japan, a variety that boosted rice yields by 25 percent. By 1901 it had become the leading rice strain in Louisiana. Yet Wilson and Galloway saw greater promise in Knapp's centrality in southern planter networks than in his talents in growing rice. After Knapp journeyed once more to East Asia and to Hawaii, returning in the summer of 1902, Galloway appointed him "Special Agent for the Promotion of Agriculture in the South." Knapp's new position encompassed rice work, seed and plant introduction for other crops, experimentation, and demonstration of rational farm management on selected farms. Seed work was now being combined with practical training for farmers. In short, Wilson and Galloway employed Knapp to extend the department's reach into southern agrarian society. Knapp would act as "the Department's representative in the South."[32]

Of course, agricultural education was hardly virgin territory in the late 1800s. County fairs and farmers' societies—led by "gentleman cultivators" such as Elkanah Watson and Jesse Buel—helped to disseminate new farming practices in the 1830s. After the Civil War, the itinerant lecturers of the antebellum period gave way to farmers' institutes that invited agrarians to land-grant college campuses (or to towns nearby) for a weekend. By 1901, 2,772 farmers' institutes were held in thirty-eight states, with a total attendance of 819,995 (a figure inflated by the fact that many farmers attended several institutes annually). "Practical education for farmers" was also a principal aim of the Grange and later the Farmers' Alliance. Disappointed by the turn of land-grant colleges to liberal arts education, the Grange and the Alliance supported institutes and organized educational meetings of their own, such as the Alliance clubs of the early 1890s.[33]

The demand for farmer education efforts was strong, but the forces impelling that demand worked only to hamper the movement. Farmers' educational difficulties stemmed from low incomes and high illiteracy rates, particularly in the South, where public education was too meager to remedy these problems. The problems of income and literacy, in turn, were magnified by farmers' high mobility. According to the Thirteenth Census, 54 percent of the farm population in 1910 lived on tracts they had occupied for five years or less. As Fred Shannon summarizes the problem, "There was not the remotest chance of [farmers'] getting acquainted with the soil in that interval." For this predicament the farmers' institutes—with their general principles of cultivation—were of little value. Farmers learned less by studying than by doing and imitating. So, too, poverty and illiteracy constrained farmers' learning. Outside the institutes, the Grange and the Farmers' Alliance contributed little to practical farm education, as they were interested primarily in political education. Louisiana farmer Wayman Hogue said of his weekly meetings with the Alliance club Brothers of Freedom in the early 1890s: "I do not recall [that] any of us ever discussed any subject connected with better farming. We said nothing that would give any enlightenment on such subjects as how to reclaim worn out land, or how to cultivate the land so as to obtain a better yield of crops." By 1900, anyway, the educational programs of the Alliance and the Grange lay dormant.[34]

The department was involved, to a small degree, in these fledgling education efforts. It supported farmers' institutes through its Office of Experiment Stations, particularly after 1903. The USDA also sent millions of farmers' bulletins throughout the South and received the cooperation of southern and western railroad companies, which eagerly sought the bulletins as trumpets of information.

By 1900, however, Knapp, Galloway, and Wilson were convinced that the path of progress lay outside the farmers' institutes and outside the land-grant colleges in particular. Knapp saw A & M colleges not as "agricultural and mechanical" but as "academic and military." Their increasing emphasis on classroom training and liberal arts education poorly served cash-crop farmers.[35]

Knapp still faced the difficult obstacle of funding. Consequently, Galloway devised a clever scheme to support the different facets of Knapp's work through several offices in the Bureau of Plant Industry. He funded plant testing and seed development from the Congressional Free Seed Distribution office, experimentation from the Division of Agrostology, and seed exploration and purchases from the Section of Foreign Seed and Plant Introduction. Proven seed varieties were to be sent to Washington for use in the congressional seed distribution program. This arrangement had the distinct advantage of broadening the range of seeds available to Congress, though no legislator had ever suggested it. In a 1903 visit to Texas farmers, Knapp publicly touted the discretionary basis of the department's funding as a USDA advantage over state institutions.

> The department . . . is better prepared to deal with [the southern cotton] question than State institutions, because there is a great deal of "cast iron" in the appropriations for State institutions, while there is considerable elasticity in the appropriations of the department. Congress, having confidence in the Secretary of Agriculture, has already left it largely to his discretion how the money appropriated through his department shall be used.[36]

With his funding diverse but momentarily secure, Knapp set out in 1903 to transform agricultural education in the South. The teaching of agricultural practice, he felt, must be extended to the farms of ordinary southern planters. He persuaded Galloway to fund the creation of experimental demonstration farms in Texas and later Louisiana. Beginning in the towns of Greenville and Terrell, Texas, in February 1903, Knapp established an experimental farm managed according to his methods: the use of extended and new varieties, deep plowing, liberal fertilizer use, and systematic crop rotation. Terrell farmers cultivated the plots themselves. The township offered them a guaranty fund compensating them for any loss, and the USDA provided only advice and information. Early results were impressive; even while the Mexican boll weevil trimmed the cotton crop, the Terrell demonstrator Walter Porter announced a $700 profit on his experimental land.[37]

After Knapp's success at Terrell, two forces—the crop losses caused by the Mexican boll weevil and the rapid spread of the gospel of demonstration—contributed to the explosion of his program. Losses incurred by the boll weevil infestation prompted Wilson and Galloway to tour Texas and Louisiana in the fall of 1903. The two visited the Terrell farms, and upon their return to Washington, they immediately secured an emergency appropriation for the boll weevil campaign. Brilliantly, Wilson secured the funding with vague terms for its expenditure. Knapp was granted $40,000 to determine the feasibility of "bringing home to the farmer on his own farm information which would enable him to grow cotton despite the presence of the weevil." Emergency funding to combat the weevil was, in Wilson and Knapp's thinking, a grant to expand the community demonstration farm. Most of the boll weevil money was subsequently spent on general education under the demonstration farm, including courses in crop diversity and canning.[38]

Combined with an ambitious speaking tour by USDA officials from 1902 to 1905, the force of observed example generated strong interest in demonstration farms in the towns and counties surrounding Terrell. Neighboring farmers rapidly adopted Porter's methods, and the community demonstration farm proliferated from county to county. As Knapp told Galloway in a November 1903 letter, "The tidal wave for demonstration farms is just beginning." In 1904, after Knapp had established headquarters in Houston, the demonstration work expanded into Louisiana and Arkansas, twenty-four new demonstration agents were employed, and more than seven thousand demonstration farms were created. Knapp used his ties to southern railroad executives to secure free travel for his agents, and the agents used the southern railroad network to launch thousands of new demonstration farms, most of which were located near or on rail lines. At Knapp's suggestion, the agents used an explicit network strategy based on the guaranty fund when arriving to a new community. Instead of trying to persuade conservative local planters to adopt Knapp's system, the agents would typically contact leading merchants and bankers and ask them to arrange a community meeting where a guaranty fund could be raised to protect experimental farms from losses. According to Knapp, the key to winning over local communities was "the support of the press and the co-operation of the best farmers and the leading merchants and bankers." The guaranty fund became the mechanism for local cooperation within the planter communities and between farmers and commercial elites. Knapp used a similar strategy in hiring extension agents, preferring people with "Northern training and Southern experience," with emphasis on men and women who could parlay their familiarity with local elites into legitimacy for his program.[39]

Knapp's continuing cultivation of academic, entrepreneurial, and agrarian networks paid off handsomely in 1905 and 1906. Knapp secured a cooperative agreement between the USDA and the Agricultural and Mechanical College of Texas and had made an earnest friend in the college's president, D. R. Houston. That year Houston introduced Knapp to Frederick T. Gates, chairman of the General Education Board (GEB), a philanthropic group with more than $50 million in funding from John D. Rockefeller Jr. Knapp arranged a meeting with Gates and Wilson in Washington, and the board began to bankroll southern demonstration work in states unaffected by the boll weevil. The board contributed funds for hiring demonstration agents and left Knapp and Wilson in full control of the administration of the program. By 1908 Knapp's agents had taken the gospel of scientific cultivation to more than 14,000 farms; two years later, 460 workers under Knapp's direction reached 100,000 farms in all the southern states. By 1910 Galloway had authorized Knapp to distribute more than 1 million USDA circulars and thousands of farmers' bulletins throughout the South.[40]

Galloway and Wilson were at once pleased and ambitious for program expansion. Cooperative demonstration was establishing a department foothold in the cotton-growing South. The USDA, through the Bureau of Plant Industry, remained the largest contributor of funds to the demonstration program. And Knapp now resided in Washington, D.C., and worked out of department headquarters, showering the cotton states with extensive publicity. As Knapp wrote in 1908, "The initial move is an aroused public sentiment in favor of doing better." Wilson and Galloway kept in daily contact with Knapp, seeing in his work a department-directed transformation of southern institutions.

> In addition to the general line of increased crop production, the work of Doctor Knapp has been instrumental in reforming rural conditions and directing public sentiment in the right lines over a large extent of territory. His agents have been thoroughly drilled along proper lines of effort to be made to aid the people. *It is absolutely necessary in his work that he should reach and control public opinion.* To this end it has been necessary for Doctor Knapp to influence any great force that is operating in the states in which he is working. For instance, he is cooperating with the National Farmers' Union . . . and he has been more or less influential in directing their energies to the ameliorating of some of the common evils, such as the advance money system and the condition of rural homes, the improvement of schools, etc. The agents under Doctor Knapp have been instructed to drop in, from time to time, as they are passing through the country, and talk to the children in these rural schools for five or ten minutes, and they are told definitely what to say and how to get at the people. Last summer Doctor Knapp spent the entire portion of warm weather addressing State meetings of teachers and Summer Schools that have been organized by Universities throughout the South. In that way he was able to reach nearly 8,000 teachers and secure their cooperation in redirecting rural matters in the South.[41]

Even though the cooperative demonstration program depended on favorable southern opinion, Knapp's diverse coalition of support for extension left him politically independent. General Education Board money insulated Knapp and Galloway from southern agrarian demands articulated through Congress, and lump-sum funding from Congress, in turn, insulated Knapp from the board's demands. State and local money protected Knapp's demonstrators from board and agrarian demands. Consistent with this logic, neither the General Education Board nor Congress ever placed procedural limitations on the program. The program was Knapp's alone to run as he wished. The only constraints envisioned by Congress or the board were procedural protections for Knapp's demonstration work.

Beginning in 1907, Knapp took the extension idea in new and unpredictable directions. As Galloway had hoped, Knapp set out to transform southern agriculture through the systematic education of farm youth. Knapp had watched with growing interest the fledgling organization of boys' clubs in Mississippi under William H. Smith. Smith's clubs provided children with literature, seeds, and experimental plots where they could raise staple crops, usually corn. Smith also organized southern girls into "culture study clubs," where they were taught sewing, bread making, and baking. Knapp hired Smith as a collaborator in 1907, and the school superintendent quickly enrolled three thousand boys and six hundred girls in "corn clubs" in a single year. After visiting Smith in 1908, Knapp resolved to take control of Smith's program and create a comprehensive youth education system to parallel the southern cooperative demonstration program. Knapp lined up support from the General Education Board, hired county school superintendents as USDA employees, and designed a curriculum that favored the concept of cost efficiency over brute productivity.[42]

In many respects, Knapp's children's clubs reinforced prevailing gender and race hierarchies in the South. Boys studied "agricultural science," and girls were taught "domestic science." Moreover, "Negro clubs" were organized separately from groups for white youth. In other ways, by introducing southern girls to schooling with established curricula and by tapping into the broader Progressive movement of domestic science, Knapp's system gave new momentum to public education for southern women. Knapp also overcame southern resistance to boys' clubs for blacks and succeeded in recruiting black clergy into the clubs. The cultural legacy of Knapp's club system was a mixture of traditionalism and progressivism.[43]

After 1910, Knapp's clubs proliferated throughout the South. Corn clubs were met by pig clubs in which children raised animals for county fairs under the tutelage of USDA agents, potato clubs in Tennessee, poultry clubs in Mississippi, and "baby beef," mutton, and dairy clubs in Texas. In 1908 10,300 southern boys were enrolled in corn clubs as "boy demonstrators"; by 1912 there were 70,000. Knapp achieved this expansion with only $40,000 in funding, just over half from the USDA. Critics disagreed over whether the children were making a material difference in southern farming, but Knapp knew that the impact of the program was not economic and short-term but cultural and long-term. He was teaching a generation of southern rural youth that their future livelihoods depended on a progressive understanding of their trade and that the department was an institution friendly to their culture and welfare.[44]

Knapp delegated USDA work with girls' clubs to Mississippi teacher Marie Cromer, whom he had met on one of his many southern lecture tours. Together with O. B. Martin, a department agent, Cromer immediately began recruiting southern women to lead girls' clubs in various states. The department named organizers in Virginia, Mississippi, North Carolina, and Tennessee in 1910. Enrollment shot from 3,000 girls in 1911 to 30,000 in fourteen states by 1913. The clubs taught canning and the rudiments of domestic science. By 1913 the department's girls' clubs had developed a simple emblem that stands today as a hallmark of rural life in twentieth-century America: the 4-H symbol, representing "head, heart, hands, and health." This symbolism demonstrated a holistic approach to the education of women and, more broadly, a comprehensive scientific practice of farm life. In the Progressive Era, it united the girls' clubs and gave them a unified movement identity.[45]

Involvement with domestic science circles was hardly foreign to the department. Although the movement's leadership consisted primarily of upper- and middle-class white women from New York and Chicago, USDA officials figured centrally in the formation of the American Home Economics Association. Nutrition specialist C. F. Langworthy chaired the 1908 committee that wrote the association's constitution. Assistant Secretary Willet M. Hays addressed the Lake Placid Women's Conference in 1908, and farmers' institute expert John Hamilton and experiment station expert A. C. True addressed the association's first annual meeting in Washington in 1909. The association's women also lobbied Congress vigorously for increased funding for USDA nutrition research.[46]

As southern extension grew, it became increasingly clear that one traditional USDA ally—the land-grant college—did not view the program favorably. Land-grant officials, with their mission of educating the cultivators of their states, rightly regarded cooperative demonstration as a threat to their institutions. Knapp's early overtures to the colleges for participation in the extension program were met with silence. USDA county agents who tried to cooperate with the North Carolina College of Agriculture encountered such an icy reception that they relocated their office to another town. In 1912 officials of the Bureau of Plant Industry achieved a breakthrough, contracting with Clemson College in South Carolina to cooperate fully in demonstration work. Five other state colleges followed Clemson's lead that year. The fact that the department cracked land-grant resistance in Clemson is hardly surprising, given that USDA division chiefs had established a hiring conduit from the college in the 1880s. Clemson alumni in the department included county agent Harmon Benton, chemist and Wiley associate James Breazeale, cotton specialist George E. Carr, and plant disease expert Haven Metcalf. The 1912 agreement laid a foundation for more formal cooperation between the states and the USDA in the Smith-Lever Act of 1914. Nonetheless, the historical implications of the early land-grant resistance are significant. Scholars such as Kenneth Finegold and Theda Skocpol rightly regard land-grant colleges as central players in the "nexus of institutions" in early-twentieth-century agriculture. Yet in cooperative extension, arguably the most profound institutional transformation in American agriculture from the Populist Revolt to the New Deal, land-grant colleges came late and reluctantly to policy development.[47]

Seaman Asahel Knapp died in 1911. The sheer numerical weight of his achievement was astonishing. He had left more than 30,000 demonstration farms superintended by the department's traveling agents, representing more than 70,000 cooperating farmers. He also had 50,000 boy demonstrators working in School Corn Clubs. At his passing, he was supervising 550 employees and had sent out more than 2 million circulars annually throughout the southern states. In all, the department counted more than 100,000 cooperating farms in the southern states by 1912. All of this germinated from a single county experiment in Terrell, Texas, in 1903. Upon his death, William Taylor, chief of the Bureau of Plant Industry, proclaimed Knapp "the highest type of our service." In his combination of science with folkish democratic vision, Knapp had sculpted in his own person the model USDA bureaucrat as well as creating the model USDA program. The department could hardly have done better, then, when it hired Knapp's son Bradford to replace him.[48]

Southern Extension: Outgrowth of Populism or Bureaucratic Innovation?

How should one interpret the evolution of southern extension? Was it the outgrowth of the post-Populist education movement in southern agriculture, refracted through growing assertiveness among southern agrarians in Congress? In some respects, one can interpret Knapp's system as a response to demands for farmer education that grew out of the didactic agenda of the Grange and the Farmers' Alliance. Yet in most respects, this rendering misleads. The Alliance and the Farmers' Union may have favored education, but none of its leaders had ever envisioned the farm-to-farm demonstration method that Knapp and Galloway had championed. Elizabeth Sanders renames Knapp's momentum as "the intensely popular rural education movement," but no organizational basis for the diffusion of county demonstrators existed outside the USDA until the northern farm bureaus after 1910. Only when Knapp commenced the cooperative demonstration program did southerners begin to perceive its value. If anything, Alliance remnants at first favored the dominant alternative to Knapp's county-based system: the farmers' institute. Beyond this, Knapp's agents consciously shied away from the political and cooperative organizing that lay at the center of the Alliance vision.[49]

Was agricultural extension yet another legacy of the corporate liberalism that Gabriel Kolko and Martin J. Sklar have eloquently detailed? After all, the General Education Board funded it. Knapp's cooperative demonstrators eschewed political radicalism, and for many southern planters and landowners the demonstration system was seen as a helpful counterweight to the radical tendencies of former Alliance organizers and the Farmers' Union. Nor did southern railroads mind the increased production that extension was sure to effect among cotton and rice farms. Yet the General Education Board could hardly control the program, and the very structure of cooperative demonstration defied the hierarchical social structures favored among southern elites. Knapp's program succeeded in the South precisely because it eschewed paternalism: farmers demonstrated to other farmers.

What cries out for narrative explanation in the evolution of southern extension is the peculiar institutional forms that it bequeathed to twentieth-century agriculture. From 1903 through the entire twentieth century, agricultural education in the United States was organized on a county basis. Why? After 1900, the predominant form of American agricultural education consisted not of rote instruction but of demonstration, assisted diffusion, and imitation. Why? The answer lies in Knapp's invention of the cooperative demonstration technique and its advocacy by Galloway and Wilson. Without Knapp, no county-based system of cooperative demonstration would have appeared in the South before 1910, perhaps not until after the First World War. Without the backing of Galloway and Wilson, and the administrative home that the Bureau of Plant Industry provided for Knapp's vision, it is difficult to see how Knapp's program could have achieved the meteoric growth that it did. By 1910 lump-sum appropriations dominated GEB money in extension funding. In summary, southern cooperative demonstration is an example of bureaucratic autonomy conditioned upon reputation. It was a program that no one demanded and that some interests actively opposed. It was a southern program funded at first with monies intended not for education but for seeds and for boll weevil eradication. It grew in funding only when a Republican Congress, whose constituents could hardly be said to be the main beneficiaries of the program, began to perceive the program's general value. Finally, the USDA's leeway in running extension grew only as fast and as far as Galloway and Knapp could demonstrate the worth of their experiment.

By cementing the department's reputation in the South, the Farmers' Cooperative Demonstration Work (FCDW) also paved the way for future autonomy. As early as 1908, southern farm leaders were convinced that Knapp's cooperative demonstration model was far superior to the farmers' institutes. As Mississippi Agricultural College president John C. Hardy admitted, Knapp's program "is even better than institute work, for [Knapp's agents] are in touch with the actual farmer for 365 days in the year." USDA surveys of southern farmers supported Hardy's judgment, although they also showed the limits of any educational campaign in the South. When C. C. Anderson surveyed fifty-three farmers in Tallapoosa County, Alabama, in September 1912, he found only three members of the Farmers' Union and three who had attended a farmers' institute (see table 7.4). He also found that just over one-third of the number of cultivators read a farm newspaper. What Anderson did find was wide readership—about two-thirds of Tallapoosa County farmers—of the USDA farmers' bulletins that Knapp had been sending throughout the South. He also found that twelve had been instructed by extension agents, eight having changed their farming practices after the lessons. Although these were not astounding numbers, they dwarfed the comparative reach of the institutes or the NFU.[50]

TABLE 7.4

The Relative Influence of the USDA in Tallapoosa County, Alabama, 1912

	Number	Percentage of Total
Total farmers surveyed	53	100
Farmers owning land	34	64
Farmers renting	19	36
Schooling		
Number having some public schooling	45	85
Number having attended high school	1	2
Readership		
Number receiving *Farmers' Bulletins*	35	66
Number receiving them directly from the USDA	29	55
Number reporting that they read the *Bulletins*	31	58
Number receiving at least one farm paper	19	36
Number receiving *Southern Cultivator*	9	17
Number receiving *Home and Farm*	7	13
Practical Education		
Number reporting farmers' institutes within "easy reach"	22	42
Number attending farmers' institutes	3	6
Number reporting changed practices as a result of farmers' institutes	0	0
Number receiving instructions from extension agents	12	23
Number reporting changed practices as a result of extension	8	15
Number belonging to Farmers' Union	3	6

Source: "Summary of Tabulation," in "Tabulation of Influence Survey Reports for Sept. 4, 5 and 6, 1912," in C. C. Anderson File, Records of the Bureau of Agricultural Economics; NA II, RG 83, E 133, B1, F "Anderson, C. C."

Note: Survey results of 53 farmers. Only aggregates are reported on the worksheet. Cross-tabulations are not available.

In the aggregate, the USDA was nowhere less entrenched than the South be-fore 1900, and nowhere *more* established after 1910. Of the department's 1,773 field offices in February 1912, more than half (904) were in the states of the former Confederacy. This southern shift had occurred *before* Democratic con-trol of the House in 1910, and it occurred despite the fact that most USDA em-ployees came disproportionately from the northern Plains (see figure 6.2). It was an administrative invasion, surely not one induced by Congress or by Theodore Roosevelt. Read in the light of economic history, the southern ex-tension program was, for its time, a massive redirection of human capital from the land-grant colleges of the Midwest to the cotton and rice fields of the South.[51]

Legitimacy in Congress: Grass-Roots Entrepreneurship and Cooperative Extension, 1910–17

By the time Rep. Asbury Lever penned his first bill for a national system of agri-cultural extension in 1911, the Department of Agriculture had been running an extension system for eight years. Continuing to manage demonstration work out of lump-sum funds with broad expenditure powers, USDA officials ex-panded the system into the North and mixed extension with economic analyses and management studies. When Congress finally passed the Smith-Lever Act in 1914, hundreds of thousands of farmers were already under the cooperative demonstration system, and the number of visitors to the department's experi-mental farms probably exceeded 10 million. In the Smith-Lever Act, Congress had simply given statutory recognition to a system of the USDA's making.

William Spillman and the Northward Migration of Extension

When Bradford Knapp replaced his father as director of the Farmers' Cooper-ative Demonstration Work in 1911, extension was purely a southern program. It received little better than ridicule from northern farmers and agricultural col-lege officials. Extension, after all, had grown in direct response to the boll wee-vil crisis. Northerners questioned the value of Knapp's program outside the cot-ton-growing South.

Not William Spillman. Raised in Missouri, and having taught at Washington State College until 1902, Spillman shared other northerners' ignorance of southern agriculture. Nonetheless, he was deeply persuaded of the wisdom of Knapp's methods for transforming agricultural practice. Spillman became more than simply the founder of government extension in the northern states. He also effected the lasting marriage between extension and agricultural economics in America, the institutional fusion of central planning and local learning.

Spillman was hired in the classic bureau-based recruitment style that marked the Department of Agriculture after the 1880s. Delivering a paper before the Association of American Agricultural Colleges and Experiment Stations (AAACES) in 1901, he caught the attention of Galloway, then chief of the Bureau of Plant Industry. Spillman had all the credentials of the upwardly mobile USDA official. He had received bachelor's and master's degrees at the land-grant University of Missouri, served as professor of agriculture at Washington State, and directed the Washington state experiment station. He was also a widely popular farm institute lecturer. Seeking an analyst for studies of grasses and hays in the West, Galloway eagerly offered a new position to Spillman, who quickly took the job.[52]

Spillman was driven by an enduring fascination with the variation in productivity across farms and across regions. If the factors separating productive farms from poorer ones could be systematically studied and drawn out, he reasoned, American agriculture would unlock a key to economic progress. Spillman suspected that a crucial variable in agricultural productivity was "the organization of the farm," which he considered "an important managerial function." Galloway agreed with Spillman and employed numerous sources of lump-sum funding to allow him to begin management studies. Galloway then placed Spillman in charge of the new Office of Farm Management in 1905. Spillman directed his agents to study the practices and organization of "successful" farms. Fred G. Allison saw his task as "locating successful farmers in Iowa." Charles L. Goodrich published his study, *A Profitable Cotton Farm*, as a USDA farmers' bulletin in 1909. Typical of the reports was G. J. Abbott's "Description of the Farm of Earle A. Blakelee," an Ohio cultivator. Abbott's study was painstaking, detailing the full acreage, stock, and soil conditions of Blakelee's farm and listing Blakelee's annual expenses and receipts for everything from fertilizer ($72.70) to chicken feed ($3.10). Yet Abbott saved his closest scrutiny for Blakelee's "strong personality."

> He is a careful buyer, a good salesman, shrewd in making a bargain, having the Yankee trait of dickering well developed. He takes pride in doing all his work well and his farm is a model of neatness. His financial success is, we believe, due to several causes: first, his system of cropping seems well adapted to the conditions; second, he is a good buyer and salesman; third, he attends carefully to the details of his business; fourth, he is a hard worker.[53]

Spillman's office quickly grew in size and reputation. His agents were known as "Agriculturists," and Spillman as "Agriculturist in charge of Farm Management," titles that reflected the uneasy status of farm management studies in the department and in social science in general. He hoped to advance the prestige of his calling by creating a professional organization and by demonstrating the value of his studies to Congress. He succeeded in the first goal by founding the American Farm Management Association in July 1910. Spillman ran the association, serving as its first president. In 1910, three years after the association had begun annual meetings in Iowa, its membership reached seventy-one officials and agronomists, including the leaders of thirty-four state colleges. The land-grant luminaries included C. W. Pugsley of Nebraska University, G. F. Warren of Cornell University, and William Jardine of Kansas State University. Soon members of Congress were privately asking him to detail his agents to farms in their districts. Yet Spillman knew that by 1912, his fledgling farm management program stood at an administrative impasse. Studies were mounting but little used in the field. Spillman could not find a way to reproduce Knapp's success in disseminating information.[54]

Just as Knapp achieved his successes in the heart of the National Farmers' Union in Texas and Louisiana, Spillman saw his breakthrough in northern New York, the stronghold of the Grange after 1900. In the spring of 1910 the Binghamton Chamber of Commerce joined with the Delaware, Lackawanna, and Western Railroad to create a model farm. Northern New York had suffered from a depressed agricultural economy for three decades—typified by erosion and abandoned farms—and the Lackawanna Railroad and Binghamton Chamber were interested in means to boost the county economy. Before implementing their plans, officials of the chamber and the Lackawanna visited the Department of Agriculture in Washington and sought advice. Spillman met the men and persuaded them to abandon the model farm in favor of a single USDA agent who would advise Binghamton farmers on improved management practices. With a memorandum of understanding signed on March 20, 1911, the Broome County experiment was begun. Spillman appointed John H. Barron to supervise farms in the Binghamton area, and the county's farmers organized the Broome County Farm Improvement Association to assist Barron in disseminating information.[55]

The Broome County experiment established a county-level linkage between the USDA adviser and organized farmers. Similar arrangements began to spread through the Ohio Valley and northern Plains states. County farm organizations cropped up in Pettis County, Missouri, in Minneapolis and Saint Paul, in South Dakota, and in Kankakee County, Illinois. Many groups expressed the hope that their institutional arrangements would translate the department's research into better farm outcomes. The Better Farming Association of North Dakota wanted to transmit "personally to the individual operating his own farm the results of investigations as obtained by the Department of Agriculture, the Experiment Stations, and similar agencies." The forces propelling the spread of county agents received two further boosts from industrial philanthropists, both with significant ties to USDA officials. Julius Rosenwald of Sears, Roebuck, and Company raised funds for 110 counties in Illinois. By August, Galloway was meeting regularly with the comptroller of the Rosenwald fund. Meanwhile, Seaman Knapp had focused the attention of the General Education Board on New England just before his death in 1911, and board money helped fund farm agent work in New Hampshire that year.[56]

At this time Spillman took a new interest in unifying the scattered and disparate extension efforts in the North. He outlined his new vision in letters to Liberty Hyde Bailey, one of the nation's most famous scientific agrarians, and Director J. L. Hills of the Vermont experiment station. Spillman took Knapp's Farmers' Cooperative Demonstration Work as a template for his efforts. He sought to place a farm adviser, paid by the department, in each congressional district in the nation. The department and the state agricultural college would jointly supervise the agents, who would visit farms, demonstrate scientific agriculture, and advance to farm-institute lecturing after several years. While adopting Knapp's ideas, Spillman also knew that farm advising in the northern states would need to be adapted to the larger, more capitalized agriculture of the region. He envisioned not the practical teachers of Knapp's system but "men whom college graduates on the farm will be glad to have visit them." By early 1912 Spillman had hammered out an agreement with Bradford Knapp so as not to intrude in the southern states. He and Galloway also signed an agreement for field studies in Iowa that spring. Spillman abandoned the congressional district as a unit of organization and now sought to place one agent per county. He also secured funding from nonfederal sources, including the International Harvester Company, maker of the revolutionary McCormick reaper. By 1913, International Harvester faithfully subscribed to the principles of county-based cooperative demonstration and agreed to help Spillman create "county improvement associations." Spillman also warmed to the idea of local financial assistance in supporting his agents, committing the department to paying half of the agents' salaries.[57]

In selecting its extension agents, Spillman's office relied on many of the same institutional selection principles that had governed the department for almost three decades. Starting extension work in California, C. B. Smith contacted university officials and business leaders in the hope of recruiting agents who could travel among fruit growers to demonstrate the most experimentally successful seeds, machines, and methods of cultivation and management. In a letter to E. O. McCormick of the Southern Pacific railroad, Smith outlined his criteria.

> The idea in this work is to secure men who have had the best possible training in agriculture which is afforded by our best agricultural institutions; men who in addition to having been born and brought up on a farm have, since graduation, had three or four years' practical agricultural experience, and place these men permanently in counties, with the understanding that they shall devote their whole time to a study of the agricultural problems of the county and to advising with the farmers with reference to the handling of crops, stock, and the organization of the farm.[58]

Spillman's plans found support in Congress. In August 1912 Congress appropriated $300,000 for the USDA to "investigate and encourage the adoption of improved methods of farm management and farm practice, and for farm demonstration work." The appropriation was noteworthy for two reasons. First, as aggrieved southerners would admit years later, the August 1912 bill was the first *explicit* federal expenditure for extension work, even though Knapp's system had been running for nine years in the South. Second, the language of the bill explicitly reflected Spillman's vision of linking "farm management" with "farm demonstration." The Agriculture Committees were clearly taking cues from Spillman and his Office of Farm Management.[59]

Yet it was this very coziness between Congress and the department that many land-grant officials found insufferable. Whereas state college officials had previously muted their uneasiness about the department's plans, now they offered vociferous opposition. New Jersey's J. G. Lipman questioned the very "right" of the department to venture into the college's extension territory, and Dean Eugene Davenport of the University of Illinois saw in Spillman's plans a "gigantic scheme" that would subjugate the land grants to the department. The USDA overcame these objections only by securing support from the figurative dean of the land-grant community: Liberty Hyde Bailey at Cornell. Bailey warmly endorsed Spillman's Broome County work in New York and committed Cornell resources toward its growth. Having split the land-grant community, the northern extension program proceeded state by state, into Iowa, Pennsylvania, New Jersey, and most Great Lakes states by the end of 1912. Spillman offered advice to any state interested in extension, guiding New Jersey away from model farms to a county agent system in 1913. By the time of Wilson's inauguration, Spillman's program had become so popular that he could override state-level opposition. When resistance from the Agricultural and Mechanical College of Oklahoma and the State Board of Agriculture became intense, Spillman threatened to pull his forces out of the state entirely. Oklahoma farmers were so distraught at the prospect that Rep. Robert L. Owen was reduced to supplication. Admitting "injurious political influences" in the state colleges and promising to "get things in much better condition," Owen pleaded with the USDA to keep its agents in his state.[60]

From 1912 to 1914, operating from a broad appropriation and a reservoir of trust in Congress, Spillman dispersed extension agents to 234 counties in the northern and western states. In the Great Lakes and northern Plains where academics had joined business-wary farmers in opposition to his plans, Spillman planted the seeds for a nationwide system. He also ignited an enduring fascination among northerners for combining county extension with the scientific study of farm management. More than anything else, this fusion of programs was Spillman's lasting achievement.

Legitimacy in Congress: A Reputational Perspective on the Smith-Lever Act of 1914

When the Sixty-second Congress began in 1911, support for some form of agricultural extension was strong. Legislators introduced sixteen bills providing for federal funding of extension work. In the following two years, Congress struggled to agree on a unified program for extension that would appeal to farmers and officials of all regions and levels of government. The popularity of extension was a truly public and Progressive phenomenon. Business and university groups, agrarian organizations, and the Progressive and Democratic Parties showered their favor on the plan. Yet the broad political embrace of extension during the Sixty-second Congress is misleading in two respects. First, as several historians have recognized, the breadth of support obscures the fact that by 1911 many politicians had jumped on the extension bandwagon. Business federations, professional associations, and Congress came late, not early, to the extension movement. Second, agreement on the need for a national extension system masked sharp discord over what kind of extension should be practiced. Land-grant colleges and farmers' groups favored the nineteenth-century "institute model" whereby traveling agents visited farm shows and county fairs. The USDA found the institute model useless and supported a "county-agent model" whereby information was disseminated not through traveling lecturers but through agents residing in counties and local farmers organized into county-level bureaus. Whereas the Grange and the NFU favored extension in *concept* before 1910, their support of the county-agent plan did not precede but followed the USDA's experiments. Only when Spillman and Knapp—without any help from the major farm groups, and with much of their funding independent of Congress—had displayed the value of the cooperative demonstration model in the North and the South did national agreement on a unified extension program become possible. In its timing and especially in its form, the Progressive system of agricultural extension reflected a broad and conscious pattern of deference to the Department of Agriculture.[61]

After 1910, proposals for federal funding for extension flourished, and they received unprecedented support from national parties, elite politicians, and business interests. The new voices for federal extension lay in three organizations. The first and most powerful of the three was the Association of American Agricultural Colleges and Experiment Stations. The association created an extension committee in 1904, and by 1910 the committee was under the leadership of Kenyon Butterfield, one of the leaders of the institute movement before 1900. After 1910 Butterfield's committee was an important venue of legislation drafting and coalition building. The second group, the National Soil Fertility League, was established by prominent industrialists and included Taft, William Jennings Bryan, and Samuel Gompers in its advisory committee. The league had the unique role of securing national business support for agricultural extension. A third voice, largely dormant by 1911 but still influential in establishing a consensual policy agenda for the Progressive period, was Theodore Roosevelt's Commission on Country Life. The commission suggested a "nationwide extension network" in its highly influential 1909 report.[62]

The AAACES, the Soil Fertility League, and the Commission on Country

Life were starkly distinct organizations. They reflected different, and frequently opposed, interests in Progressive American society. Yet they were united in two crucial respects. First, all three organizations were heavily influenced by USDA officials. The AAACES took numerous cues from its consultation with USDA dairy expert B. F. Rawl. Gifford Pinchot was among the most vocal and powerful members of the Commission on Country Life, and "Uncle" Henry Wallace of Iowa, another member of the commission, was a lifelong friend of Secretary Wilson. Not surprisingly, then, the other factor uniting the three groups was their slow but steady convergence upon the USDA's county-agent model as the preferred form of extension. The Soil Fertility League, led by Howard Gross of Chicago, became "a powerful exponent of the Knapp demonstration technique." The commission's support of a unified network in its 1909 report was in sharp contrast to proposals to let the land-grant colleges run a system as they wished. Even the AAACES, which favored the greater land-grant autonomy of the institute model in 1910, came to support the Knapp-Spillman program by 1914.[63]

In Congress legislators' attention usually focused on one extension bill among numerous alternatives. After Michigan representative James McLaughlin's bill died in the House Agriculture Committee in 1909, supporters shifted their efforts to two bills introduced by Iowa senator Jonathan Dolliver in 1910. Dolliver's proposals were noteworthy for two reasons. Initially, Dolliver chaired the Senate Committee on Agriculture and Forestry, and his first bill reflected the preferences of land-grant college officials and agrarian organizations. It provided not for the county demonstrators of the Spillman-Knapp program but for lump-sum grants to agricultural colleges, without federal oversight of state expenditures. In a noticeable slap to the USDA and a bow to the concerns of land-grant officials such as Illinois's Eugene Davenport, Dolliver's bill transferred all administration of federal extension to the Interior Department. Despite these provisions, Dolliver's bill received the unanimous support of the greater farmers' organizations, including the National Farmers' Union, the National Grange, and the National Farmers' Congress.[64]

The other feature of Dolliver's proposals reflected the peculiar convergence of agrarian and labor interests during the Progressive period. Dolliver's second bill provided for federal funds for vocational education. The Senate Agriculture Committee report merged the extension and vocational education bills, creating a single "practical education" measure for farmers and laborers. Dolliver's design for vocational education drew heavily on a popular bill first introduced in 1907 by Rep. Charles R. Davis of Minnesota. Davis sought federal funding for vocational education at high schools and agricultural "normal" schools. The growing popularity of Davis's plan, peaking with Dolliver's adoption of it, tapped into a larger "industrial education" movement dating from the 1880s. Animated by business concerns that American schools lagged behind Europe's classrooms in skill training, and by working-class disaffection with the liberal arts curricula of the grammar school, "industrial education" was the dominant educational ideal of the Progressive Era. Its broad array of backers found an organizational voice in the National Society for the Promotion of Industrial Education (NSPIE), an odd amalgamation of industrial betterment enthusiasts (Jane Addams), union leaders (John Golden of the United Textile Workers), and scientific management ideologues (Frederick Taylor himself). The movement's figurative leader was NSPIE secretary Charles Allen Prosser, a student of education reformer and Columbia professor David Snedden.[65]

In combining extension with vocational education, Dolliver's hybrid offered something for everyone. It provided $5 million for vocational education in city schools, $5 million for agricultural high schools, $1.5 million for extension departments in land-grant colleges, and $1 million for the training of vocational teachers by state normal schools. In addition to major farm group advocacy, the Dolliver bill received endorsements from the American Federation of Labor and the National Education Association. Appealing to interests across classes and regions, the Dolliver bill seemed a strong candidate for passage in the progressive Sixty-first Senate. Yet in June 1910 the higher chamber flushed it. Initially, Dolliver failed to secure favor from some of industrial education's stronger backers. Prosser, Snedden, and others weighed in with skepticism. The reason for this lukewarm reception, however, had much to do with the bill's administrative details. Dolliver's embrace of the institute model of extension—and the bill's dumping of funds on land-grant colleges with few strings attached—raised fears about the colleges' ideology and their capacity to carry out a national system. Further, the Interior Department's reputation as the captured "agency of the West" buttressed Snedden's complaint that the Dolliver plan was crafted "with a view to the needs of the southern and western portions of the country." Snedden made plain the NSPIE's wishes. It rejected the "liberal" institute model of the land-grant colleges. It desired a system independent of Interior yet under centralized control, a strong hint of favor for management by the USDA. Finally, the NSPIE wanted federal monitoring of state college expenditures, preferably by the USDA. The Dolliver bill flew in the face of these demands. Little wonder that extension's esteemed architect, the USDA, was silent on the proposal.[66]

Dolliver died unexpectedly in October 1910. From 1911 to 1913, his bill was reincarnated in numerous measures introduced before Congress by Vermont senator Carroll S. Page. Page's bills consciously reflected the now lucid preference of Congress and the NSPIE for a turn toward the USDA's county-agent model. His 1912 measure gave administration of the vocational and extension programs to the Agriculture Department and replaced the flat grant of $1.5 million to the land-grant colleges with a sequence of annual outlays monitored by the USDA. Then Page's bill began to take a downward course similar to Dolliver's. With the Interior Department and blanket authority for state colleges removed from the cauldron, the difficulties of the vocational-extension marriage rose to the surface. The NSPIE had clearly influenced Page's 1912 proposal—Snedden and Prosser drafted it—and pushed hard for the bill. The Grange and NFU also fell solidly in line behind it. Yet AAACES members wanted vocational education and extension separated, and they pulled their support from Page.

At this point a new figure—Rep. Asbury Lever, Democrat of South Carolina—took center stage in the extension debate. With the Democratic takeover of the House in 1910, Lever ascended to the position of second in command in the House Agriculture Committee. The department was already deeply embedded in South Carolina agriculture, but Seaman Knapp's strong relationship with Lever would prove of inestimable value for the USDA in securing an extension system of its fashioning. Long before the Democratic takeover, Knapp had met Lever and won the legislator over to his methods. Simply put, Lever worshiped at Knapp's altar. He praised Knapp's incremental approach and his broader aims of economic and social transformation, remarking that Knapp "was laying the foundations firmly and cautiously for a new agriculture and a new rural life in the South." Knapp, meanwhile, had been shrewdly placing a disproportionate share of FCDW agents in Lever's district, amounting to three of South Carolina's ten agents by 1910. Little wonder that Lever later announced himself Knapp's "devoted disciple." Of his role in the process, he claimed only that he "had some small part in crystallizing the ideals of Doctor Knapp into permanent law."[67]

Beginning in 1911, Lever introduced a series of extension measures into the House, but it was his 1912 bill, also backed by Senator Hoke Smith of Georgia, that won approval from the House committee. "Your committee," its members wrote, "is informed and believes that [Knapp's] system brings home to the actual farmer upon his actual farm the best methods of agriculture." The full House quickly approved the bill without a roll-call vote on August 23. The only amendment to Lever's bill was an expression of faith in the USDA's efforts: no national program could disrupt the department's southern demonstration work.

When Lever's bill reached the Senate, it lacked any mention of vocational education. Senator Page quickly changed that. He ingeniously substituted his combined vocational-extension bill for the Smith-Lever measure, having added some of Lever's provisions to appease agrarian members who increasingly favored the USDA's county-agent system. Although Smith and others warned of troubles in reconciling the House and Senate versions, the major farm groups joined with the NSPIE in universal support of Page's hybrid measure. Page then surprised the opponents and supporters of national extension by replacing the hybrid with his original bill, which excluded key elements of the Lever measure. Page's bill barely passed the Senate on January 29, 1913, but his measure died in the House-Senate conference, just as Smith had warned.[68]

The decline of Page's bill sounded the death knell for efforts to fuse vocational education with agricultural extension. The issue was not simply fusion.

Page had not paid sufficient respect to the growing appeal of the existing extension program, a respect that was encoded in Lever's House bill. The plank of Page's substitute that most angered southern congressmen was the one that deleted their most cherished guarantee: assurance that the Agriculture Department's program of southern demonstration would be unscathed by any national effort.

As the Sixty-second Congress convened in the spring of 1913, then, many emboldened legislators began to insist on a Knapp-Spillman system. Still, most legislators knew little, if anything, about the various proposals. Many had heard of the USDA's burgeoning program, however, and they turned increasingly to the department for information and advice. Iowa senator William Kenyon's letter to USDA secretary David Franklin Houston in April 1913 is exemplary.

> Dear Mr. Hueston [sic]:
>
> I am very desirous of securing some information relative to the "Farm Demonstration Work" being carried on by the Bureau of Plant Industry. I refer to the co-operation of the Government with County organizations in the employement [sic] of county farm demonstrators.
>
> I would appreciate it very much if you would give me full history of this work as carried on by your department through the office of Mr. Spielman [sic], also the appropriations that have been asked for and the different amounts granted by Congress. . . .
>
> Yours very truly, [signed] Wm. S. Kenyon

Kenyon's letter strikingly reveals the limits and the substance of what Congress knew about extension in 1913. Consider first that a powerful senator—Kenyon later chaired the vaunted Farm Bloc of the early 1920s—sought information about *congressional appropriations* from an *executive* agency. The request indicates just how severely Congress had begun to depend on the department for information about agricultural policy in the Progressive Era. Beyond this, Kenyon tacitly acknowledges that the USDA was managing extension according to its own initiative. To begin with, had Congress been setting parameters for the program, Kenyon could surely have received the facts he sought from the Senate Agriculture Committee. Yet the letter suggests more. Kenyon knew little when he wrote to Houston, but he knew that the program was Spillman's brainchild, that the Bureau of Plant Industry was managing it, and that the program involved county-level cooperation between localities and the department. Finally, Kenyon's silence about the land-grant colleges suggests that many legislators did not associate the program with the states. In summary, Kenyon's letter shows clearly that Congress equated extension with the USDA, and that extension's appeal depended on legislators' favorable impression of its history in the department.[69]

With vocational education out of the picture, congressional debate now split over policy details. Funding, and who would control it, became the central issue. The AAACES, formerly an energetic proponent of federal extension, now began to rehearse Eugene Davenport's worries about colleges losing their autonomy to the department. Congress had sharply boosted funds for Spillman's northern extension work in 1913 and 1914, portending further trouble for the colleges' hatchling efforts. The boost for the Knapp-Spillman program was driven by strong congressional perceptions of its efficacy. As Senator Sam Sells, a Democrat from Tennessee, said in favor of the new monies, "[T]he farmer has no time, equipment, nor training for questionable experimentation. . . . Our Department of Agriculture has undertaken this work for him, and its investigations have proven of *inestimable value.*" Emboldened by these events, USDA officials resolved in the spring of 1913 to ensure that any extension bill would mandate departmental control over state programs. When Galloway and Houston met with the AAACES, they proposed a cooperative venture in which the state colleges would receive federal funding but would agree to manage a county-agent system with the Knapp-Spillman demonstration model as the basic template.

Houston's proposal was no idle sketch. With trifling modifications, it became Lever's final extension bill, introduced in September 1913. Lever changed it only to guarantee southerners that the Knapp program would remain in place, and Galloway (now assistant secretary of agriculture) calmly assured members of Congress that the Lever bill would perpetuate all existing departmental efforts. The act encoded the USDA's demand that all state extension programs be approved by the department. It also required each college receiving extension funding to transmit an annual statement to the secretary of agriculture detailing the state's expenditures. Lever's Agriculture Committee then reported the bill favorably in December. The committee's report evinced neither agrarian radicalism nor the weight of national farmers' groups. Instead, it was evidence of a body convinced of the utility of the department's county-agent model. Testifying loudly to Knapp's wisdom, the committee admitted that "the farmer is naturally conservative," and that any successful education program must include "personal appeal and ocular demonstration." The House quickly passed the Lever bill by a vote of 177 to 9. The House resounded its confidence in the Bureau of Plant Industry in an amendment stipulating that "nothing in this Act should be construed to discontinue either the farm management work or the farmers' cooperative demonstration work." When Smith dropped his own extension bill for Lever's in the Senate, the push for national extension was complete. Woodrow Wilson penned the Smith-Lever Act into law on May 8, 1914.[70]

Interpreting the Evolution of Extension

Scholars have interpreted the Smith-Lever Act of 1914 as the triumph of a seamless "farmers' movement" stemming from antebellum America. Elizabeth

Sanders regards the act as having "inaugurated a large-scale system of practical education for farmers." Sanders also attributes the act to the broader energies of nineteenth-century agrarian radicalism. I argue in chapter 9 that to impute such influence to a broad, unitary, and single-minded "farmers' movement" after 1900 risks serious historical inaccuracies. For now, however, I believe that the evolution of the act casts doubt on any broad ascription of federal extension to organized agrarians.[71]

The Smith-Lever Act was first and foremost not an inauguration of any "new" system but the statutory framing of a decade-old program. As table 7.5 shows, the sequence of bills from the 1909 McLaughlin measure to the act of 1914 marks a slow but steady congressional acceptance of the USDA's demands for statutory recognition of its existing system. The McLaughlin bill provided no role for bureaucracy whatsoever. It simply funded the land-grant colleges directly, a brute affirmation of the institute model. The Dolliver bill was scarcely more favorable to the USDA, creating bureaucratic administration by the Interior Department. The Page bill wised up to congressional sentiment favoring the Knapp-Spillman approach, but only halfway. It switched administration to Agriculture yet left the institute model in place. With the defeat of the Page bill in 1912, the USDA knew that all serious alternatives to its system had been scuttled. Thereafter the department took control of the policymaking process. Galloway and Houston now insisted that any national extension bill exclude the institute model and incorporate cooperative demonstration by county agents. Most critically, the draft bill from the May 1913 AAACES-USDA conference—a conference dominated by the department—became the final Lever bill. In summary, the USDA was the literal author of modern agricultural extension.

The Demise of the Farmers' Institute

The form as well as the sequence of policy evolution in agricultural extension also points to bureaucratic innovation over movement-driven change. The farm groups and the land-grant colleges, it is important to recall, favored not cooperative demonstrators but farmers' institutes and college-based programs. This fact offers two significant lessons. First, it renders problematic the common claim that the colleges and the department were joined at the hip. Finegold and Skocpol's "nexus of institutions" metaphor remains useful as a general portrait of government institutions in agriculture, yet it encounters stark limits in the case of extension. Extension split the colleges as no issue before or perhaps since. Not only did some colleges—North Carolina and Illinois—display outright resistance to cooperative demonstration, but the mouthpiece of the colleges, the AAACES, sought state control of extension programs and funds. The second lesson is captured in table 7.5. From 1909 to 1914, Congress moved

TABLE 7.5
How the Sequence of Extension Bills Leading to the Smith-Lever Act Progressively Encoded the USDA's Plans

Plan/Bill	Knapp-Spillman USDA System (as of 1909)	McLaughlin Bill (1909)	Dolliver Bill (1910)	Page Bill (1912)	Lever Bill (1913)	Smith-Lever Act (1914)
Institute model or extension-agent model?	Agent model	Institutes	Institutes	Institutes	Agent model	Agent model
Basis of organization	Counties	State colleges	Districts	Counties	Counties	Counties
Vocational education?	No	No	Yes	Yes	No	No
Administering department	USDA	No agency	Interior	USDA	USDA	USDA
Land-grant funding control or USDA control?	USDA veto power over state expenditures	Land-grant control	Land-grant control	Land-grant control	USDA control	USDA control
Method of extension	Cooperative demonstration	Institutes	Institutes	Institutes	Cooperative demonstration	Cooperative demonstration
Farm management work?	Yes	No	No	No	Yes	Yes

steadily and surely *away* from land-grant control, *away* from the institute model, and *toward* a cooperative demonstration system under the USDA. So strong was legislative trust in the Knapp-Spillman system by 1913 that the only meaningful amendments to the Smith-Lever Act were protections for the *existing* programs of the department, both northern and southern.[72]

Whereas the Smith-Lever Act enshrined the Knapp-Spillman system, the subsequent path of extension under the USDA's control all but buried the institute model. As Roy Scott summarizes, "Farmers' institutes tended to disappear in the new scheme of things." The USDA, acting on "its general belief that they were ineffective, an opinion that was widely shared," sought the elimination of the farmers' institutes, and "with few exceptions they had faded from the scene by the World War years." In 1915–16 all 48 states held farmers' institutes, with 31 states allowing the agricultural colleges to conduct the work. By 1922 only 23 states were conducting institutes, and by 1927 they remained in only 11 states (and nine colleges). The administrative asphyxiation of an institution assembled by the Alliance and supported at every turn by the Grange and the NFU stands as strong evidence of the USDA's autonomy in extension policy.[73]

A Counterfactual: Extension without the Smith-Lever Act

Perhaps the best evidence that bureaucratic innovation was the decisive force behind Smith-Lever comes when we consider the following thought experiment: suppose Congress had never passed the act. What would have happened in its absence? Imagine first that without Smith-Lever extension would not have grown at all beyond its reach in the spring of 1914. Even under this pessimistic forecast, the Knapp-Spillman system would still have covered 41 of 48 states, with 236 county agents in the North and 859 in the South. More than 120,000 farm youth would have been enrolled in boys' and girls' clubs, with as many as 50,000 demonstration farms in the South and more than 100,000 cooperating farmers. As many as 12 million visitors would have laid eyes on demonstration farms in the ensuing decade. Moreover, virtually all of the features of extension that eventually were incorporated in the Smith-Lever Act and were already in place by 1914—the county basis of organization, cooperative relations between the USDA and the land-grants, traveling demonstrators with specified demonstration farms, and the county farm bureau—would have remained as mainstays of the system.

A more realistic scenario is to assume that federal extension would have continued growing without statutory help from Smith-Lever, funded instead by the highly discretionary lump-sum monies from Congress, combined with state spending and General Education Board largesse in the South and in New England. Even under the most conservative assumption, as figure 7.1 shows, some

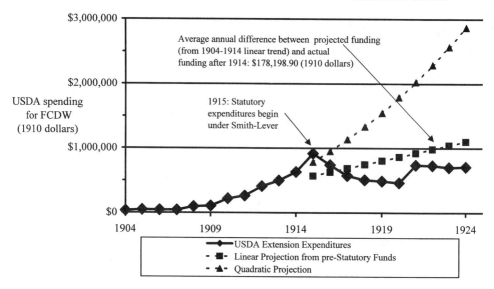

Figure 7.1 The growth of USDA expenditures for Farmers' Cooperative Demonstration Work (FCDW) from 1904 to 1924. (Data from NA II, RG 16, E 17, B 1106, Appropriations File)

aspects of extension would probably have grown faster in the absence of Smith-Lever. Figure 7.1 displays FCDW funding in 1910 dollars from 1904 to 1924. The figure also includes two projections based on the counterfactual that Smith-Lever had not passed and that the pre-1914 funding mechanisms had remained. The first projection is a linear extrapolation. It assumes that the rate of growth in funding after 1914 would have been equal to the average rate of increase from 1904 to 1914. Under these assumptions, FCDW funding would have been larger by an average of more than *$150,000 per year* in 1910 dollars. Put differently, the department would have employed an average of three hundred more demonstrators per year without Smith-Lever. An alternative projection takes account of the exponential growth pattern of extension funding before the Smith-Lever Act. If this pattern had continued, by the 1920s the USDA would have spent millions of dollars more per year than it actually spent.[74]

In the end, agricultural extension was an achievement neither of warmed-over agrarian radicalism nor of a federalist "policy nexus" among national and state institutions. The Department of Agriculture first built a system of its own design with funding from seed exploration, boll weevil eradication, industrial philanthropy, and state-level contributions. Both Knapp's and Spillman's plans were unprecedented in Congress, and the department's progress in spreading its system through the North and the South was frequently in opposition to the wishes of state colleges. Only when USDA officials, working at the grass roots of southern and Plains agriculture, had convinced 10 million cultivators of the worth of its system did the Grange, the Farmers' Union, the AAACES, and finally Congress jump on the bureaucratic bandwagon. Far from the legislative inauguration of a national extension system, the Smith-Lever Act of 1914 did little more than give the imprimatur of statute to a system that Knapp, Spillman, and the Bureau of Plant Industry had already built. Indeed, Smith-Lever probably slowed extension's growth even as it gave the program a happy permanence.

Extension as Evidence of Reputation and Autonomy

Two questions remain. Why, initially, did the Sixty-third Congress pass an agricultural extension law in 1914 but neglect vocational education? Sanders offers an intriguing explanation based on the power of farmers' groups to account for the disparity, pointing to the entrenchment of agrarians within the Progressive Era Democratic Party while labor's political influence with the major parties languished. Yet an account based on bureaucratic innovation and agency reputations fares far better. It accounts both for the timing and, most critically, for the form of the Smith-Lever Act. First, in 1914 Congress had no established federal agency in which to place a vocational education program outside the widely discredited Bureau of Education in the Department of Interior. The newly created Labor Department was hardly a repository of trust from Congress or even the AFL. Alternatively, placement of extension in the USDA was a straightforward matter in 1913. Indeed, by 1912, Congress had no other realistic option. Second, and more important, Congress had a successful bureaucratic model of agricultural extension; it lacked any such experiment for vocational training. Nor did the Agriculture Committees select some elements of the USDA's model and discard others. Lever adopted the Knapp-Spillman program wholesale. In this respect, we can explain why extension passed in 1914 without any reference to the Democratic Sixty-third Congress. By 1913, after all, Spillman had made cooperative extension a possibility in the North. USDA officials had also fomented county farm bureaus as an organized voice favoring a federally funded national system. With a strong program reputation embedded firmly in county-based farmers' networks, the elements for a cross-regional and cross-commodity coalition for national extension finally materialized, with participation (but not control) by the Grange and the Farmers' Union.

Why, in summary, does the evolution of agricultural extension provide strong evidence for bureaucratic autonomy conditioned upon legitimacy? I claim it sufficient for a demonstration of autonomy if a politically distinct bureaucracy can effect a nontrivial policy shift that would not have occurred in the absence of agency action (see chapter 1). Chapter 6 established a case for the ideological uniqueness of the department, yet it is worth remarking here that the history of extension powerfully clarifies the divergence of the USDA's policy preferences. In the case of extension, the preferences of the USDA were reducible neither to the land-grant colleges', nor to the major farm groups', nor to those of Congress or Republican presidents. Some of these actors may have defended extension as a concept, but only the department pressed for the county-agent cooperative demonstration model. And not until 1911 did other actors jump on board. As Roy Scott summarizes, "In both the North and the South, observers were aware that these popular programs had been launched and carried forward by the Department of Agriculture, often with little encouragement and less understanding from the agricultural colleges." Moreover, it was the USDA that had the greatest hand in drafting the final Lever bill. The second condition—nontrivial policy shifts—can be demonstrated by means of another counterfactual: in the absence of Knapp and Spillman and their subordinates, would there have been a statutory national extension program by 1914? Would it have been based on the county-agent system, and would it have assisted in the organization of county farm bureaus? There is simply no historically reasonable affirmative answer to these questions.[75]

The evolution of extension was conditioned upon the legitimacy of the Department of Agriculture. This reputation consisted not merely in beliefs about the department's efficacy but also in beliefs that were embedded in the multiple network ties that USDA officials had to the different interests involved in the extension debate. The following chapter offers an expanded discussion of this pattern of affiliations, yet in the rise of extension the breadth of the department's networks was impressive. With ties to state college leaders, to Sears, Roebuck, to the General Education Board, to the Farm Management Association, to hundreds of county farm bureaus, to the Farmers' Union, and to Asbury Lever, the USDA occupied a central place in the discourse of extension as did no other participant. Multiple networks—at once spanning the North and the South, farm and industry, revolting agrarians and corporate philanthropists, domestic science advocates and farm college skeptics—sustained bureaucratic autonomy in agricultural education.

Eight

Multiple Networks and the Autonomy of Bureaus: Departures in Food, Pharmaceutical, and Forestry Policy, 1897–1913

[T]he Chief of the Bureau of Chemistry of the Department of Agriculture . . . has had more influence in bringing about this legislation probably than any one man, he in fact aiding in drafting the House bill we are now considering.
> —Rep. Charles L. Bartlett (D–Georgia), speaking of USDA bureau chief Harvey Wiley in the debate over the Pure Food Act of 1906

This country's forests are being made a gigantic funeral pyre to solemnize the passing of our timber supply and the demoralization of our water resources.

Our hope of retrenchment lies with the Forest Service. Its right to public confidence rests on two things: Responsibility and the genius of an organization of able young men, guided in their work by scientific foresight, trained for their duties and inured to the rigors of work in the field.
> —"Save the Forests," *Maxwell's Talisman*

THE CREATION OF the twentieth-century agricultural extension system under the leadership of Seaman Knapp and William Spillman was an impressive demonstration of the USDA's power. Yet Progressive-Era contemporaries would hardly have characterized the extension system as the Department of Agriculture's most noteworthy achievement. The USDA also fostered lasting change in food and pharmaceutical regulation and in forest conservation policy. In the struggle for the Forest Reserve Transfer Act of 1905 and the Pure Food and Drugs Act of 1906, the Department of Agriculture displayed its mezzo-level strengths. Here the department's bureau leaders—Harvey Wiley and Gifford Pinchot—assembled lasting coalitions behind their favored policies and spurred Theodore Roosevelt and Congress into action on issues that would otherwise have attracted little notice. The USDA began to grab programs and jurisdictions from other departments. By 1910 political legitimacy and bureaucratic autonomy were nowhere established more solidly than in the bureaus of the Department of Agriculture.[1]

Whereas the transformation of seed policy and the evolution of the extension program were changes that Secretary of Agriculture James Wilson welcomed, the Forest Reserve Transfer Act of 1905 and the Pure Food and Drugs Act of 1906 were forged with much less help (and at times severe opposition) from Wilson and Republican party elites. Wiley and Pinchot were political forces in their own right. Unlike Knapp and Spillman, they crusaded with little help from organized agrarians and with opposition from major party figures.

At the core of these transformations was the political reputation of the USDA, a renown for expertise that was embedded in numerous affiliations with economic, political, and social organizations of the Progressive period. Food and drug regulation and forestry policy show decisively that the power of the Department of Agriculture lay not simply in its well-known ties to land-grant colleges and agrarian organizations. Bureau chiefs and program leaders also curried rare favor from women's federations, organized professionals, manufacturing groups, budding conservationist leagues, and associations of state and local government officials.

In two ways, these multiple network ties allowed the USDA to achieve a rare form of bureaucratic autonomy. First, they prevented the reduction of the department's interests to one or another of the contending factions in Progressive politics. The department could claim allies from numerous quarters of American society, across lines of class, gender, and region. Its officials could enter confidently into Progressive debates over a variety of legislative topics, robustly able to deflect claims that the department simply represented farmers or merely doled out seeds. In short, multiple networks supported a newfound political legitimacy for USDA officials. More significantly, multiple networks allowed the entrepreneurial officials of the department to engage in coalition building, a necessary exercise for autonomy in the federalist institutional structure of the United States, with its variegated economy and society.[2]

These networks were fastened to the USDA at its organizational middle. The connections so critical to the department's political success were maintained not by local-level agents, nor primarily by secretaries of agriculture, but by bureau chiefs and program leaders. In figures such as Harvey W. Wiley, Beverly Galloway, Seaman Knapp, Gifford Pinchot, and C. Hart Merriam, bureaucratic autonomy was fleshed out. While county-level associations between extension agents and farm bureaus emerged in 1910 and were cemented from 1914 through the war, the capacities and reputations of primary importance emerged at the bureau level (see table 8.1).

By extending its administrative reach deep into American communities, the department broke free from nineteenth-century localism. Through the proliferation of county offices under the extension system, the expansion of meat, food, and drug regulation in cities, the appropriation of western forest reserves, and other measures, by 1913 the USDA was able to place at least one employee (usually many) in virtually every county in the nation. The department vastly extended its presence in the South, the region whose representatives had long favored a distributive seed policy and administrative submission from the USDA.

Finally, the triumphs of the Bureau of Chemistry and the Bureau of Forestry show that the rise of bureaucratic autonomy and capacity at the USDA had less to do with the organized agrarian movements of the late nineteenth century than historians have commonly supposed. The Pure Food and Drugs Act of 1906 and the Forest Service transfer of 1905 were episodes in which organized agrarians were hardly involved. The crucial supporters of the pure food and drug legislation, it turns out, were activists in the Progressive women's movement, most prominently in the General Federation of Women's Clubs and the Women's Christian Temperance Union. Significantly, Pinchot drew on some of the same political organizations in his fight for a national conservation policy. Yet none of the organizations that supported either food and drug regulation or national forest policy came to their positions alone. It was Wiley who brought not just the GFWC but also the American Medical Association and state government officials into the fold of his coalition. Similarly, the Transfer Act of 1905 was not simply a "Progressive" or "conservationist" achievement. Instead, it was a triumph of bureaucratic entrepreneurship, as Pinchot built an alliance of conservationists, scientists, western logging and mining interests, and other organizations that frequently found themselves opposed on issues of national resources. In these episodes of the Progressive Era, at least, it was less the case that social movements built the bureaucratic state than that bureaucracy built social movements.

Harvey Wiley, the Bureau of Chemistry, and the Struggle for Pure Food and Drugs

Bureaucratic entrepreneurship in the USDA opened the twentieth century where it closed the nineteenth, with Wiley's efforts to build the model scientific bureau. Wiley's frustration with his campaigns for beet sugar and sorghum led him to look elsewhere in his search for an issue of empowerment for his division. His efforts to build a coalition around pure food and drug legislation propelled the 1906 Pure Food and Drugs Act into law, a lasting achievement for which the USDA chemist still receives primary credit. Nor did Wiley abandon entirely his interest in beets, and he continued his wide-ranging public speaking tour during which he proclaimed the virtues of beets and sorghum as alternatives to price-depressed grains. He also kept a close eye on the personnel of his bureau and continued publishing basic and applied research with colleagues

TABLE 8.1
The Multiple Network Affiliations of USDA Officials

USDA Official	Political Affiliations	Scientific and/or Professional Affiliations	Economic Affiliations	Agrarian or Conservationist Affiliations
Harvey W. Wiley, chief chemist	Alice Lakey, GFWC Martha Allen, WCTU Samuel Hopkins Adams, *Collier's Weekly* writer	Association of Official Agricultural Chemists R. M. Allen, Association of State Food and Dairy Departments AAAS, Cosmos Club	Charles A. L. Reed, AMA president National Canners' Association Louisiana Sugar Growers' Association	Alexander Wedderburn, Virginia Grange
Gifford Pinchot, chief of forestry	Theodore Roosevelt Lydia Phillips Williams, GFWC Urban journalists	Bernhard Fernow, German foresters Charles F. Sargent, Harvard Arboretum	F. E. Weyerhaueser, Timber Company E. H. Harriman	John Muir, Sierra Club Audubon Society Sir Horace Plunkett

C. Hart Merriam, chief of biological survey	Theodore Roosevelt "Major" John Lacey (Iowa), chairman House Public Lands Committee	T. S. Palmer, Harvard University biologist AAAS, Washington Academy of Sciences		John Muir, Sierra Club State game wardens Gilbert Grosvenor, National Geographic
Seaman Knapp, director of southern extension	Iowa Republicans (C. C. Carpenter)	Iowa Agricultural College (formerly president)	Frederick T. Gates, General Education Board	Southern rice and cotton planters Wallace Family
James S. Wilson, secretary of agriculture	House Agriculture Committee Iowa politicians, (e.g., House Speaker David Henderson)	Iowa Agricultural College Iowa Agricultural Experiment Station	Foreign seed companies (Vilmorin-Andrieux), through David Fairchild	Farmers' Protective Association (anti-monopoly) Wallace family Sir Horace Plunkett
Beverly T. Galloway, chief of Bureau of Plant Industry		Missouri Agricultural College	Foreign seed companies (Vilmorin-Andrieux)	

young and old. In short, Wiley maintained a ubiquitous presence in Progressive-Era America. He could whip up moral radicalism, inspire populist hopes for a renewal of the Plains, conduct detailed policy discussions with members of Congress, and calmly assure business representatives that their best interests lay in regulation. In the campaign for pure food and drugs, Wiley energized a bureau and founded a social movement, uniting the political and administrative energies of state building.[3]

The passage of the 1906 Pure Food and Drugs Act has been subjected to varying constructs over the twentieth century. Save for a few meat industry journals, contemporaries viewed the bill as a landmark piece of legislation. Most of the early historiography of the bill was written with a favorable view of Wiley. Thomas A. Bailey's article in the *American Sociological Review* of 1930 pitted Wiley against a reluctant Congress and the increasingly concentrated food industry. Oscar E. Anderson's *Health of a Nation* (1946), the first comprehensive historiography of the 1906 act, proclaimed Wiley "the central figure" in "the long struggle for legislation." In *Pure Food*, the most exhaustive primary-source-driven work on the legislation, James Harvey Young took a neoprogressive approach to the bill, lionizing Wiley's accomplishments and pointing to his alliance with Progressive anti-adulteration movements. In *The Age of Conservatism*, Gabriel Kolko interpreted the act as struck from the vein of producerist legislation that dominated the Progressive period. Kolko tied the increasing power of the USDA to packers and canning interests. Clayton A. Coppin and Jack High partly concurred with Kolko in *The Politics of Purity*, noting Wiley's ties to canners and packers but also suggesting that Wiley's chief aim was expanding the power of his bureau.[4]

The common failure of these narratives is their attempt to reduce the motives and interests of Wiley and of his bureau officials to one faction or another in the complex Progressive debate over food regulation. Wiley did in fact communicate frequently with canners, packers, and large pharmaceutical firms. He also sought favor from Progressive moralists and women's federations. He even curried support from agrarian groups and farm papers. The very multiplicity of Wiley's ties defies modern historians' attempts to pigeonhole his motives, just as it confounded any easy reading of his interests from 1901 to 1906. The only charge against Wiley that stuck was that he was interested in expanding the power of the federal government over interstate commerce in foodstuffs and pharmaceuticals. His multiple affiliations and the diverse social ties of his bureau officials eased the coalition-building effort so necessary for success in 1906.

From a Congress to a Coalition

The budding interest in the hazards of adulteration crystallized at the National Food and Drug Congress in Washington in March 1898. The congress was the first national gathering to focus attention on the misbranding of foods and drugs. Indeed, the congress united pure food activists and those who focused on pure drugs for the first time. Held at Columbian University Hall (now George Washington University), the conference included representatives of professional associations, state and local public health agencies, women's federations, and farmers', canners', and grocers' organizations. The conference even received the social imprimatur of President McKinley, who hosted a White House reception for the delegates.[5]

The lasting effect of the Pure Food Congress was to give unity and legitimacy to the anti-adulteration movement and to establish Wiley as its unquestioned leader. The nominal organizer of the congress was Alexander Wedderburn, a Virginia planter. Some historians have argued that Wedderburn competed with Wiley for leadership of the nascent movement. Although the two men may have had different visions of enforcement—Wedderburn later favored a separate food commissioner, whereas Wiley sought enforcement by the Bureau of Chemistry—in fact Wedderburn closely cooperated with Wiley. The conference was as much Wiley's brainchild as it was Wedderburn's. It was no coincidence that the meetings were held on the Columbian campus, where Wiley was teaching and still recruited and trained many of his division's chemists. There is also reason to believe that the two men spent late 1897 discussing the congress while Wedderburn was Wiley's employee in Washington, for Wiley had hired Wedderburn as an "Investigator" in the Division of Chemistry in September 1897, just six months before the Pure Food Congress. Wedderburn's second appointment brought him $2,400 annually, a salary exceeded only by Wiley's in the division.[6]

Wiley delivered the central address at the convention and struck a chord of moderation. He offered a restrained analysis of adulteration in chemical terms and announced his fervent opposition to "any prohibitory measure against the manufacture of goods of any description." He merely wanted "honesty" in a free market and protection for "the innocent consumer." Yet as the chief chemist spoke cautiously, he quietly engineered more concrete results in his favor. Wiley was at the helm of the legislative committee of the congress, and the meetings concluded with the endorsement of a regulatory measure written by the AOAC. Wiley had chaired the AOAC committee that drafted the bill, and he succeeded in getting Rep. Marriott Brosius of Pennsylvania to introduce it in the House in December 1897. Predictably, the AOAC bill placed all responsibility for food and drug analysis, and much of the enforcement, in the USDA Chemistry Division. It also permitted precious few exemptions to the food and adulteration standards that would also be determined by the department, with assistance from Wiley's division. Wiley's aim, codified as closely as possible by the AOAC draft, was a bill that did not privilege one product over another, favoring neither butter nor oleomargarine, or one brand of whiskey over another. His aim was truth in advertising. As Wiley asked the readers of *Collier's Weekly* in 1903,

What should the public require?

1. Good laws, state and national, forbidding the addition of deleterious substances to foods:—

2. And requiring each label to convey to the consumer a correct and complete list of all the substances not natural to the food in question which the package contains.

In other words:—

No added injurious substance!

No false labels![7]

The Pure Food and Drug Congress met twice more, in 1899 and 1900. Wiley's old employee and friend William Frear of Pennsylvania was chairman of the executive committee of the congress, and together they steered the meeting's attention toward the Wiley draft bill. At the 1900 meetings, however, sentiment shifted toward an enforcement measure that reduced the Chemistry Division's power. Wiley quickly lost interest in the institution, and it did not survive into the twentieth century. Nonetheless, the congresses had served Wiley's purposes. The organizational bases of a national anti-adulteration campaign were now in place. Through the congresses Wiley and his subordinates at the Division of Chemistry commenced alliances with farmers' organizations, the Women's Christian Temperance Union, and civic leagues and business associations. These ties would serve Wiley's bureau well in the ensuing five years.[8]

The other legacy of the congresses was to establish the AOAC draft as the operative template for national food and drug legislation. From 1898 to 1900, Wiley succeeded several times in prompting Brosius and other legislators to introduce various versions of the AOAC draft. Other measures, whether introduced by reformers or opponents, were viewed as weaker substitutes for Wiley's measure. The chief chemist also played a role in the few anti-adulteration measures that did pass the national legislature before 1906, providing information crucial to the writing of the mixed-flour prohibitions of 1898. As the Chemistry Division's stature on Capitol Hill grew, Wiley and his subordinates were called upon to provide information to committees investigating food and drug issues. When William E. Mason, chairman of the Senate Committee on Manufactures, held fifty-one days of hearings on food adulteration in New York, Washington, and Chicago in 1902, his committee hired Wiley as an analyst. Wiley analyzed 428 food samples and interviewed many of its witnesses. More significant, Wiley had the ear of the Manufactures Committee for two months. He gave senators what amounted to a daily lecture on the nuts and bolts of adulteration and the extent of the problem in the nation. The hearings established Wiley as the authority on adulteration and placed him at the center of congressional attention. "I think if there is any one man in this country who deserves great credit for trying to furnish the facts for the benefit of the people of this country," intoned Mason on the Senate floor, "that man is Harvey Washington Wiley."[9]

Mason's hearings were an important agenda-setting step. They marked the first sustained attention that Congress had given to food and drug adulteration since Paddock's efforts a decade earlier. The legislators and their newly attentive public, reading of the Mason hearings in newspaper excerpts, now learned of metallic salts in vegetable preservatives, coal-tar matter in food coloring, condensed skim milk passed off as whole milk, and an imported-wine dealer who admitted to a Chemistry Division investigator that he routinely took "Chateau Lafitte, Burgundy, and Bordeaux all out of the same cask and [labeled] them to suit." The momentum for legislation quickly built, and Wiley drafted the bill that Mason introduced in the Senate. At the point where the discussion turned to the prospect of law, however, the bill's rapidly coalescing opponents came to the fore. Baking-powder manufacturers who relied on alum and cream of tartar, two compounds that had not fared well in the publicity of the hearings, organized to fight the bill. Neither chamber brought the measure to a vote.[10]

By December 1902 the House of Representatives passed a broad pure food and drug bill introduced by William P. Hepburn of Iowa. Porter McCumber of North Dakota, succeeding Mason as chair of the Senate Manufactures Committee, introduced a similar bill in the Senate and began hearings. Cognizant of the Department of Agriculture's expertise in the area, McCumber asked Secretary Wilson for a draft of the bill, and Wilson set Wiley to the task. Before Wiley could put pen to paper, the Senate took up the Hepburn bill. With the favorable House vote and increasing public attention, Wiley expressed his strongest expectations yet that national legislation would pass: "At last we are in sight of food legislation!" His hopes were dashed when the Senate balked at the measure, refusing to bring it up for a vote. Wiley was perplexed by the defeat, without a ready explanation. Frank Barrett of the *American Grocer* had one. The political movement for pure food legislation still lacked any national identity or force. "Public sentiment in favor of the bill needs to crystalized [*sic*] and centralized," wrote Barrett, "and its influence brought to bear upon Congress."[11]

Wiley knew that he needed to demonstrate the costs of inaction to congressional Republicans, and he set out to do so in two ways—boosting the publicity of his cause and eliminating by co-optation the strongest of the bill's opponents. The first task he accomplished by means of an unprecedented administrative experiment. Wiley asked Congress for $5,000 to conduct research with human subjects on the effects of preservatives on the human body. Taking cues from the Book of Daniel, he assembled a group of twelve young men, a mix of bureau employees and chemistry students, and fed them a controlled diet of foods laced with borax. At moderate levels of borax ingestion, the subjects reported severe discomfort and "inability to perform work of any kind." More troubling results were obtained with salicylic acid, sulfurous acids, benzoate, and formaldehyde, all of which were commonly used as commercial food preservatives. Wiley broadcast the results of his experiments in *Bulletin 84: Influence of Food Preservatives and Artificial Colors on Digestion and Health*. He concluded that even small daily doses of boric acid "create disturbances of appetite, of digestion, and of health."[12]

Wiley's experiments elicited the nation's morbid curiosity, and *Washington Post* reporter George Rothwell Brown dubbed the subjects the "Poison Squad." Popular reaction ranged from genuine concern about Wiley's treatment of his subordinates to comical depictions of the group. Wiley earned the moniker "Uncle Borax" in popular cartoons. Poet S. W. Gillilan penned a tongue-in-cheek *Song of the Pizen Squad*, in which the subjects lunched "on a morphine stew" and dined "on a matchhead consommé." Lyricist Lew Dockstader's minstrel show was jokingly titled "They'll Never Look the Same." For all of the concern and comedy, however, Wiley had attracted the public's attention as never before. Whether they showed amusement or sympathy for the subjects, middle-class Americans were increasingly persuaded of the peril inherent in food preservatives.[13]

The other legacy of the Poison Squad is that it further demonstrated, albeit brutally, that the Bureau of Chemistry was the organization best equipped to discern the hazards of foods and drugs. In this sense, Wiley's use of congressional appropriations to create the Poison Squad was as much a political experiment as a scientific one. Could an executive bureau be trusted with money to conduct unprecedented scientific tests? Was Congress ready for the implications of Wiley's findings? What if Wiley had squandered the money or, worse, killed one of his subjects? For these reasons, the 1902 appropriations act, even at a low level of expenditure, was a risky venture. It boosted the funding in the 1901 appropriations act. It also contained new grants of discretion, authorizing the secretary of agriculture, in collaboration with the AOAC, to set standards for food purity "for the guidance of the officials of the various States and of courts of justice." As the Poison Squad grabbed more press attention and Wiley's campaign progressed, Congress expanded the department's mandate again. The 1903 appropriations act authorized the Bureau of Chemistry to inspect imported goods for mislabeling and for restrictions placed on the goods by the country of origin. Wiley took his expanded funds and established branch offices in six cities ranging from New York to San Francisco. The appropriations of 1902 and 1903, owing to increasing congressional trust in Wiley's mission, augured favorably for pure food legislation.[14]

Still, Wiley's dream faced entrenched opposition. Among those dedicated to the defeat of any strong pure food law were blended-whiskey manufacturers, dairy interests, and baking-powder interests. Wiley knew he could not bring these groups into the fold. Worse yet was the fact that these interests had gotten Secretary Wilson to side with them on some matters. Wilson favored a bill in general form, but he secretly desired restrictions on Wiley's enforcement power. He was largely unsupportive of the Chemistry Bureau's efforts to study food adulteration; Wiley's Poison Squad was in part an inexpensive attempt to circumvent Wilson. Dairy interests wrote Wilson asking to have Wiley dismissed, and for a time Wilson considered the request seriously. Wilson also disdained Wiley's allies in the Progressive media who were exposing the dangers of adulterated food and drugs. Wilson knew, however, that he lacked the political legitimacy to go toe-to-toe with his subordinate.[15]

The disfavor of one group—the National Association of State Dairy and Food Departments—still hinged on its rejection of any legislation giving enforcement to the USDA. The association's experienced state commissioners were wary of organized grocers who tried to use state-level food laws to weed out small competitors. Fearful of the grocers' potential alliances with a department dedicated to farmers, they initially endorsed a bill with a presidentially appointed food commissioner in their 1903 meetings. Again Wiley turned to acquaintances in his bureau to turn opponents into supporters. The association's secretary was R. M. Allen, an employee of Melvill A. Scovell, a friend of Wiley's hired in the bureau as a special agent in June 1902. Allen needed support to publish the association's annual proceedings, and Wiley tendered it on the condition that Allen steer his group toward favoring the McCumber bill. Allen helped Wiley devise a strategy for persuading the association's members at the next annual convention in Saint Paul, Minnesota. Wiley quickly rallied a group of supporters to travel with him to Minnesota to speak for the bill. He wrote detailed letters to Scovell, Frear, and others, arguing that the USDA had the full organizational machinery for enforcing the law and noting that Congress had already approved of the department's role as primary enforcer of any pure food law. Relishing his public stance of neutrality, however, Wiley again adopted a low-key tone in his speeches to the conference. He spoke in very general terms, favoring the Hepburn and McCumber bills only as the simplest and most likely to pass. The joint campaign of Allen and Wiley worked. The association concluded its 1904 meetings with an endorsement of the Hepburn-McCumber legislation.[16]

The final push for organized support came before the Fifty-ninth Congress convened in December 1905. During this time, Wiley brought two more forces solidly behind his bill. The first and most significant force was the two principal women's federations of the period, the Women's Christian Temperance Union and the General Federation of Women's Clubs. More than a decade before suffrage, women's federations were central organizations in Progressive social and political change. As Theda Skocpol has argued, the GFWC provided the organizational substrate for the early development of child and women's welfare programs in the United States. The federation provided the decisive support for mothers' pensions and the Sheppard-Towner Act of 1923. Wiley was shrewdly aware of the political strength of women's groups. He had sought their support since the first pure food congress in 1898, and now he added women's clubs to his busy lecture circuit. He consistently supplied information on his bureau analyses to Martha Allen, head of the WCTU's campaign against alcoholic nostrums. He also converted New Jersey activist Alice Lakey to his cause. Lakey became a whirlwind force for Wiley's effort, securing the endorsement of the New Jersey chapter of the GFWC and persuading the General Federation to create its pure-food committee. She then approached the National Consumer's League in support of Wiley's campaign and chaired its food adulteration committee. Wiley would later conclude that Lakey and the GFWC provided the most prodigious support he had witnessed in favor of food legislation; he found the GFWC "the most efficient organization now existing."[17]

Wiley also rounded up the laggard support of the American Medical Association. He continued a strong campaign for the riddance of patent medicine ads in *JAMA*, witnessing success in 1905 when the journal forbade all proprietary advertising. Wiley had struck up an important alliance in 1901 with Cincinnati physician Charles A. L. Reed, AMA president during its rebuilding period. Reed rallied his members behind the McCumber bill, urging them to write thousands of letters to Senator Heyburn and keeping them informed of the bill's progress in *JAMA*.[18]

The dominant institutional fact about pure food legislation in the Fifty-ninth Congress (like those of the Fifty-eighth and Fifty-seventh Congresses) was one that could hardly have warmed the optimism of Wiley and other USDA officials. Neither the House nor the Senate Agriculture Committee ever saw the legislation. Before 1900 all pure food measures had been considered by the Agriculture Committees, which sought to give jurisdiction over the legislation to the USDA. Beginning in 1902, when Senate Agriculture Committee chairman Redfield Proctor of Vermont asked to be excluded from consideration of any pure food bills in the Senate, the Senate Committee on Manufactures took authority over the legislation. The House leadership referred the Hepburn bill to the Interstate and Foreign Commerce Committee, chaired by Rep. James R. Mann, an Illinois Republican. Mann had already pronounced his skepticism of USDA enforcement of any pure food law. Moreover, the developing trust between Wilson, Wadsworth, and Proctor would not figure in the USDA's favor. For this reason, committee-based explanations of the USDA's power under the 1906 act are inadequate. In each chamber, the bill was referred *away* from the one committee most favorable to USDA discretion. Both committees reported the bill.[19]

The floor debates over the Hepburn-McCumber bill were protracted, at times comical and at times rancorous. The most steadfast opponents were southern states-rights enthusiasts such as William C. Adamson of Georgia and Charles L. Bartlett of Texas. Adamson twice ridiculed the measure as the "pure foolishness" bill, admonishing supporters that "the Federal Government was not created for the purpose of cutting your toe nails or corns." The debate boiled down to two issues—whether the law was a constitutional entry of the federal government into market policing and whether the Department of Agriculture was to be trusted with numerous grants of authority. For this reason, the development of the bill cannot be explained by any "iron triangle" relationship between the department, interest groups, and the committees that considered it.[20]

The Senate debate covered more pages and more turf. The best evidence that the bill contained broad discretion for the USDA emerged in the repeatedly expressed fears that the Chemistry Bureau was being given a regulatory carte blanche. Senator Hernando DeSoto Money of Mississippi worried aloud to a *Washington Post* reporter that the legislation would give arbitrary power to the bureau over food and drugs. Money introduced a substitute measure that gave enforcement to the newly established Department of Commerce and Labor. Money thought his bill would please critics who worried that the USDA and the Post Office had become too powerful in recent years. Significantly, he never expressed doubt about the ability of the Agriculture Department to enforce the bill, arguing instead that the new responsibilities of the McCumber measure would overburden a department already weighted down by Congress's love affair with its abilities. "The Secretary of Agriculture, as I have said, is a very efficient administrative officer ... but notwithstanding this the Secretary has great difficulty. ... I know something of the requirements and duties in [the Agriculture] Department, and I know we are always overloading it."[21]

Once the issue of administrative capacity had been raised, however, McCumber quickly took the Senate floor to remind his colleagues that authority could reliably be placed nowhere else but the USDA. Even the courts, the economic regulators of the nineteenth century, could not administer a pure food law with the expertise and efficiency of the department. McCumber referred to the prosecutions and inspections made by the Chemistry Bureau under the appropriations acts of 1902 through 1905. In 1903 alone, with just several chemists working part-time on inspection, the bureau examined more than 2,200 samples of imported wine, meat, olive oil, and other goods. They found 108 violations of law and remanded numerous products to their countries of origin. McCumber then boldly asked aloud on the Senate floor:

> Has anyone heard any complaint about the enforcement of this law? ... [T]he Agricultural Department to-day has the examining of all articles that pertain to food products. ... We have had a provision in every appropriation bill ... since I have been here appropriating a certain sum of money for the use of the Secretary of Agriculture to determine what are proper standards of food products. Has anyone heard of that power having been abused in the slightest degree? Has it not been beneficial to the country?[22]

Over weeks of debate and hundreds of pages of testimony, not one member of Congress rose to rebut McCumber's query. The senator from North Dakota had settled the issue of organizational capacity. The bill's skeptics were left to argue that the Chemistry Bureau's blend of moderation and expertise actually offered a rationale for *rejecting* the measure and retaining the status quo. They argued either that the USDA would be so effective as to trample on individual liberties and state prerogatives or that the department already had sufficient power to police the industry in its continuing appropriations powers, making the bill unnecessary.[23]

The Senate passed the McCumber measure by 63 to 4. Recognizing the popularity of Wiley's campaign, Spooner abstained and Money voted for the bill. The scene of battle shifted to the House, where in the spring of 1906 two noteworthy developments characterized the debate. First, Hepburn allowed Mann of Illinois to lead the floor debate in favor of his bill. Mann had already invited Wiley to his office in March for a "cut-and-paste session" in which Wiley took the Hepburn bill and hammered out a revision more in accord with his own wishes. Mann's conversion marked a stunning reversal of judgment, one undertaken in a matter of months. Mann had voiced some of the most vociferous objections to USDA enforcement of pure food legislation, even sponsoring a bill in the Fifty-seventh Congress that kept jurisdiction away from the department. After repeated visits from Wiley, Mann led the pure food coalition on the House floor, and Adamson justifiably felt betrayed.[24]

Adamson was also sore over Wiley's role in drafting the bill. This feature of the debate is noteworthy for its historical significance. Adamson charged that the bill was "not of [Hepburn's] origination" but of Wiley's. "Another man fomented it, and worked on it, and the gentleman from Iowa took it up." Bartlett echoed Adamson's charge, proclaiming that Wiley "has had more influence in bringing about this legislation probably than any one man, he in fact aiding in drafting the House bill we are now considering." In their minority report on the bill, Adamson and Bartlett lamented the fact that "Wiley has been most ardent, insistent, and influential in advocating the passage of a national law." Mann and Hepburn sought to play down Wiley's influence, but they never directly denied Adamson's charge. Certainly Wiley's influence did not mark the first time a bureau chief wrote legislation for Congress. Among bills of the significance of the Pure Food Act of 1906, however, Wiley's drafting role, and the intimacy of his cooperation with McCumber and Hepburn, was unprecedented. The spoken displeasure of many members over Wiley's role is a strong indicator that the chief chemist had single-handedly broken one of the principal nineteenth-century assumptions about bureaucracy: that bureaucrats were not to be heard in the making of legislation but only to be seen enforcing it.[25]

As the House considered the bill, Wiley's coalition building paid handsome dividends. The National Consumer's League, an umbrella group of women's organizations, medical professionals, and state food and drug regulators, strongly lobbied the House Commerce Committee for the bill. The league clearly reflected the breadth of Wiley's alliance. Led by Florence Kelley and Alice Lakey, it included women's organizers Sarah Platt Decker of Denver, Edith Payne Parson of Des Moines, and May Alden Ward of Boston. On the league's advisory board were numerous Wiley allies in the states—R. M. Allen of Kentucky, Julius Hortvet of Minnesota, E. F. Ladd of North Dakota, and Charles Reed of the AMA.[26]

The nail in the coffin of the status quo came with two wrenching feats of Progressive journalism. In early 1906 Upton Sinclair published *The Jungle*, an exposé of the Chicago packinghouses that was read by more than 1 million Americans in its first year. Americans everywhere read Sinclair's sensational accounts of rats running wild in packinghouses, of "potted chicken" made of meat by-products, and of packing workers falling into processing vats, their bodies converted to lard. For all of his fame and horrific details, however, Sinclair had less apparent influence on food and drug regulation than Samuel Hopkins Adams. It was Adams who struck the decisive blow against adulterated medicines in his *Collier's Weekly* series in October 1905. In two articles, "The Great American Fraud" and "Peruna and the 'Bracers,'" Adams outlined the severity of drug adulteration by compiling a list of adulterated medicines and enumerating deaths and injuries associated with their use. Adams's contribution was to explain medicinal adulteration as a problem of consumer information. The problem with adulteration, claimed Adams, lay in misleading advertising.

> Gullible America will spend this year some seventy-five million dollars in the purchase of patent medicines. In consideration of this sum it will swallow huge quantities of alcohol, an appalling amount of opiates and narcotics, a wide assortment of varied drugs ranging from powerful and dangerous heart depressants to insidious liver stimulants; and, far in excess of all other ingredients, undiluted fraud.

Adams did not come unaided to the battle against patent medicines. He visited Wiley frequently and consulted at length with the chief chemist in preparing his *Collier's* articles. The American Medical Association published and praised Adams's pieces, and the outcry over patent medicines soon rivaled that over meat. The coordinated efforts of Wiley, Assistant Bureau Chief Willard Bigelow, Adams, and the AMA established what the *New York Times* called a "vast fund of practical information" about the hazards of adulterated food and medicines. For the first time, Congress had a series of reports that quantified (albeit roughly) the hazards of patent medicines and unsafe foods. Politicians could now refer to carefully documented cases in which the toxins of adulterated or misbranded medicines and foods had led to death, malformed babies, or unnecessary hospitalizations.[27]

Wiley's bill received support from surprising quarters in the House. Two members from Alabama played crucial roles. Oscar Underwood helped defeat a weakening amendment, and William Richardson served as the bill's shepherd in the House debate. After considering several minor amendments—including a strict states' rights substitute offered by Adamson—the House passed the Wiley-Hepburn bill by 241 to 17. Only strong federalists rejected the measure. In the House-Senate conference, McCumber and Mann took leading roles, and Adams later observed that Mann's preference for the tight regulation of patent medicines won out. After both chambers passed a joint version of the legislation on June 29, Roosevelt signed the Pure Food and Drugs Act of 1906 into law the next day. In addition to capacity, Wiley had cemented the reputation of his bureau for neutrality, a rare trait during the era of "responsible parties."[28]

Enforcement of the Pure Food and Drugs Act

The Bureau of Chemistry quickly set to work enforcing the provisions of the act. In some respects, the fears of eastern processors were realized. The bureau investigated whiskey manufacturers, preservative makers, and sellers of patent medicines, attacking many companies that were powerful constituents in the Republican fold. The whiskey controversy of 1906–7 began when an AOAC committee, at Wiley's prompting, held that "rectifier" firms could no longer mix whiskey with other spirits under the label "blended whiskey." The bureau followed suit with Food Inspection Decision 45, which held that "blended whiskey" was to be applied only to mixtures of pure whiskeys. Opposition to the bureau's ruling came from the most powerful politicians, including House Speaker Cannon—the nation's most powerful distillers were located in Peoria—who personally took the rectifiers' case to President Roosevelt. Yet after a yearlong battle against Cannon and the rectifiers, Wiley's bureau succeeded not only in maintaining Inspection Decision 45 but also in strengthening it. By April 1907 whiskey sellers were required to name their product under one of four allowable names. Moreover, many former "blends" now became either "compounds" or "imitations" under the bureau's standard. So popular was the Chemistry Bureau that whiskey manufacturers began touting its approval of their products in national advertisements. The Sunny Brook Distillery Company ran newspaper advertisements that depicted Wiley's inspectors holding a bottle of their product and saying "O.K."[29]

Wiley also ended the commercial use of benzoate of soda (a preservative) and copper sulfate (a greening agent for peas). Yet his most famous tilt with industry involved another beverage: Coca-Cola. Before 1900 Wiley was convinced that cocaine and caffeine were harmful food additives, and he played a leading role in the successful struggle to ban cocaine from foods, including Coca-Cola. Yet caffeine presented different problems altogether because food chemists and medical professionals disagreed over its effects. Still, Bureau of Chemistry analyses after 1905 showed trace amounts of caffeine and cocaine, and Wiley began a public campaign to rid the popular product of these additives. Even before the bureau prosecuted the Coca-Cola Company, its analyses had led the War Department to prohibit the sale of Coke on army posts. In 1908 Wiley further decided to prosecute the company under the Pure Food and Drugs Act. Department solicitor George McCabe reluctantly agreed to prosecute but chose to try the case in Chattanooga, Tennessee, home to a major Coca-Cola bottling facility. The prosecution tried the company on two charges—adulteration of product by adding caffeine and misbranding—and Wiley served as an expert witness for the government. The trial came to an unexpected close when Judge Edward Terry Sanford decided against the government's case because he found no caffeine in the drink.

Wiley had lost the case on legal grounds, but in two other ways the Coca-Cola affair was a victory. First, the case built more esteem for his bureau, especially among moral reformers who increasingly demanded purity in all products and who distrusted caffeine and other additives. Second, Wiley forced a major change in Coca-Cola's policy, particularly after the Supreme Court overturned Sanford's decision in *U.S. v. Twenty Kegs and Forty Barrels of Coca-Cola* (1915). Justice Charles Evans Hughes found in favor of the USDA. Backed by an 8 to 0 vote expanding the bureau's authority, he pointed several times to the "evidence" presented by the bureau in rendering his decision that a jury should have been allowed to pass judgment on Coca-Cola. The company, seeking no further trial, settled with the Chemistry Bureau and reduced by half the amount of caffeine in its product. Considering the global presence of Coca-Cola in the twentieth century, Wiley's eventual victory left a mammoth regulatory legacy for consumers throughout the world.[30]

Wiley did not win all of his battles. When he argued that the Corn Products Company, in which John Rockefeller's Standard Oil Company had invested heavily, was mislabeling a glucose product as corn syrup, Roosevelt and Wilson disagreed and allowed the trade name to continue. Roosevelt also ended Wiley's campaign against saccharin—"Anybody who says saccharin is injurious is an idiot," he hissed—in part because the president's personal physician had sanctioned the preservative for Roosevelt's personal use long before Wiley ever attacked it.[31]

Yet the chemist was clearly winning most contests—Cannon, Roosevelt, Wilson, and his most entrenched opponents realized that Wiley's bureau had an effective lobby. As Wiley later reminisced, "I had won, under countless handicaps and against terrific opposition, all the big battles I had been in for the public welfare." Wiley was now doing two things that even the sponsors of the act had not intended. First, he was succeeding in establishing regulatory standards through the decisions of his bureau, precisely the fear of the act's opponents in 1906. Second, he was aiming his regulatory effort at well-established industries with major investment backing.[32]

The Chemistry Bureau's assault engendered grumbling among Republicans, including Secretary Wilson, who increasingly thought of Wiley as the rascal in his otherwise well-behaved department. Wilson and George McCabe, the department's solicitor general, set out to curb Wiley's authority. In 1907 McCabe ruled that the bureau could not advance with food inspection decisions without his consent. Wilson then convened the Board of Food and Drugs, chaired by Wiley and including McCabe and Frederick T. Dunlap of the University of

Michigan. McCabe and Dunlap often voted in tandem against Wiley and prevented him from some prosecutions, but the board always made its decisions after Wiley had first conducted (and publicized) his own. With Wiley setting the agenda and making the first strike, Dunlap and McCabe were often reluctant to overrule the chemist. After the saccharin debacle, Roosevelt tried another stratagem, appointing the Referee Board of Consulting Scientists, headed by Ira Remsen of Johns Hopkins University, to repeat Wiley's analyses. The board angered Wiley, but he set out to influence its decisions as he had previously done with Congress.[33]

With a ready-made lobby behind him, Wiley nonetheless circumvented Wilson's and McCabe's restraints. Wilson had blocked publication of Wiley's analyses on benzoate, pending the Remsen board's findings, but in July 1908 Wiley took advantage of Wilson's summer vacation to publish his analyses in *Chemistry Bulletin 84*. More important, members of a burgeoning pure food movement were writing and petitioning Wilson, Roosevelt, and Congress to grant Wiley his freedom. When Rep. James Tawney, a Republican from Minnesota, offered an amendment to the 1908 agricultural appropriations bill that would have prohibited cooperation between the bureau and state food and drug regulators, Wiley enlisted the help of Lakey and Henry Needham, head of the People's Lobby, to defeat the amendment. Women's groups lobbied aggressively in opposition to any effort to restrict the bureau's leeway. Their petitions usually mentioned Wiley by name. In 1909 the New York Legislative League, headed by Mrs. Richard Mitchell Bent, entreated the Senate Committee on Manufactures:

> Whereas, the New York Legislative League is very much interested in the valuable work for the protection of the public health done by Dr. Harvey Wiley, Chief of the Bureau of Chemistry of the Agricultural Department at Washington; and
>
> Whereas, certain manufacturers are seeking to discredit his work in order that they may use certain preservatives deleterious to the health of the inmates in the homes of our land; be it
>
> Resolved that we, the New York Legislative League[,] respectfully urge you to do all in your power to uphold Dr. Wiley in his unselfish work for the good of helpless women and children who would be the first to suffer if his labors for Pure Food were interfered with.

The league's characterization of Wiley as "unselfish" marked a significant facet of the bureau's national reputation—its public mindedness. Americans from many circles viewed Wiley and his bureau as protecting the national interest. A frustrated Roosevelt reportedly confided to one businessman who wanted Wiley dismissed, "You don't understand, Sir, that Dr. Wiley has the grandest political machine in the country."[34]

Wiley departed the bureau in 1912. Some have argued that his departure reflected the increasing constraints that Wilson and the board were placing on him. I find this interpretation unwarranted. There are other reasons for Wiley's departure. He had recently married for the first time, and one month before his departure, he had learned that his wife was expecting. Moreover, whatever resistance Wiley encountered from Wilson and Taft was minuscule in comparison with the overwhelming favor he received from Congress. An otherwise conservative legislature responded favorably to Wiley's requests for additional funds and authority. In the six years following the act, Wiley's staff expanded from 110 inspectors to 146. Congress also increased Wiley's funds more than sixfold (from $155,000 to $963,780) by 1912, a rate of growth that doubtless inspired jealousy among other executive officials, even in the USDA. Wiley's legacy in food and drug regulation was powerful. First, he had established strong internal networks that bolstered the capacity of the USDA for decades to come. Of the four individuals who led federal food and drug regulation from 1912 to 1951—Carl L. Alsberg (1912–21), Walter Campbell (1921–24 and 1927–44), Charles A. Browne (1924–27), and Paul Dunbar (1944–51)—Wiley personally had hired and supervised every one before 1908. Moreover, in the immediate aftermath of Wiley's departure, much of the bureau was run by Bigelow, a Wiley disciple who secured far more loyalty and cooperation among the bureau's workers than even Alsberg.

Second, Wiley established a long-lasting national esteem for his bureau, an esteem thoroughly grounded in ties to public health advocates, state regulators, consumer groups, women's federations, and journalists. The USDA's Bureau of Chemistry had arguably become the dominant public health agency of the federal government before the New Deal (and possibly for some time thereafter). Simply put, no government agency that laid claim to health policy was better established in the public esteem, even after Wiley's departure. With the institutional weakness of the federal government in the public health sphere—the movement to establish a national health department failed, and neither the Children's Bureau nor the Public Health Service had the capacity or the reputation of the Chemistry Bureau—the USDA was able to take the lead. The leaders of the movement for women's pensions and women's health issues understood this. Julia Lathrop, the first head of the Children's Bureau, repeatedly cast the USDA as a model for her own agency. She admired the department's embedment in numerous networks, including those of the Progressive women's circles in which she traveled.[35]

Taking Steps, Changing Minds, Forging Coalitions: Bureaucratic Autonomy in National Food and Drug Regulation. In the end, the forces behind national food and drug regulation were politically reducible neither to organized processors, nor to canners and grocers, nor to professional associations, nor to moralist Progressives, nor to women's federations, nor to agrarians, nor to state and local public health officials, nor to partisan strategies. The bill passed because these diverse and often conflicting interests converged to form a coalition. At the center of the pure food nexus stood Wiley and his associates at the Bureau of Chemistry. Wiley and Bigelow nurtured relations with all of these groups. It is significant, likewise, that the organizations Wiley gathered together would come to oppose each other frequently in the Progressive period, much as they had before the 1906 act. Indeed, nothing like the pure food coalition would appear in favor of (or opposition to) other legislation during the period. Business groups versus agrarians, the GFWC versus the AMA—these groups would find themselves on opposite sides of public health, regulation, and welfare issues until the New Deal. Wiley's unique and stunning feat was to mediate among these numerous and frequently contentious factions. Wiley's political brokerage, secured in and legitimized by the Bureau of Chemistry and the Association of Official Agricultural Chemists, accounts more than any other factor for the passage of the Food and Drug Act of 1906.[36]

The narrative of the Pure Food and Drugs Act of 1906 also bears the telltale characteristics of bureaucratic policy innovation—incrementalism, relative unanimity, and the changing of minds. Wiley slowly built capacity within his bureau and cleaved to a public rhetoric of moderation. (His break with Roosevelt in 1908 came when Roosevelt began to see the chemist as extreme.) As USDA chemists slowly built their case, public sentiment coalesced behind a radical transformation of the government's relationship to the food processing, beverage, and pharmaceutical industries of the United States. The 1906 act passed both chambers nearly unanimously, with votes that were uncharacteristic of other regulatory bills in 1906 (for example, the Mann-Elkins act). Finally, a reputational account of policy innovation explains one crucial facet that no other theory can hope to explain: *minds were changed*. There is no better explanation for Mann's conversion—from an opponent of USDA authority to a fervent supporter of department discretion in 1906—than Wiley's painstaking demonstration of the bureau's capacity to the congressman. Reputation also best accounts for why legislative debate about the USDA's capacity ended on February 19, after Porter McCumber challenged his colleagues to produce a single instance of inefficient regulation by the Bureau of Chemistry.

Does the evolution of food and pharmaceutical regulation provide evidence of bureaucratic autonomy? Although the Chemistry Bureau did not operate in a political vacuum or push alone for the bill, its actions (consistent with its own policy preferences), its capacity, and its reputation are necessary conditions for the historical emergence of national food and drug regulation. The *New York Times* reasoned in 1911 that Wiley "was the prime mover in *all* the pure food legislation that has been placed on the statute books." The two most thorough historians of the 1906 act agree with this assessment. James Harvey Young argues that Wiley "established himself beyond question as the generalissimo of the pure-food coalition to press for the passage of a law," and Oscar Anderson concludes that "Wiley was in large part responsible for the fact that food and drug legislation came when it did and in the form that it did." Moreover, the bureau used its newfound authority to prosecute numerous firms with the political backing of the nation's most powerful politicians—including House Speaker Cannon (*before* the revolt of 1910), Roosevelt, and Taft.[37]

The Centrality of the Bureau in the Social Movement: The USDA, Conservationists, and the National Forests

> Nothing permanent can be accomplished in this
> country unless it is backed by sound public senti-
> ment. The greater part of our work, therefore, has
> consisted in arousing a general interest in practi-
> cal forestry throughout the country and in gener-
> ally changing public sentiment toward a more
> conservative treatment of forest lands.
> —Gifford Pinchot, 1903

Whereas Wiley and Galloway built programs that were entirely new to the federal government, Gifford Pinchot and his associates in the Division of Forestry aimed to take an existing program—national forest management—out of the Interior Department. The battle over the national forest reserves was a competition over turf and over warring visions of the public domain. Rarely were the administrative choices facing Congress so stark. Pinchot pitted his agenda of planned harvesting and regulated grazing against the laissez-faire operations of the General Land Office. Yet the stark clarity of the alternatives hardly eased the decision-making process. The transfer of 1905, largely ignored by historians of conservation, was a painful triumph of network-based entrepreneurship.[38]

Concern about deforestation and sheep grazing on national forest reserves intensified at the turn of the century. Newspapers and journals across the country turned their attention to the new crisis. The California monthly *Wood and Iron* lamented in 1897 that "our forests are disappearing under fire and axe." The *Montpelier Journal* decried the "murderous, obliterating harvesting" of the logging companies and the "match trust." John P. Brown, secretary of the International Society of Arboriculture, predicted in a 1901 tour of New England that "the forests of America will become extinct in 50 years at the present rate of consumption" and warned that the trees might disappear as early as 1925. Bernhard Fernow, at Cornell's State College of Forestry, echoed Brown's more pessimistic forecast two years later, predicting forest exhaustion by 1930. The *Sacramento Record* took note of the emerging consensus: "[T]he interior press, with remarkable unanimity, has taken up the forest preservation and water storage question." These worries were fueled by the extended droughts of the late 1890s, a problem for which forestry experts offered an alluring hypothesis. Because forests attracted cloud cover and rain, deforestation was ruining watersheds on both coasts and disrupting climatic patterns. Secretary Wilson offered a widely quoted judgment in 1900 linking drought with deforestation, and the *Pittsburgh Dispatch* noted that Wilson's judgment was "echoed by many journals in editorial comment on the subject." The *Pottstown (Pennsylvania) Ledger* reported the current wisdom to its readers in 1901: "Students of forestry all agree that the droughts from which the country has suffered in recent years . . . are in a large measure due to the reckless destruction of the forests." Deforestation also brought a new deluge of petitions and letters to numerous congressional committees, including the House Committee on Public Lands and the House and Senate Agriculture Committees.[39]

Fernow, Pinchot, Wilson, and Herman von Schrenk's role in pointing to these hazards placed the department at center stage in the forestry debate. USDA officials received frequent and favorable mention in the pages of Progressive-Era newspapers and journals. As the *Philadelphia Item* noted in July 1901, "The present Department of Agriculture seems to command the confidence of the country and it is generally conceded that Secretary Wilson is trying to make it an extremely useful annex to the Government. The long prevailing drought in the middle West is receiving special attention from the Department." Papers like the *Quincy (Illinois) Whig*, the *Portland (Maine) Advertiser*, and the *Los Angeles Times* and *Herald* wrote repeatedly of "Mr. Pinchot," "Secretary Wilson," and "the Bureau of Forestry" without having to remind readers of their identities or full titles. The regard for the department was particularly strong in California. There a group of state administrators formed the radical Water and Forest Society to enforce two bills that had been pocket vetoed by Governor Samuel Tifft Gage in 1899. The society cooperated openly with the Division of Forestry, an accord that the *San Francisco Call* hoped would "[ensure] a plan of campaign that will finally save our mountain forests from destruction." Elsewhere, Californians welcomed the department's growing presence in the state. The optimism of the *Daily Chico Record*, the leading Democratic paper of the upper Sacramento Valley, was representative.

> Inspector Shinn says that Secretary of Agriculture Wilson is one of the most capable and progressive men who have ever occupied that responsible office, and the results of his work are everywhere manifest. Gifford Pinchot, his chief of the Forestry Division, has energetic young men out in the forests in all parts of the country, and particularly on the Pacific Coast. . . . California has been very fortunate this past summer, for besides the Convention of Experiment Stations men she has had visits from Secretary Wilson and many of his chiefs of divisions, and the relations between California institutions and the Agricultural Department at Washington are in consequence closer, more cordial and more effectual than ever before. The results are also becoming manifest in lines of publication. Dr. Merriam, chief of Biological survey, has just issued a very readable and scientific bulletin upon the animals and plants of Mt. Shasta; Dr. Pinchot's' last bulletin, "A Primer of Forestry," is crowded with Pacific Coast allusions.[40]

In sounding their warnings, USDA scientists participated in a larger community of dialogue and political action. The soldiers of American conservation included John Muir, Charles S. Sargent, Henry S. Graves, and Frederick H. Newell, among others. Recent historians have rightly emphasized the movement's life outside the government. Conservation had roots in the Reconstruction period, long before the Forestry Division arose. It also had a private organizational mouthpiece after 1909 in the National Conservation Association, as well as an active presence in state legislatures. Yet no organization was more centrally positioned in Progressive conservation than the Bureau of Forestry, and no individual knew and led more of the movement's adherents than Pinchot. Pinchot came to the USDA two years before Roosevelt had influence in government forestry, and he moved with familiarity and confidence among conservationists. Fernow, Merriam, and botanist Frederick Coville, who led the effort to establish national arboretums in Washington, D.C., and California, were also recognizable figures in conservation circles. Even anti-conservationists such as Senator Charles S. Thomas, a Democrat from Colorado, generally placed Pinchot at the center of the movement. As Indiana Progressive Albert Beveridge reminded Pinchot in 1921, "The whole Conservation system is yours, dear Gifford." Indeed, in a 1907 meeting between Pinchot, Roosevelt, and USDA forester Overton Price the term "conservation movement" was coined.[41]

To the problem of deforestation, conservationists offered a wide range of solutions. The most severe option, advocated by Muir and Sargent, was to prohibit grazing on national forest reserves and to foreclose the lands to further logging. Pinchot thought differently. He proposed not prohibition but regulation. Pinchot and his associates in the Bureau of Forestry pioneered the concept of planned management. Pinchot wanted planned logging with the goal of a "sustained yield" in the reserves. He wanted the government to lease water-power sites (in lieu of private ownership), to prohibit sheep grazing only where it was not already established, and, where permitted, to impose per-animal fees on livestock companies. Pinchot also continued Fernow's advocacy of the "multiple use" concept, the late-nineteenth-century precept that the forests were as much for the hunter, farmer, fisherman, and shipper as for the logging companies. In its philosophy of "use" combined with "regulation," the Forestry Bureau avoided the "preservationist" extremes of Muir and Sargent and wiggled securely into the middle of Progressive debates.[42]

Pinchot's administrative preferences, however, were not as diluted. By the late 1890s he was convinced that the General Land Office—"the Government's real estate office," he scoffed—was incapable of managing the national forest reserves. He marveled at the fact that the GLO, "without a single forester on its pay roll," controlled 46 million acres of reserves, whereas the forester-rich USDA "hadn't a single acre of public forest under its jurisdiction." The contradiction grew only clearer when Interior Secretary Ethan A. Hitchcock sought the assistance of Pinchot's division for planned timber harvesting in 1899. Pinchot appointed an Interior Forestry adviser from the ranks of his division and drew up plans for regulated timber harvests. Given this radical arrangement, Hitchcock's support in 1901 for a transfer of the reserves was rather unsurprising.[43]

Well before Roosevelt's ascendancy in 1901, Pinchot built a multifaceted strategy for the acquisition of the national forests. He cultivated the support of western business groups, Progressives, women's groups, and academics. As early as 1898 he had persuaded the American Forestry Association and the National Board of Trade to petition McKinley and Congress in favor of the transfer. He also took a page from Wiley and secured the loyalty of the General Federation of Women's Clubs, which created a forestry committee in 1904. Lydia Phillips Williams, chairwoman of that committee, adored Pinchot and wrote to ʰim frequently. With Williams's energy, the GFWC voted several resolutions ᵤring the transfer and supporting increased bureau funding. Beyond this, Pinchot, like Wiley, had developed a skilled publicity program. The government circulated 1 million copies of his *Primer of Forestry*. By 1905 the Forestry Bureau was mailing out 5 million circulars annually and showering weekly forestry reports on newspapers with a combined circulation of 50 million readers. Finally, Pinchot brought his alluring persona to the campaign by speaking widely in support of the transfer and lecturing before western state legislatures, lumbering associations in Oregon and Canada, and wool growers' associations in Washington, D.C.[44]

Roosevelt's ascension in 1901 brought a powerful new ally to conservationists. Yet his support for the transfer was not certain; the new president did not wish to offend his party's Old Guard. Congressional Republicans had proposed the Forestry Division's abolition in 1898, and their leaders were still in power. It was not until Pinchot urged on Roosevelt the necessity for the transfer that the president spoke in favor of the move in 1901, even adopting Pinchot's draft speech for the occasion. After 1901, Roosevelt's support for the transfer was strong, and the two men were intimate friends. The president was impressed with the nonpartisan nature of Pinchot's ideas. The forester became one of Roosevelt's most trusted confidants—the "Adonis of the tennis cabinet," as the press called him—surpassing most of Roosevelt's other advisers. In 1919 Senator Charles S. Thomas of Colorado remembered Pinchot as "chief adviser to President Roosevelt."[45]

Pinchot is widely credited for the "greening" of Roosevelt, but in fact more credit is due to the USDA's other famous conservationist, C. Hart Merriam of the Biological Survey. Merriam and Roosevelt corresponded for four decades, from 1877 until 1917. By 1895, even with Roosevelt as police commissioner of New York City, the two men carried on an intimate friendship. After 1901, Merriam dined and corresponded regularly with the president, edited his speeches, and performed character appraisals for his nominees. In Merriam, Roosevelt found a partner for the appreciation and study of the outdoors. Merriam also brought his affiliations with urban journalists to the department, including Walter Hines Page at Doubleday, Page, and Co., which featured the Biological Survey in its first issue of *The World's Work*. And when T. S. Palmer, a former Merriam disciple, became assistant vice president of the Audubon Society after 1910, the USDA had another powerful ally in the naturalist leagues. Roosevelt, Merriam, and Pinchot also participated in the emergent sportsmen's association movement, a gendered outgrowth of Progressive Victorianism whose organizations played an important role in conservation. All three were members of the naturalist Boone and Crockett Club. From a broader vantage point, the position of the Department of Agriculture was enviable. No other domestic agency before or since had two such intimate associates of the president as division chiefs *before* the president assumed office.[46]

With Roosevelt on board, Congress creaked into motion. As with pure food and drug legislation, the Agriculture Committees never saw the transfer bill. It was "Major" John Lacey of Iowa, chairman of the House Public Lands Committee, who introduced the first measure in 1901 giving the president transfer authority. Newspapers were supportive and fully expected the transfer to pass. Lacey's bill contained more than a transfer, however. It also proposed to create gaming reserves in the national forests. Members of Congress found this combination odd, John Shafroth of Colorado noting that the gaming and transfer planks had "no more relation to each other than night has to day." But this is exactly what Roosevelt and Lacey wanted. A transfer bill to create gaming reserves suited not simply Pinchot but Merriam as well. In addition, it displayed the political allure of the USDA's multiple use theory, as sportsmen strongly supported the game reserves. Lacey's committee reported the transfer bill by a 12-to-4 vote.[47]

It did not take long for opposition to materialize. When debate began in the House in 1902, Lacey was met by western representatives and Joseph Cannon, then chairman of the House Appropriations Committee. The Land Office was an important resource for the Republican Party. It provided party leaders with patronage, and its laissez-faire attitude toward forest access provided low-cost inputs for western logging, mining, and grazing concerns. The GLO was one of those rare agencies, then, whose distributive largesse reached across sections. Cannon feared that if the reserves were transferred, the rapidly disappearing patronage would dry up. Although Interior Secretary Hitchcock endorsed the transfer, moreover, GLO commissioner Binger Hermann did not.

On the House floor, the opposition was spearheaded by Wyoming representative Frank W. Mondell. Mondell wrote the minority report of the Public Lands Committee and offered several arguments against the transfer. He rightly noted that only those forest lands whose boundaries had been fully drawn would be eligible for transfer to the USDA. The transfer hence created dual jurisdiction over the reserves, leading Populist representative John Calhoun Bell of Colorado to complain that westerners would "be a shuttlecock between the two departments." Mondell also assailed the transfer as a "radical change in policy," a signifier for the limits on access to the reserves that westerners feared from the USDA. Mondell even suggested that the Interior Department was as capable of forest management as the USDA. On this point numerous representatives, including western and southern Democrats, attacked the committee minority. Edward Stevens Henry of Connecticut found the USDA equipped with "a more competent corps of foresters" than the Interior Department. Rudolph Kleberg of Texas agreed, saying that "[t]hese forest reserves ought to be placed . . . under a body composed of scientific men, such as we have now in the Forestry Bureau of the Agricultural Department." Lacey pulled the trump card in the capacity debate when he noted that the states, private woods owners, and the Interior Department itself had sought the counsel of the Forestry Bureau for planning and management advice. In concluding the supporters' case, John Sharp Williams of Mississippi waxed homiletic.

> The interests of agriculture will be the object when the Agricultural Department comes to designate and manage the forestry reserves. They will have in control and management men who have been trained as foresters, not trained as mere special agents; men who will know just how to mark the trees to be cut, just how much cutting to permit, just how much grazing should be permitted, and still at the same time keep the forests at the head of the streams what God evidently intended them to be— an ever-living and ever self-renewing thing.[48]

The minority quickly backed down from the capacity issue. Shafroth admitted that the USDA would manage the reserves well, so much so, he thought, that the bill should be scuttled because it split jurisdiction. All meaningful dialogue on the bill ceased, however, when Cannon took the floor and asked for thirty minutes. Cannon lionized the Land Office as "a great service," one "thoroughly organized" from the birth of the Republic. He announced his skepticism of government scientists who were "industrious to fasten upon the public teat." He insulted Pinchot as having been "born with a gold spoon in his mouth" and lambasted the Forestry Bureau as "a fraud and a cheat." Cannon concluded his speech by offering a motion to strike out the Lacey bill's enacting clause. The House passed the motion by 100 to 73, and the transfer was dead. Cannon had brandished the power of czar rule. As forester Arnold Hague later wrote, "Cannon's blast seems to have fallen on the House very much as the poisonous asphyxiating atmosphere from Pelee fell upon St. Pierre. . . . It's rather hard to see the Land Office methods commended for being practical."[49]

Making Policy by Changing Minds: The Conversion of Frank W. Mondell

In response to the defeat, Pinchot embarked on a risky strategy. He might have appeased Cannon by allowing political appointments in his bureau. Yet instead of capitulating, he outflanked "Uncle Joe" and went right to the source of the opposition: to the West and to Frank Mondell. As he recalled,

> Wherever I went, and I traveled thousands of miles each year, I preached USE, just as I did at Portland—conservative use of every forest resource. *Group by group we were convincing people that forestry meant the opening of land to systematic use*, as opposed to exercising the flat-footed shut-out policy so often attributed to it.
>
> During the summer of 1903 Mondell and I met and traveled together through the Yellowstone region. There's nothing like a mutual experience in the great outdoors for clarifying conflicting views. Mondell and I thus came to understand each other.

Over the summer Pinchot waged his silent campaign with Mondell and rehearsed the "use" argument in speeches throughout the West. He summarized his efforts to Roosevelt on September 4.

> One of my principal objects in making the trip in Wyoming with Mondell was to discuss with him the question of the transfer, and, if possible, to get him to change his mind on the subject. While he was not willing to express himself definitely when I left him, nevertheless I think I succeeded. . . . I explained to him that . . . I should not be surprised if he were willing, when the time comes, not only to withdraw his opposition, but to make the initiative himself in bringing the transfer about.[50]

It was perhaps Pinchot's greatest achievement that his brash dare came to fruition. On November 12, 1903, Mondell introduced H.R. 1987—"A bill providing for the transfer of forest reserves from the Department of Interior to the Department of Agriculture"—to the Committee on Public Lands. Pinchot had written the following to the president on September 21: "Mondell, you will be glad to know, has withdrawn his opposition entirely, and says that 'We' will have no trouble whatever in getting the transfer made at the coming session." As Samuel Hays admits, Mondell's conversion remains "a curious feature of the transfer legislation." Hays surmises (without any supporting evidence) that Pinchot favored a land-use program in line with the desires of Wyoming groups. Yet Pinchot promoted "use" before 1900, and California interests were no less enthusiastic about his position than were Mondell's Wyoming associates. More important, Hays mistakenly ignores Pinchot's extended political courtship of Mondell in the summer and fall of 1903. The fact that Mondell changed his mind in September 1903 points more to Pinchot's suasion than to a land-use policy developed six years earlier.[51]

With Mondell not merely removed from the opposition but actively promoting the transfer, momentum turned decisively in favor of USDA authority. By 1904 Pinchot had signed on numerous business organizations to his cause, including the National Live Stock Association, the National Wool Growers' Association, the American Mining Congress, the National Irrigation Congress, and the National Board of Trade. Cannon met with Mondell and fumed that the transfer was now "inevitable." Pinchot then made one final legitimizing step.

In a March 1904 Bureau of Forestry meeting he presented a plan for an annual "Forest and Water Convention" to be held under the auspices of the American Forestry Association. Roosevelt called the first American Forestry Congress in early January 1905. As the president remarked, it brought together "the great business and forest interests of the nation," including lumber magnate F. E. Weyerhaeuser, Lydia Phillips Williams of the GFWC, J. E. Defebaugh (editor of the *American Lumberman*), James J. Hill (president of the Great Northern Railway), Frederick Newell of the Reclamation Service, and the patent imprimatur of the Republican leadership. The tacit purpose of the Congress was to unify the budding conservation movement behind the transfer, which the meeting affirmed with a resolution. By January 1905 the House and Senate had passed the transfer bills almost without discord. Roosevelt signed the Transfer Act on February 1, 1905.[52]

Pinchot as Planner and as Legislator: The Meaning of Autonomy in Forestry

The 1905 law was pathbreaking in several ways. First, it released the Forest Service from dependence on congressional appropriations, dedicating all revenues from the forest reserves to the service rather than to the general treasury. Second, the act was followed by a law on February 6, 1905, granting Pinchot the right to make rules governing the service. Within two years, western interests acutely perceived that he was transgressing his mandate under the legislation. Pinchot had struck on the February 6 law and begun implementing his "conservative use" doctrine. Under this plan, designed to impose on users some share of the costs of USDA management, the Forest Service charged a per-mile fee for the lengths of any ditches, a per-acre fee for any land occupied, and a per-occupant fee for water conservation. Nowhere in the January 1905 legislation were such fees even contemplated. Pinchot asked Congress for explicit authorization, but Cannon's allies would not budge, so Pinchot sought and received a favorable interpretation of existing law from Attorney General William Moody and began administering fees and regulating grazing and timber sales. Western senators and representatives bristled at Pinchot's brazen assumption of legislative power. Colorado's Henry Moore Teller said, "I have never doubted that the Government of the United States could take any measures necessary to protect its property by Congressional act, but I do deny that an individual executive officer of the Government has any right to legislate as to how lands shall be preserved." Senator Charles W. Fulton of Oregon slandered the bureau as "composed of dreamers and theorists." A counterattack from the West was under way, culminating in the 1907 appropriations bill, which abolished the service's "special fund" from timber sales and curtailed and returned to Congress the president's authority to create forest reserves.[53]

The thrust of the Old Guard was met by the parry of Progressives, conservationists, and the national press. Senators from all areas—Jonathan Dolliver of Iowa, George Clement Perkins and Frank Putnam Flint of California, Fred Dubois of Idaho, Albert Beveridge of Indiana, John Coit Spooner of Wisconsin, Redfield Proctor of Vermont, and Francis Newlands of Nevada—rose up in Pinchot's defense. Whether or not he deserved it, Pinchot quickly took on the aura of an official dedicated to the common good, beleaguered by the "special interests" arrayed against him. As Minnesota's Knute Nelson reasoned, "I wish to say about Mr. Pinchot that while in some respects I think he has been a little too radical, has gone a little hastily and too far, yet I recognize the fact that in that line of work he is an expert of the very highest order, and that he is actuated by the highest and best possible sentiments—sentiments that every public man in this country could well be proud of." The GFWC also rallied to Pinchot's side, with Williams offering him the full publicity power of the federation's membership. She bluntly requested in 1906: "Would you kindly draft any resolution that you would like the G.F.W.C. to pass in support of the Forest Service or forestry." Outside of the mountain West, newspapers everywhere were indignant, and adoring portraits of Pinchot and the bureau filled their pages. The *Sioux Falls Press* lambasted Mondell for "a disgraceful attack." Hewitt Thomas responded to Fulton's attack in the *Review of Reviews*: "Call [Pinchot] a dreamer if you will; he dreams for the welfare of the people. Say he is an enthusiast, but an enthusiast seeking to safeguard the people's rights." The *North American*, whose endearing portrait appears in figure 8.1, cast Pinchot and Wiley as defenders of the "common man." Observing the emergence of pro-Pinchot sentiment in its paean "A Knight of the Twentieth Century," the *St. Louis Star* noted that "Pinchot also recognizes the power of publicity, and he has the periodicals and newspapers with him."[54]

Supported by the popular press, Pinchot deftly resisted Congress's attempts to rein in his policy. None of the western interests was able to repeal Pinchot's user fee policy of 1906. Immediately after the appropriations bill passed, moreover, Pinchot got Roosevelt to declare more than 40 million acres of reserve lands as national forests before the bill could go into effect. In a letter to his forester, Wilson expressed his concern that the department was "seriously breaking faith with the Congress" and that "a good deal of trouble" would result, but Pinchot went ahead with the land grab. The new reserves were in Oregon, Washington, Idaho, Wyoming, and Colorado, precisely those states where Fulton's amendment forbade executive reserve creation. In all respects Fulton's measure had been administratively nullified. Fulton was outraged but could do nothing. Nor did the abolition of the special fund restrain Pinchot, as the appropriations bill compensated entirely for the loss of timber money. The establishment of a budget floor, below which the service's appropriations would never again dip, more than made up for the inconvenience (combined with the greater certainty) of the appropriations process. As Pinchot later reminisced, the

Figure 8.1 Pinchot and Wiley: "Government Officers Whom the Special Interests are Assailing"

fund "accomplished its purpose," and the funding repeal came "too late to destroy" the organization he had "firmly established." Nor did the bill alter the service's spending patterns, as it continued spending millions of dollars for research and continued its implicit publicity campaign by "dissemination of valuable information among the people."[55]

With the inauguration of President William Howard Taft in 1909 came new controversy. In April of that year Taft issued an order for the removal of nonforested lands from the forest reserves. Pinchot dragged in complying with the order, provoking Taft's frustration and earning the animosity of J. Arthur Eddy, then president of the logging-friendly National Public Domain League. "To be at the mercy of such a vacillating, unreliable personality [as Pinchot]," Eddy huffed, "justifies apprehension relative to the proper execution of the President's order." Eddy also aimed his ire at user fees. In testimony before the Colorado legislature in March 1909, Eddy denounced this "radical change from the principles which had governed the Interior Department" and lambasted Pinchot's usurpation of legislative power.

> History is challenged to instance anything, approaching such audacious Departmental assumption of power in a leigislative [*sic*] capacity. With one swoop the whole government policy of the Forest Reserves is changed; our land laws and practices materially modified and a whole code of new laws pertaining to the public domain within the Forest Reserves . . . absolutely new and unique are prescribed.

Eddy declared the Forest Service a "new institution, *made without Congressional assistance.*" Congress created the Forest Reserves, Eddy implied, but it was Pinchot who created the Forest *Service*. The fact that Pinchot's policies had broad public support was due to his scurrilous "publicity machine," which in Eddy's estimation mailed out more than 9 million circulars annually. Eddy lamented Pinchot's ability to shape public opinion: "Congress usually undertakes to ascertain what the people want and legislate accordingly—Pinchot reverses the proceeding."[56]

Rethinking the Ballinger-Pinchot Controversy and the Cannon Revolt

Pinchot's brazen disregard for the Old Guard of his party reached its zenith in his public dispute with Interior Secretary Richard A. Ballinger. In August 1909 Land Office agent L. R. Glavis discovered evidence that Ballinger, who was promoted from GLO commissioner, had admitted numerous questionable private claims in the lands of the Alaskan coal reserves and had received payments from the claimants after being promoted to secretary. Overton W. Price and Alexander C. Shaw of the Forest Service assisted in the investigation of Ballinger, as the coal reserves lay in the Chugach National Forest. When Glavis reported his charges to Taft, the president dismissed him. Taft then issued a gag order preventing government employees from communicating with Congress and the press. Taft hoped to squelch word of Ballinger's misdeeds, but Price and Shaw publicized the evidence, launching a congressional investigation of the Interior Department. Pinchot then defended the actions of his foresters in a letter to Jonathan Dolliver, chairman of the Senate Agriculture Committee. Wilson implored Pinchot not to send it, as it would violate Taft's order, but Pinchot planned to "induce" Dolliver to read his letter on the Senate floor. Taft then seized on Pinchot's behavior as mutinous and promptly dismissed the chief forester, Price, and Shaw.

Taft's firing established Pinchot as a martyr for bureaucratic regulation and only strengthened the Forestry Bureau. For in dismissing Pinchot, Taft set two forces in motion that would destroy the electoral prospects of the Old Guard. First, Pinchot's dismissal was the last straw for Insurgents who had grown wary of the president from 1909 onward. As the *Philadelphia Inquirer* noted, the dismissal "started a fight against the renomination of William H. Taft." The firing enraged Roosevelt, who soon resolved to unseat Taft in the 1912 election. The second legacy of the firing arguably had a greater effect: it started the infamous Cannon revolt of 1910, which decentralized power in the twentieth-century House of Representatives. In response to the dismissal, House insurgents voted to strip Cannon of his power to name members of the joint special committee to investigate Ballinger. It was the first of three times that the Insurgents would curtail Cannon's power in the winter of 1910. It is critical that the three-vote margin of victory in the first revolt was provided by *non-Insurgent* Republicans who were outraged by their party's treatment of Pinchot and the Forest Service. In light of the larger narrative here, the Cannon revolt was not simply a decentralization of power in the House. It was also a sustained institutional revulsion to the Republicans' attack on a popular and legitimized government bureau. This reading of the Cannon revolt certainly was not foreign to the *Inquirer*, whose writer noted that "the dismissal of Pinchot has lent fuel to the flame of [the Insurgents]." Decades later, John Hicks also interpreted the revolt as coming "hard on the heels of the Pinchot-Ballinger controversy." As if to express strongly its support for the forester, the House sharply rejected New York representative Frank Fitzgerald's amendment to eliminate the Forestry Bureau by a vote of 226 to 65.[57]

The Power of Organizational Culture. Pinchot's departure did little to alter conservation policy in the Forest Service, for he had hired its entire personnel—including Henry S. Graves, his replacement—thereby securing a generation of successors who were fiercely loyal to the conservationist legacy. The "Pinchot generation" was long lasting. In 1940 Pinchot collected the memoirs of the individuals he had recruited into the service. He sent out requests to all the regional supervisors of the Forest Service and published a call for memoirs in *American Forests*. Pinchot received fully 227 memoirs, almost a fifth of the service in 1910. Of these 227 individuals, all hired between 1898 and 1910, 91 had served past 1920, 63 had served past 1930, and 33 were still working in the Forest Service. These figures doubtless exclude hundreds of men who had died or retired involuntarily (due to mandatory retirement laws) during the intervening three decades. The Pinchot generation also included the lion's share of the Forest Service's leaders and regional supervisors from 1910 through the New Deal, including Graves, Paul G. Redington, and George B. Sudworth.

As Herbert Kaufman has detailed, moreover, the culture established during the Pinchot period centralized power within the service and maintained loyalty to the conservationist legacy. As Kaufman argued in 1960, "[T]he Forest Service enjoys . . . an environment conducive to an almost automatic tendency to conform to [the leadership's] decisions. That environment is a set of conditions promoting identification of the members of the Forest Service with the organization, linking their own positions and welfare and futures with those of the agency, fusing their perspectives with those of their colleagues and superiors."

With Pinchot having hired three decades of service leaders, the organizational permanence of planning was secured.[58]

Loggers, Committees, and Movements: Explaining the Forest Service Transfer

What accounts for the transfer of the national forest reserves and the emergence of a conservation policy in the United States? Why did a consensus of near unanimity emerge in favor of the transfer? Some of the standard forces in Progressive legislation—agrarian organizations and "corporate liberal" business interests—played little or no role in the move. The Grange and the Farmers' Union were virtually absent from the struggle, and aside from logging and mining firms, business coalitions were silent. The transfer could have been a distributive ploy designed to ease restrictions on western lumber firms. Yet this interpretation is inconsistent with the historical course of the transfer. Mining and logging interests may not have been hurt by the transfer, but they hardly saw greater protection for their interests in the Forestry Bureau than in the General Land Office.

Another possible explanation for the transfer is institutional and centered in Congress: the Agriculture and Forestry Committee was expanding its jurisdictions from 1880 onward, and USDA control of the national forest reserves translated into Agriculture Committee power over the reserves. The transfer would therefore have been in the committee's best interest. (The Committee on Agriculture, it is useful to recall, was renamed the Committee on Agriculture *and Forestry* in 1884.) With turn-of-the-century legislators facing greater incentives to specialize and gather programs under their committees, the transfer may have helped turf-hungry representatives from farm states whose party status mattered less and less to their electoral futures. Yet in light of the ease with which the Agriculture Committee's eagerness for the transfer can be explained, the Public Lands Committee's initiation and approval of the transfer becomes all the more puzzling. It was Lacey (the committee's chairman) who first led the transfer campaign, and it was Mondell (the minority leader) who took up the aegis after the Lacey bill's demise in 1902. Moreover, the Agriculture Committee received forestry jurisdiction in 1884, more than two decades before the transfer. Why then did the committee not seek the transfer in the turbulent 1890s, when the sheep depredations were hitting the national press, when farm-state politics were getting more volatile, and precisely when individual members of Congress began to embrace committee-specific careers?[59]

Undoubtedly the transfer must be narrated and explained in the context of the turn-of-the-century conservationist movement. As Hays and others have shown, however, the conservationist movement was in no way independent of the USDA. Indeed, the permanence and prestige of the Bureaus of Forestry and

Biological Survey gave to the conservationist movement a stable home at a time when serious disagreements were arising among Sargent, Graves, Muir, Pinchot, and others.

As with other bureau chiefs and program leaders at the Agriculture Department, moreover, Pinchot drew his power and influence not from an association with the conservationist movement alone but from his unique standing in the multiple networks of Progressive society. Pinchot and his bureau had the trust of Republican Party leaders (he was later elected governor of Pennsylvania and served from 1923 to 1927 and 1931 to 1935). The bureau was lionized by the national press (who had come to depend on it for environmental news), and it received the unwavering support of the General Federation of Women's Clubs. Almost uniquely among the conservationists, Pinchot strode confidently among these very different and frequently opposed quarters of American politics.[60]

The most compelling account of the transfer is that emergent conservationists, loggers, and both the Agriculture and Public Lands Committees settled on the Forestry Bureau's esteem and Pinchot's planning ideology as the best course for national forest management. This is not to deny that the transfer and Pinchot's subsequent policy did not ruffle feathers and encounter fierce opposition in Congress. It did. Yet the terms of debate by 1907 and afterward were vastly different from the terms of debate in 1903, and it was Pinchot and his associates at the Bureau of Forestry who changed them. In the creation of a national forest policy, the new rationality of planning came powerfully to the fore of western resource politics. Here the very *concept* of policy—of planning and managing forest utilization for long-term use—was a novelty. By 1910 and for decades afterward it was an established principle of forest administration, a triumph driven by the agenda setting of Gifford Pinchot and the USDA Bureau of Forestry.[61]

Conclusion: Networks and Bureaucratic Culture in the Agricultural State

The forging of bureaucratic autonomy in the U.S. Department of Agriculture stands as perhaps the single most impressive state-building development of the early twentieth century. Nowhere was the federal government more liberated from the strictures of local control and congressional consignment to distributive policies. Nowhere else did administrative entrepreneurs such as Harvey Wiley, Seaman Knapp, C. Hart Merriam, and Gifford Pinchot find themselves with the means and the mandate to launch enduring programs with stable and significant grants of leeway from Congress. Only in the Department of Agriculture did a bureaucracy command such identification with and attachment from its scientific and administrative employees. Only then—through an emerging administrative network of county agents, traveling scientists, and committed foresters and regulators—did the USDA establish a presence in urban and rural communities that was only partly mediated by state and local elites. By building bureau-based reputations that were grounded in multiple networks, the department won liberation from its nineteenth-century servitude.

Through the strategies of its autonomous bureaus, the USDA transformed federal policy in agriculture, in industrial regulation, and in national resources planning. These were administrative rather than legislative innovations. Pharmaceutical regulation in the United States was the achievement not of a capturing industry, not of a consumer lobby, but of a coalition built and centered by a bureaucrat and his bureau. Agricultural extension was introduced first by USDA administrators on an experimental basis, then expanded through the use of discretionary funds, and only later given the authorizing imprimatur of legislation. The Transfer Act of 1905 and its ensuing policy were not conservationist achievements per se, but the result of multifaceted coalitions. All three policy innovations brought together voices of numerous organizations in Progressive politics. And the organizational nexus of this effort—the site of action where these forces converged—was the USDA.

Nine

Brokerage and Bureaucratic Policymaking: The Cementing of Autonomy at the USDA, 1914–28

> The Official of this United States are supposed to
> be servents of the people but instead they are
> making Slaves of the people. . . . I believe the
> only way for the farmers to get out of this condi-
> tion is to organize and reduce their acreage one
> half for a term of 5 years. he will make more with
> one half of the expence. Mr. Wallace as you are at
> the head of agriculture I should thik it your duty
> to inaugurat something of the kind.
> —Oregon farmer Squire Innis [*sic* throughout]

> The county agent is the strong right arm of the
> American Farm Bureau Federation.
> —James R. Howard

THE FIRST WORLD WAR and the decade that followed it are commonly regarded as a harsh interlude in the evolution of a national state in America. Even in 1914 observers knew that "war is the mother of all states," yet American involvement in the European conflict of 1914–18 added little to existing state capacity. In military purchasing and economic mobilization, the War Department was displaced by the War Industries Board (WIB), a council of industrialists led by financier Bernard Baruch. Bureaucracies also played a small role in the mobilization of allegiance and domestic unity. And unlike the Civil War, the Second World War, and the various conflicts of the cold war, World War I did not make lasting additions to America's social welfare state. If anything, socialist opposition to the war effort only enfeebled and delegitimized whatever statist radicalism remained from the Progressive Era. Nor did the postwar period offer any solace to state builders. The return of Old Guard Republican conservatives to the presidency and to congressional majorities in the 1920s left most agencies scrambling to maintain their existing jurisdictions and budgets.[1]

The Department of Agriculture marked a steady exception to this pattern. The USDA achieved a remarkable level of political insulation after 1910, and its strength continued through the reactionary 1920s. The department emerged from the war with a bolder presence in rural America and with new capacities to plan and regulate. Whereas many agencies floundered under the Harding and Coolidge administrations, the USDA adopted a more aggressive regulatory posture and successfully repelled two Republican attempts to have its functions transferred to other departments. Whereas farmers' organizations waxed and waned through the war and legislative coalitions such as the Farm Bloc were short-lived, the department's Extension Service and its political twin, the Farm Bureau, grew steadily with age.

The foundation of the USDA's autonomy after the Progressive period lay in its unique position of organizational brokerage. By *brokerage* I mean organizational centrality combined with a relative monopoly on agricultural policy information. Empowered and legitimized by multiple network affiliations from 1890 to 1910, the department took its place as the central representative organ of American agriculture. Although the USDA hardly represented every farmer in the nation, arguably it laid claim to the political trust of millions of American farmers, perhaps more than any single producer group. The department was closely involved with all but the most radical farmers' organizations, and in many cases it provided the only conduit through which farmers of different regions and groups could dialogue and trade information with one another. In advancing this claim, I contend neither that the farmers' movements of the late 1800s were dead nor that the newer forces of agrarian unrest (the National Farmers' Union, for example) were muted. Indeed, it was precisely the *multiplicity* of agricultural organizations during the Progressive period that empowered the department as a broker among so many competing interests, for nothing so characterizes agricultural organization from 1896 to the New Deal as its balkanization. In a system where more than eight thousand organizations competed for farmers' allegiance at all levels of government, the USDA stood as the single national organization that garnered the political trust of farmers of all commodities and all regions. Department officials provided information and advice to numerous interests in American agriculture and positioned themselves away from the extremes of agrarian debates, thereby gaining legitimacy from numerous quarters.[2]

My explanation for the power of the Department of Agriculture before the New Deal differs materially from two other accounts. In *State and Party in America's New Deal,* Kenneth Finegold and Theda Skocpol attribute the powers of the department as "an island of state strength in an ocean of weakness" to its unique positioning in the "nexus" of state land-grant colleges and experiment stations. Elizabeth Sanders advances a movement-centered explanation for the department's growth, arguing that organized farmers—taking hold of the Democratic Party from 1910 to 1920—had been the principal movers behind the department's creation, behind its expansion, and behind the legion of statutory responsibilities placed on it under Woodrow Wilson. I believe that a legitimacy-centered account fares better than either the Finegold-Skocpol or the Sanders alternative. It accounts for the *incremental* growth of the department's capacity and autonomy, and it draws on the strengths of the movement and "policy-nexus" narratives. The department's legitimacy in farm circles lay in its near-universal favor with and close ties to the major farm groups. It is fair to say that not a single major organization opposed the department's agenda during this period, not even the much-weakened National Farmers' Union after the war. Indeed, the most powerful postwar farm movement was one that the department helped to create: the Farm Bureau. In addition, although the USDA undoubtedly drew on the capacities and talents of the land-grant colleges and experiment stations—as I show in previous chapters—by 1915 the department was the figurative center of this network.[3]

The USDA also solidified its cross-regional and cross-class foundations in Progressive American society. Under the leadership of William J. Spillman, the department's extension system, previously restricted to the South, spread into the northern Plains. The USDA bolstered its weak presence in the burgeoning agriculture of the Pacific Coast, cementing lasting alliances with citrus farmers, nut growers, and state officials in California. The department's emerging program of economic analysis and planning gave it newfound legitimacy in social scientific circles, creating talents that would serve New Deal Democrats well in their search for rationality and planning in farm policy.

As under James Wilson, however, the department secured a political foothold outside of "agriculture" narrowly construed. The USDA continued to press successfully for the governance of national forests and the regulation of food and pharmaceuticals. It also took a central place in the campaign for improved public roads. In forestry and food and drug regulation, the department's policies were advanced with little assistance from organized agrarians. Instead, postwar health and environmental reformers converged on the USDA as the dominant conservationist and public health agency of Progressive-Era American government.

The Establishment of Geographic Legitimacy:
Extension and Research in California

After 1914, the department secured an institutional presence in virtually every nook and cranny of the nation. Its work in meat and drug regulation placed thousands of USDA inspectors in New York, Chicago, Saint Louis, Philadelphia, Detroit, San Francisco, Atlanta, and other urban centers. The department's renown among urban journalists, professional and civic associations, and philanthropists was equal to no other federal agency. Knapp's Farmers' Cooperative Demonstration Work positioned the department in the cotton- and rice-growing South. Pinchot's grab of the national forest reserves in 1905 meant that

TABLE 9.1
Percentage of Counties with Extension Agents, Selected States (1914)

State	Counties Reporting Agricultural Products	Counties with Extension Agents	Percentage of Counties Covered
Alabama	67	67	100
Indiana	92	27	29
New York	57	25	44
Texas	250	98	40
California	45	4	9

Source: USDA, *Cooperative Extension Work in Agriculture and Home Economics, 1916* (Washington, D.C.: GPO, 1917), p. 397.

thousands of conservationist USDA forest officials populated forest terrain from the Adirondacks to the mountain West. Spillman's push northward and the department's growing presence in experiment stations work after the Adams Act of 1906 further rooted its prestige in the Great Lakes, the Plains, and the Ohio Valley.

The clear exception to the department's geographic embedment in American society lay on the Pacific Coast, and nowhere more so than in California. There the department placed few personnel outside San Francisco and the forests. By 1914, as table 9.1 shows, departmental extension agents resided in fewer than one in ten California farm counties. This ratio compared poorly with those of other states, even in the North, where Spillman's system had just begun to make headway. Yet personnel numbers tell only half of the story, for California exhibited two unique features of American agriculture over which the department had little influence before 1910: fruit farming and the agricultural marketing cooperative. The cooperative was the dominant form of farmers' organization, splitting agrarian interests down commodity lines and creating truly cross-sectional coalitions of cultivators for perhaps the first time. Whereas department officials traveled well in Grange circles and among county farm bureaus, at first they had little influence on Pacific cooperatives. Because cooperatives were commodity specific, the USDA's political weakness in California was in large measure equivalent to its citrus problem. The department had long employed experts to study grains, cotton, and tobacco, but its capacities in fruit and nut studies were questionable. Further, almost none of the USDA's regulatory work before 1910 concerned these commodities. As a result, the USDA was not able to parlay its vaunted reputation with dairy and grain interests into a lasting esteem with Californian farmers' organizations. The organizations quite simply lay in other products. Indeed, the state's dominant cooperative from 1880 to

1920, a marketing organization as strong as any in the country, was the California Fruit Growers' Exchange (later Sunkist). With fruit culture assuming a greater profile in American farming, and with California fast becoming the dominant economic and political power of the West, the department's weakness there represented a growing threat to its national prominence.[4]

The department's absence from California's citrus industry is especially puzzling in light of the fact that the USDA had imported the nation's first navel orange tree to Riverside, California, in 1867. Notwithstanding this legacy, the department strayed to other problems in the 1880s and 1890s, among them meat and food inspection, seed importation, grain and cotton standardization, forestry, beet sugar agriculture, and the boll weevil problem. With so little political and scientific payoff in fruit research, the USDA mounted few efforts to include citrus in its policy agenda. In this light, it is worth remembering that the mother agency of federal extension—the USDA's Bureau of Plant Industry— was little concerned with fruit. Bureau experts David Fairchild, Mark Carleton, and Seaman Knapp made their mark by importing rice and wheat varieties. It fell to other bureaus—principally the Bureaus of Entomology and Chemistry— to study citrus problems, yet even the talented and well-connected individuals in these bureaus had limited influence. One exception was the Division of Entomology's work on the citrus pest known as cottony-cushiony scale, an effort that introduced new tensions between California state officials and USDA scientists. William Scott of the Bureau of Plant Industry had conducted novel studies of orchard spraying and fruit diseases. Like many other chemists of the Progressive period, however, Scott left in 1914 for the higher pay of an eastern chemical concern. Another USDA expert was Edward McKay Chace, a student of Harvey Wiley at Columbian University who had published widely on lemon oils and navel oranges before 1910. Chace's usefulness, too, was limited because Wiley detailed him to food inspections, a line of work that did not lend itself well to networking with growers. Galloway's bureau devoted more resources to fruit problems when it took over fruit disease work after the Insecticide Act of 1910. Yet of six scientists on the bureau's lump-sum roll for Fruit Disease Investigations in 1914, only Merton B. Waite devoted any time to California, and Waite's interest amounted to a side fancy with pear-blight eradication.[5]

Whatever influence the department did have in California farming before 1900 was limited to seed introduction. Galloway, Fairchild, and Carleton found in California the variegated soils and conditions necessary to conduct rigorous tests of European and Asian seeds. Yet seed introduction consisted mainly in the mailing of seed packets from Washington and in postal correspondence between departmental personnel, the growers, and the College of Agriculture at Berkeley. It meant little visitation of USDA officials with California growers or state officials. Seed work did, however, inform some of the most elite farmers and agribusiness firms of the department's research prowess. In *Seed Bulletins* distributed throughout the state by the Berkeley experiment station, Director

Eugene Hilgard regularly trumpeted the quality of the USDA's seeds as the "best in the world."[6]

The department's eventual inroad came in its developing ties to California's two main agricultural research institutions: the College of Agriculture at Berkeley (and its experiment station) and the Citrus Experiment Station at Riverside. Berkeley was the dominant center for agricultural research on the Pacific Coast at the time, and Spillman and his associate C. B. Smith began making contacts there after 1910. Spillman struck up a long correspondence with Thomas Forsyth Hunt, dean of the college after 1912, which continued into the 1920s. Beginning in 1910, Spillman placed numerous farm management projects in Berkeley. As early as 1913 Spillman had so ingratiated himself with the dean that Hunt promised to spend more than California's share of the needed funds for demonstration: "You have always assumed such a liberal attitude in our cooperation with you that we are more than anxious to meet you halfway in this work." Smith, meanwhile, took a more managerial role, coaching Hunt on how best to establish a program of farm management and cooperative extension in California. Smith's influence gradually grew to the point where he was naming extension personnel in the state and urging Hunt (and other college leaders) to provide special courses for training county agents and other extension personnel.[7]

The experiment station at Riverside held less national prestige than its Berkeley counterpart, yet it carried high esteem among fruit farmers. F. Q. Story, president of the California Fruit Growers' Exchange in 1918, credited the Riverside station with twice saving "the life of the citrus industry" in his state. Although the USDA had few contacts with Riverside personnel before 1910, two men who figured critically in the station's evolution were G. Harold Powell and Herbert J. Webber, department alumni and close associates of Galloway and Spillman. Powell was the department's expert on citrus diseases during the James Wilson years. When California growers suffered unprecedented shipping losses from fruit decay in 1904, they turned not to Berkeley but to Washington, transmitting an "urgent request" for department expertise in the matter. Galloway sent Powell, who discovered that the decay was caused by cuts to the fruit from stem clippers and handlers' fingernails. Powell led an industry-wide effort to introduce modern methods of packing. One year later Galloway remarked, "I was assured by some of the most prominent citrus growers in the southern part of the State that Mr. Powell's efforts that season alone had resulted in the saving of several hundred thousand dollars." By February 1911 Powell, who was still a consulting pomologist with the USDA, was named secretary and manager of the Citrus Protective League in Los Angeles. Later that year, he became manager of the Fruit Growers' Exchange, vacating his position as assistant chief of the BPI. He remained with the bureau as a collaborator until December 1912 and occupied a central role in the 1912–13 campaign to press the California legislature to enlarge the Riverside station.[8]

The department had another loyal friend in the accomplished Nebraskan Herbert J. Webber, who in 1913 became director of the Riverside station and dean of California's Graduate School of Tropical Agriculture. Galloway hired Webber to the Plant Physiology Division in September 1892. Webber quickly ascended the division's ranks, taking charge of the BPI's plant-breeding laboratory in 1899. He also spent five years at Cornell (all the while on Galloway's payroll) before taking the Riverside job.[9]

The department's ties to Hunt, Powell, and Webber resulted in an increasing flow of USDA officials through Berkeley and Riverside. At Riverside's First Horticultural Assembly in November 1913, which gathered prominent growers from throughout the state, Powell and Webber invited USDA experts Lyman Briggs, R. S. Woglum, and L. B. Scott to discuss fumigation and bud-selection techniques. At the California State Fruit Growers' Convention in 1914, USDA official A. D. Shamel lectured and rubbed shoulders with Governor Hiram Johnson, an enthusiastic proponent of Powell's plans for the Riverside station in 1913. In 1916 USDA scientists outnumbered University of California professors at Webber's Five Days' Citrus Institute, with five of the seventeen lecturers visiting from Washington and two more being department collaborators. Department officials and their lectures and exhibits showed up at university beekeeping courses, conventions of California farm institute workers, and even the annual meetings of California boys' clubs.[10]

With relations to California academic leaders stabilizing, several bureaus in the department focused their efforts on citrus issues. The attack on citrus began in the Bureau of Chemistry, where headquarters scientists were conducting more and more research on citrus problems. Chace and Calvin Church began publishing the results of their citrus work in leading trade journals such as *Pacific Coast Packer, American Fruit Grower,* and their favorite venue, the *California Citrograph,* established in 1916 as the organ of the California Fruit Growers' Exchange. Between 1918 and 1924, Chace and Church published eight articles in the *Citrograph* alone. The Bureau of Plant Industry sent Shamel and Harry S. Smith to work at Riverside. Shamel and Smith helped Webber coordinate citrus institutes, and Shamel lectured widely in the state, acquiring repute as an unparalleled expert in citrus problems. When Tulare County plant pathologist P. A. Bocquet (whose work was being upstaged by Shamel's) criticized Shamel as a glorified "palmist" in 1920, California growers came vociferously to Shamel's defense. J. A. Prizer, superintendent of the Merryman Fruit Land and Lumber Company, called Bocquet's writings "despicable" and reminded the readers of the *Exeter Sun* that "A.D. Shamel of the U.S. Department of Agriculture . . . is said to have accomplished more for the citrus grower than any other one man" in the state.[11]

By World War I, USDA officials had established a commanding esteem among citrus growers and state officials in California. Helped by their fortuitous ties to Powell and Webber, and sagely redirecting their studies to citrus and related problems, officials had transformed a weakness into strong geographic legitimacy. Among growers, demand for USDA county agents was vigorous and growing to the point of "embarrassment" for university officials, who could not meet the demand. With Webber taking over as director of the Berkeley station in 1918, agricultural research in California increasingly became a cooperative venture in which the USDA took the lead. Webber acknowledged the irony that his station, the dominant center for agricultural research in the western states, could not rival the USDA's analyses in something so intrinsic to California as dates. The station "could not hope to make much headway in an independent study of [dates]," Webber admitted, "and while we could assist the work somewhat in a close cooperation with them, we could not expect to have more than a minor part in the investigation and would really be of little service as the work on varieties is already so far advanced." Whatever research on dates would be conducted in California, Webber concluded, would be of the USDA's choosing. Some USDA scientists even took to criticizing state officials for their lack of a "proper" research atmosphere. Pathologist H. B. Humphrey warned C. M. Haring, director of the California Experiment Station in 1920, that "until the State of California sees fit to build up a department of plant pathology that is commensurate with teaching and research needs of that great State it will be difficult for any [USDA] research agency to cooperate advantageously in the investigation of pathologic problems of any kind." If date studies and pathology are indications of the USDA's leverage with California officials, then the breadth of the department's influence through "cooperative research" is astonishing. A university newsletter reported that seventy-three members of the Berkeley faculty had engaged in cooperative investigations with the department in 1923 alone.[12]

One might wonder whether the Department of Agriculture's newfound legitimacy in California was the result of political efforts on the part of vote-hungry Democrats or Progressives. After all, with California governor Hiram Johnson making waves in national politics and the growth in his state's population, it would have made sense for politicians to cultivate votes in the state by spreading departmental largesse there. Yet if such an electoral motive prevailed, there is no evidence for it in administrative records. Nor would it make sense that the USDA would focus on citrus problems. The political stronghold of California during the Progressive period, it is important to recall, lay not in the South but in San Francisco and the North. There the department was doing little besides meat and food inspection. Finally, distributive politics played a small role in the USDA's presence in California. The Department was not in the business of awarding huge contracts or doling out subsidies before 1933. And the only pork program of the Department—free seed distribution—had played a small role in the state, even declining after 1905.[13]

The most compelling account of the USDA's Pacific aspirations lies not in the distributive strategies of politicians but in the reputation-building strategies of bureau chiefs. Officials knew that the surest way of obtaining the autonomy and security they desired for their programs was to convince farmers in numerous regions of their value. The chiefs also knew that developing contacts with cooperatives and other organizations was the best way to cement these reputations. Accordingly, Galloway, Wiley, Chemistry Chief Alsberg, and others rewarded their workers for developing ties to growers. When Alsberg recommended John Breazeale for promotion, he called attention less to Breazeale's publications than to his political and social prowess: "He is very popular with the citrus growers, takes an active personal interest in their cultural problems, and is doing much local work in this connection, which does not appear in his printed papers." William A. Taylor, chief of Plant Industry after 1914, pointed to James Morrow's numerous connections to California canners, orchard firms, and state officials when he suggested him for advancement in 1919. Galloway found a valuable asset in George Husmann's esteem with vineyard owners, including Leland Stanford: "[Husmann] is the best trained man in technical viticulture connected with the Department or any of the State experiment stations in the country. He meets people well and delivers interesting talks before grape growers." From 1910 onward, bureau chiefs actively promoted the careers of well-connected scientists. In this respect, the advance into California was a bureau-level campaign.[14]

The department's California ties paid off handsomely in postwar budgetary battles. In 1919, when the Senate eliminated the appropriation for the Bureau of Soils in the USDA, the department used its Extension Service contacts and the experiment stations to foment opposition to the measure. The principal contact for California farmers was Hiram Johnson, now a senator who served on the Senate Committee on Foreign Relations in 1920. Johnson had known Powell and Shamel from before his ascension to the governorship. Strategically, in March 1920 Webber sent Johnson the results of the Soil Survey, as well as numerous petitions and letters favoring its continuance. Webber had also sent them to William Kettner, representative for California's rural Eleventh District. As a result of the lobbying of Johnson and Webber and other experiment station leaders, much of it done at the behest of Secretary of Agriculture Edwin Meredith, the Soil Survey was restored to the Senate appropriations bill.[15]

The culmination of the USDA's reputation-building efforts came in its long affiliation with the California Fruit Growers' Exchange and Charles Collins Teague. From 1913 to 1922, Powell had built the exchange into the largest cooperative in California and perhaps the nation's most powerful one. By 1920, as Joseph G. Knapp remarks in *The Rise of American Cooperative Enterprise,* the exchange had "more influence on the character of the entire American cooperative movement than any other single cooperative organization." Teague's elevation to president of the exchange in the 1920s gave the USDA a second ally at the helm of California citrus farming. Teague was a grower from Santa Paula who became, with the possible exception of cooperative legal theorist

Aaron Sapiro, the dominant figure in California agribusiness after 1910. Teague grew in prominence through his profitable lemon business (the Limoniera Association), his participation in citrus institutes, and his growing role in the exchange. He had interacted with the department from the earliest days of James Wilson's tenure. He received the department's first shipments of fenugreek seeds in 1901, and he had known Powell since 1905. It was Teague who showcased the Limoniera packing methods that Powell used to reduce fruit decay losses after 1906. Teague's loyalty to the department's ideology of extension and cooperative organization was a crucial asset to USDA officials, for Teague not only commanded the exchange but also assumed leadership of the cooperative marketing movement in California after 1922. In the late 1920s, Teague chaired the American Institute of Cooperation, the national umbrella organization for cooperative production and marketing. He ushered the department into the center of his state's cooperative organization efforts. At the American Institute's meetings in Berkeley in 1928, which he arranged and brought to California, Teague showcased the department's expertise in cooperative marketing. Lloyd Tenny, then chief of the Bureau of Agricultural Economics and treasurer of the American Institute, gave the opening lecture. Seven more USDA officials addressed the conference, USDA officials were named to every major committee of the institute, and Tenny chaired its Finance Committee.[16]

By the time of the Great Depression, then, there was scarcely a feature of California agriculture in which the department was not materially involved. The USDA had chartered a cultural and institutional presence on the Pacific Coast. Although resistance to departmental ingression surfaced among Grange loyalists in Washington and to a lesser extent in Oregon, and although the National Farmers' Union retained some allegiance in California, the USDA had secured a lasting influence in western states' farming. As table 9.2 shows, the department was now placing agents in 71 percent of California's farm counties, on a par with its presence in many other northern and southern states.[17]

TABLE 9.2
Percentage of Counties with Extension Agents, Selected States (1927)

State	Counties Reporting Agricultural Products	Counties with Extension Agents	Percentage of Counties Covered
Alabama	67	56	86
Indiana	92	81	88
New York	60	55	92
Texas	254	164	65
California	58	41	71

Source: USDA, *Cooperative Extension Work, 1927* (Washington, D.C.: GPO, 1928), p. 121.

War and the Expansion of Extension

The push into California embodies the broader geographic legitimacy that the department built after 1914. The pressure for increased crops during the First World War provided the extension and farm bureau movements with added momentum. Indeed, the enlargement of extension after 1914 owes less to the Smith-Lever Act than to the war. Boosting farm production was a central part of the domestic war mobilization of the United States. Congress passed the Food Production and Control Acts on August 10, 1917, giving the president the authority to control food production, distribution, and conservation. The act was named after Asbury Lever but written by USDA official Charles Brand. On the same day, President Wilson created the U.S. Food Administration by an executive order, placing Herbert Hoover (then chairman of the Commission for Relief in Belgium) in charge. Under a cooperative agreement, the Food Administration took direction of distributing and conserving food, whereas the USDA's main task was boosting production.[18]

The official war effort in agriculture was under way, but in fact the USDA had quietly launched it seven months earlier. From January through March 1917 the department used its network of extension agents to appeal for an increase in crop production throughout the South. In April the department held a conference in Saint Louis, gathering state commissioners of agriculture and land-grant officials to orchestrate efforts to press western farmers to increase corn and hog production. By May the department and the land-grant colleges had identified labor shortages as the greatest threat to increased production. Extension surveys had shown that ethnic divisions and growing industrial-employment alternatives had drawn many farm workers away from the fields. By late summer the department had struck an agreement for emergency farm labor agencies to regulate the labor markets so that a scarce supply would meet an artificially induced demand. Many extension agents now acted as "state farm labor agents," coordinating their recruitment of workers (particularly women) through county farm bureaus.[19]

The department also put together a national speaking tour through the States Relations Service, the bureau managing federal extension. SRS officials arranged the effort along county lines, organizing countywide mass meetings of farmers arranged through the county agent and the local farm group. In other words, the 1917–18 production campaign came rather easily to the USDA because, as Robert Howard has remarked, the USDA's ties to county farm organizations meant that "the machinery for reaching farm communities was already in place." The speakers included USDA officials from Washington, state college leaders, and county agents. To all of these individuals the States Relations Service distributed a list of fifteen speaking points. The tour aimed to encourage farmers' identification with American agriculture and to reinforce the notion of increased production as "America's obligation." To impress upon farmers the national character of this initiative, the department asked state agricultural leaders to speak outside their state, thereby carrying a "fresh point of view" and promoting vigorous production in other regions.[20]

In retrospect, it is difficult to tell whether the department's efforts in the spring of 1917 to boost farm production worked. (The Food Production Act of 1917, passed in August, came too late in the growing season to make any difference.) Gross farm product increased across most commodities in 1917, but much of the growth was surely due to farmers' expectations that commodity prices would continue to increase, as they had for years. Whatever the war effort's economic effect, however, its institutional legacy is undeniable. The war energized the extension service by orchestrating agricultural mobilization through the county agents in cooperation with the farm bureaus. The effort also bolstered the USDA's representative stature. In the county meetings of the 1918 tour, USDA officials were presented to farmers as "representatives of the Government direct from Washington." Another effect of the production campaign was to boost farm bureau membership. Speakers in 1918 were instructed to stress the "importance of the local farm bureau as a means of membership in the State and National agricultural campaigns" and a "necessity for war production and marketing." Last, in perhaps the most noticeable legacy of all, the war effort fueled an explosion of county agents across the northern and southern states. Congress appropriated millions of dollars in emergency funding for cooperative demonstration work, and the department scattered its personnel throughout the countryside. As of 1915 there were 1,136 white county agents in the United States. By June 30, 1917, 1,434 counties had white county agents and 66 others had "Negro agents." By June 30, 1918, there were 6,725 agents at work, with "agricultural agents" residing in 2,435 counties and demonstration agents in 1,715. By the early 1920s, the USDA had positioned its agents in virtually every county in the United States. The department now suffused the political geography of America as only the Post Office had previously done.[21]

The Farm Bureau, the Farm Bloc, and the Bureaucratic Suffusion of Agrarian Representation

Discretion, activity, and spending declined precipitously for military and civilian agencies alike after the Armistice of November 1918. Congress quickly rid itself of the patchwork war state it had hastily created just two years earlier. Yet the Department of Agriculture stood out among bureaucracies in its ability to protect its existing activities while growing in others. The main force propelling the 1920s expansion of the USDA was the legacy of wartime extension: the multiplication of farm bureaus and agents cooperating in tandem. When commodity prices plummeted after 1918, the meteoric ascent of the American Farm

Bureau Federation irreversibly changed national politics. The AFBF—the "Farm Bureau" writ large—is rightly regarded as the most innovative pressure group of its time, perhaps of the twentieth century. It succeeded, where other groups had failed, in coalescing farmers across regions and commodities. It also brought to Washington an integrated lobby with an active membership base of one-half million voters.

The anomaly of the Farm Bureau stemmed not from its movement base but from its institutional roots in thousands of American communities. The Farm Bureau was linked as no movement before (or perhaps since) to an already established bureaucracy. Its growth gave the USDA an organized pressure group committed to its policy agenda of applied science and management ideology. The Farm Bureau was a group that the department had explicitly and consciously fostered, a group with USDA members serving as ex officio governing members, a group with USDA alumni in its highest positions of leadership. Its components—county farm associations—owed their very existence to the department's extension program. Indeed, the explosion of county agents during the First World War made possible the meteoric rise of the Farm Bureau. Little wonder that the AFBF rarely departed from the department's wishes during its first decade.

The Farm Bureau was a coalition of coalitions. Its voting members were usually leaders of state farm bureau federations. These federations crystallized less than five years after the birth of the county farm bureau. Extension agent M. C. Burritt helped form the New York State Federation of County Farm Bureau Associations in 1917, and West Virginia farmers, led by extension agent Nat T. Frame, followed in January 1918 with a federation of their own. By 1920 thirty-two states either had statewide federations or were creating them. As in New York and West Virginia, county extension agents were at the center of state federation drives.[22]

Along with the emergence of state federations, two developments impelled farmers toward a nationwide organization. The first was the standardization of county farmers' associations. Before the war, the county farm groups that had sprung up alongside the extension agents were diverse in their identity and structure. Some were "improvement associations" whose members met only occasionally with the agents, others were tight-knit "farmers' clubs," and still others were commodity-specific groups. In 1917 the USDA mounted a public campaign through its Office of Extension Work to transform all county associations into inclusive farm bureaus with separate committees for different commodities and extension projects. The wartime expansion of extension did the work of homogenization. By 1919 virtually all county associations were farm bureaus with the committees envisioned by the office.

A second force leading to national organization was the increasing faith of northern farmers in the county bureau as an educational and political tool. In November 1917 a group of county farm bureau presidents from New York and

New England traveled to Washington to complain of their labor shortages. Four county presidents met with L. R. Simons of the USDA's States Relations Service. Long Island grower E. V. Titus argued that a national farm bureau was needed, and Simons agreed. Simons then consulted with other departmental officials and advised Titus that one of the state federations, preferably New York's, should sponsor a meeting to discuss a national federation. Simons also recommended that any national organization should have a "high-class manager." The New York farmers acted quickly, mailing out invitations to a multistate conference in Ithaca in February 1919.[23]

The Ithaca meeting displayed farm leaders' diverse motives in forming a national organization. Many state delegates wanted unified advocacy for policies that would ameliorate wartime disruptions in agriculture. Delegates from New England and the Ohio Valley, where labor shortages were worst, made up the bulk of the conferees: Delaware, Massachusetts, Michigan, New Hampshire, New York, Ohio, Pennsylvania, Vermont, and West Virginia. Western state delegates had a different focus. Led by Illinois farm journal editor Clifford V. Gregory, they called for less emphasis on production and more attention to a national program of marketing. The meetings also reflected the growing wish of USDA leaders and state federation presidents for more farm bureaus. C. B. Smith, one of William Spillman's original agents in the Office of Farm Management and now an extension chief with the USDA's States Relations Service, made the first speech at the meeting. He warned the audience that of eight hundred farm bureaus in the northern and western states, fewer than four hundred were well organized and active. A national organization could "get real local associations established in every county," and it could create resources, momentum, and identity that would strengthen existing county bureaus. Whatever their concerns, the delegates were united in favor of a national association. The Ithaca meeting concluded with a resolve to hold a national meeting in Chicago later that year, and the delegates appointed an organization committee to plan the gathering. Smith and his USDA associates submitted a draft constitution for a "national farm bureau" to the committee, outlining the objects of a national group, namely to "develop, strengthen and correlate the work of the State farm bureaus . . . through the adoption and promotion of a definite national program of work."[24]

Approximately five hundred delegates from thirty states descended on Chicago on November 12, 1919, for a two-day meeting. The conference assembled more farmers from more states than ever before. Compared with the Ithaca gathering, the Chicago meeting received greater press but was less visionary. The principal issues of discussion were the title of the federation, the election of its leadership, and the thorny question of whether and how to organize the South. The first two issues were resolved quietly. The conference agreed on the American Farm Bureau Federation for its title, and it surprised observers by electing James R. Howard of Iowa as its first president. The federation's adopted constitution uncannily echoed C. B. Smith's draft. The organization's stated objects were

> to correlate and strengthen the State farm bureaus and similar State organizations of the several States in the national federation, to promote, protect, and represent the business, economic, social, and educational interests of the farmers of the Nation, and to develop agriculture.

USDA officials also attended the Chicago meeting, and they liked what they saw in the federation's constitution and its elected leadership. The federation had declared the goal of advancing the USDA's preferred form of farm organization: county bureaus federated at the state level. Moreover, the secretary of agriculture and the director of the States Relations Service were made ex officio (though nonvoting) members of the AFBF executive committee. The constitution was ratified at a second Chicago conference, in March 1920, where a Washington lobbyist, Gray Silver of West Virginia, was appointed. The nation's first institutionalized farm lobby had begun.[25]

Naturally, the spring of 1920 brought far more to farmers than new organizations. It also launched the infamous "price toboggan" that carried American farmers unwillingly into their worst depression since the 1890s. With hostilities ending in Europe, Congress had terminated loans that supported European grain purchases, and the demise of the Food Administration removed the dominant conduit through which grain had reached foreign markets. Farmers were unable to predict the timing of these events, and having invested heavily in technology and learning, they had little ability, much less incentive, to scale back planting. The resulting agricultural surplus was, in percentage terms, the largest in American history to date. The wheat acreage of the nation reached a record high, which was unsurpassed until World War II. Yet falling European purchases and an explosion of South American imports were pushing grain prices ever lower.[26]

With commodity prices falling and the federation movement growing, the county farm bureau spread like prairie fire. By November 1921, at the federation's annual meeting, AFBF secretary James W. Coverdale could report 46 state federations comprising 1,486 farm bureaus and 967,279 members. In states across the land—California, Delaware, Illinois, Indiana, Iowa, Michigan, Minnesota, New Jersey, Nevada, Ohio, Utah, and all of New England—more than 90 percent of agricultural counties had farm bureaus. Only in the South were bureaus scarce, though in Georgia, Kentucky, Texas, and West Virginia a majority of farm counties had them.[27]

In 1921 a rift developed in the Farm Bureau between members who favored its marketing and educational promise and those who favored political pressure. At first, the federation took both paths. In a May 1921 meeting in Silver's office, nine farm-state senators from both parties agreed to form the Farm Bloc. At its height, the Senate Farm Bloc comprised a majority of the Senate Agriculture Committee and claimed up to thirty members. Its leader was William Kenyon, an Iowa Republican known for neither conservatism nor radicalism. Its House counterpart was much weaker, enlisting the allegiance of twenty-eight members, most of them junior. Together, the federation and the Farm Bloc mounted a legislative campaign that evinced the feeble hold of the Republican and Democratic Parties over agrarians. When the Senate tried to adjourn in June 1921 without having passed any of the federation's twelve suggested bills, Silver wired state-level farm bureau leaders and an avalanche of telegrams buried the Senate. The Farm Bloc would brook no adjournment. Embarrassed and desperate, Harding and Republican leaders threw together an eleventh-hour deal with the Farm Bloc. Before adjourning, the Senate passed six agricultural bills that were pending from the House, the most noteworthy being the Packers and Stockyards Act, the Grain Futures Trading Act, and an extension of War Finance Corporation loan authority.[28]

The June triumph of the Farm Bloc shocked politicians. The farm lobby had defied party leadership and established its independence. Observers pronounced the Farm Bloc "the dominant force in Congress" and noted that the Farm Bureau had displaced the Grange at "the center of this complex of [farm] organizations." Yet outside of the loan authority measure, the farm lobby had also quietly served the USDA's interests. The lasting Senate actions of June 1921—regulation of meat packers, grain exchanges, and milk distributors—forked over considerable new authority to the department. Moreover, these were activities in which USDA officials had already developed expertise before 1910, giving them vested turf interests. On all three measures, USDA officials brokered information and staked out a middle ground. They eschewed both the conservative inertia of the Harding Republicans and the radical animus of some Farm Bloc members, but they provided information and advice to all interests involved in the legislation.[29]

Packing regulation was a mixed policy victory for the Farm Bloc but a clear reputational triumph for the USDA. By empowering the secretary of agriculture to issue "cease and desist" orders to packers engaging in restraint of trade, it gave the department regulatory power previously restricted to the Federal Trade Commission. Farm interests had long complained of collusive practices in the nation's meatpacking oligopoly, or the "Big Five." Together the Big Five had established full vertical control over the industry—dominance over livestock marketing, transportation to stockyards, meatpacking, and retail outlets. An FTC investigation in 1918–19 found that the packers' collusion prevented competitive bidding on livestock, making the Big Five price setters. After the Justice Department brought an antitrust suit against the packers in August 1919, the Big Five agreed to divest themselves of retail interests and stockyard connections. Farmers opposed the "consent decree," however, and when the packers showed reluctance to abide by the agreement, the threat of regulation became reality with the Kenyon-Kendrick bill. The bill would have established

USDA authority over the packing industry by federal licensing of packers. Secretary of Agriculture Henry Cantwell Wallace, formerly a strong antitrust proponent, struck a tone of moderation on the bill in hearings before the House Agriculture Committee. Unlike other agrarian progressives, Wallace doubted the efficacy of antitrust, tolerating oligopoly only "under thorough supervision and regulation." Wallace's testimony evinced clear favor for the Kenyon-Kendrick bill, but his ultimate aim was enhanced USDA governance over meatpacking. The end result in Congress satisfied Wallace and USDA officials even as it left Farm Bloc members forlorn. The meat industry lobby blocked passage of Kenyon-Kendrick, but a substitute without the licensure provisions passed and became the Packers and Stockyards Act of 1921. As Thomas McCraw argues, the act *could* have vested regulatory authority in the FTC. Yet the USDA's long experience with meat inspection, dating from the 1880s, led Congress to bow to the expertise at Wallace's command. James R. Howard considered packer regulation the Farm Bureau's chief achievement that year. The act also further tied the department to the livestock cooperatives, who worked closely with USDA personnel in enforcing the act.[30]

Grain markets had also occasioned long-standing agrarian laments, and they provided further opportunity for the department to intrude on commodity markets. The Capper-Tincher bill of 1921 proposed strict federal regulation of futures markets to quash speculation. Wallace quietly approved but also detailed USDA grain expert Chester Morrill to study the measure and suggest changes to the House Agriculture Committee. In hearings in April 1921, Wallace proposed Morrill's changes, most of which were incorporated into the June version of the bill. Subsequently, in *Hill v. Wallace* (1922), the Supreme Court declared the Grain Futures Trading Act of August 1921 unconstitutional. The Court found that Capper-Tincher's section 3—which enacted a levy on grain sold for future delivery by anyone other than the producer—exceeded Congress's taxation power. The department sprung into action and helped draft another version of the bill, one without the tax, which was passed in September 1922. The Grain Futures Act gave the secretary of agriculture power to regulate commodity exchanges and prevent monopolistic practices and price manipulations. The second act survived legal challenges.[31]

The department exhibited a shrewd silence on other measures that the Farm Bloc favored. Wallace praised the Capper-Volstead Act of 1923, which exempted farm cooperatives from prosecution under antitrust laws. The act was in keeping with Wallace's moderate views on economic concentration, and he left the work of legislative pressure to the Farm Bureau. The department also sat quietly while the federation launched its two most ill-fated initiatives of the 1920s: the United States Grain Growers (USGG) and the Muscle Shoals campaign. The U.S.G.G. was the Farm Bureau's foray into cooperative marketing. Taking cues from legal theorist Sapiro of California, in July 1920 the federation appointed the Grain Marketing Committee of Seventeen to investigate the possibility of a nationwide grain cooperative. The department's role in the cooperative push was to provide information and to participate silently in the committee's deliberations. The department did provide statistics to the committee, reaping brief criticism from the Grain Dealers' National Association. The committee resolved to form a national grain sales agency, and the U.S.G.G. was begun in April 1921. State farm bureaus and the national federation dedicated hundreds of thousands of dollars in seed capital to the U.S.G.G. It was all for naught. The Grain Growers encountered stiff resistance from grain dealers, railroads, and banks, and the federation proved a feeble instrument of cooperation. Wracked by debt and unable to persuade farmers to switch from their existing marketing conduits during the price plunge, the Growers folded in June 1922. The federation had been embarrassed politically and enervated financially.[32]

Muscle Shoals, Alabama, was home to the nation's largest nitrate plant, developed during the war. When Henry Ford concocted a plan to convert the plant to fertilizer production in order to subsidize fertilizer costs for farmers, the Farm Bureau quickly threw much of its legislative time and energy behind the effort. Its annual "Memorandum on Agricultural Legislation" regularly listed Muscle Shoals first among its suggested bills. Senator George Norris halted the campaign by refusing for two years to report a Muscle Shoals bill from his committee, leading Ford to rescind his offer in 1924. By 1925 the Farm Bureau had sunk five years into Muscle Shoals, with no apparent payoff. Together, the Grain Growers debacle and Muscle Shoals persuaded Farm Bureau leaders to stride irreversibly into politics.[33]

Rethinking the Legacy of the Early Farm Lobby

After the victories of 1921, the Farm Bloc quickly declined, and it never formed in the Sixty-eighth Congress. The early crisis had invigorated the farm bureau movement, but by 1923 the national federation was reeling. What, then, was the legacy of the farmers' postwar frustration?

There were many legacies, of course. Cooperative marketing was now a political and economic reality. And the Farm Bureau did revive in the mid-1920s. Yet the obvious residue of the postwar crisis lay in administrative state building. The USDA was strengthened by the farm lobby's victories yet was never sullied by its defeats. It emerged from the Sixty-seventh Congress with new regulatory authority over three separate industries. As following sections will reveal, it also garnered new capacities in public roads planning and economic analysis. All of these policies were areas in which USDA officials had been vitally interested before the war. By 1923 the department's budget again was growing rapidly, defying the trend of cuts that had winnowed other agencies. The department had participated quietly in the U.S.G.G., yet aside from eliciting disgruntlement from the Grain Dealers' Association—which only occasioned more loyalty from despairing grain farmers in the Midwest—it was not weakened by the Growers' demise.

If the Farm Bureau's early history indicates anything, it is just how thoroughly agrarian organizations were suffused by the personnel and alumni of the USDA. Department officials were deeply involved in the federation's formation at every step. Nor did USDA involvement with the Farm Bureau stop with its founding. From 1919 to 1923, Extension Service director Alfred Charles True attended every executive committee meeting of the federation as an ex officio member. After 1923, the USDA's "visitor" in these meetings was L. G. Michael and often Secretary Wallace himself. Coverdale, the federation's secretary, had worked for the department as an extension agent leader in Iowa, and after 1920 he traveled regularly to USDA headquarters in Washington to discuss policy with officials. Although he did not have the power of Farm Bureau president James R. Howard, he frequently set the federation's policy agenda, and Howard later recalled that he could not remember a single instance in which he and Coverdale had ever disagreed. C. E. Gunnels had served as the USDA's chief of extension work (North and West) in Washington before joining the federation as assistant secretary. Such leadership ties only continued the deep ingression of the farm bureau movement by USDA personnel at the state and county level. As C. B. Smith noted in 1920, "[T]he extension director and county-agent leader of practically every State is on the executive board of the State federations." The state-level ties were rooted in even closer patterns of cooperation at the county level. As Howard proclaimed in 1921,

> The county agent is the keystone of the federation. . . . The American Farm Bureau Federation is exactly what the individual county farm bureaus make it. And the county farm bureau, I have found again and again, is just what the county agent makes it. . . .
>
> I would urge every county agent in America to assume a position of real leadership in his county and to stand or fall on his record as an organizer of farmers into a strong and effective county farm bureau. . . .
>
> The county agent is the strong right arm of the American Farm Bureau Federation.

Howard's confidence in the agents may have been excessive, yet USDA officials hardly backed away from his statement. W. A. Lloyd of the States Relations Service declared that "[t]he county agent has been the John the Baptist of the farm-bureau movement. Without him it would never have existed and without him it is doubtful if it could longer endure." Smith of the SRS agreed with Lloyd in a paper entitled "Cooperation of Agricultural Forces," released in December 1920. He called the farm bureau "practically a public institution, developed at the direct suggestion of agents of the Government." As Grant McConnell characterized the early farm lobby in *The Decline of Agrarian Democracy,*

[U]ntil the Farm Bureau had adopted a narrowly focused program of its own, there was good reason for discontinuance of the congressional farm bloc. One obstacle to the formulation of the necessary program was that the Farm Bureau Federation had not been formed around an idea but around a bureaucracy.[34]

The cooperation between the department and the Farm Bureau was not limited to farm organizing. The Farm Bureau became an enthusiastic proponent of a discretionary role for the USDA in numerous policy arenas, including many in which the federation's membership was not materially interested. When the Harding administration tried to scale back the USDA in 1922—proposing to transfer the Bureau of Markets to Herbert Hoover's Commerce Department and the Forest Service back to the Department of Interior—the federation mobilized its membership to defeat the initiative, and it was dropped in Congress. Although the federation might have had a stake in the Bureau of Markets, it had not shown interest in the Forest Service. The Coolidge administration also tried to shuttle some programs out of the USDA, but federation resistance again killed the attempts. As the Executive Committee instructed farm bureau leaders in 1925, "[I]nasmuch as we understand there is a move being made to transfer certain branches or bureaus from the Department of Agriculture to other Departments . . . we direct our Legislative Committee to use every effort to prevent such transfers." The Farm Bureau also helped to expand the department's discretion in the administration of the Packers and Stockyards Act. After 1921, the federation steadfastly insisted that all inspectors hired in meat stockyards be USDA employees, to the exclusion of the packers' own inspectors or state employees.[35]

So knit together were the department and the Farm Bureau that as early as 1921 observers in the farm press and in Congress began complaining of the coziness. Howard's "keystone" statement alarmed members of Congress, and he was called before the House Committee on Banking and Currency to explain it. Rumors that county agents were pushing farmers into the federation and away from other groups outraged the Farmers' Union. Assistant Secretary of Agriculture C. W. Pugsley issued a warning to county agents in March 1922, telling them to be "careful so that no complaint can stick." The Extension Service also took steps to distance itself, at least officially, from the federation's pressure politics. In California, Extension Service leader B. H. Crocheron resisted farmers' attempts to have the service and the Farm Bureau engage in joint publicity, arguing that the service's aim lay in "information, not propaganda." In Washington, Howard and the Extension Service's True acted quickly to dispel any confusion, signing a "memorandum of understanding" on April 21, 1921. The agreement promised to "differentiate" the farm bureau from the county agent by authorizing a distinct committee in each bureau to interact with the agent. True and Howard also tried to clarify the agents' role in farm bureau work, claiming that the "extension service . . . is as much interested in the marketing, distribution, production and utilization of farm products as it is in production, and it may properly give information and help in all these lines." The agreement concluded by acknowledging "much advisory consultation between representatives of the farm-bureau federation and officers of . . . the department with reference to plans for advancing the agricultural interests of the States and the Nation."[36]

The Farm Bureau as the Institutionalization of Bureaucratic Legitimacy. The True-Howard agreement bore a mixed legacy. The memorandum, and the impetus of political caution that produced it, undoubtedly put an end to the most egregious collusion between the federation and the service. Secretary Wallace followed the concord with a statement in August 1922 prohibiting county agents from membership campaigns or from acting in cooperative commercial activities. Yet in other ways the True-Howard memorandum legitimated and cemented an unprecedented relationship in American political development. It established a legal basis for the department to offer cooperation and advice to the Farm Bureau. A national bureaucracy had publicly recognized patterns of cooperation with an interest organization, and these patterns were acknowledged at the county, state, and national levels. Moreover, the complaints of NFU leaders and others after 1921 showed that some activities Wallace and True intended to prohibit had continued. The continued intimacy of the Farm Bureau and the USDA was best revealed in Secretary of Commerce Herbert Hoover's courtship of the federation after 1922. After his campaign to grab the USDA's Bureau of Markets failed—in large part because the Farm Bureau had opposed it—Hoover tried to divorce the Farm Bureau from the USDA. His plan was simple. He tried to build the esteem of the federation for Commerce while weakening the USDA's reputation, speaking repeatedly to the AFBF Executive Committee about the "work that the Commerce Department is doing for the farmer." The federation's obstinate resistance to any and all transfers of jurisdiction from the USDA in 1925–26 showed the futility of Hoover's scheme.[37]

The lasting result of the early farm crisis, then, was the development of an integrated political and economic organization that assisted extension work in the states and defended the department's interests with unprecedented force in Washington. Put differently, the department had fostered a new organizational structure of bureaucratic legitimacy in America: an organization conceptually separate from the state but knit together with bureaucratic officials at the local, state, and national levels in both formal and informal patterns of mutual support. Was the Farm Bureau in the department's pocket? Certainly not in all respects. The federation proposed many policies in the 1920s, some of which (McNary-Haugen, for example) the department disliked. Nor could the department have had the policy successes it enjoyed in the decade without the federation. Yet to conclude that the Farm Bureau captured the USDA in the 1920s would also be inaccurate. The federation was less than a decade old and took many of its cues from USDA officials, particularly Smith and True. Capture would await the 1940s.[38]

Brokerage and Legitimacy: The USDA through Crisis and Conservatism

In some ways, the Farm Bureau and the Senate Farm Bloc simplified the agricultural picture in national politics. The federation represented farmers of all regions and products, and it engaged the cooperative movement in ways that eluded the Grange and the Farmers' Union. The Farm Bloc represented the explicit creation of a farmers' congress in Washington; observers could now point as never before to a recognizable farm lobby. In other ways, the Farm Bureau and the Farm Bloc only furthered the balkanization of the agrarian organization that had begun in the 1890s. The Grange and the Farmers' Union, after all, had not disappeared. The AFBF drew membership from each, though many farmers belonged to multiple groups. The cooperative movement, however, weakened agrarians politically as much as it helped them economically. Farmers flocked eagerly to marketing collectives, leaving less political time and energy for the major organizations. The failure of the Grain Growers, for instance, stemmed in part from the resistance of the Equity Cooperative Exchange of Saint Paul. Many other farmers' organizations also emerged after 1900 and remained through the war. The American Society of Equity (with numerous ties to the cooperatives) and the more radical "progressive Grange movement" (represented in Washington by the Farmers' National Council) vied with the Grange, Farm Bureau, and NFU for agrarians' loyalty. Radical third parties with an agrarian base proliferated in the states, including the Minnesota Farmer-Labor Party (1918–44), the North Dakota Nonpartisan League (1915–56), the Washington Farmer-Labor Party (1920–24), the Idaho Progressive Party (1920–26), and the Oklahoma Farmer-Labor Reconstruction League (1922). Though fierce, the farmers' postwar anger was never politically channeled.[39]

For all of the diffused energy, farmers had not lost their disdain for the status quo. In the 1922 midterm elections, agrarians wreaked havoc on the legislative majorities that Republicans had secured in 1920, handing the party of Harding a loss of seventy-six House seats and eight Senate seats. They elected the first third-party senator since the 1890s, Henrik Shipstead of the Minnesota Farmer-Labor Party. They deposed entrenched Republicans such as Harry S. New of Indiana, Porter McCumber of North Dakota, and A. B. Cummins of Iowa.[40]

Whereas politicians and parties paid dearly for the postwar depression, the Department of Agriculture did not. To the degree that the department succeeded in boosting production during the war, it certainly contributed to the surpluses generating the crisis. Yet by 1920, the department's reputation as the paternal organization of American agriculture—one bent on transforming farming, and one with a claim to the providence of the national and agricultural interest— was firm. The crisis provided a severe test of this reputation, with continual beatings taken by the national parties in farm states—first the Democrats in 1920, then the Republicans in 1922. Yet a systematic review of letters sent to Wallace, Harding's secretary of agriculture from 1921 to 1924, reveals that western farmers were not so much inclined to blame the department for the crisis as to plead for programmatic assistance. The onus for the apparent price disparities in the 1920s was placed not on the department but on elected officials and private institutions. L. D. Seass wrote to Wallace in February 1922, blaming depressed grain prices on speculation at the Chicago Board of Trade: "[S]ince the government turned the Board of Trade loose on the farmer and let them gamble his prices down to one-fourth of what it has cost him to produce them and he is forced to sell at these ruinous prices, his stuff is being sold under the hammer, and he is moving to town or wherever he can get a place to stick into."[41]

Midwestern agrarians also felt that the fundamental status of agriculture entitled farmers to governmental protection in much the same way that other industries had received it. Kansas farmer Fred Weaver wrote to Wallace in January 1922 lamenting the workings of the ICC and other organs of the national state.

> Henderson Martin item tells a big truth we are aware of viz. that protection to American industry helped put us in first place industrially, also our railroads have Government protection through the Inter-State Commerce Commission and the Railway Board.
>
> Our National Banks Federal Reserve [sic] have abundant protection for carrying on their business.
>
> The farmers the corner stone of our national well being now need it. You see Mr. Martin can easily start the tide that will sweep the country as conditions are ripe— the same are actual and the state of mind universal. Prices should be set for farmers principal crops for a term of ten year until proper system of handling could be worked out.[42]

In addition, much of the agrarians' antagonism was directed at Harding Republicans and at the East in general. Farmers excluded Wallace from this ire, as he governed the department and was the scion of the famous Wallace family of Iowa, influential in agrarian politics and journalism. Clinton, Illinois, grower James Baker wrote to Wallace in February 1922 with deep suspicions of the Harding administration and with a clear expectation that Wallace was not one of the lot: "I am satisfied Harding & Co. is not friendly to the farmers. He appears to be 'holding with the Hare and running with the hounds' so he says the farmers must help themselves. You must expect a hard fight for the east are [sic] not for the farmers. . . . Give them a black eye if you can." Baker's sentiments were echoed by Montana farmer T. E. Richards: "My Dear Mr. Wallace. The farmers appreciate very much what you have done and are trying to do in their behalf but it seems you are alone. . . . I have been farming for a long while never saw conditions like this. Clevelands last administration was fine compared to this."[43]

In fact, the reputation of the department and that of the position of secretary of agriculture weathered the crisis rather well. Western agrarians looked to Wallace for guidance and for policy solutions, seeing the department as their genuinely representative organ. Oregon farmer Squire Innis wrote to Wallace in January 1922 offering his dark impressions of a national conspiracy, but in so doing he requested the programmatic assistance of the secretary and haphazardly expressed the corporate idiom of agricultural representation established from 1900 to 1920.

> The Official of this United States are supposed to be servents of the people but instead they are making Slaves of the people. They know they have to keep them in Poverty so they can keep them under subjection so the monopolies can rob them of their living and the education of their children. . . . I believe the only way for the farmers to get out of this condition is to organize and reduce their acreage one half for a term of 5 years. he will make more with one half of the expence. *Mr. Wallace as you are at the head of agriculture I should thik it your duty to inaugurat something of the kind.*[44] [*Sic* throughout]

Similar sentiments were voiced in the South, where many felt that the USDA could save them from financial distress. North Carolina planter B. F. Keith wrote to Wallace in disgust in 1922.

> I have just returned from the farmers conference that was called by the President and yourself which I think the wisest move that the Administration has made since taken hold of reign of the defunct Wilson, and his international bankers administration. . . . What I wanted to write you was to please try to divorce us from the influence of the money trust (ie) National Bankers. They controlled by Morgans and cabinet of international banks that will finally destroy our Government if they dominate any longer. . . . They own or control most of the large daily papers.
> . . . *We look to our Sec. to help us out of the mire.* all of the different [interests] must know that when the farmer is prosperous all other classes are, even the national and commercial banks will be more prosperous as a whole.[45] [*Sic* throughout]

The letters demonstrate the immense transformation that had taken place in agrarian political culture in the course of twenty years. Farmers saw their universe as composed of three industries—commerce, manufacturing, and agriculture. It was this tripartite vision of the American political economy that served as the rhetorical basis for the parity plans of the middle and late 1920s. And this parity concept, grounded in agricultural fundamentalism, established the USDA as the organ of state for farmers. For agrarians like Innis and Keith, the department could embody the interests of distressed farmers as no other political organization or party figure could hope to do.

The Meaning of Brokerage

Who, then, represented farmers after 1900 and through the years of war and crisis? To whom did farmers look for solutions to their problems? Which organizations claimed their trust?

The best answer is that no single organization or alliance of groups garnered wide allegiance among farmers after 1900. If any did, it certainly was not the parties, from whom the agrarians had bolted repeatedly since the 1880s. Nor did the established farm groups have wide adherence. By 1900 the Grange was a pale shadow of its former glory. According to Robert Tontz, who has completed the most exhaustive study of farm organization memberships, Grange family membership fell from 450,000 in the 1880s to less than 25,000 by 1910. Although Grange numbers rebounded after the war, its membership was much more heavily concentrated than before in the Ohio Valley, with scattered pockets in Washington and Oregon. Among radical agrarians the movement was discredited, so much so that Progressive Granges broke away from the national Grange in several states.

As an organization, moreover, the Grange after 1900 was internally divided and decentralized. Martin Sklar's discussion of Rep. William Hepburn's corporate regulation bill of 1907—one requiring federal licensing of corporations and strong antitrust provisions—is illustrative. When National Civic Federation president Seth Low asked Nahum Bachelder, head of the national Grange, to speak in favor of Hepburn's bill, Bachelder declined, saying, "I am frank to say that I think the organization which I represent will be divided upon this question and that I would have no authority to speak for it in this matter." On the most sweeping antitrust bill before Congress in a generation, one favored by Samuel Gompers and numerous statist progressives, the Grange could not even summon the unity to weigh in.[46]

Whatever void was left by the decline of the Grange was filled at best temporarily by the National Farmers' Union. Led by Charles S. Barrett of Georgia, the NFU mushroomed after 1904. By 1907, its secretary claimed 935,837 members, but Tontz places the total at 134,886 families in 1908. Thereafter the Farmers' Union stagnated, dropping to just over 100,000 families by wartime and fewer than 80,000 in the 1920s. Its numerical strength aside, the geographic limits of the NFU are undeniable. Before 1913, more than 80 percent of the NFU's membership was in the southern states. By wartime it retained less than one-third of its southern membership of 1912 and was limited to the western Great Plains. Even here it fell prey to the split identity that enervated the

Grange, as the Nebraska Union adopted a laissez-faire stance toward national political issues after 1915. Generally, the union's political obstinacy left it on the sidelines of national policy debates after 1910. In landmark laws such as the Smith-Lever Act, the Grain Standards Act, and the Packers and Stockyards Act, the NFU played a minute role, if any at all. As Wallace, then head of the Corn Belt Meat Producers' Association, declared in 1920, the Grange was "impotent," the NFU "irresponsible."[47]

The political debility of farmers after 1900 was not due to their failure to join organizations but to the fact that they had joined so many. The dominant pattern of agrarian organization after 1900 was balkanization. Before 1917, as John Mark Hansen notes, "[L]awmakers seeking to target appeals specifically to farmers had a bewildering 8,600 organizations from which to choose, including 559 in Illinois, 449 in California, 93 in North Dakota and 2,203 in New York." The multiplicity of organizations divided farmers' loyalties, most commonly along crop lines. Since commodity-specific cooperatives had the greatest impact on farmers' lives, they drew energy from political organizing and pressure lobbying. As Orville Kile argued, the NFU's sponsorship of cooperatives prevented it from becoming a national organization. A farm group based on cooperatives, he opined, "can be sectional at best, since crop interests are sectional." Only the Farm Bureau was able to overcome this predicament, with a combination of local entrenchment and cross-regional strength. After 1921, the Farm Bureau served to connect the Department of Agriculture more strongly to thousands of farm cooperatives throughout the nation.[48]

My claim that farmers were balkanized after 1900 is hardly new. Kile characterized the 1896–1910 period as one of agricultural "disorganization": "No broad general organization comparable to those of earlier days existed." Theodore Saloutos and John D. Hicks offer a similar portrait. They review the different organizations that arose between 1900 and 1930—the American Society of Equity, the Nonpartisan League, the Farmers' Union, and the Farm Bureau—and conclude that the western Plains farmers led the way in farmers' unrest. Yet their review is notable for the attention they give to the organizational difficulties and divisions of the different groups. The Farmers' Union "suffered greatly from the want of cohesion," they note, and "only in North Dakota was the League program put into operation." Meanwhile, the American Society of Equity directed farmers' attention much more toward economic cooperation than political cooperation. Just as important as the internal divisions among the groups was their lack of cooperation with each other. The Farmers' Union made a furtive try at absorbing the equity in 1910, but nothing came of it. Little wonder that when farm organizations set up shop in the capital during the war, they established not one office but four.[49]

In the 1910s and 1920s, then, agricultural organization presented a vacuum into which the USDA moved decisively. As figure 9.1 shows, the major farm groups had lost membership during the 1910s. Precisely as the Farmers' Union

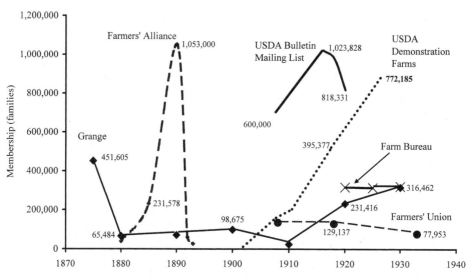

Figure 9.1 Filling the Progressive vacuum (the USDA and the national farm organizations from 1870 to the 1930s).

stagnated and the Grange lagged, the department's county agent system surged. Figure 9.1 offers some indication of the comparable number of farmers in whose lives the department was engaged. It shows that demonstration farms and the USDA mailing list—both enumerated in family units and thus directly comparable with the group memberships—numbered in the millions by the 1920s. Although receiving USDA publications was hardly the equivalent of joining an organization and paying dues, converting one's land to demonstration use was arguably a far more costly (and risky) undertaking than group membership during this period.

More broadly, the Department of Agriculture achieved *political brokerage* in the early-twentieth-century domain of agricultural policy. Brokerage, again, implies centrality in the universe of organizations in agricultural policymaking, combined with a relative monopoly on policy information. The centrality of the USDA stemmed from two facts. First, the USDA was connected to farmers of all sections and was closely tied to most of the major groups. The department was deeply engaged with the farm bureau movement, with the Grange, with southern agriculture (under the Knapp demonstration system), with the cooperative movement (in California, in dairy states, and in stockyards regulation), with Pinchot and the conservationists, and, of course, with the land-grant colleges and experiment stations. Second, farmers of different sections and groups were only weakly connected to each other. Only through the Farm Bureau Federation did farmers of all regions unite in a single organization after 1900, and this organization was built on the backbone of the USDA's county agent system. Relations among the Grange, the equity, the league, and the Farmers' Union, to say nothing of thousands of cooperatives, were passive at best, distrustful at worst.[50]

What the numerous organizations of American agriculture did share after 1900 is a common dependence on the USDA for the provision of information and advice. Farm groups and their representatives rarely dropped a bill in the legislative hopper without first passing the idea by department officials to get their support and to establish the bill's feasibility. Cooperatives and farm bureaus actively engaged USDA officials for suggestions and assistance on political and economic organization. It is crucial, moreover, that before 1933 almost none of the department's assistance to cooperatives or farm bureaus came in the form of cash, loans, or other explicitly distributive transfers. The USDA's centrality in American agriculture was a function not of patronage but of policy legitimacy. Postpopulist agrarian politics harbored many parties, many groups, but one bureaucracy.

Science, Economics, and the Planning Imperative

In light of the department's brokerage position in postwar agriculture, it is worth remarking that its reputation for scientific expertise grew stronger during the 1920s. At a time when administrative capacities were under attack from Harding-Coolidge Republicans, the USDA moved decisively into roles that would later characterize its preeminent place in New Deal economic planning.

Throughout the decade, USDA scientists continued to receive accolades and occupy positions of prominence that were the envy of any other bureaucracy, in America and elsewhere. Frederick Coville served as president of the Botanical Society of America and then of the Washington Academy of Sciences, and he headed the prestigious Cosmos Club after 1915. He also chaired the National Geographic Society's Research Committee. Karl F. Kellerman founded the *Journal of Agricultural Research* and was named to Woodrow Wilson's National Research Council in 1917. David Fairchild received the Plant Introduction Medal of the *Journal of Heredity* in 1920 and contributed regularly to *National Geographic*. Charles A. Browne, who ran the Bureau of Chemistry after October 1923, was the world's dominant authority in the analysis of sugars. Browne served as associate editor of the *Journal of the American Chemical Society* from 1911 to 1922 and wrote *A Handbook of Sugar Analysis* (1912). A German sugar industry journal lauded the text as "the most extensive and complete of any [book] at the present time not only in English but in any other language." Bacteriologist Erwin Smith was among the most celebrated American scientists of the 1920s. He worked at the department from 1886 until his death in 1927, authoring more than 120 articles and the first textbook on plant bacteriology—*An Introduction to the Bacterial Diseases of Plants* (1920). From

1904 to 1925, Smith's work pointed boldly to similarities between animal and plant cancers. The book attracted significant attention in American and European laboratories and elevated Smith to the presidency of the American Society for Cancer Research in 1924. Numerous other USDA scientists—seed analyst Edgar Brown, biochemist J. J. Skinner, pathologists Florence Hedges and Cornelius Shear, and dozens more—achieved national and international acclaim in their fields.[51]

Another index of the department's capacity was the vigorous outside demand for its scientists. Firms such as E. I. Du Pont de Nemours, Armour Chemical, and Liggett and Myers Tobacco Company and institutions such as Harvard and the Smithsonian readily offered USDA analysts salaries that were 50 to 75 percent above their government salaries. As Herbert Bailey, a departed inspector, told his former USDA colleagues in 1919, "From my experience in commercial and Govt work, I do not know of a single Food & Drug Inspector who could not make more money in commercial work than he is now making." The problem was especially acute before the Classification Act of 1923, the first conscious attempt of Congress to tie civil service salaries to inflation. Calculations in 1920 by Mary Conyngton of the Bureau of Labor Statistics implied that scientists in the USDA's Bureau of Markets could, on average, boost their salaries by 69 percent by departing for private firms; for the Forest Service, the increase was 54 percent.

Yet on the whole, the department was able to retain its researchers. During the highly inflationary years of 1915 to 1917, the USDA Bureau of Markets lost only 5 percent of its scientists per year to voluntary separation, and the Forest Service lost 8 percent annually. Even the USDA's clerical workers left at a higher rate (7.9 percent in the Bureau of Markets and 11.8 percent in the Forest Service). By comparison, state agricultural experiment stations experienced an annual average turnover rate of 80 percent. By 1928 the USDA was the only federal department outside the Post Office with a voluntary turnover rate of less than 10 percent—9.7 percent annually compared with 15 percent for the Interior Department and 19 percent for the Treasury Department. Simply put, scientists knew that the USDA's cohesive scientific culture could be found nowhere else. As David Fairchild wrote Wallace in 1922, "Quicker advancement may come in smaller organizations but I doubt if it would bring with it any fuller satisfaction than that which comes in the improving of this great Governmental machine which, when it is perfected, should become the greatest tool of discovery in the biological sciences (indeed I think that it is now) which the world has ever seen." One scientist tersely pronounced himself "not willing to move individually. If organization moves, will go with it."[52]

One aspect of the USDA's cultural cohesion was a highly gendered cultural division of labor. Scientific work was defined as the province of men, and women were not eagerly welcomed to research. For USDA bureau chiefs, younger men were ideal hires as scientists. Where no one of sufficient leadership ability was available, the department sought men with the prized tandem of virtues for government research: "virility" and "vigor." After 1910, these terms became codes for quality research. When up for reappointment in 1922, USDA artist Walter Chaloner was nearing mandatory retirement age, but his superior wrote that Chaloner "is a man of great virility and endurance, and can do far more work than any of the younger artists who are his associates in the work." Pest expert Nathan Cobb was promoted in part because his vigor compared well with that of the department's younger researchers. Bureau of Plant Industry chief Taylor wrote that Cobb was "an indefatigable investigator, in full intellectual and physical vigor." For many departmental scientists, women were not capable of these traits. When E. Alberta Reed was credited with discovering a new method for discovering tea adulteration in 1915, an unnamed USDA official awkwardly pronounced to the *Washington Times* that "Dr. Reed is the only woman in the Government service who ever really discovered anything of real economic value." The scientists' social activity only cemented this culture. The Cosmos Club, a gathering place for many USDA scientists, admitted no women or blacks.[53]

Agricultural Economics and the Fruits of Expertise

Scientific prowess, of course, did not translate easily into political capital. Yet urban and rural newspapers regularly trumpeted the department's accomplishments and called for boosts in its scientific funding. Typical of the paeans was the 1927 editorial "More Farm Relief" in the Philadelphia-based *Saturday Evening Post.*

> The appropriation at the command of the Department of Agriculture ranges around $160,000,000 a year. . . . Only 6 or 7 percent of the entire sum is spent upon scientific research calculated to take the guesswork out of farming and to evolve correct procedures which will do away with cut-and-try methods. Bureau scientists are not [to] be blamed if certain of their studies are not of the widest application and do not noticeably hasten the farmer's millennium. They are surrounding and edging up on problems whose solution will mean hundreds of millions a year in the pockets of the American people.

To grant more research funds to the USDA, the *Post* reported, "would be to grant one form of farm relief against which nothing can be said, for it would be a relief sound in theory, simple in practice, far from costly, and lasting in its results."[54]

After the war, the department was known less for its biological and chemical research than for its strides in agricultural economics. Historians commonly attribute the emergence of agricultural economics in the USDA to the creation of the Bureau of Agricultural Economics in 1923. Yet on their own, department analysts such as Spillman were turning to economic questions before 1910. Spillman's work on the cost of production stimulated the interest of other USDA officials, some of whom—including Extension Service chief True— joined the American Farm Management Association when Spillman formed it in 1910. Many others joined the Rural Economics Club, a gathering of more than fifty USDA researchers formed in 1911. The club met monthly, and its members gave papers and discussed policy problems in agriculture. As table 9.3 shows, the club included some of the chief luminaries of agricultural poli- cymaking in the 1920s. Charles J. Brand, author of the first McNary-Haugen bill and later administrator of the Agricultural Adjustment Administration (AAA) during the New Deal, was one of its leaders. Other members included Assistant Secretary of Agriculture Willet Martin Hays, Logan Waller Page (head of the Bureau of Public Roads and leader of the Progressive movement for a federal highway system), Bradford Knapp, and statistician Nat C. Murray. Of the officials at the helm of the federal government's work in agricultural pol- icy in the 1920s and early 1930s, at least one-third belonged to the USDA's Rural Economics Club in 1912.[55]

Well represented in the Rural Economics Club were three strands of research

TABLE 9.3

Selected Members of the USDA's Rural Economics Club in 1912 and Their Positions in the 1920s and 1930s

Member	Position
Eldon Ball	Assistant Secretary of Agriculture, 1920– 21 Director of Scientific Work, USDA, 1921–25
Charles J. Brand	Director, Agricultural Adjustment Administration Author, Lever Food Control Act (1917) Author, first McNary-Haugen bill (1923)
C. C. Clark	Federal Crop Reporting Board
Bradford Knapp	Director of Southern Extension, USDA, 1911–20
Nat C. Murray	Head, Division of Crop Estimates, USDA
B. F. Rawl	Chief of Dairy Division, Bureau of Animal Industry, USDA, 1920s
Clarence B. Smith	Director of Agricultural Extension Work, the North and West, 1915–21 Director of Extension, USDA, 1921–23
Carl W. Thompson	Director, Rural Organization Service, USDA
Werner Stockberger	Director of Personnel, USDA, 1925–38

that informed the emergent movement in economic planning: statistical crop reporting, marketing research (including commodity standardization), and production-control theory. All three disciplines had adherents in the land-grant colleges, but with the possible exception of the University of Wisconsin, none of these was better established elsewhere than the USDA. Crop reporting concerned the central question of information. It dated from Jacob Dodge's work as USDA statistician from 1866 to 1893. Crop data were crucial to farmers because they formed a necessary basis for rational planting decisions. Analysts knew that farmers could not plant shrewdly without information on the size of the current year's crop, along with an estimate of future crop sizes. Until 1910, however, the department's crop reports were often late and full of inaccuracies. Under the leadership of Minnesota professor Willet Martin Hays and Leon M. Estabrook, the department's practices began to improve. At Estabrook's urging, the USDA copied the crop-reporting systems of western Europe. By the early 1920s, the department had invented several new instruments with which to gauge farmers' decisions: "intentions-to-plant" surveys, yield inquiries, and annual livestock counts that were gathered by the Post Office from rural free delivery carriers. Like other USDA officials, Estabrook pressed for exhaustive crop reporting out of his ideological hatred of speculation: "Crop statistics . . . lessen speculation, because speculation thrives on lack of public information, doubt and uncertainty."[56]

The USDA quickly won worldwide recognition of its forecasting expertise. In 1929 the International Institute of Agriculture in Rome elected Estabrook director of the World Census of Agriculture. In the United States, the department's reputation spread via the rural press and radio broadcasts. On its own initiative, the department launched two programs to disseminate information and forecasts to farmers. The first was a series of "outlook conferences" designed to publicize the USDA's yield and price forecasts. The first conferences were held in April and July 1923 and annually thereafter during spring planting. The second program was the federal government's most sustained entry into nonmilitary radio broadcasting before the 1950s. In 1921 the Bureau of Markets and Crop Estimates began broadcasting daily market reports. Two years later 117 commercial and 46 military radio stations were carrying the forecasts to hundreds of thousands of farmers. Combined with newspaper readerships, consumption of the department's reports was as high as 15 million readers per year. In 1923 the editor of *Radio Broadcast* remarked that the USDA had a market broadcasting service unparalleled in the world. With a national medium for dissemination, the department's analyses had a widespread economic and political impact. The USDA correctly forecast lower cotton prices in 1927, leading many southern planters to scale back their plans. The forecast (and its accuracy) so angered exchanges and speculators that Republicans prohibited cotton price forecasting in the next appropriations act. Yet the prohibition was as ineffectual as it was meaningless. The department simply supplied the raw numbers with which farmers could make their own forecasts, and the official USDA forecasts resumed in 1930 under intense demand for them.[57]

Winning Reputations and Organizing the South, Again

Two aspects of marketing—commodity standardization and cooperatives—had fascinated department personnel before 1910. A decade before Congress became interested in the problem, New York market grades for cotton were based entirely on the USDA's "Official Grades." In standardization work, the department could satisfy two constituencies. It could address the demand of international traders for unified standards and appease agrarian concerns that exchanges were allowing low-quality foreign commodities in the back door of domestic markets to depress prices. Accordingly, USDA officials were fiercely protective of their reputation in grain research. As Plant Industry chief Taylor remarked to associates in 1914, "It has been very important to the reputation of the Department that the manner of preparation of the Official Grades be above criticism." Congress recognized the department's talents in the Grain Standards Act of 1917 and the Cotton Standards Act of 1923. Passed by quite different congresses, the acts were strikingly similar in their establishment of the USDA's grades as binding in national markets. In June 1923 representatives of the leading European commodity exchanges also adopted the USDA's standards as authoritative in international exchanges.[58]

Cooperative marketing was the other area of fascination for USDA analysts. One of James Wilson's last acts as secretary was to follow through on Spillman's request and ask Congress for an office of markets. Congress obliged in 1913. The USDA was little involved with cooperatives before this period, but with the wartime expansion of the Extension Service and the interest of cooperatives in commodity standardization, the department was able to put two of its most highly developed skills to use. Between 1921 and 1923, the Office of Markets (which later folded into the BAE) and the Extension Service began to assist cooperative organizing in southern cotton. With the help of Sapiro, the cotton cooperatives flourished, relying on the "iron-clad contract" that bound co-op farmers to the market only through the cooperative's "pool" for five years. In 1924, with the co-ops controlling up to 25 percent of the cotton market in some states, the USDA took a different tack. Henry Taylor sent Guy Meloy on a "Cotton Special" train tour to advocate cotton standardization and warehousing to the southern co-ops. The tour stopped in eighty-seven towns, and at least sixty thousand farmers, perhaps as many as seventy-five thousand, met Meloy and toured his exhibit train. By the summer of 1924 nearly all of the co-ops had adopted Meloy's recommendations. The department had taken its research in plant pathology and put it to economic use in the South, establishing a lasting trust among the cotton cooperatives.[59]

From Production Control to Domestic Allotment

Researchers of production control asked the most profound question of all: given reliable information about current and future crops (and prices), and given a fair marketing network with commodity standards, how should farmers behave in order to stabilize their income and remain profitable? Spillman was convinced that the answer lay in "price adjustment." Successful farmers responded to price incentives, he held, but they did so through planning and cost accounting. Spillman turned the research of his offices to these questions. In so doing, he drew on a rich vein of research by luminaries such as Thomas Forsyth Hunt (at the University of California), Willet Martin Hays, Henry C. Taylor, and many of the analysts in the USDA's Office of Farm Management (OFM). Spillman focused on cost-saving measures with which farmers could respond to price drops. The most notable strategy concerned fertilizer, a large variable cost wherever it was used. In work with Emil Lang, Spillman showed that there were decreasing marginal returns to fertilizer use. This finding was a considerable novelty in the 1920s, when many farmers faithfully dumped nitrates on their plots without restraint. Spillman also advanced the cost-of-production studies that had been developed in the OFM before 1910.[60]

These three streams of research—forecasting, marketing, and production-cost studies—were organizationally fused in 1923. Secretary Wallace wanted a bureau devoted less to science than to "policy," and he found it in the Bureau of Agricultural Economics. To head the BAE, Wallace tapped the figurative dean of agricultural economics, the USDA's own Henry C. Taylor. Taylor made his academic mark in Wisconsin and joined the department as head of the new Office of Farm Management and Farm Economics in 1919. Taylor had trained a generation of Wisconsin students in the "institutional economics" of his mentors, John R. Commons, Richard T. Ely, and William A. Scott. Taylor was at the center of a network of farm scholars that included Spillman, Hunt, Harvard's Thomas Nixon Carver, and Cornell's George N. Lauman. His emergence coincided with the popularity of "the Wisconsin idea" of bringing academic experts to policy positions.[61]

The BAE already lay at the center of Wallace's plans for a policy-oriented department, but with the Purnell Act of 1925 it arguably became the USDA's dominant bureau. The act gave the department control over a program to disseminate production-control theory among the states. The act also gave the USDA power over the definition of American agricultural economics, as officials in the Office of Experiment Stations henceforth pressed scholars in that field to focus their research efforts. All told, the Purnell Act left the BAE an impressively powerful and diversely active organization, one that regulated academic research, produced crop and livestock statistics, studied marketing and distribution, established and enforced commodity standards, and investigated foreign production and demand.[62]

Slowly, the department shifted away from making "two blades of grass grow where before grew one" to focusing on "production control." Spillman, Taylor, and their subordinates were now convinced that cooperatives were only part of the solution to the farm crisis. Incentives had to be created for farmers to refrain from producing surpluses. Their thinking diverged strikingly from the popular income-support measure of the time, the export corporation bill best known for its congressional cosponsors, Senator Charles L. McNary of Oregon and Rep. Gilbert N. Haugen of Iowa. The McNary-Haugen bill was the brainchild of George N. Peek of the Moline Plow Company, who with Hugh Johnson authored a tariff-based plan for farm relief in the pamphlet *Equality for Agriculture*. Peek's idea was simple but radical. By creating a government corporation to purchase surplus crops at the "fair" domestic price and dump the remainder on the world market, it would rid farmers of the surplus problem. The domestic price of American commodities could then rise behind the wall of the tariff. The Peek-Johnson plan received little attention until the USDA's National Agricultural Conference of January 1922, at which Peek was a delegate. Peek's plan gained adherents and eventually won the recommendation of Taylor, Wallace, Gompers, and others. By 1923 it was the rallying cry for disaffected farmers, shrewdly couched in terms of "parity" for agriculture.

Peek and Johnson then presented the plan to the USDA for a legislative draft. Most of the key details of the first draft of McNary-Haugen were written by Charles Brand, earlier the leader of the Rural Economics Club. The USDA's work on the bill earned it the enmity of Hoover, who accused the BAE of socialism and argued that the bureau "had originated the McNary-Haugen Bill and would not support legislation favorable to cooperatives." The battle for McNary-Haugen intensified after the 1922 midterm elections, in which many grain-belt Republicans lost their seats to agrarian insurgents. Because the bill could not procure southern support, it failed in Congress until 1927. The end of the USDA's official advocacy came much earlier. After Wallace's death in 1924, Coolidge tabbed McNary-Haugen opponent William Jardine of Kansas as his replacement. Jardine promptly dismissed Taylor and Brand, and the USDA's McNary-Haugen campaign came to an end.[63]

In a different department, Jardine's purge of 1925 might have spelled the end of bureaucratic planning. Not in the USDA. With McNary-Haugen no longer monopolizing attention, Spillman offered a different policy. He developed the outlines of "the domestic allotment plan," published in *Balancing the Farm Output* (1927). Spillman saw the Achilles' heel of McNary-Haugen; it contained no reliable incentive for farmers to reduce production. His alternative included a tariff but changed the terms of payments to the farmer. Farmers would receive the free trade price plus the tariff duty for the portion of their crop consumed domestically. They would receive a free trade price *without* the tariff duty for the part of their consumption that was exported. Under Spillman's plan, then, farmers would receive a price "allotment" only for domestic production.

Whenever the free trade price did not cover the costs of production, farmers had an incentive to scale back planting. Spillman's plan was taken up by Montana's Milburn Wilson, who overlapped with Spillman in the BAE from 1924 to 1926 and who shared Spillman's devotion to production-control theory. Wilson, a former county agent with the Extension Service, pressed for the domestic allotment plan from the late 1920s into the New Deal, joining John D. Black of Harvard in advocating modifications of Spillman's original plan.[64]

The domestic allotment plan became the basis for President Franklin D. Roosevelt's agricultural policy in the 1930s. Unlike McNary-Haugen, it envisioned a clear role for bureaucratic administration, for it was the Agricultural Adjustment Administration of the USDA that would allot payments and payment rights to farmers. The domestic allotment plan also cemented the USDA's role in a permanent planning capacity for the federal government. Walter Lippman would later call Spillman's project "the most daring economic experiment ever seriously proposed in the United States." Upon the passage of the AAA in 1933, Russell Lord declared that "a month from now it will be useless to duck the fact that it compels national planning." In this respect, it is useful to recall that the twin strands of New Deal agriculture policy—production-control theory and cooperative marketing—were firmly entrenched in the department before 1920. If nothing else, the development of planning capacities in the Department of Agriculture shows that neither Congress nor presidents nor groups ever hardwired a capacity for agricultural economics into the USDA. The capacity evolved through networks of study like the Rural Economics Club, the affiliation of M. L. Wilson with Spillman, and the ties that Henry C. Taylor brought to the department. From the BAE's network-based amalgam of sciences came the federal government's most sustained entry into centralized economic planning.[65]

All things told, it is useful to reflect that the outlines of Progressive agricultural policy—and the bases of New Deal policymaking—were profoundly shaped by two individuals. The first was Spillman, who reinvented federal extension, fostered the organizational bases of the nation's first farm lobby, and authored the fundaments of New Deal agricultural policy. His absence from Progressive historiography is unfortunate. The second is Gilbert Haugen, whose long rein as chair of the House Agriculture Committee gave the department a stable and enthusiastic ear for its proposals. The influence of these two individuals is a profound demonstration of the power of administrative reputations in policy innovation.

Ten

Structure, Reputation, and the Bureaucratic Failure of Reclamation Policy, 1902–14

DESPITE THEIR LIBERATION from nineteenth-century politics—the strictures of patronage and purely distributive programs—executive departments in the Progressive Era still lacked a central component of modern statehood: a genuine degree of independent planning capacity. The development of discretionary program administration in the U.S. Department of Agriculture and the Post Office Department remained exceptions to the rule of limited capacity and diminished bureaucratic reputation. Never was this pattern more visible than in the evolution of American reclamation policy—those collected governmental attempts to "reclaim" the West for habitation and agriculture through irrigation.

Reclamation policy started as a bold experiment in bureaucratic planning. The Department of Interior, given hold of more than $100 million in a "reclamation fund" bankrolled by public land sales, possessed virtually unlimited authority to inaugurate new projects, spend monies without justification to Congress, and displace landowners to advance its designs for remaking the arid West. The Reclamation Act of 1902 and its surrounding case law granted broad discretion to the Interior Department's Reclamation Service; its decisions were only partly contestable in federal courts. As Alabama representative Oscar Underwood, chairman of the House Ways and Means Committee, remarked in 1914, "I do not know of any other place in the Government where such a large sum is being left to the discretion of a bureau chief." On paper, there was no more autonomous bureau in the American state than the Reclamation Service.[1]

Yet this administrative bliss was not to endure. By wartime, the Interior Department retained only a bare residue of its former liberty with the program. The secretary's ability to choose projects without presidential approval had disappeared. The service, having outspent the reclamation fund by more than $20 million, lost control over the fund, as Congress now controlled project monies through regular appropriations mechanisms. To top it off, Congress now subjected all of the service's projects to review and oversight by a board of army engineers. The service had been put under restraint by a Congress no longer tolerant of its rampant cost overruns and project failures, and this institutional leash would loosen only slightly by 1930.

What happened in the interim—the early years of reclamation—is the subject of this chapter. The failures of early American reclamation lay primarily in the administrative debility of the U.S. Reclamation Service from 1902 to the Depression. The missteps of the service were legion. The Reclamation Service overcommitted its resources, launching more projects than it could maintain, monitor, or finish. Shackled by the Interior Department and the restrictions it placed on its own bureaus, the service administered projects with multiyear delays in construction and contracting and regularly transgressed its early cost estimates by 300 or 400 percent. With a myopic focus on dam and reservoir construction, service engineers failed to plan for sustainable agriculture on their projects, neglecting soil analysis, drainage, and farm advising. They also failed to develop political affiliations in the West. Finally, the service never followed through on the Progressive dream of community planning. One of the prized aims of Francis Newlands, the planning of neo-Jeffersonian communities of small farms, was abandoned by the service's leaders in favor of purely numerical program expansion: more dams, more settlers, more farms.

None of these failures escaped congressional or public notice. The service's reputation sank quickly and irreversibly through the Progressive Era. The despair of project settlers mounted even while American agriculture was in its golden age, and letters of complaint rained down on the service's Washington headquarters. Interior Department officials were called repeatedly before Congress to account for the hapless state of their western operations. The stagnation of a national program to which members of Congress had surrendered tens of millions of public dollars further eroded the service's reputation. As a result, the Interior Department slowly forfeited its opportunity to build ties to professional associations, western Republicans, and arid-lands farmers. In retrospect, this was a monumental loss. The western water users' associations that organized on irrigated lands might have become the service's staunchest allies in Congress and the Republican Party. By wartime, however, they greeted the Interior Department's reclamation proposals with public skepticism if not outright disdain. The service lacked a broad-based support coalition capable of transcending American sectionalism.

The saga of American reclamation offers instructive lessons precisely because the Interior Department began the century with a degree of formal autonomy almost unimaginable to nineteenth-century agencies. The contrast with the Post Office and the USDA could not be clearer. Whereas the history of American bureaucracy provides numerous examples of agencies where discretion never developed, the story of the Reclamation Service is one in which discretion was possessed, then lost. The possibility for autonomy in the service not only existed, but for a time it was realized. For political scientists, then, this chapter addresses the question: under what conditions is broad administrative discretion taken away? The tragedy of the service demonstrates that lasting discretion is based on reputation and locally based legitimacy. As the reputation of the service declined, it became progressively more encumbered by Congress and organized interests. The fact that the Reclamation Service developed neither durable policymaking capacity nor a lasting presence in western arid lands suggests that even in its heyday it did not exhibit genuine bureaucratic autonomy founded on a strong organizational reputation.

The plummeting reputation of the service during the Progressive Era was a collective judgment about the service's capacity. Reclamation was an exacting program from an administrative vantage point, and the service fell short of its demands. Nothing crippled the service's efforts more than the administrative structure of the Interior Department, for the service was organized not by Congress but by the secretary of interior under the 1902 law. And the Interior Department's deep structural faults—its bureau-stifling procedures, its deep embedment in lateral ties of distribution to western interests, its leaders' stubborn resistance to communication with other agencies of the government, and its lack of scientific capacity—combined to haunt the reclamation program from its inception. The problems of reclamation were not purely structural, however. The service's leaders systematically launched more projects than they could start, committing to twenty-five in the program's first five years. The abandonment of incremental project development was a conscious strategy of the service's first leaders, Frederick Haynes Newell and Arthur Powell Davis, who received enthusiastic support for this path from a chorus of reclamation engineers. The early choices of Newell and Davis decisively limited the subsequent development of reclamation.[2]

Indeed, a focus on the reputation and capacity of the Interior Department differentiates this analysis of reclamation's failures from those of several other important scholars, namely Donald Pisani, Donald Swain, and Louise Peffer. Swain and Peffer have attributed the early troubles of the service to legislative pressures for distribution, as well as the "exuberance" of Newell and Davis. Yet as I show here, distributive and partisan accounts for the failures of reclamation do not meet well with the actions of the Reclamation Service or Congress. They do not explain, for instance, why so much discretion was granted to the service in 1902, why the service made the decisions it did, and why discretion was so quickly and decisively encumbered after 1910. Moreover, what Swain and Peffer see as the "personalities" of reclamation officials were in fact shaped by the organizational structure within which these officials worked and the political networks in which they were embedded. Pisani, one of the most accomplished historians of the West, has discussed bureaucratic factors in reclamation more than others, though he emphasizes the legal constraints on the program in accounting for its troubles. In short, historians of the reclamation program have attributed reclamation's early troubles to either the personalities of its leaders or to distributive politics, and both explanations, as I discuss later, are fraught with shortcomings.[3]

The Newlands Act and the Reclamation Service

The idea to reclaim the arid West through water drew on long-standing agrarian dreams, but only a unique combination of federal advocacy and western farmer organization brought the idea to fruition. Private efforts to construct reservoirs and divert river waters were common but limited in the late 1800s. Congress tried to provide incentives for homesteaders to take up private irrigation efforts in the Desert Land Acts of 1877, 1890, and 1891. Yet large-scale reclamation demanded two things—planning capacity and plentiful capital—that neither settlers nor private water companies possessed. In the 1880s, then, western farmers and state officials began organizing Irrigation Congresses to discuss and orchestrate broader efforts toward federal involvement. In the end, it was no western interest but a federal official who concretized the possibility of large-scale irrigation projects. Major John Wesley Powell's "Report on the Lands of the Arid Region of the United States" provided a powerful argument for a federal reclamation program. Powell, head of the Interior Department's Geological Survey, set the agenda by advocating the construction of large storage reservoirs. Without a large reserve of water, Powell reasoned, western irrigation projects would remain forever dependent on the vagaries of annual rainfall and unable to cope with flooding.[4]

Powell's message caught on. In the 1880s and 1890s, the Senate repeatedly called on the major to study a broad policy of western irrigation. In February 1889, the Senate created the Select Committee on Irrigation and Reclamation of Arid Lands. Armed with analyses from Powell's survey, the Select Committee drafted a model reclamation law. With resistance to large-scale federal efforts high, however, Congress first offered money to the states to address the problem. The Carey Act of 1894 granted 1 million acres of federal land to each of ten states for the purpose of promoting settlement and irrigated farming on plots of no more than 160 acres. Yet the Carey Act proved dramatically insufficient. By the turn of the century, only Wyoming had taken advantage of its provisions to start systematic irrigation. Federal officials such as Frederick Haynes Newell, Powell's successor as head of the Geological Survey, joined with western farmers in advocating a more aggressive federal role in reclamation.[5]

The pressure for a more comprehensive program started to build. In 1900 both the Republican and the Democratic Party platforms featured a plank favoring a national system of western reclamation. Reclamation bills drafted by Nevada representative Francis Newlands won support from all ideological quarters and all geographic sections. At the core of Newlands's plan lay a shrewd and innovative fiscal mechanism. Large-scale reclamation projects would receive funding from the receipts of public land sales in the West. Although some rural eastern representatives feared agricultural competition from western states, and although the minority of the Arid Lands Committee was concerned about the constitutionality of a federal program, neither of these fears aggregated to create sufficient opposition to Newlands's bill. Perhaps the most important factor was the support of President Theodore Roosevelt, who was advised throughout by Francis Newell and Gifford Pinchot. With support from all sections and an impressive array of federal officials, Congress passed the Newlands measure in July 1902.[6]

The Reclamation Act (or "Newlands Act") of 1902 established western irrigation on a theoretically self-sufficient basis. The act funneled all monies received in the sale and transfer of western public lands into a reclamation fund, which would support irrigation efforts. This fund, predicted by congressional investigators to yield $3 million annually, established the operational autonomy of the department in irrigation policy. The Newlands Act vested sole discretion over the expenditure of this fund with the secretary of interior. The secretary possessed unique and full authority to select project sites and to withdraw lands from the public domain for irrigation. Moreover, early court decisions removed most of the secretary's discretion from judicial review. To establish the lands to be irrigated under any project, the secretary was given full authority to acquire lands by purchase or by condemnation. These condemnation powers were broad, transcending state statutes and enjoining the full power of the U.S. attorney general whenever the secretary wished to use it.[7]

The role of the department under the Newlands Act was to construct storage reservoirs for water by damming major western rivers. The act also charged the department with the construction and maintenance of diversion canals for carrying waters to project lands. More generally, Congress wanted the department to support and create the conditions for sustainable and profitable agriculture. Once viable farming was established on projects, the maintenance of the irrigation works was to be transferred to the farmers.[8]

The allure of the Newlands Act to western and eastern interests alike was its cleverly self-contained funding scheme. Under the act, the costs of any irrigation works would be assessed on the farmers themselves, in ten annual installments. Where the reclaimed lands were productive, the irrigated land values would rise accordingly, and the reclamation fund would benefit. Upon the assurances of the Interior Department's Geological Survey, Congress believed the program would pay its own way. Charles Walcott, director of the survey in 1902, had predicted that the requirement of settler repayment rendered the reclamation program a potentially profitable enterprise for the federal government. Among the many believers in the immortality of the reclamation fund was Senator Henry C. Hansbrough.

> The cost of the works is to be assessed against the lands benefited, . . . the moneys thus going into the reclamation fund. By this method the fund will be constantly replenished, making irrigation practically a self-sustaining enterprise and, according to the Geological Survey, ultimately putting money into the Treasury.

The act was a truly Progressive creation. In a departure from the sobriety with which westerners received earlier irrigation programs, the *Genoa (Nevada) Weekly Courier* claimed of Newlands's measure that "[i]t is perhaps the only bill ever passed which furnishes so complete, comprehensive and automatic a plan of action."[9]

The passage of the 1902 act was a shadow triumph for the Interior Department. On one hand, its funding was discretionary and its responsibilities were limited. On the other hand, Interior Department officials had played little role in designing the program that they would administer. This would turn out to be a serious political handicap. In the western areas into which officials of the Interior Department eagerly charged with abundant funds lay a political vacuum, without any networks that the department might have mobilized into action around the 1902 act. The department attempted to create a clientele basis when it fostered water users' associations, but its success in nurturing these groups was limited.

The Leadership of the Service: The Rejection of Incrementalism and Planning

The tragedy of reclamation policy cannot be told without reference to Frederick Haynes Newell and Arthur Powell Davis. Newell, head of the U.S. Geological Survey's hydrographic branch since 1890, ascended to his new perch as director of reclamation in 1902. A trained civil engineer, Newell brought genuine expertise and administrative resources to the fledgling program. He had helped to found the National Geographic Society and served as its first secretary. He had served as an early president of the American Forestry Association, and his friendships at the Smithsonian Institution strengthened his ties to the Washington scientific community. Davis, who would serve as Newell's deputy until 1914, also brought erudition and political clout to the service. Like many of the ascendant bureau chiefs of the Progressive period, he was educated at Columbian (now George Washington) University. Before his arrival to the service, Davis had been employed as topographer and hydrographer for the Geological Survey from 1884 to 1894, and he worked as a consulting engineer for the construction of the Panama Canal. As a result, he brought an intimate familiarity with modern construction practices. Along with Newell, Davis occupied an integral place in Washington's professional and scientific circles, serving as president of the American Society of Engineers and the Washington Academy of Sciences. In short, like Harvey Wiley, Gifford Pinchot, and August Machen, Newell and Davis seemed the ideal political architects for launching Progressive policy ambitions.[10]

Despite the strengths Newell and Davis brought to the service, their leadership failed to materialize. Both men suffered from a peculiar aversion to comprehensive planning for irrigated farming, focusing instead on brute construction. Unlike the USDA's Ellwood Mead, whom the architects of reclamation overlooked, neither Newell nor Davis had coordinated a reclamation project before 1902.[11] In some respects, Newell's penchant for measuring program success in terms of construction made sense. For an administrative monopoly over irrigation works was one of the driving desires of Newell in his push for the program, and reservoir construction was his organization's greatest talent. The service was building large dams the likes of which had not been seen in the Western Hemisphere. Newell and Davis relentlessly promoted these functions at the expense of smaller but critical details such as drainage, soil preparation, farm advising, and community planning. Moreover, their ambition for a purely numerical program expansion and large blockbuster projects crowded out forethought.

The demise of community planning provides one example. The sponsors and supporters of the 1902 act, including Newlands himself, saw in reclamation the possibility of creating new Jeffersonian utopias: administratively planned communities with small homesteads, supporting a collective identity. The service engaged briefly in planning these communities, especially after the Town-Site Act became law in April 1906. Eventually, however, community planning gave way to Newell's preference for building larger and costlier irrigation works. Even though township planning would have helped to attract settlers to projects, Newell was concerned with the short-term bottom line. Except for the Bard township on the Yuma project, township plans never figured in Newell's projects, and when in 1912 the American Civic Association offered the services of its members for free, Newell simply ignored its generosity. In the end, Newell relegated planning to servile status. The director gauged the success of his program in terms of the number of dams built, the number of potentially irrigable acres, and the number of families on project farms—however well or poorly these families fared.[12]

The Administrative Organization of Reclamation. Critically, there was no mention of a reclamation service in the 1902 legislation. The act left administration to the secretary of interior. Like the secretary of agriculture, secretaries of interior possessed broad authority—continuing from the nineteenth century—to reorganize their department. Yet this structural liberty proved to be the decisive flaw of the reclamation program. Initially, Interior Secretary E. A. Hitchcock placed the Reclamation Service under the auspices of the Geological Survey. By 1905 the service had become a separate organization with bureau status. And like all other Interior bureaus, the Reclamation Service was smothered by the department's organizational structure (see figure 2.1).

The structural defects of the department, reviewed in chapter 2, wreaked havoc on the Reclamation Service's attempts to plan and conduct punctual operations. The twelve divisions of the Secretary's Office closely scrutinized the service. All service decisions involving legal issues (even tangentially) required review and approval by the department's assistant attorney general. All operations requiring expenditure required approval by the Finance Division. The Publications Division reviewed at length all of the service's scientific studies requiring publication. Most critically, the divisions conducted these reviews *before* the secretary could weigh in on any decision. The only way for the service's directors to speed up administrative reviews was to lobby the secretary personally, a tactic used ever more frequently after 1905. Because the secretary's schedule was constrained, however, lobbying was an unreliable strategy. On a daily basis, the divisions ruled the Reclamation Service.

The Costs of Clerical Hierarchy: Truckee-Carson and Klamath Falls. As James Garfield discovered in 1906, multiyear project delays were the most distressing effect of Interior's shackling of the service. Ever impeded by the divisions of the Secretary's Office, the service showed considerable difficulty in communicating and announcing cost estimates, in agreeing to contracts, and in deciding on applications. At the otherwise fast-completed Truckee-Carson project in Nevada, where farmers were applying for water rights as early as February 1905, the Interior Department delayed water delivery for more than a year. Water users' groups at Truckee-Carson had submitted two applications on February 27, and Newell requested early approval of these applications, as the water would be ready for delivery by April. Unfortunately for Newell and the farmers of Truckee-Carson, a critical structural flaw stood in the way of approval. As a standard operating procedure, the Interior Department passed all contracts and signed papers through the Office of the Assistant Attorney General. The office sat on the applications for a year while Newell brought repeated complaints to Hitchcock. Finally, on February 9, 1906, Hitchcock arranged a meeting between two service engineers and two assistant attorneys from the office. So minuscule were the matters of decision on the applications that the four men approved them after one hour of discussion. The expansion of one hour's decision to one year had denied water to Nevada farmers for a full growing season.[13]

The crippling effect of clerical supervision on reclamation administration was also on display in the service's efforts in the Klamath project on the California-Oregon border. To construct dams and to open a greater expanse of land for irrigation, the service used reclamation monies to purchase tracts of land from private companies, usually small-scale private irrigation firms. In June 1905 Hitchcock approved the service's purchase of the entire holdings of the Klamath Falls Irrigation Company. Before the service could purchase the Klamath property, however, it required approval of the Office of the Assistant Attorney General. In October the office advanced an opinion against the purchase, finding certain reservations of water rights objectionable. In a letter of November 18, Newell's officers replied that the objectionable reservations of rights were common to many of the service's land-purchase contracts, including one that the department had approved in December 1904. The office failed to answer the service's communications, even after Newell's officers wrote additional letters on December 8 and January 2, 1906. Finally, the service got Hitchcock to reverse the decision of the office on January 9, but the matter was far from over. On March 14, 1906, the Office of the Attorney General put forth more objections. Again the service speedily answered the office, and Hitchcock again sided with Newell's organization. Undaunted, however, the Office of the Assistant Attorney General advanced another opinion on July 10, requiring the service to obtain quit claim deeds from the land owners at Klamath Falls. Two weeks later Davis, the service's chief engineer, personally visited Hitchcock and impressed upon him the necessity for Klamath properties to vest in the United States government as soon as possible. Hitchcock assented and approved the Klamath purchase on September 20. The clerical supervisors of the service had delayed the Klamath Falls purchase for a year and a half, during which the price of the purchased lands had risen and western speculators had descended on Klamath Falls to buy the remaining properties.[14]

As Garfield knew, the source of administrative delays lay in the clerical supervision of the Interior Department, particularly with the Office of the Assistant Attorney General. Project by project, the clerical supervision of the service added months (quickly accumulating to years) to construction and project-completion times. In its struggle to build lasting relations with western water users' associations, the service was crippled by its own department.

Networks without Local Knowledge: Recruitment and the Capacity of the Service. The Newlands Act placed heavy demands on the department. Selection of project locations, surveying for reservoir construction and diversion of waters, laying out comprehensive canal networks, and systematic planning for agriculture on irrigated lands—each of these functions required scientific capacity, but the combination of them required a diverse force of personnel who could claim familiarity with the unique problems of construction and agriculture in the West. Secretary Hitchcock first placed the Reclamation Service under the auspices of the Geological Survey. From the survey's hydrographic branch the service drew its early personnel, including Newell and many of the highest-ranking engineers. More than 70 percent of the employees of the service were classified as scientific workers. On paper, it was among the most learned of federal agencies.

The stellar résumés of the service's engineers cloaked deeper weaknesses in its scientific capacity, however. The bureau lacked the embedment in professional networks needed to recruit a cadre of officials with experience in government irrigation. Newell and Davis monopolized the early recruiting. Four of the service's top engineers hailed from Los Angeles, where Powell had made both his name and his home. Yet California was behind most western states in irrigation, and southern California most of all. Indeed, it was the dearth of private irrigation efforts in the Imperial Valley that recommended to Newell the desirability of the Imperial Valley (Yuma) project in 1903. So although many of the service's leaders were trained in reservoir construction, few had experience in reclamation, either privately or as administrators of state or foreign government programs. Among those who did have government experience or ties to state or local administrators, such as Davis, their enmeshment in the distributive politics of western states hindered as much as helped Newell's efforts to rationalize the program. Although the service drew some of its employees from land-grant colleges where irrigation systems were discussed and explained as a matter of course, in reality it was only distantly connected to these colleges. And perhaps most troublesome of all, scarcely any of the early engineers came from the very states and localities where reclamation projects were under way. Outside of Los Angeles, few of the service's engineers hailed from west of the Mississippi. For a program that required both knowledge of arid soils and an ability to understand and relate to western farmers, this proved to be a critical shortcoming.

Moreover, service officials were both powerless and unwilling to draw on the expertise of other agencies, including some within the Interior Department. Some of the capacities necessary for a successful reclamation policy—soil analysis, plot planning, and canal construction—lay with the Agriculture Department and the Army Corps of Engineers. Principally because Newell fought for full administrative control over the program, the Newlands Act ignored these fonts of scientific research and engineering talent in the federal government. The service's relationship to Agriculture was tense, due in part to the Ballinger-Pinchot controversy. Even when mandated by Congress, administrative cooperation between Agriculture and Interior was minimal. The administrative gulf separating the service from these agencies was principally a function of the Interior Department's procedural restrictions on communicating and contracting with other bureaus of the government. These factors combined to isolate the survey from some of the best talents of government irrigation, particularly the USDA's Ellwood Mead, who had served as Wyoming's state engineer in the 1890s. Whatever handicaps the Newlands Act or Interior Department organization gave to the service were exacerbated by Newell's stubborn refusal to draw on the expertise of other agencies.[15]

Indeed, clerical restrictions eventually impeded official cooperation between the Reclamation Service and the Geological Survey, the very bureau that had provided the service with its early administrative shelter. For after 1905, the two bureaus were placed under separate clerical supervisors in the department (see figure 2.1). Even though a neglected and withering plant under the care of Interior, the survey still possessed expertise in surveying and project location, and it had assisted many of the service's early efforts. Yet the isolation of the service from the survey after 1905 left it distanced from the best minds and energies of the Interior Department.[16]

The constraints of service recruitment emerge from an analysis of the geographic origins of the service's employees. As in chapter 6, I tabulate the number of Reclamation Service employees appointed from a given county, using Interior Department employee rosters in the *Official Register of the United States*. I then regress the counts upon a set of variables measuring the political, social, and economic characteristics of the county. I attempt to parcel out the effect of land-grant recruitment by including a variable for land-grant counties. Further, to assess the hypothesis that the service's recruitment was driven by its early leaders and by the Geological Survey, I include a variable tabulating the number of Geological Survey employees from the county as of 1905. To measure network-based recruitment by chief engineers, I include a variable scored one for all counties of origin of chief engineers. Finally, I test whether service personnel were more likely to come from states where reclamation projects were under way by assigning to each county the log of the value of reclamation expenditures in that state. In a similar way, I assign to each county the log of the value of public lands receipts from that state.[17]

The results of the statistical analysis appear in table 10.1, which displays both the coefficient estimates of the negative binomial model and the marginal effects on county matriculation of a one-unit change in each variable. Four results are worthy of note. First, the service's recruitment patterns did not favor Republican members of Congress, unlike the practices of other agencies. Republican representation is in fact *negatively* associated with recruitment to the service on a county basis. Second, much of recruiting appears to have been done through the networks of the Geological Survey and the head engineers of the service. Matriculation rates are higher in those counties that sent more employees to the Geological Survey, and higher as well in those counties from which the service's chief engineers arrived. Third, service personnel were more likely to come to the department from land-grant counties than from others, suggesting that the service did recruit through land-grant colleges and experiment stations. However, the substantive effects of this variable are diminutive. When summed across the number of land-grant colleges, the land-grant county variable accounts for only three employees, or 1.3 percent of the service's workforce in 1905. In contrast, the same variable accounted for 2.7 percent of the total USDA workforce in 1905, and because the USDA hired more nonscientific employees than the service, at least 40 percent of USDA scientific hiring was done through land-grant colleges. Although a measurable degree of land-grant college recruitment prevailed in its first decade, the service's ties to the land grants were insubstantial. What this analysis shows is that the construction of analytic capacity in the service followed predictable lines. As in other departments, there is evidence of network-based recruiting at the service that was less influenced by partisan forces. Yet the service was unable to create a pipeline from the land-grant colleges to its doors in the same way that the USDA had.

Finally, the service did not, on balance, attract more employees from those states where its projects were located. There is a negligible association between reclamation expenditures in a given state and the number of employees from

TABLE 10.1

Zero-Inflated Negative Binomial Regression Analysis of County-Level Matriculation into the Reclamation Service, 1905

Variable	Negative Binomial Estimates	Marginal Effects (one unit Δ in X)
Constant	-18.423^{**} (7.6933)	—
ln(County population)	0.1705 (0.1268)	0.0327
ln(Capital in manufacturing)	0.1620* (0.0743)	0.0311
Percentage of farms rented for cash	-0.0162^{**} (0.0062)	-0.0031
Percentage of farms rented for crop (tenancy)	-0.0055 (0.0049)	-0.0011
ln(Average farm land values) [valuation per acre]	1.5437 (0.9575)	0.2967
(ln(Average farm land values))^2 [valuation per acre]	-0.0533^+ (0.0318)	-0.0102
ln(Total value of livestock)	0.2244* (0.1086)	0.0431
House Republican representation, 1893–1905 (number of congresses, maximum = 6)	-0.0586^* (0.0289)	-0.0118
South	-0.4151^* (0.1989)	-0.0798
Land-grant county	0.5164* (0.2248)	0.0993
Chief and consulting engineers' counties of origin	1.2852** (0.1824)	0.2470
Number of employees entering Geological Survey from county	0.1150** (0.0350)	0.0221
ln(State reclamation expenditures)	0.0325 (0.0214)	0.0062
ln(State public land sale receipts)	0.0049 (0.0224)	0.0009
Dispersion	0.2245 (0.1518)	—
Zero-inflation parameter (tau-model)	-1.4901^{**} (0.4520)	—
Number of observations	2605	
Log-likelihood	-603.615	
Vuong statistic for zero-inflation	1.8643$^+$	

Note: Dependent variable is number of Service employees from county i. Mean count = 0.113.

Source: Census of 1900, ICPSR County Election Data, Official Congressional Directories, and Official Interior Department Roster, 1905.

Standard errors appear in parentheses after coefficient estimates.

*Significance at $p < .05$.

**Significance at $p < .01$.

$^+$Significance at $p < .10$. (All tests are two-tailed).

Marginal effects are calculated at dependent variable mean.

the counties of that state. Concretely, the Interior Department lacked personnel who knew the land, the agriculture, and the communities of the arid West. At the Carlsbad, New Mexico, project in 1905, Newell forsook the advice of W. M. Reed, an engineer who knew well the geology and soils of Carlsbad. Instead he designated two Washington-based engineers—E. W. Myers and B. M. Hall— as supervisors of the Carlsbad project. As implementation proceeded and problems arose, the service's lack of local knowledge impeded its efforts to build good reputations with local water users' associations. At Carlsbad, the president of the water users' association doubted the competence of the two engineers Newell had chosen to replace Reed, complaining that Myers "had no experience, was stubborn, obtuse, and never planned ahead." The poor rapport of the service's engineers with the Carlsbad water users haunted the service over the ensuing decades.[18]

The Failures of Reclamation Policy

The early troubles of American reclamation were traceable to the Interior Department's stifling administrative structure, exacerbated by program leadership that emphasized administrative isolation and extreme centralization. Among these failures, three were most critical: (1) the overcommitment of service resources, (2) massive cost overruns, and (3) the systematic neglect of planning for sustainable agriculture.

The Overcommitment of Reclamation

The act of 1902 gave the Reclamation Service, through the authority of the secretary of interior, the authority and discretion to launch projects as it pleased. Almost impulsively, Newell and his officials broke ground on as many projects as they could start. The service had initiated twenty-four projects by 1907 and twenty-seven by 1914. Theodore Roosevelt, a fan of the program, later admitted that "the work was pushed forward at a rate previously unknown in Government affairs." Although this early pace seemed an astute strategy to reclamation officials, the rapid and simultaneous construction hid two fatal flaws. First, it was self-defeating. The inauguration of multiple projects diluted the resources that the service could bring to any one project, delaying the completion of all of them. Thus, by attempting to please as many western interests as possible, the service ensured that all would be infuriated. Second, overcommitment thwarted learning by doing. It prevented service administrators from taking the lessons of one project and applying them to the next. Almost all of the work of surveying, project location, and construction was under way by 1910, and from 1906 to 1911 no new projects were started. As a result, the service was never able to develop any guidelines or standard operating procedures for these activities that made sense in light of its previous experience. In Donald Pisani's synopsis, "[B]y rushing to open as many projects as possible in the years from 1902 to 1907, [the Reclamation Service] severely limited the effectiveness of national reclamation."[19]

Historians of western irrigation such as Donald Swain have often attributed project overcommitment to the strictures of the Newlands Act. Section 9 of the 1902 act required that the service "expend the major portion of the funds arising from the sale of public lands within each state or Territory . . . within the limits of such State or Territory." Swain argues that section 9 led the service to undertake "too much, too soon." Indeed, in the first decade of the reclamation program, this argument proved alluring. In 1914 Rep. Carl Hayden, a defender of the reclamation program, offered an early version of Swain's argument, hypothesizing that because public land monies were coming from sixteen states, section 9 had forced the service to build more projects than it might have wished.[20]

Although plausible, Hayden's (and later Swain's) explanation for overcommitment in reclamation is flawed. Reclamation officials never interpreted section 9 so literally as to think that it required the service to spend at least 51 percent of the land receipts from a given state in that state. And even if the service had read the act in this way, this stricture would explain the existence of only sixteen projects, not twenty-seven. Beyond this, a closer examination of the relationship between public land sales and project spending across states suggests that section 9 could not possibly have caused the service to overcommit. As many western congressmen complained, and as table 10.2 shows, the service's construction patterns did not reward those states where public land sales were greatest. Indeed, public land receipts and reclamation expenditures were *negatively* correlated across states in 1914. States such as North Dakota, which provided more than $11 million to the reclamation fund, received less than $2 million in irrigation expenditures. And Texas, which had generated no public land monies, was home to almost $3 million in irrigation projects by 1914. Had section 9 operated to demand 51 percent in-state expenditure, the service's actions in North Dakota, South Dakota, Oregon, Kansas, and Oklahoma would have been in violation of the Newlands Act. Newell and his lieutenants, far from abiding by section 9, literally flouted the requirement in their administration of the program.

The pattern of project initiation also seems irreconcilable with partisan and distributive explanations. To begin with, reclamation was a western program, and most of the arid western states had been solidly Republican since their entry into the Union. Accordingly, the correlation across states of reclamation expenditures and Republican voting patterns is low, whether one measures voting patterns as House victories or as a fraction of the general election vote. Nor does table 10.2 provide evidence for the suggestion that service officials spent

TABLE 10.2
Public Land Receipts and Reclamation Expenditures Across 16 States, 1914

State	Receipts from Sales of Public Lands	Reclamation Service Expenditures on Irrigation Projects
Arizona	$1,455,000.00	$17,049,211.31
Idaho	5,039,708.90	16,181,170.51
Washington	6,433,299.73	9,475,583.36
Colorado	6,680,991.93	8,837,577.56
Montana	8,588,290.73	8,334,430.39
Nevada	541,596.96	6,781,272.03
Wyoming	4,320,900.46	6,614,027.90
New Mexico	3,939,790.95	6,531,423.80
Nebraska	1,664,013.83	5,797,553.83
Utah	1,890,479.34	4,652,949.61
Oregon	10,413,928.22	4,371,791.08
South Dakota	6,823,778.66	3,219,007.83
California	5,358,943.03	3,073,542.59
Texas	0.00	2,817,928.90
North Dakota	11,921,898.43	1,947,467.20
Kansas	963,080.07	376,471.29
Oklahoma	5,783,557.84	72,512.10

Correlation between sales and expenditures across states: -0.11.

Correlation between expenditures and farm product (1900) across states: -0.48.

Correlation between expenditures and fraction of House seats won by Republicans, 1896–1931: 0.04.

Source: CR (House), July 22, 1914, p. 12492.

more in those states where electoral competition was tighter: California, Colorado, and Oklahoma. Expenditures are also barely correlated with state populations and negatively correlated with farm productivity, casting doubt on any incentives to spend monies where votes, people, or organized farmers resided. Although there exists some evidence that Newell and his officials fretted over the completion of projects in election years, it is not clear that reclamation officials found the partisan incentive to complete projects more compelling than the administrative necessities of completing them. Indeed, the service exhibited great difficulty in completing projects.[21]

If neither partisan calculation nor institutional incentives led the service to plunge into too many projects, then what did? Historians have yet to provide an answer. In addition to section 9, Swain notes the "exuberance" of the service's early leaders as a contributing factor to the number of projects started. Members of Congress, too, blamed the service's "iridescent dreams" for overcommitment. Yet whether historians' preferred culprit lies in politics, in law, or in exuberance, these explanations miss the ineluctable connection between overcommitment and the service's other troubles: endless cost overruns, persistent overestimation of the returns to irrigated farming, and administrative delay. In 1902 Newell and his subordinates honestly believed that twenty or more simultaneous projects were possible. They expected sufficiently low average project costs and sufficiently high average project returns to justify the inauguration of numerous reclamation efforts at the same time. That there were no cautionary voices in the service to constrain Newell's plans speaks only to its dire organizational dilemmas. Service engineers shared Newell's belief that rapid, simultaneous construction would establish a vigorous "perception of efficacy." Overcommitment, then, flowed from a broader administrative fabric of infirmity in policy formulation.[22]

Riddles of Cost: The Yuma, Salt River, and Carlsbad Projects

The Reclamation Service encountered its greatest difficulties in maintaining cost-effectiveness in the Southwest. In California, after a long search for appropriate sites, Newell and his team of engineers chose a project for the Imperial Valley. This project—at Yuma, near the Mexico border—would be the largest in the service's first decade. In May 1904 Newell persuaded Secretary Hitchcock to allot $3 million for the Yuma project. Shortly thereafter, the service began construction of the Laguna Dam, the project's main reservoir. Newell's lieutenants in California then set out to sign up as many Imperial Valley farmers as possible. They secured nine-tenths of the private lands within the project's boundaries, and they purchased most of the existing irrigation canals within the valley. They promised Yuma settlers more water than ever before, even though the hydrographic branch of the survey had not systematically measured the flow of water on the Colorado River for almost two decades.[23]

A similar rush to settlement was evident at the service's Salt River project in Arizona. Here the service relied on the local water users' association to subscribe farmers to 200,000 acres, even though Davis (the chief engineer for the project) predicted that a maximum of 180,000 acres would be irrigable under the service's best efforts. At sites throughout the arid West, service officials at once threw open all of the project lands to cultivation by settlers before the lands had been developed, before the excess private lands had been bought, and before the storage waters were available. A decade later, the service's Central Board of Review would offer a stiff recommendation against this nonincremental policy.[24]

The service expected and publicized low per-acre costs on its projects—$35 per acre at Yuma, and $18–$20 at Salt River—but several factors conspired to make a mockery of these guesses. First, service officials systematically undercalculated the costs of project construction and maintenance. In most cases, reservoir construction was not the principal activity inflating costs, as the service was able to build complex dams rather easily. Even here, however, an independent board of army engineers found that the service had built more complex dams than necessary; at Laguna and the Lower Yellowstone, "equally suitable structures could have been constructed at less cost." So, too, reservoir construction was subject to the administrative delays plaguing the program in its first decade; even the best-constructed reservoirs (including the Laguna Dam) were finished several years behind schedule, delaying the arrival of irrigation waters to eager settlers. And several of the service's early construction projects failed or broke, including an important levee at Yuma and a particularly embarrassing case of seepage at the Hondo project in New Mexico. At Hondo, the service failed to check for gypsum in the reservoir basin. The reservoir's gypsum deposits dissolved, allowing the water to seep through the rock. So complete was the failure of the reservoir that the Hondo project had to be abandoned altogether, at a deadweight loss of more than $1 million.[25]

Much more than damming major rivers, however, reclamation required preparing project lands for sustainable farming. Reclamation officials were dimly aware of this fact and seemingly incapable of incorporating it into their plans and actions. Newell saw the service's mission under the Reclamation Act as the construction and maintenance of "works." The planning and management of a project seemed beyond the ken of his organizational imagination. By their own admission, service officials fallaciously assumed that "as soon as water was provided this was practically the end of necessary expenditures. Little consideration was given to the large cost of leveling, subduing, and cultivating the soil and of providing the fertilizers which are necessary in an arid region." Indeed, before 1910, the service had not engaged in project-wide surveys for computing its cost estimates; it had studied dam construction but neglected studies of land productivity, soil viability, and property ownership, relying on the limited (and often biased) studies of local water users' associations. In his early studies at the Salt River project, Davis said nothing about the viability of the valley's soils. And at Carlsbad in New Mexico, the service conducted soil analyses only *after* having bought the project lands and irrigation works. Had the service undertaken such studies, it would probably have discovered conditions that made mere reservoir construction grossly insufficient for the success of settlers. In areas such as the Imperial Valley, where private irrigation efforts were already under way—or more likely, where these efforts had failed—the land was frequently cut up by old water channels and covered with shrubbery, making plot preparation even more costly. Had the service properly surveyed the plots and soils to be irrigated on its projects, it might have made some provision for these costs in its estimates. The incorporation into reclamation planning of soil analysis, of the sort developed in the USDA before 1900, would become one of Ellwood Mead's material innovations to the program in the 1920s. Its absence from reclamation before the 1920s crippled many projects from the start. Beyond this, the service failed to anticipate the costs of constructing drainage systems to combat seepage, soil water-logging, and alkali buildup, an undertaking that added $5 to $6 per acre. As Pisani summarizes, the "miscalculations of Reclamation Service officials contributed to the fact that project construction costs usually ran far higher than initial estimates."[26]

Speculation and preexisting land ownership combined as a second force inflating project costs. Speculators descended in droves on reclamation projects, purchasing project lands and holding out on the service officials who intended to buy them. The service had purchase and condemnation rights, but even condemnation required repayment of value to the landowner. And because the Newlands Act gave no legal procedure for the determination of property values in irrigation districts, the service faced daunting legal and delay costs if it wished to divest a recalcitrant (and speculative) landowner of his plot. The service had also failed to account for the degree of private land ownership on its projects. Where a high fraction of the project lands were already owned, the strain on the service's water supplies would increase, and the benefits of reclamation would accrue to private landowners in greater proportion than it would to homesteaders. Unfortunately, Newell's officials never undertook systematic surveys to assess the degree to which private demand would exist for its waters. Instead, the service relied on the limited (and biased) surveys of local water users' associations. Ironically, neither speculation nor private ownership was as problematic at Yuma as it was elsewhere. For Newell and Lippincott, two of the alluring features of the Imperial Valley were its lack of development and its large cache of public and Indian lands. These features combined to minimize the extent of speculation once the project was announced. In the end, however, these advantages were only of academic significance. The relative absence of speculation at Yuma left the service with one less excuse for its cost overruns.[27]

The plethora of sites to which the service had committed its resources only worsened the problem of cost estimation. The simultaneity of twenty-four projects prevented learning by doing. Had the service begun one or two projects per year instead of the twenty-four launched between 1902 and 1907, it could have updated its cost estimates as it went along. Instead, it replicated the same

set of errors for the first decade after the Newlands Act. As Rep. William LaFollette, a Republican from Washington, recognized in 1914, the service had systematically "misled" the settlers, not out of dishonesty, but out of a faulty
method. "The engineers made their estimates no doubt honestly, but each project was of a different nature practically. They could not judge one by the other,
and they had no precedents to go by." What LaFollette neglected to mention is
that the service had denied itself the possibility of precedents, at least until funds
permitted a trickle of new projects after 1914. That the service did learn lessons
is evident from its annual reports to Congress, beginning as early as 1905. The
service's eleventh report (1911–12) contained a section called "Fallacies Entertained," which included the early administration of the Reclamation Act.
Newell ran systematically through the service's mistakes: optimistic cost estimates, neglect of land preparation activities and costs, the difficulties of finding markets for new supplies, land drainage, and settler recruitment. By 1911
the service had even updated its cost estimates for completing the remaining
projects. The grand irony of Newell's confession, however, is that overcommitment had deprived the service of any opportunity to put these lessons to use.
The service had not commenced a project in six years.

> During the first four years a considerable number of surveys and examinations were
> carried on, with the result that selection was made of one or more projects in each
> State where the conditions were most favorable for immediate construction. Practi-
> cally all of the enterprises which have been entered upon were examined at that time,
> and since 1905 or 1906 no new projects have been taken up and very few investi-
> gated.[28]

Miscalculation, speculation, and inefficiency combined to explode per-acre
reclamation costs. The service's constant transgression of its initial estimates
was hardly a marginal affair; the overexpenditure ranged from 50 to 300 percent across projects. On no single project did the service finish at or under its
initial estimates. The Yuma project, for which Newell and Lippincott had envisioned costs at only $35 an acre, proved no exception. By 1909, with the La-
guna Dam completed, the per-acre cost at Yuma had risen to $55. By 1911 this
had reached $65 an acre, settling at $75 an acre after the war. Even with this
added expense, the service did not formally provide water from Laguna until
1914, when Secretary Franklin Lane tentatively granted to the Imperial Valley
Irrigation District the right to secure water from Laguna Dam upon a flat payment of $500,000.[29]

None of these early troubles would have bothered the settlers or Congress
much had the reclamation projects spawned sufficiently profitable agriculture
to compensate for them. Instead, the opposite happened. Irrigated agriculture
failed throughout western reclamation projects, and settlers deserted the service's planned communities en masse. At Yuma, the service overestimated the

amount of water it could provide, having failed to take measurements of the Colorado River when making its estimates. In addition, Newell and Lippincott's dreams of profitable citrus crops never materialized. Instead, Yuma farmers turned to fields of alfalfa, timothy, and grains, all commodities with a lower market value. The service's irrigation canals became clogged with silt, and alkali buildup in the topsoil reduced yields even after the service constructed drainage ditches at additional expense.[30]

The abiding defect of federal reclamation, however, lay in the limited farming abilities of the settlers. Except for experienced farmers who were already living on project lands, most of the farmers making homes at Yuma and other projects were eastern and Plains states transplants with little knowledge of agriculture. They brought scarcely any capital to their newly acquired lands, and they generally knew little about the crops they would plant. Early reclamation projects failed to attract settlers, and where settlers did arrive, their farms rarely attained the level of productivity to which reclamation officials had aspired. Among those who did come, many abandoned their farms within a few years of beginning farming. When the Reclamation Service opened lands in the Yuma Indian Reservation in March 1910, it provided 173 homesteads to eager settlers. Of these, 68 were forfeited later that year, and another 31 were abandoned by 1913. At Carlsbad settlers began a two-year exodus much earlier, in 1905. By the close of its first decade, the service had made a marginal contribution to western irrigation. By 1908 the service had irrigated 7,500 acres at Carlsbad, but a private company was already irrigating 13,000 acres. And at Yuma, most of the 10,500 acres under cultivation in 1912 were already being irrigated privately when the Newlands Act passed in 1902.[31]

Abandonment went hand in hand with delinquency. The Newlands Act required settlers to repay their loans and the value of reclamation to the fund within ten years of their arrival. The service enforced the ten-year rule whether or not it had provided water upon the arrival of settlers. Among those who stayed on the projects, only a few met their payment schedules. To make matters worse, Newell blamed the fiscal crises of his organization on the settlers, even though the service's failure to provide water on a timely and reliable basis stunted the settlers' yields. Indeed, reclamation officials seemed only dimly aware of the settlement and abandonment problems on their projects. They continued to build construction works, irrigation canals, and drainage ditches, without paying attention to the genuine financial and informational problems the settlers were facing. Instead of attending systematically to farming viability, the service simply constructed more works. From 1912 to 1915, it boosted fourfold the acreage of Yuma lands served by irrigation ditches, but at the end of this period only 27,000 of these 71,000 acres were under cultivation. As Pisani writes, "[T]o government engineers, half a project was no project at all, and the canal network expanded much faster than the rate of settlement."[32]

The Descent of Reputation and Discretion

The administrative transgressions of the service soured its relations with water users' associations and with Congress. From 1905 onward, the service's reputation in congressional debates and among western clienteles took a continuous beating. In the West the service lost a number of potential supporters by its failure to inform settlers of mounting cost increases until their bills were due. At the Bellefourche project in South Dakota, the service gathered independent estimates that the per-acre costs of construction and maintenance would amount to $34. In a 1913 lawsuit against the service, however, settlers charged that reclamation officials had promised a $22.50 per-acre cost, a 1907 completion date, and no payments until the project was completed. By 1914 the per-acre cost estimates exceeded the original $34, the project was still unfinished, and the service had already levied per-acre construction charges on the settlers. The service's misdeeds led Bellefourche's representative, Republican Charles Burke, to complain not that the reclamation program was flawed but that the service was. "The whole trouble with the Reclamation Service," he lamented, "is that there is too much jurisdiction and too much power in the service itself."[33]

Newell and his lieutenants also managed to infuriate the water users' association at the Salt River project in Arizona. Here the service had published an original cost estimate of $3.75 million in 1903. As elsewhere, however, Salt River project costs ballooned, reaching $10.5 million in 1912. Throughout the intervening decade, even as they knew that completed project costs would vastly exceed their original projections, reclamation officials kept Salt River farmers in the dark. When the Roosevelt Dam, the reservoir for the Salt River project, was completed in March 1912, the service announced that mandatory repayments would be required from project farmers that year. So began a decade-long struggle between the service and local farmers, who permanently lost trust in the Interior Department. So infuriated were Salt River water users that they pressed for a congressional investigation of the service's expenditure patterns. The investigation, conducted by a subcommittee of the House Committee on Expenditures in the Interior Department, issued a scathing (though little noticed) report on the department's practices. In Arizona, according to the subcommittee, the department had been "accountable to no one" and conducted its operations "in the twilight zone."[34]

The laments of western farmers did not suffer from lack of focus or clarity. In most instances, settlers aimed their political ire directly at the perceived incompetence of the service. A consulting engineer of the Geological Survey visited the Carlsbad project in 1906 and found "that the community was divided on the question of the professional ability of the engineers representing the Reclamation Service at Carlsbad." The settlers harbored doubts about every aspect of the service's operations, including "the efficiency of the proposed work on the Avalon Dam," which had failed one year earlier. When the newly reconstructed Avalon Dam was completed in July 1907, local officials organized festivities and invited officials of the service and the Interior Department. Yet their requests were ignored, leaving Carlsbad settlers "bitterly disappointed." The service could not have offended its clients more efficiently.[35]

As the settlers' troubles compounded, and as project after project fell subject to delay and cost overruns, the service's reputation in Congress began to suffer irreversible damage. First and foremost, the service had, by the time of the Taft administration, established a reputation for fiscal profligacy. As of 1910 the service had already outspent the reclamation fund by $20 million, compelling Congress to advance Treasury funds to cover this discrepancy. The bond act of 1910 authorized Interior to draw on Treasury funds for the completion of existing reclamation projects and any "proper and necessary" extensions to those already under way. In granting this fiscal reprieve to the service, however, the Republican majority took direct aim at the Interior Department's fiscal lifeline. The secretary lost discretion over project extensions, which now required approval by the president. Any funds taken from the Treasury were later to be returned to it by the service. Congress further prohibited the service from spending any Treasury monies upon the inauguration of new projects. Finally, as if to add jurisdictional insult to discretionary injury, section 1 of the bond act stated that

> no part of this appropriation shall be expended upon any existing project until it shall have been examined and reported upon by a board of engineer officers of the Army, designated by the President of the United States, and until it shall be approved by the President as feasible and practicable and worthy of such expenditure.

In one brief paragraph, Congress had put the service under severe restraint. Presidential approval of new projects and extensions reduced the service's operational leeway to the level enjoyed by other agencies. To subject *existing* projects to a review by officers of the Army Corps of Engineers, however, was to express broad disapproval of the service's choices from 1902 to 1910. The Board of Army Engineers would now choose the allocation of reclamation monies from 1910 to 1914. Newell found his once expansive grip on the service weakened.[36]

Despite its infusion of funds, the bond act hardly seemed to solve the service's problems. As early as 1914, the service had spent the $20 million allowance from the 1910 act and was estimating that $50 million more would be needed to complete the projects under way. And even while many projects were incomplete and settlers fell ever more behind on their repayments, Newell had new sites in mind for reservoir construction, diversion, and farming. Members of Congress began to suspect that Newell and other service officers were pushing to create a slew of new projects based on slim evidence. And at the service's headquarters in Washington, the incoming mails were filled with complaints from settlers and water users' associations. Finally, western community newspapers, which had been supportive of other departments and their efforts, began to target their ire at the service. At the Salt River project after 1910, the *Arizona Republican* and the *Chandler Arizonan* turned against the service and began to advocate reduced authority for Newell, even while supporting the continuation of Salt River. From every conceivable corner, the service's reputation was under attack.[37]

Newell's intransigence in the face of settlers' complaints served only to further sour the Interior Department's reputation in Congress. Settlers received little more than contempt in Newell's annual reports. Newell complained in the 1911–12 report that the service could not "secure the right kind of farmers to handle the reclaimed land, and utilize it to advantage." He found the project settlers utterly unlike the pioneers of the storied West.

> The characteristics of present settlers are in many respects entirely different from those of the older pioneer communities; there is not the spirit of cooperation which ruled the early pioneers; the class of people now attracted to the lands are not as capable of adapting themselves to existing conditions and initiating the building of distributing works.

Members of Congress, naturally, placed the blame for abandonment on different shoulders. As Harvey Fergusson enjoined, Newell's service had deceived arid-lands farmers with misguided optimism.

> The Government engineers mistook the time they could finish the work. The people who went on the lands, seeking and hungry for homes, were misled partly by these Government engineers and by their own hopefulness that they would get a home, and so undertook it.[38]

Newell's rhetoric did not serve his organization well. In the summer of 1914 the department came to Congress asking for a measure that would give project settlers an extra ten years to repay their loans. The reclamation extension bill would thus bring the total repayment period to twenty years. Although most representatives in Congress agreed that the ten-year repayment period of the Newlands Act was shortsighted, supporters and detractors of the act concurred that the service was principally responsible for the program's early failures. As a result, arguments for and against reclamation extension invoked the hapless administration of the service. Western representatives pleading for a ten-year extension blamed overcommitment and administrative profligacy for having placed undue burdens on settlers. As Rep. Edward Taylor, a Democrat from Colorado, complained in 1914, the service "has simply gone out and tried to build 32 Government reclamation projects, and has told them they could get the land for $10 to $15 an acre. Now the overhead charges have mounted from $20 to $50 an acre, and they are asking the poor people there to pay it, and they cannot do it." For Taylor and his western colleagues, the service's administrative incompetence necessitated a generous repayment extension.[39]

Opponents of the repayment extension argued that the service's (and Interior's) incompetence was the best reason *not* to extend repayment. The extension would let the secretary off the hook and continue a program whose administration doomed it to failure. The service had already spent $100 million on the twenty-seven projects (with few tangible results), and by its own estimates it would need $50 million more to complete the projects under way. Rep. Martin Madden of Illinois wondered whether a $50 million cost overrun would eventually reach $100 million: "[I]f that should be true, we would find ourselves having expended $200,000,000 for the development of 3,000,000 acres of land." In this respect, members of Congress regarded overcommitment and cost overruns as evidence of the same phenomenon of profligacy. For how could the explanation for cost overruns lie in labor shortages or the vagaries of commodity markets when the number of projects was purely an administrative choice? No price shock, no labor shortage, and not even a distributive-minded Congress had pushed the service to begin twenty-seven projects. As the debate unfolded, the lack of congressional trust in the service became ever clearer. Beyond the fiscal costs of the program, Congress had spent valuable time and administrative resources of its own to monitor and correct the flaws of the service's efforts. As Madden lamented,

> [W]e allowed the Department of Interior to accept the money coming from the sale of public lands and to expend that money for the development of these irrigation projects. And we found ourselves in the predicament of having begun projects that were impossible of perfection, and we had to appoint a committee of the Senate and of the House and a commission of Army engineers to go out and overlook and revise the work of the Department of the Interior, where it failed, either by lack of knowledge or because of its lack of patriotism, and we were obliged to call a halt.[40]

In expressing his reluctance to trust the Interior Department, Madden made note of its crowning embarrassment, the bond act of 1910. The experiment with irrigation policy had taught Congress a bitter lesson. Whether in forest management or in irrigation projects, the Interior Department was not to be trusted. For reclamation enthusiasts as well as skeptics—for Madden as well as Taylor—the problems of reclamation lay not in the secretary but in the department.

> And now we are asked again to continue our confidence in the Department of Interior and to continue to authorize the Secretary of Interior to expend moneys received from the sale of public lands in the development of irrigation projects without coming to Congress to tell us why or where or when.
>
> Now, personally, I have the greatest confidence in the Secretary of the Interior, no matter who he may be. But he is human, and he has too much to do, and he can not know; and whoever he may be himself he undoubtedly has men under him who are not always filled with that degree of patriotism which permits the economic expenditure of the public funds, and they have not been expended economically on these irrigation projects. On the contrary, there has been reckless extravagance with the public funds, without the accomplishment of the kind of work that we had the right to hope for.[41]

Madden's statement, attributing reclamation's faults to a lack of "patriotism" and a "reckless extravagance," evinced a dim knowledge of Interior's actual defects. Like most members of Congress and other political elites, however, he could perceive that the failures of reclamation lay not with the appointees of one president or another but with the Interior Department itself. Members could see that reclamation's problems were embedded within the administrative structure of the department and resulted especially from the weak capacity of the service. For this reason, Franklin Lane's demotion of Newell and his eventual appointment of Davis as director of the service did little to calm legislative (or western) nerves about the program's troubles.

In 1914 Congress approved the Reclamation Extension Act. This act and its aftermath provide the clearest evidence of congressional distrust of the service. In approving the extension bill, Congress affirmed the basic principles of the Newlands Act. The extension act doubled the repayment period to twenty years and paved the way for new appropriations for existing projects. Yet even as the Progressive-Democratic coalition shored up the program with one hand, it placed a tight procedural grip around the service with the other. The act of 1914 prevented the secretary from increasing construction charges for any project without prior consent of the water users, whether organized or not. This was a signal departure from the Newlands Act, which granted to the secretary broad powers over charges and water pricing. Beyond this, the 1914 act also allowed water users' associations to relieve the service of project maintenance. Western water users quickly took advantage of this provision to minimize the service's control over their operations.[42]

Finally, in the last section of the Reclamation Act, Congress tucked in a provision that essentially ended the fiscal autonomy of the service. Section 16 decreed that after July 1, 1915, "expenditures shall not be made for carrying out the purposes of the reclamation law except out of appropriations made annually by Congress therefor." The secretary of interior would now have to justify reclamation spending in the annual book of estimates, just as was required of every other executive department. In addition, all monies from the reclamation fund returned to congressional control. Confronted repeatedly with the failures of the service, Congress took away the very taproot of discretion on which Newell had thrived. As Underwood, the sponsor of section 16, argued for the necessity of compelling the service to present its program before Congress for annual appropriations, he pointed again to overcommitment, reminding members that "the bureau has overreached itself and will continue to do so in the future. More than that, I think the bureau has at times entered upon projects that were unwise, and has expended more money on projects than conditions authorized or warranted." Democrats and Progressives of the early Wilson administration, otherwise imbued with a faith in the bureaucratic form, could agree to discipline the Reclamation Service. Section 16 was approved by a vote of forty to twenty-one.[43]

Conclusion: Structure, Reputation, and the Demise of Autonomy

In the end, Congress approved the Reclamation Extension Act of 1914 because its hands were tied. Having sunk $100 million into the program, and having held out the promise of watered farmland to tens of thousands of settlers, there was no going back. The significant fact about the act, in retrospect, is not that it gave new life to governmental irrigation in the west. Rather, the legacy of the bill lay in its fine print. Underwood's amendment quashed one of only several experiments in American history with open-ended spending discretion for an agency. Indeed, the demise of fiscal autonomy for the service came during a period of economic growth, a time of agricultural prosperity, a time of increasing discretion for other government bureaus, and a time when new agencies were created for new functions of state.

In short, administrative debility best explains the demise of the service's discretion from 1910 to 1914. This factor, and the painful process by which Congress became aware of it, account first for the arguments used to justify the increasing encumbrance of the service's activities after 1910. For Republicans, Democrats, and Progressives alike pointed to overcommitment and cost profligacy when advocating greater restrictions on the Interior Department's western operations. Second, Congress's growing concerns about the service's haplessness explain the particular form of the reclamation legislation that was passed after 1910—the full project review by the Army Board of Engineers, the wresting of project selection from the secretary of interior, and the death of the department's control over the reclamation fund. Finally, the Reclamation Extension Act's combination of program expansion and liberalization, on the one hand, with the procedural shackling of Interior's officials, on the other, points to a consensual judgment (repeated at length in congressional debates in 1914) about the service's irreversible faults. For Congress's nagging doubt in 1914 was not about the reclamation program but about the service.

It is important to remember, though, that the failures of the service after 1902 were not random mistakes. As Garfield presaged in 1906, and as members of Congress knew ever more lucidly in the first decade of the Newlands Act, the Reclamation Service was fundamentally constrained by the structure of the Interior Department and the limits of its organization. The demise of bureaucratic autonomy in early reclamation therefore illustrates the significance of administrative structure, planning capacity, and incremental program building.

It is also worth reflecting once again on the network bases of the service's reputation. Like much of the Interior Department, the Reclamation Service was deeply embedded in the western states (though not with any degree of popularity or favor) but had few allies in conservationist circles, in academic and professional organizations, and in other sections of the country. The contrast

with the USDA's Forest Service—which claimed allegiance from women's organizations, from academics, from conservationists on both coasts, and among
a sizable portion of western interests—could not have been clearer. Contrast-
ing reclamation with federal extension at the Agriculture Department raises a
set of more dramatic polarities: Where in the history of federal reclamation were
the industrial philanthropists? Where were the land-grant colleges, whom the
Interior Department partly regulated? Where were the farm organizations, both
the national lobbies and the producer cooperatives that increasingly populated
the West? Where were the railroads? The large-scale absence of these organizations from the story of reclamation says more about the political debility of
the Interior Department than it says about reclamation itself or about any of
these organizations in particular. Put simply, Interior officials were powerless
to bring these voices into the fold of a policy coalition.

Bureaucratic autonomy in Progressive-Era resource policy was premised not
upon capture, not upon section, but upon broad-based alliances centered in middle-level bureaus. It was this possibility that Newell's hasty program expansion,
and the clerical structure of the Interior Department, defeated.

    It is possible, in light of the autonomy of the Post Office and the USDA, and
in light of the theory guiding this narrative, to imagine a different history for
federal reclamation. Consider a counterfactual history of reclamation. Had the
service nursed the reclamation fund through a selective choice of projects, it
surely would not have exhausted its funds so quickly, and it might have been
able to survive early project failures, in part by highlighting and building on a
few early successes. Had the service developed lasting and stable political ties
to water users' associations and professional groups, it would have been able to
defend itself against congressional and executive-branch critics more effectively after 1907. The most fascinating counterfactual scenario comes when we
ask how reclamation would have evolved had the Interior Department looked
more like the USDA. Had the service been led by the USDA's Ellwood Mead
or a similar official with broad affiliations in Progressive society, and had it retained a corps of officials capable of developing legislative and partisan trust in
the service and with broad support outside the department, then political attacks
on the service would have been much more costly for politicians to launch. Indeed, the promise of the reclamation program was larger than even these separate counterfactuals will allow. With careful project selection, incremental development, stronger ties to water users' associations, stable and knowledgeable
personnel, and diverse network support, the Interior Department would probably have housed in its Reclamation Service the most autonomous bureau in the
federal government.

Conclusion _____

The Politics of Bureaucratic Autonomy

Bureaucrats are politicians, and bureaucracies are organizations of political actors. Autonomy arises when bureaucrats successfully practice a politics of legitimacy. It occurs when agency leaders build reputations for their organizations—reputations for efficacy, for uniqueness of service, for moral protection, and for expertise. It occurs, further, when they ground this reputation in a diverse coalition wrought from the multiple networks in which they are engaged. These coalitions, suspended in beliefs and in networks, and uncontrollable by politicians, are the stuff of autonomous bureaucratic policy innovation. This, I submit, is the basic lesson of the forging of bureaucratic autonomy in the United States. *Bureaucratic autonomy is politically forged.*

Contemporary political science—including an entire literature on bureaucracy that depends on "principal-agent" models of bureaucratic politics—assumes that the linkages between voters and policies occur through parties, elections, representatives, and the legislature. Yet the decisive steps in forging bureaucratic autonomy occurred when federal bureaucrats broke free from the traditional model of politics and established links directly to citizens and the new associations that increasingly claimed their allegiance. Long before the "iron triangles" of the New Deal Era, bureaucracies began to aggregate citizens and voters precisely when parties and politicians were having a difficult time doing so.

Because some agencies did this more successfully than others, the state-building achievement of the Progressive Era was concrete but limited. What emerged in the 1910s and 1920s was not a uniformly more powerful bureaucracy than existed three decades earlier. In pockets of the American state, relative autonomy conditioned upon political legitimacy materialized. Most other agencies lay dormant. Therein lies the puzzle of American state building. Why was the Department of Agriculture able to establish a foothold in writing significant legislation? Why was the Interior Department, with authority over public lands and ties to numerous western interests, unable to capitalize on the movements for conservation and western reclamation? Why were reformers in the Post Office Department able to eliminate systematically the positions of strong Republican identifiers in fourth-class offices at the very time when Republicans enjoyed hegemony in electoral politics? Why were postal officials able to grab all of the moral policing powers they wanted and resist political control of their use? Why was the USDA able to take its newfound authority in food and drug regulation and turn its fire on the very firms who most supported Republicans during the Progressive period?

The answer lies in the organizational properties of executive agencies at the turn of the century. Bureaucratic autonomy cannot exist apart from the organizational characteristics of the agencies that experience it. If it exists, bureaucratic autonomy *must* be premised not upon the popularity of a policy, not upon occasional administrative fiat, not upon a single well-heeled lobby, but upon the stable political legitimacy of the bureaucracy itself. To focus on organizational reputations is not, as I have emphasized, to divorce bureaucracies from politics. Instead, it is to reconceive politics as a process of coalition building and to acknowledge that in some circumstances bureaucrats can take the decisive initiative (at times, the *only* initiative) in building them. It is to these reputations—and the capacities and coalitions that supported them—that autonomous bureaucracies in America owe their origins.

Is Autonomy the Right Metaphor?

> A bureau . . . can coerce the legislators through its powers of propaganda. The procurement of apparent popular support through skillfully conducted publicity may so fortify its position that Congress would hesitate to abolish the bureau or reduce its appropriation.
>
> A group becomes dependent on the existence of the bureau. . . . Moreover, the bureau builds a place for itself in the community and makes demands of Congress in the name of the "public welfare." New fields of possible usefulness are outlined. Perspicacious, aggressive, well-meaning, the officials, supported by the public benefiting from their services[,] bring forward plans for expansion.
>
> —E. Pendleton Herring, 1934

Can bureaucratic autonomy be a meaningful concept? E. Pendleton Herring discovered half of the answer more than six decades ago. *Autonomy lies not in fiat but in leverage.* Autonomy does not really consist in the ability of bureaus to take clandestine, undetected actions against the wishes of elected authorities. It exists most powerfully when bureaus have acquired lasting esteem and durable links to social, political, and economic organizations, links that rival or surpass those of politicians. For this reason, bureaucratic autonomy arises less in the administration of policy than in its *emergence.* Only a weak autonomy is observed when agencies shirk while administering a law or policy that was of politicians' design. Genuine bureaucratic autonomy exists when agencies take the decisive first moves toward a new policy, establishing an agenda or the most popular alternative that becomes costly for otherwise recalcitrant politicians and organized interests to ignore. It exists when agencies can *alter* the preferences of the public, of organized interests, of presidents, of members of Congress, of media organizations, and of partisan elites. When agencies—by virtue of their recognized legitimacy in a policy area, by virtue of their superior ties to voters or their superior publicity, by virtue of their established reputations for impartiality or pursuit of the national good—can make it politically costly to oppose or restrain their innovations or deny them leeway, they have achieved a form of autonomy that modern political science fails to recognize.[1]

It makes little difference for the present account whether these reputations are deserved or well founded. Did the Forest Service protect national forests better than did private landowners? Did the Post Office truly enhance the nation's morals, or did it do the country a profound and lasting disservice by reversing advances in Americans' (especially women's) personal liberty? Did agricultural extension actually improve farm productivity? All of these questions might be answered skeptically. Yet in the early twentieth century, most politically active Americans—citizens active in organizations of all kinds, across geographic sections, across parties, across gender and even class lines—believed that the Post Office and Agriculture Departments offered unique services and protections of lasting value. Not only did Americans view the departments favorably, but they also were clearly enthusiastic about Harvey Wiley, August Machen, Carter Keene, Gifford Pinchot, Anthony Comstock (to a lesser extent, for many civil libertarians), Seaman Knapp, and other officials.

A skeptic might suggest that *innovation* better describes the narratives in this book than autonomy. Clearly not all bureaucratic innovation entails autonomy, but the episodes of policy initiation in this book were, frequently enough, opposed or little sought by presidents, the major parties, congressional committees, and others. Progressive-Era politicians supported bureaucratic innovations only after autonomous agencies made it politically costly to oppose them. Consider then the following episodes of bureaucratic policy reform after 1900:

- the Post Office Department's massive closure of fourth-class offices after 1900 (in which Republicans were not spared);
- the Chemistry Bureau's unyielding prosecution of whiskey firms supported by House Speaker Joseph Cannon;
- the Forest Service's creation and administration of controversial "user fees" when none were contemplated in the 1905 Transfer Act (even by the act's western supporters);
- the Post Office's redirection of postal savings banks from agrarian regions to immigrant-laden areas;

- the USDA's systematic elimination of farmers' institutes—the mode of farm education most favored by the Grange, the NFU, and the states—from the American landscape and their replacement by the Knapp-Spillman county extension system;
- the Post Office's single-handed expansion of arrest powers in the 1890s and its brazen resistance to politicians' attempts to use its inspection authority for partisan ends.

These and numerous other episodes are only weakly described as "innovations." They were undertaken within the broader energies of Progressive reform, of course, but they were fundamental departures from existing and favored policies. They were first and foremost counter-majoritarian, often initiated against the wishes of the dominant Republican Party (including its Progressive and agrarian wings), and against the dominant institutional actors of the period: congressional committees and their chairs, presidents, and party leaders, except when these actors were subsumed into the agency's coalition. More generally, by shaping the parameters of Progressive legislation itself—by writing laws and amendments that were accepted wholesale by presidents and leaders in Congress—federal bureaucrats in the early 1900s transcended the legacy of clericalism. This often painful break with the past was itself an instantiation of autonomy.[2]

It merits repeating, however, that Progressive-Era autonomy was not a pan-bureaucratic love affair with the state. If it was, the Interior Department was institutionally forlorn. Nor is it the case that reputations must be universal; not every organization in the early 1900s supported expansions of postal and USDA discretion, and not every group opposed an autonomous Interior Department. The key to strong organizational reputations lay not in their unanimous hold but in their broad social basis.

The Poverty of Procedural Politics

The argument elaborated here poses several challenges to contemporary erudition on bureaucracies. Following the highly influential work of Mathew McCubbins, Roger Noll, and Barry Weingast, a generation of scholars has argued that an agency's "enacting coalition" of politicians can use administrative procedures to induce the agency to take exactly those actions that the coalition desires. These "procedural politics" theories suggest that most of the political action in bureaucratic politics occurs when the methods and processes for a given policy are set by politicians and the interests to which they respond. Hence bureaucratic politics does not really involve bureaucracies at all; "the administrative system is automatic."

The theory elaborated here suggests that procedural politics is unlikely to control agencies with stable political legitimacy. Agencies with esteemed officials who have publicly recognized capacity and expertise, and who have independent access to organized citizens, exercise power over the procedures of their agency. Autonomous agencies are powerful bargaining agents in procedural design. The more powerful constraint on administrative procedures is that legitimated agency officials can make it politically costly for politicians to constrain them. Partisans of the procedural-politics school of bureaucracy have discussed all sorts of mechanisms for controlling the bureaucracy without recognizing that these strategies have costs. In some respects, these amount to forfeiting the benefits of agency specialization. The argument here, however, is that when agencies have political legitimacy, the costs of control are *explicitly political and electoral.* William Howard Taft, Joseph Cannon, Eugene Loud, and other Progressive-Era politicians learned this lesson the hard way.

Empirically, procedural accounts are powerless to explain the narratives of this book. Most of the administrative procedures to which political scientists point emerged after the Second World War and the Administrative Procedures Act (APA) of 1946. Indeed, the very passage of the APA came in response to patterns of autonomous action that worried national politicians during a time of bureaucratic expansion. Yet would the narratives of autonomous policy innovation in this book have turned out differently if the Administrative Procedures Act had been in place in 1880? Surely not. Nothing in the APA would have prevented officials in the Post Office and the USDA from developing the experimental programs that they later launched into fully statutory activities of the national government. Beyond this, procedures were then (and are now) powerless to prevent agency coalition building. Nothing in the APA would have prevented Anthony Comstock, Gifford Pinchot, August Machen, Harvey Wiley, and Seaman Knapp, among others, from building reform coalitions of their own making.

The argument here also suggests a counterintuitive criterion for assessing agency independence. In a shrewd argument, McCubbins and colleagues have noted repeatedly over the last two decades that agencies can appear to be taking all of the important actions even when they are fully controlled by their legislative principals. Yet the theory here suggests an appropriate counter to this methodological point. Because autonomous agencies can shift electoral and representative preferences by virtue of their political legitimacy, bureaucracies can be autonomous even when it appears that they are in perfect political alignment with politicians and the public mood. *Political harmony and the appearance of control can mask autonomy.*

The Poverty of Structural Politics

The narratives in this book also reveal difficulties with a related theory of bureaucracy championed by Terry Moe. Moe and other "structural politics" scholars argue that the characteristics of an agency are the product of strategic design on the part of politicians and all of those interests that are affected by what the agency does. Hence an agency's personnel, its capacities, its turf, and its procedures are subject to a chaotic politics of design that frustrates policymakers' goals. In the politics of procedure, legislators get their way; in the politics of structure, no one does.

Agency structure undoubtedly shapes the potential for bureaucratic autonomy. The stranglehold that clerical organization placed on the Interior Department is an important factor differentiating the political debility of the Interior Department from the autonomy of the USDA. Still, this structure was not the result of systematic design, even by a pluralistic chaos of forces. Clerical organization evolved over five decades as bureaus were lumped onto the department.

The first problem with the structural politics argument is that for the past 150 years, at least, much policy innovation in the United States has occurred within agencies that were created long ago. The bearing of agency design is therefore questionable at best. The narratives here bear out this irrelevance. Stark differences in capacity across the Post Office, Agriculture, and Interior Departments emerged only decades (in the case of the Post Office, a century) after their creation, and ten to twenty years after institutional reforms in the federal civil service and congressional appropriations. Nor was capacity a function of agency size. When Reconstruction ended, the Post Office was the largest government agency; the USDA, by contrast, had a workforce of less than 1 percent of that of the Post Office.

Moreover, agency design in no way predetermined the particular roles that agencies assumed for themselves in forging bureaucratic autonomy. Nothing in the design of the Post Office Department in 1792 (or in the reforms of the early 1860s) intimated the agency's potential as a moral police force, an operator of savings banks, or a rural service machine. Nothing in the design of the U.S. Department of Agriculture in 1862 suggested that the agency would function as a conservation agency, a consumer protection agency, or an education outfit that would take the school to the farm (especially to the southern farm).

The weakness of agency design in shaping Progressive bureaucracy stems in part from the realities of bureaucratic politics. In part, delegation of new laws to agencies more often takes the form of delegation to *existing* agencies than delegation to agencies created *ex nihilo*.[3] Yet just as often, new policies come about because agency officials have created the policies in the first place—along with a coalition that favors the policy in the form that bureaucrats created it—and it will therefore be costly for politicians to structure the agency in ways that the agency does not favor. Agencies may not get their way entirely when they innovate, but they will sometimes get their way more than politicians get theirs.

Another problem with design-based theories is that agencies have reasons to depart from the structure they are given. James Q. Wilson has advanced an interesting typology in which agencies are established to be one of four kinds: coping, craft, procedural, and production. Wilson's categories are wonderfully helpful, but they also mislead. The point is not simply that agencies can cross these boundaries but that agencies may have *incentives* to sell themselves as "coping" and "production" agencies (or more) at the same time. Surely no provider of abortion or publisher of erotic literature from 1870 to 1920 would have thought the Post Office a "production agency" alone.[4]

Organizational design also poorly accounts for the emergence (or nonemergence) of capacity—both programmatic and political—in Progressive-Era agencies. The genesis of bureaucratic capacity was primarily an evolutionary outcome. The problem with Moe's argument is that designing constraints is easier than designing capacities. Although Moe is certainly correct when he states that many agencies are "literally designed to fail," it is evident from the history of American bureaucracy that agencies *cannot* automatically be designed to succeed even when politicians want them to. Innovation and planning capacity arose only when long-tenured bureau and division chiefs could draw on the technical and programmatic expertise in their offices. Whereas weak-tie networks were instrumental in bureaucratic recruitment, strong-tie networks within these agencies heightened the attachment of skilled managers and employees. Organizational design was, furthermore, irrelevant to the emergence of these networks. As in many agencies today, collaborative work patterns and information flow were orthogonal to the formal command structure.

The Promise and Failure of State-Building Scholarship

The argument here also speaks to the burgeoning literature in American state building. My principal disagreement is with scholars who ascribe institutional change primarily to "societal" pressures that are embedded in geographic sections, in parties, and in congressional coalitions (Bensel, Sanders, Kernell, and James). I have dealt with some of these arguments in the foregoing chapters. Yet generally, would the sectionalist framework of Bensel and Sanders have forecast these reforms? Would the party-system accounts of James have predicted the occurrence, form, and timing of these changes?

The diverse timing and sequence of these reforms suggest not. A striking feature of the cases of bureaucratic autonomy in this book is their consistent occurrence over a pattern of fifty years—from the Comstock statute of 1873 to the stockyard laws of the early 1920s. These reforms transpired under unified Democratic control of government, under unified Republican control, and under divided government. They happened both when national elections were highly competitive and when one party regularly trounced the other. Most of the innovations—from the Pure Food and Drugs Act of 1906 to the rural free delivery system—occurred *before* the Cannon Revolt of 1910 and the decentralization of power in Congress. Some important ones—the Postal Savings Act, the Smith-Lever Act, and the parcels post system—occurred afterward.

The emergence of sectionally embedded movements and party constituencies also poorly explains the narratives of innovation here. Many of the policies counted "periphery" agrarians among their coalition partners and intended beneficiaries. Yet many others, including the forest reserve transfer of 1905, the Pure Food and Drugs Act of 1906, the antipornography laws of the 1870s, and the antilottery laws of the 1890s, did not. Moreover, a close historical analysis of two other policies previously thought to be "agrarian"—the twentieth-century farm extension system and the postal savings system—shows that agrarian and populist organizations did not receive their preferred form of policy but rather saw the agency's own wishes codified into law.

Business-centered accounts also weakly explain bureaucratic policy innovation. Victoria Hattam, Daniel Rodgers, and Kim Voss, in strikingly different narratives, all point to business opposition to state activity as a recurrent force in American political development, and Gabriel Kolko and others gesture to business "capture" of the state as an explanation for Progressive policy. It is remarkable, in this light, how frequently business associations lost out to diverse, bureaucratically centered coalitions in the early twentieth century. In every conceivable respect, business associations suffered defeat in battles over forest conservation and postal savings banks, and in food and drug regulation, parcels post service, and stockyard regulation in the 1920s organized business was beaten in important respects.

Narratives of bureaucratic autonomy have greater concord with "state-centered" theories of institutional change in the United States, notably Skowronek's *Building a New American State* and Skocpol's *Protecting Soldiers and Mothers*. These authors rightly identify government officials at the center of institutional change during the Progressive period, and they rightly point to state capacity as a central variable in explaining policy change. Skowronek's state-building narrative helps to explain the reorientation of Progressive politics around bureaucracy and suggests, appropriately, that arrangements of the "party period" and Gilded Age constrained and enabled the achievements of the Progressive period. Skocpol's "polity-centered" argument is a powerful addition to Skowronek's, and it helps point the way to associations between state and society that drive policy reform. In particular, women's activism—whether in explicitly gender-based federations such as the GFWC or the WCTU or in broader organizations such as moral reform and consumerist leagues—was an important part of the institutional changes detailed here.

At the same time, neither Skowronek's nor Skocpol's account accurately and completely points to these changes. Skowronek's narrative is notable for the *lack* of variation across policy domains in state building. It also has difficulties with instances of bureaucratic autonomy that occurred before 1896, including

Comstockery and the early experience with free delivery. The most promising alternative theory that might explain these reforms is Skocpol's. Yet to conceive of the agency-driven, policy-specific coalitions that emerged in the Progressive period as "polity-based" is a less accurate explanation than a theory that focuses squarely on bureaucratic autonomy and the historically specific conditions under which it emerges.

Whither Presidents?

In separate strains of scholarship, Skowronek, Moe, and James have pointed to presidential action as a crucial force in bureaucratic and regulatory politics. Since all three departments studied here are executive agencies, it warrants asking whether and in what way presidents influenced bureaucratic autonomy. Surely bureaucratic autonomy is more stable when presidents do not actively oppose agency initiatives. Presidential appointment powers are also an important avenue of political control over the bureaucracy. Notwithstanding these powers, agencies that have stable political legitimacy will be able to resist the control strategies of presidents, at least in the short run, as the postal inspection service and Wiley's Bureau of Chemistry were both able to do after 1900. Even a hostile secretary at the helm cannot derail a legitimated agency for long, as the cases of Agriculture Secretary Julius Sterling Morton and Postmaster General Wilson Bissell show. The postal inspection and agricultural extension cases show, moreover, that lower-level program leaders in autonomous bureaucracies who lie beyond the reach of presidential appointment—Anthony Comstock and Seaman Knapp, respectively—can nonetheless shape policy in significant ways.

Autonomy in Time and Space

In this light, the narrative here is not merely a story of autonomy, of "success" for Progressive administrators desiring greater freedom from politicians. The theory laid out in chapter 1 explains the political "dominance" of bureaucracies as much as it accounts for their independence. When agencies in democratic regimes have nothing unique to offer to politicians, and when agencies lack an independent power base, autonomy is not to be expected even if political, economic, and social conditions are highly variable and chaotic. The argument here explains not only why autonomy *did* emerge in the USDA and the Post Office but why it did *not* emerge in these agencies until the *time* that it emerged, and why it did not emerge *at all* in the Department of Interior and many other agencies.

The "panel" character of this study—the narrative analysis of bureaucratic autonomy that varied across agencies *and* over time—offers an important window into the jointly necessary conditions for bureaucratic autonomy. These dual domains of change ensure that the degrees of historical variation in autonomy exceed the number of explanatory factors I have invoked. As the following points show, the theory here does not overdetermine history from the standpoint of causal inference.

- Before 1900, the USDA had capacity and unique preferences (chapter 6) but *not an embedded reputation.* Not until the USDA's networks were synthesized and its reputation was politically grounded did autonomy emerge.
- The Post Office in the 1890s possessed the social bases of reputation—ties to moral reform leagues, agrarian and business groups—but *lacked demonstrated capacity* in postal operations (chapters 3 and 4). Program autonomy outside of moral policing (where the department had shown considerable capacity as well as network ties) awaited the reduction of the department's operations deficit.
- Any number of agencies in the Progressive period—the Children's Bureau under Julia Lathrop, the Reclamation Service, the Bureau of Corporations—possessed unique preferences but *lacked capacity and the social and reputational bases of legitimacy.*
- A host of other agencies—the Department of Justice, the Department of Treasury, and the ICC—had formal capacities but were *not politically differentiated* from the dominant party coalitions of the Gilded Age and Progressive period.

Organizational Change and the Progressive Achievement

It is useful, in light of this narrative, to rethink what was unique about Progressive politics. Consider the dominant interpretations of Progressivism over the last several decades. Skowronek has narrated American state building as a response to a crisis that, most critically, was mediated by preexisting institutional arrangements. Presidents in particular assume a central role in Skowronek's narrative. Scott James has extended Skowronek's argument to focus on the coalition-building strategies of party leaders, including presidents. Skocpol and Linda Gordon have, from different perspectives, gestured powerfully to the role of gender and women's political organization in Progressive institutional change. In more recent interpretations, Bensel and Sanders have argued that sectional tensions, particularly the antagonism of periphery agrarians, drove numerous Progressive reforms, mediated less through presidents than through Congress. Kolko and Sklar have traced developments from 1890 to 1920 to the interests and ideologies of "conservative" corporate liberalism. Eileen McDonagh and Nicola Beisel, among others, have emphasized the culturally reactionary themes of Progressivism. Samuel Hays and a generation of succeeding scholars have pointed to the emergence of new movements and organizational forms during the Progressive Era.[5]

The account of Progressive state formation in this book partakes of the riches of these diverse narratives and offers a way of reconciling many of their differences. My intention has been to narrate Progressive reform less as a story of bureaucratically driven change and more as a story of how agency leaders were central actors in coalitions, coalitions hewn from the elements of Progressive political society to whom other historians have given the status of "prime mover" in American political development. The role of reputation in this coalition-building process is crucial. Agency leaders assembled coalitions for their bureaus and their programs not by doling out pork but by building a socially grounded esteem for the activities of their organization. Put differently, congressional leaders, social movements, business groups, presidents, and other actors were all participants in the forging of bureaucratic autonomy in the United States. Yet by pointing to the political centrality of agency leaders, this account offers a clearer view of coalition formation than do other recent studies that focus on coalitions (Sanders and James). Again, the power of bureau officials lay in the *multiplicity* of their ties to political organizations. Multiple networks did not refract power. They rather reduced the dependence of agencies on any one group, putting the agency in the role of broker among numerous interests seeking access to the state.

Congress, the Media, and Multiplicity

In addition, the role of general beliefs about agencies in bureaucratic reputations points to important changes in Congress and the media that enabled agencies to erect reputations. The building of bureaucratic reputations between Congress and executive departments found fertile soil in the Progressive period. Not only were bureau chiefs serving longer tenures, but members of Congress were investing more and more time in committees. As a result, agency officials and their overseers in Congress began to develop a mutual familiarity. The institutional memory of Congress grew, the abilities and interests of bureaus became clearer and more consistent, and uncertainty over the bureaucracy declined. The stability of these relations gave bureau chiefs an incentive to cultivate the trust of committee chairs and congressional party leaders, and some Progressive-Era program leaders adopted this strategy to great advantage.[6]

Perhaps the most important venue of bureaucratic reputation lay in the rapidly expanding media. At a time when broadcast news remained only an imaginary possibility, Americans received their political information from a highly variegated print industry. In this market the critical split was between the larger urban newspapers and related syndicates and the rural farm weeklies. In the urban newspapers arose the "muckraking" of Progressive reformers, whereas farm editors remained committed to a mix of populist and pro-agrarian sentiments. In part because these papers depended increasingly on the USDA and the Post Office for information and rate classification, both agencies were treated with favor by urban and rural presses. Yet the network advantages of the two agencies transcended mere resource dependence. Numerous Agriculture Department officials were close acquaintances with one or more rural newspaper editors. And newspaper editors, urban and rural, interacted frequently with postal officials over matters of rate classification. As a result of these ties, Progressive-Era citizens were better (and more favorably) informed about the USDA and Post Office than any other agencies in American government.

Reputations for Neutrality and Moral Protection

Traditionally, political scientists have expected greater autonomy where agencies can lay claim to expertise—especially where agencies possess a monopoly on information in a given area. A more interesting case of "policy" in this book emerges from "moral politics" during the culturally conservative Progressive Era. A key component of both the USDA's and the Post Office's march to autonomy was their linkages to Victorian moral reformers and their anti-adulteration campaigns, both in the adulteration of food and the adulteration of morals (through pornography and gambling). The Interior Department lacked any such connection to anti-adulteration themes. These moral reputations, and the framing of policy campaigns in terms of "protection" from "the evils of adulteration," served to enhance the agencies' esteem for national service. A core component of strong agency reputations is the mien of neutrality, impartiality, or orientation toward the public good. Where an agency's innovations appear patently to serve its own interests or those of a selected group or region, the political legitimacy necessary for autonomy is less likely to emerge.

In the case of postal state building, coalition building combined moralist Progressives, media organizations, agrarians, and corporate business. Each of these interests sought something different from the Post Office. Progressive Victorians wanted moral policing in the form of Comstockery, agrarians wanted expanded services in rural America and an alternative to institutions dominated by corporate industry, and business interests and the media (for different reasons) wanted an efficient national communications infrastructure. Each saw their interests met in the same programs. Without all four (and more) of these organizational forces, programs such as rural free delivery, parcels post, and postal savings would not have marked Progressive change as they did. More critically, without Anthony Comstock, August Machen, John Wanamaker, and other postal officials to bridge these forces and to create a multifaceted coalition, the possibility of institutional change would have been trifling.

The logic of multifaceted coalitions was demonstrated nowhere more powerfully than in the Department of Agriculture. Republican presidents, women's organizations, conservationists, congressional committees, agrarian organizations—all of these interests converged to influence policy change in areas as diverse as pharmaceutical regulation, forest preservation, and agricultural extension. The central point, again, is that the coalitions were nursed and maintained not by elected politicians but by middle-level bureaucrats. Far more than in Herbert Hoover's Department of Commerce, the "associational state" in America was established in the early-twentieth-century USDA. Unlike Commerce, moreover, the USDA exerted an immense influence on the groups in its coalitions.

The unprecedented multiplicity and diversity of civic and voluntary associations during the period 1880–1920 enabled bureaucratic officials to enter and occupy these unique positions. As Theda Skocpol, Marshall Ganz, and Ziad Munson have recently argued, the period from the Civil War to the New Deal was a high point of organizing activity in the United States. Gerald Gamm and Robert Putnam have emphasized the local character of these associations, and Skocpol and her colleagues have echoed Elizabeth Clemens and emphasized their federated and institutionalized character. These organizations permeated numerous sectors of American life. Martin Sklar, Gabriel Kolko, and Daniel Rodgers have, in different ways, documented the rise of corporate political activity during the Progressive period. Other scholars have drawn attention to unprecedented organizing activity in rural America, pointing to the Grange, the Farmers' Alliance, and thousands upon thousands of local groups and farm cooperatives. Skocpol and other scholars have pointed to new energies on the part of women's groups, and Paul Boyer and Nicola Beisel have focused on moral reform organizations. Bureaucratic autonomy, in this view, is enabled not so much when economic tension arises among tightly defined classes—as in Skocpol's *States and Social Revolutions* or Skowronek's *Building a New American State*—but precisely when cross-cutting networks allow state officials to achieve multiple embedments in a complex society. These embedments create the possibility for coalition building from diverse elements, and they enhance the agency's appearance of neutrality. When agencies' favored innovations drew support from agrarians, business organizations, women's groups, and moral reform associations, it became much harder for politicians to resist them or to stall.[7]

The organizational flourishing that was characteristic of Progressive society offers one reason that the patterns of bureaucratic autonomy witnessed in this book are less likely to be observed in contemporary politics. To be sure, modern America is rife with organizations in the formal sense. Yet if Putnam, Skocpol, and other analysts of American society are correct, the day-by-day embedment of Americans in organizations has waned, not strengthened, over the last few decades. The challenge of contemporary American state building, in this view, may demand more than "reinventing" American government—although as Paul Light has argued in *Thickening Hierarchy,* it may demand a reduction in the "layers" of political appointments that separate the most talented career officials from status-laden discretionary positions. Future state building may depend as much on societal change as on governmental reform.[8]

Contemporary Examples, Future Possibilities

Although contemporary American politics has reduced the likelihood of bureaucratic autonomy founded on legitimacy, at least one case in recent years accords more or less with the theory presented here. The Food and Drug Administration (FDA)—no longer a child bureau of the USDA but an agency under the Department of Health and Human Services—is a highly legitimized actor in contemporary American politics. Although its detractors have been growing in recent years, the FDA has held tremendous power over the pharmaceutical industry since the Food, Drug and Cosmetic Act of 1938 and the Kefauver-Harris Amendments of 1962. The reputational bases of these policy reforms are striking. Both occurred after the FDA had acted to stem vast consumer crises in adulterated medicines, first in the sulfanilamide scandal of 1937, then in the thalidomide tragedy of 1960–61. In both cases, and especially in the second, the FDA received public credit for protecting the American public from the hazards of consumer goods. Moreover, the agency has long profited from its placement at the crossroads of a diverse set of interests—pharmaceutical companies, consumer safety advocates, the American medical profession, farmers and organic food growers, academic scientists, and other groups. In recent years the FDA has maintained its unique presence in American politics, successfully pressing for expansions of its budget in the Prescription Drug User Fee Act of 1992 and radically (though as yet unsuccessfully) proposing authority over tobacco products in the last decade.

From the Civil War to the Great Depression, in pockets of the American state, genuine bureaucratic autonomy was forged on the anvil of agency reputations. The primary actors in this saga were bureau chiefs and program leaders driven by maximal control over their programs and organizations. These leaders took direction of the hiring process in the Gilded Age, using weak-tie networks and internal socialization to transform their agencies into politically distinct entities. They built capacity by assembling talented offices where turnover was minimized, and they used inspection and other intermediary institutions to reintegrate their organizations. They completed the process by participating in the construction of lasting legitimacy in the form of organizational reputations, forms of institutional trust that were embedded in elite and local networks. In bureaucratic entrepreneurship the policy fruits of this process came to shape decisively the parameters of the American state.

The patterns of bureaucratic policy innovation observed in this narrative may or may not be praiseworthy. Autonomous policymaking does not necessarily translate into successful policy. Yet the autonomy narrated here is one in which bureaucratic power grew not at the expense of democratic participation but in a symbiotic relationship with it. Precisely because federal agencies shrewdly orchestrated the participatory energies of American politics, they cleared a unique policymaking place for themselves in the American institutional order, at least for a time. If the stories of statehood in this book offer promise, the challenge of American state building may be to reengage state bureaucracies with the very civic organizations and social networks in which they once flourished.

Notes

Introduction

1. Stephen L. Skowronek, *Building a New American State: The Expansion of National Administrative Capacities, 1877–1920* (New York: Cambridge University Press, 1982).

2. Theda Skocpol, *States and Social Revolutions: A Comparative Analysis of France, Russia, and China* (New York: Cambridge University Press, 1979); *Protecting Soldiers and Mothers: The Political Origins of Social Policy in the United States* (Cambridge, Mass.: Harvard University Press, 1992); see also Kenneth Finegold and Theda Skocpol, *State and Party in America's New Deal* (Madison: University of Wisconsin Press, 1995). Skocpol's argument has some similarities to my emphasis on multiple networks; see her conclusion in *Protecting Soldiers and Mothers*, 526–31. I interpret Richard John's *Spreading the News: The American Postal System from Franklin to Morse* (Cambridge, Mass.: Harvard University Press, 1995) as a capacity-based argument inasmuch as John focuses on the postal system not simply as an arena of political action but as an agent of change in the early Republic.

3. Richard Bensel, *Yankee Leviathan: The Origins of Central State Authority in America, 1859–1877* (New York: Cambridge University Press, 1990); Elizabeth Sanders, *Roots of Reform: Farmers, Workers, and the American State* (Chicago: University of Chicago Press, 1999); Martin Shefter, *Political Parties and the State: The American Historical Experience* (Princeton: Princeton University Press, 1994); Scott C. James, "A Party System Perspective on the Interstate Commerce Act of 1887," *Studies in American Political Development* 6 (1992): 163–210 (this includes a reply by Elizabeth Sanders and a rejoinder by Scott James); Scott James, "Building a Democratic Majority: The Progressive Party Vote and the Federal Trade Commission," *Studies in American Political Development* 9, no. 2 (fall 1995): 331–85; Ronald Johnson and Gary Libecap, *The Federal Civil Service System and the Problem of Bureaucracy* (Chicago: University of Chicago Press, 1994); Brian Balogh, *Chain Reaction: Expert Debate and Public Participation in American Commercial Nuclear Power, 1945–1975* (New York: Cambridge University Press, 1991); Terry Moe, "Interests, Institutions, and Positive Theory: The Politics of the NLRB," *Studies in American Political Development* 2 (1987): 236–99; Terry Moe, "The Politics of Structural Choice: Toward a Theory of Public Bureaucracy," in *Organization Theory,* ed. Oliver Williamson (New York: Oxford University Press, 1995).

4. For a recent narrative that situates American state building in the context of New Deal politics, see Edwin Amenta, *Bold Relief* (Princeton: Princeton University Press, 1998).

5. Skowronek, *Building a New American State;* Skocpol, *Protecting Soldiers and Mothers;* Bensel, *Yankee Leviathan;* Sanders, *Roots of Reform.*

6. Skowronek, *Building a New American State,* 248. Skocpol's and Bensel's books are exceptions to this focus on commissions, though each devotes only brief discussions to the executive departments of the period (Interior, Agriculture, Post Office, and Treasury).

7. In their recent book on congressional delegation, David Epstein and Sharyn O'Halloran claim that 81 percent of all delegating laws from 1947 to 1992 gave policymaking authority to executive departments, and 38.1 percent of these laws gave authority to independent regulatory agencies (of which commissions are a subset); *Delegating Powers: A Transactions-Cost Approach to Policy Making under Separate Powers* (New York: Cambridge University Press, 1999).

8. Ari Hoogenboom and Olive Hoogenboom, *A History of the ICC: From Panacea to Palliative* (New York: W. W. Norton, 1976), 117. By the close of the 1920s, the commission fully acknowledged its utter inability to plan: "Unaccustomed to planning and unable to break habits of more than three decades, the ICC tried to relinquish its responsibility to plan consolidations" (107). I. L. Sharfman, *The Interstate Commerce Commission: A Study in Administration Law and Procedure* (New York: Commonwealth Fund, 1931–37), 5 vols., 1:119–32.

9. A similar interpretation guides Johnson and Libecap, *Federal Civil Service System*. Both Bensel and Skowronek suggest that merit reform was, given genuine partisan competition, a historically sufficient condition for the emergence of state autonomy. As Bensel writes, "Once it became possible for the 'rebel' South to participate in a winning presidential coalition, the state bureaucracy became a potential balance-wheel between rival political-economic coalitions. With that possibility of a balance-of-power position in national politics *and the emergence of civil service protection from partisan influence,* the state could at last begin to develop a 'statist' sensibility, an identity and interest apart from any class or partisan interest" (*Yankee Leviathan,* 3; emphasis added). Bensel later states this argument more explicitly: "Because no public policy, no matter how well designed in law, would [succeed] if executed by an incompetent or corrupt bureaucracy, civil service reform was a fundamental requirement for almost all government intervention in the political economy (including active management of the nation's money market)" (342). Skowronek suggests that "[c]ivil service reform promised to rebuild the autonomy and prestige of [federal executives'] offices" (*Building a New American State,* 55). He summarizes the historical process: "By 1920, American national government had broken from the grip of local politics and had assumed a more independent role in American society" (211). This is not to deny that the Progressive period left American bureaucracy largely "attuned to the interest of organized labor and of the Institute for Government Research" (211), but the repoliticization of American bureaucracy around constitutional control is still interpreted as an emancipation from partisan and social control.

10. In addition, many of the postal employees "covered in" under the Roosevelt and Taft administrations were originally patronage appointees and thus Republican party loyalists. So in several areas of the federal civil service, the preferences of administrative employees did reflect those of a national party (Skowronek, *Building a New American State,* 192–94).

11. The appointment of railroad sympathizer Winthrop Daniels to the ICC by President Wilson in 1914 presented an early example of the potential force of presidential appointments, as Daniels and colleague Henry C. Hall provided the decisive votes for the commission's first decision to allow railroads to raise rates (Hoogenboom and Hoogenboom, *A History of the ICC,* 170–76). As Sanders (*Roots of Reform,* 210) summarizes, "Daniels' pro-railroad stance pointed up the vulnerability of discretionary regulation to a sharp change in personnel." As Skowronek admits (*Building a New American State,*

270–71), the commission interpreted its new Hepburn and Mann-Elkins mandates narrowly, the result of a "timid and narrow outlook." Just how broadly it could have construed its mandate is a matter of debate (see Sanders, chapter 6), but Hoogenboom and Hoogenboom argued that the commission could have attempted to rationalize the rate structure during this period, reducing idiosyncratic regional disparities. Among contemporary agencies, the influence of appointment power on regulatory decision making has been most thoroughly studied at the National Labor Relations Board. Terry Moe, "Control and Feedback in Economic Regulation: The Case of the NLRB," *American Political Science Review* 79 (1985): 1094–1116.

Chapter One

1. I distinguish between *influence* and *control*. Political scientists and historians often deny the possibility of sustained agency discretion by pointing to evidence of social and political influence over agency decisions. Yet such evidence is insufficient to show that no degree of bureaucratic autonomy exists. When agencies carry political legitimacy, they can build coalitions of different interests which allow for influence but in which the agency retains significant leverage over the course of policy development. Under such conditions, bureaucratic autonomy can coexist with the influence of politicians and social interests. As Ronald N. Johnson and Gary D. Libecap remark, "showing that Congress had sufficient power to control a 'runaway' agency does not deny the existence of independent bureaucratic behavior"; *The Federal Civil Service System and the Problem of Bureaucracy* (Chicago: University of Chicago Press, 1994), 158.

2. Sanders has argued that the primary mechanism of legislative control is "explicit and discretion-limiting" statutory specification. "State Theory and American Political Development," *Studies in Law, Politics, and Society* 10 (1990): 93–99; also Sanders, *Roots of Reform*, 12–13; Richard Bensel, *Sectionalism and American Political Development, 1880–1980* (Madison: University of Wisconsin Press, 1984), 139; Samuel Kernell and Michael McDonald, "Congress and America's Political Development: The Transformation of the Post Office from Patronage to Service," *American Journal of Political Science* 43, no. 3 (July 1999): 792–811.

3. Eric A. Nordlinger, *On the Autonomy of the Democratic State* (Cambridge, Mass.: Harvard University Press, 1981), 26, 27–38. I depart from Nordlinger's argument that bureaucratic actors, at least, can "ignore and circumvent" the demands placed on them by elected representatives. This happens only when the agencies have an independent power base, and strategic agencies that care about their public legitimacy will do it rarely.

4. Among students of American political development, Elizabeth Sanders and Barry Weingast are best known for this "legislative dominance" argument, whereas Terry Moe has developed a somewhat broader theory of political control, which emphasizes the strategies of presidents and interest groups. Moe has advanced a "structural politics" argument in which "public bureaucracy is not designed to be effective" because so many different interests converge in the design of agencies. See "The Politics of Bureaucratic Structure," in *Can the Government Govern?* ed. John E. Chubb and Paul E. Peterson (Washington, D.C.: Brookings Institution, 1990); "The Politics of Structural Choice: Toward a Theory of Public Bureaucracy," in *Organization Theory,* ed. Oliver Williamson (New York: Oxford University Press, 1995). For formal arguments, see Mathew

McCubbins, "The Legislative Design of Regulatory Structure," *American Journal of Political Science* 29 (1985): 721–48. Barry Weingast and Mark Moran offered an early empirical argument in "Bureaucratic Discretion or Congressional Control? Regulatory Policymaking by the Federal Trade Commission," *Journal of Political Economy* 91 (1983): 765–800. Moe locates political control instead with the president. See his exhaustive "Control and Feedback," 1094–1116. On budgetary control, see Daniel P. Carpenter, "Adaptive Signal Processing, Hierarchy, and Budgetary Control in Federal Regulation," *American Political Science Review* 90 (June 1996): 283–302. An argument that legislative dominance can hold even in administrative rule making appears in Mathew McCubbins, Roger Noll, and Barry Weingast, "Administrative Procedures as Instruments of Political Control," *Journal of Law, Economics, and Organization* 3, no. 2 (Fall 1987): 243–77.

5. Definitions of bureaucratic discretion in positive political theory focus on a bureaucracy's "ability and desire to depart from the policy expected by the elected authorities," or divergent actions that "no political coalition can overturn." Mathew McCubbins, Roger Noll, and Barry Weingast, "A Theory of Political Control and Agency Discretion," *American Journal of Political Science* 33, no. 3 (August 1989): 588–611. Yet there is a difference between (1) politicians' preferences over agency actions and (2) politicians' willingness to overturn or prevent agency actions. For some agencies, there may be actions *not* preferred by a political coalition yet that the coalition would not *wish* to overturn or to *prevent* in the future. Restated, bureaucratic autonomy occurs when a preference-irreducible agency takes self-consistent policy-shifting action that political authorities do not strictly prefer and that they cannot or will not overturn or prevent in the future.

I mean *preference* here in its decision-theoretic usage: politicians would prefer that the agency take an action different from the one that it is taking, and hence the agency's action, once taken, is an outcome that represents a political loss for politicians and organized interests.

This definition admittedly risks redundancy. Self-consistent action following unique preferences implies that the agency's action is also irreducible. Hence the clause that the agency's actions are ones that neither politicians nor organized interests prefer may be superfluous. I choose to retain this clause, however, because some scholars argue that politicians can shape agencies culturally to act consistently with politicians' objectives even though the agency in "false consciousness" thinks otherwise. Roger Noll and Barry Weingast, "Rational Actor Theory, Social Norms, and Policy Implementation: Applications to Administrative Processes and Bureaucratic Culture," in *The Economic Approach to Politics,* ed. Kristen Renwick Monroe (New York: Harper Collins, 1991).

6. Roderick Kiewiet and Mathew McCubbins have argued that the success of legislative delegation in complex policy arenas depends in part on "the creation and maintenance of good faith relationships. *This is something that cannot be achieved through statute. Indeed, the specification of precise strictures and guidelines may do more to impede such understandings than to facilitate them.*" *The Logic of Delegation* (Chicago: University of Chicago Press, 1991), 214; emphasis mine. Unfortunately, political science lacks a genuine theory of "good faith relationships" between Congress and the bureaucracy. I envision my theory of reputation-conditioned delegation as a starting point and a necessary component of such a broader theory. The narrative in this book is a styl-

ized account of the evolution of "good faith relationships" in two policy domains at the turn of the century.

7. Skowronek, *Building a New American State,* 10–13. Robert Wiebe, *The Search for Order, 1877–1920* (New York: Hill and Wang, 1967). For similar arguments, see Morton Keller's *Regulating a New Economy: Public Policy and Economic Change, 1900–1933* (Cambridge, Mass.: Harvard University Press, 1990); Balogh, *Chain Reaction;* and Junko Kato, *The Problem of Bureaucratic Rationality: Tax Politics in Japan* (Princeton: Princeton University Press, 1994). For formal models embodying this intuition, see Kathleen Bawn, "Control versus Expertise," *American Political Science Review* 89 (1995): 62–73; David Epstein and Sharyn O'Halloran, "Administrative Procedures, Information, and Agency Discretion," *American Journal of Political Science* 38 (August 1994): 697–722.

8. This argument has a few similarities to "informational" theories of legislative organization, developed most clearly by Keith Krehbiel and associated scholars. According to these theories, legislatures will tolerate discretionary committees only when the costs of discretion are surpassed by the value of information or problem solving that committees provide. Keith Krehbiel, *Information and Legislative Organization* (Ann Arbor: University of Michigan Press, 1992). For applications to bureaucratic politics, see Bawn, "Control versus Expertise," and Epstein and O'Halloran, "Administrative Procedures." I likewise believe that politicians, in delegating authority to agencies, barter control over policy outcomes for the gains of agency innovation and expertise. Yet this intuition forms only a bare tendril of my argument, for delegation to agencies is fundamentally unlike delegation to committees. Congress charges agencies with tasks that no committee could undertake on its own, including scientific analysis, forecasting, comprehensive planning, program administration, distribution of goods and services, and others. Because agencies are far less unitary than committees (that is, because they are more complex organizations), and because politicians can appoint only a fraction of agency membership, delegation to agencies requires political trust. Beyond this, agencies as separate political actors can forge links with voters in their own right.

9. In his book *Democracy and Its Critics* (New Haven: Yale University Press, 1989), Robert Dahl presents autonomy as a continuous rather than a binary variable (pp. 48–49).

10. Skocpol, *States and Social Revolutions,* 29; and *Protecting Soldiers and Mothers* ("any set of relatively differentiated organizations" that include "the administrative, judicial and policing organizations"), 43. Skowronek, *Building a New American State,* 5. Charles Tilly, "Reflections on the History of European State-Making," in his edited volume *The Formation of National States* (Princeton: Princeton University Press, 1975), 70. Even articulants of the "organizational synthesis," such as Louis Galambos, generally pay little attention to social science organization theory. See Balogh, *Chain Reaction.* Organizational aspects of the state do not figure prominently in Bensel's *Yankee Leviathan* or in Sanders's *Roots of Reform.* Nor do they appear in Nordlinger's *Autonomy of the Democratic State.* Among recent books, an exception is Bartholomew Sparrow's *From the Outside In: World War II and the American State* (Princeton: Princeton University Press, 1996).

11. Four structural concepts are central to any definition of bureaucracy: (1) a well-defined division of administrative labor among persons and offices; (2) a personnel system with consistent patterns of recruitment and stable linear careers; (3) a hierarchy

among offices, such that authority and status are differentially distributed among actors; and (4) formal and informal networks that connect organizational actors to one another through flows of information and patterns of cooperation. I discuss all four in this chapter. The first three concepts are core properties of the definition of bureaucracy in Max Weber's "Bureaucracy," chap. 11 of *Economy and Society* (*Wirtschaft und Gesellschaft*), ed. Guenther Roth and Claus Wittich (Berkeley: University of California Press, 1978), 956ff. For Weber, the division of administrative labor is "stable" and "strictly delimited by rules." The administrative career is a "vocation" (*Beruf*), and hierarchy—"a clearly established system of super- and sub-ordination in which there is a supervision of the lower offices by the higher ones"—is indispensable to modern bureaucratic organization.

12. Although my narrative ignores the legal and coercive aspects of states, features emphasized by Hegel, Tocqueville, and many other scholars, it achieves a more accurate focus on bureaucratic organization. No modern state is defined apart from its bureaucracy. And many theorists define the state primarily (some almost exclusively) in bureaucratic terms. Among social theorists, see Claus Offe, *Contradictions of the Welfare State* (Cambridge, Mass.: MIT Press, 1984), 52ff.; Gianfranco Poggi, *The State: Its Nature, Development, and Prospects* (Stanford: Stanford University Press, 1990), 30ff. Stephen Krasner suggests that "[t]he dominant conceptualization in the non-Marxist literature is the state as a bureaucratic apparatus and institutionalized legal order in its totality"; "Approaches to the State: Alternative Conceptions and Historical Dynamics," *Comparative Politics* 16, no. 2 (1984): 224.

13. For a similar classification, see James Q. Wilson's concepts of executives, managers, and operators in *Bureaucracy: What Government Agencies Do and Why They Do It* (New York: Basic Books, 1989). Unlike Wilson, I group managers and program monitors together in my concept of mezzo-level administration.

14. It is true that Cabinet secretaries often have had symbolic connections to the department they managed and the industry or sector governed by the department—agriculture secretaries being appointed from farm states, treasury secretaries hailing from Wall Street, and labor secretaries having connections to organized trade unions. These connections do not connote expertise in the associated area of law or regulation, however. As an example, see Bensel's discussion of the incompetence of treasury secretaries in the 1860s and 1870s in *Yankee Leviathan,* 364–65. And in many cases, department secretaries have had no ostensible connection (symbolic or otherwise) to the departments they have governed. Consider Woodrow Wilson's choice of the populist orator William Jennings Bryan as his secretary of state (1913–15), or Theodore Roosevelt's choice of Republican loyalist George Cortelyou as postmaster general (1904–7), then secretary of treasury (1907–9).

15. These properties of bureau chiefs have changed little in the twentieth century, even with the eclipse of patronage. In this light, it is regrettable that, with Herbert Kaufman and several other scholars as rare exceptions, political scientists and other students of bureaucracy have neglected these actors. See Herbert Kaufman, *The Administrative Behavior of Federal Bureau Chiefs* (Washington, D.C.: Brookings Institution, 1981). For evidence that bureau chiefs have not been targets of partisan appointment strategies, see Nolan McCarty and Rose Razaghian, "Advise and Consent: Senate Responses to Executive Branch Nominations, 1885–1996," *American Journal of Political Science* 43, no. 4 (October 1999): 1122–43.

16. The concept of program control as the maximand of bureau chiefs is intended to

include the pursuit of policy aims or political ideology. Program control was in this sense a proximate goal for bureau chiefs; whatever else they desired, program control was necessary to achieve it. David Mayhew has made a similar argument for the primacy of the reelection incentive governing congressional behavior; *Congress: The Electoral Connection* (New Haven: Yale University Press, 1974), 16.

17. I rely here on a particular definition of *hierarchy*, which embeds two concepts: authority and communication. Gary Miller confines his recent analysis of hierarchy to two-player principal-agent relationships, focusing only on authority: "Hierarchy can be defined as the asymmetric and incompletely defined authority of one actor to direct the activities of another within certain bounds." See *Managerial Dilemmas: The Political Economy of Hierarchy* (New York: Cambridge University Press, 1992), 16. The concept of hierarchy in the present book corresponds more to Roy Radner's definition of a "ranked tree" or a ranked network. See "The Organization of Decentralized Information Processing," *Econometrica* 61, no. 5 (September 1993): 1109–46. Hierarchy is not simply a Weberian tree of authority relations; it is also a tree of communication ties, which constrains patterns of information flow.

18. Herbert A. Simon, *Administrative Behavior: A Study of Decision-Making Processes in Administrative Organization* (New York: Macmillan, 1957), 26–28. Simon also argues (with James March) that the "stability of attention" to specific problems declines as one's position in the hierarchy rises. *Organizations*, 2d ed. (New York: Blackwell, 1993), 220. Of course, either monitoring technology or information-revealing "mechanisms" can reduce the information asymmetries between superior and subordinate and thus increase the effective span of control. Still, the "bounded span of control" result holds whenever technology improvements are held constant, and the problem of efficient mechanism design is not an easy one, as Gary Miller has argued ("Hidden Information in Hierarchies: The Logical Limits of Mechanism Design," chap. 7 of *Managerial Dilemmas*, 138–58). See also Theodore Groves, "The Impossibility of Incentive-Compatible and Efficient Full-Cost Allocation Schemes," in *Cost Allocation: Methods, Principles, Applications*, ed. Peyton Young (Amsterdam: Elsevier, 1985), 95–100. Moreover, no hierarchical design can rid an agency of these problems. See Thomas Hammond and Paul Thomas, "The Impossibility of a Neutral Hierarchy," *Journal of Law, Economics, and Organization* 5 (spring 1989): 155–84.

19. An ecological control pattern is one in which control over the various premises of choice rests at different levels or sites of the organization. Formal authority—the ability to direct and command—is greatest at the top executive levels of an agency, but control over information is greatest at the lower-level operations units. See March and Simon, *Organizations*, and Darwin Cartwright, "Influence, Leadership, Control," in *Handbook of Organizations*, ed. James G. March (Chicago: Rand McNally, 1965). The clearest exposition of the concept appears in John F. Padgett, "Hierarchy and Ecological Control in Federal Budgetary Decision Making," *American Journal of Sociology* 87, no. 1 (July 1981): 75–129.

20. This precept implies that bureaucracies that are well enough structured to yield policy innovation will not be fully centralized. Instead, as March and Simon argue, "[M]ost program elaboration will take place within the unitary subdivisions [or bureaus] of the organization" (*Organizations*, 219). A strongly centralized bureaucracy will not generate learning when information enters the organization at the roots or when information processing is already decentralized. However, such agencies will not necessar-

ily be fully decentralized. An innovative agency may center program elaboration in subdivisions, but these subdivisions may themselves be highly centralized. In other words, if learning and innovation are more likely to occur at the mezzo level, then the "best" organizational structure is a mixture of centralization and decentralization. Information processing is decentralized, final approval for programs and decisions is centralized, but planning and the authority to innovate must lie with middle-level managers and monitors.

My argument that efficient structures for organizational information processing must have intermediate nodes is consistent with recent findings in organizational studies. These studies have cast doubt on Oliver Williamson's argument that centralized spoke-wheel networks are efficient for processing information (*Markets and Hierarchies: Analysis and Antitrust Implications: A Study in the Economics of Internal Organization* [New York: Free Press, 1975], 47). Kenneth Arrow had made a similar argument in *Limits of Organization* (New York: W. W. Norton, 1974), 68. Among the many works that debunk this claim, see Radner, "Organization of Decentralized Information Processing."

21. Alfred D. Chandler, *The Visible Hand: The Managerial Revolution in American Business* (Cambridge, Mass.: Harvard Belknap Press, 1974), 7, 170, 182. Chandler focused on innovation, but he largely neglected organizational learning. Inference from trial-and-error experimentation plays little role in his narrative.

22. Bureaucratic culture is not something merely internal to the agency. External "reputation" and internal "culture" are only analytically separable. By implication, the distinctive style or styles of operation and language that characterize an administrative agency are influenced by those institutional actors who interact with and oversee the agency, such as executives, legislators, interest groups, professions, and parties. This understanding of agency culture departs from a more traditional account in which agency culture is effectively insulated from external political and social forces (see Wilson, *Bureaucracy,* chap. 6, for a contemporary example).

In a similar vein, economic theorists have recognized the inseparability of "external" and "internal" culture. In David Kreps's analysis, culture is a principle undergirding an agency's reputation with both internal and external trading partners (that is, employees and clients). It "is the product of evolution inside the organization," but "[v]iolation of the culture will generate direct negative externalities insofar as it weakens the organization's overall reputation" (Kreps, "Corporate Culture and Economic Theory," in *Perspectives on Positive Political Economy,* ed. James E. Alt and Kenneth A. Shepsle [New York: Cambridge University Press, 1990], 93, 126). Transactions-cost theorists have also noted the language- and symbol-based nature of culture. Douglas North, *Institutions, Institutional Change, and Economic Performance* (New York: Cambridge University Press, 1990), 37.

23. Mary Douglas, *How Institutions Think* (Syracuse: Syracuse University Press, 1986). An earlier account of this argument appears in Daniel Carpenter, "The Corporate Metaphor and Executive Department Centralization in the United States, 1880–1920," *Studies in American Political Development* 11 (Spring 1998): 162–203.

24. This argument marks a further point of departure from the characterization of culture in Wilson's *Bureaucracy,* in which each organization has one unique culture. Wilson's portrait of culture is to agencies what Almond and Verba's concept of civic culture is to advanced industrial democracies.

25. In this respect, one of the chief results of organizational metaphors is to give to

the prevailing division of administrative labor a natural representation. The most powerful organizational metaphors thus express an economic fact in noneconomic terms.

26. Skocpol, *Protecting Soldiers and Mothers,* 42. In *States and Social Revolutions,* Skocpol argues that "a state's involvement in an international network of states" generates these divergent preferences (24). Similarly, Offe has argued that "the political-administrative system must be sufficiently isolated from its environment—the economic system and the process in which political demands and support are formed—in order to be relatively independent of its functional requirements or specific political demands" (*Contradictions of the Welfare State,* 58). Skowronek equates independence with capacity, arguing that "[e]ffective regulation presupposed a governmental capacity to resist the immediate interests of groups in conflict and to transform these conflicts, through mediation and authoritative direction" (*Building a New American State,* 125, also 133). Finally, formal theorists commonly assume that the divergence of agency preferences from those of the legislature is a necessary condition for bureaucratic "drift." Bawn, "Political Control versus Expertise"; Epstein and O'Halloran, "Administrative Procedures."

27. As John Brehm and Scott Gates argue in *Working, Shirking, and Sabotage* (Ann Arbor: University of Michigan Press, 1997), "[T]he process of selecting and indoctrinating bureaucrats is the process that matters. Bureaucrats select themselves into bureaucracies, but management also has considerable control over the kinds of bureaucrats they hire" (202).

28. For a similar argument, see John F. Padgett and Christopher K. Ansell, "Robust Action and the Rise of the Medici, 1400–1434," *American Journal of Sociology* 98 (1993): 1259–1319; and more generally, Ronald Burt, *Structural Holes: The Social Structure of Competition* (Cambridge, Mass.: Harvard University Press, 1992).

29. As Wilson has noted, "By passing the civil service laws [Congress] has lost the power to choose or replace individual bureaucrats" (*Bureaucracy,* 238; see also 139–42). Similar arguments have been advanced by Murray Horn, *The Political Economy of Public Administration: Institutional Choice in the Public Sector* (New York: Cambridge University Press, 1995); and by Johnson and Libecap, *Federal Civil Service System.*

30. Philip Selznick, *Leadership in Administration* (Berkeley: University of California Press, 1957), 104–7. Wilson, *Bureaucracy,* 66–67. Kreps, in "Corporate Culture and Economic Theory," makes a similar argument about the screening mechanism role of culture. As I detail in the chapters that follow, this culture can also legitimate racially and gender-discriminatory employment practices.

31. Herbert Kaufman, *The Forest Ranger: A Study in Administrative Behavior* (Baltimore: Published for Resources for the Future, by Johns Hopkins University Press, 1967), 170–75 (esp. 175). The concept of a career—of government employment as a calling or vocation, a position demanding partial devotion to the intrinsic value of its work—was foreign to most federal agencies before 1920. The modern notion of a bureaucratic career is that of a sequence of positions for which an individual with specific training or experience is eligible. The career structures this sequence as a linear progression in status, authority, and income wherein officials move steadily up the "ladder" of command. Unique duties and status attach to each of these positions and create expectations about performance (and incentives) at each position. Bureaucratic attachment is then the process of "buying into" a sequence of positions within a single agency. Career ladders render this sequence more "natural" and thus enhance agencies' ability to recruit and retain analytic talent.

The idea of a career as a peculiarly late modern concept appears in Chandler, *The Visible Hand*. Chandler argues that with "the coming of the modern business enterprise, the businessman, for the first time, could conceive of a lifetime career involving a climb up the hierarchical ladder" (9). On federal "career ladders," see Thomas DiPrete in *The Bureaucratic Labor Market: The Case of the Federal Civil Service* (New York: Plenum Press, 1989), esp. 99–109. See also Andrew Abbott, *The System of Professions* (Chicago: University of Chicago Press, 1988). Abbott argues that the concept of a career in British and American societies emerged within the larger development of professions (129–34). Paul Van Riper, *History of the United States Civil Service* (Evanston, Ill.: Row, Peterson, 1958); Johnson and Libecap, *Federal Civil Service System.*

32. Bernard Silberman suggests that the *Ecole Libre des Sciences Politiques,* begun under private auspices in the Third Republic, became, "in essence, one of the *grandes ecoles.*" *Cages of Reason: The Rise of the Rational State in France, Japan, the United States, and Great Britain* (Chicago: University of Chicago Press, 1993), 152. During this period, the *Ecole Libre* (or "Science Po") trained more than 80 percent of entrants to the *grand corps,* the higher civil service. Ezra Suleiman, *Politics, Power, and Bureaucracy in France: The Administrative Elite* (Princeton: Princeton University Press, 1974), 48; Suleiman, "From Right to Left: Bureaucracy and Politics in France," in *Bureaucrats and Policy Making,* ed. Ezra Suleiman (New York: Holmes and Meier, 1984), 132. Thomas R. Osborne, *A Grand Ecole for the Grand Corps: The Recruitment and Training of the French Administrative Elite in the Nineteenth Century* (Boulder, Colo.: Social Science Monographs, 1983), and Silberman, *Cages of Reason,* chaps. 4 and 5.

33. As Silberman suggests, "[T]he men now holding positions of power in the new [Meiji] government, especially after 1873, had common social origins, values and norms, thus radically increasing the possibility of agreement." *Cages of Reason,* 187 (also 174, 180–84, 212).

34. Unlike the French system of recruitment, no formalized education-career tracks emerged in nineteenth-century Britain. Yet by 1880, most historians agree, the Northcote-Trevelyan and Macaulay reforms of the 1850s had fashioned a civil service with a high degree of social cohesion and a "generalist" educational outlook. The Northcote-Trevelyan report of 1853 championed a system of selection and promotion by merit (determined by competitive examination) but also espoused the utility of general education in the humanities and mathematics to produce a civil servant highly mobile among diverse occupations. See the "Northcote-Trevelyan Report" (1853), appendix B, in the *Fulton Report on the Civil Service* (London: Her Majesty's Stationery Office, June 1968), 1:114.

On the Victorian public school system (actually a network of private boys' schools), see Rupert Wilkinson, *Gentlemanly Power: British Leadership and the Public School Tradition* (New York: Oxford University Press, 1964), 110–22. Silberman, *Cages of Reason,* 288–90, 408. Leonard D. White, Charles H. Bland, Walter R. Sharp, and Fritz Morstein Marx, *Civil Service Abroad: Great Britain, Canada, France, Germany* (New York and London: McGraw-Hill, 1935), 9. Margaret Weir and Theda Skocpol, "State Structures and the Possibilities for 'Keynesian' Responses to the Great Depression in Sweden, Britain, and the United States," in *Bringing the State Back In,* ed. Peter Evans, Dietrich Rueschemeyer, and Theda Skocpol (New York: Cambridge University Press, 1985), 126–29.

35. Hugh Heclo, *Modern Social Politics in Britain and Sweden* (New Haven: Yale

University Press, 1974), 305–6. Silberman, *Cages of Reason.* Offe offers a similar argument: "The political system must have at its disposal sufficient information about the processes that take place in its environment, and which are relevant both for safeguarding the system and for avoiding conflicts. . . . Finally, the state must exhibit a forecasting capacity whose chronological range is congruent with its own 'planning horizon' " (*Contradictions of the Welfare State,* 58–59).

36. See the assessment of Dietrich Rueschemeyer and Peter Evans that "[e]ffective bureaucratic organization as well as the issue competence and factual knowledge required for intervention are perhaps nowhere more put to the test than in attempts at income redistribution" ("The State and Economic Transformation: Toward an Analysis of the Conditions Underlying Effective Intervention," in *Bringing the State Back In,* ed. Evans, Rueschemeyer, and Skocpol, 53–57).

37. There is a significant difference between the *formal specification* of agency powers (through statutes and appropriations) and the *organizational development* of capacity. Unfortunately, many books on state building equate these two forms of capacity. This equation appears in Bensel's argument in *Yankee Leviathan* that the Civil War and Reconstruction generated an enhanced (though still constrained) administrative state. This assumption also lies at the core of Sanders's argument that Progressive state building was driven primarily by populist agrarian social movements that championed the ICC. More recently, Sparrow's book on American state development in World War II focuses heavily on the budgets and personnel levels of domestic agencies; *From the Outside In.*

38. Bensel, *Yankee Leviathan,* 125.

39. The difficulty is that the skills required for government labor are not exclusively firm-specific and can be easily transferred to private-sector firms.

40. Emphasis added to Skocpol quotation. Network ties may be crudely divided into strong and weak ties, a distinction first developed by sociologist Mark Granovetter. Strong ties are relations involving greater trust, reciprocity, and frequency of interaction. Weak ties, analogous to acquaintances, are "cheaper" than strong ties in these dimensions. Granovetter's argument is simple but forceful. If societies are composed of tight clusters of strong ties, or "cliques," then weak ties are the conduits for information flow because they link these cliques together. See Mark Granovetter, "The Strength of Weak Ties," *American Journal of Sociology* 78 (1973): 1360–80; Granovetter, *Getting a Job* (Cambridge, Mass.: Harvard University Press, 1974); Scott Boorman, "A Combinatorial Optimization Model for Transmission of Job Information through Job Contact Networks," *Bell Journal of Economics* 6, no. 1:216–49. Skocpol surmises that "[t]he best situation for the state may be a regular flow of elite university graduates, including many with sophisticated technical training, into official careers that are of such high status as to keep the most ambitious and successful from moving on to nonstate positions" ("Bringing the State Back In," 16). I thank Nancy Burns for helping to clarify this argument.

41. As Simon argues, "In time, the actual system of relationships [in an organization] may come to differ widely from those specified in the formal organizational scheme" (*Administrative Behavior,* 160). For the classic demonstration that information flow in bureaucracy is only weakly constrained by formal lines of authority, see Peter Blau, *The Dynamics of Bureaucracy: A Study of Interpersonal Relationships in Two Government Agencies* (Chicago: University of Chicago Press, 1955). In a mathematical model of or-

ganizational networks, Roy Radner has shown that "efficient networks for information processing need not coincide with hierarchies of authority" ("Organization of Decentralized Information Processing," 1116). See also Mark Granovetter, "Economic Action and Social Structure: The Problem of Embeddedness," *American Journal of Sociology* 91 (1985): 481–510.

42. Even in programs whose purpose is the distribution of tangible benefits, or "pork," politicians' doubts about agencies will play an important role. Bureaucratic inefficiency can thwart the distribution of services to targeted constituencies.

43. Bensel, *Yankee Leviathan,* 110.

44. John Kingdon, *Agendas, Alternatives, and Public Policies* (Boston: Little, Brown, 1984). Deborah A. Stone, "Causal Stories and the Formation of Policy Agendas," *Political Science Quarterly* 104 (1989): 281–300.

45. Students of bureaucracy have long noted the value of incrementalism as a problem-solving strategy. Charles Lindblom offered the classic contribution in "The 'Science' of Muddling Through," *Public Administration Review* 19 (1959): 79–88. More recently, Jonathan Bendor has modeled Lindblom's claims mathematically and has attenuated some of his findings. "A Model of Muddling Through," *American Political Science Review* 89 (December 1995): 819–40. The point here has little to do with bureaucratic risk aversion. Incremental strategy is a wise way of building up programs, given that reputation is key to future autonomy.

46. In their pathbreaking study of the rise of the Medici family in Florence, John Padgett and Chris Ansell point to Cosimo Medici's unique positioning in Florentine social and political networks as a central condition underlying his political power; "Robust Action." See, more generally, Burt, *Structural Holes.*

47. R. Douglas Arnold, in *Congress and the Bureaucracy: A Theory of Influence* (New Haven: Yale University Press, 1979), also discusses bureaucratic coalition building (40–41). My theory differs from Arnold's in that it suggests that bureaucrats have incentives to take coalition-building strategies directly to the electorate. Gary Becker, "A Theory of Competition among Pressure Groups for Political Influence," *Quarterly Journal of Economics* 98 (August 1983): 392.

48. The method of historical demonstration is frequently a counterfactual, which I discuss in more detail later. This means that not all instances of bureaucratic policy innovation indicate bureaucratic autonomy.

49. Gary King, Robert O. Keohane, and Sidney Verba, *Designing Social Inquiry: Scientific Inference in Qualitative Research* (Princeton: Princeton University Press, 1994), 217–28. See also Ira Katznelson, "Structure and Configuration in Comparative Politics," in *Comparative Politics: Rationality, Culture, and Structure,* ed. Mark Irving Lichbach and Alan S. Zuckerman (New York: Cambridge University Press, 1997), 99. Jacob Hacker, "The Historical Logic of National Health Insurance: Structure and Sequence in the Development of British, Canadian, and U.S. Medical Policy," *Studies in American Political Development* 12, no. 1 (spring 1998): 57–130. Hacker's otherwise trenchant comparative analysis of national health insurance fails to take advantage of counterfactuals, not simply to generate new cases but also to clarify the importance of historical path-dependence and policy feedback. On the role of "surprise" in historical narrative, see Daniel P. Carpenter, "What Is the Marginal Value of Analytic Narratives?" *Social Science History* 24, no. 4 (winter 2000): 647–61.

50. By *counter-institutional* I mean that the action was *not* preferred in either of the

following two senses: (1) politicians and/or organized interests (in the form of the governing majority, the median voter in the electorate or Congress, or the enacting coalition of a relevant statute) preferred the status quo to the action, or (2) they preferred to change the status quo, but with a policy alternative that was nontrivially different from the one that the agency preferred and that became the final result. *Counter-institutional* thus implies *counter-majoritarian, counter-"committee," counter-presidential*, and the like.

These counterfactual departures from actual history must surpass triviality. If, for instance, the prodding of a "reputable" agency leads Congress to adopt a measure one month earlier than if the agency had not publicly advocated it, such action hardly indicates reputation-conditioned autonomy.

51. On explicitness and cotenability, see James D. Fearon, "Counterfactuals and Hypothesis Testing in Political Science," *World Politics* 43, no. 2 (1991): 169–95. Also, Philip E. Tetlock and Aaron Belkin, eds., *Counterfactual Thought Experiments in World Politics: Logical, Methodological, and Psychological Perspectives* (Princeton: Princeton University Press, 1996). Fearon's condition of "proximity" appears in "Causes and Counterfactuals in Social Science," chap. 2.

Chapter Two

1. Article 2, section 2, contains the only mention of the word "Opinion" in the Constitution. Whereas department heads offer their "Opinion" (on so nominal a subject as their own duties), the president provides Congress with "Information on the State of the Union, and [recommends] to their Consideration such measures as he shall judge necessary and expedient" (article 2, section 3). Congress, meanwhile, provides "advice and consent" concerning presidential appointments. So while the president and Congress barter in "judgment," "information," and "advice," the offerings by executive departments have less value as mere "Opinion." This phraseology was significant in light of the "philosophy/opinion" distinction still prevalent in eighteenth-century thought.

2. At the Massachusetts Ratifying Convention in 1788, Fisher Ames warned that "a pure democracy . . . would be a government not by laws, but by men" (Massachusetts Ratifying Convention, January 15, 1788, in *The Debates in the Several State Conventions on the Adoption of the Federal Constitution as Recommended by the General Convention at Philadelphia in 1787 . . .* , edited by Jonathan Elliot, 5 vols., 2d ed. [1888; reprint, New York: Burt Franklin, n.d.], 2:8–9). Nineteenth-century polemicists reversed Ames's ordering and championed "a Government of laws not of men" (Richard E. Ellis, *The Jeffersonian Crisis: Courts and Politics in the Young Republic* [New York: Norton, 1971], 204). Hamilton expressed a similar vision of the ideal republic under the Constitution in *The Federalist Papers* 33, edited with an introduction by Clinton Rossiter (New York: Mentor, 1961), 204. Scholars have disagreed with Tocqueville on this very point; see the discussion on bureaucratic reputation below.

3. John, *Spreading the News;* William Novak, *The People's Welfare: Law and Regulation in Nineteenth-Century America* (Chapel Hill: University of North Carolina Press, 1996); Colleen Dunlavy, *Politics and Industrialization: Early Railroads in the United States and Prussia* (Princeton: Princeton University Press, 1994); Patricia Nelson, *The Legacy of Conquest: The Unbroken Past of the American West* (New York: W. W. Norton, 1987); the citations to Donald Pisani are in the notes to chapter 10; Merritt Roe Smith, *Harpers Ferry and the New Technology: The Challenge of Change*

(Ithaca: Cornell University Press, 1977). For a fine survey of this new strain of argumentation, see Richard John, "Governmental Institutions as Agents of Change: Rethinking American Political Development in the Early Republic, 1787–1835," *Studies in American Political Development* 11, no. 2 (fall 1997): 347–80.

4. Stanley Elkins and Eric McKitrick, *The Age of Federalism: The Early American Republic, 1788–1800* (New York: Oxford University Press, 1993), 50.

5. Leonard White, *The Jeffersonians: A Study in Administrative History, 1801–1829* (New York: Macmillan, 1959); John, *Spreading the News.*

6. Dorothy Ganfield Fowler, *The Cabinet Politician: Postmasters General, 1829–1909* (New York: Columbia University Press, 1943), 306–7.

7. I believe Martin Shefter was the first to demonstrate the incentives for political control of bureaucracy during the Jacksonian period. See "Party, Bureaucracy, and Political Change," chap. 3 in *Political Parties and the State: The American Historical Experience* (Princeton: Princeton University Press, 1994), 68–69. See also Matthew Crenson, *The Federal Machine: Beginnings of Bureaucracy in Jacksonian America* (Baltimore: Johns Hopkins University Press, 1975); Richard McCormick, *The Party Period and Public Policy: American Politics from the Age of Jackson to the Progressive Era* (New York: Oxford University Press, 1986), 157–66. On the postal suppression of abolitionist mailings, see John, *Spreading the News,* esp. 268–72, 278–79. On party politics and pension distribution, see Skocpol, *Protecting Soldiers and Mothers,* chap. 2, esp. 112ff. See also William W. Savage Jr., *The Cherokee Strip Live Stock Association: Federal Regulation and the Cattleman's Last Frontier* (Norman: University of Oklahoma Press, 1973); Leonard D. White, *The Republican Era, 1869–1901: A Study in Administrative History* (New York: Macmillan, 1958), 196–231; Roy M. Robbins, *Our Landed Heritage: The Public Domain, 1776–1936* (Princeton: Princeton University Press, 1942; Lincoln: University of Nebraska Press, 1962), 268–69.

8. "Recapitulation of Appointments in the Department of the Interior," received August 9, 1887; "Colored Employees of the Department," October 14, 1884; "Number of Women Employed in the Dep't of the Interior," November 21, 1884; "Persons from Indiana (Who Served in the Union Army)," June 21, 1888; all in NA II, Records of the Secretary of Interior (RG 48), Records of the Appointments Division (E 67), V 2. More generally, see Skocpol, *Protecting Soldiers and Mothers,* 118–19; Everett Dick, *The Lure of the Land: A Social History of the Public Lands from the Articles of Confederation to the New Deal* (Lincoln: University of Nebraska Press, 1970), 24, 30.

9. Alexis De Tocqueville, *Democracy in America,* ed. J. P. Mayer and Max Lerner, trans. George Lawrence (New York: Harper and Row, 1966), vol. 1, pt. 1, 90. On the equivalency of rotation in office and a revolution of state that "takes place every four years in the name of the law," see vol. 1, pt. 1, 130–31. On impediments to the popular will, see vol. 1, pt. 2, 262–63. This state of affairs was, to be certain, much to Tocqueville's liking, as he feared a "tyranny of the majority" if administrative centralization took too much hold. Still, he was quick to point out the potential defects in American arrangements, such as institutional threats to order and the defeat of the popular will.

As Skowronek observes, this refraction of national authority was hardly different in military affairs. In *Building a New American State,* he notes that the renaissance of the state militia in the late 1870s and early 1880s thwarted "hopes for enhancing the army's presence downward through American society" (109).

10. In James D. Richardson, *A Compilation of the Messages and Papers of the Presidents, 1789–1910* (New York: Bureau of National Literature, 1911), 2:448–49.

11. John, "The Wellspring of Democracy," chap. 6 in *Spreading the News*.

12. Some of the most acute historians of Jacksonian politics—Arthur Schlesinger and Leonard White among them—have ignored the import of this passage in Jackson's inaugural address and have focused instead on the president's democratic idealism: his belief that all citizens should have access to administrative employment. White (*Jacksonians,* 319) even agreed with Jackson that nineteenth-century administrative duties were indeed as perfunctory as he claimed. The novelty of this sentiment in administrative history seems to have been lost on these authors.

13. Hill's statement appears in the congressional *Register of Debates,* 23d Cong., 2d sess., 569 (February 20, 1835), quoted in White, *Jacksonians,* 320. Bancroft's statement appears in M. A. DeWolfe Howe, *The Life and Letters of George Bancroft* (New York: G. Scribner's Sons, 1908), 1:197, quoted in White, *Jacksonians,* 328.

14. McLean's statement appears in the *Proceedings* of the Massachusetts Historical Society, 3d ser., 1:366, quoted in White, *Jacksonians,* 321.

15. On the Pendleton Act, see Skowronek, *Building a New American State,* chap. 3; Johnson and Libecap, "Replacing Political Patronage through Merit," chap. 2 in *Federal Civil Service System.* On the weakness of the winnowing effect of civil service examinations, see Secretary of Interior, *Annual Report* (1892–93), xvii. For examples of appointments by "presidential recommendation" in the Land Office, Pension Office, and Patent Office, see the list of clerical employees "Recommended by President Arthur," in Records of the Appointments Division, NA II, RG 48, E 67, V 2, p. 9.

16. In a 1913 review of the Land Office removals, Clarence Allen found that few "are definitely based on authenticated and investigated charges of misconduct" and surmised that the removals were for "political reasons." Clarence G. Allen, Appointment Section, Interior Department, to Assistant Attorney General Cobb, April 30, 1913 (with accompanying statistics), NA II, RG 48, E 67, B 1, F "Terminations." There were 110 registers and 110 receivers in 1888, and the number of "for cause" removals amounted to 30 to 50 percent of the force in any given administration.

17. I discuss the limited capacity of the late-nineteenth-century Post Office in chapter 3.

18. Skowronek, *Building a New American State,* 81–82.

19. Robert A. Ferguson, *Law and Letters in American Culture* (Cambridge, Mass.: Harvard University Press, 1984), quoted in Christopher Tomlins, *Law, Labor, and Ideology in the Early American Republic* (New York: Cambridge University Press, 1993), 27.

20. Skowronek, *Building a New American State,* 32.

21. John, *Spreading the News,* 335 n. 117. White, *Jacksonians,* 327–29, 329–32. Tocqueville, "Concerning Place-Hunting in Some Democratic Countries," chap. 10 in *Democracy in America,* vol. 2, sec. 1, p. 633. Hawthorne's "guillotine" metaphor appears in his essay "The Custom House" (quoted in White, *Jacksonians,* 330).

22. "Changes in Special Examiners in the Pension Office from March 4, 1889 to June 18, 1889," manuscript document, Appointments Division, Department of Interior, NA II, RG 48, E 67. Charles F. Diggs to Commission of Pensions, December 19, 1902, Appointments Division files, Records of the Secretary of Interior, NA II, RG 48, E 67. Diggs went into private practice and represented claims of debt before the Interior Department.

Skocpol, *Protecting Soldiers and Mothers,* 118–19. The bureau rejected 28 percent of applications received between 1862 and 1875 (108), but as the system grew, this percentage fell, and just over one-half of 1 percent of pensioners' claims were rejected for fraud by the late 1870s (143–44); Secretary of the Interior, *Annual Report* (1892–93), xvii.

23. "Recapitulation of the Number of Officials and Employees in the Department of Interior, October 12, 1888," Records of the Appointments Division, Department of the Interior, NA II, RG 48, E 67. "Statement Concerning Special Agents of the General Land Office," June 11, 1889, NA II, RG 48, E 67. The office employed 16 of a possible 35 agents for "fraudulent land entries," 12 of 26 agents investigating "timber depredations," 2 of 6 for "swamp lands" work, and none of the 3 slots for "examination of surveys." White, *Republican Era,* 196–208; Dick, *Lure of the Land,* 24, 30; Bartholomew Sparrow, "Fragmented and Uneven: Public Lands and the Rule of Law in the Nineteenth-Century United States" (paper presented at the annual meetings of the Social Science History Association, Fort Worth, Texas, November 1998).

24. U.S. Senate, Committee on Public Lands, Senate Report 362, 47th Cong., 1st sess. (December 27, 1881), p. 9, quoted in White, *Republican Era,* 199; see also 207. Dick, *Lure of the Land,* 31; Sparrow, "Fragmented and Uneven," 14.

25. I am indebted to John Padgett for this point. White, *Republican Era,* chaps. 9 and 10.

26. Although Congress added external bureaus, the organization of the Secretary's Office was not a congressional prerogative but an administrative one. The first clerical supervisory division was the Division of Appointments, and discussion of clerical supervision first occurred in 1850; see "The Division of Appointments in the Office of the Secretary, Department of the Interior, Notes Concerning Its Origin and Development," RG 48, E 67, B 1, F "Appt. Div."

27. Garfield served as a civil service commissioner in Roosevelt's first term and then steered the Bureau of Corporations. Skowronek, *Building a New American State,* 183–85. The report was untitled but was referred to as "Methods of Administration in the Department of Interior," hereafter "Methods," James R. Garfield to Theodore Roosevelt, October 22, 1906, C 143, F "Department of Interior, 1903–1907," James R. Garfield Papers, Library of Congress.

28. Ibid., p. 40.

29. Ibid., p. 6.

30. Ibid., pp. 4–5.

31. Ibid., pp. 15, 40. For a criticism of organizational structure in the contemporary federal bureaucracy that echoes Garfield's, see Paul Light's *Thickening Hierarchy* (Washington, D.C.: Brookings Institution Press, 1995).

32. Although Roosevelt did implement the recommendations of Garfield and of the Keep Commission by executive order, in reality the clerical supervision of bureaus continued for two decades after Garfield's tirade. Roosevelt merely reduced the number of divisions of the Secretary's Office from eight to four; nothing in the 1906 reorganization of Interior changed the fundamental principle of clerical supervision. Skowronek, *Building a New American State,* 183–85. Bensel, *Yankee Leviathan,* 110; see a related discussion in chapter 1 of this book.

33. Garfield to Roosevelt, October 22, 1906, p. 26.

34. "Officers and Employees of the Department of the Interior" (February 4, 1885),

"Recapitulation of the Number of Officials and Employes in the Department of the Interior, Oct. 12, 1888," and "Statement Concerning Special Agents of the General Land Office" (June 11, 1889); all in NA II, RG 48, E 67. Dick, *Lure of the Land,* 30–31; Malcolm J. Rohrbough, *The Land Office Business: The Settlement and Administration of American Public Lands, 1787–1837* (New York: Oxford University Press, 1968), 34; Sparrow, "Fragmented and Uneven," 14–15.

35. "Changes in the Force of Employees in the Dep't of the Interior Necessitated by the Appropriations for 1887–8," in Appointments Division Records, NA II, RG 48, E 67.

36. Reginald McCrane, *The Panic of 1837: Some Financial Problems of the Jacksonian Era* (Chicago: University of Chicago Press, 1924), 45, quoted in Robbins, *Our Landed Heritage,* 64. Fred A. Shannon, *The Farmer's Last Frontier: Agriculture, 1860–1897* (New York: Farrar and Rinehart, 1945), 54; White, *Republican Era,* 205ff.

37. Dick, *Lure of the Land,* 44. Rohrbough concludes that "[l]and offices differed widely in their interpretation of the act's general intent as they did in their administration of it" (*The Land Office Business,* 206). For the Cockrell Committee's report, see Report of the Senate Select Committee on Methods of Business and Work, Senate Report 507, 50th Cong., 1st sess. (March 8, 1888); White, *Republican Era,* 203–4.

38. U.S. Senate, *Report of the Senate Select Committee on Methods of Business and Work,* 507; White, *Republican Era,* 203–4.

39. U.S. Senate, *Report of the Senate Committee on Public Lands,* 362, 47th Cong., 1st sess. (December 27, 1881), 9, quoted in White, *Republican Era,* 199. Donald J. Pisani, *Water, Land, and Law in the West: The Limits of Public Policy, 1850–1920* (Lawrence: University Press of Kansas, 1996), 109.

40. "Brief of Inspector Hobbs' Report on Charges against T. F. Singiser, Receiver of Public Moneys at Mitchell, Dak." (July 28, 1888); also records of cases against Harry King and Frederic Metzger, chief and assistant chief of the Drafting Division of the General Land Office, December 26, 1902; both in NA II, RG 48, E 67, B 1, F "Precedents, Memos, Etc." "Mr. Conrad's Dismissal" and "Angry with Mr. Noble," *Washington Post,* October 26, 1889.

41. Donald J. Pisani, "Forests and Conservation, 1865–1890," chap. 7 in *Water, Land, and Law.* Charles Sargent, "The Protection of Forests," *North American Review* 135 (October 1882): 386–401; Bernhard Fernow, "Our Forestry Problem," *Popular Science Monthly* 32 (December 1887); both quoted in Pisani, *Water, Land, and Law in the West.* "Forest Destruction," *Norfolk (Virginia) Landmark,* September 11, 1891; "A Treeless Country," *Farm Implements News,* June 1891; "Deforestation," *The Weeks Sport,* October 8, 1890; "Forstfrevel in Amerika," in the German-American *Buffalo (N.Y.) Democrat,* January 5, 1891; "Clearing Away the Forests," *Rockville (Ill.) Herald,* February 8, 1891; John L. Shawver, "American Forests—Their Destruction and the Evident Result" (paper read before the Logan County Annual Institute, January 1, 1889), reprinted in *The American Register* 1889, 12–13.

On the increasing flow of petitions to congressional committees, see the Records of the House Agriculture Committee (NA I, RG 233), subject "forest lands" (45A-H2.5, 50A-H1.3); Records of the Committee on Public Lands, subject "forest reservations and timber lands" (RG 233, 37A-E16.11, 53A-F38.3); Records of the Senate Committee on Agriculture, subject "forest reserves" (RG 46, SEN 43A-H1, 45A-H1); Records of the Senate Committee on Agriculture and Forestry (50A-J1.1).

42. For discussions of the Forest Transfer Act and Reclamation Act, see chapters 8 and 10, respectively. James Muhn, "Early Administration of the Forest Reserve Act: Interior Department and General Land Office Policies, 1891–1897," in *Origins of the National Forests,* ed. Harold K. Steen (Durham, N.C.: Forest History Society, 1992), 259–75. Robbins, *Our Landed Heritage,* 291–95; White, *Republican Era.*

43. The account here relies heavily on Skocpol, *Protecting Soldiers and Mothers,* 118–20.

44. John William Oliver, "History of Civil War Military Pensions, 1861–1885," *Bulletin of the University of Wisconsin* 844 (History Series 1) (1917): 43–45, cited in Skocpol, *Protecting Soldiers and Mothers,* 119–20. Skocpol argues that the French experience with centralization in pension administration resulted in a reduced rate of pension expansion (120).

45. Richard McCormick, *The Party Period and Public Policy: American Politics from the Age of Jackson to the Progressive Era* (New York: Oxford University Press, 1986), 206. Novak, in *People's Welfare,* challenges McCormick's portrait, though only with respect to state governments.

46. Jackson's veto message appears in Glyndon G. Van Deusen, *The Rise and Decline of Jacksonian Democracy* (New York: Van Nostrand Reinhold, 1970). See also Arthur M. Schlesinger Jr., "Veto," chap. 8 in *The Age of Jackson* (Boston: Little, Brown, 1945).

47. Schlesinger, *Age of Jackson,* 105, 123.

48. In 1834, after the demise of the recharter proposal, Taney and Thomas Hart Benton worked to create a policy of specie revaluation. As a result, the coinage of national mints increased immensely from 1834 to 1836. To suppress the competing form of currency—small paper notes issued by banks—Benton wrote the famous "Specie Circular," instructing federal land agents to accept payments for western properties only in specie. Jackson quickly adopted the policy by issuing the circular as an executive order and later vetoed a congressional attempt to repeal the circular. Brownson's statement appears in Schlesinger, *Age of Jackson,* 514.

49. Bensel, *Yankee Leviathan,* 276–81. With the establishment of the national banking system under the supervision of the comptroller of the currency in 1863, the Treasury Department was given authority to regulate the supply of paper currency.

50. Bensel, *Yankee Leviathan,* 275ff., 294, 315–16, 365; Gretchen Ritter, *Goldbugs and Greenbacks: The Antimonopoly Tradition and the Politics of Finance in America* (New York: Cambridge University Press, 1997), 175; Irwin Unger, *The Greenback Era: A Social and Political History of American Finance, 1865–1879* (Princeton: Princeton University Press, 1964); Walter Nugent, *The Money Question during Reconstruction* (New York: Norton, 1967).

51. Skowronek, "Patching Civil Administration," chap. 3 in *Building a New American State.* The role of business concerns is highlighted by Ronald N. Johnson and Gary D. Libecap, *The Federal Civil Service System and the Problem of Bureaucracy* (Chicago: University of Chicago Press, 1994), chap. 2.

52. Richard Ellis, *The Jeffersonian Crisis: Courts and Politics in the Young Republic* (New York: Oxford University Press, 1971). The quotation is from p. 249.

Chapter Three

1. Quotations are from John, *Spreading the News,* 8, 10–11.

2. Wayne Fuller, *R.F.D.: The Changing Face of Rural America* (Bloomington: Indiana University Press, 1964), 9; White, *The Jeffersonians,* 329.

3. The 1792 law appears at 1 Stat. 232, section 6 (February 20, 1792). John, *Spreading the News,* 31. John depicts the postal system of the late 1700s as "little more than a mirror image of the royal postal system for British North America" (25). The government monopoly in postal affairs was established under the Continental Congress, first by a general assumption of control over intercolonial postal distribution in 1775, and then more formally in the ordinance of 18 October 1782, granting to Postmaster General Ebenezer Hazard the sole right to collect and distribute mail matter as defined by acts of the legislature. The 1782 ordinance recognized, however, the prerogative of private carriers to distribute newspapers and pamphlets. Carl H. Scheele, *A Short History of the Mail Service* (Washington, D.C.: Smithsonian Institution Press, 1970).

4. John, *Spreading the News,* 5, 37, and chap. 2, "The Communications Revolution," passim.

5. Ibid., 46–49, 82–83, 244 (evidence of the system's first debt). White, *Jeffersonians,* chap. 21, esp. 313–19.

6. John, *Spreading the News,* 65–69, chaps. 5–7, passim; White, *Jeffersonians,* 313–19.

7. John, *Spreading the News,* 75.

8. Steamboats also transported mail. Like stagecoaches and antebellum rail transport, however, river transport was under contract, not under official department auspices. The steamboat's role in postal transportation grew steadily until the 1880s, then began a long, slow decline as rail transport expanded (Scheele, *Short History,* 96). Even antebellum postal officials believed that managerial authority should remain centralized. John quotes Peter Washington in 1851, who regarded any decentralizing scheme as "a great evil" (*Spreading the News,* 76).

9. James Holbrook, *Ten Years Among the Mail Bags; or, Notes from the Diary of a Special Agent of the Post Office Department* ([1855]; New York: Loomis National Library Association, 1888); In *Spreading the News,* John links Holbrook to the modern detective genre (77). P. H. Woodward, *The Secret Service of the Post Office Department, as Exhibited in the Wonderful Exploits of Special Agents . . .* (San Francisco: A. L. Bancroft, 1886). David B. Parker, *A Chautauqua Boy in '61 and Afterward* (Boston: Small, Maynard, 1912).

10. Even the antebellum inspectors, writes White, did little, if any, monitoring of the operations of local post offices, instead confining their endeavors to the suppression of mail theft (*Jeffersonians,* 329). Alan H. Patera, ed., *Your Obedient Servant: The Letters of Quincy A. Brooks, Special Agent of the Post Office Department, 1865–1867* (Lake Oswego, Ore.: Raven Press, 1986). Quincy A. Brooks to Alex W. Randall, December 28, 1865 (Patera, *Your Obedient Servant,* 23); Brooks to Randall, January 27, 1866 (Patera, *Your Obedient Servant,* 44). Of the 239 letters printed in Patera's edition, 130 (or 54 percent) were written to officials in Washington. Brooks wrote most frequently to McLellan (69 letters, or almost 30 percent of the total). He also wrote 46 letters (19 percent) to Randall, who succeeded Dennison as postmaster general in 1866. The Washington office was also slow to inform special agents of specific instructions. Duff Green

to Postmaster General Charles Wickliffe, Jan. 1, 1842, NA I, RG 28, A1 E 228A, "Correspondence and Reports of Special Agents, 1836–1845," F "1842."

11. Howard Kennedy [Baltimore] to John Marron, chief clerk of the POD, October 6, 1842; George Plitt to John Marron, chief clerk of the POD, January 8, 1842; H. W. Orburn, U.S. deputy marshal for northern district of N.Y., to E. Whittlesby, POD, July 23, 1842; all in NA I, RG 28, A1 E 228A, "Correspondence and Reports of Special Agents, 1836–1845," F "1842."

12. Jacob Collamer, in Special Agent Circular, October 8, 1850, p. 1; copy in Inspection Service Vertical Files, USPSL. George Plitt to Charles Wickliffe, October 27, 1842, October 22, 1842, November 20, 1842; all in NA I, RG 28, A1 E 228A, "Correspondence and Reports of Special Agents, 1836–1845," F "1842."

13. On the number of inspectors, see the 1861 *Annual Report*, p. 4. Holbrook, *Ten Years Among the Mail Bags*, 409. John B. Furay to P. H. Woodward, August 6, 1875, Inspection Service Vertical Files.

14. Oliver W. Holmes and Peter T. Rohrbach, *Stagecoach East: Stagecoach Days in the East from the Colonial Period to the Civil War* (Washington, D.C.: Smithsonian Institution Press, 1983). John, *Spreading the News*, 99. Postmaster General, *Annual Report* (1853), 10–11. John B. Furay to P. H. Woodward, July 25, 1875, Inspection Service Vertical Files. Parker, *Chautauqua Boy*, 205–10. *Opinions of the Solicitor General for the Post Office Department, 1868–1897*, volume for 1873–76, opinion no. 42, p. 249, May 28, 1874 (NA I, RG 28, E 48 [Office of the Postmaster, Division of the Solicitor]). Hereafter cited as *Opinions*. The worst abuses of the awarding system are commonly acknowledged to have occurred under the tenure of Jackson's postmaster general, William T. Barry (1829–35). See John, *Spreading the News* (216–17), and the memoirs of Barry's successor, Amos Kendall (1835–40), *Autobiography of Amos Kendall*, ed. William Stickney (Boston, 1872), 337, 343. Kendall encountered a number of collusive practices in private bidding, such as the submission of straw bids and the maintenance of favoritism toward stage companies who were faithful Jackson supporters. On Brooks's efforts, see Patera, *Your Obedient Servant*, 21, 31, 33. The argument of T. A. Spence, assistant attorney general for the department, appears in *Opinions*, opinion no. 4, p. 34, July 11, 1873. Inez E. Kirkpatrick, *A Postal History of Sioux City* (Crete, Neb.: J-B Publishing, 1976), 24.

15. Kendall, *Autobiography*, 337, 343. John, *Spreading the News*, 241–45. John concludes that "there can be little doubt that the Jacksonians' contracting policy quickly ran the enterprise into debt" (242). Kirkpatrick, *Postal History*, 24–25. On "extra allowances," see 4 Stat. 102, section 10 (March 3, 1825), and 4 Stat. 102, section 43 (March 3, 1825). Wayne E. Fuller, *The American Mail: Enlarger of the Common Life* (Chicago: University of Chicago Press, 1972), chaps. 2 and 5.

16. In recognition of the increasingly distributive and partisan role of the department, in 1829 Jackson elevated his postmaster general, William Barry, to the Cabinet and placed the Post Office outside the institutional confines of the Treasury Department. Fuller, *American Mail*, 56–57, and White, *Jacksonians*, 265–66. John, *Spreading the News*, 216. Marshall Cushing, *The Story of Our Post Office: The Greatest Government Department in All Its Phases* (Boston: A. M. Thayer, 1893), 286.

17. John, *Spreading the News*, 102–6; Plitt's quotation is on p. 104. Parker, *Chautauqua Boy*, 198–99. Even McLean's apparent successes were based less on the department's ability to monitor local operations than on the purported esprit de corps that

he instilled (John, *Spreading the News*, 48–49). Brooks reported that in "a number of small offices on [the Oregon] coast . . . the incumbents act in the double capacity of Postmaster and Express Agent" (Brooks to first assistant postmaster general, September 16, 1866, in Patera, *Your Obedient Servant,* 164). Quincy A. Brooks to Col. A. H. Markland (special agent, San Francisco), December 26, 1865, in Patera, *Your Obedient Servant,* 18. In letters to First Assistant Postmaster General St. John B. S. Skinner (November 4, 1867) and Alexander Randall (undated), Brooks bemoans the difficulty of removing postmasters (ibid., 210, 214).

18. John Frey to David B. Parker, June 12, 1879, [p. 12]; August 13, 1879, [pp. 63, 83]; September 1, 1879, [p. 88]; September 15, 1879, [p. 99]; September 12, 1879, [p. 100]; September 15, 1879, [pp. 102, 105, 107–9]; September 17, 1879, [p. 146] (on express agents); all in Frey-to-Parker Letterbook, NA I, RG 28, Accession Records of the Postal Inspection Service, B 14, F 53. These records, which survived a recent postal headquarters fire, are stored separately from other entries in RG 28. Parker to Sen. S. B. Maxey, January 24, 1878, Parker Letterbook, David Parker Collection, University of Delaware. (I thank Richard John for the use of his notes on this letterbook.) Special Agent J. N. Nichiger to A. N. Zevely, March 31, 1868; W. D. Maxey, postmaster at Alexandria, to George W. McLellan, March 27, 1868; NA I, RG 28, Correspondence and Reports of Special Agents, B 2, 1861–69. See also document, "Violation of Law by Express Cos," initialed by A. N. Zevely.

19. John Frey to David M. Key, December 3, 1879, [p. 301], in Frey-to-Parker Letterbook, NA I, RG 28, Accession Records B 14, F 53. West, in *Annual Report* (1886), p. 119.

20. White, *Jacksonians,* chap. 13, and *Republican Era,* chap. 12. Joseph Bristow, *Fraud and Politics at the Turn of the Century* (New York: Exposition Press, 1952), 35. Mulroney, *Montgomery Blair,* 15–16.

21. James H. Bruns, *Mail on the Move* (Polo, Ill.: Transportation Trails, 1992) and *Horse Drawn Mail Vehicles* (Washington, D.C.: National Postal Museum, 1996). From still pictures in the latter book, it is evident that not until the advent of Concord coaches did "U.S. Mail" appear with any regularity on the sides of stages. Even numerous late-nineteenth-century coaches did not bear the insignia (for example, pp. 22–25). Postmasters were legally restricted from administering oaths of office (or even of loyalty) to contractors. See opinion of T. A. Spence, assistant attorney general of the Post Office Department, in *Opinions,* no. 7, p. 51, July 30, 1873.

22. Skowronek, *Building a New American State,* chap. 4. Fred A. Shannon, *The Organization and Administration of the Union Army, 1860–1865* (Gloucester, Mass.: Peter Smith, 1928).

23. The secession of the Southern states in 1861 led to dual postal systems in the Union and Confederacy. The Confederacy usurped the previous structure of operations in the South, and under Confederate Postmaster General John Reagan of Texas, it administered with much less efficiency the same routes and delivery network that a unified government had managed just months earlier. Bensel, *Yankee Leviathan,* 101, and Scheele, *Short History,* 86–90.

24. Private activity in mail delivery reflects a much larger commercial role in mail transportation in the antebellum period, particularly on the East Coast, where postal rates were higher and commercial activity was more intense, creating opportunities for shrewd firms to cut into the department's business. Richard R. John, "Private Mail De-

livery in the United States: A Sketch," *Business and Economic History,* 2d ser. 15 (1986): 131–43.

25. Blair, *Annual Report* (1862); Rita Lloyd Mulroney, *Montgomery Blair: Postmaster General* (Washington, D.C.: GPO, 1963), 23–24. Special delivery was authorized at 12 Stat. 701 at 703 (March 3, 1863). See Blair's arguments in the 1862 *Annual Report* and 1864 *Annual Report* (pp. 24–25); Mulroney, *Montgomery Blair,* 24. The money-order system is authorized at 13 Stat. 76 (May 17, 1864).

26. See Hezekiah Niles's description of the route agents in his *Niles Register,* May 18, 1838. H. L. Johnson, principal clerk, Mail Equipment Division, Office of Second Assistant Postmaster General, to Hon. Walter Q. Gresham, postmaster general, July 22, 1884, RMS Vertical Files, USPSL. "One Hundred Years of Railway Mail Service," *Railway Age,* July 9, 1938. Armstrong's concerns about distributing post offices appear in the recollections of John Montgomery, superintendent of mails, in George B. Armstrong Collection. Montgomery wrote, "I have heard [Armstrong] say repeatedly, that the time was not far distant when the great D.P.O. offices of the country would be like any other way station along the line of a Railway Post Office." Armstrong railway mail prospectus sent to A. N. Zevely, Post Office Department, Washington, D.C., May 1864, quoted in William J. Dennis, *The Traveling Post Office: History and Incidents of the Railway Mail Service* (Des Moines: Homestead Printing Co., 1916), 21–22. Parker, *Chautauqua Boy,* 268–70.

27. *Sioux City Sunday Journal,* November 23, 1867, excerpted in Kirkpatrick, *Postal History,* 25. The series in figure 3.1 is calculated by dividing the total annual postal miles covered by railroad by the total annual postal mileage for that year. Because data are not available for the year 1865, 1864 data appear instead. After the collapse of the Confederacy in 1865, Lincoln's second postmaster general, William Dennison, dispatched department officers to the South to devise plans for the reestablishment of southern post offices and transport networks. Yet by 1866 the department's officers had been able to open only 2,778 of the nearly 9,000 post offices of the antebellum system. Moreover, the department reconfigured many of the southern transport networks, relying much more heavily on new and repaired railroad lines to achieve a universal distribution of mails. As a result, the mail system in the postbellum southern states was characterized and integrated by the railroad postal service to a degree unwitnessed before the Civil War. See Paul Buck, *Road to Reunion* (Boston: Little, Brown, 1937), 157; Bensel, *Yankee Leviathan,* 101; Fuller, *American Mail,* 102–3.

28. Before 1882, Congress did not welcome the older route agents into the railway mail cars, limiting their appointments through an appropriations cap. Many route agents had been appointed under Democratic administrations, and congressional Republicans preferred to legitimize the department's practice of appointing Union veterans with railroad experience. The 1882 law authorized the RMS to appoint all route agents as railway mail clerks. Dennis, *Traveling Post Office,* 22ff.; Clark E. Carr, *The Railway Mail Service: Its Origin and Development* (Chicago: A. C. McClurg, 1909).

29. "Workings of Railway Mail Car Prove Interesting to Thousands," *Springfield (Mass.) Union,* September 19, 1923, p. 7. R. F. Valentine, "Railway Mail Service Is Nation's Santa Claus," *Richmond Times-Dispatch,* December 16, 1923; Valentine wrote that "[m]any clerks carry in their mind and at their finger ends 5,000 to 10,000 post offices, comprising several states and the schedules of hundreds of trains."

30. Dennis, *Traveling Post Office,* 76–77.

31. *Peoria Star,* April 26, 1904, reprinted in *Railway Post Office* (hereafter *RPO*), November 1904, p. 6.

32. H. W. Strickland, "History of the Railway Mail Service Divisions," *RPO,* September 1933, 53.

33. According to RMS regulations, at least one copy of *The Black Book* was to be carried in every mail car on every run. The book's instructions helped to establish procedural control over RMS employees, reducing reliance on postal inspectors, whose numbers were too restricted at this time to survey the mail cars with any regularity. "The Great Seal in the Railway Mail Service," RMS Vertical Files, file 5. The quotation is from Dennis, *Traveling Post Office,* 44. As Dennis (28) describes the "fast mail" cars, "At the lower sides were ovals corresponding to those containing the name [of governors for whom the cars were named], in which were painted landscape scene backgrounds [of the governors' states], and in the relief was an all-seeing eye, beneath which was a pyramid inscribed in gilt 'MDCCCLXXV' and the motto 'Novus Ordo Secularum.'"

34. Editorial of RMA secretary George A. Wood, *RPO,* February 1905, 12. Letter of H. M. Ormsby, March 6, 1905, in *RPO,* March 1905, 9. Carr, *Railway Mail Service,* v. The clerks' association was known as the National Association of Railway Postal Clerks until 1904, when its name was changed to the Railway Mail Association. The precursor of the *RPO* is the *R.M.S. Bugle.*

35. Thomas Schlereth, *Victorian America: Transformations in Everyday Life, 1876– 1915* (New York: Harper Collins, 1991). Herbert Gutman, *Work, Culture, and Society in Industrializing America* (New York: Alfred A. Knopf, 1976), esp. chap. 1. Joel Silbey, *The American Political Nation, 1838–1893* (Stanford: Stanford University Press, 1991); see also Edward T. Linenthal, *Changing Images of the Warrior Hero in America: A History of Popular Symbolism* (Toronto: Edwin Mellen Press, 1982).

36. Letter of J. V. O'Toole, of the New York and Chicago RPO, printed in *RPO,* September 1904, 20–21.

37. Clark E. Carr to the editor, January 23, 1905, printed in *RPO,* February 1905, 1– 4. Carr, *Railway Mail Service,* p. 40.

38. W. H. Coulter to RMA secretary George Wood, November 5, 1904 (printed in *RPO,* November 1904), entitled, "All Hail the R.M.A."

39. Speech of D. W. Young, November 18, 1904, Saint Louis, Missouri (reprinted in *RPO,* January 1905, 9).

40. Two aspects of the antebellum postal system had a quasi-divisional organization—the "divisional" system of the general office that McLean established (John, *Spreading the News*, 79) and the hub-and-spoke distribution system—yet neither approached the division of labor that Armstrong envisioned and established. The control of regional RMS superintendents over railway post offices was much greater than the corresponding control of distributing postmasters over local offices and stage operations.

41. With the civil service protection afforded by the Pendleton Act of 1883, postal workers had greater interest in their working conditions, and letter carriers in New York briefly joined the radical Knights of Labor in the 1880s. Soon after, several trades in the department formed labor associations in the 1880s and 1890s, including the National Association of Letter Carriers (NALC) (formed with help from the Knights of Labor) in 1889 and the National Association of Post Office Clerks (NAPOC) in 1890. The railway

clerks organized a mutual benefit association in November 1880, well before any labor association had formed in the department. Yet no labor organization would form for a decade. Cushing, *Story of Our Post Office,* 804–50.

42. David B. Parker to George M. Butler, May 7, 1877; Parker to Charles Devons, August 10, 1877; both in Parker Letterbook, David Parker Collection. Frey to Parker, November 1, 1879, Frey-to-Parker Letterbook, 252; Frey to Parker, March 9, 1880, [p. 617], NA I, RG 28, Accession Records, B 14, F 53. "Monthly Report of D. E. Brainard," December 1864, in NA I, A1 E 228A, Correspondence and Reports of Special Agents, B 2, 1861–69, F "1865."

43. Fuller, *American Mail,* 247. Fuller writes, "[T]he post office inspectors were, as a group, the most competent men in the postal service. Chosen with care, usually from the elite corps of railway mail clerks, they were experts on postal law" (256). Furay to Woodward, August 6, 1875, p. 2.

44. Estimates of the fraction of inspectors hired from the RMS are calculated from the inspectors' "Rosters 1898–1909," NA I, RG 28, E 234, which include data from 1897 until 1910. The figure of 34.8 percent is a lower bound on the portion of inspectors from the RMS, for the rosters reported only the most recent service or occupation from which individuals were appointed. Hence inspectors who first worked for the RMS, then worked in another section of the department, and then came to the inspection service were not counted as RMS appointments. R. T. Mayhew, "Post Office Inspection Service, History of Organization," May 1, 1951, Inspection Service Vertical Files; Woodward, *Secret Service.*

45. There were in fact two Comstock laws, one passed in 1872 (28 U.S. Statutes 302, section 148) and the more famous version passed in 1873 ("An Act for the Suppression of Trade in, and Circulation of, Obscene Literature and Articles of Immoral Use," 28 U.S. Stat. 598, section 258, passed March 3, 1873). Comstock fought hard in 1873 to strengthen the 1872 law; Anna Smith Bates, *Weeder in the Garden of the Lord: The Life and Career of Anthony Comstock* (Lanham, Md.: University Press of America, 1995), 69–95. Heywood Broun, *Anthony Comstock: Roundsman of the Lord* (Boston, 1927); Nicola Beisel, *Imperiled Innocents: Anthony Comstock and Family Reproduction in Victorian America* (Princeton: Princeton University Press, 1997); Cushing, *Story of Our Post Office,* 617ff.; Paul W. Boyer, *Urban Masses and Moral Order in America, 1820–1920* (Cambridge, Mass.: Harvard University Press, 1978), 120.

46. Beisel, *Imperiled Innocents,* chaps. 2–4; Cushing, *Story of Our Post Office,* 613, 621; Fuller, *American Mail,* 252–54. The Comstock quote is from his *Traps for the Young* (1883; reprint, Cambridge, Mass.: Harvard University Press, Belknap Press, 1967).

47. On the use of the federal anti-obscenity statute to arrest Heywood, see Beisel, *Imperiled Innocents,* 98–99. R. W. McAfee to Chief Inspector W. J. Vickery, November 30, 1906, NA I, RG 28, Accession Records, B 3.

48. David B. Parker to Anthony Comstock, September 24, 1876, Parker Letterbook, David Parker Collection. Comstock to Parker, June 1, 1878, November 24, 1877 (Parker writes back on the same stationery, asking Comstock to keep him informed of a case in New Jersey state court), September 30, 1876, April 19, 1877, November 17, 1877; Comstock to P. H. Woodward, February 19, 1876 (indecent exposure arrest); Comstock to C. Cochran Jr., Division of Mail Depredations, August 21, 1875; Comstock to William A. West, chief inspector, May 28, 1887 (typescript reproduction); all in NA I, RG 28, Accession Records, B 27. *Arrest Book, 1868–1874,* in NA I, RG 28, UD E 229A.

49. Comstock to West, May 28, 1887. "Crusade Against Lotteries," *New York Times,* March 14, 1877. Comstock to Woodward (Hallenbeck arrest), April 27, 1876; Comstock to Parker (Gaulier arrest), November 27, 1876; all in NA I, RG 28, Accession Records, B 23.

50. Fuller, *American Mail,* 273–77; Cushing, *Story of Our Post Office,* 617. James C. Mohr, *Abortion in America: The Origins and Evolution of National Policy, 1800–1900* (New York: Oxford University Press, 1978), 197; Beisel, *Imperiled Innocents,* chap. 2. On congressional proposals to vitiate the inspectors' corps, see Parker, *Chautauqua Boy,* 231–32. The Chicago arrest figures are from the Division of Post Office Inspectors, *Arrest Book, 1868–1874,* NA I, RG 28, UD E 229A. Postmaster General, *Annual Report* (1886–87), 315.

51. Dorothy Ganfield Fowler, *Unmailable: Congress and the Post Office* (Athens: University of Georgia Press, 1977), 68–70; Beisel, *Imperiled Innocents,* 89–92. Heywood was convicted in June 1878 and sentenced to two years' hard labor but was pardoned by President Hayes. After four more arrests, Heywood was convicted and sent again to prison in 1890. On criticism of Comstock's methods in these cases, see Beisel, *Imperiled Innocents,* 93–94, 100. On the Harman arrest (by McAfee), see Cushing, *Story of Our Post Office,* 612. On the YMCA and anti-Tammany forces and their ties to the department, see Boyer, *Urban Masses,* 115, 120, 134, 176. On Wanamaker's religiosity, see William Leach, *Land of Desire* (New York: Pantheon Books, 1993), 194–215.

52. Bissell's statement appears in his *Annual Report* to Congress (1892–93), pp. xxix–xl, quoted in White, *Republican Era,* p. 267. Wanamaker's appears in *Annual Report* (1888–89), p. 8.

53. On Wanamaker's business career, see Leach, *Land of Desire,* passim. The authoritative biography is Herbert Adams Gibbons's *John Wanamaker* (New York: Harper, 1926), 2 vols. See also Fuller, *RFD,* 17–35, and Dorothy Fowler, *The Cabinet Politician: The Postmasters General, 1829–1909* (New York: Columbia University Press, 1943), 207–23.

54. Midlevel officials customarily served through several changes in presidential administrations; see Parker, *Chautauqua Boy,* 213–16. Throughout his tenure Wanamaker pressed to expand the inspectors' corps; Cushing, *Story of Our Post Office,* 316. Tyner was appointed postmaster general on July 12, 1876, and served until Hayes appointed David M. Key on March 12, 1877. On Tyner's duties and outlook, see Cushing, *Story of Our Post Office,* 613ff.

55. *Annual Report* (1888–89), 8–9.

56. Gibbons, *John Wanamaker,* 1:253–337. Wanamaker envisioned a system of "apprenticeship": "The post-office should be a school for the railway mail, the railway mail for the Department, the Department for the division chiefs, and the highest places in the service." See *Annual Report* (1889), 3–5, 6–8, 9 ("venerable clerk"), 17–18 ("apprenticeship," "school"), 24 ("spinal column"). See also Cushing, *Story of Our Post Office,* 68–100. Cushing was Wanamaker's private secretary.

57. Fuller, *American Mail,* 182.

58. *Annual Report* (1889), 34–35.

59. Bissell, in White, *Republicans,* p. 267 n. 34; Postmaster General, *Annual Report* (1892–93), xxxix–xl.

Chapter Four

1. Cushing, *Story of Our Post Office,* 435–37.

2. The postmasters were B. Wilson Smith of LaFayette, Indiana; F. T. Spinney of Medford, Massachusetts; L. H. Beyerle of Goshen, Indiana; James P. Harter of Hagerstown, Maryland; O. H. Hollister of Meadville, Pennsylvania; J. F. Sarratt of Steubenville, Ohio; and Archibald Brady of Charlotte, North Carolina. Cushing, *Story of Our Post Office,* 454–55.

3. Ernst was educated at the famous Klosterschule in Ilfeld, Germany. He was also a member of Phi Beta Kappa and the American Philological Society. Hughes had edited the *Pittston Gazette* and the *Wyoming Valley Journal.* Field emigrated from Ireland and served as president of the Philadelphia Hibernian Society and a trustee of the local Young Men's Christian Association. Cushing, *Story of Our Post Office,* 747–66, quotation on 747.

4. G. H. Slaughter, *Stage Coaches and Railroads; or, The Past and the Present* (Nashville, Tenn.: Hasslock and Ambrose, 1894). Copy in NA I, RG 28, E 25, B 2.

5. Cushing, *Story of Our Post Office,* 25, 51.

6. Speech of D. W. Young on November 18, 1904, in Saint Louis, Missouri (reprinted in *RPO,* January 1905, p. 9, emphasis added). Cushing, *Story of Our Post Office,* 744.

7. The image of an organic machinery was widespread in the Railway Mail Service, particularly as it concerned the train and its locomotive engine, the "machine" to which the service was most often compared. Clerks frequently assigned gender to the daily train, calling it "she" (Dennis, *Traveling Post Office,* 89–90).

8. Daniel T. Rodgers, *The Work Ethic in Industrial America, 1850–1920* (Chicago: University of Chicago Press, 1978), chap. 3. Wood's advocacy is in *RPO* editorial, November 1904, 11, emphasis added.

9. Clarence E. Votaw, *Jasper Hunnicutt of Himpsonhurst* (Chicago: Union Book and Publishing Co., 1907). Votaw entered the RMS on the Chicago, Richmond, and Cincinnati RPO in 1881, ascending to the position of assistant superintendent in 1906.

10. Cushing, *Story of Our Post Office,* 18–19, 21–22. White announced the competition in the *Daily Bulletin of Orders Affecting the Postal Service,* March 16, 1892 (copy in RMS Vertical Files). The use of exemplary performances as standards for other workers was a staple feature of the "stopwatch" methods of Taylor's scientific management school. Frederick Taylor, *The Principles of Scientific Management* (1911; reprint, New York: Norton, 1967). Dennis, *The Traveling Post Office,* 48.

11. Postal uniforms became official when Postmaster General Alexander Randall prescribed them and Congress authorized them on July 27, 1868 (15 Stat. 197). In 1894 the department attempted to standardize these for the first time, letting a single contract for all twelve thousand carriers' uniforms. *Records Relating to the History of Postal Carriers' Uniforms, 1868–1957,* NA I, RG 28, UD E 179. See the portraits in Daniel P. Carpenter, "From Patronage to Policy: The Centralization Campaign in Iowa Post Offices, 1890–1910," *Annals of Iowa* (summer 1999): 273–309. The recollections of New Orleans mail carrier Ozenine Kinler appear in "Oldest Postman Still Spry After Forty-one Years' Service," *The Times-Picayune,* November 15, 1925, Louisiana Collection, Howard-Tilton Memorial Library, Tulane University. *Cedar Rapids Gazette,* April 5, 1959; see also Postmaster W. G. Haskell, *United States Post Office, Cedar Rapids, Iowa;* both in Records of the Cedar Rapids Post Office, Iowa State Historical Society of Iowa, Iowa City.

12. RMA secretary Wood, editorial in *RPO,* November 1904, p. 11. On gendered categorizations and the feminization of government clerical work in the early twentieth century, see Cindy Aron, *Ladies and Gentlemen of the Civil Service* (New York: Oxford University Press, 1990).

13. H. T. Newcomb, *The Postal Deficit* (Washington, D.C.: Ballantyne and Sons, 1900). Moody presented his statistics in *CR,* 56-1, March 27, 1900, pp. 3612–13. Adams's testimony appears in Report of the Joint Commission to Investigate the Postal Service, *Railway Mail Pay* (1901), House Report, 56th Cong., 2d sess., vol. 1, no. 2284. Cushing, *Story of the Post Office,* 49; Charles Emory Smith, *Greatest Business Organization in the World: The United States Postal Service* (n.p., 1899).

14. Forrest Crissey, "The Traveling Post-Office," *World's Work* (September 1902): 2873–80. Earl Mayo, "Post Office Work and Methods," *The Outlook,* October 3, 1903, 298–309. "A National Opportunity: A Business Postal Department," *World's Work* 19 (March 1910): 12643–44. George W. Norris, "Why Not Take the Post Office Out of Politics?" and Editors, "Timely Topics," *The Editorial Review* 6, no. 3 (March 1912): 198, 189, respectively. David Gates, "The Railway Mail Service," *Watson's Magazine* 5, no. 4 (October 1906): 76.

15. Wayne Fuller, *The American Mail: Enlarger of the Common Life* (Chicago: University of Chicago Press, 1972), 277. Vern K. Baxter, *Labor and Politics in the U.S. Postal Service* (New York: Plenum Press, 1994), 61; after the protest of the National Association of Letter Carriers (NALC), the department stopped the practice of "spotting" in 1896.

16. Postmaster General, *Annual Report* (1905), 148.

17. Statistics in this paragraph are calculated from inspectors' rosters in Records of the Division of Post Office Inspectors, NA I, RG 28, E 234, "Rosters 1898–1909," which include inspector data from 1897 until 1910. I emphasize again—see chapter 3—that the actual fractions and percentages were probably higher.

18. Bates, *Weeder,* 173–201. On the Enloe bill and the department's substitute, see Fowler, *Unmailable,* 80–81. WCTU petitions are in Records of the House Committee on Post Office and Post Roads, NA I, RG 233, F HR52A-H18.3. The WCTU attached a clipping showing that Comstock coordinated the letter-writing and petition campaign around H.R. 5067.

19. Charles A. L. Reed to George Cortelyou, November 4, 1905 (italics added); Cortelyou to Reed, January 12, 1906; NA I, RG 28, E 36, B 1, file "American Medical Association." Allan Brandt, *No Magic Bullet: A Social History of Venereal Disease in the United States Since 1880* (New York: Oxford University Press, 1985).

20. Division of Post Office Inspectors, *Arrest Book, 1891–1902,* NA I, RG 28, E 162. In 1891 alone, arrests were made in Alabama, Arkansas, Iowa, Virginia, and West Virginia.

21. Card index to General Records, Division of the Solicitor, Post Office Department, 1905–21, NA I, RG 28, E 35. Of a random sample of 144 correspondents in the case file, 128 cases were alcohol related. Jack S. Blocker Jr., *Retreat into Reform: The Prohibition Movement in the United States, 1890–1913* (Westport, Conn.: Greenwood Press, 1976); K. Austin Kerr, *Organized for Prohibition: A New History of the Anti-Saloon League* (New Haven: Yale University Press, 1985); Boyer, *Urban Masses,* 212–13. For correspondence with the Washington-based lobby, the Anti-Saloon League of America, see cases 46951, 46901, 54352, and 54800. For correspondence with Prohibi-

tion United, see 48686. For correspondence with Anti-Saloon Leagues of Idaho, Maryland, and Texas, see 47179, 47015, and 47113 respectively.

22. John Wanamaker to Benjamin Harrison, June 28, 1890, enclosing "Memorandum Concerning Lotteries" (probably Tyner), in the files of the House Committee on Post Office and Post Roads, RG 233, B 71, HR51A-F30.4. Harrison's handwritten letter to the Senate, July 29, 1890, in same files. Leonard V. Huber and Clarence A. Wagner, *The Great Mail: A Postal History of New Orleans* (State College: American Philatelic Society, 1949), 190; Fowler, *Unmailable,* 81–84.

23. Hayes, in *CR,* 51-1, S. 568, S. 2768, S. 4323, H.R. 177, H.R. 241, H.R. 242, H.R. 3321, H.R. 8981, H.R. 11569, H.R. 12150, pp. 8439, 8698–8721, 9510, 10085, in Fowler, *Unmailable,* 82–84. Comstock's biographer Charles Gallaudet Trumbull argues that the 1890 legislation was a successor to a bill that Comstock had drafted in 1885. Trumbull, *Anthony Comstock: Fighter* (New York: Fleming H. Revell, 1913), 114. Cushing (*Story of Our Post Office,* 524) argues that Tyner was the original author.

24. Henry A. Castle, "Abuses in Our Postal System," pt. 2, *The North American Review,* July 1902, 122. Division of Post Office Inspectors, *Arrest Book.*

25. Fowler, *Unmailable,* 86–90. *Ex parte Rapier,* 143 U.S. 110 (1892); *Stokes,* 157 U.S. 187 (1895); *Streep,* 160 U.S. 128 (1895); *Durland,* 161 U.S. 305 (1896); *Public Clearing House,* 194 U.S. 497 (1904). See also *Fitzsimmons v. United States,* 156 Fed. 477 (1907), where Judge Gilbert cites *Public Clearing House.*

26. Cushing, *Story of Our Post Office,* 313.

27. Second Assistant Postmaster General J. Louis Ball to J. M. Masten, March 3, 1894, NA I, RG 28, E 102, B 1, V 2/27/1894–1/28/1898, p. 4. G. F. Stone, acting second assistant postmaster general, to J. M. Masten, May 9, 1894, ibid., p. 67. The department generally distrusted subletting. W. S. Shallenberger to Irvin W. Mayfield, January 10, 1903, NA I, RG 28, E 102, B 1, V 1, p. 6. G. F. Stone to W. C. Heckman, assistant superintendent, RMS, December 20, 1895, NA I, RG 28, E 102, B 1, V 2/27/1894–1/28/1898, p. 355.

28. As Cushing noted in 1893, "The great bulk of an inspector's work consists of simple irregularities in the mail service. The fourth-class postmasters do not carefully observe the rules and regulations, and hence much carelessness, where there is no dishonesty, results" (*Story of Our Post Office,* 313). West's statement is in *Annual Report* (1888), 39. *Postmasters' Advocate,* August 1904, 18. G. F. Stone to W. C. Heckman, November 3, 1894, NA I, RG 28, E 102, B 1, V 2/27/1894–1/28/1898, pp. 185–86. Second Assistant Postmaster General J. Louis Ball [?] to W. C. Heckman, assistant superintendent, RMS, St. Louis, Missouri, February 27, 1894, ibid. The department questioned postmasters' preferences to hire through kin and friendship networks. G. F. Stone to J. M. Masten, May 26, 1894, ibid., p. 92. Terry, in *CR,* 54-2, February 25, 1897, p. 2351.

29. G. F. Stone to W. C. Heckman, May 11, 1894, NA I, RG 28, E 102, B 1, V 2/27/1894–1/28/1898, p. 74. Stone to Heckman, May 15, 1894, p. 90 (same volume). RMS agents were also required to assess independently railroad companies' claims that new "transfer" services were needed between adjacent but unconnected lines. Second assistant postmaster general to W. C. Heckman, January 26, 1895, ibid., p. 225.

30. See the case of messenger bids for Oshkosh, Wisconsin; Mulrose, second assistant postmaster general, to J. M. Masten, February 2, 1895, NA I, RG 28, E 102, B 1, V 2/27/1894–1/28/1898, p. 233.

31. G. F. Stone to W. C. Heckman, September 27, 1895, NA I, RG 28, E 102, B 1, V 2/27/1894–1/28/1898, p. 333.

32. Anthony Comstock to R. A. Maxwell, September 25, 1895; John Ashe to M. D. Wheeler, chief post office inspector, November 20, 1895; John Mouros to R. A. Maxwell, February 17, 1896, February 21, 1896; all in Inspection Service Vertical Files.

33. "A Bill to Increase the Efficiency of the Postal Service," 54th Cong., 2d sess., H.R. 4808. Judiciary Committee, "Efficiency of the Postal Service," January 30, 1897, *CR,* 54-2, February 25, 1897, 2348–55.

34. The equation estimated is *Vote = probit(constant + β1*Republican + β2*[D-NOM1] + β3*[D-NOM2])*, where *probit* signifies the standard normal distribution link function, D-NOM1 is a "first-dimension" ideological score, and D-NOM2 is a "second-dimension" ideology score. For the construction of these ideology scores, see Keith Poole and Howard Rosenthal, "Patterns of Congressional Voting," *American Journal of Political Science* 35 (1993): 228–78. The coefficient estimates for this equation (with standard errors in parentheses) are *constant = -0.4532* (0.3308); *β1 = -0.5246* (0.5332); *β2 =* 1.1815 (0.5671); *β3 =* 0.4713 (0.5978). The first-dimension ideology score *is* significantly associated with the vote, but the approximate percentage of variance explained by this model is quite low: 22.9. David Brady and Philip Althoff, "Party Voting in the U.S. House of Representatives, 1890–1910: Elements of a Responsible Party System," *Journal of Politics* 36 (August 1974): 753–74.

35. Heywood Broun and Margaret Leech, *Anthony Comstock: Roundsman of the Lord* (New York: Literary Guild of America, 1927), 220; Bates, *Weeder,* 180.

36. The author of the codified statutes was probably Henry D. Lyman, who served as chief clerk of the second assistant postmaster general. Lyman's codification was celebrated as the first attempt to compile and index numerically the criminal laws of the United States. It became the basic procedure for indexing statutes after 1890, including those of the U.S. statutes at large; Parker, *Chautauqua Boy,* 283–84. See HED 12, 53d Cong., 2d sess.; HED 13, 54th Cong., 1st sess.; HED 11 54th Cong., 2d sess.; HED 13, 55th Cong., 3d sess.; HED 16, 56th Cong., 1st sess.; HED 4, 56th Cong., 2d sess.; summary statistics from these are given in Fowler, *Unmailable,* 223. On the Crumpacker bill, see ibid., 94–95.

37. George Cortelyou, "Frauds in the Mail: Fraud Order and Their Purposes," *North American Review* 184 (April 30, 1907): 808–17; Fowler, *Unmailable,* 95–96.

38. Fowler, *Unmailable,* 93–97.

39. Roosevelt reluctantly agreed to the rationale behind the department's repudiation; Fowler, *Unmailable,* 96–101.

40. Brookline selectmen's petition (undated); petition of Philadelphia Bourse, Grocers' and Importers' Exchange, January 19, 1898; "Resolutions" of Wilkes-Barre Board of Trade, January 22, 1898; petition of Rochester Chamber of Commerce, January 24, 1898; "Protest of the People of New York," January 25, 1898; all in the files of House Committee on Post Office and Post Roads (NA I, RG 233, B 246, HR55A-H21.6).

41. Robert J. Stets, *Street Car R.P.O. Service in Philadelphia* (Mobile, Ala.: Mobile Post Office Society, 1978); Richard S. Clover, "The Street Railway Post Office in Philadelphia," *The American Philatelist* (December 1937). The department also tried an experiment with horse-drawn collection and distribution wagons, but wagon service withered by the summer of 1900, leaving the streetcar service as the principal mechanized alternative to traditional delivery systems. See James H. Bruns, *Collection and*

Wagon Distribution Service, 1896–1904 (Mobile, Ala.: Mobile Post Office Society, 1986).

42. Formal account books existed throughout the nineteenth century, but in many offices they were not used in standard fashion until the era of centralization (1890–1910). See *Cash Book,* George M. Howlett, postmaster, Cedar Rapids, Iowa, 1870; *Cash Book,* J. T. Urice, postmaster, Garrison, Iowa, 1887–88; *Accounts and Records,* Cedar Rapids Post Office, 1898–1900; *Account and Record Book,* Cedar Rapids Post Office, 1916; *Cash Book,* Cedar Rapids Post Office, 1916–17; in Records of the Cedar Rapids Post Office and Records of the Garrison Post Office. Perry S. Heath, "Official Instructions in Relation to Postmarking and Backstamping" (Washington, D.C., May 14, 1897). Cushing, *Story of Our Post Office,* 432ff.

43. A minor adjustment came in 1905, with a substantial one in 1910. M. L. Thomas, "What Is the Credible Truth About Railway Mail Pay?" *Uncle Remus' Home Magazine* (March 1911): 16–18. For evidence on the institutional constancy of railway payments during this period, see Reports of Payments for Railway Mail Transportation, 1876–1928, NA I, RG 28, UD E 68. See also "Laws Respecting Pay for the Transportation of Mails on Railroad Routes and for Railway Post Office Cars," appendix A (pp. 19–20), in *Letter from the Postmaster General, Submitting a Report Giving the Results of the Inquiry as to the Operation, Receipts, and Expenditures of Railroad Companies Transporting the Mails, and Recommending Legislation on the Subject* (Washington, D.C.: GPO, 1911). HED, 62-1, 105.

44. "The Post-Office and the Deficit," *The Outlook,* December 14, 1907, 794–95; "Conditions of the Postal Service," *The American Review of Reviews,* March 1910, 266; "A Plain Word About the Postal Service," *World's Work,* February 1911, 13949; "Cause and Cure of Deficits," *The American Review of Reviews,* March 1911, 269; Norris, "Why Not Take the Post Office Department Out of Politics?" *The Editorial Review,* March 1912, 198–205.

45. A different analysis in which costs are first regressed upon receipts also shows marked declines. I mention here two measurement concerns. First, to account for inflation, I include the office's free delivery receipts as a denominator or control in all analyses. Whatever national, regional, and local monetary factors are inflating cost aggregates should also be inflating receipts aggregates in nearly the same fashion. In the absence of annual local-level price indices for 1896–1910, this procedure offers the only reasonable control for price inflation. Second, the postal "cost function" may not be stable over time, in part because, as figure 4.3 shows, the standard errors for cost and operations variables decline over time, suggesting that the panel is not "variance-stationary." Hence regime shifts in the denomination or coefficient value of receipts may render any estimates inconsistent.

46. I include the second three variables because I am interested in indices that correlate with the probability and the severity of local inspection. Intuition and anecdotal evidence suggest that longer-tenured agents who had better learned the procedures of inspection were more likely to crack down on city offices.

47. James E. Rauch, "Bureaucracy, Infrastructure, and Economic Growth: Evidence from U.S. Cities during the Progressive Era," *American Economic Review* 85 (September 1995): 968–79. Rauch finds that the adoption of merit reform in urban civil service administration increased municipal bond ratings and stunted spending on infrastructure.

In some respects, the findings of this chapter suggest that Rauch's results do not transfer easily to national politics.

48. Wayne Fuller, *RFD: The Changing Face of Rural America* (Bloomington: Indiana University Press, 1964); Samuel Kernell and Michael McDonald, "Congress and America's Political Development: The Transformation of the Post Office from Patronage to Service," *American Journal of Political Science* 43, no. 3 (July 1999): 792–811.

49. Fuller's description of the rural postmasters appears in *RFD,* 84. Lena Hecker finds the fourth-class postmasters and star route contractors to be the most vocal enemies of the new system. Hecker, "The History of the Rural Free Mail Delivery in the United States" (master's thesis, University of Iowa, 1920), 25–26.

50. Bruns, *Mail on the Move.* The Georgia congressman's statement appears in Fuller, *RFD,* 54 (italics added).

51. For Wanamaker's initial proposal, see *Report of the Postmaster General,* HED 1, pt. 4 (Washington, D.C., 1889), 27. Beckwith wrote Wanamaker on February 20, 1890, enclosing a copy of House bill 3322, entitled "A Bill to Extend the Free Delivery System of the Post Office Department, and for Other Purposes" (NA I, RG 233, HR51A-F30.1, B 71). Beckwith also asked for Wanamaker's "opinion as to the advisability of its passage, and an estimate of the increased expense incident thereto." Wanamaker responded two weeks later with enthusiasm: "[T]he Bill meets with my entire approval in every feature, and its passage would, in my judgment, accommodate a large number of people with additional postal facilities." To document the latter point, Wanamaker enclosed a calligraphic script list of all post offices still without free delivery, yet which had garnered revenues of $5,000 or more in the fiscal year ending June 30, 1890 (John Wanamaker to Hon. C. D. Beckwith, March 4, 1890, ibid., B 71). Bingham sent his proposal—Senate bill 925—to Wanamaker on December 16. In his letter of December 23, Wanamaker dissuaded Bingham from the broader expansion (ibid.). He informed Bingham that the Senate's plan would result in an extension of free delivery to at least 573 post offices, perhaps as many as 700. Many of these offices "will not have the requirements as to lighted streets, good side-walks, numbered houses and names of streets at intersections." Wanamaker reasoned that the Senate would be lucky if 400 such towns were even to apply for the service. He concluded that "300 or 350 offices having the necessary requirements, will be the maximum number which will apply and can be properly inspected and established."

52. *Annual Report of the Postmaster General* (1890–91). Wanamaker "was the first to suggest officially through his annual report of 1891 that a rural delivery department be added as a branch of the United States Post Office" (Hecker, "History of the Rural Free Mail Delivery," 20). Wanamaker lamented the fact that by 1889, only one in six post offices in the United States delivered mail to its patrons. Fuller also argues that Wanamaker was the main progenitor of the RFD idea (*RFD,* 17, 22).

53. Rural experience with stage and star route contractors in the late nineteenth century had been painful. For star route frauds, see Cushing, *Story of Our Post Office,* 30–32, 351, 439. The statement in the *Farm Journal* appears in Wanamaker's voluminous report "Free Delivery System," May 3, 1892; SED 92, 52d Cong., 1st sess., p. 180. Gibbons, *John Wanamaker,* 1:279–80. The *Farm Journal's* opposition was ironic because Wanamaker had helped to establish the journal; James Bruns, *Reaching Rural America: The Evolution of Rural Free Delivery* (Washington, D.C.: National Postal Museum,

1998), 16. Hal Barron, *Mixed Harvest: The Second Great Transformation in the Rural North, 1870–1930* (Chapel Hill: University of North Carolina Press, 1997), 174–88. *Proceedings of the Twentieth Annual Meeting of the National Board of Trade, 1888* (Boston: Crosby, 1888), 159–62. The board also favored one-cent postage in succeeding years.

54. For a broadcast repetition of Wanamaker's call for rural petitions, see *Spokane Spokesman*, February 5, 1892, "Free Delivery System," 144–45. Grangers' support for RFD was not universally enthusiastic; at the 1891 convention, a minority of the Grange's Committee on Resolutions proposed that the National Order shelve the RFD resolutions and wait upon the matter for a few years. The eventual resolution was adopted by only a 27-to-19 vote; National Grange of the Patrons of Husbandry, *Journal of Proceedings,* 25 (1891) (Philadelphia: J. A. Wagenseller, 1891), 99. *Philadelphia Bulletin,* October 20, 1891; *Baltimore American,* October 20, 1891; "Free Delivery System," 52–53. Bruns, *Reaching Rural America,* 11–12, esp. 15.

55. As Fuller argues: "Perhaps because they could visualize no practical substitute for their antiquated postal system, farmers had never demanded a change in their mail service before 1891" ("Rural Free Delivery in Hardin County," *Annals of Iowa* 41, no. 6 [fall 1972]: 1050). The *Louisville Home and Farm* printed blank petitions with its November 15, 1891, edition, vowing to send to "Brother Wanamaker a Christmas present of a petition with 4,000,000 names, that his name may resound down the vista of time, through countless generations, as the greatest benefactor the country people ever had"; excerpted in "Free Delivery System," 98. The Summit County Farmer's Alliance resolution appears in ibid., p. 7. Fuller also makes it clear that Wanamaker's announcement was decisive in stimulating congressional support for RFD (*American Mail,* 105; Fuller, "Rural Free Delivery in Hardin County," 1050). On the unprecedented volume of RFD petitions, see *Free Delivery of Mail in Rural Districts,* House Report 1352, 52d Cong., 1st sess., p. 1. Hecker, "History of the Rural Free Mail Delivery," 20.

56. On Wanamaker's lobbying efforts, see Gibbons, *John Wanamaker,* 1:281; *Milwaukee News,* September 22, 1891, "Free Delivery System," 32. William Leach, *Land of Desire: Merchants, Power, and the Rise of a New American Culture* (New York: Vintage, 1993), 182–85. Bruns, *Reaching Rural America,* 15–16.

57. The revenue statistics appear in "Free Delivery System," 8–9. The quotes appear on pp. 63, 59, respectively. Whether the general revenue boosts are attributable to RFD or something else is difficult to discern from the department's data. Departmental statisticians tried to control for "natural" revenue growth in the post offices by calculating the average annual increase in earnings for the two years preceding the experiments. Whether or not the controls were proper, contemporary newspapers noted the care with which the department had calculated and presented the revenue data. See the discussion of reputation formation in this chapter. The vast majority of newspaper editorials advocating RFD mentioned the experiments in some way. Although I have not made an exact tabulation of those mentioning the department, the figure of 340 is probably a lower bound on this number (see table 4.4).

58. For the Accotink Farmers' Club resolution, see Senate, *Letter from the Postmaster General in Response to Senate Resolution of January 13, 1892, Relative to the Extension of the Free Delivery System to Rural Districts,* Exec. Doc. 92, 52d Cong., 1st sess. (May 3, 1892), p. 7; for the Luzerne and Summit county resolutions, see pp. 5, 7.

59. *Minneapolis Journal,* August 24, 1891; "Free Delivery System," 21. *New York*

Press, September 9, 1891, ibid., 27. *Butler (Miss.) Record,* October 10, 1891, ibid., 43. For extracted editorials, see ibid., 56, 60, 66, 130, 144–45.

60. I offer two caveats on this brief statistical exercise. First, the tabulation of editorial credit assignment is not a particularly interpretive matter. Those editorials assigning credit to the department almost universally fail even to mention Congress or any of the farm organizations of the day. Second, the editorials do not constitute a properly construed random sample, though they might. It is possible that Wanamaker selected only those editorials that assigned credit to his department. This explanation seems implausible for two reasons. First, Wanamaker had an incentive to select from as broad a collection of editorials—politically and geographically—as possible. Second, the preponderance of editorials crediting Wanamaker over those that do not is large; the department would have had to go to extreme lengths to locate more than two hundred editorials to skew the results.

61. See "Free Delivery System," 83, 116, 103, 90, 121, respectively.

62. On Wanamaker's request, see Fuller, "Rural Free Delivery in Hardin County," 1051. Fuller also points to congressional uncertainty as "the greatest obstacle to establishing a system" (1051 n. 4). For instances of editorial concern about the postal deficit, see "Free Delivery System," 173, 123, respectively. See also the excerpted editorial of the *N. E. Homestead* (Springfield, Mass.), November 7, 1891, ibid., 92.

63. Newspaper editorials concurred that the sum of $10,000 was insufficient for genuine experimentation. The *Harrisburg Telegraph* complained that "the amount was not sufficient to give the movement a comprehensive test" (12), and the *Chicago Inter-Ocean* described it as a "very small appropriation" ("Free Delivery System," 12, 40, 59, respectively). Kernell and McDonald, "Congress and America's Political Development," 795. See Machen's remarks in "Rural Free Delivery in Carroll County, MD," House Document 691, 56th Cong., 1st sess., 2. For a discussion of Bissell's reasons for refusing to spend the experimental RFD funds, see Gibbons, *Wanamaker,* 1:281.

64. Fuller, *RFD,* 56, and "Rural Free Delivery in Hardin County," 1051.

65. Gary explicitly cleaved to incrementalist growth, arguing that RFD should be expanded "not immediately, or in all districts at once, but in some gradual and gradated form, the character of which might be regulated by the tenor of the reports herewith presented as to the experimental service." Gary's report is in "Free Rural Delivery," SED 171, 55th Cong., 2d sess. (March 3, 1898), 3. Fuller, *RFD,* 34–35.

66. For the department's announcement suggesting petitions, see *Annual Report of the Postmaster General* (1898), 155, 246. Fuller, "Rural Free Delivery in Hardin County," 1053; Fuller, *American Mail,* 76.

67. For sample petitions, see NA I, RG 233, B 175, F 18.7. A number of the petitions were sent out by *The Homestead,* Springfield, Massachusetts. On the volume of letters and petitions received by the department regarding RFD, see Postmaster General, *Annual Report* (1900–1901), unpaginated; (1898), 155; (1899), 203; also Fuller, *RFD,* 41–43. Even petitions to the House Committee on Post-Office and Post Roads mentioned the department as the primary proponent of the RFD system. Pomona Grange petition (Vandergrift, Pennsylvania) to Hon. E. E. Robbins, March 4, 1898, NA I, RG 233, HR55A-H21.5, B 246. Meigs County (Ohio) Farmers' Institute petition from Racine, Ohio, HR56A-H21.9, B 110.

68. Machen, "Rural Free Delivery in Carroll County, MD," 1–3. Because Machen commenced the experiment in December, skeptics complained that the department was

trying to sabotage the RFD by starting operations in the most difficult month. So convinced was Machen of the inherent efficiency of his division and of the sure profitability of the RFD program, however, that he decided to demonstrate its value in the most difficult delivery months of winter.

69. Machen, "Rural Free Delivery in Carroll County, MD," 1, 11–12.

70. W. Frank McClure, "The Countryman Has the Better of It," *World's Work,* October 1901, 1309. Act of April 21, 1902, Ch. 563, 32 Stat. L., 1237. M. G. Cunniff, "The Post-Office and the People," *World's Work,* December 1903, 4246. Leach, *Land of Desire,* 183.

71. Machen, "Rural Free Delivery in Carroll County, MD," 4–5.

72. *Preliminary Report of the Joint Commission on the Business Method of the Post Office Department and the Postal Service,* Senate Reports, 60th Cong., 1st sess., vol. 4 (December 2, 1907–May 30, 1908), p. 39. Examples abound of rural agents defying Congress in the belief that they held local power. When an RFD agent in Georgia had planned some route changes that met with the dissent of Senator Alexander S. Clay, the route alterations nonetheless went through. Clay was concerned that the department was exerting too little control over the agent, who "thinks he is the Post Office Department" (Fuller, *RFD,* 45–46). The department had granted this authority to its rural agents in part because it was so informationally dependent on them (Fuller, *RFD,* 46).

73. Guttersen and Olson were based in the Indianapolis office of the Western Division of the Rural Free Delivery Service. Gilbert Guttersen to Gilbert N. Haugen, June 16, 1900, on stationery of the Merchant's Hotel, Osage, Iowa (Gilbert N. Haugen Papers, State Historical Society of Iowa, B 120, June 1900 file). For Guttersen's request for Haugen's backing on a decision to close a small post office and discontinue a star route, see Guttersen to Haugen, July 11, 1900. On third-class appointments, see C. P. Grandfield, first assistant postmaster general, to Haugen, August 7, 1908; and Grandfield to Haugen, August 21, 1908, Calmar file, Haugen Papers. On Guttersen's promotion of Haugen, see Guttersen to Haugen, June 2, 1900, B 120. See also Guttersen to Haugen, June 9, 1900, May 28, 1900, B 120, May 1900 file.

74. Eaton wrote to Haugen informing the congressman of Guttersen's favorable report on a route application for Orchard, Iowa. See Willard L. Eaton to Haugen, February 21, 1900, Haugen Papers, B 120. Olson filed his report on the Calmar and Ossian cases using the stationery of the National Bank of Decorah (Olson to Machen, September 29, 1900, Haugen Papers, RFD Correspondence, Calmar file). Ole P. Ode, the cashier for the Winneshiek National Bank, knew Haugen well and later served on the Republican Central Committee of Winneshiek County. In a 1907 petition for the reappointment of Decorah postmaster J. J. Marsh, Decorah bank officials, including three cashiers, were the first private officials listed in a petition of more than one thousand names (Haugen Papers, Decorah file). Rural agent John T. Boylan was a coeditor of *The Herald* at Eldora and a friend of Charles Albrook, president of the Hardin County Republican Central Committee. See Fuller, "Rural Free Delivery in Hardin County," 1058.

75. Ole P. Ode, the cashier for the Winneshiek County Bank in Calmar, submitted Calmar's petition (Ode to Haugen, July 18, 1900). Machen acknowledged the petitions in a return letter to Haugen (August 10, 1900). Six weeks later, Olson filed his report on private stationery (see above); Olson to Machen, September 29, 1900. All three letters are in Calmar file, RFD Correspondence, Haugen Papers. As an indicator of his status and that of other cashiers, Ode later served, as mentioned, on the Republican Central

Committee for Winneshiek County. Two decades later, he served as president of Calmar's First State Bank. See letter of Sigvart T. Kittlesby to John H. Bartlett, first assistant postmaster general, February 23, 1928, Calmar file. For the decision on the Calmar and Ossian cases, see Johnson to Haugen, January 9, 1901, Calmar file (department file "Rural-F-118-HAB"). Machen's initials appear at the top right corner of the letter. Two weeks later, the department approved RFD for the Decorah post office, a second-class office; Johnson to Haugen, January 22, 1901 (department file "S-F-39-FH"). Calmar later became a third-class ("Presidential") office and received RFD. See C. P. Grandfield, first assistant postmaster general, to Haugen, August 7, 1908, Calmar file. On Osage route case, see Guttersen to postmaster of Osage, July 7, 1900, Haugen Papers, RFD Correspondence, July 1900 file.

76. Graham Romeyn Taylor, "At Your Door-Step: The Neighborly Service of the United States Post Office," *The Survey,* May 6, 1916. Machen to Haugen, February 21, 1901, Decorah file, Haugen Papers (department file "Rural-F-992-O"). Peter V. DeGraw to Haugen, July 7, 1905, RFD Correspondence.

77. "Proposed Plan for the Civil-Service Administration of the Rural Free Delivery Service," Garfield Papers, C 123, files 1–3, p. 2. Questions about alcohol consumption appear on p. 7 of the sample carrier questionnaire in this document. Fuller, *RFD,* 108–9.

78. For Washington officials the relationship between literacy and revenues was an ineluctable fact. City free delivery revenues provided the best indication; revenues were sharply higher where patrons were more literate. In a statistical analysis of the revenue data used in tables 4.2 and 4.3, I find that city revenues plummeted where illiteracy was high, that is, they were low precisely in those southern states where Republicans were weakest after 1896. The statistical relationship is robust ($t = -6.1$). For Olson's reasoning in the Calmar and Decorah cases, see Olson to Machen, September 29, 1900. Fuller, "Rural Free Delivery in Hardin County," 1054. Kernell and McDonald also find a positive association between route allocations after 1898 and allocations from 1895 to 1898. This is consistent with the revenue maximization incentives of the department and the experimental nature of RFD. The department was more likely to approve routes next to those with established revenue streams. For the quote on Kansas and South Carolina, see Fuller, *RFD,* 64. Quoted in Kernell and McDonald, "Congress and America's Political Development," 799. For summary statistics showing the differential in routes across Republican and Democratic districts, see ibid.

79. For Olson's reasoning in the Calmar and Decorah cases, see Olson to Machen, September 29, 1900. For the Hardin County RFD petition, see Fuller, "Rural Free Delivery in Hardin County," 1054.

80. On the English consolidation example, see Thomas L. James, "Needed Postal Reforms," *The Forum,* December 1889, 128. Smith's order is in Postmaster General, *Annual Report* (1901), 11–12. Fuller, "Rural Free Delivery in Hardin County," 1061. C. P. Grandfield to Haugen, December 22, 1908, Haugen Papers. The department also asked Haugen for information and gave him the chance to object.

81. Carroll County, Maryland, for instance, had ninety-four fourth-class postmasters and dozens of star-route (horseback) mail carriers. They "vigorously denounced" Machen's experiment and "succeeded in creating in some quarters a strong but temporary opposition to the service." See Machen's report, "Rural Free Delivery in Carroll County, MD," 4; Fuller, *RFD,* 51–52, 100ff.

82. Fuller, "Rural Free Delivery in Hardin County," 1049–72.

83. Roy Alden Atwood, "Routes of Rural Discontent: Cultural Contradictions of Rural Free Delivery in Southeastern Iowa, 1899–1917," *Annals of Iowa,* III, 48, nos. 5, 6:264–73, 269, and n. 14.

84. Aggregate statistics are from "Statistics of the Postal Service from 1862 to 1912," in Daniel Roper, *Postal Policies and Problems* (Washington, D.C.: GPO, 1914). See Kernell and McDonald, "Congress and America's Political Development," fig. 1. Congressional Republicans were keenly aware of the immense political value of the rural carriers (Fuller, *RFD,* 59).

85. Fuller, *RFD,* 87–88.

86. For a summary of the scandal, see "The Real Meaning of the Postal Scandal," *World's Work,* January 1907, 4280; Fowler, *Cabinet Politician,* 273–78. Bristow's report appears in Senate Doc. 151 (1903), House Report 383 (1903), U.S. Congress, 58-2. Tyner denied wrongdoing and was never convicted of a crime.

Chapter Five

1. The epigraph to this chapter is from "Postal Savings," *The Survey* 23, no. 3 (October 16, 1909).

2. *The Outlook,* June 10, 1911; "A Check on Postal Efficiency," *The Outlook,* September 7, 1907, 13–14; "Working under Difficulties," *American Review of Reviews,* March 1910, 266. Graham Romeyn Taylor, "At Your Door-Step: The Neighborly Service of the United States Post Office," *The Survey* 36, no. 6 (May 6, 1916): 133. See also Frank B. Lord, "A Practical Reform," *Baltimore Sun,* June 22, 1914.

3. James Babcock, "More Light on Postal Matters," *Twentieth-Century Magazine* (June 1911): 222.

4. Daniel T. Rodgers, *Atlantic Crossings: Social Politics in a Progressive Age* (Cambridge, Mass.: Harvard University Press, 1998), 182, 262, 267, 552 n. 69. In an otherwise admirable work, Rodgers's *Atlantic Crossings* sidesteps powerful transnational currents of Victorian moral reform that infused early-twentieth-century discussions of "social work," the cult of "thrift," the rise of the "Progressive physician" movement, and other central forces of Progressive social politics. Clarke A. Chambers, *Paul U. Kellogg and the* Survey: *Voices for Social Welfare and Social Justice* (Minneapolis: University of Minnesota Press, 1971). "The Gist of It," *The Survey* 36, no. 6 (May 6, 1916): 1.

5. "List of Friends Associated with James L. Cowles in His Postal Progress Work" (n.d.), and Postal Progress League letterhead, B 4, James Lewis Cowles Papers, Manuscripts and Archives Division, New York Public Library. Samuel Gompers to James Cowles, July 12, 1906; John Mitchell to James Cowles, July 11, 1906; both in "Promotional Material of the Postal Progress League and the World Postal League, 1909–1918," Cowles Papers. Richard Kielbowicz, "Government Goes into Business: Parcel Post in the Nation's Political Economy," *Studies in American Political Development* 8 (spring 1994): 164. Leach, *Land of Desire,* 183. James Cowles to Postmaster General George von Lengerke Meyer, August 16, 1907, and March 13, 1909, F 15, George von Lengerke Meyer Papers, Massachusetts Historical Society, Boston, Massachusetts.

6. On postal cooperation with Wiley, see B 3, Office of the Solicitor, General Records, 1905–21, NA I, RG 28, E 36. James Harvey Young, *Medical Messiahs: A History of Quackery in the Twentieth Century* (Princeton: Princeton University Press, 1967). The very *Survey* issue of May 1916 that noted the progressive mind of the department

just two paragraphs later worried about the dangers of "gonorrheal infections of brides." On liberal support, see Fowler, *Unmailable,* 127.

7. "Fighting the Fraudulent Promoters," *World's Work* 46, no. 3 (July 1923): 251; Harry S. New, "Closing the Mail Box to Frauds," *World's Work* (August 1923): 255; "Better Sentences for Crooked Promoters," *World's Work* (August 1923); "Making Crooked Promotion Unprofitable," *World's Work* (August 1923): 384–88; Rush Simmons, "How Uncle Sam Protects Your Mail," *The American Magazine,* May 1924, 62. P. V. DeGraw, "Uncle Sam's Postal Service," *The Outlook* (April 18, 1914): 839–43.

8. As Jean Keith Schroedel and Richard Snyder report, "[N]o [postal savings] bills were seriously debated on the floor until 1908"; "People's Banking: The Promise Betrayed?" *Studies in American Political Development* 8, no. 1 (1994): 173–93, 177. Edwin Kemmerer, *Postal Savings* (Princeton: Princeton University Press, 1917). For a brief treatment of the Panic of 1907–8, see John Hicks, *The American Nation,* 2d ed. (New York: Houghton Mifflin, 1949), 414–16.

9. Schroedel and Snyder, "People's Banking." Kenneth W. Hechler, *Insurgency: Personalities and Politics of the Taft Era* (New York: Cambridge University Press, 1940).

10. M. La Rue Harrison, quoted in "Postal Savings Depositories," report submitted February 21, 1882 [to accompany H.R. 4198] by Mr. Lacey, from the House Committee on Post Office and Post Roads, in *To Establish Postal Savings Depositories,* Senate Report 525, 60th Cong., 1st sess., April 17, 1908, p. 87 (emphases added). See also John A. G. Creswell, in Postmaster General, *Annual Report* (1873), xxxiii–xliii. Schroedel and Snyder report that postal savings were "first proposed in Congress only a decade after the end of the Civil War" ("People's Banking," 174), but they neglect to mention the department's advocacy four years before, in 1871.

11. In Harrison's day money-order inspectors were organized under the money-order system itself, outside Comstock's division.

12. Rodgers, *Atlantic Crossings;* see pp. 21–32 for a general characterization. On Meyer's interest in Italian postal savings, see "The Hon. George von Lengerke Meyer," *The Roman World: A Weekly Journal of Art, Archaeology, Literature, Society, and General News* (March 4, 1905): 1. Wanamaker, in Postmaster General, *Annual Report* (1890), 12–14. J. H. Gore, "Holland's Care for Its Poor," *The Forum,* April 1896, 228; "The Post-Office and Thrift," *The Outlook* (December 12, 1908): 802; Alfred Henry Lewis, "The Political Round-Up," *The World To-Day* 21, no. 7 (January 1912): 1688.

13. It appears that immigrants were *not* using the money orders primarily to transmit funds to family and friends in their countries of origin. This alternative hypothesis is, however, impossible to test with individual data. I do, however, undertake a test using aggregate data below. If the money orders were used for transmission to family, then first-generation immigrants should have been no more likely to use postal savings banks in the United States after 1910 than native-born citizens. I report such a test in table 5.1 and discuss the results. The statistic on European money-order transmissions is in *Annual Report of the Postmaster General* (1907), cited in Marcus M. Marks, "For Postal Savings Depositories," *Charities and the Commons,* January 23, 1909, 720.

14. U.S. Congress, House of Representatives, Committee on Post Office and Post Roads, *Postal Savings Depositories,* Report 125 (January 28, 1910), 27, 60–61.

15. *Postal Savings Bank,* Hearings before the Committee on Post Office and Post Roads, House of Representatives (March 16, 1910), 4; Committee on Postal Savings Banks, "Some Considerations Concerning the Postal Savings Bank Question," Ameri-

can Bankers' Association, Savings Bank Section, December 27, 1909, quoted in *Postal Savings Bank,* 68; Schlereth, *Victorian America,* 77–85.

16. Rep. John Small of North Carolina admitted that "the main purpose of the postal savings bank is to encourage saving and national thrift." Thomas Carter, in *To Establish Postal Savings Depositories,* p. 1. Kemmerer, *Postal Savings,* 62; testimony of E. R. Gurney, vice president of the First National Bank of Fremont, Nebraska, in *Postal Savings Bank,* 15–16; ibid., 15–16, 75, 88, 156.

17. S. 6484 also authorized a one-time appropriation of $100,000 to assist the department in establishing the system. Under all the bills, postal savings that were deposited by postmasters in private banks had the full guarantee of the federal government.

18. Creer, in *Postal Savings Bank,* 39, 53. See also the testimony of Fred E. Farnsworth, ABA secretary, in ibid., 106–7. "Postal Banks and Other Things," *American Review of Reviews,* March 1910, 267.

19. Gurney, in *Postal Savings Bank,* 26–27; L. B. Caswell, "Do We Want the Postal Savings Banks?" speech introduced into the record by Senator Knute Nelson, January 13, 1909, in *Postal Savings Banks,* 60th Cong., 2d sess., Document 65, 1–4. John Harsen Rhoades, "Postal Savings Banks," *The Outlook* (January 16, 1909): 118.

20. Committee on Postal Savings Banks, "Some Considerations Concerning the Postal Savings Bank Question," quoted in *Postal Savings Bank,* 70; Gurney, in ibid., 29.

21. F. D. Wimberly, in *Postal Savings Bank,* 167–80, esp. 173. Nahum Bachelder, Master National Grange, to George von Lengerke Meyer, January 27, 1908, Meyer Papers.

22. James Cowles, in *Postal Savings Bank,* 185–95. Cowles to Meyer, March 13, 1909.

23. Lucius Teter, in *Postal Savings Bank,* Hearings (March 16, 1910), 3–4; Albert Shaw, editor, *American Review of Reviews,* to George von Lengerke Meyer, February 1, 1909, Meyer Papers. Shaw personally lobbied Iowa senator Albert Cummins on the issue.

24. For House committee petitions, see Records of the House Committee on Post Office and Post Roads, NA I, RG 233, HR 41A-F19.1, HR 45A-H18.5, HR 47A-H18.1. Florence Kelley, "Postal Savings Banks," *Charities and the Commons,* January 23, 1909, 717–19; Marcus M. Marks, "For Postal Savings Depositories," ibid., 719–21. On Kelley's lack of support for pensions, see Rodgers, *Atlantic Crossings,* 240. Marcus M. Marks to George von Lengerke Meyer, January 25, 1908, January 2, 1908, Meyer Papers. Frederick W. Coburn, "Postal Banks as Savings Bank Stimulators," *The Survey* (March 19, 1910): 947–49.

25. Frank Hitchcock to Thomas Carter, January 3, 1910, in *CR,* 61-2 (February 4, 1910): 1519. Rep. Martin B. Madden saw the money-order business as "a postal savings-bank business . . . to a limited extent" (*Postal Savings Bank,* 157). Finley statement during Joseph W. Fordney testimony, in ibid., 127. Money-order revenue statistics in report of the Penrose Commission, *Business Method of the Post-Office Department,* Senate Report [60–61] (December 2, 1907–May 30, 1908), 4:15 and exhibit 2c. Committee statement in *Postal Savings Depositories,* Senate Report 125, 61st Cong., 2d sess. (January 28, 1910).

26. Edwin. W. Kemmerer, "The United States Postal Savings Bank," *Political Science Quarterly* 26, no. 3 (September 1911): 495–96. Hitchcock to Carter, January 3, 1910, in *Postal Savings Depositories,* 1519.

27. John Weeks and William Creer, in *Postal Savings Bank,* 49. Second to having no bill at all, Teter of the ABA favored depositing the funds with the Treasury Department (ibid., 95). Cowles's remark is in ibid., 193. In its report, the Senate committee produced very few original arguments for the bill, relying instead on copious citations of the Post Office Department's annual reports and other documents (*Postal Savings Depositories,* 9, 30–31). Kemmerer, *Postal Savings,* 22.

28. The most significant amendment in the Senate was a measure attached by Republican William Borah of Idaho. Desiring to prevent the investment of postal savings funds in eastern banks saddled with 2 percent bonds, Borah offered an amendment to prohibit investment of postal savings monies in any bonds paying less than 2.25 percent annually. Borah's amendment passed. For more detailed treatments on the passage of the 1910 act, see Schroedel and Snyder, "People's Banking," 186–93; Kemmerer, "The United States Postal Savings Bank," 465, and the remarks of Rep. David Foster, *CR,* 61-2 (June 9, 1910): 8753. The "exigency" provision of the House bill struck fear among eastern banking interests and agrarians alike. Agrarians feared that if the word *exigencies* were defined loosely enough, the funds would be transferred to major eastern banks, whereas banking officials and many Republicans worried that the monies would be used for all sorts of purposes. Indeed, numerous proposals to lend the money for public purposes were received, ranging from public school loans to a bailout of the troubled reclamation program. Records of the Postal Savings System, NA I, RG 28, E 172, B 2; untitled typescript, 2 (1903), Ellwood Mead Collection, Water Resources Library, University of California, Berkeley. Testimony of Rep. Joseph Fordney, a Republican from Michigan, at the Weeks hearings, in *Postal Savings Bank,* 127–28.

29. Post Office Department Appropriation Act of March 4, 1911, section 5; Kemmerer, *Postal Savings,* 50.

30. The department's profit on the postal savings system was $172,421.67 in 1914 and leapt to $421,028.44 in 1915. Senate, Committee on Post Office and Post Roads, *Postal Savings System,* January 25, 1916, 64th Cong., 1st sess., Report 65, pp. 13–15 (committee quotation, 15). Carter B. Keene, in *Commercial and Financial Chronicle,* ABA Convention Supplement, October 14, 1916, 195. Harvard banking professor O. M. W. Sprague offered a similar argument in the Weeks committee hearings of 1910, *Postal Savings Bank,* 107. Kemmerer, *Postal Savings,* 57ff.; "Six Years of Postal Savings," *American Economic Review* 7, no. 1 (March 1917): 46–90. Schroedel and Snyder, "People's Banking," 192. Albert Burleson, "Postal Thrift," *The Independent,* March 29, 1915, 453–54; Alexander Monroe Dockery, "Postal Savings," *American Leader,* October 14, 1915, 11112–15.

31. Sharecropping is a good marker for areas where southern radicalism ran high. I include the residuals from the postal savings regression in the second (depositors) and third (deposits) regressions because the other variables in these estimations are correlated with the distribution of postal savings banks. The residual variable captures the effect on deposits of savings banks in each state whose presence is not explained by the variables that correlate with savings banks in the first regression. The "percentage rural" variable is significantly associated with savings banks, but its effect (an increase of 3.15 savings banks per population of 100,000 for every standard deviation increase in this variable) is still less than the increase associated with a standard-deviation jump in foreign-born citizens (3.3 additional banks). Moreover, the "percentage rural" variable is not associated with either depositors or deposits.

32. Kemmerer, *Postal Savings*, 57.

33. Scott James, "Building a Democratic Majority: The Progressive Party Vote and the Federal Trade Commission," *Studies in American Political Development* 9, no. 2 (fall 1995): 331–85. Irish, Italian, and Jewish immigrants often created their own savings banks. Stephen Erie, *Rainbow's End: Irish-Americans and the Dilemmas of Urban Machine Politics, 1840–1985* (Berkeley: University of California Press, 1988). For evidence that Progressive-Era Democrats did not heavily court Italians and Eastern European immigrants, see David Sarasohn, *The Party of Reform: Democrats in the Progressive Era* (Jackson: University Press of Mississippi, 1989), esp. chap. 7.

34. Skocpol, *Protecting Soldiers and Mothers*, 465–79; Gwendolyn Mink, "The Lady and the Tramp: Gender, Race, and the Origins of the American Welfare State," and Barbara Jean Nelson, "The Origins of the Two-Channel Welfare State: Workmen's Compensation and Mothers' Aid," both in *Women, the State, and Welfare*, ed. Linda Gordon (Madison: University of Wisconsin Press, 1990), 92–122 (Mink) and 123–51 (Nelson). See also Deborah A. Stone's discussion of Skocpol's book in "Conference Panel: On Theda Skocpol's *Protecting Soldiers and Mothers: The Political Origins of Social Policy in the United States*," *Studies in American Political Development* 8, (spring 1994): 111–18.

35. Kemmerer, *Postal Savings*, 6. The postal savings system continued until 1966, when it was discontinued. It achieved its greatest popularity during the Depression, with more than 1 million depositors in 1932 (and $1 billion in deposits in 1933) and peaking at 4,196,517 depositors (and $3.3 billion in credit) in 1947. By this time, most depositors were native-born.

36. Bills introduced for parcel post generally allowed the department to classify and transport all articles not exceeding eleven pounds, though early proposals allowed for a weight limit of sixty. See "A Bill for the Consolidation of Third and Fourth Class Mail Matter," S. 1020, 56th Cong., 1st sess., read December 11, 1899, House Post Office Committee files, NA I, RG 233, HR56A-H21.9. See also "Proposed Extension of Parcel Post," S. 5115 (March 6, 1908), reprinted in SED 366, 60th Cong., 1st sess. Kielbowicz, "Government Goes into Business," 150–72. Kielbowicz contends that parcel post was "arguably the deepest federal thrust into public enterprise in the early 1900s" (150 n. 2).

37. Barron, *Mixed Harvest*, 182–84.

38. Editorial, *Chicago Dry-Goods Reporter*, February 26, 1900; also March 3, 1900, p. 11. See also the petitions of Hills, Minnesota, and Pana, Illinois, in "Parcel Post," House committee files, HR56A-H21.9. Albert N. Merritt, "Shall the Scope of Governmental Functions Be Enlarged so as to Include the Express Business?" *Journal of Political Economy* 16 (July 1908): 417–35, quoted in Kielbowicz, "Government Goes into Business," 166. Charles William Burrows, "Thoughts upon Some Proposed Parcels Post Legislation," an address delivered at the Union Club, Cleveland, October 30, 1906, pp. 1, 12, Firestone Library, Princeton University. Undoubtedly, Burrows's alliance with wholesalers underlay this argument, which was more ideologically oriented than authentic, but the fact that Burrows relied on the standard rhetoric of postal inefficiency and incapacity points to the power of this idiom. David Lewis's remarks appear in *CR* (House), June 8, 1911, p. 1771. Resolutions of National Hardware Association and National Board of Trade in *Proceedings of the Thirty-sixth Annual Meeting of the National Board of Trade, January 1906* (Philadelphia: John McFetridge & Sons, 1906), p. 115.

39. "The Post-Office and the Deficit," *The Outlook,* December 14, 1907, 794–95; "Conditions of the Postal Service," *The American Review of Reviews,* March 1910, 266; "A Plain Word About the Postal Service," *World's Work,* February 1911, 13949; "Cause and Cure of Deficits," *The American Review of Reviews,* March 1911, 269.

40. As Kielbowicz reports, the rural carriers' "unplanned test," though stopped by Congress, "heartened parcel post advocates and strengthened claims that the postal system's underutilized capacity could efficiently accommodate additional services" (158). See also the remarks of S. R. Miles, *Parcels Post,* Hearings before the Committee on Post Office and Post Roads, April 1910 (Washington, D.C., 1910), 189. A 1910 survey by the National Hardware Retail Association found that the average rural carrier admitted to carrying one package per month.

41. Whatever the postmasters general felt about parcel post, "a growing cadre of postal bureaucrats saw merits in the proposal" (Kielbowicz, "Government Goes into Business," 158). Assistant postmasters general had been pressing for a parcel post program since Wanamaker's first advocacy in 1889. Meyer floated a rural parcel post bill to key members of Congress and the Roosevelt Cabinet in 1908. George von Lengerke Meyer to James R. Garfield (then secretary of the interior), February 29, 1908, with enclosed bill, Garfield Papers, C 128, file 44. On Meyer's 1907 speech, see the remarks of S. R. Miles, in *Parcels Post,* 187. See *Data Relative to Proposed Extension of Parcel Post,* SED 366, 60th Cong., 1st sess., pp. 8ff. Meyer planned addresses in Philadelphia and Chicago after his visit to Boston.

42. Albert A. Pope spearheaded the league's campaign, calling the department "the People's Mutual Transportation Company" and maintaining that "the Post Office is the only mechanism that can guarantee equal rights and privileges to all." See the Postal Progress League, *Col. Albert A. Pope's Parcels Post Bill,* pamphlet of 1906 [?], in Haugen Papers. Kielbowicz, "Government Goes into Business," 164. Leach, *Land of Desire,* 183. Cowles to Meyer, March 13, 1909; John Stahl to Meyer, February 26, 1908 (enclosing mass mailing); Stahl to Meyer, February 27, 1908; E. H. Clement, Editorial Rooms, *Boston Evening Transcript,* to Meyer, January 25, 1908; M. M. Simpson of *Advertiser's Magazine* to Meyer, March 10, 1909; all in Meyer Papers.

43. See Kielbowicz, "Government Goes into Business," 164. "Abuses in Our Postal System," *North American Review,* June 1902, 812. Leach, *Land of Desire,* 183–84.

44. See the remarks of Lewis, *CR* (House) (June 8, 1911): 1770, 1784. See also Lewis's book-length monograph, *The Express Companies: An Economic Study* (Washington, D.C., 1912), esp. 389.

45. See the remarks of Britt in Senate Committee on Post Office and Post Roads, *Parcel Post,* Hearings before the Subcommittee on Parcel Post, November–December 1911 (Washington, D.C., 1912), 1:27.

46. Kielbowicz, "Government Goes into Business," 170. The rate decisions were subject to review by the ICC, but in the period under study such a review never occurred. On the economic development of the program, see Chin Hock Ow, "The Economics of the United States Parcel Post, 1913–1970" (Ph.D. diss., Vanderbilt University, 1973). It would also be inaccurate to trace the fate of parcel post to shifting coalitions in Congress after the midterm elections of 1910. As Kielbowicz maintains, "Long before the last round of hearings concluded in April 1912, public opinion had crystallized in favor of parcel post."

47. Sterling Denhard Spero, *The Labor Movement in a Government Industry: A Study*

of Employee Organization in the Postal Service (New York: Macmillan, 1927), 125–30.

48. Given the numbers and the geographic dispersion of postal workers, their unions should have been stronger than those of other government agencies (usually organized within the National Federation of Federal Employees [NFFE]). In fact, postal unions were no stronger than the NFFE and arguably weaker. Not until the 1960s did postal employees present a united front under the umbrella of the AFL-CIO. Baxter, *Labor and Politics,* 67–75, 201–22; DiPrete, *Bureaucratic Labor Market.*

49. Spero, "The Early Years of the 'Gag Rule,'" chap. 7 in *Labor Movement;* Skowronek, *Building a New American State,* 180–82; Johnson and Libecap, *Federal Civil Service System,* 79–81.

50. Dennis, *Traveling Post Office,* 60–62; Spero, *Labor Movement,* 123ff., 141–46, 173–76; Skowronek, *Building a New American State,* 191–92. The Lloyd-LaFollette Act made statutory what had prevailed by custom before, namely that federal employees had no right to strike. On the Taft-LaFollette fight, see Spero, *Labor Movement,* 167–73.

51. My interpretation of the relationship of the department to the Reilly Act differs considerably from that of Spero (*Labor Movement,* 179), whose account is premised entirely on published sources. Although Hitchcock did write to Senate Post Office Committee chairman Jonathan Bourne opposing some of the features of the Reilly bill (Frank Hitchcock to Jonathan Bourne Jr., January 10, 1912, in Spero, *Labor Movement,* 179 n. 60), Hitchcock ultimately favored a salary increase and a boost in travel expenses for the clerks. As evidence, RPO clerks sent Hitchcock a resolution of gratitude after the reclassification passed in 1912, seven months after Bourne's letter. See "Expression of Appreciation for Reclassification of Railway Mail Service by Clerks of the Second Division, Railway Mail Service to Honorable Frank H. Hitchcock, Postmaster General, Washington, D.C.," petition letter of December 3, 1912, signed by A. J. Driscoll, "C in C" (clerk in charge), New York and Washington RPO, Frank H. Hitchcock Papers, B 2, Library of Congress.

52. For biographical accounts, see newspaper clippings, Albert S. Burleson Papers, Library of Congress. Roper's statement is in Spero, *Labor Movement,* 214; see also 186–92, 210–21. "Railway Mail Clerks Ask Burleson's Removal," *St. Louis Republic,* June 21, 1919.

53. Burleson executed the department's responsibilities under the Espionage and Trading with the Enemy Acts. "A Proper Question," *The Providence Journal,* December 3, 1919; "Loco-Mindedness Mr. Burleson's Way," *Philadelphia Ledger,* October 15, 1920; "Investigate the Whole Postal Service!" editorial, *World,* May 17, 1919; "Incompetence of Burleson Brings Storm of Disapproval from All Classes in Nation," *World,* July 14, 1919; "Burleson Should Go," editorial, *World,* July 14, 1919.

54. Gibbons, *John Wanamaker,* 1:276–320.

55. Kielbowicz, "Government Goes into Business." R. J. Harris's letter to W. H. Riddell was written from Atlanta, Georgia, on June 25, 1923, and appears at NA I, RG 28, E 120, B 1, F "1923, June." R. M. Birch, Fifth Division superintendent, Cincinnati, Ohio, to Riddell, February 3, 1923, NA I, RG 28, E 120, B 1, F "1923, Feb." Superintendent, Sixth Division, Chicago, to Riddell, February 3, 1923, NA I, RG 28, E 120, B 1, F "1923, Feb."

56. Hays was succeeded by Hubert Work, who was replaced by Henry A. Taylor in

March 1923. Work became secretary of interior. Newsletter of S. A. Cisler, superintendent, Fourteenth Division, Omaha, Nebraska, July 7, 1923, NA I, RG 28, E 120, B 1, F "1923, July." "Organization of Post Office Department. Postmaster General's Office," a note to the *Postal Bulletin,* in NA I, RG 28, E 112, B 1, F "1922."

57. Joseph Formanck, superintendent, Ninth Division, Cleveland, Ohio, to the General Superintendent's Office, February 10, 1923, NA I, RG 28, E 120, B 1, F "1923, Feb." *New York Times,* February 11, 1923, p 12. The RMA's Georgia Branch Committee stated that it was "gratified at the great meetings that have been held . . . by the Post Office Department," believing that the meetings promoted "good feeling and improved conditions for the employees" ("Resolutions, Adopted by the Georgia Branch Committee, July 5, 1923," NA I, RG 28, E 120, B 1, F "1923, July"). Newsletter of John F. Bradley, acting superintendent, Fourth Division, July 28, 1923, ibid. Undated form letter of February 1923, NA I, RG 28, E 120, B 1, F "1923, Feb." S. L. Erwin, postmaster, Honey Grove, Texas, to E. H. Hon. Shaughnessy, second assistant postmaster general, October 19, 1921, NA I, RG 28, E 112, B 1, F "1921." W. M. Collins to Will H. Hays, March 17, 1921, NA I, RG 28, E 114, B 5, F "1921, March." Spero, *Labor Movement,* 244ff.

58. Skowronek, *Building a New American State,* 177–211; Silberman, *Cages of Reason,* chap. 9. *Atlanta Constitution,* January 20, 1923. An almost identical program was followed for the Postal Conference Convention of South Carolina, January 18, 1923 (NA I, RG 28, E 120, B 1, F "1923, Jan"). Edward McGrath, superintendent, Eighth Division, RMS, to W. H. Riddell, March 1, 1923, in ibid., F "1923, March."

59. Kringel, from Fourteenth Division headquarters in Denver, January 24, 1922, NA I, RG 28, E 114, B 5, F "1922, Jan." Collins to Hays, March 17, 1921.

60. Significantly, Kringel delegated the clerical labor of the postal "business" to the post office clerks. E. H. Shaughnessy to R. S. Regar, appointment clerk, POD, September 16, 1921, NA I, RG 28, E 112, B 1, F "1921." Newsletter of Joseph Formanck, superintendent, Ninth Division, Cleveland, Ohio, October 13, 1923, NA I, RG 28, E 120, B 2, F "1923, October." Newsletter of R. S. Bramer, superintendent, Sixth Division, August 18, 1923, NA I, RG 28, E 120, B 1, F "1923, August." "Railway Mail Service Is Nation's Santa Claus," *Richmond Times-Dispatch,* December 16, 1923.

61. Kringel, from Fourteenth Division headquarters in Denver, January 24, 1922.

62. Newsletter of S. M. Gaines, superintendent, Eleventh Division, Fort Worth, Texas, July 21, 1923. Fourth Division superintendent R. J. Harris lauded the "conservative action" of Georgia branch RMA meetings in his newsletter of February 9, 1923. June 1923 newsletter of W. H. Remington, superintendent, First Division, Boston. On the RMA's unwillingness to affiliate with the AFL, see "Unwise Agitation," editorial, *RPO,* September 1902, 8. S. M. Gaines, superintendent of the Eleventh Division stationed in Fort Worth, helped the local RMS branch to find a new meeting place; see his newsletter of June 9, 1923. For an endorsement of the department's "plan of co-operation," see the report of the resolutions of the Fourth Division branch of the RMS in the *Chattanooga News,* July 25, 1923. All in NA I, RG 28, E 120, B 1, F "July," "Feb.," "June," and "July," respectively.

63. Joseph Formanck, superintendent, Ninth Division, to general superintendent, Washington, D.C., March 10, 1923, NA I, RG 28, E 120, B 1, F "1923, March." "Gets Mail Squad to Aid Post Office—Railway Clerks to Serve Here for Relief of Congestion," *Cleveland Plain Dealer,* March 15, 1923.

Chapter Six

1. Gladys L. Baker et al., *Century of Service: The First One Hundred Years of the Department of Agriculture* (Washington, D.C.: USDA, 1963), 1–12; Lyman Carrier, "The United States Agricultural Society, 1852–1860: Its Relation to the Origin of the United States Department of Agriculture and the Land-Grant Colleges," *Agricultural History* 11:278–88. The opposition to the USDA in the Midwest was paralleled by midwestern opposition to the terms of the Morrill Act. Indiana, for instance, refused to accept its Morrill land grant until 1865; Kenneth M. Stampp, *Indiana Politics during the Civil War* (Indianapolis: Indiana Historical Bureau, 1949), 258. John Y. Simon, "The Politics of the Morrill Act," *Agricultural History* 37, no. 2:103–11.

2. Act of May 5, 1862, 12 Stat. L., 387; Bensel, *Yankee Leviathan,* 376–77; Eric Foner, *Free Soil, Free Labor, Free Men: The Ideology of the Republican Party Before the Civil War* (New York: Oxford University Press, 1970). Baker et al., *Century of Service.* On Morrill's cuts, see *Congressional Globe,* 38-1: 1019–1021; William Belmont Parker, *The Life and Public Services of Justin Smith Morrill* (Boston: Houghton Mifflin, 1924), 147.

3. Act of March 1, 1862, 12 Stat. L., 348, 350 (emphasis in original).

4. Eastman was the department's consul in Bristol, England, from 1864 to 1868. See Isaac Newton, first commissioner of agriculture, to Zebina Eastman, December 12, 1864, Zebina Eastman Collection, B 1 of 2, 107a, F 2, Chicago Historical Society. See also J. M. Stokes to Zebina Eastman, June 28, 1867, August 20, 1867 (letter 226); both in ibid. Sorghum, wheat, rye, and common grains were the primary crops in the experimental farm; Baker et al., *Century of Service,* 16. Harold Faulkner, *The Decline of Laissez-Faire, 1897–1917: The Economic History of the United States,* vol. 7 (New York: Rinehart, 1951), 342.

5. The bulk of "scientific work" in the early stages of the department consisted in answering farmers' queries by mail—analyzing soil samples and specimens and making recommendations as to agricultural practice ("Journal of the Division of Chemistry, 1862–1867," NA II, RG 97, E 1; see also the Division of Chemistry's "Laboratory Journal, 1868–1878," NA II, RG 97, E 2). See also "Journals of Townend Glover," 1853, NA II, RG 54, E 61. Even in the 1890s, Division of Chemistry chief Harvey Wiley subscribed in part to the view that a prompt response to farmers' questions was the central function of the division. In an 1891 letter to a Staunton, Virginia, farmer, Wiley saw it as in the purview of the Chemistry Division not to advocate growing certain crops but only to provide information about them; NA II, RG 97, E 17, V 1, p. 349. On the education of early USDA scientists, see Baker et al., *A Century of Service.*

6. Glover appeared at the New York Convention in 1849, the Ohio Convention in 1848, the Buffalo Convention in 1848, the Genesee Valley Horticultural Society Convention in 1847, and the Pomological Congress of 1852 in Philadelphia. He had also attended the Maine Horticultural Society's convention, the Massachusetts Horticultural Society's convention of 1851, the Pennsylvania Horticultural Society's convention, and the Rochester (N.Y.) exposition of 1851. Most of these fairs were held in late summer or autumn (August through October), during the harvest season. The catalog of fruits examined and collected at fairs from 1851 to 1853 contained more than fifteen hundred entries. For each fruit, Glover listed the donor and his or her residence, allowing the department to establish a linked network of scientific donors. "Directions to Find Fruit

from Catalogue," NA II, RG 54, E 61, Catalogue, p. 1. He turned over his notes to the department in 1859, returning to add to the stock of knowledge when he resumed service as an entomologist for the department in 1863. Other scientists and bureaus in the department used his notes and references for decades, and the USDA took legal possession of his personal museum in 1897. *Scientific American,* September 28, 1897, p. 197.

7. In December 1857 Glover visited the Vilmorin-Andrieux seed interest in Paris and purchased $6,500 worth of seeds and plant specimens. And in November 1856 he visited Charlwood and Cummins Seedsmen of Covent Garden, England, purchasing 450 English pounds' worth of seeds and cuttings. "Notebooks and Related Papers of Townend Glover, 1853," NA II, RG 54, E 61. On antebellum institutions in American agriculture, see Wayne Caldwell Neely, *The Agricultural Fair* (New York: Columbia University Press, 1935); Clarence H. Danhof, *Change in Agriculture: The Northern United States, 1820–1870* (Cambridge, Mass.: Harvard University Press); Albert Lowther Demaree, *The American Agricultural Press, 1819–1860* (New York: Columbia University Press, 1941); Tamara Plakins Thornton, *Cultivating Gentlemen: The Meaning of Country Life among the Boston Elite, 1785–1860* (New Haven: Yale University Press, 1989).

8. Margaret Rossiter, *The Emergence of Agricultural Science: Justus Liebig and the Americans, 1840–1880* (New Haven: Yale University Press, 1975); William H. Brock, *Justus von Liebig: The Chemical Gatekeeper* (New York: Cambridge University Press, 1997). Edgar Fahs Smith, "Charles Mayer Wetherill," *Journal Chem. Ed.* 6:1461–77, 1668–80.

9. Watts was clearly displeased with Brown's resignation and subtly suggested that Brown owed the department at least a stint of public service. Yet in so doing Watts implicitly recognized that for most of his employees private pursuits carried greater importance and legitimacy than government service. He wrote to Brown that "[w]hilst I dare not interpose a wish that you should sacrifice your private interests for the sake of the place you now hold, yet I can but help the feeling of regret that the Department of Agriculture is about to lose the valuable [services] advantages of your Science and industry." Frederick Watts to Ryland T. Brown, December 4, 1872; see also Brown's resignation letter, December 2, 1872; both in NA II, RG 16, E 184, B 1, Ryland T. Brown file.

10. Thomas A. Woods, *Knights of the Plow: Oliver H. Kelley and the Origins of the Grange in Republican Ideology* (Ames: Iowa State University Press, 1991). Historians usually ignore the fact that all but one of the seven recognized founders of the Grange were federal civil servants (Edwin Wiest, *Agricultural Organization in the United States* [Lexington: University of Kentucky Press, 1923], 374). The first Grange was organized in Washington, D.C., and in 1868 Kelley organized another one in Fredonia, New York. After Kelley's second trip, agricultural journals began promoting the organization throughout the Midwest. Wiest reports that in Kelley's plan "[l]ecturers from the Department of Agriculture were to address members of the organization from time to time" (399). On Kelley's disillusionment, see Woods, *Knights of the Plow,* 85.

11. As Commissioner Norman Colman wrote to Henry Cabot Lodge in April 1888, "I herewith enclose a list of our Garden Seeds. These seeds comprise the great majority of those in common use throughout the country." Norman Colman to Henry Cabot Lodge, April 5, 1888, NA II, RG 16, E 4, B 1, V 10, p. 264. Colman to H. Goff, March 9, 1888, USDA-congressional correspondence, 1886–93, in NA II, RG 16, E 4, B 1, V

3, p. 188; Colman to James Blount, February 4, 1888, NA II, RG 16, E 4, B 1, V 10, p. 89. If the USDA-congressional correspondence in the National Archives is illustrative of the seed program's dynamics, one can conclude that the political demand for seeds tended to spike in national election years. As Colman wrote to Senator J. B. Beck in February 1888, "The demand upon me this year for seed is beyond precedent, and the proportion allotted the Department is insufficient to fully meet it" (Colman to Beck, February 23, 1888, NA II, RG 16, E 4, B 1, V 3, p. 135). As Colman wrote Rep. John R. Brown, "I find that I have received 25 per cent. more requests for seed this year than ever before in the history of the Department" (Colman to Brown, April 7, 1888, NA II, RG 16, E 4, B 1, V 10, p. 270). The department allotted each member a quota, but these were regularly transgressed; Colman to N. C. Blanchard (Fourth District, Georgia), March 17, 1888, B 1, V 10, p. 209.

12. See the aggregate cross-program budgetary estimates for each year in Department of Agriculture, "Finances of the Department for Seventy-One Years," *Annual Report* (1910), 591–619. The seed distribution program comprised more than 30 percent of the total departmental budget until 1883, when the Bureau of Animal Industry, a regulatory division, was established. In 1896 it remained the third largest program (behind Animal Industry and the Weather Bureau), requiring $150,000 in expenses, equivalent to more than 70 percent of the department's total scientific budget (which included many nonscientific expenditures such as publications and regulation). Secretary of Agriculture, *Annual Report* (1896), xiii. Contemporary reports indicate that the program was widely abused; John M. Gaus and Leon O. Wolcott, *Public Administration and the United States Department of Agriculture* (Chicago: Social Science Research Council, 1940), 8. The estimate of 3 million is based on an average expenditure of $0.07 per shipment per farmer (or fifteen shipments per dollar)—the approximate cost prevailing in 1893—assuming a budget of $200,000 for seeds in 1900. See also Jack R. Kloppenburg Jr., *First the Seed: The Political Economy of Plant Biotechnology, 1492–2000* (New York: Cambridge University Press, 1988), 60–65.

13. Mary Summers argues that Grange and Alliance members were consistent supporters of agricultural science, as well as of "every major bill that increased the resources of the Department of Agriculture" ("Putting Populism Back In: Rethinking Agricultural Politics and Policy," *Agricultural History* 70, no. 2 [Spring 1996]: 395–414). Yet like other neo-Populist historians, Summers relies almost entirely on secondary sources to establish her account. I am unaware of any primary-source-based narrative that demonstrates Alliance or Grange support for science *as against seeds* with the sort of evidence needed to establish the point—not the proclamations of Grange and Alliance members themselves, not the summaries of Solon Buck and Grant McConnell, but petitions, voting data, and the actual engagement of these groups with the USDA and the agriculture committees. An extensive consultation of such sources is a primary aim of this chapter.

14. On Grange and Alliance support for seed distribution, see *Country Gentleman* 22 (December 17, 1863): 401, cited in Woods, *Knights of the Plow,* 28–29, 82. Norman Colman to Hon. H. G. Turner (Georgia) , March 1, 1889, NA II, RG 16, E 4, B 2, V 11, p. 232. Jeremiah Rusk to Sen. John H. Reagan, December 31, 1889, B 2, V 11, p. 435 (in response to the secretary of the Smith Springs Alliance No. 2531). Rusk to Rep. J. A. Pickler, April 10, 1890, ibid., p. 272. Rusk to Pickler, May 1, 1890, ibid., p. 343; Rusk to Pickler, May 3, 1890, ibid., pp. 360–62. The May 1890 shipment was not the only distribution of seeds to South Dakota Alliances that year. A separate shipment of

sugar beet seeds was also sent in late April to E. P. Hoover, president of the Farmers' Alliance in Blunt, South Dakota (Rusk to Pickler, April 30, 1890, p. 351). Grange petitions for reduced rates on seeds and bulbs appear in the Papers of the Senate Committee on Post Office and Post Roads, NA I, RG 46, 49A-H19.1, 50A-H20.2, 52A-J20, 56A-J31.4.

15. These regressions are intended to establish not causation but only association. The proper inference is not that the demand for seeds led to more votes for Weaver but that voters with a higher demand for seeds were also more likely to vote for Weaver. All calculations are from the database of the USDA-congressional correspondence (1886–93), which I collected from NA II, RG 16, E 4.

16. Werner Stockberger, *Personnel Administration in the United States Department of Agriculture: The First Fifty Years* (Washington, D.C.: USDA Office of Personnel, 1947), 11–12. Consider as well the op-ed sentiments of the *American Agriculturalist* (1872), perhaps the leading journal of the national agricultural press: "One of these days the farmers will make themselves heard; then the Department of Agriculture will be quite different from what it has ever been" (quoted in Stockberger, *Personnel Administration,* 10).

17. The department stopped distributing coffee plants in 1889 after discovering that its imports were not adding to coffee production in Florida. A similar choice was made with turnip seed. Jeremiah Rusk to Charles O'Neill, September 12, 1889, NA II, RG 16, E 4, B 2, V 11, p. 355. See Gaus and Wolcott, *Public Administration,* 17. Leonard White, *The Republican Era: A Study in Administrative History, 1859–1901* (New York: Macmillan, 1958), 246.

18. The divide between applied and basic science was an especially American one, and the conflict informed much of nineteenth-century agrarian culture. Even Tocqueville wondered "Why the Americans Are More Addicted to Practical Than to Theoretical Science" (*Democracy in America,* 1835, vol. 2, sec. 10, chap. 10). Although elite cultivators had embraced some principles of agricultural chemistry as early as the 1830s, most nineteenth-century farmers continued to look with either suspicion or outright disdain upon "book farming." Their reluctance to embrace scientific agriculture can be explained in part by the lack of any reliable, observable gains to be had from it. See Deborah Fitzgerald, *The Business of Breeding: Hybrid Corn in Illinois, 1890–1940* (Ithaca: Cornell University Press, 1990). For book farmers as for others in the 1800s, farming success was volatile and unpredictable. The cultural stability of farming according to generationally transmitted precepts also accounted for the distrust of science. See Rossiter, *Emergence of Agricultural Science,* xii–xiii, 7. In contrast, Mary Summers has argued that mass political organizations occupied a central role in the rise of scientific agriculture in the nineteenth century, particularly in the attempt to establish land-grant colleges and experiment stations. See Summers, "People's Universities and Experiment Stations: Visions, Conflict, and Forgetting in the Development of Agricultural Science and Education" (paper presented at the annual meetings of the Social Science History Association, New Orleans, October 1996). Summers's arguments are intriguing, but I contend that although mass organizations helped establish educational institutions for scientific farming, they did not successfully alter the practices of the majority of nineteenth-century farmers. As Roy Scott has argued in his exhaustive book on the evolution of agricultural education, nineteenth-century farmers "listened but they were little moved" by agricultural science (*The Reluctant Farmer: The Rise of Agricultural Extension to 1914* [Champaign: University of Illinois Press, 1970], x).

19. Gaus and Wolcott, *Public Administration*, 17, and White, *Republican Era*, 250. See also the complaints of Secretary Jeremiah Rusk in the department's 1890 *Annual Report*, 540.

20. At first the department distributed farmers' bulletins to localities through their representatives in Congress (see Secretary of Agriculture, *Annual Report* [1897], 30). Later, when the volume of bulletins became too large for congressional staff to handle, distribution was accomplished through direct mailings from the department to local USDA offices (experiment stations) and regional farmers' associations.

21. Assistant Secretary Edwin Willits, in the department's 1890 *Annual Report*, 59; also Secretary Jeremiah Rusk in his 1889 *Annual Report*, 11. It appears that the publications room assumed divisional status in 1895. Secretary James Wilson (1897–1913) saw the yearbook as a "popular form of annual report" (*Annual Report* [1897], lii). For a general review of the publications strategy, see White, *Republicans*, 241.

22. Statement of Isaac Newton in his 1862 *Annual Report*, 1. Three decades later, Assistant Secretary Edwin Willits rehearsed some of the same rhetoric in the 1890 *Annual Report*, 59.

23. For a discussion of the matriculation patterns at Michigan Agricultural College in the nineteenth century, see Madison Kuhn, *Michigan State: The First Hundred Years* (East Lansing, Mich.: Michigan State University, 1955), 80.

24. Stockberger, *Personnel Administration*, 12–14. Letter from Norman Colman, commissioner of agriculture, to Rep. Milo White of Chatfield, Minnesota, October 6, 1886, NA II, RG 16, E 4, B 1, bk. 8, p. 393.

25. That is, GSR = [(USDA state total)/(USDA total)]/[(state population)/(U.S. population)].

26. Skowronek lists the USDA as covered under the merit law from 1894 to 1896 (*Building a New American State*, 70), but Stockberger's more detailed review of the history suggests that the 1890s classifications had little effect. The vast majority of the department's workers (excluding temporary laborers) were already classified under the merit law (*Personnel Administration*, 19, 99).

27. See Frederick Coville, chief of the Division of Botany, to Secretary James S. Wilson, February 24, 1900, Jesse B. Norton Personnel File, NA I. Stockberger, *Personnel Administration*, 19, 27. On the pattern of deference, see ibid., 61.

28. Emphasis added. Lyman Briggs Personnel File, E 185, B 1.

29. Milton Whitney to Charles Dabney, July 3, 1896, p. 2, Frank D. Gardner File, NPRC. Briggs later led a number of scientific studies and ascended to the leadership of the National Bureau of Standards.

30. This is consistent with a recent article on Senate confirmations of executive agency nominees; see Nolan McCarty and Rose Razaghian, "Advise and Consent," *American Journal of Political Science* 43, no. 4 (October 1999): 1122–43. The authors find little evidence that the early USDA was subject to the political confirmation dynamics affecting other departments (tables 1 and 5). On the norm of deference for bureau chiefs, see Stockberger, *Personnel Administration*, 36.

31. In summary, as Gaus and Wolcott remark, administrative selection created "a characteristic personnel, derived from the increasing number of civil servants recruited from the land-grant institutions." USDA employees were literally "farm-bred," and they shared a heritage as "natural scientists by training" (*Public Administration*, 15–16).

32. There are two shortcomings of this analysis that warrant discussion here. First,

my choice of the county as the unit of analysis may leave the geographic estimations vulnerable to ecological fallacies or biases. For a thorough discussion of this issue, see Gary King, *A Solution to the Ecological Inference Problem* (Princeton: Princeton University Press, 1997). A second problem is that the county data elide two important stages of the recruitment process: self-selection and agency selection. Ideally, one would want data on those individuals who applied to the USDA but who were not selected for employment. As Thomas DiPrete (*The Bureaucratic Labor Market,* 120) suggests, and as far as I am aware, no such data exist. Moreover, as I have argued, there is good reason to believe that self-selection patterns reinforced the bureau chiefs' preferences.

I analyze these counts in a negative binomial regression model that accounts for the overdispersion of the data from a baseline Poisson distribution (for a discussion, see Gary King, *Unifying Political Methodology: The Likelihood Theory of Statistical Inference* [New York: Cambridge University Press, 1989], 51–52). Overdispersion may follow from contagion and communication networks: within any county, recruitment begets more recruitment. Tests show that the employee counts are consistent with these assumptions.

33. The Republican and Populist voting percentages were created using an instrumental variables procedure. Each raw voting percentage was regressed upon the following set of variables: log of county population, size of county, effective tax rate on manufacturing, percentage of farms rented for crop and cash, average county farm values (logged) and their square, total fertilizer and machinery spending on farms (both logged), percentage of county population of African Americans, and literacy rate, plus East, Midwest, and South dummies. The principal instrument used here is the county's effective tax rate on manufacturing income, the sum of collected taxes on manufacturing divided by the total manufacturing product for the county. This variable is negatively correlated with Republican voting patterns (rho $= -0.18$; *t*-stat in the regression $= -6.29$), as expected, but insignificantly correlated with USDA recruitment (rho $= -0.06$). It is also uncorrelated with manufacturing capitalization (rho $= -0.06$), which means that it is not correlated with industrialization-related variables that may be associated with USDA recruitment.

If the instrumental substitutes are replaced by the actual voting aggregates, two results change. First, the Republican percentage vote estimates positive and robust but remains substantively insignificant. The estimated marginal effect of a one-standard deviation increase in Republican voting is 0.174 additional USDA employees from a county. In other words, a full five-standard-deviation increase in Republican voting is insufficient to yield a mere additional USDA matriculant from a county. Second, the coefficient on the seed demand variable declines but remains negative.

34. The state-level memberships for these groups were taken and, for each county, were multiplied by the fraction of the state's population in the county. This adjusted aggregate was then regressed upon the following variables—the percentage of families on farms, machinery and fertilizer expenditures, average agricultural productivity, the percentage of farms rented for crop, and the log of average farm land values and its square— and the predicted county memberships were retrieved for use as instruments.

35. Another caveat is in order: many of these patterns may be driven by cross-county variation in the probability of passing the civil service examination. Assuming this probability was increasing in average skill levels, then by any definition of such skill, this variable was probably higher in advanced (mechanized and fertilizer-prone) farming

communities, in the North, and in areas that were likely to demand informational goods from the government. Yet if cross-county variation in passage of the merit examinations is driving the results here, we would expect the relationships to hold for other departments that had a civil service examination. In a separate analysis I have taken the same set of independent variables used in table 6.3 and analyzed Department of Treasury selection in 1905. I find that most of the factors that affect USDA selection either do not affect Treasury selection or have the opposite effect. Treasury employees in 1905 were *more* likely to come from the South, *less* likely to come from farming communities with higher mechanization and fertilization, and *less* likely to come from districts with high informational demand.

36. These recruitment patterns would continue well into the twentieth century. By 1944 an internal USDA newsletter could properly remark that an employee without farm experience or land-grant education was "[set apart] in a Department where farm and 'ag' college backgrounds are often regarded as basic requirements for policy-making and many technical jobs" (*USDA* [department newsletter], October 16, 1944, p. 2). For a more general argument that USDA personnel were turning to science in the late 1800s, see Gaus and Wolcott, *Public Administration,* 15–16. The actual effects of the land-grant county variable are probably larger, for many land-grant graduates did not switch their legal residence to the land-grant county. Indeed, National Archives personnel data suggest that 34 percent of the USDA's employees and 57 percent of its college-educated employees came from land-grant institutions (calculations from a database collected by author).

37. See Rusk's response in the 1890 *Annual Report,* 56; White, *Republicans,* 237.

38. Norman Colman to Rep. Jos. Wheeler, April 2, 1886, USDA-congressional correspondence, 1886–93, NA II, RG 16, E 4, B 1, F 8, p. 146. Colman to Rep. H. S. Van Eaton, Sixth District, Mississippi, April 16, 1886, NA II, RG 16, B 1, bk. 8, p. 162. Colman to Senator Wm. B. Allison, July 22, 1886, ibid., p. 344. In contrast, writing to Sen. William Hearst of California two days later, Colman did not use "Your obedient servant" (Colman to Hearst, July 24, 1886, ibid., p. 3471/2). White summarizes the tension as follows: "Despite the dominant interest of many Congressmen in the free distribution of seeds to their constituents, the departmental personnel was primarily concerned with science, not seeds; with experimentation, not partisanship; with long-run, not merely immediate gains" (*Republican Era,* 243).

39. Morton felt that the Seed Division had grown to "unwieldy, unnecessary, and extravagant proportions." He proposed its abolition in 1894, citing its failure to demonstrate "any appreciable advantage" to American agriculture (1893–94 *Annual Report,* 19–20). White offers a concise review of the conflict (*Republican Era,* 238–39). Morton's relationship to the department was strained. A conservative antisilver ideologue, he was hostile at times to the department's very existence. Morton also reduced USDA expenditure in other areas; Baker et al., *A Century of Service,* 34. Oscar Anderson, *The Health of a Nation: Harvey W. Wiley and the Fight for Pure Food* (Chicago: University of Cincinnati Press, 1958), 87–89. Morton also earned the enmity of western agrarians. See the generally favorable biography of James C. Olson, *J. Sterling Morton* (Lincoln: University of Nebraska Press, 1942), chap. 23, "Secretary of Agriculture," and chap. 24, "Cleveland's Stormy Petrel," esp. 356–63. Morton's argument against seed distribution appears in his 1893 *Annual Report,* 69. See the proposed estimates for fiscal year 1895 (*Annual Report* [1893–94], 412–13).

40. Henry C. Hansbrough's statement appears in *CR,* 54-1, 487. In keeping with his preference for greater economy, Morton did not protest the reduced scientific monies. Between 1893 and 1897, for example, the funding for the Bureau of Animal Industry was reduced by more than $200,000, and research monies for "[b]otanical investigations and experiments" (mainly for the Division of Botany) were reduced by half, from $30,000 to $15,000 over the same period ("Finances of the Department for Seventy-One Years," *Annual Report* [1910], 600–602). The funding cuts doubtless affected research and regulatory functions, as the department remained highly dependent on yearly congressional appropriations (rather than statutory authority) to perform even the most basic operations during this period (William L. Wanlass, *The United States Department of Agriculture: A Study in Administration* [Baltimore: Johns Hopkins University Press, 1920], 30). Morton frequently impounded congressional funds; it was only the seed impoundments that brought congressional protest. In fiscal year 1892, $2,303,655.75 was appropriated, and $2,253,262.29 was spent. In fiscal year 1895, $2,506,915.00 was appropriated, and only $2,021,030.38 was spent (Baker et al., *Century of Service,* 34). Kloppenburg, *First the Seed,* 60–65.

The available data show that White (*Republican Era,* 239) erred in his judgment that Morton was able to maintain the department's research funding during his tenure. White suggested that Morton's economies did not impair the USDA's analytic capacities, but White relied on Morton's own statements (in the 1895 *Annual Report*) in drawing this conclusion, whereas the budgetary data cited earlier suggest that funding was cut for a number of programs from 1893 to 1897. In no case did research monies increase for any program during Morton's four years.

41. Stockberger (*Personnel Administration,* 84, 97–100) documents the high turnover and resentment of the department's scientists. Throughout Morton's tenure, USDA employees continued to work out of their homes in open disobedience of executive orders by Rusk and Morton (73). Among these were A. W. Harris, director of the department's experiment stations, Major B. F. Fuller, chief of the Accounts and Disbursing Office, and C. V. Riley, the department entomologist. On executive orders, see ibid., 72.

42. Wiley agreed with Collier that abundant sugar could be produced from sorghum and that sorghum, which unlike cane could be grown in numerous climates in the United States, could become a large-scale crop in America. Harvey Washington Wiley, *An Autobiography* (Indianapolis: Bobbs-Merrill, 1930); Anderson, *Health of a Nation,* 29. Before Wiley's arrival, the department's only effort with sugar beets lay in seed distribution. See Colorado governor B. H. Eaton's request for beet seed; Norman Colman to Sen. H. M. Teller, April 23, 1888, NA II, RG 16, E 4, B 1, V 10, p. 298.

43. John Alfred Heitmann, *The Modernization of the Louisiana Sugar Industry, 1830–1910* (Baton Rouge: Louisiana State University Press, 1987). For southern praise of Wiley's "friendly" efforts toward sugar interests, see *New Orleans Picayune,* July 15, 1897; *New York Sun,* July 3, 1897; *American Agriculturist,* September 11, 1897. Wiley details the experiments in USDA Division of Chemistry, *Bulletin 17: Record of Experiments Conducted by the Commissioner of Agriculture in the Manufacture of Sugar from Sorghum and Sugar Canes* (Washington, D.C., 1888). Theodore Wilkinson, "The Sugar Question, with Certain Allegations on the Subject, Considered," House speech, July 9, 1888, copy in "Sugar Industry," Vertical Files (2), Louisiana Collection, Howard-Tilton Memorial Library, Tulane University, New Orleans, Louisiana. See also Clayton A. Coppin and Jack High, "Entrepreneurship and Competition in Bureaucracy: Harvey

Washington Wiley's Bureau of Chemistry, 1883–1903," in *Regulation: Economic Theory and History,* ed. Jack High (Ann Arbor: University of Michigan Press, 1991), 95–118.

44. When sugar production began to decline mysteriously in the 1910s—even while commodity prices were rising across agricultural products—the USDA's E. W. Brandes diagnosed the problem as the dread mosaic disease. Along with Arthur Rosenfeld of the Louisiana State Experiment Station, the department developed several mosaic-resistant cane varieties known as P.O.J. strains. Whatever the USDA's actual contribution, state analysts and sugar officials commonly credited the department with saving the Louisiana sugar industry in the 1920s. See "Louisiana Sugar Comes Back," *New Orleans Item-Tribune,* January 29, 1928. See also the South Coast Company, *The Story of the South Coast Company* (1928); Arthur Rosenfeld, *The Decline and Renaissance of Louisiana's Sugar Industry,* reprint (1929); both in "Sugar Industry," Vertical Files (1 and 2), Louisiana Collection. See also the "Address by R. E. Rose, State Chemist, at the Second Annual Convention of the Inter-State Cane Growers Association, Jacksonville, May 4–6, 1904," ibid. (file "Sugar, J-Z").

45. Rural communities welcomed Hines with enthusiasm; *Auburn (N.Y.) Advertiser,* November 13, 1897. Six hundred people attended Wiley's Rochester, New York, lecture (*Syracuse Standard,* December 24, 1897). Successful beet agriculture required that refining factories be located nearby beet fields, creating in Wiley's vision a truly industrialized agriculture. As Wiley held, "[T]he beet industry . . . is one of the agricultural industries with which manufacture is indissolubly united. The factory is as necessary as the field." See Wiley's speech "The Sugar Beet: The Ideal Crop for Irrigated Areas," NA II, RG 97, E 27, B 1, V "1903," pp. 16ff.

46. *Elmira Advertiser,* October 5, 1897. The *Indianapolis Journal* called Wiley "Chemist of the United States" (October 20, 1897), and the *Saginaw Evening News* named Wiley the nation's "highest authority" on the sugar beet question (October 28, 1897). The reports of the Division of Chemistry also made their way to eastern trade and finance journals interested in the viability of the sugar beet industry; *Manufacturers' Record (Baltimore),* October 15, 1897. See also *Cultivator and Country Gentleman,* November 11, 1897. For an example of the recognition Wiley received in Florida and Louisiana, see Reginald Dykers, "In the Louisiana Sugar Belt," *The Southern States* (May 1983): 126–27 (quoting an article on Wiley in the *Florida Farmer*), "Sugar Industry," Vertical Files (2), Louisiana Collection. The status of the beet sugar industry after Wiley's campaign is summarized in a 1917 Federal Trade Commission monograph, *Report on the Beet Sugar Industry in the United States* (Washington, D.C.: GPO, May 24, 1917). Annual investigations of the industry and its status were also conducted by the Bureau of Plant Industry, for example, *Progress of the Beet-Sugar Industry in the United States in 1907,* Department of Agriculture Report no. 68 (Washington, D.C.: GPO, 1908).

47. *Troy Daily Times,* December 13, 1897; Anderson, *Health of a Nation,* 13–21. Wiley, "The Sugar Beet," pp. 16ff.

48. Rossiter, *Emergence of Agricultural Science,* 149–71; Alan Marcus, "Setting the Standards: Fertilizers, State Chemists, and Early National Commercial Regulation, 1880–1887," *Agricultural History* 61 (1987): 47–73; Anderson, *Health of a Nation,* 68–69; James Harvey Young, *Pure Food: Securing the Pure Food and Drug Act of 1906* (Princeton: Princeton University Press, 1989), 123–24.

49. The NBT's support for a *national* measure was weak at best, usually coming in the form of a vague resolution for a "judicious" law against food adulteration; *Proceedings of the Nineteenth Annual Meeting of the National Board of Trade, 1889* (Boston: George Crosby, 1890), 98; *Proceedings of the Twenty-second Annual Meeting of the National Board of Trade, 1892* (Boston: George Crosby, 1893), 250. Mitchell Okun, *Fair Play in the Marketplace: The First Battle for Pure Food and Drugs* (De Kalb, Ill.: Northern Illinois University Press, 1986), 149–54. See also p. 177 for a discussion of New York's 1884 pharmacy reforms. Okun argues that "the NBT was the dominant nationwide organization representing the interests of middle-sized business firms" (121). Young discusses the fertilizer debates in *Pure Food*, 123, and the AMA advertising controversy on p. 141.

50. Department of Agriculture, *Division of Chemistry Bulletin 13: Foods and Food Adulterants,* pts. 1 through 13 (Washington, D.C., 1887–93). Anderson, *Health of a Nation,* 70–74; Young, *Pure Food,* 103–6. Beer was analyzed in pt. 3, *Fermented Alcoholic Beverages, Malt Liquors, Wine, and Cider* (1887), and baking powders were discussed in pt. 5, *Baking Sodas* (1887). The discovery of sulfurous and salicylic acid and copper sulfate in canned vegetables was reported in pt. 8, *Canned Vegetables* (1893).

51. Algernon Paddock's remarks are in *CR* (52-1), 1717; Young, *Pure Food,* 99.

52. Wedderburn was formerly the editor of *National Farm and Fireside* and served as secretary of the legislative committee of the Virginia Grange. For Wedderburn's appointment, see USDA Appointment Records, NA II, RG 16, E 185. See Wedderburn, *Division of Chemistry Bulletin 25: A Popular Treatise on the Extent and Character of Food Adulteration* (Washington, D.C., 1890). Wedderburn revised and updated *Bulletin 25* two years later, in *Bulletin 32: Special Report on the Extent and Character of Food Adulterations* (Washington, D.C., 1892); Anderson, *Health of a Nation,* 74–75; Young, *Pure Food,* 106.

53. On the patent medicines and their advertisements, see James Harvey Young, *The Toadstool Millionaires: A Social History of Patent Medicines in America before Federal Regulation* (Princeton: Princeton University Press, 1961). Young discusses "quackery" in the twentieth century in *The Medical Messiahs: A Social History of Health Quackery in Twentieth-Century America* (Princeton: Princeton University Press, 1967). Anderson, *Health of a Nation,* 121–22; Young, *Pure Food,* 187–88.

54. The figure on bills introduced in Congress is in Thomas A. Bailey's "Congressional Opposition to Pure Food Legislation, 1879–1906," *American Journal of Sociology* 36 (July 1930): 52; Okun, *Fair Play,* 3. The National Grange and the Farmers' National Congress also supported a federal food law; Anderson, *Health of a Nation,* 124. On the Paddock bill, see Stephen Wilson, *Food and Drug Regulation* (Washington, D.C.: American Council on Public Affairs, 1942), 15.

55. On Fernow's leadership role in the 1891 AAAS meetings, see "Economics and Statistics," *Washington Star,* July 23, 1891. Fernow presented his speech "Need of a National Forest Administration" at this meeting. See also *New York Nation,* July 30, 1891. Fernow also began the USDA's push for a national arboretum, a campaign that would utilize the energies of several department scientists, including Pinchot, Merriam, and Frederick Coville. Harold K. Steen, "Origins and Significance of the National Forest System," in *The Origins of the National Forests,* ed. Harold K. Steen (Durham, N.C.: Forest History Society, 1992), 5. Of the association and the division, Steen argues that "it is no coincidence that the driving force in both institutions was Bernhard Eduard Fer-

now" (5). On Fernow's training and early career, see Andrew Denny Rodgers III, *Bernhard Eduard Fernow: A Story of North American Forestry* (Princeton: Princeton University Press, 1951; Durham, N.C.: Forest History Society, 1991). See also Char Miller, "Wooden Politics: Bernhard Fernow and the Quest for a National Forest Policy, 1876–1898," in *Origins of the National Forests*, ed. Steen, 287–300.

56. Samuel Hays gives short shrift to Fernow's career and incorrectly suggests that "Fernow believed that the Forestry Division should merely dispense information and technical advice to those who sought it, and not promote sustained-yield practices" (*Conservation and the Gospel of Efficiency: The Progressive Conservation Movement, 1890–1920* [Cambridge, Mass.: Harvard University Press, 1959], 29). When starting their state forestry association, the citizens of Louisville, Kentucky, invited Fernow to give a lecture. Colman to Hon. Asher G. Caruth, House of Reps., April 7, 1888, NA II, RG 16, E 4, B 1, V 10, p. 269. In 1891 the University of Nebraska at Lincoln asked Fernow to organize a set of lectures for forestry students on its campus; *Annual Report* (1891), 195–96. See also Commissioner Jeremiah Rusk to H. Clay Evans (Tennessee), March 22, 1890, NA II, RG 16, E 4, B 2, V 12, p. 190.

57. John Ise, *The United States Forest Policy* (New Haven: Yale University Press, 1920), 115. Ise accepts Fernow's later claim that he and Edward A. Bowers, of the American Forestry Association, "had educated Noble up to the point" of demanding the insertion of the forest-reserve clause of the 1891 law, referring to Interior Secretary Edwin Noble. Gifford Pinchot, *Breaking New Ground* (New York: Harcourt, Brace, 1947), 85; Pinchot argues (84–85) that Fernow's 1888 draft "was the ancestor of many bills that followed," and he gave credit for the 1891 act to Secretary Edwin Noble of the Interior Department and Edward A. Bowers of the General Land Office. Harold K. Steen, *The Beginning of the National Forest System* (Washington, D.C.: USDA Forest Service, 1991). See also Miller, "Wooden Politics," 290. The literal author of section 24 was probably Congressman William Holman of Indiana; see Ron Arnold, "Congressman William Holman of Indiana: Unknown Founder of the National Forests," in *Origins of the National Forests*, ed. Steen, 301–13. Bernhard Fernow, Forestry Division, *Annual Report* (1891), 223, 226–27; Fernow pointed out the system of the thorough inspection of local offices by the Prussian Forestry Department as a practice worthy of American emulation (227).

58. Pisani, "Forests and Conservation, 1865–1890," chap. 7 in *Water, Land, and Law*, 137. Pisani makes a persuasive case that the federal government did not achieve the genuine "rationality" that Hays attributes to it in *Conservation and the Gospel of Efficiency*. Yet whether or not the Division of Forestry achieved rationality from the historians' perspective, it certainly achieved the veneer of rationality at the time. See Rodgers, *Bernhard Eduard Fernow*.

59. Pinchot, *Breaking New Ground*, 147–53; Hays, *Conservation and the Gospel of Efficiency*, 29–31; Miller, "Wooden Politics," 297; Harold T. Pinkett, *Gifford Pinchot: Public and Private Forester* (Champaign: University of Illinois Press, 1970), 47–48.

60. Merriam worked for the Department of Interior in 1872 and for the U.S. Fishing Commission in 1875. Like Pinchot, he was a Yale graduate (1877) who received his M.D. from the New York College of Physicians and Surgeons (C. Hart Merriam Personnel File, NA II, RG 16, E 184). Baker et al., *Century of Service*, 23–24. Merriam's report on the sparrow plague was widely sought by foreign governments dealing with the problem. See Secretary for Agriculture, Government of Nova Scotia, Office for Agri-

culture, Halifax, to Charles Hart Merriam, September 2, 1887, BANC FILM 1958, reel 75, frame 89ff., C. Hart Merriam Papers, Bancroft Library, University of California, Berkeley.

In his first letter to Merriam, Roosevelt reported that in his brief hunting career he had shot at least one of each species of birds that Merriam had studied; Roosevelt (in Cambridge, Massachusetts) to Merriam, March 7, 1877, BANC FILM 1958, reel 78, frame 2. Merriam and Roosevelt dined frequently in the 1880s; Herbert G. Ogden to Merriam, May 21, 1889, BANC FILM 1958, reel 75, frame 97. Roosevelt also lobbied fellow party members on behalf of Merriam's favored bills. Roosevelt to Merriam, February 18, 1896, BANC FILM 1958, reel 78, frame 39. "I have written to a dozen Senators and Congressmen, including Tom Reed, and urging as strongly as I could the passage of that bill."

61. See the petitions as follows: House Agriculture Committee, "forest lands" (RG 233, 45A-H2.5, 50A-H1.3); Committee on Public Lands, "forest reservations and timber lands" (RG 233, 37A-E16.11, 53A-F38.3); Senate Committee on Agriculture, "forest reserves" (RG 46, SEN 43A-H1, 45A-H1). Herbert D, Kirkland, "The American Forests, 1864–1898: A Trend toward Conservation" (Ph.D. diss., Florida State University, 1971); J. A. Miller, "Congress and the Origins of Conservation: Natural Resource Policies, 1865–1900" (Ph.D. diss., University of Minnesota, 1973).

62. See Fairchild's autobiography, *The World Was My Garden* (New York: Charles Scribner's Sons, 1939), esp. chap. 7, "The Lathrop-Fairchild Odyssey Begins." See also the fascinating correspondence between David Fairchild and Jared Smith of the Office of Seed and Plant Introduction (established in 1898), in Fairchild's mounted letters (NA II, RG 54, E 15).

63. Jim Patrico, "Mark Carleton: Wheat's Johnny Appleseed," *Progressive Farmer,* November 1999, 20. Unfortunately, Carleton's import was all but ignored in the congressional Free Seed program, which continued to dispense garden varieties. Instead, Russian winter wheat was diffused through the land-grant colleges to which Galloway's section gave free samples. For figures on the extent of durum wheat cultivation, see Fairchild, *The World Was My Garden,* 115–16. Mary W. M. Hargreaves discusses the "diligent research" of Carleton in *Dry Farming in the Northern Great Plains, 1900–1925* (Cambridge, Mass.: Harvard University Press, 1957), 328. See also the National Archives photos of Carleton's trip (RG 16, 16-G-2-218-BPI-714), in *Farmers, Bureaucrats, and Middlemen,* ed. Trudy Huskamp Peterson (Washington, D.C.: Howard University Press, 1980), 184. T. Swann Harding, *Two Blades of Grass: A History of Scientific Development in the U.S. Department of Agriculture* (Norman, Okla.: University of Oklahoma Press, 1947).

64. On the popularity of the *Yearbook* in Europe, see David Fairchild (at Turin) to Ernst Bessey, May 24, 1901, NA II, RG 54, E 15, V 2. On the procurement of Semsch hops, see Fairchild to Jared Smith, March 8, 1901, NA II, RG 54, E 15, V 2.

65. Jamie Cole, "Marion Dorset"; Karl Wolfshohl, "Mark Francis"; both in *Progressive Farmer,* November 1999, 31, 34.

66. As Summers argues, the Grange also helped elevate the USDA to Cabinet status in 1889, as the first demand of its 1879 national platform was the elevation of the USDA (see "People's Universities and Experiment Stations"). Still, this is hardly surprising, given that many of the Grange's early leaders were current or former USDA employees, and it was not entirely significant, given that Cabinet status was not achieved for another

decade. Moreover, the effect of Cabinet status on the department has been overstated; Wiley, Galloway, Fernow, and many of the department's most famous scientists came to the department several years before the elevation (see table 6.2). For petitions to elevate the USDA to Cabinet status, see the Records of the Senate Committee on Agriculture and Forestry (NA I, RG 46, SEN 45A-H1, A-H1.1).

As Thomas Woods argues of the early Grange, it was animated by "a new desire to contain individual liberty through legislative controls on monopoly capitalism," and it also sought "legislative remediation of the problems of farmers" (Woods, *Knights of the Plow*, xv, xx).

Chapter Seven

1. Horace Plunkett, "Better Farming, Better Business, Better Living," *The Outlook* 94 (1910): 497; paraphrased from Keller, *Regulating a New Economy*, 150. A. Frank Lever, "Origins and Objects of Agricultural Extension Work," South Carolina Agricultural Extension Service, Circular 143 (Clemson, S.C., 1935), n.p.; quoted in Scott, *Reluctant Farmer*, 298. In terms of the important distinction drawn by sociologist Mark Granovetter, the department was characterized by officials webbed together by collaborative "strong ties" on the inside, with numerous and overlapping "weak tie" affiliations on the outside. Mark Granovetter, "The Strength of Weak Ties," *American Journal of Sociology* 78 (1973): 1360–80. In the early 1900s the Cosmos Club was composed entirely of white males, usually government scientists. In recent years, it has come under criticism for its racially and sexually exclusive membership.

2. Willard L. Hoing, "James S. Wilson as Secretary of Agriculture, 1897–1913" (Ph.D. diss., University of Wisconsin, 1964). Russell Lord, *The Wallaces of Iowa* (Boston: Houghton Mifflin, 1947), 90–93. I thank Mary Summers and Jess Gilbert for impressing upon me the importance of these early ties to the Wallace family and to the antimonopoly campaigns. White, *Republican Era*, 239; Gaus and Wolcott, *Public Administration*, 16.

3. Secretary of Agriculture, *Annual Report* (1897), p. v. Contrast the certainty of mission expressed in this statement with the dubious prelude of Morton in the 1893–94 *Annual Report:* "This Department . . . is . . . the youngest in the Executive branch of the Government of the United States, and not yet perfectly emerged from the period of formation. Even its objects, its duties, and its possibilities are only dimly defined or vaguely surmised. It is difficult to deduce clearly from the law which created it the functions that the lawmakers designed it to exercise. It is still more difficult to determine where duty in the management and direction of this Department begins and where it ends, under existing statutes" (7).

4. Wilson crafted the department as a repository and producer of information: "This Department differs from the others. Appropriations for its use are investments. It makes direct returns by adding to the wealth of the country. It gathers facts and spreads information" (*Annual Report* [1900], ix). As Wilson stated in his first report: "The Department is now the most comprehensive repository of scientific facts regarding agriculture in all its relations to mankind, and a publisher of this kind of information more extensive than is found anywhere else" (*Annual Report* [1897], liv). See also the 1900 *Annual Report*, 31. On later "rehearsals" of this message, compare the 1900 *Annual Report*, ix, and 1910 *Annual Report*, 158.

5. See the 1912 *Annual Report,* 114; Gaus and Wolcott, *Public Administration,* 16. On the "corps of experts," see the 1897 *Annual Report,* vii–viii; 1912 *Annual Report,* 114, 258. "Uncle Sam's Work for the Farmer," *Chicago Record Herald,* November 14, 1903. See Wilson's speeches, "Agricultural Education," "Agricultural Education in the United States," "Education for the Farmer" (to the University of Missouri), "The Education of the American Farmer" (to the National Education Association), all in James S. Wilson Papers, Iowa State University, hereafter *JSW.* Harding, *Two Blades of Grass.*

6. See the 1900 *Annual Report,* lxxvi.

7. Secretary of Agriculture, *Annual Report* (1893–94), 7.

8. See the 1897 *Annual Report,* v, xiii, and 1900 *Annual Report,* 31. Wilson's advocacy of domestic science intimates a rather tight connection between the corporate metaphor and gendered divisions of labor: "Now, what has been done for the boy in agriculture and engineering needs to be done for the girl in domestic art and science" (*Annual Report* [1897], xiv). James S. Wilson, "The Education of the American Farmer," *Proceedings of the National Education Association, 1902* (Washington, D.C., 1902), 93–100.

9. Employees' self-descriptions on personnel forms provide perhaps the best evidence of the transformation of departmental discourse under Wilson, because one can compare 1890s, 1900s, and 1910s self-descriptions for the same employees. For instance, on his 1898 personnel form, USDA plant physiologist Mark A. Carleton listed himself as having been trained and educated in "Teaching," but by 1912 he felt he was trained to be an "Agriculturist." From USDA personnel questionnaires, NA II, RG 16, E 184, Mark A. Carleton Personnel File. Completing the very same forms as Carleton, Charles Richard Dodge, curator of the department's Agricultural Museum, having described himself as an "Economic Scientist" in 1898, proclaimed devotion to "Agricultural Science" in 1907.

On Wilson's use of "American Agriculture," see his diplomatic greeting letter for traveling physiologist Mark A. Carleton, July 1, 1898, NA II, RG 16, E 184, B 2, Carleton Personnel File. Wiley's prophecy of an "empire of Agriculture" appears in a 1903 lecture tour speech, "The Sugar Beet," pp. 16ff.

10. Emphasis mine. See Secretary of Agriculture, *Annual Report* (1897), p. liv. The USDA's seal was arguably the most widely used and ornate imagery in the federal bureaucracy of the early 1900s. Stockberger (*Personnel Administration,* 92) reports that "from 1895 to 1913, the seal was impressed upon all notifications of appointments, promotion, or other personnel actions, each of which bore in addition the holographic signature of the Secretary." Interestingly, the seal embodied the tension between populist and progressive visions of agriculture. In Wilson's vision, a progressive agriculture could embrace the modern industrial economy even while retaining its status as the font of virtue in the republic. In fact, he envisioned the USDA as the "vessel" of this new farming.

11. Beverly T. Galloway, chief of the Bureau of Plant Industry (BPI), to JSW, December 21, 1903, personnel file SFTUV318, NPRC. Other recommendations are in William A. Taylor, chief of BPI, to Secretary David F. Houston, January 7, 1914, NPRC, personnel file NCXBJUF362, p. 24.

12. Willet Martin Hays, later assistant secretary of agriculture, was praised for combining progressive sentiments with classic research vigor: "[Hays] is an enthusiastic student of agricultural science, understands very well, I think, the progressive movements

in modern agriculture, and is in general a vigorous and loyal worker." On the appointment of Hays, see W. H. Jordan, director of the New York Agricultural Experiment Station, to Theodore Roosevelt, July 14, 1904, NA II, RG 16, E 184, B 3, Willet Martin Hays Personnel File. See also the promotion recommendation for E. W. Nelson, the chief of the Bureau of Biological Survey, October 9, 1924, NA II, RG 16, E 184, B 7, Nelson file.

13. Margary Davis, *A Woman's Place Is at the Typewriter: Office and Office Workers, 1870–1930* (Philadelphia: Temple University Press, 1982); Elyce J. Rotella, *From Home to Office: U.S. Women at Work, 1870–1930* (Ann Arbor: University of Michigan Research Press, 1981); Carole Srole, "A Position That God Has Not Particularly Assigned to Men: The Feminization of Clerical Work, Boston, 1860–1915" (Ph.D. diss., University of California, Los Angeles, 1984); Angel Kwolek-Folland, *Engendering Business: Men and Women in the Corporate Office, 1870–1930* (Baltimore : Johns Hopkins University Press, 1994). Joseph P. Cutter to JSW, December 14, 1900, NA II, RG 16, E 184, B 2, Josephine A. Clark file.

14. For Wilson's "university" remark, see Secretary of Agriculture, *Annual Report* (1912), p. 114. I undertake a more thorough investigation of the university idiom in "The Corporate Metaphor and Executive Department Centralization in the United States, 1888–1928," *Studies in American Political Development* 12 (spring 1998): 162–203.

15. The fight for Cabinet status for the USDA had a strong proponent in Missouri congressman William Hatch, chairman of the House Agriculture Committee, who had strong ties to Agriculture Commissioner Norman Colman. The advancement of the department to Cabinet status was the number-one demand of the Grange platform of 1879. See Summers, "People's Universities and Experiment Stations," 54.

16. Wilson spent almost 90 percent of the seed funds ($133,000 of $150,000). Unexpended program funds in the range of 10 percent were quite common during this time. Compare this with Morton's $100,000 impoundment in 1895. Secretary of Agriculture, *Annual Report* (1897), vii.

17. Jesse Macy, "The National University of Agriculture," *Iowa Journal of History and Politics* 2 (July 1904): 394–98. *New York Times,* November 8, 1902; "Secretary Wilson's Report," *Pittsburgh Gazette,* December 4, 1902; "Secretary Wilson's Report," *Philadelphia Press,* December 4, 1902; "Progressive Agriculture," *Pittsburgh Gazette,* December 5, 1902; "The Mainstay of the Nation," *Colorado Springs Gazette,* December 11, 1903; "A Cabinet Officer Praised," *Daily Express,* September 10, 1902.

18. The department's organic legislation in 1862 and 1889 left the department's organization to the secretary (Gaus and Wolcott, *Public Administration*, p. 9). For Wilson's request for salary increases for "expert assistants," see *Annual Report* (1900), lxxvii. Stockberger, *Personnel Administration,* 110–11.

19. Gaus and Wolcott, *Public Administration,* 14, 19. It is important to recognize that the development of organizational forms in the American industrial economy of the early 1900s does not closely track this narrative. See the case studies of Alfred D. Chandler in *Strategy and Structure: Chapters in the History of the Industrial Enterprise* (Cambridge, Mass.: MIT Press, 1962). The management-sales-production schematization witnessed in so many of Chandler's case studies (for example, General Motors under DuPont) stands as a sharp contrast to Wilson's USDA.

Clientele-based organizations did not disappear from the USDA but instead were tucked inside scientific bureaus. In the summer of 1904, Wilson created three laboratories—among them the Sugar Analysis Laboratory (with strong connections to Louisiana sugar growers)—in the Bureau of Chemistry. See Wilson's Special Orders of July 1, 1904, Records of the Chief Clerk, Memoranda and Circular Letters, 1903–5, NA II, RG 16, E 153, B 1, F 1.

20. Stockberger, *Personnel Administration,* 119–21.

21. In an exchange with the Agriculture Committee in 1904, Wilson discussed his department's attempts to render the personnel of the Bureau of Plant Industry as homogeneous as possible in outlook. House Committee on Agriculture, January 16, 1904, p. 423.

22. Gaus and Wolcott, *Public Administration,* 15–16.

23. Letter of June 15, 1917, file Chem78, and letter of December 1, 1916, file Chem19, NPRC.

24. White (*The Republican Era,* 252) suggests that the department's scientists were webbed together by a pattern of shared ties to professional organizations in their line of research. For a brief survey of the Washington intellectual community of the period, see Michael Lacey, "The World of the Bureaus: Government and the Positivist Project in the Late Nineteenth Century," in *The State and Social Investigation in Britain and the United States,* ed. Michael Lacey and Mary O. Furner (New York: Cambridge University Press, 1993).

25. Finegold and Skocpol, *State and Party in America's New Deal,* 60.

26. Letter of June 6, 1920, file Chem186 (emphasis mine). Statistically, these historical trends imply that for USDA employees, the "hazard rate" of turnover—more specifically, the probability or instantaneous rate of leaving the agency to take another job in a given month, given that the employee had not done so before that month—constantly increased over an employee's career. This would imply a Weibull duration distribution, as the hazard rate increased steadily over time.

27. I collected membership totals from a personnel database I maintained. Personnel files are from NPRC and NA II, RG 16, E 184. Because employees were not required to divulge their organizational memberships, these numbers are a lower bound on the true number of employees who were members in these societies.

28. Skowronek, *Building a New American State,* 189.

29. John A. Stevenson, "Plants, Problems, and Personalities: The Genesis of the Bureau of Plant Industry," *Agricultural History* 28 (1954): 155–62. Kloppenburg, *First the Seed,* 66ff.

30. Carleton's imported variety of Red Russian wheat had a high yield at the Kansas Experiment Station; Mark Carleton to Beverly T. Galloway, July 23, 1897, NA II, RG 54, E 58, F 7. Galloway to JSW, January 2, 1906, NA II, RG 16, E 184, B 2, Carleton Personnel File. Mark Hufstetler and Lon Johnson, *Watering the Land: The Turbulent History of the Carlsbad Irrigation District* (Denver: National Park Service, 1993), 54. In the early 1890s cooperative relations were established between the USDA's Division of Pomology and the Berkeley station under E. W. Hilgard. The early system of agricultural extension education was thus extremely decentralized; many of the experiments in California were conducted not on the premises of the experiment station grounds but on the plots of private farmers. See William A. Taylor, acting pomologist, to E. W. Hilgard, April 12, 1892, BANC, CU-20 (Archives of University of California Experiment Station), B 2, F "Seeds 1890's." From the 1890s onward, the USDA assigned a four-

digit number to each experimental seed (or "scion") sent to an experiment station. State experiment station investigators called this the "USDA number" of the sample. A. V. Stubenrauch to J. W. Mills, March 2, 1904, BANC, CU-20, B 16, F "Seeds 1904." *New York Nation,* August 28, 1902.

31. Seaman A. Knapp to JSW, November 17, 1899, December 8, 1900; both in *JSW.* The department's awareness of Knapp's social connectedness is revealed in correspondence between Galloway, Wilson, and other bureau officials. G. H. Powell, acting chief of the bureau, to JSW, June 8, 1910, NA II, RG 16, E 184, Seaman A. Knapp Personnel File. Joseph C. Bailey, *Seaman A. Knapp: Schoolmaster of American Agriculture* (New York: Columbia University Press, 1945), 128–33; A. C. True, *A History of Agricultural Extension Work in the United States, 1785–1923* (Washington, D.C.: GPO, 1928), 58–59; Scott, *Reluctant Farmer,* 208–9; Rodney Cline, "The Life and Work of Seaman A. Knapp" (Ph.D. diss., George Peabody College for Teachers, 1936), 32–43.

32. Seaman A. Knapp to JSW, April 18, 1898, July 23, 1898, July 30, 1898, October 23, 1899, November 17, 1899, and December 8, 1900; all in *JSW.* Knapp served in Lake Charles, Louisiana, for the Division of Statistics. He was recommended to the USDA by ex-governor Warmoth. See John Hyde, USDA statistician, to JSW, April 28, 1898, Knapp Personnel File. Wilson selected Knapp himself from a list of four applicants for the position. The idea to gather Japanese rice strains was Fairchild's. David Fairchild to JSW, July 27, 1898, Knapp Personnel File. On the boosting of rice production, see USDA Division of Botany, Inventory no. 8 (1900), 60; cited in Bailey, *Seaman A. Knapp,* 143. On Wilson's and Galloway's aims, see Beverly Galloway to JSW, July 1, 1902, and June 30, 1903, Knapp Personnel File. Galloway referred to Knapp as "the Department's Representative in the South," authorizing him "to represent the Department of Agriculture in Louisiana, Texas, and such other states as may be necessary at agricultural and other meetings; locate, manage and direct demonstration experiments and secure cooperation for such work wherever inaugurated." Powell to JSW, June 8, 1910. Bailey, *Seaman A. Knapp,* 134–38; True, *History of Agricultural Extension,* 59; Scott, *Reluctant Farmer,* 209–10.

33. James S. Ferguson, "The Grange and Farmer Education in Mississippi," *Journal of Southern History* 8 (November 1942): 497–512; Theodore R. Mitchell, *Political Education in the Southern Farmers' Alliance, 1887–1900* (Madison: University of Wisconsin Press, 1987); Homer Clevenger, "The Teaching Techniques of the Farmers' Alliance: An Experiment in Adult Education," *Journal of Southern History* 11 (November 1945): 504–18; Steven Hahn, *The Roots of Southern Populism: Yeoman Farmers and the Transformation of the Georgia Upcountry, 1850–1890* (New York: Oxford University Press, 1985); Scott, *Reluctant Farmer,* chaps. 3 and 4, and pp. 3–4.

34. Fred A. Shannon, *The Farmer's Last Frontier* (New York: Farrar & Rinehart, 1945), 8–9; Michael Schwartz, *Radical Protest and Social Structure: The Southern Farmers' Alliance and Cotton Tenancy, 1880–1890* (Chicago: University of Chicago Press, 1976), 114; Wayman Hogue, *Back Yonder: An Ozark Chronicle* (New York: Minton, Balch, 1932), 194–97; Julius Rubin, "The Limits of Agricultural Progress in the Nineteenth Century South," *Agricultural History* 49, no. 2 (April 1975); Stephen J. DeCanio, *Agriculture in the Postbellum South: The Economics of Production and Supply* (Cambridge, Mass.: MIT Press, 1974); Gilbert C. Fite, *Cotton Fields No More: Southern Agriculture, 1865–1980* (Lexington: University Press of Kentucky, 1984).

35. The Knapp quote is in Russell Lord, *Agrarian Revival: A Study of Agricultural*

Extension (New York: American Association for Adult Education, 1939), 71; Scott, *Reluctant Farmer,* 173.

36. Knapp's statement is quoted in *Dallas Morning News,* November 6, 1903. Bailey, *Seaman A. Knapp,* 136–39.

37. As of July 1903, Knapp had established four testing and demonstration farms, "and will establish more," according to Galloway. Galloway to JSW, June 30, 1903. Cline, *Life and Work,* 53–57; Bailey, *Seaman A. Knapp,* 148–60; Scott, *Reluctant Farmer,* 210–11; True, *History of Agricultural Extension,* 59–60.

38. For coverage of Wilson and Galloway's visit to Terrell and other southern visits, see *Terrell (Texas) Star,* November 6, 1903; *Dallas News,* November 7, 1903; *Philadelphia Press,* November 10, 1903; clippings in *JSW.* On the aims of Wilson and Knapp in securing the boll weevil appropriation, see Scott, *Reluctant Farmer,* 215–16: "But Knapp wanted to do more than simply retard the spread of the boll weevil, dangerous though it was. . . . The demonstrators and cooperators were the instruments through which Knapp hoped to reach ultimately all southern farmers, showing them the most satisfactory methods of producing the standard farm crops in their areas." See also True, *History of Agricultural Extension,* 60. An internal USDA report in 1924 found that little of the boll weevil money was used to combat the pest; C. W. Warburton, director of extension work, to William Jump, March 17, 1924, NA II, RG 16, E 17, B 1035, March appropriations file.

39. "Secretary Wilson Coming to Visit Louisiana," *New Orleans States,* October 6, 1902; "Secretary Wilson," "Keynote Rung Clearly by Secretary Wilson," *Macon (Ga.) Telegraph,* May 8, 1903; *Southern Farm Magazine,* April 12, 1903; Seaman Knapp to JSW, March 10, 1904, *JSW.* By February 1905 Knapp had an annual budget of almost $40,000 for demonstration, based on the estimated $19,513.33 allotted for January to June 1905. Beverly Galloway and Leland O. Howard (Division of Entomology) to JSW, February 27, 1905, Knapp Personnel File. In 1906 Knapp had a staff of fifty-six workers whom he supervised for the cotton boll-weevil investigations alone; Galloway to JSW, June 29, 1906, Knapp Personnel File. By June 1908 this staff had grown to more than two hundred members (201, to be precise, including Knapp, using calculations in a letter from Galloway to JSW, June 17, 1908, Knapp Personnel File). For the number of new demonstration agents and demonstration farms, see USDA, *Yearbook* (1904), 505–6. Knapp to Galloway, November 26, 1903, cited in Bailey, *Seaman A. Knapp,* 159; True, *History of Agricultural Extension,* 60–61; Cline, *Life and Work of Seaman A. Knapp,* 59–62. Scott, in *Reluctant Farmer,* 214–15, discusses the local network strategies of the agents and their use of guaranty funds as organizing tools. Knapp's statement is in *Farmers' Cooperative Demonstration Work and Its Results,* proceedings of the Ninth Conference for Education in the South, May 1906, Richmond, Virginia, 8, in Bailey, *Seaman Knapp,* 180. On hiring criteria, see Galloway's appraisal of F. L. Stevens, August 21, 1911, NARPC. USDA Special Agent Anton V. Swaty to Seaman Knapp, July 23, 1906, in files of Texas Agricultural Extension Service, Cushing Memorial Library, Texas Agricultural and Mechanical University.

40. G. H. Powell, acting chief of the Bureau of Plant Industry, to JSW, June 8, 1910. Powell wrote that Knapp "has 23,000 demonstrators, that is, specific farms that are superintended by our traveling agents, and over 70,000 cooperating farmers, who agree to meet at demonstration farms for instructions and follow our plans, besides about 46,000 boy demonstrators, working in school corn clubs" (Knapp Personnel File, NA II, RG 16,

E 184, B 6; see also Beverly Galloway to JSW, December 26, 1908, ibid.). C. Vann Woodward, *Origins of the New South, 1877–1913* (Baton Rouge: Louisiana State University Press, 1971), 403.

41. Powell to JSW, June 8, 1910. For other evidence of southern support, see JSW to George T. Williams, August 23, 1905; to B. D. Campbell, August 9, 1905; to C. J. Bier (president of the Louisiana and Texas Rice Millers' Association), August 9, 1905; all in JSW Letterbooks, *JSW.* Cline, *Life and Work of Seaman A. Knapp,* 67–68. Galloway to JSW, December 26, 1908, emphasis added.

42. "Remarks of the Secretary of Agriculture to the Prize-Winning Boys from the Southern States," December 10, 1910, in *JSW.* Scott, *Reluctant Farmer,* 240–42; Edmund de S. Brunner and E. Hsin Pao Yang, *Rural America and the Extension Service* (New York: Teachers College, Columbia University, 1949), 10–11.

43. Scott, *The Reluctant Farmer,* 245. Debra Ann Reid, "Reaping a Greater Harvest: African Americans, Agrarian Reform, and the Texas Agricultural Extension Service" (Ph.D. diss., Texas Agricultural and Mechanical University, May 2000).

44. William A. Taylor to JSW, March 30, 1911, NA II, RG 16, E 184, B 6, Knapp Personnel File. General Education Board, *The General Education Board: An Account of Its Activities, 1902–1914* (New York: General Education Board, 1915), 59; Bailey, *Seaman A. Knapp*; Cline, *Life and Work of Seaman Knapp,* 51–82; Scott, *Reluctant Farmer,* 246.

45. Franklin M. Reck, *The 4-H Story: A History of 4-H Club Work* (Ames: Iowa State University Press, 1951); Gladys Baker, *The County Agent* (Chicago: University of Chicago Press, 1939), 30; Scott, *Reluctant Farmer,* 251–53.

46. Other leaders of the association included Illinois professor Isabel Beveir, Mrs. Melvil Dewey of the Lake Placid Club, Columbia University professor Adelaide Nutting, MIT professor Ellen H. Richards, and Maurice LesBosquet, director of the Chicago-based American School of Home Economics. Galloway himself arranged the decorations for the 1909 meeting. See "Organization of the Home Economics Association," *The Journal of Home Economics* 1 (February 1909): 7–39. See also "Lake Placid Conference on Home Economics, 1899–1908," *The Journal of Home Economics* 1 (February 1909): 3–6; Alice Ravenhill, "The Scope of Home Economics and Its Subject Matter in Universities and Colleges," *The Journal of Home Economics* 9 (September 1917): 393–404; Linda Hull Larned, "The National Household Economic Association, 1893–1903," *The Journal of Home Economics* 1 (April 1909): 185–87. Generally, see Sarah Stage and Virginia B. Vincenti, eds., *Rethinking Home Economics: Women and the History of a Profession* (Ithaca: Cornell University Press, 1997).

47. William A. Taylor to DFH, July 10, 1914, NA II, RG 16, Secretary's Files. For a discussion of Breazeale's work in California, see chapter 9. Baker, *County Agent,* 32–33; Finegold and Skocpol, *State and Party in America's New Deal,* 59. Finegold, "From Agrarianism to Adjustment: The Political Origins of New Deal Agriculture Policy," *Politics and Society* 11 (1981): 1–27.

48. Taylor to JSW, March 30, 1911. For Taylor's eulogy, see Taylor to JSW, April 4, 1911, Knapp Personnel File.

49. Sanders, *Roots of Reform,* 324.

50. The heart of the extension movement lay not in Alabama but in Texas, Louisiana, and South Carolina. Hardy's statement is in Scott, *Reluctant Farmer,* 235–36.

51. See "Summary of Tabulation," report in "Tabulation of Influence Survey Reports for September 4, 5, and 6, 1912," by C. C. Anderson, NA II, RG 83, E 133, B 1, F "Anderson, C. C." "Distribution of the Field Service," February 1, 1912, NA II, RG 16. The department began mailing *Farmers' Bulletins* directly to farmers after 1900, when the volume became too large for congressional staff to handle; the *Bulletins* were an important linkage between the USDA and local communities.

52. William J. Spillman Personnel File, NA II, RG 16, E 184, B 11. E. H. Thomson, "The Origin and Development of the Office of Farm Management in the United States Department of Agriculture," *Journal of Farm Economics* 14 (January 1932): 10–16; Scott, *Reluctant Farmer,* 254–55.

53. Spillman, "Farm Management in the United States" (Records of the Bureau of Agricultural Economics, NA II, RG 83, E 145, B 1, F 1). C. B. Smith, "The Origin of Farm Economics Extension," *Journal of Farm Economics* 14 (January 1932): 17–18; Scott, *Reluctant Farmer,* 259. Fred G. Allison (Sac City, Iowa) to the Office of Farm Management, August 6, 1906, RG 83, E 133, B 1, F "Allison, F. G., Reports for July 31, Aug 6, and 20, 1906." Charles L. Goodrich, *A Profitable Cotton Farm,* U.S. Department of Agriculture, *Farmers' Bulletin* 364 (Washington, D.C.: GPO, 1909). G. J. Abbott, "A Description of the Farm of Earle A. Blakelee" (NA II, RG 83, E 133, B 1, F 1, "Abbott, G. J.").

54. Galloway appointed Spillman as "Agriculturist in charge of Farm Management" in 1906, transferring him from the lump-sum fund for Grass and Forage Plant Investigations to the "General Expenses" Roll for the bureau (Designation of Secretary of Agriculture, June 30, 1906, RG 16, E 184, B 11, Spillman Personnel File). Galloway secured a different source of lump-sum funding less than a year later when he transferred Spillman from the roll for Cotton Boll Weevil Investigations to the "General Expenses" Roll (Designation of Secretary of Agriculture, May 25, 1907, Spillman Personnel File). See the American Farm Management Association, "Report of the First Annual Meeting" (July 1910) and "Report of the Third Annual Meeting" (September 30, 1913), NA II, RG 83, E 133, B 1, F 11. For an optimistic review of the office's accomplishments during this period, directed to a financial audience, see J. H. Arnold, "Has Scientific Farming Been Profitable in the United States?" *The American Banker,* September 19, 1913, 2276–78.

55. Gould Colman, "Government and Agriculture in New York State," *Agricultural History* 39 (January 1964): 41–50; True, *History of Agricultural Extension,* 73–74, 77–80; Orville Merton Kile, *The Farm Bureau Movement* (New York: Macmillan, 1921), 78ff., 96; Robert P. Howard, *James R. Howard and the Farm Bureau* (Ames: Iowa State University Press, 1983), 71; Scott, *Reluctant Farmer,* 263–64.

56. Galloway's memorandum to Chief Clerk Reese, August 2, 1912, NA II, RG 16, E 17, B 47, F "Disease." Howard, *James R. Howard,* 74; Scott, *Reluctant Farmer,* 262–63.

57. "Memorandum of Understanding between the Iowa State College of Agriculture and Mechanic Arts and the Bureau of Plant Industry, U.S. Department of Agriculture, Relative to Farm Management Field Studies and Demonstrations in the State of Iowa" (NA II, RG 16, E 17, B 47, F "Disease"). Spillman's agents, namely Fred G. Allison, had been working in Iowa since at least 1906. Kile, *Farm Bureau Movement,* 80, 94ff.; Scott, *Reluctant Farmer,* 268–69. P. G. Holden, director, Agricultural Extension De-

partment, International Harvester Company, memorandum entitled "Suggestions for the Organization [of] County Improvement Association," NA II, RG 83, E 133, B 1, F "Suggestions . . ."

58. C. B. Smith (Bureau of Plant Industry, USDA) to E. O. McCormick of the Southern Pacific Company, San Francisco, December 20, 1912, BANC, CU-20, B 13, F 3 (C. B. Smith).

59. 37 U.S. Stat., pt. 1, 277. Scott, *Reluctant Farmer,* 270–71.

60. Colman, "Government and Agriculture in New York State," 44–45; Gould Colman, *Education and Agriculture: A History of the New York State College of Agriculture at Cornell University* (Ithaca: Cornell University Press, 1963), 170, 195–97. See Assistant Secretary, USDA, to Edward Leavitt Howe, Princeton, New Jersey, March 20, 1913, and Spillman's accompanying memorandum of March 19, NA II, E 17, B 47, F "Disease." Scott, *Reluctant Farmer,* 271–77. On Oklahoma, see Rep. Robert L. Owen to secretary of agriculture, April 10, 1913; also telegram from John T. Burns (Tulsa) to Beverly Galloway, April 10, 1913; both in NA II, E 17, B 47, F "Disease."

61. Sanders, *Roots of Reform,* 314–15. Scott, in *The Reluctant Farmer,* argues that most extension supporters in the Sixty-second Congress had jumped on a "bandwagon" of the USDA's making (288–91).

62. Butterfield successfully led the drive for land-grant colleges to establish extension departments while in Michigan. Scott, *Reluctant Farmer,* 76–77. By 1910 he was president of the Massachusetts Agricultural College. Howard W. Gross, *The National Soil Fertility League* (Chicago, 1911); Clayton S. Ellsworth, "Theodore Roosevelt's Country Life Commission," *Agricultural History* 34 (October 1960): 155–72.

63. True, *History of Agricultural Extension,* 100–103; Scott, *Reluctant Farmer,* 290–93.

64. Senate Committee on Agriculture and Forestry, "Agricultural Colleges and State Experiment Stations," *Hearings on S. 4676,* 61st Cong., 1st sess.; *CR,* January 5, 1910, 311; *CR,* June 22, 1910, 8713; True, *History of Agricultural Extension,* 103; Scott, *Reluctant Farmer,* 294–95.

65. Davis was prodded to introduce his bill by Willet Hays, his former teacher at Minnesota and assistant secretary of agriculture at the time; True, *History of Agricultural Extension,* 104–5. Of industrial education, Rodgers contends that between 1906 and 1917 "no other educational topic approached it in vitality" (*Work Ethic in Industrial America,* 84, see generally 83–87). See also Lawrence A. Cremin, *The Transformation of the School: Progressivism in American Education, 1876–1957* (New York: Alfred A. Knopf, 1961), chap. 2; Sol Cohen, "The Industrial Education Movement, 1906–1917," *American Quarterly* 20 (1968): 95–110; Bernice M. Fisher, *Industrial Education* (Madison: University of Wisconsin Press, 1967). Marvin Lazerson, *Origins of the Urban School: Public Education in Massachusetts, 1870–1915* (Cambridge, Mass.: Harvard University Press, 1971).

66. True, *History of Agricultural Extension,* 104–5; Scott, *Reluctant Farmer,* 294–95; Sanders, *Roots of Reform,* 324–31.

67. Asbury F. Lever, "Extension the Most Universal University," *Texas Extension Service Farm News* 16, no. 12 (September 1931): 7. Scott, *Reluctant Farmer,* 298; Sanders, *Roots of Reform,* 331–32.

68. House committee report at *CR* (April 4, 1912), 4318; (April 13, 1912), 4764;

quoted in Scott, *Reluctant Farmer,* 300 (see generally 299–302); Sanders, *Roots of Reform,* 332–33.

69. William Kenyon to David Franklin Houston, April 15, 1913, secretary's files, NA II, RG 16, E 17, B 47, F "Disease."

70. Sells's remarks are in *CR,* 63-1 (appendix) (March 5, 1914), 206. Smith's remarks on the conference are in *CR,* 62-2 (September 6, 1913), 4330. True, *History of Agricultural Extension,* 111; Scott, *Reluctant Farmer,* 306–10. Kile, *Farm Bureau Movement,* 88; Brunner and Yang, *Rural America,* 14–15.

71. Sanders, *Roots of Reform,* 314–21.

72. Finegold and Skocpol, *State and Party in America's New Deal,* 59. One might surmise that Congress turned toward the USDA model only when agrarian Democrats took control of Congress in 1912. Unfortunately, this explanation cannot account for the fact that Republican congresses from 1904 to 1910 allowed the USDA to build the southern FCDW. Moreover, the Democratic House of 1911–12 supported the institute model in the particulars of the extension bills it passed. The USDA also used its veto power to corral straying state programs into line; A. C. True, chairman, USDA States Relations Committee, to G. S. Fraps, Texas Agricultural and Mechanical College, June 20, 1914, Records of the Texas Agricultural Extension Service.

73. U.S. Department of Agriculture, *Cooperative Extension Work in Agriculture and Home Economics, 1916,* pt. 2 of *Report on Experiment Stations and Extension Work in the United States* (Washington, D.C.: GPO, 1916), 373–75; USDA, State Relations Service, *Cooperative Extension Work, 1922* (Washington, D.C., 1924), 8; USDA, Office of Cooperative Extension Work, *Cooperative Extension Work, 1927* (Washington, D.C., 1929), 52. Scott, *Reluctant Farmer,* 312; True, *History of Agricultural Extension,* 41–42.

74. The series for figure 7.1 is from "Expenditures of U.S. Department of Agriculture Funds in States for Farmers' Cooperative Demonstration Work, 1904 to 1924, inclusive," NA II, RG 16, E 17, B 1106, F "Appropriations, July." Three caveats need to be mentioned here. First, I have removed World War I emergency expenditures from the series. In 1918 Congress appropriated $2,949,072.48 in emergency FCDW funds, followed by $4,598,243.13 in 1919. This does not affect the projections, as Congress would certainly have allocated emergency monies to extension in the absence of Smith-Lever. Indeed, Smith-Lever funding fell in nominal dollars (and quite steeply in real dollars) after the war. Second, there is the possibility that FCDW expenditures were raised in 1914 in expectation of the act. Yet even if projections are based on FCDW growth from 1904 to 1913, USDA spending would still have been larger than under Smith-Lever, with an average overexpenditure of greater than $50,000 (in 1910 dollars) from 1914 to 1924 (see figure 7.1). Finally, skeptics might regard the figure as evidence of *strict congressional control,* given that growth in program funds *declined* in real dollars after Smith-Lever. Yet reputation-based autonomy is a far better explanation. To begin with, a congressional-control interpretation of the growth patterns after 1914 presupposes that all expenditures from 1904 to 1914 were fully autonomous. It also awkwardly posits that Progressive Congresses wanted *less* extension than did the USDA. In addition, there are reasons to believe that the department preferred the reduced program growth after 1914, mainly because Smith-Lever reduced the USDA's uncertainty over the program's future even as it reduced the rate of growth.

75. Scott, *Reluctant Farmer,* 302.

Chapter Eight

1. Bartlett, *CR* (House), June 23, 1906, 9050. "Save the Forests," *Maxwell's Talisman,* July 15, 1907.

2. See chap 1 n. 27 for citations to Padgett and Ansell, and Burt. I thank Nancy Burns and Elizabeth Clemens for their criticism of the multiple-networks argument in this chapter.

3. On Wiley's shift of attention, see Coppin and High, "Entrepreneurship and Competition," 113.

4. Bailey, "Congressional Opposition to Pure Food Legislation," 52–64; Anderson, *Health of a Nation,* 195; Young, *Pure Food;* Clayton A. Coppin and Jack High, *The Politics of Purity* (Ann Arbor: University of Michigan Press, 1998); Wilson, *Food and Drug Regulation.*

5. *Journal of Proceedings of the National Pure Food and Drug Congress Held in Columbian University Hall, Washington, D.C., March 2, 3, 4, and 5, 1898* (Washington, D.C., 1898). Anderson, *Health of a Nation,* 124–25; Young, *Pure Food,* 125–27.

6. As Anderson explains, "Whatever Wiley's role in calling the congress may have been, he quickly became its central figure" (*Health of a Nation,* 124). Young, *Pure Food,* 125–30; Coppin and High, "Entrepreneurship and Competition," 113–14. Alexander Wedderburn appears twice in 1890s appointment records of the Bureau of Chemistry, NA II, RG 16, E 185, Appointment Records, 1907–8. Both of Wedderburn's appointments were temporary; he left the department for the last time in December 1897. Wiley had also hired Wedderburn's brother Augustus, who served from September 1892 to September 1893.

There is another reason to believe that Wedderburn was cooperative with the department. Wedderburn operated a newspaper out of the Grange Camp called the *National Farm and Fireside.* Postal inspectors charged him with fraud in 1890, but Secretary Jeremiah Rusk intervened with Wanamaker to prevent the initial filing of charges. From that point onward, the department had a major farm journal in its back pocket; Records of the U.S. House of Representatives, House Committee on Post Office and Post Roads, RG 233, B 71, F HR51A-F30.4.

7. *Journal of Proceedings of the National Pure Food and Drug Congress,* 1898. Anderson, *Health of a Nation,* 124–28. Wiley, "Dangers in Food Adulteration," for *Colliers' Weekly,* manuscript in NA II, RG 97, E 27, B 1, V "1903," 158ff.

8. Wiley hired Frear as a special agent in July 1903; NA II, RG 16, E 185, Appointment Records. As Young summarizes, "If Wedderburn strove to defeat Wiley for leadership of the crusade, he failed. At the congress itself, Wiley outmaneuvered Wedderburn and enhanced his own stature" (*Pure Food,* 126). Anderson, *Health of a Nation,* 126; Coppin and High, "Entrepreneurship and Competition," 113–14.

9. Wiley prompted Brosius and Senator Charles J. Faulkner of West Virginia to introduce a revised draft of the AOAC bill in 1898, and he got Brosius to introduce another version in December 1899 (Anderson, *Health of a Nation,* 125–31). See Senate, *Adulteration of Food Products,* 56th Cong., 1st sess. Mason's statement appears in *CR,* 56-1, 4963, remarks on S. 2426; quoted in Young, *Pure Food,* 140.

10. *Adulteration of Food Products,* 396; cited in Young, *Pure Food,* 140–45.

11. Hepburn chaired the House Committee on Interstate and Foreign Commerce. Anderson, *Health of a Nation,* 141. Barrett, cited in ibid., 146. It is possible that Wiley came

to accept Barrett's explanation of the 1902 failures through their correspondence. Boxes 7 and 8 of the Harvey W. Wiley Papers, Library of Congress, contain numerous letters from Wiley to Barrett; see Coppin and High, "Entrepreneurship and Competition," 114–15.

12. Harvey Wiley, *Influence of Food Preservatives and Artificial Colors on Digestion and Health,* Department of Agriculture, Bureau of Chemistry, *Bulletin 84* (Washington, D.C., GPO, 1904–8). Young, *Pure Food,* 151–55; Anderson, *Health of a Nation,* 149–52.

13. Gillilan's poem and Dockstader's lyrics appear in Wiley, *Autobiography,* 217, 219, respectively. Anderson, *Health of a Nation,* 151.

14. Young, *Pure Food,* 160–64. Young reported on Wiley's inspections and prosecutions in 1903 and 1904: "[F]oreign exporters quickly learned the lesson that Wiley meant business. The United States ceased to be a dumping ground for shoddy foods and liquors sent from abroad. No importer took one of the bureau's restrictive decisions to court" (164). Another law that indicated an increasingly favorable climate for food and drug regulation was the 1902 Biologics Act, a law passed in response to two tragedies with antitoxins that killed twenty-one children in Saint Louis, Missouri, and Camden, New Jersey. Ramunas A. Kondratas, "The Biologics Control Act of 1902," in *The Early Years of Federal Food and Drug Control,* ed. James Harvey Young (Madison: University of Wisconsin Press, 1982); Young, *Pure Food,* 148–49.

15. R. James Kane argues that Wiley's experiments were "nearly throttled" by Wilson; "Populism, Progressivism, and Pure Food," *Agricultural History* 38 (1964): 162–64. Wilson was aghast at Upton Sinclair's *Jungle,* writing that Sinclair was "grossly misrepresenting conditions in our packing houses"; JSW to Sen. Redfield Proctor, May 22, 1906, *JSW,* letterbooks 12/368. Charles Knight, secretary and treasurer, National Dairy Union, to JSW, September 8, 1905, *JSW.*

16. Anderson, *Health of a Nation,* 135. Wiley hired Scovell for the bureau in June 1902; see USDA Employee Data, Bureau of Chemistry. Coppin and High, "Entrepreneurship and Competition," 115–17.

17. Young, *Pure Food,* 184–87; Anderson, *Health of a Nation,* 145–47. For Wiley's discussion of the effectiveness of the GFWC, see *Annals of the American Academy of Political and Social Science* 28 (September 1906): 82, quoted in Young, *Pure Food,* 185. Skocpol, *Protecting Soldiers and Mothers,* 328–33; Paula Baker, "The Domestication of Politics: Women and American Political Society, 1780–1920," *American Historical Review* 89 (1984): 620–47.

18. Harvey Wiley to the editor of *Science,* January 18, 1904, and essays, "The Attitude of the Medical Profession towards Food Preservatives" and "Federal Control of Drugs," Records of the Bureau of Chemistry (NA II, RG 97, E 27, B 1, V "1903," 51–55, 68–72, 81–88). Young, *Pure Food,* 188–89.

19. On the Senate Agriculture Committee's preference for USDA enforcement in the Fifty-first Congress, see *Report to Accompany S. 3991,* Senate Report 1366. Young, *Pure Food,* 97–98.

20. Adamson speech, *CR* (House), May 7, 1906, 6465.

21. Wilson, *Food and Drug Regulation,* 32. McCumber responded: "There is nothing in the bill . . . to justify the suggestion . . . now, nor has there been anything to justify it for the last four years" (*CR,* 59-1, 1923). Money speech, *CR,* 59-1, February 19, 1906, 2657.

22. On the role of courts in nineteenth-century economic regulation, see Skowronek, *Building a New American State,* chap. 2. On the Chemistry Bureau's activities in 1903, see the manuscript "Report of the Work of the Bureau of Chemistry for the Fiscal Year Ended June 30, 1904," NA II, RG 97, E 27, B 1, V "1903," pp. 208ff. McCumber's speech was given on February 19, 1906, *CR,* 59-1, 2663.

23. On congressional fear of USDA power, see Sen. Money's speech on Feburary 19, 1906, *CR,* 2656–57. See also Senator Hemenway's speech at 2724–25 and Spooner's remarks at 2734. Wiley, of course, wanted the institutional permanence that came with statutory authority.

24. Anderson, *Health of a Nation,* 138; Young, *Pure Food,* 255.

25. Adamson speech, *CR,* 59-2, May 7, 1906, 6465.

26. Florence Kelley, general secretary, National Consumers' League, to Hon. Jesse Overstreet, House of Representatives, March 16, 1906, files of House Committee on Interstate and Foreign Commerce, NA I, RG 233, HR 59A-H11.6.

27. Upton Sinclair, *The Jungle* (New York: Doubleday, 1906). Young, *Pure Food,* 221–52. Taking the estimates of the Armour Packing Company at face value, meat sales declined by 50 percent in the year following Sinclair's book. Samuel Hopkins Adams, "The Great American Fraud," *Collier's Weekly,* October 7, 1905, 14; "Peruna and the 'Bracers,' " *Collier's Weekly,* October 21, 1905. Young, *Pure Food,* 203, 219; *New York Times,* July 13, 1911, pp. 1–2.

28. William Richardson, one of the shepherds of Wiley's legislation in the House debates, referred to Wiley as "the distinguished gentleman at the head of the Chemical Bureau of the Government" (*CR* [House], June 22, 1906, 8962). On Underwood's assistance, see Evans C. Johnson, *Oscar W. Underwood: A Political Biography* (Baton Rouge: Louisiana State University Press, 1980).

29. Anderson, *Health of a Nation,* 201–3. Wiley wrote to Sunny Brook and demanded that it change or discontinue the advertisements; Harvey Wiley to Sunny Brook Distillery Co., Louisville, Kentucky, May 17, 1907; Sunny Brook to Wiley, May 22, 1907; both in NA II, RG 97, E 8, B 33, F 2310.

30. Mark Pendergrast, *For God, Country, and Coca-Cola* (New York: Basic Books, 1993), 107–22. A different explanation for Wiley's successes in the cases of whiskey and Coca-Cola might be that Republicans were willing to allow him to pursue prosecutions because these were southern interests. Such an explanation would commit historical and logical errors. First, many powerful whiskey distributors were located in the Midwest (especially Indiana and Illinois), which is why Cannon, more than southern politicians, headed the opposition to the Chemistry Bureau's whiskey regulations. Second, the explanation would not suffice to account for Wiley's other successes, namely against the use of benzoate of soda and copper sulfate, which were manufactured almost exclusively by northern firms. "Caffein: An Insidious, Dangerous Drug," in HWW, C 200, F "Bureau of Chemistry"; "Is Coca-Cola a Menace to the Public Health?" *Town Topics,* November 20, 1913, 15; "Trial Brings Many People," *The (Chattanooga) Daily Times,* March 13, 1911; Anderson, *Health of a Nation,* 236–37. Sanford's decision in *U.S. v. Twenty Kegs and Forty Barrels of Coca-Cola,* 191 Fed. 431; circuit appeal in U.S. Circuit Court of Appeals, case no. 2415, at 215 Fed. 535; Hughes's majority opinion at 241 U.S. 265 (1916).

31. Wiley was insulted by the president's tongue-lashing over saccharin—which came in front of several ketchup manufacturers—but I believe that several biographers

(including Wiley) have overemphasized this episode; Wiley, *Autobiography,* 240–41. The insult came just after Roosevelt had handed Wiley a major victory in supporting the USDA's stance on benzoate, which was used much more widely than saccharin. For Roosevelt to allow Wiley to prohibit benzoate while holding the line on saccharin was to give the visiting businessmen a cheap symbolic victory. Wiley also made the rare mistake of interrupting Roosevelt before the comment. Anderson, *Health of a Nation,* 210; Gladys Baker, "The Face of the Bureaucrat: A Profile of USDA Leadership," in *Farmers, Bureaucrats, and Middlemen,* ed. Peterson, 71.

32. Wiley, *Autobiography,* 288. Rep. Edgar G. Crumpacker had worried that the bill would establish "department-made law" (*CR,* June 22, 1906, 9002).

33. Anderson, *Health of a Nation,* chaps. 10 and 11.

34. Harvey Wiley to Alice Lakey, February 8, 1907, NA II, RG 97, E 8, B 33, F 2303; "Joker in Food Law: People's Lobby Denounces Tawney Amendment," *Washington Herald,* February 4, 1907. Petition of January 20, 1909, in Records of the Senate Committee on Manufactures, 60th Cong., NA I, RG 46, SEN 60A-J80 [B 122]; written and sent by Helen M. Bent, the league's first vice president. Business groups were enraged by *Chemistry Bulletin 84.* See E. C. Johnson, secretary of the National Food Manufacturers' Association, to Theodore Roosevelt, July 23, 1908: "The National Food Manufacturers' Association regards the giving out by Dr. Wiley this week of his article condemning benzoate of soda as a food preservative extremely unfortunate and inopportune." Wilson had previously assured the manufacturers' association that no interference would come from the department in 1908; JSW to E. C. Johnson, secretary, National Food Manufacturers' Association, March 21, 1908; correspondence in NA II, RG 16, E 17, B 12, F "Charges and Criticism." Roosevelt's statement is in Coppin and High, *Politics of Purity,* 87.

35. The interpretation of Wiley's departure as stemming from his frustration with the Remsen board appears in James Harvey Young, "Food and Drug Administration," in *Government Agencies,* ed. Donald R. Whitnah (Westport, Conn.: Greenwood Press, 1983), 251–57. On Wiley's personal reasons for departing, see Clayton Coppin, "James Wilson and Harvey Wiley: The Dilemma of Bureaucratic Entrepreneurship," *Agricultural History* 64, no. 2:180. The long-standing tradition in the FDA of hiring commissioners from within the agency or the Public Health Service, broken only in 1977 when the commissioners came from academic posts, began under Wiley. In a separate analysis of copublication networks in the Bureau of Chemistry before 1913, I have found Bigelow to be the most centrally located employee—the employee who served to tie more individuals together through collaborative research than any other employee in the bureau. On the failure of the campaign for a national health department, see Skocpol, *Protecting Soldiers and Mothers,* 302–4. Skocpol discusses Lathrop's admiration of the USDA in chap. 9, pp. 486–87.

36. On the opposition between women's federations and the American Medical Association on Progressive-Era welfare programs and other matters, see Skocpol, *Protecting Soldiers and Mothers,* chap. 9.

37. "Taft Is Advised by Wickersham to Oust Wiley," *New York Times,* July 13, 1911, 1–2, italics added; Anderson, *Health of a Nation,* 133, 196. Even Gabriel Kolko, who has tied most Progressive regulatory efforts to business influences, admits that "the history of the pure food movement is the history of Harvey W. Wiley" (*The Triumph of Conservatism* [Chicago: Quadrangle Books, 1967], 108). T. Swann Harding, in *Two*

Blades of Grass: A History of Scientific Development in the U.S. Department of Agriculture (Norman: University of Oklahoma Press, 1947), pronounced Wiley "a one-man movement all by himself" in the battle for regulation, one who "carried others with him" (48).

38. Gifford Pinchot to R. C. Melward, May 20, 1903, Office of Forest Reserves correspondence, quoted in Pinkett, *Gifford Pinchot,* 53. Conservation historians have largely dismissed the USDA's seven-year campaign for the Transfer Act of 1905. Hays spends one page on the transfer (*Conservation and the Gospel of Efficiency,* 42–43) but ignores most of the relevant sources. Robbins, in *Our Landed Heritage,* ignores the transfer altogether, and E. Louise Peffer (*The Closing of the Public Domain: Disposal and Reservation Policies, 1900–1950* [Stanford: Stanford University Press, 1951], 62–63) devotes two paragraphs with nothing of detail. Pinkett's biography of Pinchot allocates less than one paragraph (*Gifford Pinchot,* 57), and Pisani (*Water, Land, and Law,* 151–52) focuses on the aftermath of the transfer. In contrast, Pinchot himself devotes a self-idolizing chapter to the transfer in *Breaking New Ground,* 254–62.

39. "California Forestry," *Wood and Iron,* February 1897. See the interview of Brown in the *Rockland (Maine) Gazette,* August 27, 1901. J. Sterling Morton was the society's president. "The Forest Preservation Question," *Sacramento Record,* December 1, 1900. On the deforestation-drought hypothesis, see W. C. Bartlett, "The Tree and the Fountain," *The Citrograph (California),* January 11, 1902; *Pottstown Ledger,* August 27, 1901. See also the judgment of the *Roanoke World* (July 20, 1901) that "[f]orests conserve rainfall, which prevents drouth within their confines during rainless periods." Bernhard Fernow, "Outlook of the Timber Supply in the United States," *Forestry and Irrigation* 9 (May 1903): 230, quoted in Pisani, *Water, Land, and Law,* 235. For coverage of Fernow's statement, see the *Scranton (Pa.) Truth,* April 20, 1903; "Making New Forests," *New York World,* May 28, 1903. For a contrary view among newspapers, see "Forests and Heat," *Pittsburgh Gazette,* July 30, 1901. Petitions descended on the House Committee on Public Lands (NA I, RG 233, HR 53A-F38.3), the Senate Committee on Agriculture and Forestry (NA I, RG 46, SEN 50A-J1.1, SEN 60A-J2, SEN 60A-J8, SEN 62A-J3), and the Senate Committee on Forest Reservations and the Protection of Game (NA I, RG 46, SEN 54A-J13, SEN 60A-J52, SEN 61A-J36).

40. See the report of von Schrenk's April 17, 1903, speech before the New York Railroad Club in "Blame for Forest Destruction Placed," *New York Commercial,* April 18, 1903. See also "Forest Denudation," *Boston Evening Transcript,* July 29, 1901; "Forest Destruction and Climate," *Quincy Whig,* July 27, 1901; "Studies of Maine Trees," *Portland Advertiser,* June 29, 1903; "Repairing Ravages of Mountain Fires: Bureau of Forestry Replanting Mountain Slopes," *Los Angeles Times,* October 28, 1902; "To Replant Forest," *Los Angeles Herald,* October 27, 1902; "Causes of the Drought," *Philadelphia Item,* July 29, 1901. On California, see "Water and Forest Society Goes Ahead," *San Francisco Call,* April 8, 1899; "Save the Forests," *San Francisco Call,* February 25, 1899; "Yerba Buena Island to Have Chico Trees," *Daily Chico Record,* November 11, 1899. See also the *Scranton (Pa.) Truth,* April 20, 1903, and the *Bridgeport (Conn.) Standard,* April 8, 1903.

41. J. Leonard Bates, "Fulfilling American Democracy: The Conservation Movement, 1907 to 1921," *Mississippi Valley Historical Review* 44, no. 1 (June 1957): 29–57; Albert Beveridge to Gifford Pinchot, September 2, 1921, in Bates, "Fulfilling American Democracy," 32 (also GP, B 236). Charles S. Thomas, in *CR,* 66-1, August 23, 1919,

4255–56, in ibid., 43. "The World's Trees," *Washington Star,* April 6, 1901; "Arboretum at Santa Barbara," *San Francisco Chronicle,* October 1, 1899.

42. I use "extreme" here not to delegitimize Muir and Sargent but only to locate them historically on one end of the forestry spectrum in Progressive politics and to characterize Pinchot's views as "moderate" in relation to theirs. It is undeniable that at the turn of the century Pinchot's ideology was more legitimate, in the sense of gaining wider acceptance. One may, nonetheless, criticize Pinchot's stance as opportunistic, as Kolko and several of Muir's biographers have done. See Kolko, *Triumph of Conservatism,* 111; Linnie Marsh Wolfe, *Son of the Wilderness: The Life of John Muir* (New York: A. A. Knopf, 1946), 275–76. Wolfe is cited in Char Miller, *Gifford Pinchot: The Evolution of an American Conservationist* (Milford, Penn.: Grey Towers Press, 1992), who reviews much of the Muir-Pinchot correspondence. Still, I agree with Miller that Pinchot held a sincere belief in the multiple-use concept. See generally Bates, "Fulfilling American Democracy," 34.

43. Much of the material for the following narrative is taken from Pinchot, "The Transfer of the Reserves" (1938), 1, 4, 8–26; GP, B 974, F "Transfer." Pinchot saved a large amount of material related to the Transfer Act of 1905 for his 1947 autobiography *Breaking New Ground,* but he left most of it out of the book, and as far as I know it has not been systematically used by historians to narrate the transfer. See also Peffer, *Closing of the Public Domain,* 63; Pinchot, *Breaking New Ground,* 172–73; Hays, *Conservation and the Gospel of Efficiency,* 38–39.

44. On Pinchot's complex strategy to influence public opinion, see Pinkett's excellent chapter "Publicist and Educator," in *Gifford Pinchot,* 81–88, also 53. Steven Ponder, "Federal News Management in the Progressive Era: Gifford Pinchot and the Conservation Campaign," *Journalism History* (summer 1986): 42–48; Steven Ponder, "Gifford Pinchot: Press Agent for Forestry," *Journal of Forest History* (January 1987): 26–35; Steven Ponder, "Conservation, Community Economics, and Newspapering: The Seattle Press and the Forest Reserves Controversy of 1897," *American Journalism* (1986): 50–60. Lydia Phillips Williams to Gifford Pinchot, May 18, 1906, NA II, RG 95, E 22, B 3.

45. Charles S. Thomas, in *CR,* 66-1, August 23, 1919, 4255–56, in Bates, "Fulfilling American Democracy," 43. Robbins reports that "it was said that the President consulted [Pinchot] more than any other man in Washington" (*Our Landed Heritage,* 337). Pinkett, *Gifford Pinchot,* 54. Dale White, in *Gifford Pinchot: The Man Who Saved the Forests* (New York: Julian Messner, 1957), reports that Roosevelt's 1901 speech in favor of the transfer was adopted wholesale from Pinchot's draft (152–53).

46. For an argument that Pinchot deserves less credit than he has received for the "greening" of Roosevelt, see Paul Cutright, *Theodore Roosevelt: The Making of a Conservationist* (Urbana: University of Illinois Press, 1986), 234–35, cited in Miller, *Gifford Pinchot.* As Miller (75) suggests, however, Cutright pins his argument on the National Wildlife Conservation Hall of Fame. Theodore Roosevelt (at 16 Winthrop St., Cambridge, Massachusetts) to C. Hart Merriam, March 7, 1877, BANC FILM 1958, reel 78, frame 2. Roosevelt to Merriam, July 9, 1907, ibid., frame 123; see also frame 97. William Loeb [Roosevelt's personal secretary] to Merriam, November 26, 1908, ibid., frame 136. All in Merriam Papers. Merriam was invited to contribute to *The World's Work.* Of the first issue, Page said, "There is nothing to which we look forward with greater eagerness than to this article." Walter Hines Page to Merriam, July 18, 1900

(frame 305), July 27, 1900; frame 307; both in BANC FILM 1958, reel 75. On the Boone and Crockett Club, see Roosevelt to Merriam, December 20, 1892, and January 4, 1893, BANC FILM 1958, reel 78, frames 25 and 26. Merriam's role in Roosevelt's conservationism suggests that even if Cutright is correct, USDA officials still had an independent influence on the policy preferences of the president. J. F. Reiger, *American Sportsmen and the Origins of Conservation* (New York: Winchester Press, 1975). George Bird Grinnell, ed., *A Brief History of the Boone and Crockett Club with Officers, Constitution, and List of Members for the Year 1910* (New York, 1910), 20.

47. Constitutionally, an administrative transfer was the prerogative of the president, but no clear authority for such a move existed before the act. Hays, *Conservation*, 42–43. On newspaper optimism, see the *Wellsville (N.Y.) Democrat,* January 23, 1901: "The government, instead of letting [the forest] all be cut down by private individuals [,] is waiting until it can be scientifically taken in hand by the forestry experts now being trained by the agricultural department." Shafroth's argument is in *CR,* 57-1 (June 2, 1909), 6521.

48. On Binger Hermann's opposition, see Pinchot, "Transfer of the Reserves," 59–60; Hays, *Conservation,* 42. The majority report appears in "Forest Reserves Administration, Etc.," Report of the Committee on the Public Lands, 57th Cong., 1st sess., House Report 968. For the minority report, see "Proposed Transfer of Forest Reserves to the Agricultural Department" (March 26, 1902), 57th Cong., 1st sess., House Report 968, pt. 2. Bell's argument: *CR* (House), 57-1, 6202. McRae's argument: ibid., 6203. Lacey's argument: ibid. (June 9, 1902), 6513. Henry: ibid., 6513. Kleberg: ibid., 6524.

49. Shafroth's reversal is in *CR,* 57-1, 6204; see also *CR,* 57-1 (June 9, 1902), 6512–13. Cannon, *CR,* 57-1 (June 10, 1902), 6567–70. Hague's comment is quoted in Pinchot, "Transfer of the Reserves," 27 (GP, B 974).

50. Gifford Pinchot (in San Diego, California) to Theodore Roosevelt, Sept. 4, 1903, in Pinchot, "Transfer of the Reserves" (GP, B 974).

51. *CR* (House), 58-1 (November 12, 1903), 224. Mondell introduced another version (H.R. 8460) on December 19, accompanied by a committee report. Pinkett (*Gifford Pinchot,* 44) shows that Pinchot was dedicated to a multiple-use policy that split him from Sargent as early as 1897. Hays makes other errors as well. From Pinchot's records it is clear that Mondell told the forester of his conversion by September 21 at the latest, whereas Hays, citing a Pinchot letter to Henry Graves, suggests October 3. Gifford Pinchot to Henry S. Graves, October 5, 1903, GP, B 79, quoted in Hays, *Conservation and the Gospel of Efficiency,* 43; Gifford Pinchot (from Billings, Montana) to Theodore Roosevelt, September 21, 1903, GP, B 974.

52. See act of March 3, 1905 (33 Stat. 872). Pinchot, "Transfer of the Reserves," 105, 108; Pinkett, *Gifford Pinchot,* 56–57.

53. For the opinion, see William Moody to Gifford Pinchot, May 31, 1905, in U.S. Forest Service, *1905 Use Book* (Washington, D.C., 1905), 130. Pinkett (*Gifford Pinchot,* 80) concurs that the grazing and waterpower fees were "issued without specific statutory authority." Pisani, *Water, Land, and Law,* 151. As Pisani remarks, the funding provision was in some respects a slap to the Department of Interior, as it prevented the Reclamation Service from acquiring more reclamation funds by more land sales of the forest reserves. Teller, *CR,* 60–1, May 8, 1908, 6187; Nelson, ibid., 6185. Pinchot, *Breaking New Ground,* 334–38; Pinkett, *Gifford Pinchot,* 61.

54. *CR,* February 23, 1907, 3722ff. Hewitt Thomas, "Gifford Pinchot and His Fight

for Our Natural Resources," *American Review of Reviews,* 1907, 89; "For the Love of the Work," *Milwaukee Free Press,* May 13, 1907. The *Springfield (Mass.) Republican* lauded Pinchot as one of those "disinterested men" in public service (June 11, 1907); "A Knight of the Twentieth Century," *St. Louis Star,* November 24, 1909. *Maxwell's Talisman* reported (perhaps incorrectly) that Pinchot's bureau had "practically eliminated fire loss on its reserves" ("Save the Forests," July 15, 1907). Lydia Phillips Williams to Gifford Pinchot, May 18, 1906, NA II, RG 95, E 22, B 3. "A Disgraceful Attack," *Sioux Falls Press,* April 2, 1908.

55. JSW to Gifford Pinchot, February 28, 1907; Pinchot to Hon. Henry C. Hansbrough, January 20, 1908; both in GP, B 974, F "Congressional Attack, 1908." Pinchot, "Transfer of the Reserves," GP, B 974, p. 117; Pinchot, *Breaking New Ground,* 338.

56. J. Arthur Eddy, "Eliminations of Unforested Lands from the Forest Reserves," National Public Domain League Bulletin 1, June 26, 1909 (my italics), and "The Forest Service Operating the Forest Reserves as It Affects the Welfare of the People" (March 18, 1909, typescript), p. 10, NA II, RG 95, E 22, B 3. For a similar argument, see Rep. Heyburn's complaints of the Forest Service's entry of unforested lands into the reserves in 1906; *CR* (Senate), January 29, 1906, 1681; Pinkett, *Gifford Pinchot,* 75–76.

57. Alpheus Thomas Mason, *Bureaucracy Convicts Itself: The Ballinger-Pinchot Controversy of 1910* (New York: Viking Press, 1941). See also *CR*, 61-2, January 6, 1910, 369–79. Gifford Pinchot to William Howard Taft, January 7, 1910, NA II, RG 16, E 184, Pinchot file. As Bates concludes, "[M]any progressives never forgave Taft" for Pinchot's dismissal, and the event "helped to precipitate . . . the revolt of Republican progressives" to Roosevelt's "Bull Moose" Party in 1912 ("Fulfilling American Democracy," 45). The former president's entry spelled the end of Taft's tenure, as no Republican could win in 1912 with Roosevelt running as an independent. See Hoing, "James S. Wilson as Secretary of Agriculture," 210ff. Pinchot, *Breaking New Ground,* 447–58. *Philadelphia Inquirer,* January 7, 1910. Several scholars have noted the connection between the Ballinger-Pinchot affair and the Cannon revolt, including Kenneth William Hechler, *Insurgency: Politics and Personalities of the Taft Era* (New York: Columbia University Press, 1940), and Skowronek, *Building a New American State,* 191. None, to my knowledge, have made the proper inference, namely that the revolt was as much about Taft's attack on a legitimized bureau as about intraparty ideological dissensus. Hicks, *American Nation,* 427. A brief account of Roosevelt's anger after the Pinchot dismissal appears in John Milton Cooper Jr., *The Warrior and the Priest: Woodrow Wilson and Theodore Roosevelt* (Cambridge, Mass.: Harvard Belknap Press, 1983), 143–44.

58. See the "Old Timers" Collection, GP, B 1001–6; calculations are from a list of the "old timers" in the Library of Congress inventory of the collection, Manuscript Reading Room. Sudworth Personnel File and Redington Personnel File, NA I, RG 16, E 184. Herbert Kaufman, "Developing the Will and Capacity to Perform," chap. 5 in *The Forest Ranger: A Study in Administrative Behavior* (Baltimore: Johns Hopkins University Press, 1960; Washington, D.C.: Resources for the Future, 1986), 175–76.

59. Indeed, *before and after* the Agriculture Committee's change in title it had received petitions on forest matters (Records of the Senate Committee on Agriculture, NA I, RG 46, SEN 43A-H1, 45A-H1, 50A-J1.1, 60A-J2, 60A-J8, 62A-J3). Moreover, although the Committee on Agriculture and Forestry had jurisdiction over forestry matters, other committees considered many of the same issues. The Committee on Forest Reservations and the Protection of Game was established by a Senate resolution on

March 19, 1896, and was terminated by S. Res. 43, 67th Cong. (1921). The Committee on Forest Reservations and the Protection of Game was preceded by the Select Committee on Forest Reservations in California, established on July 28, 1892, and that select committee's successor, the Select Committee on Forest Reservations, was established on March 15, 1893. Unfortunately, few records—less than one-inch thick in the National Archives—remain from these committees.

60. Skowronek inaccurately regards Pinchot as "the dominant figure in the Agriculture Department" during the Progressive period; *Building a New American State,* 184–85. If such a distinction existed, it would surely have gone first to Wiley and probably then to Wilson.

61. Organizational reputations are never without blemish. The USDA found itself embroiled in several controversies over scandals in the Wilson period, including Weather Bureau chief Willis Moore's dismissal in 1913 over charges that he leaked crop and climate reports to futures market speculators. For a general review, see Willard Hoing, "Corruption in the Crop Reporting Service," chap. 7 in "James S. Wilson as Secretary of Agriculture." In the Forest Service, California Forest supervisor Everett B. Thomas was convicted of ten counts of fraudulent expenses on March 15, 1906. Yet aside from a petition drive in California to get Thomas pardoned after paying a fine, there was little political fallout from the Thomas scandal. Pinchot and USDA inspector R. H. Charlton, who had assisted the prosecution, rejoiced. Both were afraid that Thomas's iniquities would tar the bureau's reputation. The reason, in light of the narrative here, is easy to understand. Unlike the case of Albert Fall in the 1920s, the Forest Service scandal was limited to lower-level personnel, and it was discovered by one of Pinchot's inspectors. See R. H. Charlton to Gifford Pinchot, March 16, 1906, which lays out the conviction and the associated penalties. Pinchot felt that "Mr. Thomas was not a good officer," and he was happy to see him convicted; see also Pinchot to William G. Kerekhoff (Los Angeles), April 29, 1907, NA II, RG 95, E 22, B1.

Chapter Nine

1. Squire Innis, Creswell, Oregon, to H. C. Wallace, January 1, 1922, NA II, RG 16, E 17, B 875, file "Agricultural Situation." James R. Howard's remark is cited in Hearings before the Committee on Banking and Currency of the House of Representatives, *Farm Organizations,* pt. 5 (1922), quoted in True, *History of Agricultural Extension,* 166. Robert Cuff, *The War Industries Board: Business-Government Relations during World War I* (Baltimore: Johns Hopkins University Press, 1973); James Weinstein, *The Corporate Ideal in the Liberal State, 1900–1918* (Boston: Beacon Press, 1968), 214–54; Skowronek, *Building a New American State,* 234–41. In *America in the Great War: The Rise of the War Welfare State* (New York: Oxford University Press, 1991), Ronald Schaffer argues that New Deal state building borrowed materially from the institutions and personnel of the Wilson administration during the war. Although Schaeffer helpfully enriches our understanding of wartime mobilization, none of the state organizations he studies lasted through the 1920s until the New Deal. Even Hoover's Reconstruction Finance Corporation, built on the model of Wilson's War Finance Corporation, was built from scratch in 1930.

2. John Mark Hansen, *Gaining Access: Congress and the Farm Lobby, 1919–1981* (Chicago: University of Chicago Press, 1991), 28.

3. Finegold and Skocpol, *State and Party in America's New Deal,* 57–59; Sanders, *Roots of Reform,* 394.

4. Steven Stoll, *The Fruits of Natural Advantage: Making the Industrial Countryside in California* (Berkeley: University of California, 1998). The Fruit Growers' Exchange grew out of California fruit growers' conventions that began in 1881. E. J. Wickson, *Rural California* (New York: Macmillan, 1923), esp. 292ff.; Clarke A. Chambers, *California Farm Organizations* (Berkeley: University of California Press, 1952). Donn E. Headley, "The Cooperation Imperative: Relationships between Early Forest Administration and the Southern California Metropolis, 1892–1908," in *The Origins of the National Forests,* ed. Harold K. Steen (Durham, N.C.: Forest History Society, 1992).

5. William Scott was appointed plant pathologist in January 1903. He published widely cited studies of apple blot and peach rot, detailing methods for their control. See "Apple Blotch: A Serious Disease of Southern Orchards," *Bureau of Plant Industry Bulletin 144* (1909); "Control of Peach Brown-Rot and Scab," *Bureau of Plant Industry Bulletin 174* (1910). Scott left the department in January 1912 to join Baltimore's Thomsen Chemical Company, manufacturer of fungicides and insecticides for fruit trees. The department tried unsuccessfully to recruit him back in its attempt to launch new citrus studies in 1916. Edward McKay Chace published seven articles on citrus products before 1910, among which were "Saccharine in Wine," *Journal of the American Chemical Society (JACS)* (1898); "A Method for the Determination of Citral in Lemon Oils and Extracts," *JACS* (1906); and "Italian Lemons and Their By-products," *Bureau of Plant Industry Bulletin 160* (1909). On the cottony-cushion scale problem, see Richard C. Sawyer, *To Make a Spotless Orange: Biological Control in California* (Ames: Iowa State University Press, 1996); Ian Tyrell, *True Gardens of the Gods: Californian-Australian Environmental Reform, 1860–1930* (Berkeley: University of California Press, 1999), chap. 9. On Merton B. Waite, see the promotion letter of William A. Taylor to DFH, July 10, 1914, NPRC.

6. E. W. Hilgard, director of the University of California Experiment Station, "Additional Seeds for Distribution," Berkeley, California, December 11, 1901, BANC, CU-20, B 22 [Printed Materials, Publications], F 1. Among the new seeds were barleys, of which Hilgard's pamphlet stated: "Nos. 5590 and 5592 were superb brewing barleys from Bavaria, grown one year at Paso Robles. They were obtained by Mr. D. G. Fairchild of the Department of Agriculture. He says of No. 5590: 'The Bavarian brewers consider this Kitsing Barley the best in the world.' "

7. Smith was formerly Spillman's agent in the Office of Farm Management, but by 1914 he had become the chief of Field Studies and Demonstrations for the Bureau of Plant Industry. Thomas Forsyth Hunt to William J. Spillman, April 2, 1913: "Your Bureau, as well as other divisions of the Department of Agriculture, have always manifested such a liberal attitude toward financing cooperative enterprises that we will not hesitate to cooperate in the most cordial manner, even though we may be furnishing more than half of the expenses of the enterprise." Spillman to Hunt, April 16, 1913: "I regret very much that we haven't more money this coming year to use in California. . . . I hope another year we will get an appropriation that will enable us to be liberal with you"; BANC, CU-20, B 13, F 7 (W. J. Spillman, outgoing). For Smith's recommendation of Stanley F. Morse—"a man of medium build, not at all handsome, but a live wire"—for extension work, see C. B. Smith to Hunt, February 27, 1913, January 8, 1915; both in BANC, CU-20, B 13, F 3 (C. B. Smith).

8. F. Q. Story, "The Dedication of the Citrus Experiment Station and Graduate School of Tropical Agriculture, Riverside, California, March 27, 1918," *University of California Chronicle* 20, no. 4:28–29. G. Harold Powell, "The Decay of Oranges While in Transit from California," *USDA Bulletin No. 123* (1908); Beverly Galloway to JSW, June 13, 1906, NA II, RG 16, E 184, B 9, Powell file. Greetings letter from JSW, February 23, 1911, ibid. G. Harold Powell, *Letters from the Orange Empire* (Los Angeles: Historical Society of Southern California, 1990).

9. *Amador Dispatch,* July 13, 1889 (also July 15). Webber was raised on a Michigan farm but received bachelor's, master's, and doctoral degrees from the University of Nebraska, along with a doctorate from Washington University in 1900; Herbert J. Webber file, NPRC. Story, "Dedication of the Citrus Experiment Station," 4–31.

10. See the flier for the First Horticultural Assembly, November 15, 1913, at the Riverside station, BANC, CU-20, B 22, F 36. Attending the assembly were growers Ethan Allen Chase and Nathan W. Blanchard. See also Report of California Fruit Growers' Convention, June 1914, BANC, CU-20, B 22, F 13; Programme of Five Days' Citrus Institute, Riverside, November 20–24, 1916, BANC, CU-20, B 22, F 17; Second Annual Convention of High School Agricultural Clubs of California, October 14–17, 1915, BANC, CU-20, B 22, F 34; program of the twentieth annual meeting of the American Association of Farmers' Institute Workers, August 12–14, 1915, BANC, CU-20, B 22, F 28; "Beekeeping Short Courses," *Supplement to University of California Bulletin,* 3d ser., vol. 11, no. 13. See also "Programme Outlines for the Boys' Agricultural Clubs of California: University of California College of Agriculture and United States Department of Agriculture Co-Operating" (Berkeley: University of California Press, 1917), BANC, CU-20, B 22 [Printed Materials, Publications], F 9. B. H. Chocheron, state leader for California, wrote the "Programme," whose outlines for meetings refer most commonly to USDA agricultural *Bulletin*s.

11. Edward Chace and Calvin Church, "Notes on California and Arizona Grape Fruits," *California Citrograph* 3 (1918): 200; Edward McKay Chace, "The Detection and Elimination of Frosted Fruit," *California Citrograph* 4 (February 1919); Edward McKay Chace and Calvin Church, "The Composition of California Lemons," Department Bulletin 993 (1921); "Maturity Test for Salmon Tint Melons," *Pacific Coast Packer* 13 (1922): 8AA. See also *American Fruit Grower* 40, no. 7 (July 1920), in BANC, CU-20, B 16, F 25 (viticulture). A. D. Shamel to Herbert J. Webber, January 2, 1920, BANC, CU-20, B 15, F 39 (A. D. Shamel). Harry S. Smith [at California Department of Agriculture, under G. H. Hecke, director] to Webber, January 13, 1920, BANC, CU-20, B 15, F 41 (Harry S. Smith). See J. A. Prizer, "The County Plant Pathologist," *The Exeter Sun,* Tulare County, California, November 18, 1920, BANC, CU-20, B 15, F 30 ("P miscellaneous").

12. "The University of California Promotes Agricultural Research," BANC, CU-20, B 15, F 14 (newsletters). Herbert J. Webber to C. M. Haring, December 26, 1922, BANC, CU-20, B 16, F 28. *Agricultural State Letter,* November 27, 1922, p. 1: "[T]he University of California College of Agriculture has been embarrassed by the number of counties which have requested agents in excess of the supply available under the funds appropriated," BANC, CU-20, B 15, F 14 (newsletters). H. B. Humphrey, pathologist in charge of Cereal Disease Investigations for the Bureau Plant Industry, to Haring, September 13, 1920, BANC, CU-20, B 14, F 35 (H. B. Humphrey). Sawyer, *To Make a Spot-*

less Orange, 22–27. Biological control appears to be one area in which the capacities of California outgrew those of the USDA; ibid., 82–86.

13. Martin Shefter, *Political Parties and the State* (Princeton: Princeton University Press, 1994), 179–84; George Mowry, *The California Progressives* (Berkeley: University of California Press, 1951); Alexander Saxton, "San Francisco Labor and the Populist and Progressive Insurgencies," *Pacific Historical Review* 34 (1965): 421–38.

14. Carl L. Alsberg's recommendation letter, undated but probably 1918, is in Breazeale Personnel File, NPRC. William A. Taylor, "Recommendation to the Secretary," January 18, 1919, Morrow file, NPRC. Acting chief of Bureau of Plant Industry to JSW, June 18, 1910, Husmann file, NPRC. "Prof. George C. Husmann, Viticulturist, Retires from Department of Agriculture," April 1, 1931, ibid.

15. Charles F. Shaw, professor of Soil Technology, to L. R. Cady, chairman, Board of Supervisors, Susanville, Calif., March 24, 1919; Hiram Johnson to H. J. Webber, April 3, 1920; William Kettner to Webber, March 26, 1920; Edwin Meredith to Webber, March 27, 1920; all in BANC, CU-20, B 16, F 12 (U.S. Congress, Agriculture Committees).

16. Joseph G. Knapp, *The Rise of American Cooperative Enterprise, 1620–1920* (Danville, Ill.: Interstate, 1969). On the USDA's shipment of fenugreek (an annual Asian herb) to thirty-one California farmers, including Teague, see document (dated "1902") entitled "Trifolium Foenum Graecum Was Sent to the Following Persons Last Year," BANC, CU-20, B 2, F "Seeds 1902–03." Teague made his early money in the lemon business. Charles Collins Teague to Waldo A. Harrison, July 12, 1902, Teague Papers, BANC MSS, C-B 760, B 1, V 1, p. 165. Stoll, *Fruits of Natural Advantage,* 45–46. Teague enthusiastically promoted the state's experiment stations, regarding them as the only institutions in California that provided "entirely disinterested" information. See *Official Program,* The American Institute of Cooperation, 1928, BANC, CU-20, B 15.

17. Marilyn P. Watkins, *Rural Democracy: Family Farmers and Politics in Western Washington, 1890–1925* (Ithaca: Cornell University Press, 1995). Clarke A. Chambers, *California Farm Organizations* (Berkeley: University of California Press, 1952).

18. David F. Houston, *Eight Years with Wilson's Cabinet, 1913–1920,* vol. 1 (Garden City, N. Y.: Doubleday, Page, 1926), 260–61; William Clinton Mullendore, *History of the United States Food Administration, 1917–1919* (Stanford: Stanford University Press, 1941). Baker et al., *Century of Service,* 88–89.

19. William J. Breen, *Labor Market Politics and the Great War: The Department of Labor, the States, and the First U.S. Employment Service, 1907–1933* (Kent, Ohio: Kent State University Press, 1997). R. L. Adams, state farm labor agent for the University of California and the USDA, "Emergency Farm Labor Agencies," July 1918, BANC, CU-20, B 13, F 3 (C. B. Smith). True, *History of Agricultural Extension,* 134–51.

20. Howard, *James R. Howard,* 67; C. B. Smith, States Relations Service, to Dean Thomas F. Hunt, March 21, 1918, BANC, CU-20, B 13, F 3 (C. B. Smith). See also the enclosed "Memorandum of Matters Which Should Be Mentioned at Farmers' Mass Meetings, March–April 1918."

21. USDA, *Cooperative Extension Work in Agriculture and Home Economics, 1917* (Washington, D.C.: GPO, 1919), 26, 169. USDA, *Cooperative Extension Work in Agriculture and Home Economics, 1918* (Washington, D.C.: GPO, 1919), 20–22; Baker et al., *Century of Service,* 82. Lloyd P. Jorgenson, "Agricultural Expansion into the Semi-

arid Lands of the West North Central States during the First World War," *Agricultural History* 23 (January 1949): 30–40.

22. Kile, *Farm Bureau Movement,* 111–12; Howard, *James R. Howard,* 79–96; True, *History of Agricultural Extension,* 154–59.

23. R. K. Bliss, *A History of Cooperative Agriculture and Home Economics Extension in Iowa* (Ames: Iowa State University Press, 1960); True, *History of Agricultural Extension,* 157–58; Howard, *James R. Howard,* 74, 78.

24. Kile, *Farm Bureau Movement,* 113–14; True, *History of Agricultural Extension,* 160. Clifford V. Gregory was the editor of *Prairie Farmer,* based in Chicago. James R. Howard of Iowa, who was voted the first AFBF president one year later, also attended the meeting; Howard, *James R. Howard,* 102–5.

25. Howard, *James R. Howard,* 108–19; True, *History of Agricultural Extension,* 160–62. Most observers (and many delegates) had expected Oscar E. Bradfute of Ohio to be elected the federation's first president. In 1923 Bradfute became the second president of the AFBF.

26. The total farm product in 1919 was more than 150 percent above its 1913 level. Farmers were also far more indebted than before. Between 1910 and 1920, the amount of mortgage debt on owner-operated farms in the United States grew from $1.7 billion to $4 billion, an increase of 131.9 percent. James H. Shideler, *Farm Crisis, 1919–1923* (Berkeley: University of California Press, 1957), 39–40.

27. True, *History of Agricultural Extension,* 162; Kile, *Farm Bureau Movement,* 126–27. Other estimates place the federation membership at fewer than five hundred thousand, but whatever the actual total, by 1921 the Farm Bureau carried greater weight and diversity of membership than any other organization.

28. Howard reports that "several [USDA] departmental specialists" were on hand at Silver's office when the formational meeting occurred (*James R. Howard,* 167). Arthur Capper, *The Agricultural Bloc* (New York: Harcourt Brace, 1922); George W. Norris, *Fighting Liberal* (New York: Macmillan, 1945); Hansen, *Gaining Access,* 31–32; Donald Winters, *Henry Cantwell Wallace as Secretary of Agriculture, 1921–1924* (Champaign: University of Illinois Press, 1970), 75–82. Alice M. Christensen, "Agricultural Pressure and Government Response in the United States, 1919–1929," *Agricultural History* 11 (1937): 33–42; Patrick O'Brien, "A Reexamination of the Senate Farm Bloc, 1921–1933," *Agricultural History* 47 (1973): 248–63.

29. John K. Barnes, "The Man Who Runs the Farm Bloc," *World's Work,* November 1922, 52, quoted in Hansen, *Gaining Access,* 32. Ralph Gabriel, *North American Review,* July 1921. The department had been asking for regulatory authority over the stockyards since at least Secretary Houston's tenure. See his *Address before the American National Live Stock Association,* January 22, 1919 (Washington, D.C.: GPO, 1919), 12–13.

30. The Big Five were Armour, Morris, Cudahy, Swift, and Wilson. Winters, *Henry Cantwell Wallace,* 76–81. Thomas McCraw, *Prophets of Regulation* (Cambridge, Mass.: Harvard University Press, 1984); Howard, *James R. Howard,* 168; Theodore Saloutos and John D. Hicks, *Twentieth-Century Populism: Agricultural Discontent in the Middle West, 1900–1939* (Lincoln: University of Nebraska Press, 1964), 327–28.

31. Grain Futures Act at 43 Stat. 653. See also *Hill v. Wallace,* 259 U.S. 44. A copy of the department's redraft of the 1921 act is in the files of Gilbert N. Haugen, chairman of the House Agriculture Committee in the early 1920s, GNH, Legislative Files (USDA). Jonathan Lurie, "Regulation of the Commodities Exchanges in the 1920s: The

Legacy of Self-Government," in *Farmers, Bureaucrats, and Middlemen,* ed. Peterson, 233–61. Winters, *Henry Cantwell Wallace,* 80–82; Baker et al., *Century of Service,* 109–10; Shideler, *Farm Crisis,* 159.

32. Shideler, *Farm Crisis,* chap. 4, esp. 104–11; Kile, *Farm Bureau Movement,* 150–54; Howard, *James R. Howard,* 142–56. The Committee of Seventeen included George Livingston of the USDA's Bureau of Markets.

33. See, for instance, the federation's "Memorandum on Agricultural Legislation," press release, January 14, 1924, NA II, RG 16, E 17, B 1035, AFBF file. For a review of the legislative struggles over Muscle Shoals, see Bensel, *Sectionalism and American Political Development,* 130–35; Shideler, *Farm Crisis,* 172–74; Hansen, *Gaining Access,* 29, 40.

34. The other departmental participant in AFBF executive committee meetings was the president of the National Association of County Agricultural Agents. On James Coverdale's experience as a USDA employee—from 1912 to 1918—see Samuel R. Guard (Director of Information, AFBF, in Chicago) to Nellie V. Price (AFBF, Washington, D.C.), August 16, 1921, enclosures, NA II, RG 16, E 17, B 802, AFBF file. On Coverdale's trips to Washington, see Howard, *James R. Howard,* 89–91; see 119 for Howard's memory of complete agreement with Coverdale. The statements of Howard, Lloyd, and Smith appear in True, *History of Agricultural Extension,* 166–67. On Michael's and Wallace's participation, see Minutes, Executive Committee Meetings, AFBF, General Offices, Chicago, Illinois, December 5, 11, and 12, 1924, RG 16, E 17, B 1035, AFBF file. Grant McConnell, *The Decline of Agrarian Democracy* (Berkeley: University of California Press, 1953), 59.

35. *AFBF Weekly News Letter,* October 5, 1922, p. 4, NA II, RG 16, E 17, B 875. See also *AFBF Advance Weekly News Service* 83, October 3, 1922, NA II, RG 16, E 17, B 875, AFBF file. Among the strongest opponents of the Forest Service move was the California Farm Bureau. W. H. Heileman, secretary/treasurer, California Farm Bureau Federation, to C. M. Haring, January 19, 1922: "I beg to advise that both the national and state Farm Bureau Federations have already taken action protesting against the disturbance of any of the bureaus in the Department of Agriculture" (BANC, CU-20, B 14, F 22 [W. H. Heileman]). Resolution carried by the Executive Committee of the AFBF, Minutes, January 31, 1925, Chicago, Illinois, RG 16, E 17, B 1106, AFBF file. On the stockyard inspection issue, see ibid., January 29, 1925, Chicago, Illinois, NA II, RG 16, E 17, B 1106, AFBF file.

36. "Just Criticism of County Agents Worries Department of Agriculture," in GNH, Legislative Files (USDA); *Daily Drovers Journal-Stockman (Omaha),* March 28, 1922. See B. H. Crocheron's undated bulletin "Information Not Propaganda the Aim of U. C. Extension Service," BANC, CU-20, B 15, F 14 (newsletters). Christiana McFayden Campbell, *The Farm Bureau and the New Deal* (Urbana: University of Illinois Press, 1962), chaps. 1–3.

37. In December 1921 Pinchot wrote a number of letters in protest of the proposed transfers. Gifford Pinchot to C. M. Haring, December 31, 1921, BANC, CU-20, B 14, F 22. Winters, *Henry Cantwell Wallace,* 161–89; Orville Merton Kile, *The Farm Bureau through Three Decades* (Baltimore: Waverly Press, 1948), 140–41.

38. Gregory Hooks, "From an Autonomous to a Captured State Agency: The Decline of the New Deal in Agriculture," *American Sociological Review* 55, no. 1 (February 1990): 29–43.

39. Richard M. Valelly, *Radicalism in the States: The Minnesota Farmer-Labor Party and the American Political Economy* (Chicago: University of Chicago Press, 1989); Saloutos and Hicks, *Twentieth-Century Populism;* Hansen, *Gaining Access,* 35–36.

40. Shideler, *Farm Crisis,* 217–27; Vallelly, *Radicalism in the States,* 41; Hansen, *Gaining Access,* 35–36.

41. L. D. Seass to HCW, February 10, 1922, NA II, RG 16, E 17, B 875, F "Agricultural Situation."

42. Fred W. Weaver to HCW, January 15, 1922, ibid.

43. James Baker to HCW, February 3, 1922; T. E. Richards to HCW, January 14, 1922. The popularity of the Wallace name and the fond memories of the Roosevelt administration for many western agrarians are evinced in a letter from W.S.A. Douglas, Excelsior, Minnesota, to HCW, September 27, 1921: "We farmers do have confidence in our Secretary of Agriculture because of the great confidence engendered through your grand old father who always fought for a square deal for the farmers. . . . We need another fearless Teddy." All letters are in NA II, RG 16, E 17, B 875, F "Agricultural Situation."

44. Squire Innis, Creswell, Oregon, to HCW, January 1, 1922, in ibid.

45. B. F. Keith (Keith Farm, Currie, N.C.) to HCW, January 28, 1922, ibid.

46. Robert M. Tontz, "Membership of General Farmers' Organizations, United States, 1874–1960," *Agricultural History* 38 (July 1964): 143–52; Martin Sklar, *The Corporate Reconstruction of American Capitalism* (New York: Cambridge University Press, 1988), 254; Hansen, *Gaining Access,* 29.

47. Charles S. Barrett, *The Mission, History, and Times of the Farmers' Union* (Lincoln: University of Nebraska Press, 1960); Commodore B. Fisher, *The Farmers' Union* (Lexington: University of Kentucky Press, 1920); Wiest, *Agricultural Organization,* 499–502; Saloutos and Hicks, *Twentieth-Century Populism,* 219–54, 227; William P. Tucker, "Populism Up-to-Date: The Story of the Farmers' Union," *Agricultural History* 21 (October 1947): 198–201. Although Tontz does not provide NFU membership data for the 1920s, he estimates that by 1933 the NFU counted fewer than eighty thousand families ("Membership of General Farmers' Organizations," 155). Wallace's remark is reported in Howard, *James R. Howard,* 119.

48. Hansen, *Gaining Access,* 28; Kile, *Farm Bureau through Three Decades,* 21–22. Barron, *Mixed Harvest,* 141–45.

49. Kile, *Farm Bureau Movement,* 52: Saloutos and Hicks, *Twentieth-Century Populism,* 224–25, 545–47; Hansen, *Gaining Access,* 27.

50. Noah E. Friedkin, "Theoretical Foundations for Centrality Measures," *American Journal of Sociology* 96 (1991): 1478–1504. I thank Michael Heaney for a penetrating criticism of my brokerage argument in this chapter.

51. Kellerman's obituary is in *Science,* October 26, 1934, 373–74. Fairchild also received the Public Welfare Medal of the National Academy of Sciences in 1933; USDA press release, May 19, 1933. Charles A. Browne, *A Handbook of Sugar Analysis* (New York, 1912). For its review, see *Deutsche Zuckerindustrie,* November 6, 1912. Browne was a member of the Association des Chimistes de Sucrerie de France and associate editor of *Industrial and Engineering Chemistry* from 1911 to 1917. By 1925 he was president of the AOAC and author of more than three hundred papers, books, and pamphlets. On Smith, see Frederick V. Rand, "Erwin F. Smith," *Mycologia* 20, no. 4 (July–August

1928): 181–86; "Dr. Erwin F. Smith, Scientist, Is Dead," *The Official Record* (USDA), April 20, 1927, p. 5. In November 1924 Brown was elected honorary foreign fellow of England's National Institute of Agricultural Botany in Cambridge.

52. Herbert Bailey left the department for Du Pont in 1918. Bailey to Dr. C. O. Johns, Washington, D.C., April 12, 1919, Bailey file, NPRC. Mary Conyington, "Separations from Government Service," *Monthly Labor Review* 11 (1920): 1131–44; David Fairchild to HCW, August 21, 1922, Fairchild file, NPRC; Paul F. Brissenden, "Labor Turnover in the Federal Service," in *Report of Wage and Personnel Survey,* Field Survey Division, Report of the Personnel Classification Board (Washington, D.C.: GPO, 1929), 337–38. On experiment station turnover, see Joel Kunze, "The Purnell Act and Agricultural Economics," *Agricultural History* 62, no. 2 (spring 1988): 133.

53. A summary of Reed's method, along with the USDA official's statement, is in the *Washington Times,* Sunday, October 23, 1915. Reed's discovery was the subject of considerable controversy in the department, for chemist Aida M. Doyle claimed that she had invented the method and had used it for several years in tea inspection work. The method was simple and entailed using only a fine-meshed sieve, a piece of white paper, and a spatula or knife blade to determine whether tea leaves had been dyed.

54. "More Farm Relief," *Saturday Evening Post,* September 17, 1927.

55. "Minutes of the First Organization Meeting of Men Interested in Rural Social Sciences" (undated [1912]), which called for a gathering on May 4, 1912 (in NA II, RG 16, Records of the Office of the Secretary, F "Employee Organizations"). On June 13 the first meeting of the Rural Economics Club was held, complete with a constitution and a board of officers. See "Memorandum Concerning the Organization of a Society to Be Known As the Rural Economics Club" (in ibid.). The most thorough membership list of the club appears in an untitled meeting announcement containing fifty-two names.

56. NA II, RG 16, E 185, Jacob R. Dodge file; Henry C. Taylor and Anne Dewees Taylor, *The Story of Agricultural Economics in the United States, 1840–1932: Men, Services, Ideas* (Ames: State College Press, 1952), 169–99, 239–49. See the profile of Estabrook in T. M. Kingsbury, "Uncle Sam's Hired Men Who Serve You," USDA press release, April 18, 1921, NA II, RG 16, E 185, Leon M. Estabrook file.

57. On Estabrook's appointment, see G. DeMichaelis, president, International Institute of Agriculture, to William Jardine, secretary of agriculture, December 16, 1929, NA II, RG 16, E 185, Estabrook file. See USDA, Office of the Secretary, *Crop Report Regulations* (Estabrook file, January 3, 1921, photocopy). Joel Kunze, "The Bureau of Agricultural Economics' Outlook Program in the 1920s As a Pedagogical Device," *Agricultural History* 64, no. 2 (Spring 1990): 252–61; Taylor and Taylor, *Story of Agricultural Economics,* 447–53, 456–57. On USDA broadcasting, see HCW to Governor R. A. Nestos, North Dakota, January 26, 1924, NA II, RG 16, E 17, B 1035, January appropriations file; Reynold M. Wik, "The USDA and the Development of Radio in Rural America," *Agricultural History* 62, no. 2 (Spring 1988): 177–88; Winters, *Henry Cantwell Wallace,* 127. Barron, *Mixed Harvest,* 216–17. B. B. Smith, "Factors Affecting the Price of Cotton," *USDA Technical Bulletin* 50 (Washington, D.C.: GPO, 1928).

58. The Bureau of Plant Industry had a program in Cotton Breeding in 1909. The New York Cotton Exchange's cotton grades were based entirely on the official cotton grades of the USDA, which were developed by W. E. Chambers. See William A. Taylor to DFH, July 10, 1914, 27ff., NA II, RG 16, secretary's files. On the act of 1923, see *The United States Cotton Standards Act,* U.S. Bureau of Agricultural Economics Service and

Regulatory Announcements, 82 (1924); Baker et al., *Century of Service,* 112–13; Winters, *Henry Cantwell Wallace,* 128–36.

59. S. G. Rubinow, "The Next Organization Step in Southern Agriculture," *School and Society* (October 25, 1919): 479–85. Andrew W. McKay, "Federal Research and Educational Work for Farmer Cooperatives, 1913–1953," U.S. Farmer Cooperative Service, Service Report 40. Wilson Gee and Edward Allison Terry, *The Cotton Cooperatives in the Southeast* (New York: D. Appleton-Century, 1933); Grace H. Larsen and Henry E. Erdman, "Aaron Sapiro: Genius of Farm Co-operative Promotion," *Mississippi Valley Historical Review* 49 (September 1962): 242–68; Hansen, *Gaining Access,* 61–66. The Meloy tour was chartered with the Saint Louis Southwestern Railway Company on their "Cotton Belt line," and the resulting tour was named the Cotton Belt Cotton Train. P. T. Cole, agricultural commissioner for Saint Louis Southwestern, to Henry C. Taylor, March 26, 1924, NA II, RG 83, correspondence files (also RG 16, E 184, Meloy file). "Cotton School on Wheels at Athens," *Dallas News,* February 20, 1924; "Crowds Welcome Cotton Special," *Arkansas Gazette,* March 8, 1924; "Cotton Belt Train Heartily Received," *Arkansas Gazette,* March 11, 1924.

60. William J. Spillman and Emil Lang, *The Law of Diminishing Returns* (Yonkers-on-Hudson: World Book, 1924). Spillman also contributed to the statistical analysis of "yield curves" for fertilizer use. See his draft "Form of the Yield Curve," in NA II, RG 83, E 145, B 1, F 2. Spillman discovered that an exponential specification of the yield curve was better than the parabolic specification that some European chemists proposed. The paper was later published as "Use of the Exponential Curve in Fertilizer Experiments," *USDA Technical Bulletin* 348 (Washington, D.C.: GPO, 1933); Taylor and Taylor, *Story of Agricultural Economics,* 140–41, and more generally 388–479.

61. The organizational lineage of the BAE is complicated. The OFM had been created by Wilson in 1905. In 1913 Secretary Houston made Spillman director of the Office of Markets within the Bureau of Plant Industry. This office was combined with the Division of Crop Estimates to create the Bureau of Farm Management and Farm Economics in 1919. It was then combined with the Office of Crop Estimates (itself an outgrowth of Bureau of Statistics) in 1921 to create the Bureau of Markets and Crop Estimates, which was renamed the Bureau of Agricultural Economics in 1923. Harry McDean, "Professionalism in the Rural Social Sciences, 1896–1919," *Agricultural History* 58 (July 1984): 373–92, and "Professionalism, Policy, and Farm Economists in the Early Bureau of Agricultural Economics," *Agricultural History* 57 (January 1983): 64–82. Richard Hofstadter, *Anti-Intellectualism in America* (New York: Knopf, 1963), 199–204. See also Richard Kirkendall's concept of "service intellectuals" in *Social Scientists and Farm Politics in the Age of Roosevelt* (Columbia: University of Missouri Press, 1966).

62. Kunze, "The Purnell Act," 131–49. The USDA's leadership role under the Purnell Act grew out of farmers' recognition of the USDA's leadership in agricultural economics. As James Shideler writes, "Farmers criticized agricultural colleges and experiment stations for being slower than the Agricultural Department in developing the field of agricultural economics" (*Farm Crisis,* 133).

63. The draft was changed after Brand sent it to Peek and Johnson, but Brand had established the bill's basic outlines. "Corn and cotton" married after 1926, and the bill twice passed Congress, in 1927 and 1928. Both times it fell to Calvin Coolidge's veto, turning western farmers ever more solidly against stalwart Republicans. On Hoover's

opposition to the BAE, see William D. Rowley, *M. L. Wilson and the Campaign for the Domestic Allotment* (Lincoln: University of Nebraska Press, 1970), 27–28. For the most exhaustive legislative and administrative history of McNary-Haugenism, see Gilbert C. Fite, *George N. Peek and the Fight for Farm Parity* (Norman: University of Oklahoma Press, 1954). Jardine hired Nils A. Olsen as assistant chief of the BAE; Olsen became chief in 1928; see his *Diary of a Tamed Bureaucrat: Nils Olsen and the BAE, 1925–1935,* ed. Richard Lowitt (Ames: Iowa State University Press, 1980).

64. William J. Spillman, *Balancing the Farm Output: A Statement of the Present Deplorable Conditions of Farming, Its Causes, and Suggested Remedies* (New York: Orange Judd Publishing, 1927); John D. Black, *Agricultural Reform in the United States* (New York: Orange Judd Publishing, 1929); Theodore Saloutos, *The American Farmer and the New Deal* (Ames: Iowa State University Press, 1980), 34–35; Rowley, *M. L. Wilson,* 33–46.

65. Lippman and Lord are quoted in Rowley, *M. L. Wilson,* 185. David E. Hamilton, *From New Day to New Deal: American Farm Policy from Hoover to Roosevelt, 1928–1933* (Chapel Hill: University of North Carolina Press, 1991), 182ff.; Edwin G. Nourse, Joseph S. Davis, and John D. Black, *Three Years of the Agricultural Adjustment Administration* (Washington, D.C.: Brookings Institution, 1937), 12–20.

Chapter Ten

1. *CR* (House), July 29, 1914, p. 12964.

2. The wisdom of a less ambitious course based on a stepwise program expansion became apparent in the 1920s, when Ellwood Mead, commissioner of reclamation, explicitly cleaved to incrementalism in order to calm recalcitrant members of Congress and to learn project by project about the difficulties of irrigated agriculture. Through incrementalism, Mead had, by the time of the Depression, established a thread of legitimacy for his bureau, paving the way for its expansion in the New Deal. For this reason, Mead was one of the few Hoover officials kept by the Roosevelt administration in 1933. In his informative book on Mead's career, James Kluger notes that Roosevelt's reappointment of Mead as commissioner of reclamation in 1933 rested on Mead's "reputation" and the "positive image" he had created for the bureau. James Kluger, *Turning on Water with a Shovel: The Career of Elwood Mead* (Albuquerque: University of New Mexico Press, 1992), 128–29.

3. Peffer, *Closing of the Public Domain;* Donald C. Swain, *Federal Conservation Policy, 1921–1933* (Berkeley: University of California Press, 1963); Donald Pisani, *From the Family Farm to Agribusiness: The Irrigation Crusade in California and the West, 1850–1931* (Berkeley: University of California Press, 1981); Pisani, *Water, Land, and Law.*

4. The National Irrigation Congress, the most powerful irrigation group, held its first annual meeting in 1891. Other congresses included the Western Commercial Congress and the Transmississippi Commercial Congress. Dorothy Lampen, *Economic and Social Aspects of Federal Reclamation* (Baltimore: Johns Hopkins University Press, 1930), 28–32, 38; Pisani, *From the Family Farm to Agribusiness,* 279–82. Mark Hufstetler and Lon Johnson, *Watering the Land: The Turbulent History of the Carlsbad Irrigation District* (Denver: National Park Service, 1993), 67. Powell's report appears at House Misc. Doc. 45, pt. 4, 47th Cong., 2d sess. That the Senate supported reclamation before

the House is not surprising, given that the western states had equal footing with eastern ones in the Senate, and given that the Republicans had brought a number of territories into statehood well before population considerations would have suggested it. Charles Stewart III and Barry Weingast, "Stacking the Senate, Changing the Nation: Republican Rotten Boroughs, Statehood Politics, and American Political Development," *Studies in American Political Development* 6, no. 2 (fall 1992): 223–71.

5. Carey Act of 1894, 38 U.S. 422. Lampen, *Economic and Social Aspects,* 33–35; Smith, *The Magnificent Experiment,* 8; Pisani, *From the Family Farm to Agribusiness,* 280.

6. House of Representatives, Committee on Irrigation of Arid Lands, "Irrigation of Arid Lands," HED 446, 57th Cong., 1st sess., p. 12. For the majority and minority reports of the committee, see "Irrigation and Reclamation of Arid Lands," Report 794, pt. 1 (majority) and pt. 2 (minority), March 8 and 10, 1902, 57th Cong., 1st sess. Among the officials speaking in favor of the legislation were Secretary of Agriculture James Wilson, Sen. Benjamin F. Tillman of South Carolina, Sen. Henry C. Hansbrough of North Dakota, Sen. J. H. Gallagher of New Hampshire, and Sen. A. S. Clay of Georgia. Donald Pisani, *To Reclaim a Divided West: Water, Law, and Public Policy, 1848–1902* (Albuquerque: University of New Mexico Press, 1992), chap. 8.

7. Reclamation Act, passed June 17, 1902 (32 Stat. 388), reported with accompanying case law in U.S. Department of the Interior, *Federal Reclamation Laws Annotated* (Washington, D.C.: GPO, 1927). For a general discussion of the act's provisions as they affected settlers, see Department of the Interior, U.S. Reclamation Service, *Questions and Answers Relating to the Reclamation Act and Its Operations,* September 12, 1909 (Washington, D.C.: GPO, 1909). See also U.S. Department of the Interior, *Federal Reclamation Laws Annotated,* 10–51. The supremacy of the Interior Department's decisions over state laws was established in *U.S. v. O'Neill,* 198 Fed. 677, in which the court also held that the secretary's project-location decisions were not reviewable by federal courts.

8. The creation of irrigation works and their transfer to western settlers was supposed to involve close cooperation between Reclamation Service engineers and western water users' associations. The latter were groups of individuals claiming the right to use the diverted water and owning lands in the basin area. Critically, the secretary of interior determined the organizing principles of these associations, a denial of local autonomy that problematized the relations of the service with the West. See U.S. Reclamation Service, *Questions and Answers,* 22–23.

9. Hansbrough, in "Reclamation of Arid Lands," Senate Report 254, p. 1. The Geological Survey's predictions for the program appear in Walcott's message, pp. 2–7. The *Genoa Weekly Courier* quote is in Pisani, *To Reclaim a Divided West,* 323. See Pisani's judgment that "[u]nder the 1902 law, reclamation was largely self-contained and self-sufficient" (323).

10. Pisani, *Water, Land, and Law,* 185–86. Elements of Davis's biography appear in *CR* (House), May 22, 1928, p. 9497. Swain, *Federal Conservation Policy,* 78–79.

11. I thank Donald Pisani for this point. Mead also brought international experience to reclamation, which the Reclamation Act of 1902 ignored; Rodgers, *Atlantic Crossings,* 345–52.

12. In 1906 Newlands expressed his hope that "the Reclamation Service, in laying out the public lands under the various projects, will provide for well-planned towns, in

which the owners of the adjoining farms will gather together for social, educational, and religious purposes" (quotation from Pisani, *Water, Land, and Law,* 186). So, too, throughout Mead's decades-long critique of American reclamation policy, he consistently emphasized the importance of township planning. Once a project was selected, "[t]he town sites should be located and laid out, like the farms, according to some carefully thought out plan." Indeed, the entire evolution of an irrigated farming valley should be "planned development." See Ellwood Mead, "A Plan for Reclaiming and Peopling the Mesa Lands Bordering the Imperial Irrigation District," 3, 4, Ellwood Mead Collection, entry MEAD 3, Water Resources Library, University of California, Berkeley. As he announced in 1910, the director's measure of success for the program was the placing of ten thousand families on project lands. Newell cared much less about the viability of project farms than about the strictly numerical growth of the program in terms of number of settlers and number of acres irrigated.

13. The Truckee-Carson delay is reported in the "Garfield Report," James Garfield to Theodore Roosevelt, October 22, 1906, p. 28, Garfield Papers, C 143. On the development of the Truckee-Carson project, see the Board of Army Engineers' report, *Fund for Reclamation of Arid Lands* (Washington, D.C.: GPO, 1911), 87–91.

14. The Klamath Falls dilemma is narrated in James R. Garfield's report "Methods of Administration in the Department of Interior," Garfield to Roosevelt, October 22, 1906, p. 30. For a broader discussion of the report, see chapter 2. For a review of the Klamath project, see the Board of Army Engineers, *Fund for Reclamation of Arid Lands,* 119–26.

15. Pisani notes that "Newell and his lieutenants stubbornly, and foolishly, refused to exploit the skills and experience of the Department of Agriculture" (*From the Family Farm to Agribusiness,* 316). The USDA had two of the nation's foremost irrigation experts—Ray Palmer Teele and Ellwood Mead. On Mead's career in Wyoming, see "Wyoming Decade," chap. 2 in Kluger, *Turning on Water with a Shovel,* 14–26. Mead had authored *Irrigation Institutions* (New York: Macmillan, 1903), a tract widely read among civil engineers which discussed the economic and political implications of the rise of irrigated agriculture in the West. As a more sophisticated extension of Mead's analysis in *Institutions,* in 1915 Teele had penned *Irrigation in the United States* (New York: D. Appleton).

16. As Doris Ostrander Dawdy summarizes, "The Geological Survey was made to order for an intrinsic part of the action in the reclamation movement. So was the Department of Agriculture. Unfortunately both were improperly used in reclaiming the West, and the Corps of Engineers was not used at all." Doris Ostrander Dawdy, *Congress in Its Wisdom: The Bureau of Reclamation and the Public Interest,* Studies in Water Policy and Management 13 (Boulder, Colo.: Westview Press, 1989).

17. Because the service was rather small and the number of counties large, I analyze these counts in a zero-inflated negative binomial regression model that accounts both for the overdispersion of the data from a baseline Poisson distribution and for the appearance of more zeros than would be predicted by the negative binomial distribution. Whenever I introduce the chief engineers' variable into estimation, I subtract this variable from the dependent (matriculation) variable so that the same employees are not counted on both sides of the equation.

18. Hufstetler and Johnson, *Watering the Land,* 70–74.

19. Theodore Roosevelt, *Theodore Roosevelt: An Autobiography* (New York:

Charles Scribners's Sons, 1913), 411. In part because what defined a new project was unclear, historians of western irrigation offer varying estimates of exactly how many projects the service had started by 1907. In *From the Family Farm to Agribusiness,* Pisani reports 24 (p. 301). Swain, in *Federal Conservation Policy,* suggests 25 (p. 76). Dawdy states that the service had 30 projects under way in 1910 (*Congress in Its Wisdom,* 16), whereas an independent board of army engineers counted 32, of which 30 were "primary" (Board of Army Engineers, *Fund for Reclamation of Arid Lands,* p. 9). Members of Congress often exhibited the same confusion. In debates over the reclamation extension bill of 1914, the number of projects under way that year ranged from Frank Mondell's estimate of 27 to Edward Taylor's number of 32 (*CR* [House], July 16, pp. 12224, 12238, respectively). More generally, see Pisani, *Water, Land, and Law,* 49. On the stoppage of project initiation from 1906 to 1912, see U.S. Reclamation Service, *Eleventh Annual Report of Reclamation Service, 1911–1912* (Washington, D.C.: GPO, 1913) (in "Excerpts from Annual Reports of Bureau of Reclamation," Garfield Papers, C 134, "Excerpts from Eleventh Annual Report," p. 2); see also President Taft's message in *Fund for Reclamation of Arid Lands,* by Board of Army Engineers, p. 10.

20. Reclamation Act of 1902, 32 Stat. 388. Repealed by section 6, act of June 25, 1910, 36 Stat. 835. Quoted in Department of the Interior, *Federal Reclamation Laws Annotated,* 50.

21. Pisani, *From the Family Farm to Agribusiness,* 307. The correlations reported in the table and discussed in the text do not change under multiple regression analysis. If reclamation expenditures are regressed upon (1) land receipts, (2) fraction of House victories won by Republicans from 1896 to 1931, (3) state population in 1900, and (4) state farm productivity in 1900, only farm productivity is significantly associated with service expenditures, and this effect is negative. Indeed, the inverse association between expenditures and farm product suggests that Newell and service officials were indeed aiming their projects at those areas where agricultural production was low due to lack of water.

22. Swain, *Federal Conservation Policy,* 76. Rep J. R. Mann suggested in 1914 that the service suffered from the "iridescent dreams" of its engineers (*CR* [House], July 16, 1914, p. 12235). On the drive to establish a "perception of efficacy," see Hufstetler and Johnson, *Watering the Land,* 68.

23. For an early sense of the optimism surrounding Imperial Valley reclamation, see the report of C. E. Tait, *Irrigation in Imperial Valley, California,* 60th Cong., 1st sess., document 246. The Central Board of Review was chaired by Mead, who easily qualified as Newell's fiercest critic. In its 1916 report on the Yuma project, Mead's board recommended that the new "Mesa lands" in Arizona and California, which would be available for settlement that year, be opened incrementally in units of no more than ten thousand acres each. Mead wanted no unit opened until "at least two thirds of the preceding unit is settled, planted with fruit trees, or otherwise put under cultivation, and that the maximum sale price of excess private lands be fixed with the assent of private owners, before the project is undertaken at all" (from dissenting letter to Secretary Franklin K. Lane, March 6, 1916, p. 6, *Reports of Central Board of Review,* EMC, entry MEAD 18). Pisani, *From the Family Farm to Agribusiness,* 318.

24. Smith, *Magnificent Experiment,* 50–51.

25. The Board of Army Engineers reviewed the service's construction patterns on p. 15 of its report, *Fund for Reclamation of Arid Lands.* On the delays at Laguna, see

p. 33 of the report. For the Salt River cost estimates, see Arthur Powell Davis's analysis in the *Annual Report, 1902–1903* (Washington, D.C.: GPO, 1903), pp. 71–76. Hufstetler and Johnson, *Watering the Land,* 68; Board of Army Engineers, *Fund for Reclamation of Arid Lands,* 93–94.

The service's Ockerson levee, built in 1911 at the Yuma project, suffered numerous breaks that year and left the Colorado River flowing away from irrigation headways and down the Bee River channel. It was the only levee protecting the Imperial Valley to break consistently during the project's early years. See the report of the board of engineers appointed by Interior Secretary Franklin Lane and University of California president Benjamin Ide Wheeler, chaired by Ellwood Mead, "Irrigation and Flood Protection Problems of Imperial Valley, California" (March 1917), Exhibit A, p. 3, EMC, entry MEAD 26. Mead's board reported that the government never repaired the Ockerson levee and that additional breaches occurred due to "lack of maintenance." "Aside from the Ockerson levee," the board summarized, the levees at Yuma "have thus far fairly accomplished their object" (3).

26. In its *Third Annual Report of the Reclamation Service, 1903–1904* (Washington, D.C.: GPO, 1905), the service estimated the cost of the Yuma project at $40 per acre and stated that the project offered 130,000 irrigable acres. A decade later, the service admitted that in its early years "the average cost per acre was estimated at an extremely low figure because of the fact that the actual cost was not recorded and the acreage which might be irrigated was, as a rule, highly exaggerated" (*Eleventh Annual Report of the Reclamation Service, 1911–1912* [Washington, D.C.: GPO, 1913]). On the lack of soil analysis at the Salt River project, see the report of Arthur Powell Davis in *Annual Report, 1902–1903,* pp. 91–103; the absence of soil analysis at Carlsbad is reported in Hufstetler and Johnson, *Watering the Land,* pp. 74ff. On the service's failure to consider land preparation costs and the necessity for drainage systems, see the remarks of Rep. Frank Mondell, *CR* (House), July 16, 1914, p. 12225. Even by 1911, as the reviewing board of army engineers discovered, the service had updated its cost estimates only by previous experience of overruns, not by further study. See Board of Army Engineers, *Fund for Reclamation of Arid Lands,* 16–17. Pisani, *From the Family Farm to Agribusiness,* 317 n. 46. For examples of the service's reliance on local water users' associations, see Peffer, *Closing of the Public Domain,* 61. Newell's view of the service's responsibilities under the 1902 act appears in ibid., 60. A dissenting opinion to Mead's study of the Yuma project in 1914 provides a discussion of the obstacles left by previous irrigation efforts and farming. See Department of the Interior, United States Reclamation Service, *Reports of the Central Board of Review* [1915–16], p. 4, EMC, entry MEAD 18.

27. The service complained of speculation in its *Fourth Annual Report of the Reclamation Service, 1904–1905:* "The amount of land in these States which can be irrigated on any considerable scale is very small, in most States less than 1 percent of the area. The land is now all in the hands of a few persons" (see "Excerpts from Annual Reports.") See also the remarks of Rep. John J. Fitzgerald, a Democrat from New York and chairman of the House Appropriations Committee, in *CR* (House), July 22, 1914, p. 12498. Peffer, *Closing of the Public Domain,* 61.

28. Remarks of Rep. William LaFollette, *CR* (House), July 29, 1914, p. 12967. Reclamation Service, *Eleventh Annual Report of the Reclamation Service.* Taft's message is in the Board of Army Engineers, *Fund for Reclamation of Arid Lands,* 10. For evidence of service updating, see ibid., 16.

29. The 50 to 300 percent figure is from Rep. William LaFollette, in *CR* (House), July 29, 1914, p. 12967. See Mead, "Irrigation and Flood Protection Problems of Imperial Valley, California." Pisani, *From the Family Farm to Agribusiness,* 311–15. Pisani suggests that the per-acre cost at Yuma had risen to $75 by 1917. It appears, however, that the Reclamation Service's Central Board of Review privately estimated a $75 per-acre average project cost as early as March 1916, perhaps as early as the fall of 1915. See the dissenting letter to Franklin Lane, March 6, 1916, in the *Reports of the Central Board of Review,* by Reclamation Service, p. 6.

30. Pisani, *From the Family Farm to Agribusiness,* 316–19. The hope for sustained citrus agriculture in the Imperial Valley was not held by Newell and Lippincott alone. Even Newell's fiercest critic, Ellwood Mead, wrote that the Yuma lands were "equal to or superior to any citrus and semi-tropical fruit land in the United States." See letter to Franklin Lane, March 6, 1916, p. 7, in *Reports of the Central Board of Survey,* EMC, Entry MEAD 18.

31. Pisani, *From the Family Farm to Agribusiness,* 318–19; Hufstetler and Smith, *Watering the Land,* 98.

32. Pisani, *From the Family Farm to Agribusiness,* 319. "Excerpts from Eleventh Annual Report," in *Eleventh Annual Report of the Reclamation Service,* pp. 4–5. Hufstetler and Johnson, *Watering the Land,* 101.

33. On the troubles at Bellefourche, see the remarks of Rep. Charles H. Burke, *CR* (House), July 29, 1914, pp. 12959–60. A similar state of distrust prevailed at the Klamath project on the northern California–Oregon border, where a board of army engineers discovered that "much dissatisfaction was expressed" by settlers about the overcharging tendencies of the service (Bureau of Army Engineers, *Fund for Reclamation of Arid Lands,* 121).

34. Smith, "The Business of Irrigation," chap. 5 in *Magnificent Experiment.* The subcommittee report is quoted on p. 116. *Annual Report, 1902–1903,* 71–76; Smith, ibid., 31.

35. The consulting engineer was C. E. Grunsky, who detailed the complaints of the Pecos Valley Water Users' Association, led by F. G. Tracy. Hufstetler and Johnson, *Watering the Land,* 92.

36. Smith, *Magnificent Experiment,* 107.

37. See the act of June 25, 1910, "An act to authorize advances to the 'reclamation fund,'" 36 Stat. 835; U.S. Department of the Interior, *Federal Reclamation Laws Annotated,* pp. 97ff. On the bond act of 1910, see *CR* (House), July 16, 1914, p. 12224. Smith, *Magnificent Experiment,* 114, 141.

38. Remarks of Rep. Harvey B. Fergusson, New Mexico, *CR* (House), July 22, 1914, p. 12497.

39. Remarks of Rep. Edward Taylor, Colorado, *CR* (House), July 16, 1914, p. 12238. Exactly where Taylor obtained his figure of thirty-two projects is unclear. All available reports indicate that only twenty-seven projects were under way in 1914 at the time of the debate.

40. Remarks of Rep. Martin Madden, *CR* (House), July 16, 1914, pp. 12238.

41. Madden, *CR* (House), p. 12239.

42. See Reclamation Extension Act, August 13, 1914, ch. 247, 38 Stat. 686, in U.S. Department of the Interior, *Federal Reclamation Laws Annotated,* pp. 124ff. On the transfer of project operations to the water users' association at Salt River, Arizona, see

Smith, *Magnificent Experiment,* 141–46. As Hufstetler and Johnson note, "The passage of the Reclamation Extension Act was one reflection of an increasing congressional awareness of major problems inherent in nearly all Reclamation Service projects" (*Watering the Land,* 119).

43. Remarks of Rep. Oscar Underwood, *CR* (House), July 29, 1914, p. 12963. Underwood was the sponsor of the amendment creating section 16 of the Reclamation Extension Act, and debate over the act appears in ibid., 12963–74.

Conclusion

1. E. Pendleton Herring, "Social Forces and the Reorganization of the Federal Bureaucracy," *Southwestern Social Science Quarterly* 15 (December 1934): 7.

2. Both the postal inspection service and the USDA contradict James Q. Wilson's claim that "[b]efore the second decade of this century, there was no federal bureaucracy wielding substantial discretionary powers" ("The Rise of the Bureaucratic State," *The Public Interest* [1980]: 103).

3. In David Epstein and Sharyn O'Halloran's analysis of all acts of congressional delegation to administrative agencies from 1947 to 1992, 79 percent of delegations gave laws to existing agencies, whereas only 21 percent of delegations were to newly created agencies (*Delegating Powers,* 158).

4. Wilson, *Bureaucracy,* 158–71.

5. See the notes to the introduction. Linda Gordon, *Pitied but Not Entitled: Single Mothers and the History of Welfare, 1890–1935* (New York: Free Press, 1994). Kolko, *Triumph of Conservatism;* Sklar, *Corporate Reconstruction of American Capitalism.* Eileen L. McDonagh, "The 'Welfare Rights State' and the 'Civil Rights State': Policy Paradox and State Building in the Progressive Era," *Studies in American Political Development* 7, no. 2 (fall 1993): 225–74. Hays, *Conservation and the Gospel of Efficiency.*

6. Jonathan N. Katz and Brian R. Sala, "Careerism, Committee Assignments, and the Electoral Connection," *American Political Science Review* 90 (March 1996): 21.

7. Theda Skocpol, Marshall Ganz, and Ziad Munson, "A Nation of Organizers: The Institutional Origins of Civic Voluntarism in the United States," *American Political Science Review* 94, no. 3 (September 2000): 527–46; Gerald Gamm and Robert Putnam, "The Growth of Voluntary Associations in America, 1840–1940," *Journal of Interdisciplinary History* 29, no. 4 (spring 1999): 511–57; Elizabeth Clemens, *The People's Lobby: Organizational Repertoires and the Rise of Interest Group Politics in the United States, 1890–1925* (Chicago: University of Chicago Press, 1997). Sklar, *Corporate Reconstruction;* Kim Voss, *The Making of American Exceptionalism* (Ithaca: Cornell University Press, 1993); Kolko, *Triumph of Conservatism.* Boyer, *Urban Masses and Moral Order;* Beisel, *Imperiled Innocents.*

8. Paul C. Light, *Thickening Government: Federal Hierarchy and the Diffusion of Accountability* (Washington, D.C.: Brookings Institution and the Governance Institute, 1995).

Archival Sources ———————————————

For those interested in the primary-source record of bureaucratic development during the period 1862–1928, here are the archival sources and databases used in this book. For other primary sources (including government publications, newspapers, magazines, and pamphlets), as well as secondary sources examined, please consult the notes.

Archival and Manuscript Collections Consulted

The Post Office Department (Chapters 3, 4, and 5)

George B. Armstrong Collection, Chicago Historical Society, Chicago, Illinois

Hubert Howe Bancroft Papers, Bancroft Library, University of California, Berkeley

Wilson Bissell Papers, Library of Congress, Washington, D.C.

Lloyd Wheaton Bowers Papers, Library of Congress

Albert S. Burleson Papers, Library of Congress

Burrows Family Papers, Western Reserve Historical Society, Cleveland, Ohio

Records of the Cedar Rapids Post Office, State Historical Society of Iowa, Iowa City

Records of the Committee of Fifteen, Manuscripts and Archives Division, New York Public Library, New York, New York

Records of the Committee on Post Office and Post Roads, U.S. House of Representatives, RG 233, National Archives, Washington, D.C.

Records of the Committee on Post Office and Post Roads, U.S. Senate, RG 46, National Archives

Records of the Garrison Post Office, State Historical Society of Iowa

George B. Cortelyou Papers, Library of Congress

James Lewis Cowles Papers, Manuscripts and Archives Division, New York Public Library

Isaac Cummins Papers, State Historical Society of Iowa

George B. DeSellem Papers, State Historical Society of Iowa

Don M. Dickinson Papers, Library of Congress

Records of the Division of Railway Mail Service, NA I, RG 28

James R. Garfield Papers, Library of Congress

Records of the Garrison Post Office, State Historical Society of Iowa

Gilbert N. Haugen Papers, State Historical Society of Iowa

Edward Everett Hayden Papers, Library of Congress

Clara Hinton Family Papers, State Historical Society of Iowa

Frank H. Hitchcock Papers, Library of Congress

Hyatt Collection, National Postal Museum, Smithsonian Institution, Washington, D.C.

Records of the Inspection Service, NA I, RG 28 (Accession), Washington, D.C.

Inspection Service Vertical Files, U.S. Postal Service Library, L'Enfant Plaza, Washington, D.C.

Charles Kepler Papers, State Historical Society of Iowa

Luis Kutner Collection, Chicago Historical Society

Louisiana Collection, Howard-Tilton Memorial Library, Tulane University, New Orleans, Louisiana

George von Lengerke Meyer Papers, Massachusetts Historical Society, Boston, Massachusetts

Records of the National Consumers' League, Library of Congress

Proceedings of the National Conventions of the National Association of Railway Postal Clerks (NARPC), 1891–1905, Library of Congress

Records of the National One-Cent Postage Association, National Postal Museum, Washington, D.C.

National Postal Research Library, Various Records, National Postal Museum, Washington, D.C.

Records of the New York Society for the Suppression of Vice, Library of Congress

David Parker Collection, University of Delaware Special Collections, Newark, Delaware

Henry C. Payne Papers, State Historical Society of Wisconsin, Madison, Wisconsin

Postal Savings Records, Office of the Historian, U.S. Postal Service

Postal Savings Vertical Files, U.S. Postal Service Library

Railway Mail Service Library, Frank Scheer, Curator, Alexandria, Virginia

Records of the Railway Mail Service (Northeast), National Archives Regional Branch, Waltham, Massachusetts

Railway Mail Service Vertical Files, U.S. Postal Service Library

Theodore Roosevelt Papers, Library of Congress

Records of the Bureau of the Second Assistant Postmaster General, NA I, RG 28

Reed Smoot Collection, J. Willard Marriott Library, University of Utah, Salt Lake City, Utah

William McKendree Springer Collection, Chicago Historical Society

William F. Vilas Papers, State Historical Society of Wisconsin

Henry Haven Windsor Collection, Chicago Historical Society

The Department of Agriculture (Chapters 6, 7, 8, and 9)

Charles Albert Browne Papers, Library of Congress

Records of the Bureau of Agricultural Economics, NA II, RG 83, College Park, Maryland

Records of the Bureau of Agricultural Engineering, NA II, RG 8

Records of the Bureau of Animal Industry, NA II, RG 17

Records of the Bureau of Chemistry and Soils, NA II, RG 97

Records of the Bureau of Plant Industry, NA II, RG 54

Francis Morton Cockrell Collection, Chicago Historical Society

Richard Coke Collection, Chicago Historical Society

Records of the Committee on Agriculture, U.S. House of Representatives, NA I, RG 233

Records of the Committee on Agriculture and Forestry, U.S. Senate, NA I, RG 46

Records of the Committee on Interstate and Foreign Commerce, U.S. House of Representatives, NA I, RG 233

Records of the Committee on Manufactures, U.S. Senate, NA I, RG 46

Records of the Committee on Public Lands, U.S. House of Representatives, NA I, RG 233

Records of the Committee on Public Lands, U.S. Senate, NA I, RG 46

Dana Family Papers, Yale University, New Haven, Connecticut
Samuel Trask Dana Papers, Bentley Historical Library, University of Michigan, Ann
   Arbor, Michigan
Zebina Eastman Collection, Chicago Historical Society
John Fitzpatrick Papers, Chicago Federation of Labor Collection, Chicago Historical
   Society
Records of the Food and Drug Administration, NA II, RG 88
Records of the Forest Service, NA II, RG 95
William Frear Papers, Paterno Library, Pennsylvania State University, State College,
   Pennsylvania
Charles W. Garfield Papers, Bentley Historical Library, University of Michigan
Gilbert N. Haugen Papers, State Historical Society of Iowa
Willet M. Hays Papers, Iowa State University, Ames, Iowa
Kate Adele Hill Papers, Cushing Memorial Library, Texas Agricultural and Mechanical
   University, College Station
Harry Burns Hutchins Papers, Bentley Historical Library, University of Michigan
John Harvey Kellogg Papers, Bentley Historical Library, University of Michigan
Louisiana Collection, Howard-Tilton Memorial Library, Tulane University
C. Hart Merriam Papers, Bancroft Library, University of California, Berkeley
William Butts Mershon Papers, Bentley Historical Library, University of Michigan
Sterling Morton Family Papers, Chicago Historical Society
Frank Murphy Papers, Bentley Historical Library, University of Michigan
National Agricultural Library, various collections, Beltsville, Maryland
Records of the National Consumers League, Library of Congress
Records of the National Society for the Promotion of Industrial Education, Library of
   Congress
Alfred Noble Papers, Bentley Historical Library, University of Michigan
Nils Andreas Olsen Papers, Iowa State University
Chase Salmon Osborn Papers, Bentley Historical Library, University of Michigan
Charles Christopher Parry Papers, Iowa State University
Personnel Files of the Department of Agriculture, National Archives, Saint Louis, Mis-
   souri
Amos R. E. Pinchot Papers, Library of Congress
Gifford Pinchot Papers, Library of Congress
G. Harold Powell Papers, Special Collections, University of California, Los Angeles
Theodore Roosevelt Papers, Library of Congress
Julius Rosenwald Collection, Special Collections, University of Chicago Library
Jeremiah Rusk Papers, State Historical Society of Wisconsin, Madison
Records of the Secretary of Agriculture, NA II, RG 16
   Willard Bigelow Personnel File
   Lyman Briggs Personnel File
   Mark A. Carleton Personnel File
   Beverly T. Galloway Personnel File
   Willet Martin Hays Personnel File
   John K. Haywood Personnel File
   Seaman A. Knapp Personnel File
   C. Hart Merriam Personnel File

Julius Sterling Morton Personnel File
Gifford Pinchot Personnel File
R. M. Reese Personnel File
C. V. Riley Personnel File
Daniel Salmon Personnel File
William J. Spillman Personnel File
William A. Taylor Personnel File
Harvey W. Wiley Personnel File
James S. Wilson Personnel File
Louise Benjamin Smiley Collection, Chicago Historical Society
Reed Smoot Papers, J. Willard Marriott Library, University of Utah
Charles C. Teague Papers, Bancroft Library, University of California, Berkeley
Records of the Texas Agricultural Experiment Station, Cushing Library, Texas Agricultural and Mechanical University, College Station
Records of the Texas Agricultural Extension Service, Cushing Memorial Library, Texas Agricultural and Mechanical University
Records of the University of California College of Agriculture, Bancroft Library, University of California, Berkeley
Records of the University of California Experiment Station, Bancroft Library, University of California, Berkeley
Booker T. Washington Papers, Library of Congress
Harvey W. Wiley Papers, Library of Congress
James S. Wilson Information File, Economic Research Service, Department of Agriculture, Washington, D.C.
James S. Wilson Papers, Iowa State University

The Interior Department (Chapters 2 and 10)

Richard Achilles Ballinger Papers, Library of Congress
Hubert Howe Bancroft Collection, Bancroft Library, University of California, Berkeley
Records of the Bureau of Agricultural Engineering, NA II, RG 8, College Park, Maryland
Records of the Bureau of Reclamation, NA II, RG 115 (microfilm, M96)
Records of the Committee on Interior and Insular Affairs, U.S. House of Representatives, NA I, RG 233
Records of the Committee on Interior and Insular Affairs, U.S. Senate, NA I, RG 46
Records of the Committee on Irrigation of Arid Lands, U.S. House of Representatives, NA I, RG 233
Records of the Committee on Irrigation of Arid Lands, U.S. Senate, NA I, RG 46
Records of the Committee on Public Lands, U.S. House of Representatives, NA I, RG 233
Records of the Committee on Public Lands, U.S. Senate, NA I, RG 46
Records of the Department of the Interior, NA II, RG 48, College Park, Maryland
Records of the Forest Service, NA II, RG 95, College Park, Maryland
James R. Garfield Papers, Manuscript Division, Library of Congress, Washington, D.C.
Records of the General Land Office, NA II, RG 49, College Park, Maryland
Lucius Q. C. Lamar Papers, Library of Congress
Ellwood Mead Collection, Water Resources Library, University of California, Berkeley

Frederick Newell Papers, Library of Congress
William T. Otto Collection, Chicago Historical Society

II. Primary-Source Statistical Collections Gathered by the Author

Department of Interior Employee Data. A collection of employment data for eighty employees of the Geological Survey in 1919 and 1920. It also includes data on the county origins of all employees working in the Geological Survey and Reclamation Service in 1905.

Department of Treasury Employee Data. Data on the county origins of all employees working in the Department of Treasury in 1905, excluding employees of the U.S. Customs Service.

Haugen District Post Office Data. A collection of postmasters, status changes, and dates of termination for more than two hundred post offices in the congressional district of Rep. Gilbert N. Haugen, gathered from Haugen Scrapbook, State Historical Society of Iowa.

Post-Office City Free Delivery Operations Survey, 1896–1910. A collection of operations data for all first- and second-class post offices in Pennsylvania, Texas, and Iowa from 1896 to 1910, gathered from NA I, RG 28.

Post Office Employee Data. A collection of employment data for 2,368 postal carriers and 2,568 clerks at first- and second-class offices, as well as more than two hundred postal inspectors. From NA I, RG 28.

USDA Correspondence Data. A summary database of all letters written by the commissioner (or secretary) of agriculture to Congress from 1886 to 1893, including the recipient and the subject (usually seed distribution, scientific programs, or employment).

USDA Employee Data. A collection of employment data for 1,590 personnel of the Department of Agriculture, including data from 865 personnel files of USDA employees gathered at the National Personnel Records Center, National Archives, Saint Louis, Missouri. It includes data on the distribution of county origins of all employees working at the USDA in 1905.

Index

PRINCETON STUDIES IN AMERICAN POLITICS
Historical, International, and Comparative Perspectives